The Quest for Quality in Services

The Quest for Quality in Services

A.C. Rosander

QUALITY PRESS
American Society for Quality Control
Milwaukee, Wisconsin

QUALITY RESOURCES
A Division of Kraus-Thomson Organization Limited
White Plains, New York

First printing 1989

Printed in the United States of America

Quality Resources
A Division of Kraus-Thomson Organization Limited
One Water Street, White Plains, New York 10601

Library of Congress Cataloging-in-Publication Data
Rosander, A. C. (Arlyn Custer), 1903–
    The quest for quality in services / by A.C. Rosander.
      p.   cm.
    Bibliography: p.
    Includes index.
    ISBN 0-527-91644-7
    1. Service industries—Management. 2. Service industries—Quality control. 3. Consumer satisfaction. I. Title.
HD9981.5R66   1989
658.5′62—dc19

                                          88-36874
                                            CIP

Contents

Preface

The purpose of this book is to describe and illustrate various concepts and aspects of quality of service so that a quality program can be put on a sound foundation. It also shows the detailed knowledge necessary to have a quality program not only to succeed but to continue with improvements.

Several important aspects and techniques are described, which are not used or emphasized in a factory quality improvement program. Several fallacies connected with quality of services are treated at length. A review of the several points made by each of the authorities on quality control is made, and this book shows how they apply to the service industries. Stress is put on the widespread nature of human error and how to prevent it.

The ultimate consumer is treated in detail. Complaints are not enough; there is a need for continuous surveys of those who are pleased, dissatisfied, indifferent, or lost, as well as the reasons. The non-customer should not be overlooked. Several examples are repeated, but for different purposes, because a single example may represent several aspects of quality.

Introduction

Quality is a permanent function that permeates all aspects of the work of an organization. It therefore falls in the same class as terms like cost, expenses, assets, and budget.

Quality applies to any organization whether it is operating for profit or not. It applies not only to those persons who are working for wages or salaries, but to those volunteers who are working for nothing, because quality is concerned with what people do and how they behave toward others. It applies to the performance of people, including their decisions and actions, regardless of what level they are working at. It applies to products and services. It applies to data. It applies to decisions. It applies to actions. It applies to behavior.

Quality is a permanent function of a service organization. It is the people in this organization who determine whether or not the quality function is being carried out in an acceptable manner.

The customer is the ultimate judge of whether the quality of these goods and services is satisfactory and acceptable. This is why the customer must be at the center of any quality improvement program.

The Quest for Quality in Services

Chapter 1

Services At the Crossroads—What Next?

IS SUSPENDED ANIMATION OVER?

After decades of successful testing and application, the quality of services is just now emerging from the doldrums. Recently there has appeared some evidence of a new interest in this field:

- A few books have been published devoted entirely to services.
- More articles and papers are appearing.
- The Juran Institute is now giving seminars on quality in non-manufacturing, including services.
- Interest is being shown in the quality of services which support manufacturing.

Tom Peters is also helping by stumping the country calling for excellence, more concern for the individual customer, and quality.

This is very little progress considering the importance of services—that four times as many people are employed in services as in manufacturing, that at least one hundred million people in this country are using or buying daily some kind of service, and that the operations of governments as well as service companies could be greatly improved by using an effective quality program.

Manufacturing, however, still overwhelmingly dominates the field of quality. This includes all aspects—people, management, concepts, techniques, practices, books, articles, and thinking generally. This concentration on the quality of products has pushed quality of services into the background and kept it there. There are several reasons for this:

- Quality control started in the factory.
- Quality of products has strong engineering aspects.
- Foreign competition involves products much more than it does services.
- Many think that quality applies only to products, not to services.
- Most large organizations, outside of governments, are not in services.

THE NEED FOR A NEW APPROACH

Quality in services cannot make any real progress until some very drastic changes in approach and thinking are made. Some of these changes, which are described below, illustrate what needs to be done now; there is no reason why these changes need to be postponed any longer:

- As much attention needs to be given to the quality of services as to the quality of products.
- Quality of services has to become a full-time job of everyone in management, supervision, lower-level employment, and professional staff functions, not the passing interest of those whose real job is in the manufacturing of products.
- Services everywhere have to be studied in depth. Quality of services has to be based on actual data about various characteristics, not on the imitation of what goes on in a factory nor on some fictitious analogies with manufacturing.
- Quality of services determined by *customers* has to be given the same attention, time, and importance as quality of services determined by *professionals* in the organization. Indeed, quality as perceived by the customer should have top priority.
- Management of services is not the same as managemment of factory production because of sharp differences between the two types of organization:
  - The role of people is different.
  - The role of the customer is different.
  - The content, environment, and the knowledge involved are different.
  - The concept of quality is different in many ways.

Striking differences exist even between the management of two companies in two different service industries, due to differences in the basic function of the service company and the resulting differences in the number and nature of service operations. The following managers will find their jobs relative to quality and numerous other functions widely different:

- a manager in a bank;
- a manager in a federal tax agency;
- a manager of an airport;
- a manager of a hospital;
- a manager of a nursing home;
- a manager of a power and light company.

To be most effective, managers have to have adequate knowledge of operations, how they are conducted, procedures, professional relationships, processes, laws, regulations, functions, organization, and communication channels.

The terrible loss incurred by shifting a top-level manager from a position he is familiar with to one about which he knows nothing is illustrated by an actual case:

A top-level federal tax administrator with an excellent record was shifted to a welfare agency which was floundering. This shift was based on the false notion that an excellent manager in one large agency is going to be an excellent manager in another agency and can save another agency.

This manager's knowledge, abilities, skills, decision making, planning, and even leadership were tax-oriented and therefore not transferable. In the new job he would have to start over again. Furthermore, the tax agency lost an excellent man who had taken 10 to 15 years to advance to where he was. It takes a lot of time to learn how an organization operates, and to contribute to the direction and improvement of those operations.

The same situation exists in manufacturing. John De Lorean observed that executives whose knowledge is limited to accounting, and whose past experience was with refrigerators and railroad diesel locomotives, are not very good at making automobiles.[1]

A LONG-TERM PROGRAM

We need not only a new approach to quality of services but a long-term program developed along the lines indicated in the 10 items given below. This program outlines some of the actions we should take to improve the quality of services in all service industries during the next 10 to 15 years.

1. Develop a body of knowledge about services—their nature, scope, characteristics, components, measurement, appraisal, and peculiarities.
2. Make available to a wider audience statistical techniques and other methods which are not being used today to improve the quality of services, including elimination of the faults of the system.
3. Make comprehensive surveys periodically of *all* customers, including the lost ones and the pleased ones. A study of customers who complain is not enough; these complaints are only the tip of the iceberg.
4. Develop a body of accurate knowledge about the customer's experiences with quality of services in all of the service fields.
5. Develop a body of accurate knowledge about the organization's experiences with quality of services, both inside and outside the company.
6. Develop a body of accurate knowledge about the scope and nature of

---

[1] P.J. Wright, *On a Clear Day You Can See General Motors* (New York: Avon, 1980).

human error and its prevention, so as to improve human reliability in all of the service industries.

7. Develop a body of sound empirical knowledge on the psychology of managers, supervisors, employees, and customers relative to attitudes and behavior affecting quality performance and quality service.

8. Study service operations and service components at first hand, in depth, and continuously. The purpose is to obtain accurate and relevant data and information about quality of services and their improvement.

9. Develop knowledge showing the differences in quality characteristics within and between components of service, as well as the differences between and within service industries.

10. Develop a body of knowledge, including case studies, on the cost of non-quality characteristics of services 1) to the customer, 2) to the organization, and 3) to the public. The cost of quality, including non-quality, is described in detail in Chapter 11.

WAYS TO PUT QUALITY ON A SOUND FOUNDATION

To put quality of services on a sound foundation means that some new thinking is required, that some current ideas will have to be changed, that fallacies will have to be replaced with sound ideas and concepts. The nature of this new type of thinking is indicated in the 13 items listed below:

1. Get rid of the fallacies connected with the quality of services.

2. Put the brakes on human error. In many situations even one error cannot be condoned. In other situations errors are not to be explained away as inevitable, or else any savings by prevention of error are impossible.

3. Stop the high cost of non-quality to the customer. Simply costing out non-quality to the organization is not enough.

4. Get rid of the poor-quality services reported by customers.

5. Define quality in terms of each of the groups in the total customer group, not just in terms of those who complain. (See Point 9, ''21 Ways.'')

6. Balance the eight vectors of quality to obtain the greatest benefits.

7. Drive non-quality characteristics of Type A to zero. (See Chapter 3.)

8. Stabilize quality characteristics of Type B. (See Chapter 3.)

9. Get management under control.

10. Get the computer under control.

11. Watch out for the plateau in a learning curve situation. It may be evidence of temporary stability, not of statistical control. (See Point 20, ''21 ways.'')

12. Make the collection and analysis of good-quality data a top priority throughout the organization.

13. Get rid of the notions that

- the customer is a "bloody nuisance";
- the patient is "dumb" and therefore should be ignored;
- the consumer is "irrational";
- the company "knows what's best" for the customer;
- the manufacturer's perceptions are sound but the customer's are not;
- salesmanship is more important than quality.

21 WAYS TO IMPROVE QUALITY

1. Quality of Service is Real, Observable, Identifiable, and Improvable, and Not to be Equated to the Quality of Products

In a paper in a quality control journal the expression "product or service" appeared more than 20 times, giving the reader the impression that whatever applied to a product applied in the same way to a service. Nothing is more unfortunate and more misleading than the notion that quality concepts, ideas, and practices can be carried over willy-nilly from the factory to the operations of a service organization.

The 1985 Gallup survey for the American Society for Quality Control brought out very strikingly not only that quality of services is different from quality of products, but that quality of services is real, observable, and identifiable. The respondents could not only identify poor-quality products and poor-quality services but could select words that described quite precisely what they had in mind.

Poor-quality services were connected directly with employee behavior and attitudes, and the respondents used these words to describe them: lack of courtesy, indifference, unqualified, too slow, work not done right, lack of personal attention. This is to be expected because the quality of service in numerous companies and industries is determined by the individual clerk or salesperson who waits on the customer.

In the same survey the reasons given for poor-quality products were entirely different, concentrating on the unfavorable physical characteristics of products such as lack of durability, mechanical failures, poor workmanship, poor performance, and shortness of life. These reasons bore no resemblance whatever to those given for poor-quality services.

2. Take Measures to Insure Acceptable Quality of All Purchased Products

The service organization buys products, supplies, equipment, machinery, energy services, and the like in the same way as a manufacturing company. If attention is concentrated on this aspect, it is very easy to conclude that quality in an office is the same as it is in a factory.

If this happens, a very significant difference is overlooked. A manufacturing company makes purchases in order *to make a product*. A service company makes purchases in order *to render a service*. There is a world of difference. Even identical products are used for entirely different purposes; hence the quality characteristics are different. Oxygen and X-ray machines are used for entirely different purposes in a health agency and in a factory.

To insure quality, the service company has to work very closely with its suppliers. Some of the important points the purchasing department has to observe are the following:

- Purchase according to written specifications of what the customer wants.
- Select vendors that can meet these specifications.
- Check vendor's history for quality, reliability, and meeting schedules.
- The first requirement to meet is quality, not price.
- See that the vendor has an effective quality control program.
- Insist on evidence from vendors that they are meeting the specifications and requirements of the company.
- Use the vendor's evidence to reduce receiving inspection and record keeping to that which is necessary for shelf-life control, inventory control, or other purposes.
- Hold visits and conferences with vendors to discuss all problems related to quality of products and services.

3. Quality Defined as Meeting the Customer's Requirements Has Severe Limitations

This is not a good definition; it is incomplete. A close examination of how customers buy shows that it is inadequate. A customer is a sample of one. A company, on the other hand, sells to a mass market and sells those goods and services for which there is the greatest demand.

A clothing store carries sizes that fit most people. A shoe store carries shoes that fit most people. Both of these stores will carry sizes in the middle or the mode of the frequency distribution.

A customer's requirements are not met if the company does not carry the clothing sizes that fit the customer. This means those persons at the extremes of the distribution do not have their requirements met.

The same holds true in a shoe store. The company may not carry, and often does not carry, shoes of the proper width that meet the requirements of the customer.

Clothing and shoes are not the only commodities which fall into this nonquality classification. Insurance companies may refuse to issue an insurance policy that the customer wants. They will sell only a "package" insurance policy, which contains one or more items that do not apply to the customer. In this case the customer may have to buy what is offered because it is required by law. The "package" does not "meet the customers requirements." The companies have no intention of giving customers what they want. They want to prescribe what the customer needs, aided by state insurance departments.

It is not uncommon for the customer to go to a restaurant or hotel and discover that it is impossible to get what is wanted. The customer has no choice, but must accept an item on the menu.

Quality defined as "meeting the customer's requirements" assumes that the company is doing what the customer wants and is meeting the customer's specifications. In practice this does not occur, as pointed out above. If anything, the "requirements" are determined by the company, not by the customer.

4. The Approach to Quality Has Always Been Negative, Not Positive

The current and historical approach to quality has always been negative. The cost of quality is defined as the cost of doing things wrong. This sounds strange; one would think that quality cost was the cost of doing things right, of building quality into a product or service in the first place. We get quality by getting rid of non-quality. The current practice relative to quality costs is to reduce, if not eliminate, internal and external failures. These failures are simply admissions that products and services cannot be produced without a myriad of failures.

Quality, then, is perfection toward which we work but which we never quite reach. Indeed, the emphasis on "quality improvement" implies that it takes an indefinite time to obtain overall quality. All we ever have is partial quality.

Quality is perfection: zero defects, zero errors, zero failures, zero wasted time, zero complaints, and zero unacceptable behavior. What we do is move progressively toward better and better quality by progressively eliminating sources of non-quality. We are forever talking and writing about quality when we mean that we are trying to get rid of non-quality. This is what Shewhart did; he showed us how to get rid of non-quality in dimensions encountered in manufacturing. We work toward quality despite the implications of perfection.

These sources of non-quality surround us. They are built into organizations, they are inherent in processes, they are associated with human behavior and attitudes, they occur in policies and plans and practices, they occur because managers and professionals and persons generally lack the capabilities and motivation to get them under control or eliminate them.

The positive approach to quality would settle for no less than the cost of doing things not only right but most efficiently. Under these conditions the cost of quality would be simply the cost of doing business.

The slogan "Do it right the first time" is a positive approach. It implies, however, that 1) there is a right way, 2) the worker *knows* the right way, and 3) the worker *does* the right thing. If there are several "right" ways, then the problem is one of selecting the most effective procedure that is feasible.

5. Errors, Wasted Time, and Ill-Mannered Behavior Are to Be Reduced to Zero

In manufacturing a common problem is to stabilize some dimension at a level $y = \bar{y}$, in order that specifications will be met. A control chart of the $\bar{x}$ type is used to eliminate assignable causes and to gain statistical control. In services and even in manufacturing, there are quality characteristics in which the goal is not some set level but a continuous downward trend toward zero.

We do not set an acceptable level for errors, mistakes, and blunders. We want to avoid them. We want to prevent them. We want to drive them down persistently toward zero. We do not want to stabilize them at some value such as 5 percent, 2 percent, or even 1 percent. Zero error (ZE) is the goal, and we drive toward it even though we never quite reach it.

We do not set an acceptable level for wasted time. We do not want to accept costly delays, idle time, down time, unnecessary time. We want to drive wasted time persistently down toward zero. Zero wasted time (ZWT) is the goal.

We do not set an acceptable level for ill-mannered behavior among employees who service customers directly. We want this to be at a zero level continuously. There are to be no exceptions, no acceptable levels, no departures. Zero ill-mannered behavior (ZIMB) is the goal. Quality performance requires ZIMB constantly.

Both management and supervisors should make it very clear to both new and old employees that quality of services requires these three goals: ZE, ZWT, and ZIMB. Indeed, they are needed in manufacturing just as in service companies.

We are *not* interested in stabilizing these characteristics at some level, but in a dynamic stability where the value constantly and persistently moves toward zero. These are not just slogans, but real-world goals. Successful examples show that they are real. There are ways to prevent errors, to eliminate wasted time, and to banish ill-mannered behavior, and these will be described in detail later.

6. Stress the Positive Characteristics of Quality

Strangely enough, the cost of quality is the cost of non-quality: it is the cost of getting rid of internal and external failures of the company or organization. While this is being done, there is a real need to stress the positive approach to quality, to base quality programs not only on the negative characteristics but also on the positive characteristics. Two lists of these latter characteristics are given below; one is identified with people and the other is identified with products:

People	Products
• courteous	• work as they should
• kind	• durable

People	*Products*
• considerate	• reliable
• helpful	• long-lasting
• accurate	• low-cost
• friendly	• operate smoothly
• caring, careful	• have low life-cycle cost
• prompt	• have low repair cost
• reliable	• have low maintenance cost
• productive	• defect-free
• innovative	• error-free
• concerned	• trouble-free
• honest	• safe
• fair	• pure: no adulteration
• trustworthy	• clear instructions for use
• cooperative	• meet standards
• poised	
• truthful	
• capable	
• credible	
• efficient	
• competent	
• alert	
• taking initiative	
• thoughtful	

7. The Current Need Is to Implement Quality Using the Knowledge We Have

To implement means that the persons involved from top to bottom have to be convinced of the significance and value of quality, they have to be motivated, they have to be educated, they have to be trained, they have to accept quality improvement as a continuing program. In most organizations this is not going to be easy.

To implement means to have an ongoing program of good-quality data collection, of observing behavior, of conducting surveys and studies (sample or otherwise), of interviewing employees and customers and vendors, of making diagnoses and finding remedies.

To implement means that persons in the various divisions and departments have to cooperate to start and develop an ongoing quality program, that they need to be in close communication with one another, that they need to do their jobs with a high quality of performance, that they need to work together to resolve problems and prevent conflicts. A quality program cannot start, let alone progress, unless there is cooperation, understanding, and communication among all those engaged in the program.

To implement means to have an intensive study of all service operations, a continuous monitoring of operations to discover problems and measure progress, a continuous collection of data of all key operations to know exactly whether or not quality is being attained. Only by an in-depth knowledge of the service operations and their nature can an organization develop a sound quality improvement program. One starts with a thorough knowledge of the organization's operations, not with preconceived ideas gathered from manufacturing, the factory, or esoteric theories about human behavior.

Implementation of a study or project or plan is *a group affair* requiring a group of employees with a leader or supervisor. An individual acting as an advisor or consultant cannot do this. He or she is divorced from the operating part of the organization. An individual can be effective in implementation only if he or she not only prepares the technical instructions but also is allowed to participate in putting the plans into effect and to monitor them continuously.

When the implementation stage is reached, the situation is no longer limited to statistics or to any other technical subject matter represented by an individual specialist. It now involves human relations and psychology as well as economics. It is no longer a statistical problem.

The supervisory statistician has always worked under these conditions, although the human relations problems never received any publicity; only the statistics were publicized. Past experience shows that in implementation the statistical and other technical problems were often the easiest to solve. The hardest problems were human relations problems, especially those connected with the opposition and objections of higher-level officials and professional specialists. The technical aspects of statistical quality control and probability sampling required that in implementation certain procedures be followed very carefully and explicitly, something that many of these officials and professionals did not think was necessary. They are mistaken; if a sample study is to be implemented properly, it must be supervised, if not monitored continuously, by a statistician or other specialist familiar with probability sampling and its application. Otherwise some technical decisions will be made by high-level officials who haven't the slightest idea about the consequences of what they are doing. Such decisions may limit greatly, if not invalidate, the value and effectiveness of the study.

8. Executives Have to Do More than Talk Quality. Cheerleading Does Not Get Others to Build Quality Into Products and Services

Approval of, commitment to, or pushing for quality by top-level officials has to motivate those below to build better products and to render better services. Otherwise all of the quality policies, plans, and programs from the top will be worthless.

This statement can be documented by more than one example. Despite the exposure of automobile companies and executives to the latest in quality philosophy, steps, programs, and practice, hundreds of thousands of cars are still being produced and recalled because of a faulty gear shift or some other defects. There is still something missing. We have not implemented quality improvements to the extent necessary to prevent relatively simple defects. We overlook the fact that executives do not build quality into the final output or render services to the customer; others do.

Pronouncements from the top may *not* be effective for one or more of several reasons:

- Employees do not take management seriously.
- Preparatory steps have been inadequate to obtain the acceptance of a quality policy or program.
- Adversary relations exist; many people want to maintain the status quo.
- Managers and employees are not convinced that quality has the advantages claimed for it; they may oppose change.
- No concrete evidence or demonstration has been given to show the merits, advantages, and necessity for a quality improvement program.

Then there is another, more basic question. How are the executives going to learn about the philosophy and techniques of quality? Who will enlighten them? They will have to be convinced of the need for quality in their business before they will commit themselves to a program of quality management and improvement. In practice it will not be as easy to convince top-level management as we are led to believe. They can learn in many different ways. One way is from the seminars and videotapes of Dr. Deming and Dr. Juran. Another way may be from some official in the company who is already familiar with quality concepts. It is necessary to do this, or a quality program cannot start from the top.

The role of top-level officials relative to quality is a very difficult one to say the least. The reasons are not hard to find.

1. Their role is due to power, not to knowledge or know-how.
2. They know little or nothing about operations where quality is built in.
3. Their orientation is finance, not quality; salesmanship, not customer needs; money accounting, not quality audit.
4. They recognized the value of quality only after Japanese competition showed them that quality was important, even though quality control has been applied successful in this country for over 40 years.
5. Management was not concerned about quality between 1946 and 1975 because they were basking in a seller's market.
6. Top-level officials cannot start quality control because it is too technical. It has to be started by middle managers, supervisors, and professionals

who understand Shewhart's concepts and techniques and are in a position to apply them.

7. There is a strong tendency for top-level officials to think that quality is for lower-level persons, not for themselves, even though poor-quality performance at the top is much more serious than poor-quality performance at the bottom.

8. Pep talks, slogans, retreats to fancy resorts, and even trips to Japan may be futile *unless* management provides leadership, personal examples, and the necessary resources, and fosters the knowledge and motivation needed to improve quality.

9. The above are reasons why Dr. Deming states that "a long thorny road lies ahead" and why Dr. Juran concludes that it will take until the year 2000 for top managers to learn how to manage quality—"an agonizingly slow pace."

9. Every Quality Program Should be Balanced by Giving Adequate Consideration to Each of the Eight Vectors of Quality

The eight vectors of quality are

- management;
- supervision;
- psychology;
- statistics;
- economics;
- problem subject matter;
- processes and systems;
- time.

There has been, and still is, a tendency to latch onto a few of these and consider them sufficient. This results in imbalance and the waste inherent in such a position. At present some people are enthusiastic about management and process control. Some think they have discovered something new in "statistical process control" (SPC), apparently not knowing that what Shewhart called SQC (statistical quality control) was precisely process control; he made this clear in both of his books. (It is true that "process control" will make more sense to a worker in operations than the term "quality control".) Others want more emphasis put on people (psychology); still others stress techniques (statistics) or costs (economics).

But psychology includes more than a few employee problems; statistics includes more than a few simple methods, such as those associated with quality circles; and economics includes more than what are called quality costs.

Concentrating on a few vectors, or even on a few aspects of all eight vectors, is not enough. A company or agency which does this is simply short-changing itself. Making effective use of all eight vectors means coming near to the maximum benefits to be obtained therefrom. It means using knowledge which is already available but is scattered widely through the literature. We need books which describe the nature of the eight vectors and tell how each contributes to the improvement of quality, together with a generous sampling of actual examples, illustrations, and cases from the real world of practice.

10. Apply Psychology to Human Relations Problems in Quality

Dr. Deming's 14 points are presented as a new philosophy of quality for management. It is not only a new approach to quality; it is also a basic plan and a quality management creed. Not all of the 14 points are strictly philosophical despite the claim of a new philsophy.[2] (See also Chapter 9.)

Three points are psychological, not philosophical. Fear (Point 8) and pride (Point 12) are feelings and emotions. Also, to the extent that barriers (Point 9) are due to love of power, envy, fear, jealousy, feuds, and personality conflicts, (as they often are), they, too, are based on feelings and emotions.

These are attitudes which are often deep-seated. They cannot be changed by the usual classroom instruction. Most of the time they cannot be changed by any form of knowledge. They have to be changed by assurances from other people. They have to be changed by finding the root of the feeling or emotion, and this is not easy.

They cannot be changed as several of the other points can be changed. They are not like mass inspection (Point 3) or like buying by the price tag (Point 4). Neither are they like the statistical training given under Points 6, 7, and 13. They have no resemblance to the elimination of numerical goals (Point 10) or work standards (Point 11). There are no deep-seated feelings of emotions connected with these items or practices. They are practices, not personal feelings. This does not mean that there are no personal attachments to these practices. There are, and they will appear just as soon as management wants to change them, let alone eliminate them. But they are concepts which can be discussed in terms of knowledge and better techniques. It is very difficult, if not impossible, to approach emotions and feelings in this way. They must be approached by using personal assurances from other people, personal changes in behavior, personal negotiations, frank talks, elimination of causes, and much more.

11. We Need to Survey All Customers For Their Attitudes, Preferences, and Appraisals, Not Only Those Who Complain

By surveying all customers we obtain information on attitudes, preferences, appraisals, and suggestions for improvement. We obtain information on each of the following six situations:

---

[2]R. D. Snee, "Youden Memorial Address, October 1985," *Statistics Division Newsletter* (ASQC, March 1986).

1. Why dissatisfied customers are dissatisfied but are not complaining;
2. Why customers are already lost and what is necessary to win them back;
3. Why some customers are indifferent and what can be done about it;
4. Why some customers are satisfied;
5. Why some customers are pleased;
6. Why customers keep coming back; the loyal customers; the repeat customers.

By keeping in close touch with these six groups as well as with the seventh group—the group that complains—the organization has a fairly complete picture of the role of the customers, how they are reacting to the various quality characteristics of the service, and what actions have to be taken to improve and maintain quality.

In addition there is an eighth group—the non-customers—who are potential customers but who also have to be surveyed to determine why they are not buying this particular good or service: this is the challenge of market studies and research, and should be conducted as an integral part of a comprehensive and continuous customer-market program.

These surveys or studies are to be made periodically and staggered so that each group is contacted every two or three months. Contacting them only once a year is not enough: the information is too important to be delayed that long.

A Note On the Meaning of "Customer"

In this book the word "customer" has its usual popular meaning—an individual buying goods or services. (This is the same as the dictionary meaning.) Invariably the individuals are buying for themselves or for a household or family. The customer is the ultimate buyer, not an intermediate buyer.

"Customer" may also be used to refer, in specified places, to service companies that purchase goods and services they need to perform the services for which they were established. This is necessary because of the effects of these purchases on the quality of services both for the company and for the ultimate individual buyer.

"Customer" is *not* applied to other organizations or companies. Neither is it ever used, as it often is by speakers and writers today, to refer to those persons in any organization who are receiving the output of a preceding sequence of work. It is unfortunate that the word "customer" is applied to this situation. Some more appropriate term, such as "sequential workers," should be used instead.

Activities of customers which involve quality but which are not direct buying, although they are related thereto, include all kinds of inquiries and contacts made by telephone, mail, or in person.

12. Quality Services Require Quality Data for Quality Decisions and Quality Action

By "quality data" we mean data that are relevant, accurate, sufficient, and clear. The collection and analysis of data that meet these criteria at all key points in the organization are a "must." The reason is that inferences, conclusions, decisions, and actions are no better than the data on which they are based. This very important point is often overlooked.

More attention needs to be paid to this vital function. Examples of aspects that need close attention and improvement include

- Regular operating data; production data; learning curve data;
- Accounting data;
- Financial data and purchasing data;
- Inspection data;
- Probability sample studies; random time sampling;
- Quality control data and charts;
- Receiving inspection data.

Technical know-how including statistical capability has to be available and applied effectively. For example, there must be operating people who know how to design and test data sheets, questionnaires, control charts, and probability samples, and who know how to interpret the data in terms of the problems to be solved and the questions that have to be answered.

People can go wrong in these ways, as illustrated by the following situations:

- The data are biased so much as to render them useless and misleading.
- Data are needed but are never collected.
- Data are available but are ignored, e.g., on foreign car imports.
- Data are misinterpreted.
- Data are misused; e.g., a sample is used for a purpose for which it was not designed.
- Specialists in sample design and data analysis are ignored, although available.

13. Powerful Techniques Are Not Being Used to Correct Faults in the System

One of the major reasons why management goes out of control and the faults of the system are not eliminated is the lack of a continuous flow of good-quality data from key points and situations to management. Data have to be used to discover problems; conversely, problems have to be analyzed to collect relevant data. The following powerful techniques are rarely, if ever, used:

- Random time sampling (RTS)
  RTS can be used to detect and measure downtime, idle time, delay time, excessive time, and wasted time.
  RTS with the minute model can be used to cost out activities, jobs, and projects.
  RTS can be used to decompose joint costs, such as quality vs non-quality costs. It is the only known technique that can do this accurately.
- Learning curve analysis
  The learning curve shows individual and group capabilities.
  It shows quality improvement as errors are eliminated.
  It shows that learning can progress far beyond the point where it is often claimed that "this is the best we can do."
  It shows how effective training and retraining really can be.
  It shows what realistic production goals are, or can be.
  It shows the rate at which errors are being reduced, production increased, productivity improved, and unit costs reduced.
- Input-output analysis
  Relates man-hours of input to number of units of output such as insurance claims, bills, tax returns, invoices, checks, and accounts.
  Reflects increased productivity as learning continues.
  Gives a realistic picture of how much output to expect, given a certain amount of input, or conversely, how much input is necessary given a certain amount of output.
- Probability sample surveys on a continuous basis
  Customers divided into significant groups;
  Non-customers;
  Lost customers;
  Employees.

14. The Employee is Responsible for Quality of Services

It is generally recognized that those who build products are responsible for their quality. This responsibility cannot be delegated or transferred. A company cannot blame a government agency for the poor automobile, pacemaker, or drug it turns out.

The same principle holds true of quality of services. The company or organization that renders a service is responsible for its quality. More specifically, the individual who renders the service is responsible for its quality. A company or organization is based on the tacit assumption that the employee who waits on the customer will perform a satisfactory service. Clearly they were hired for this purpose and for nothing else.

The customer does not deal with supervisors, managers, or executives. The customer does not deal with management. The customer deals with an employee. The customer has no alternative but to hold the employee responsible for the quality of service received. The customer receiving poor service gets little comfort or satisfaction from being told that the poor quality is due to management that is absent and inaccessible, and not to the employee. To the customer, the employee, not management, represents quality or non-quality performance. This means that in services we have to reject the notion that the employee has very little responsibility for quality.

In any contact, meeting, or transaction the customer is a sample of one; so is the employee waiting on the customer. A customer may have to go through contacts with two or three persons before the right person is found. Quality is determined by the behavior and attitudes of samples of one. There is no mean, no variance. This is a psychological problem, not a statistical problem. Over time the customer may contact several persons in the same service company. The customer will distinguish the person who renders good quality service from those who do not, often for the simple reason that excellent service is so rare.

The division of responsibility for quality in industries where one employee's error is not only dangerous but fatal is at least 50/50, rather than 85/15 or 80/20. The real question is to what extent are individual workers to be held responsible for their errors, wasted time, and ill-mannered behavior? Management should reject the common notion and alibi that it is human to make errors and mistakes. Using this alibi, it is not uncommon for managers and workers to explain away not only costly mistakes but fatal ones as well. Management should announce loudly and clearly to everyone that the level of acceptable work is zero errors, zero mistakes, zero wasted time, and zero ill-mannered behavior.

Persons unwilling to accept these zero levels should not be hired. Those who are hired should be put through an orientation course which stresses the zero goals, and which shows persons how to work toward such a level. It is not enough to preach zero errors: workers must be shown how to attain, or at least move toward, such goals.

Management is to blame for poor-quality performance if it hires unqualified persons, if it does not have a continuous training program, if it does not show employees how to reach zero levels. Who is blame if technically trained persons such as technicians, engineers, scientists, specialists, and the like are hired and make errors? Who is to blame if they make a technical error that is dangerous or fatal? Who is to blame in the following actual cases?

- A nurse gives cocaine to a patient instead of phenobarbital; the patient dies.
- Medical technicians hook up a cylinder of carbon dioxide (CO_2) instead of oxygen (O_2); the patient dies.
- A pilot takes off with ice on the wings; the plane crashes; 70 die.
- Two freight trains on same track have a head-on collision: five die, with very heavy damage to trains, track, and highway overpass.

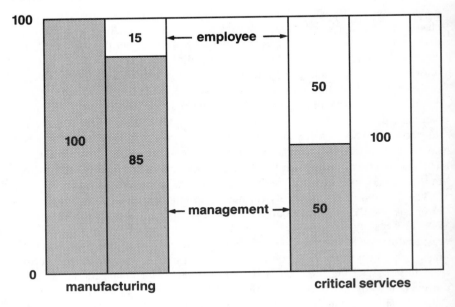

Figure 1–1. Responsibility for Quality

15. The Most Serious Out-of-Control Situation is That in Which Management Itself is Having Difficulty Maintaining Control

Drs. Deming and Juran have been pointing out for decades that the greatest need in this country is for top-level officials to learn how to manage for quality. The Number One problem is management. This bears out what many of us discovered in the early days: that the opposition to better methods and improved operations came from high-level managers and professional specialists, not from lower-level employees. This was why it was difficult to start even a single application of probability sampling and statistical quality control, let alone initiate a program across the entire organization.

There are many examples which show how and why management is having trouble with control. These examples can be documented:

· Decisions are made without data.
· Decisions are made with biased data.

- Significant data are ignored.
- Communication with lower levels is faulty or nonexistent.
- New and better methods are too technical, too refined, upsetting.
- Probability sampling runs contrary to common-sense notions of sampling or sampling used in opinion polls.
- Better methods of collecting and analyzing data are opposed as being too complicated.
- Critical information is stopped before it reaches the top-level decision makers, e.g., the Challenger disaster.
- Technical experts are overruled.
- Customer's needs, requirements, and preferences are ignored.
- Short-term goals such as profits are stressed, rather than long-term goals stressing customer satisfaction, quality, and productivity.
- Operating instructions and explanations are fuzzy and incomplete.
- Employees are blamed for what is the responsibility of management.
- Planning at the top is faulty and lacks purpose, clarity, and stability.

16. Quality Improvement is Primarily a Human Relations Problem, Not an Organizational Problem

Starting as well as maintaining a quality improvement program is primarily a human relations problem, a people problem. The success of these programs depends upon the knowledge, attitudes, and behavior of people. The people are the key, not the type of organization, not a fancy organizational chart. The people are quite independent of the type of organizational chart the company has.

If the people do not have the knowledge, the technical know-how, the attitudes, the motivation, or the cooperation for teamwork, no form of organization is going to correct these basic deficiencies. Streamlining the organization without changing the people will fail. So will quality circles, participative management, and all other kinds of organizational gimmicks. That is why so many "reorganizations" of government agencies and private companies fail to accomplish the fine-sounding goals they are supposed to achieve.

With an adequate force of employees, managers, supervisors, and professional staff, the usual form of organization will work. This assumes, of course, that the necessary technical capabilities, supervisory skills, and cooperative attitude already exist or are being developed.

It is only fair to point out that in both government and private companies there may be, and often are, too many layers of organization, and that a marked improvement in operations is obtained by simply abolishing two or three of these layers. Tom Peters and John DeLorean both cite examples of where this change was very successful.

17. Determine the Losses and Cost of Non-Quality, and Drive Them Toward Zero

Non-quality characteristics create a loss that can often be expressed in terms of money expense. Sometimes these losses are of such a nature as to make estimation of money cost difficult, if not impossible. The following are some of these major non-quality charateristics.

Errors, Mistakes, and Blunders

The loss takes the form of the time spent in making the error and the expense incurred in correcting it. Also involved are the possible losses of time and money involved if actions were taken on the basis that the error was correct. If the error is serious, then time and money are lost due to litigation in the form of damage suits or other legal action. These are losses the organization faces. The loss to the customer is described below.

Lost Time

Lost time is due to delays, downtime, idle time, or excessive time. In most instances these losses of time can be converted directly into money losses. These delay times and downtimes can also have a chain effect on other operations, and this may be very costly as well.

Anti-Customer Attitudes and Behavior

These refer to attitudes and behavior which turn off the customer. The effect is real, but it is hard to measure the consequences because they may range all the way from displeasure to a lost customer. This is a very serious matter which needs corrective action, even though the consequences may not be immediately apparent.

Lost Customers

There seems to be very little attention paid to lost customers because no studies are ever made of all groups of customers. Attention seems to be concentrated on those who complain, who are only a small part of the problem. The loss due to a lost customer can be estimated if the company has any records to show how much this customer had been buying in the past; these data will be available for charge-account customers and those using credit cards. Good customers can easily be worth $50 to $200 per week.

Customer Complaints

Customer complaints can be very expensive. Some complaints may take considerable time of one person, while others may require very little time. In many organizations of any size, including large supermarkets, handling customer complaints may be a full-time job for one person. Usually complaints in a store go to the salesperson or department where the complaint originated. It may be resolved there, or it may have to go to higher levels, even to the manager.

The trouble with customer complaints is that they may be only the tip of the iceberg. The attitudes, opinions, and dissatisfactions of other customers may be much more important.

Failures

The cost of failures can be tremendous both to the organization and to the customer. Two major kinds of failures are failure of machinery, equipment, and apparatus and failure of processes and operations. Examples include the following:

1. Equipment
   - computers
   - school buses
   - trucks
   - word processors
   - city buses
   - automobiles
   - typewriters
   - airplanes
   - electrical machinery and apparatus

2. Processes and operations
   - electricity
   - garbage collection
   - water
   - bus line
   - telephone
   - postal service

Defects In Purchased Products

The cost of defects in purchased products can be minimized by holding the supplier responsible for the quality of the product. Every shipment should contain evidence that it is of acceptable quality and that defects of any consequence have been eliminated. A hospital cannot afford to have defective anesthesia machines. One hospital had two of these machines and two deaths before it realized the trouble—an oxygen valve that sticks.

Damage

An organization wants to reduce all forms of damage to a minimum, with zero as the goal. Damage includes a wide variety of occurrences: breakage, accidents, injuries, destruction, weather, fires, and falls. Examples include the following:

- breakage: dishes in a restaurant or cafeteria, articles in shipment or transportation;
- damage due to shipping, fires, weather, handling, traveling, opening containers, weak containers, or inadequate containers;
- accidents: auto, airplane, trucks, buses, railroads; collisions, crashes, turnovers, derailments, wrecks;
- injuries: cuts, bruises, burns, falls;
- destruction: fires, floods, hurricanes, rain, snow.

Two other important sources of loss are shoplifting and employee stealing of merchandise or equipment.

18. There Are Many Ways to Start a Quality Program

There is more than one way to start a quality program. Several questions have to be answered. First, *who* are the key people who can start such a program or a project in such a program? There are four groups of key people:

- top officials;
- middle managers;
- professional specialists (staff people);
- supervisors.

How will these people obtain the necessary knowledge and orientation, assuming that no one is knowledgeable in quality control? There are four ways in which this can be done:

- Hire a full-time practitioner who knows quality control and statistics to explain, instruct, plan, advise, orient, apply;
- Hire an outside consultant in quality management and quality improvement to explain, instruct, orient;
- Send key people to outside seminars and courses in quality;
- Set up a training program in quality within the company or agency.

What forms can the first step take? An actual start can be made by any of the four key groups; it is better to start with the operating people who are familiar with problems, and who build quality into products and services:

- Top officials can issue statements of quality policies, plans, and program. This is necessary if any program is to include everybody in the company. All of the authorities in the field favor this top-down approach. From the viewpoint of quality policies and plans for the entire company, this is a sound approach. From the viewpoint of implementation, however, the problem is quite different. Managers, supervisors, and employees may take a different attitude ranging from indifference to opposition.

- Middle managers. It is possible to start with middle-level managers who are already familiar with quality control, quality programs, and quality concepts. There may be one or more who are familiar with statistical quality control and how it can be applied to problems and situations in their department. Middle managers are in operations and hence are in a key position to identify problems and set up projects for quality improvement. They can demonstrate in projects that quality control works.
- Professional specialists. A professional specialist may be familiar with quality control techniques and how they are applied to problems. If knowledgeable in this field, he or she can teach others the basic concepts and principles, and point out situations and problems to which they can be applied. This is especially true where a specialist works closely with operating managers and employees.
- Supervisors. A start may be made with one or more supervisors who are favorable to the use of quality control techniques and concepts. Supervisors are in constant contact with difficulties and problems which require the quality approach.

19. Plan and Implement Education and Training Courses to Meet Specific Needs of Employees, Supervisors, and Managers

Education emphasizes an understanding of concepts and principles which have applicability to a wide variety of problems and situations. Training focuses on specific rules and procedures. For example, in connection with a nuclear power plant, education calls for mastering and understanding the principles of nuclear physics and how these principles are applied to the operation of nuclear reactors and other equipment to generate electricity. Training concentrates on specific areas, such as the rules and procedures to follow in case of a failure or accident.

There are two aspects to the planning, preparation, and presentation of courses in the training program: courses to meet present needs, and up-dating the curriculum by changing old courses and introducing new ones. Courses have to be kept up to date because of developments in technology, changes in customer demands, changes in composition of the market, and changes in competition.

Courses needed to meet present needs will concentrate on such major aspects of quality as the following:

- Errors and their prevention;
- Customer preferences and requirements, and how to meet them;
- Customer surveys anad contacts, and how to make a better use of this important information;

- Safe practices, and how to prevent accidents and disasters;
- Employee behavior and attitudes, and their importance in dealing with customers and maintaining good customer relations;
- Problem finding, problem identification, and quality improvement;
- Reducing costs by reducing or eliminating the effects of various sources of lost time;
- How to improve relations with suppliers and reduce the cost of receiving inspection.

20. Statistical Control May Be Spurious Because It Represents a Plateau on the Learning Curve

The learning curve has been ignored in manufacturing and services in general and quality control in particular. Psychologists have known for a long time that the learning process, both for an individual and a group, is subject to leveling, which is easily spotted as a plateau on the learning curve as a function of time. During a learning process as short as 45 days, three of these plateaus may exist on the production curve.[3]

It is very easy in a production process, which often is a learning process as well, for a characteristic to reach one of these lower plateaus and result in the false conclusion that the process is under control and that this is "the best that we can do." What exists is only temporary stability, which can be broken as time passes and as learning continues. Then the process can move to another and higher plateau on the production curve. This is one way in which improvements are made—by moving from a lower plateau to a higher one. How far this process can continue has never been thoroughly studied. More will be said later about learning curve analysis. Detailed examples of learning curves in both manufacturing and data processing are given below in the reference.

In terms of the *error curve*, improvements are made as the error rate moves to lower and lower levels. One explanation of plateaus is in terms of elimination of errors; if they are eliminated in spurts, there are periods of leveling where the error rate is constant. The *unit cost curve* tends to follow the error curve.

In the data processing example given in the reference a plateau existed on the production curve at about 120 records per day, at about 150 records per day, and at about 200 records per day. It should be pointed out that the learning curve as described here is really a group capability curve, corresponding to a machine capability curve. The curve shows the actual capability of this group

---

[3] A. C. Rosander, *Applications of Quality Control in the Service Industries* (Milwaukee: American Society for Quality Control, and New York: Marcel Dekker, Inc., 1985), pp. 111–114, 206, 337–338.

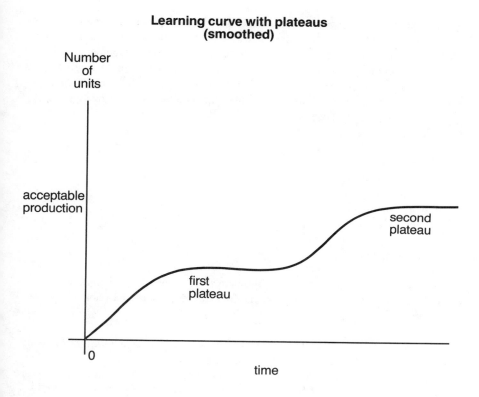

Figure 1–2. Learning Curve with Plateaus (smoothed)

in accomplishing a specified job under given conditions of management, supervision, training, physical conditions, salary level, and the like. The actual capability of this group under excellent supervision was far from the unrealistic numerical goals set by the vice-president.

21. The Quest for Quality Is the Quest for Survival

Quality is no longer an idea we argue over because it is too statistical, does not apply to my company, is too costly, is something we already have, or is of minor importance.

Foreign nations learned it from us. They have accepted it and put it into practice so that the quality of their goods is now equal, if not superior to the quality of our products. This sharp improvement in foreign production has changed drastically both domestic and foreign markets, many of which we used to dominate. Facing these new realities calls for some drastic changes.

Management cannot meet this challenge with fine phrases, slogans, and exhortations. Neither can they meet it with salesmanship, sales gimmicks, high-pressure advertising, or appeals to patriotism. Nor will recourse to political action solve the problem such as charging cheap labor, dumping products at cut-rate prices, and demanding tariffs and quotas as protection. Defending ourselves as a "superpower" and as an "affluent society" will not be of any help; this is nothing but self-deception.

We will have to learn how to

- accept quality;
- plan for quality;
- manage for quality;
- work for quality;
- concentrate for quality;
- innovate for quality;
- improve quality.

It requires no less than a basic change in attitudes toward the economic system, the education system, and government. Changes in practice must follow changes in attitude.

1. Begin by emphasizing the need to do a good job in school and the need for quality performance on the job and in one's career.
2. Make clear that good work has more than economic value. It has other emotional and psychological values as well, as the experts keep telling us.
3. The need in order to meet competition is to think and work smarter, harder, and longer.
4. Schools should concentrate on important knowledge, abilities, skills, and attitudes needed by the informed citizen on the one hand, and by the proficient worker on the other. Get rid of the "fun and frolic" philosophy.
5. Put the needs, performances, and requirements of the customer first. Listen to the customers instead of trying to dictate to them.
6. Concentrate on ways of getting rid of sources of non-quality: defects, errors, wasted time, failures, customer complaints, and lost customers.
7. Give more care and attention to the collection of high-quality data at every level.
8. Spend more time building in quality at the bottom rather than talking about quality at the top.
9. Eliminate the computer as the Number One alibi of the century. Insist on tight controls of the computer system at every step. Make the computer cost-effective.
10. Where an employee error can be dangerous, if not fatal, the division of

responsibility between management and the employee should be at least 50–50.

11. There is need to sharply reduce federal taxes and possibly other taxes in order to stimulate small businesses into making quality products and rendering quality services in local communities.

12. There is a need to stimulate new manufacturing to compete with foreign products, such as textiles, clothing, and shoes.

Chapter 2

The Scope of Service Functions and Industries

The application of statistical quality control to service functions in manufacturing and to service industries is not new. These applications, which first began in a large study in 1940, have paralleled those in the manufacturing industries, but to a very limited extent. What is new, however, is the growing realization that the quality of services is just as important, just as necessary, as the quality of products. Indeed, in many areas it is even more important to stress the quality of services, especially where a single error made by an employee may be dangerous, if not fatal, as in health or transportation.

To show that quality control is not new in services, we cite some early examples in supportive or service functions in manufacturing and some early examples in service industries:

Services in manufacturing:

- Bicking, Hercules Powder, personnel, other administrative aspects
- Buhl, Goodrich Tire, office operations
- Noble, Kimberley-Clark, marketing
- Parkin, 3M, sales and economic forecasting

Service industries, including government:

- Deming, 1940 federal census of population: key punching, other
- Rosander, 1943, War Production Board, allocation of materials
- Ballowe, 1945, Aldens Mail Order House, errors in filling orders
- Halbert, 1947, AT&T, revenue accounting
- Jones, 1950s, Illinois Bell Telephone, accounting, clerical work
- Magruder, 1950s, Chesapeake and Potomac Telephone Companies, customer surveys, property appraisals for rate cases
- Lobsinger, 1950s, United Air Lines, reservations, meals, offices
- Peach, 1950s, Sears testing laboratory
- Connell, 1960s, Blue Cross, processing insurance claims

SERVICE ASPECTS

Manufacturing companies are concerned with services in two ways, while service companies are concerned with service aspects in four ways, as shown in the following chart:

	Function	Responsibility for quality
• Manufacturing companies		
	1. In-house services	Company
	2. Purchased services	Vendor
• Service companies		
	1. Purchased products	Vendor
	2. In-house services	Company
	3. Purchased services	Vendor
	4. Services sold	Company

In both manufacturing and in services these functions are supportive or supplemental to the real purpose for which the company was established. They are building blocks. In the case of a service company it is the fourth function—selling services to customers—that predominates.

SERVICE FUNCTIONS IN MANUFACTURING

These are overhead functions not associated with direct factory production, but they are needed to make factory production possible. These functions may account for as much as 20 or 25 percent of the total cost of doing business:

purchasing	financial	transportation	accounting
personnel	auditing	training	communication
sales	storage	packaging	shipping
legal	marketing	advertising	receiving inspection
customer service	computer	administrative	travel

In general, manufacturing companies have not been greatly concerned about the quality of these services. The reason is simple. Quality control was originated for the purpose of controlling the quality of manufactured products, and the emphasis has been on products ever since. Even so, as noted above, some early successful applications of quality control were in the service functions of a manufacturing company. Furthermore, it was easier to learn how to apply statistical quality control to products whose quality was directly related to physical measurements. Also, the early books and published papers presented many successful applications of control techniques and control charts to characteristics of products.

All of these functions are found in service companies as well as in manufacturing companies. Hence quality control concepts and techniques developed for and applied to the operations of a service company can be applied to these service functions in manufacturing. Examples are error trend plots, random time sampling applied to work operations and activities, frequency distributions, and learning curve analysis. In later chapters these concepts and techniques will be discussed in detail.

These service functions involve a substantial cost to the company in the form of overhead or fixed costs. Therefore it pays to apply quality control with emphasis on preventing errors and faulty performance on the one hand, and excessive time consumption on the other. These functions can be analyzed into a number of specific jobs, components, projects, and problems for which quality performance is of the utmost importance. These aspects then become immediate candidates for a quality improvement program.

It should be noted, however, that quality improvement in the service functions may not improve product quality to the customer because the bottom line of the company is still money, not quality: sales, profit, return on investment, share of the market, dividends. This means that improving the quality of the following service operations may *not* improve the quality of the product to the customer unless steps are taken to ensure that these operations improve the quality of the product from the viewpoint of the customer: purchasing, financial, transportation, marketing, accounting, customer research, customer service, sales, and training. Improvements can be made that increase profits but do not improve the quality of the product.

Despite all the claims about improved quality that have been made during the past several years, complaints about American-made automobiles are still higher per 100 automobiles than for Japanese cars. These data come from a 1985 national study of complaints made during the first 90 days after purchasing the car. (See Chapter 5).

THE SERVICE INDUSTRIES

According to the standard industrial classification, (SIC), the following are service industries. The names are arranged alphabetically; "nec" means "not elsewhere classified":

1. Banking
2. Business services: legal, engineering, accounting, data processing, etc.
3. Education, nec
4. Entertainment, recreation
5. Finance, other
6. Government: local, state, federal

7. Health
8. Hotels and motels
9. Insurance
10. Personal service: household service, beauty, cleaning, etc.
11. Professional services, nec
12. Public utilities: water, gas, electricity, telephone, etc.
13. Real estate
14. Restaurants and cafeterias
15. Retail trade
16. Transportation
17. Wholesale trade

A considerable amount of construction work is included under "government" because of government contracts for construction projects (e.g., roads, streets, bridges, buildings, tunnels, overpasses, dams).

SERVICE INDUSTRY EMPLOYMENT

Most people do not realize that over 60 percent of the total labor force is employed in the service industries; five out of every eight workers are so employed. Furthermore, employment in the service industries is 3½ times as large as that in manufacturing—70 million as against 20 million, as the following data for 1982 show. The figures are given in millions: [1]

Trade, wholesale, and retail	20.8
Government: federal, state, local	15.8
Federal: 2.7	
State, local 13.1	
Transportation, public utilities	6.6
Finance, insurance, real estate	6.3
Business services	4.0
Personal including hotels, lodging	4.0
All other services	12.5
Total	70.0

There are as many people employed in trade alone as there are in all of manufacturing. In 1982 almost five times as many were employed by state and local governments as by the federal government—13.1 million as against 2.7 million. Between 1970 and 1982 federal employment remained constant at 2.7 million, but state and local government employment increased by 3.3 million, or about 33 percent.

---

[1] *Statistical Abstract of the United States,* 1984 (Washington, DC: Bureau of the Census), pp. 421, 425, 429. The latest total is about 80 million.

"All other services" includes employees in private hospitals, private health services, private professional services, and others not connected with government. These latter include private schools, colleges, and welfare and similar organizations and agencies.

Not included in the above are approximately seven million persons employed in agriculture, forestry, fishery, mining, and construction. These industries are considered neither manufacturing nor service, although construction may be considered as a combination of the two.

The above list shows that the industries that are considered service industries vary widely in their specific functions, a factor of great importance in considering the quality of the services rendered by companies in the different industries. In this regard, however, service industries are no different from manufacturing industries.

THE WORK FORCE, THE NON-WORK FORCE, AND QUALITY

There is a saying with a long history that is almost an axiom in quality: "Quality is everybody's business." The big question is, does "everybody" really mean everybody? In the past the meaning of the word was very ambiguous. No one has seen fit to define it specifically or operationally. In the usual context the writer or speaker appears to mean everybody in the company from the lowest-paid worker to the highest official. "The company" is a manufacturing company, not a service company. Excluded are government agencies and non-profit companies or organizations.

If "everybody" means everybody who works for money, then the scope of the term is at least the entire work force. For the United States in 1982 the numbers of persons involved (in millions) were approximately as follows[2]:

Everybody in manufacturing	20 million
Everybody in service industries	80 million
Everybody in other industries	7 million
Everybody who wants work (the unemployed)	8 million
Total work force	115 million

This means that only about 17 percent of "everybody" is employed in manufacturing. These are the persons covered by the expression "total quality control" that Feigenbaum, Ishikawa, and others mention. Their "total" includes only 17 percent of the total work force; obviously this total is limited to manufacturing and excludes all other industries and activities. The term "total" was introduced to stress the need for all the divisions of a manufacturing com-

---

[2] *Statistical Abstract*, 1984, pp. 421–429.

pany to cooperate and work together in attaining quality in a product; it may or may not include the service or supportive divisions such as marketing and finance. The term was used to counter the practice of these divisions working in isolation or in actual conflict with one another.

What about the other 83 percent? Do we not expect these workers to build quality into the products (for example, construction) and services they render? We certainly do. We talk and write about quality being everybody's business, but we do not attempt to practice it or even to move in that direction.

BALANCING THE EIGHT VECTORS OF QUALITY

Quality control in manufacturing has suffered from the beginning from imbalance, from particularism, from over-emphasis on one aspect. This one-sidedness has taken various forms at different times. Examples are engineering, statistics, quality costs, quality circles, statistical process control, and management. This imbalance should not be carried over into service operations and service industries, but there is a real danger that it will occur, if it is not already occurring.

The scope of quality in services, as well as in manufacturing, should include the eight vectors of quality. These are the major fields which have to be addressed, considered, and utilized if an effective, balanced program of quality improvement is to be attained. Balance is necessary if we are to take advantage of the unique contributions that each of these fields makes to the improvement of quality.

Vector	*Broad quality aspect*
1. Management	Direction, purpose, policy, plan, decisions, action, leadership
2. Supervision	Plan, direct, implement, coach, train, corrective action, problem analysis, leadership
3. Psychology	Behavior, attitudes, learning, teaching, teamwork, harmony, motivation, cooperation, training, customer preferences, trust, security, safety
4. Statistics	Data collection, variability, data analysis, problem detection, sampling, estimation, control
5. Economics	Cost, overhead, waste, loss, damage, profit, sales, market share, supply, demand, quality cost, price, affordability, safety
6. Subject matter of problem situation	Problem solving, corrective action, problem analysis, safety, engineering, technology
7. Process	Defects, errors, time, control, sequencing, synchronization, speed, safety, production
8. Time	Utilization, delay, service, delivery, processing, timeliness, promptness

These eight aspects are not independent; they are closely related. Provision has to be made for each of them in any program aimed at attaining or improving quality of services. (These aspects will be discussed in detail in later chapters.) For example, sampling or some other aspect of statistics is involved in measuring variability of human behavior (psychology), in overhead and other costs (economics), in control of the process (subject matter), and in measuring how well time is being utilized (time).

THE QUALITY OF GOVERNMENT SERVICES

Governments—local, state, and federal—require special attention because they are not usually considered in the same category as service industries. Nevertheless, this is where they belong because their major, if not sole, purpose is to render services to the public which they represent. We are constantly being reminded, however, that while private industry is concerned with making a profit, governments are not. This is true, but it has led to a number of false inferences and conclusions which are described and refuted below.

1. It is asserted that because of the profit motive private industry can always perform a job better than government employees.

This view ignores business failures, bankruptcies, losses, mergers, taxpayer bailouts, taxpayer subsidies in the form of tariffs and quotas, and other evidences of inefficiency and failure. This view also overlooks numerous failures when federal government functions are contracted out to private companies.[3]

This is a common delusion fostered and kept alive by the media and millions of others who haven't the slightest idea how federal agencies operate under civil service. They blithely and persistently ignore the waste, inefficiency, handsome free benefits, and low productivity of numerous companies and industries in the private sector.

2. Since government operations are not carried out for the purpose of making a profit, and since by definition are very wasteful if not useless, there is no point in applying quality control to try to improve them.

This is false. Quality is everybody's business. Quality applies to performance wherever people are working or engaged in any activity. Public or private ownership has nothing to do with this; quality performance is necessary whether profit is involved or not. It is needed in non-profit organizations and agencies just as much as in service companies operated for a profit.

3. Quality improvement does not apply to government operations. The latter cannot be improved because of the political nature of government.

False again. The political nature of government does hinder and obstruct, but

---

[3] For several examples see ''contracting out'' in the index of my book *Washington Story* (National Directions, 500 26th Street, Greeley, CO 80631, 1985).

it does not prevent the introduction and implementation of a quality improvement program into government operations. Quality improvement is precisely what the bottom line of government can and should be. It cannot be profit in the strict sense of the word, but it can be improvement of performance and operations. Quality improvement will result in the following, as actual experience shows:

- Reduction of errors, failures, trouble;
- Elimination of errors, failures, trouble;
- Reduction of wasted time;
- Elimination of wasted time;
- Reduction of time required to do a satisfactory job;
- Reduction in paperwork;
- Better service to the public;
- Better service to other government officials and staff;
- Better data, better analysis, more timely reports.

These will result in saving time, saving people, increased productivity, and reduced outlays of tax money. They will result in precisely the same gains as if the government were a private company.

The trouble with government operations is that many politicians, and the public, have a conflicting, if not confusing, set of notions about what a government function is and what it is not. Examples are easily found.

1. Economists and others state that businesses that are not profitable should be financed by the taxpayer. Examples are low-cost and low-rent housing, and hydroelectric and nuclear power plants. In these situations it may be very difficult to introduce a quality control and a quality improvement program. Nuclear power plants do have some quality control, as enforced by the Nuclear Regulatory Commission.

2. It is thought that some government ventures should *not* operate at cost. One example is the Post Office.

Several years ago the Post Office Department pointed out to a Congressional Committee that a slick-covered magazine was being subsidized to the extent of $4 million a year. It wanted to make these magazines pay the cost of mailing and handling. Congress refused to permit such a change, although paying for costs incurred would seem to be a sound business practice. If a private company takes over the postal business the public can be sure it will operate at cost, plus 8 or 10 percent profit. Then first class postage may be 50 cents, not 25 cents.

Government, including local, state, and federal government, is full of functions, projects, and jobs where a well-designed and implemented quality improvement program would pay off in very handsome benefits. The savings can be as great, if not greater, than they are in private industry. What is needed is leadership by politicians insisting that quality improvement is just as important in the public sector as it is in the private sector, but don't look for this soon.

GOVERNMENT INSPECTION DOES NOT GUARANTEE QUALITY OF PRODUCTS OR SERVICES

A common belief is that inspection assures the quality of products and services. Therefore, the argument goes, government inspectors protect us not only from a host of ills and catastrophes but from inferior products and services. Hence one of the functions of government is to provide an army of inspectors to ensure quality.

No idea is more fallacious and costly than this one. Quality engineers and others have an age-old axiom: "Quality is built into products and services, not inspected in." It is a basic truth, still not understood.

During the 1970s an inspector general's office was established in all of the major federal agencies. The purpose was to expose inefficiency, waste, mismanagement, and criminal behavior. The basic method was inspection. This guaranteed that inefficiency, waste, and mismanagement would continue. Why? Because inspectors never find the causes and eliminate them. They find faults and report them, and they will continue to do so.

Congress believes wholeheartedly in federal inspection. Senator Ribicoff publicly criticized the Food and Drug Administration for the defective heart pacemakers which were reported to be in use in this country, but nothing was said about the responsibilities of the manufacturers.

Inspectors presumably protect us from watered milk, impure food, defective scales, unsafe dams, faulty bridges, defective elevators, dangerous chemicals, and unsafe trucks. The quality of milk is the responsibility of the bottler; the impure food is the responsibility of the food manufacturers; the crooked scales are the responsibility of the store that tampers with them; the condition of dams is the responsibility of the company or agency that owns them; the faulty bridge is the responsibility of those who designed and built it; the condition of the elevator is the responsibility of the company that built it and the company that uses it; dangerous chemicals are the responsibility of the company that manufactures and sells them; the unsafe truck is the responsibility of the company that makes it and the company that uses it.

Government inspectors cannot relieve these companies or agencies of their primary responsibility for the quality of the products they make, the quality of the equipment they use, or the quality of the products they sell.

Chapter 3

The Unique Nature of Services

The first step in applying quality control to service operations is understanding the unique nature and characteristics of services, and how they vary from one service industry and company to another. Since quality control was first applied to manufactured products, practically all of the books, papers, articles, and thinking stress quality control applied to factory products. Further, it is assumed by many people that what has worked successfully in the factory can be carried over and applied willy-nilly to any and all service operations.

This is unfortunate even though some of the ideas and a few of the techniques used in the factory can be applied, with proper adaptations, to some service operations. It is unfortunate because it puts service quality control in a straightjacket; limits the area of application; does not recognize that services are not the same as physical products; does not recognize the significant differences in the quality function in different service industries; ignores many techniques which can be widely used in services but which are not widely used in manufacturing; and ignores the fact that services are dominated by subjective human elements and not by precise physical measurements.

The purpose of this chapter is to describe in detail the unique nature and characteristics of services as represented by the different service industries, and to show why the service company has to explore its operations in detail if it wants to develop a sound and effective quality control program. This means that one begins with a first-hand examination and identification of the quality characteristics of services throughout the company, not with a slavish imitation of some factory quality control plan.

Services cannot be measured, with exceptions. Services cannot be measured in the sense that the dimensions or properties of physical objects or physical products can be measured. This is because a service is dynamic, not static. It is a function, not a structure. Measurements, however, may be connected with a service operation. For example, in health services there are laboratory tests and measurements of various body and anatomical characteristics such as weight, blood pressure, and temperature, and characteristics of blood and urine such as blood count, cholesterol, uric acid, potassium, glucose, and iron. These measures, however, are indicators of whether the body is functioning properly, and consequently are the basis of medical decisions. Therefore they need to be highly accurate, or a diagnosis may be wrong. The measure of the quality of the medical service, however, is whether the interpretation of these measurements, the diagnosis, and the treatment are correct, effective, and helpful to the patient.

Services cannot be stored. Once a serivce is rendered, it is gone. It can be repeated, but not recovered. It is a process, not a product. It is a series of related activities usually dominated by human behavior. A service consists of components that can be identified.

Services cannot be inspected or examined. Services can be observed and conclusions drawn therefrom, but they cannot be inspected in the literal sense. Physical conditions and physical products associated with services rendered by a company can be inspected and appraised in connection with certain standards of performance or certain environmental standards. Examples are inspection of hotels, restaurants, and nursing homes relative to certain health standards involving sanitation, storage of food, preparation of food, and the like. These inspections are not to be confused with quality control. They occur rarely, possibly only once a year, and touch on only a very limited part of a full-coverage quality control program.

Quality cannot be determined beforehand. The nature of the service cannot be determined beforehand, except in those cases where the customer has had prior service of the same nature. There is no way of examining services, as one examines products before making a purchase in a supermarket. The customer does not know whether the service will be satisfactory or not without buying it and going through the service experience. In buying products, from apples to automobiles, the customer can look, examine, ask questions, even make tests in some cases, before making a purchase. A service cannot be bought in this way.

Services do not have a lifetime. Products have a lifetime. They can be repaired; they can be maintained. Some products fail, so a failure test can be run. Services are not like this. They have duration, but no lifetime.

Services have a time dimension. Services, unlike products, have a time dimension. That is, services take place over time. A service pattern may consist of a series of time-related activities, each component of which is subject to quality performance. In these cases a service has a beginning and an ending in time. An example is a bus ride from origin to destination, or a trip by airline which extends in time from obtaining a reservation to arriving at the destination. The trip involves not only the time required for the service but also related or associated times, delay or waiting times, unnecessary time, excessive time, idle time, and lost time.

Services are rendered on demand. Services are rendered on two kinds of demand: instant demand and scheduled demand. The former include water, gas, electric, and telephone service. These services are available on demand any time of the day or night, every day of the year. These companies must meet a standard of 100 percent availability and reliability. The latter are services rendered only at scheduled times. Examples are retail stores, doctor's offices, banks, and transportation.

Services are much more critical in some industries than in others. Public utilities, which have to give service on instant demand, must have operations running at 100 percent reliability. This means a higher level of quality than is required in other companies.

In certain companies, where one error made by an employee may be dangerous if not fatal, the goal of zero errors is a "must." These companies include those in health service, transportation, and electric power.

This is another example in which a service company not only differs radically from other service companies, but also differs radically from a manufacturing company. This is why a careful exploration and examination of all the operations of a service company are necessary in order to put a quality control program on a sound foundation.

Services involve human reliability much more than product reliability. Every service company has to buy products and services in order to sell the services for which it was created. Reliability of these purchased products, as in a hospital, nursing home, and doctor's office, is crucial, for the quality of the services rendered depends upon the trustworthiness of these products.

Services, however, are performed by people, and so the reliability of people is encountered even more often than the reliability of equipment and other products. A report in *Science* relative to the Three Mile Island disaster pointed out that this experience showed the need to give more attention to human reliability. Human reliability is the complement of human error, so the problem boils down to controlling, correcting, and preventing human error.

Services are rendered by the lowest-paid workers in the company or agency. This is literally true. The quality of the service is determined completely by the individual who is waiting on the customer. This is the case in the following service industries: retail stores, banks, post offices, hotels, motels, restaurants, cafeterias, insurance offices, bus lines, nursing homes, government, airlines, personal service, and repair services. This fact contrasts sharply with most factories, where the product is *not* made solely by the lowest-paid worker in the plant. Examples of services rendered by the lowest-paid employees are

1. Salespeople in retail stores, in supermarkets;
2. Waiters and waitresses in restaurants;
3. Servers in a cafeteria;
4. Clerks and other workers in a hotel or motel;
5. Attendants and practical nurses in a nursing home;
6. Medical assistants and clerks in a doctor's office;
7. Postal clerks;
8. Bank tellers;
9. Airline clerks and attendants;
10. Insurance agents;

11. Billing clerks in private industry and government offices;
12. Many kinds of repair workers;
13. Government office clerks for automobile licenses, taxes, other licenses;
14. Library employees.

The common exceptions are the services of doctors, nurses, lawyers, dentists, and other professional persons.

This means that the quality of service is determined by the qualifications, attitudes, and behavior of a single individual or series of individuals. Thus the quality of services is very different from the quality of products.

This does not necessarily mean that the quality of service will be poor from low-paid workers and very good from those with higher wages or salaries. It does mean that training in the elements of the jobs and training in desirable attitudes toward customers are very important for companies which hire low-salaried persons. The latter are likely to be inexperienced, not aware of how customers must be treated if the company is to stay in business, and even unaware of how to treat fellow workers. A substantial amount of orientation and training will be required.

Quality is both objective and subjective. Quality is not a technique. It is pride and passion. It is management commitment. It is people. It is innovation. It is subjective.[1] There is nothing new about the view that quality is subjective. Shewhart recognized that it is the subjective measure of quality that is of commercial value, although he concentrated on the objective aspect.[2] He called attention to the "human element involved in the wants of individuals." Obviously he saw the importance of the customer.

Peters does *not* describe those who actually build quality into products and services. Rather he describes the remarkable achievements of outstanding leaders in getting others to innovate and improve quality. It is true that he stresses concern for the customer, including courteous treatment, but this is primarily from the viewpoint of the salesman, not from the viewpoint of the buyer. This is indicated by the sales gimmicks which he cites; they have little or nothing to do with quality:

- Kleenex on a ski lift;
- Blowing feathers off a chicken;
- Putting fresh fish on ice;
- Describing an auto dealer's luxurious salesroom.

The role of knowledge, of technical skills and abilities, of professional scientific and engineering competence, of mastery of special fields, and of their role

---

[1] Tom Peters and Nancy Austin, *A Passion for Excellence* (New York: Warner Books, 1985), pp. 114–123.
[2] W.A. Shewhart, *Economic Control of the Quality of Manufactured Product* (New York: Van Nostrand, 1931), pp. 53–54.

in innovation is ignored. Peters, in *Thriving on Chaos,* lists and describes 12 traits of effective quality program. These are described in Chapter 9.

Quality is both objective and subjective. It is objective because it deals with measurements, with the observable, with facts outside personal feelings, with external material objects, with objects and events that two independent observers can agree upon, with sense perceptions. It is subjective because it is affected by what arises from the mind, by the reactions of the nervous system, by what originates from within. More traits of the objective and the subjective are listed below.

Objective	*Subjective*
• measurements	• feelings
• counts	• emotions
• data	• motivation
• formulas	• expectations
• problems	• satisfaction
• control charts	• needs
• samples	• preferences
• defects	• attitudes
• errors	• ambitions
• idle time	• pride
• downtime	• values
• delay time	• goals
• cost	• hopes
• production	• ideals
• methods	• fear
• processes	• cooperation
• graphs	• courtesy
• tallies	• manners
• techniques	• perceptions
• product	• purpose

UNIQUE CHARACTERISTICS OF SERVICE INDUSTRIES

Face-to-face relations exist between employee and customer. Services are characterized by a personal face-to-face encounter between employee and customer, between the seller and the buyer. There are no intermediaries, no middlemen. This fact puts a very important direct responsibility for quality of service on the employee, and an indirect responsibility on supervision and management. It creates a human relations situation which must be given top priority in any quality control program.

A large number of people are involved. By far the greatest number of people involved in services are the customers, but the 70 million employees themselves are customers and buyers of several kinds of services. Knowledge of a customer's preferences, likes, dislikes, desires, and needs, and the wide variation in these demands, are of paramount importance.

Many money transactions are made. The large number of people generates a large volume of transactions which can take place daily, weekly, or monthly. Most of these transactions are for relatively small amounts of money. The large volume of transactions means that the probability of making errors is substantial.

Large masses of paper are generated. The large number of transactions generates a large volume of paper records such as sales slips, bills, checks, credit cards, premiums, claims, meter readings, and tickets, all of which are subject to human error.

Service failure can be due to human failure, equipment failure, or both. This occurs because some services are subject to both human reliability and equipment reliability. Examples are found in electric power plants, health services, transportation, and service companies using computer systems. These require extra care so that human reliability and equipment reliability are both 100 percent. Safety must be at the top of the list of quality characteristics in health, transportation, power plants, and any other industry where human life is at stake.

There is no mechanical control over variation, as in a factory. All kinds of precision instruments and machinery are used to control and limit variation in a product measurement in a factory. There is no such equipment or machinery in a service industry, with some exceptions. The use of MICR checks in banking, subtracting cash registers, and the product scanning system in supermarkets all tend to reduce errors and improve service.

Computer systems require special controls. Computer systems require special controls over the input data and the computer program to prevent two major sources of errors. There are other sources of failure which can only be revealed by an intensive study of all computer operations from the collection of the input data to the examination of final readouts.

Process control should be used to improve quality, not freeze the status quo. Process control in a factory assumes the existence of a mechanically controlled system that keeps successive measurements within tolerance limits. It is tied to machine capability. Both low and high values falling outside these limits are subject to close scrutiny.

In services where processes are carried out by people, the use and interpretation are different, as the following situations reveal: human capability, not machine capability, rules.

- A low error rate may be due to a better method or an improved method.
- A reduced amount of time may also be due to employees working smarter.
- A large volume of acceptable work may also indicate the use of better procedures or improved methods.

An out-of-control point may be a winner. Adhering to some process limits may be simply accepting an inefficient procedure or a mediocre performance. The emphasis should not be on freezing process limits but on improving the process.

The following characteristics account for most of the quality problems and costs of poor quality in services: defects in products purchased, human errors and mistakes, wasted or lost time, unacceptable human behavior, too high a price, damage and loss, customer complaints, lost customers, failure, unsafe conditions or practices.

Quality as Fitness for Use and Conformance to Specifications

Quality as fitness for use and quality as conformance to specifications are concepts developed and used in manufacturing. They should be used with extreme caution even in manufacturing, and more so in applying them to services. A customer wants a car that is reliable, has a low life-cycle cost, doesn't have to be repaired every few months, and passes the pollution test. A lemon is fit for use, but who wants a lemon?

The reason why these concepts are not applicable to services is simple: Services are faced at every turn with *individual human differences;* manufacturing is not. A drug that works for one person may not work for another. A tranquilizer may be effective for one person but not for another. The same is true of pain killers, blood pressure medicines, and sleeping pills. There are wide variations in preferences for food, clothing, housing, transporation, and entertainment.

The nature and form of the service have to be adapted to age differences, size differences, sex differences, and income differences, just to name a few. The "customer" and the "market" include hundreds if not thousands of different groups of people.

Despite what Victor Kiam says on television, the Remington Micro-Screen shaver may not shave as close as a blade for all men. For some men this shaver fails, whereas a blade shaver such as the Gillette does not. This means that the manufacturer's specifications fail to meet the needs of *all* customers.

The Road to Acceptable Quality

We do not get high quality directly. High quality is obtained by getting rid of the causes of poor quality. The term "quality improvement" implies that quality is obtained by a series of progressive steps. Shewhart's assignable causes of out-of-control points are much more common than causes of random variation. This is why it is hard to obtain a condition of statistical control in which non-random variations have been eliminated. This is true for a characteristic which must be stabilized; it is not true of a characteristic whose only acceptable level is zero. Gosset (Student) put the problem succinctly in 1934 when he

Table 3–1. **How Quality of Services is Determined—Multiple Response of 1,005 Persons**

1. Courteous or polite behavior	21%			
2. Satisfy your needs	18			
3. Past experience	13			
4. Recommendations by others	12		*Condensed Table*	
5. Promptness	12			
6. Price	11		Employee behavior, attitudes,	
7. Attitude of personnel	10		competence	67%
8. Helpful personnel	9		Satisfy needs	18
9. Friendliness	8		Time (promptness, quick service)	12
10. Reputation	7		Price	11
11. Advertising	6		Experience	13
12. Personal attention	6		All other	58
13. Cleanliness	6			179%
14. Trouble-free, accuracy	6			
15. Efficiency of staff	4			
16. Dependability	3			
17. All other	27			
Total	179%			

stated that the real issue was the reconciliation of random mathematics with biased data.

Quality of Services According to a Gallup Poll[3]

Gallup's poll of 1005 persons nationwide during 1985 not only verifies what many thought about the quality of services but also throws light on several aspects. Table 3–1 shows how the 1005 persons interviewed determined the quality of a service; a condensation is shown. Tables 3–2 and 3–3 show the reasons given by 593 persons for the poor quality of services received during the past year or two.

In Table 3–1, Items 1, 7, 8, 9, 12, 14, 15, and 16 are combined because they deal directly with employee behavior, attitudes, and competence. These figures show that the respondents put the responsibility for quality of services directly on the shoulders of the employee. Other items such as "satisfy your needs," "recommendation by others," "reputation," "advertising," and "cleanliness" have implications involving employees but were left as shown

---

[3] *Consumer Perceptions concerning the Quality of American Products and Services* conducted for the American Society for Quality Control, The Gallup Organization (Princeton, NJ: September 1985), pp. 39–40.

Table 3–2. Reasons Given for Poor Quality of Service

1. Work not done right	39%	
2. Too slow	30	
3. Too expensive	20	
4. Indifferent personnel	20	*Condensed Table*
5. Unqualified personnel	12	
6. Lack of courtesy	10	Employee behavior, attitudes,
7. Poor service (unspecified)	10	competence 81%
8. Lack of personnel	5	Time (too slow) 30
9. Poor scheduling	4	Price (too expensive) 20
10. Reservation problems	2	All other 35
11. Poor food	2	Total 166%
12. Miscellaneous	11	
13. No answer	1	
Total	166%	

in the report. The catchall class includes availability, convenience, company name (which is the same as reputation), variety of services, goodness of services, length of time in business, miscellaneous, and no answer (8 percent).

The condensed table shows that employee behavior, attitudes, and competence are far out in front as criteria for determining quality of services. Time and price together are next, followed by need satisfaction and experience.

During this poll the 1005 persons interviewed were asked if during the past year or two they ever used a service of any kind that they thought was of poor quality or needed improvement. Of the 1005 persons, 56 percent answered "yes," 42 percent answered "no," and 2 percent gave no answer. This means

Table 3–3. Reasons for Poor Quality by Service Industry

Reason	Total %	Auto Rep	Bank	Insur	Govt	Hosp	Airlines
1. Work not done right	39%	63%	19%	12%	19%	9%	5%
2. Employee behavior, etc	42	15	45	39	44	60	32
3. Too slow	30	19	29	31	40	23	8
4. Too expensive	20	26	7	18	0	20	0
5. Poor service	10	5	15	8	6	6	3
6. Lack of personnel	5	1	6	1	6	12	0
7. All other	20	5	9	13	12	17	72*
Number of interviews	593	256	104	96	91	83	52

*Poor scheduling 42%, reservations 15%

that 563 individuals reported a service of poor quality or one that needed improvement. The specific reasons are given in Table 2, with a condensation showing that the great majority gave only one reason. (The publication gives 593 "interviews.")

In this same poll the 1005 persons were asked a similar question about buying poor-quality products. The number reporting poor-quality products was 534, compared with 593 reporting poor-quality services. The chief reasons for poor-quality products were not durable, fell apart or broke down, poor performance, and poor workmanship; 6 percent gave no answer. Clearly the reasons for poor-quality products are entirely different from those given for poor-quality services.

In Table 3–2, Items 1, 4, 5, and 6 are combined to give the classification "employee behavior, attitudes, and competence." It is quite likely that "poor service" also relates to a problem associated with employees, but it was not included.

The data in Table 3–2 show that the reasons given for poor quality by the 593 respondents match very closely the specific criteria used to determine quality of services given by the entire group of 1005. (See Table 3–1.)

The condensed table shows that employee behavior, attitudes, and competence as a class are overwhelmingly first, followed by time and price. The "no answers" were 8 percent for the entire group and 1 percent for those reporting examples of poor-quality service.

Table 3–3 gives reasons for poor-quality service for each of six industries. Auto repair is at the top for poor work. Under employee behavior, hospitals are first, banks and government second. For slowness, government is at the top, followed by insurance and banking. Auto repair and hospitals are too expensive. Airlines rank high in poor scheduling and employee behavior.

This information should lay to rest the insistent claim that services and quality of services are "intangible" and beyond human observation and identification, that customers have difficulty appraising the quality of service, that employees have little or no responsibility for quality of services rendered, and that services and products are identical.

This survey shows that 51% reported poor-quality products and 56% poor-quality services. Extrapolated, that means that at least 50 million persons complained about poor-quality products and at least 50 million persons complained about poor-quality services. The task of improving quality is both immediate and stupendous.

INTERPRETATION OF THE GALLUP POLL

The findings are very enlightening. The respondents had no difficulty stating what constituted poor service, thus refuting the notion that services are intangible. The reasons they give for poor service, and their view on what constituted quality characteristics of services, had no connection with the quality characteristics of products. They had no trouble sharply differentiating services from products. Some of the very important characteristics of quality of services, such as personnel, time, and price, are largely, if not entirely, ignored by those interested in product quality. This is more evidence that quality of services cannot be equated with the quality of products.

The principal ways in which quality is perceived or measured are given here in rank order. Courtesy, politeness, attitude, helpfulness, personal attention, and personality have all been combined under "personnel":

1. Personnel attitude and behavior
2. Satisfy needs (do what they're supposed to do)
3. Past experience (have to try it)
4. Promptness (quick service, time)
5. Price (affordable, good deals)

The reasons given by the 593 who report some experience with poor service match the above list quite closely:

1. Personnel behavior
2. Work not done right
3. Too slow (time)
4. Price (too expensive)

"Personnel" is placed first because it combines "indifferent personnel," "lack of courtesy," "unqualified personnel," and "lack of personnel." "Poor service" may also involve personnel. "Work not done right" largely involved auto repairs. Government, banking, and insurance were at the top of the list of those that were "too slow." Hospitals and government were at the top for indifferent personnel. Banking and insurance were at the top for unqualified personnel. Hospitals and banking were leaders among those showing lack of courtesy. Banking was at the top for "poor service."

This study shows that the customer places the most emphasis on three attributes associated with quality of service: the attitudes and behavior of personnel, including inabilty to do the work right, the time required to render the service, and the price charged.

This means that Dr. Deming's 14 points for manufacturing have to be modified for service industries to include at least the three characteristics just mentioned: personnel behavior, time, and price. The customer will not let the individual employees (personnel) hide behind the 85–15 ratio, even if it is true. The fact that management is responsible for the poor service the customer is receiving does not change the situation as far as the customer is concerned. He or she is *not* buying the service from top management or from a supervisor, but from individuals who are performing the service. Top-level management may be 1,000 or 2,000 miles away. Do we insist on a poor-quality hot line directly to top-level management wherever they are? They would never buy any such idea, regardless of how they defend quality as a major goal.

In many service operations and industries such as retail trade, repair, transportation, and health, the employee *is not responsible* for the quality of the *product* that he or she is selling or using, but *is responsible* for the quality of *service* rendered. This point seems to have been overlooked, no doubt because this situation is quite foreign to the factory.

This survey supported many statements made for years about quality of services:

- Services and quality of services are not intangible, elusive, or subtle. They are observable, identifiable, and can be explained.
- Employee behavior and attitudes are at the heart of quality of services.
- Poor-quality services can be identified as easily as poor-quality products.
- Six percent "no answer" for products; 1 percent gave "no answer" for services.
- The 85–15 percent division of responsibility for quality of products does not apply to quality of services.
- Quality of services is not equal to, nor the same as, quality of products.

Safety, a very significant quality characteristic, is not mentioned in the survey. No doubt this may be due to the relative infrequency of serious accidents and disasters. However, the fatal consequences that result when they do occur mean that safety is of vital importance in several important industries such as health, transportation, power plants, chemicals, and construction.

Nor has safety received any attention in any of the discussions of the quality of either products or services. One exception is the top priority given to safety by the Japan Air Lines.[4]

The Cost of Poor Quality in Services

The magnitude of the savings that can arise from a quality program can easily be seen by visualizing what would happen if all the losses due to the negative quality characteristics are eliminated. Nine of the major causes are listed:

- Defects in purchased products;
- Wasted and lost time;
- Customer complaints;
- Damage, warranties, lawsuits;

---

[4] A.C.Rosander, *Applications of Quality Control in the Service Industries* (Milwaukee and New York: ASQC Quality Press, Marcel Dekker, 1985), pp. 87–90.

- Human errors or mistakes;
- Unacceptable human behavior;
- Lost customers;
- High cost;
- Preventable accidents.

It would be noted that all of these losses occur in manufacturing as well as in services. In the latter, they run into the billions of dollars every year. The savings attributable to a continuous quality improvement program in all of the service industries can equal, if not exceed, the savings due to a quality improvement program in manufacturing. A continuous, not a one-shot, improvement program is needed.

Fallacies about Quality of Services

The first step is to get rid of a host of fallacies that pervade quality of services. The major ones are as follows:

- Quality of products and services are identical.
- Quality in the factory is the same as quality in the office.
- Management is responsible for employees' errors and mistakes.
- Quality of services is intangible.
- Human error is random.
- Service operations can be treated as though they were manufacturing operations.

QUALITY CHARACTERISTICS
Two Basic Types of Characteristics

In identifying and measuring characteristics of quality of services, two basic types need to be distinguished: the first type is controlled and stabilized at one level, although improvement changes this level. The second type is a characteristic whose goal is zero (0) and which is continuously being driven to that goal. It is not stabilized, although stabilization is still common practice. These two types are illustrated in Figure 3–1, Parts A and B.

The stabilized characteristic illustrated in Figure 3–1A is a measurement that often needs to be increased or decreased. It is stabilized only temporarily. Examples are absenteeism, delivery times, time to do a job, turnover, mail delivery time, time to fill a position, transaction time, time equipment is idle, percent utilization of machinery and equipment, percent utilization of workers, daily production, and daily production of acceptable product. Stability of these characteristics is rarely natural. Stability has to be created by statistical control and by elimination of assignable causes.

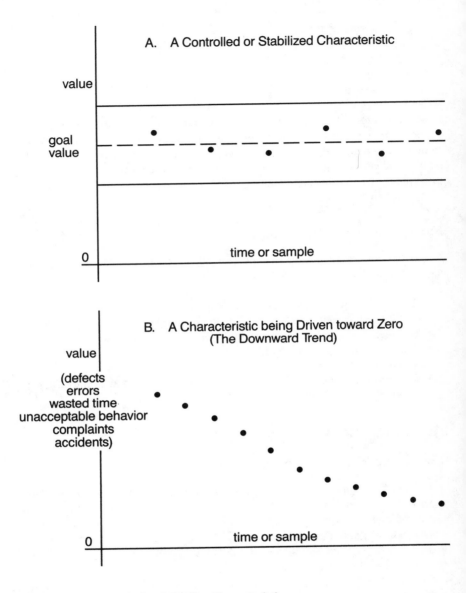

Figure 3–1. **Two Kinds of Quality Characteristics**

The second set of characteristics includes those that need to be driven to a level of zero (0). These are the negative aspects of quality that we are trying to get rid of. The major examples are the same as those given above: defects in purchased products, human errors, mistakes, and blunders, wasted or lost time, unacceptable human behavior and attitudes, customer complaints, lost customers, poor quality data, preventable accidents and unsafe conditions, too high a price, and preventable damage and loss.

The practice of trying to stabilize error rates at 5 percent, 2 percent, or even 1 percent should be stopped. Numerous examples from a wide variety of situations show that it is much easier to drive error or defective levels to zero than many persons believe. Here are three examples from three industries:

- Insurance claims 7%, down to 0.5%;
- Mail orders 5%, down to 0.7%;
- Blemished auto tires 6%, down to 1%.

In every case the 6 or 7 percent was thought to be the "best we can do."

Acceptable Quality Behavior

The Gallup Poll for the American Society for Quality Control shows that employee behavior and attitudes are the major determinant of the quality of services, based on the interviews with 1,005 persons. These traits can be divided into three classes, with examples in each class:
Behavior:

- Acting promptly
- Listening carefully
- Being attentive
- Acting with understanding
- Making to-the-point explanations
- Avoiding unusual ways of talking
- Showing ability to do the job
- Getting along with people

Attitudes:

- Courteous
- Friendly
- Mannerly
- Kind
- Conversational
- Alert
- Accurate
- Concerned
- Responsible

Appearance:

- General appearance
- Grooming generally
- Clothing—fit, color, style
    trousers
    suit, jacket
    dress, hose
    shirt
    necktie
- Shoes
- Hair
- Beard
- Cleanliness

Quality of service may also be improved not only by wearing proper clothes and by careful grooming, but by giving employees a certain prestige through unique symbols of identification:

- Uniforms;
- Special jackets;
- Special caps or hats;
- Special coveralls;
- Special smock.

This not only gives employees a feeling of importance but may also impress some customers with the distinctive and businesslike way in which services are performed.

Customers may like to do business with well-dressed and distinctive-appearing persons. Many companies stress conservative dress among both men and women. Some of us no doubt think that airline service was much better in earlier days when the stewardesses wore very distinctive and attractive uniforms. (True, the requirements that had to be met were much stiffer in those days, such as height and training.)

Who Benefits from Quality Improvements?

It is possible for a company to improve quality but not have this reflected in any gain for the customer. Eliminating all kinds of internal failures such as errors, defects, and wasted time will reduce the costs of the company but may not be reflected in any better service to the customer. Just because a manufacturing company saves $1 million annually in the cost of production by means of a quality improvement program does not mean that the customer will necessarily receive a better product at a reduced price. The company may simply glorify profits on an annual basis rather than on a quarterly basis.

Four parties can gain from a quality improvement program:

1. The company. A quality improvement program reduces the cost of production. If this is large enough,
   - Profits increase;
   - Dividends may increase;
   - Wages and salaries may increase;
   - Prices to customers may decrease, although this is not a sure thing;
   - Reputation is enhanced.
2. The employees may or may not get increases in pay due to increased productivity.
   - Morale may be improved.
   - Turnover may be decreased.
3. The customers:
   - Benefits may *not* be in form of reduced prices.
   - Benefits may be derived from a better product with lower life cycle costs (operating, repair, maintenance), higher reliability, less trouble, better satisfaction. This will happen only if the quality of the product is greatly improved.
4. The vendors gain through better, steadier market, higher profits, enhanced reputation.

Two Cases

Dr. Deming describes how the Nashua Company saved millions of dollars by reducing the thickness of the coating applied to paper. Two questions arise:

1. Was the customer conscious of a "better-quality" paper, or was "better quality" simply the manufacturer's perception? Was the "better quality" simply due to the fact that the manufacturer found a more profitable way to coat the paper?

2. Was the reduced cost of production passed on, or was it simply a way of increasing the profits of the company? Were any of the benefits of this "improved quality" passed on to customers in the form of reduced prices, to employees in the form of increased wages and salaries, to the stockholders in the form of increased dividends? The question "Who benefited?" was not answered.

The Florida Power and Light Company has hundreds of quality improvement teams. One of these teams found that the billing department was making about 60,000 errors annually. Steps were taken to reduce these errors to practically zero. When this happened, who benefited? Clearly, customer complaints due to these errors were reduced if not eliminated, but what this amounted to is not disclosed. The big money gain, however, was made by the company, not by the customer. This is bound to be the case where there is a big reduction in the internal failures made by the company. Benefits of quality improvement are centered on the company, and nowhere else.

It may very well be that we will have to be satisfied with the social benefits that result from many quality improvement programs: that the company meets competition, that it stays in business, that it keeps people employed.

THE NEED FOR A NEW KIND OF CONTROL

There are situations where statistical control should be avoided and where stabilization of some measurement at a mean value $\bar{y}$ is precisely what we do not want. These situations include errors, mistakes, blunders, and all forms of wasted time. They also include employee attitudes and behavior, which dominate the quality of most services rendered to a customer.

The only level we want to set for errors, mistakes, and blunders is zero (0). The only level we want to set for wasted time is zero (0). We will not set an acceptable level for discourtesy, rudeness, indifference, or surliness. We will not set an acceptable level for employee stealing and customer shoplifting.

It is true that every service company does purchase a variety of products such as machinery, equipment, apparatus, supplies, and chemicals, all of which should meet the levels in specifications given to the vendor. Specific quality control evidence is required to show that these levels have been under statistical control.

In the service operations of the service company, however, we are not trying to stabilize a dimension of a physical object so that it will fall within tolerances and be fit to operate in a system of interchangeable parts. We are not interested in maintaining fixed levels of characteristics that need to be improved. We are interested not in maintaining a certain level but in driving values constantly downward. Ths contrast is shown in Figure 3–1, where the goal for a factory-made product is that for the dimension $y = \bar{y}$, a horizontal straight line (Figure 3–1A). In services where we are dealing with errors and wasted time, the goal is quite different: as time goes to infinity, $y = 0$ (Figure 3–1B). Infinity does not have to be very far away. It is not hard to find examples of measures which push error levels lower and lower.

Case 1

At Aldens mail order house in Chicago, daily error rates in one mail order department were posted on a huge wall chart which everybody could see. The rate was based on the number of errors found in a random sample of 100 order tickets filled each day. Errors included items, colors, and sizes (Figure 3–2).

Within a month the error rate was reduced from 4 percent to less than 1 percent. During the month specific steps were taken to concentrate on the var-

Percent Error

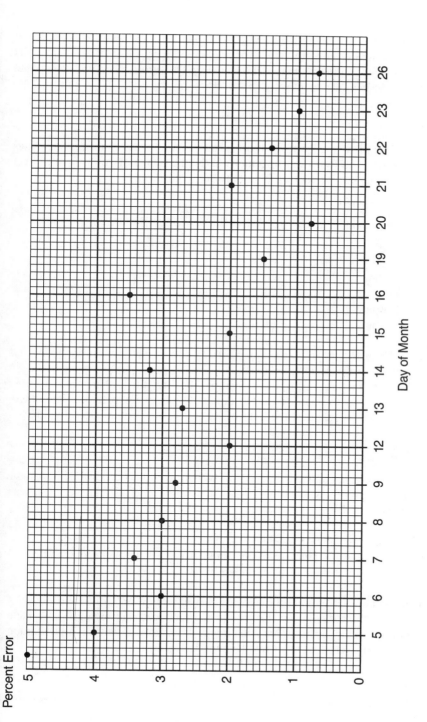

Figure 3–2. Daily Error Rate on Order Tickets for a Mail Order House for Three Weeks

ious kinds of errors being made in filling orders, and the ways to avoid them. There is no telling how low the error rate would have fallen if this effort had continued four or five months. Unfortunately the record does not show what happened during later months.

Case 2

Connell applied quality control to the reduction of errors in processing insurance claims.[5] The following operations show the reduction in error rates over a period of several weeks (see Figure 3–3):

Operation	Error Rate at Start	Error Rate at End
Coding 1	7.0%	0.5%
Coding 2	3.4	1.6
Coding 3	4.7	1.3
Refunds	8.3	2.4
Hospital 1	8.4	1.1
Hospital 2	5.0	2.3

The results of the project were time saved, money saved, productivity up, and reduction in customer complaints.

This experience revealed how to improve quality still further: Find out how the clerk with the lowest error rate is doing the job, and explain it to the others with the hope that some of the improved methods will be practiced by others.

Case 3

This is the amazing case of a young woman who was a keypunch operator in a large group of keypunch operators. Her record for 11 weeks (55 days) was as follows:

- 900 cards per day, or a total of 49,535 cards;
- An error rate of eight in 1000 cards, based on a sample of about 3500 cards drawn at random from the 49,535.

Her production was double the average, her error rate only one-fourth the average. In other words, the rest of the group produced half as much and made four times as many errors. This is an unusual example of very high production combined with very low error rate (Figure 3–4).

---

[5] A.C.Rosander, *Case Studies in Sample Design* (New York: Marcel Dekker, 1977), Chapter 10.

Percent
Error

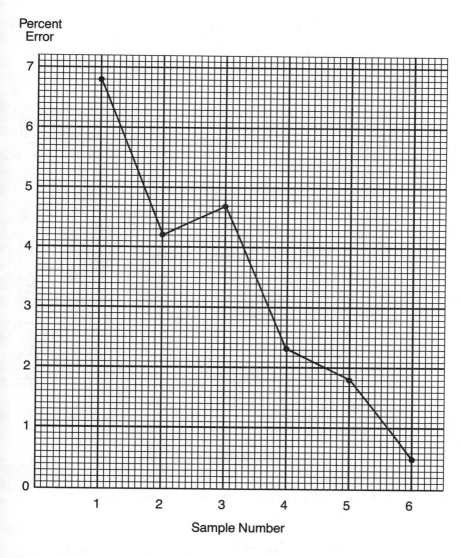

Sample Number

Figure 3–3. **Error Rate for Insurance Claims Coding**

This was very difficult work; cards were punched directly from tax returns. This young woman came to the job like the others. She received no training on the job other than an explanation of what had to be punched in the various fields on the punch card. She was in a group of keypunch operators who were paid the lowest salaries in the place. So far as we know she received no extra pay, no promotion, no recogition for her outstanding performance. On the con-

(Percent of cards in error)
Total number of cards punched = 49,535
Average number punched per week = 4,500

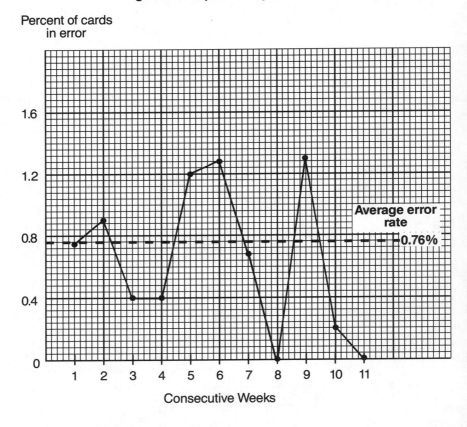

Figure 3–4. **Error Rate for a Keypunch Operator for 11 Consecutive Weeks**

trary, she was bumped from her job along with others, but later was brought back after an official interceded. Even this was little recompense for a performance which was better than two ordinary keypunch operators in her section.

We all need to learn the secret of this young woman's performance. There is no evidence that her supervisor tried to learn the secret of her high rate of production and high degree of accuracy, or to pass it on to the others.

What this performance shows is that you do not have to settle for a 5 percent error rate or a 2 percent error rate, as was being done at that time. Learning curve experience shows that it is easy to reach a temporary plateau in both errors and production, and to come to the false conclusion that ''this is the best we can do.'' Attempts to push down the error rate should be persistent and continuous, with emphasis on finding causes and removing them. It does not appear yet that we have reached the point of diminishing returns, but we need much more work on this problem. Indeed there is no evidence that eight in 1000 is the lowest error rate at which this operator can perform.

Chapter 4

Fallacies about Quality of Services

THE FALLACY OF THE FACTORY

In a recent article in a quality journal the expression "product or service" occurred no less than 20 times.[1] Obviously this meant that whatever was being written about the quality of products made in a factory applied to services in the same way. Nothing is more common or erroneous than this widespread belief that factory quality control can be applied automatically to the service industries. The point has already been discussed. There is abundant evidence to support the charge that this belief is fallacious. Consider the following format comparing a manufacturing company with a service company:

Stage	Manufacturing Company	Service Company	Remarks
1.	Buys products, materials, parts, supplies, energy, services	Buys products, materials parts, supplies, energy, services	Appear identical but are not. Purpose of purchases is different
2.	Uses purchases to *make* a product	Uses purchases to *render* a service	Different goals, processes, operations, desires
3.	Uses sales force or sales agency to sell product	May or may not use a sales force to sell services	Process of selling to customer very different
4.	Company customer buys directly; ultimate customer buys through intermediaries	Company customer buys directly or through intermediaries; ultimate customer buys directly	Great mass of services is bought directly from service company
5.	Customer is held or lost	Customer is held or lost	Follow-up on customer

---

[1] Richard A. Freund, "Definitions and Basic Quality Concepts," *Journal of Quality Technology,* Vol. 17, January 1985, 50–56.

In broad terms Stage 1 is the same for both types of companies because each is buying from vendors the same general categories of things and services. Each is concerned with purchases, vendors, receiving inspection, incoming quality, defects, products, engineering, design, meeting specifications, and production. The similarity, however, is only superficial. Stage 1 is *not* the same for services as it is for manufacturing, as the following format shows. The two use the same product or the same energy in widely different ways.

Manufacturing	*Service Company*
1. Oxygen for industrial use	1. Oxygen for medical use
2. Food for factory cafeteria	2. Food for airline, hospital, nursing home
3. X-ray for non-destructive testing	3. X-ray for medical use
4. Circuit breaker in a factory	4. Circuit breaker in a power plant or house
5. Electricity for welding, making aluminum, power motors	5. Electricity for medical apparatus, computer, toaster, dryer
6. Measuring instruments: gages, micrometers, switchboard instruments	6. Measuring instruments: clinical thermometer, blood pressure, glaucoma pressure, electrocardiograph
7. Parts for original product	7. Parts for repair

In Stage 1 quality control is applied by both companies to the vendor so that the purchased goods and services are of acceptable quality. But since the purpose is different, the quality control has to be different.

THE FALLACY THAT SERVICE = PRODUCT, THAT QC SERVICE = QC PRODUCTS

Further evidence is given below that services are not the same as products, that quality control of one is not the same as quality control of the other. Consider the following comparison:

Manufacturing	*Service Company*
1. Making an airplane	1. Using an airplane for transportation
2. Making laboratory equipment	2. Using laboratory equipment to test blood and urine samples, other chemicals
	Using laboratory equipment for other health purposes

	Manufacturing		Service Company
3.	Making a drug	3.	Using a drug in a doctor's office, hospital, nursing home, or home
4.	Making a computer	4.	Using a computer for business research, mathematical calculations; writing a program for a computer
5.	Making an automobile	5.	Renting or leasing an automobile
6.	Making a truck or bus	6.	Using a truck or bus for transportation

Quality control over the actual production of the product is entirely different from the quality control needed when the product is put into use, as the above examples show. For example the various service operations in obtaining transportation by an airplane are entirely different from those required in the construction of that airplane. The service operations and components are of an entirely different nature from the manufacturing operations required to make it. Therefore the quality characteristics are different, and the quality program has to be entirely different. Service components cannot be equated to manufacturing processes.

In Stage 2 each company is now concerned with its major purpose, with what it sells, and whether the quality is acceptable or not. *The company is now the vendor,* not the buyer. And as far as quality is concerned from the viewpoint of the customer–buyer, the company is responsible for it.

While Stage 1 is very important because it affects the quality of what occurs during Stage 2, but the real service quality problem occurs during Stage 2. Here the company must render service of such quality that it is both satisfying and affordable to the customer. In a service company Stage 1 is preparatory and supportive, because the company is a buyer. In Stage 2, which is its real business, it is a seller. Quality control must be geared to external factors, not to internal factors alone. We see persons today who are so intent on Stage 1 that they overlook or neglect Stage 2 where the real problem of quality of service lies. Furthermore by staying within Stage 1 it is easy to limit quality control to that of the factory.

THE FALLACY OF THE INTANGIBLE [2]

Products are simple or complex physical objects, or workable systems of such objects, with characteristics subject to physical and chemical measure-

---

[2] Carol A. King, "Service Quality Assurance is Different," *Quality Progress,* June 1985, 14.

ments and engineering tests. These characteristics are directly related to the quality of these products.

Services are different. Some have characteristics which can be measured or counted but rarely with precision instruments or laboratory tests. Laboratory tests of blood and urine pressure and temperature for health purposes are the exception. Other characteristics of services can only be observed. What can be measured or observed or reported is not intangible. The Gallup Survey described in the preceding chapter illustrates this statement.

A service is human behavior or activity coupled with specific objects and processes, whose aim is to help people meet immediate and continuing needs. This behavior can be measured or observed. The major needs are security, health, safety, transportation, communication, energy, food, clothing, housing, repair, appearance, and professional advice. Examples of service characteristics which relate to quality, and which can be measured or observed, are the following:

Measured	*Observed*
1. number of errors	1. courtesy
2. error rate	2. cooperation
3. delay or waiting time	3. promptness
4. idle or downtime	4. reliability
5. service time	5. responsibility
6. laboratory tests e.g., blood	6. helpfulness
7. variation of human performance	7. consideration
8. learning curve: capability	8. alertness
9. learning curve: errors	9. industriousness
10. learning curve: production	10. truthfulness
11. safety record	11. honesty
12. lost customers	12. carelessness
13. blood pressure	13. indifference
14. temperature	14. rudeness

To the extent that behavior is observable and identifiable, it is tangible. Some terms now in use are certainly difficult, if not impossible, to identify objectively by observation. Probing the individual's thoughts and feelings is necessary in some cases. Examples are as follows:

1. An intangible is a company's "good will," even though it is assigned a money value
2. Ouchi's "trust"
3. Deming's "fear" (Point 8)
4. Deming's "pride" (Point 12)

Specifications can be written for the observable. Take courtesy as an example: A courteous employee 1) Reflects "welcome" attitude; 2) Shows consideration and respect for customer; 3) Listens to customer; takes friendly, helpful attitude; 4) Talks to customer; 5) Tries to understand feelings, needs, and requests of customer; 6) Explains situation to customer; 7) Sees that customer is satisfied; 8) Offers to help customer at any time; 9) Thanks customer.

THE FALLACY THAT SAFETY IS NOT AN IMPORTANT QUALITY CHARACTERISTIC OF SERVICES

Safety is never mentioned as a quality characteristic in a factory. If quality of product = quality of service, then safety is not very important in services.

Making this assumption is a dangerous mistake. What is missed is that in those service industries involving human life, safety has to be the Number One quality characteristic whose goal always has to be zero. The critical services industries include health, transportation, power plants (including nuclear power plants), and construction, whether under government contract or not.

In these industries and many others, where one employee error can be dangerous if not fatal, zero error is not a slogan; it is a "must." Management must take steps to prevent these errors at several points: during recruitment and hiring, during initial orientation and initial steps to get familiar with operations, during the performance of the operations themselves, and during error prevention and safety training courses.

In summary, safety as a quality characteristic in services implies that 1) safety is the Number One quality characteristic; 2) the goal is zero errors and zero accidents; the goal is prevention; 3) safety and error prevention are subjects of special training courses; and 4) safety and error prevention require not only care, alertness, and sound judgments, but a workable knowledge of special conditions, technical operations, warning signs, protective devices, and preventive measures.

THE FALLACY THAT THE MANUFACTURER'S PERCEPTIONS ARE BETTER THAN THE CUSTOMER'S

There are those who talk or write about the customer's perception of quality. Quality is in the mind of the viewer. The implication is that the customer's notion of quality is irrational, vague, and hazy and not to be taken seriously. This implies also that only those who make the product know what real quality is.

The perceptions of the maker of a product are not necessarily better; they are simply different. It is the difference between the perceptions of a maker of a product and the user of the product. We have already described how the quality aspects of manufacturing a product are entirely different from the quality aspects of rendering a service with that product.

It is only fair to point out that improvements in many products came from the technical staffs of the manufacturer, not from the customer. The automobile is an example. The improvement in tires, starting, and comfort came from technical people and engineers, not from the customer. In all three of these areas quality was greatly improved, to the advantage of the customer.

There are percepts and concepts, both of which are involved in quality. A percept is an awareness or impression of an object through the senses. Examples are color, smell, noise, shape, size, touch, pressure, comfort (feeling), and taste.

Concepts are abstractions, thoughts, ideas, and mental constructs. Examples are force, cost, price, value, satisfaction, life, reliability, efficiency, productivity, and safety.

The designer no less than the customer-buyer perceives quality. The stylist may make a clay model of a new automobile contour without regard to what customers prefer. Many of the percepts and concepts of the engineer and the customer may be expressed in the same language, but the interpretations may be different.

- The color preferences may not be the same;
- The customer may prefer different arrangements of meters, instruments, controls;
- They may disagree on size and shape;
- The cost of the one may not agree with affordable price of the other;
- The life-cycle costs are very important to the customer but not to the company.

A list of percepts and concepts shows how the manufacturer and the customer may be alike in a few ways, but widely different in many other ways:

Manufacturer		Customer-buyer	
Percepts	Concepts	Percepts	Concepts
appearance	profit	color	fastness of color
color	cost	size	price
size	strength	fit	economy
shape	force	comfort	length of life
feel	length of life	appearance	life-cycle cost
noise	speed	noise	operating cost
component parts	acceleration	sound	maintenance cost
physical arrangement	torque	looks	trade-in value
assembly	temperature	smell, odor	repairability
fit	durability	taste	style

Manufacturer		Customer-buyer	
Percepts	*Concepts*	*Percepts*	*Concepts*
taste	nutrition	feel	nutrition
looks	measurement	shine	reliability
handling	functioning	handling	cost of living
smoothness	accuracy	breakage	safety

Interpretations of the same word may be very different, as in the following examples. *Color:* The customer is interested in fastness, in colors that do not fade in the sun or wash out in water. *Fit:* The customer is interested in shoes and clothing that fit. A manufacturer may not produce sizes that fit the small or large person but only the large middle group. Or if the manufacturer produces these sizes, the retail store may not carry them. Shoes are pointed, although the human foot is not this shape. Good-fitting shoes and clothing then become difficult, if not impossible, to buy ready-made. *Cost:* The producer is interested in cost regardless of the customer. May cater to the high-priced market. May cut costs and produce shoddy and poor-quality products. Customer is interested in what he or she can afford. May be forced to buy in thrift shops, second-hand stores. *Nutrition:* Producer's nutrition may be a synthetic, may be in additives, may be greatly exaggerated. Customer may be interested in more naturally nutritious foods; may find that most nutritious foods are not those highly advertised. The manufacturing process may destroy nutrition so that additives are used to put back what the manufacturing process has eliminated.

THE FALLACY THAT SALESMANSHIP AND ADVERTISING IMPROVE QUALITY

We return now to the comparison of the four stages characterizing a manufacturing company and a service company, and consider Stage 3, which deals with sales. Here we find another difference between a factory and a service. One of the major characteristics of manufacturing is the sales force, the sales agency, and the practice of salesmanship. The title of a paperback book expresses this philosophy in its most blatant and brazen form: HOW TO SELL ANYTHING TO ANYBODY. If salesmanship can overcome the resistance of the customer, of great masses of people, to various products, there is no need to pay any attention to the quality of the product. Simply produce the product that management, design engineers, and production engineers specify, and leave the selling job to the sales department or agency. Quality control, then, is simply seeing that production conforms to the specifications that the factory people prescribe. The customer must be sold, not listened to. The customer must be bombarded with sales talks and gimmicks until his or her resistance is broken down.

Stage 3 does exist in some service industries, but is found primarily in retail trade. Other examples are insurance agencies, branch banks, authorized service companies such as IBM, and chain hotels, motels, restaurants, cafeterias. The customer-buyer has always been important in retail trade. Sears Roebuck discovered the importance of the customer when it was only a mail order company, in about 1900 or even before. Detroit didn't discover it until 1985. A top-level automobile executive states: "We've redefined quality in terms of the customer's needs and wants."[3] This is what quality has meant to most service companies for a long time. Quality has been "redefined." It would be interesting to know how they perceived quality before they "redefined" it in terms of the customer's needs and wants. Walter Shewhart, originator of statistical quality control, saw quality of products in terms of human wants and needs in the 1920s and 1930s. Obviously, many people need to read Shewhart.

THE FALLACY THAT QUALITY OF SERVICE IS AN ENGINEERING PROBLEM

Shewhart originated quality control concepts and techniques to control the dimensions of physical products. This is an engineering problem to a great extent, but statistics and probability were applied to solve it. Factory production is largely engineering because it involves forces, energy, mechanisms, and physical and chemical processes and principles. It involves the use of precision instruments and machinery.

Quality of services, except in a few cases, is not an engineering problem at all. The assumption that the quality of products is the same as quality of services leads to the belief that engineering can be applied to both. This simply is not as true as experience over the last 40 years clearly shows. With a few exceptions, the quality of services is not concerned with the dimensions, forces, mechanisms, and other concepts which are associated with the quality of products.

A major reason why quality of services has developed so slowly is that probably 95 percent or more of the professionals and others interested in statistical quality control, quality assurance, and quality improvement are factory-engineering oriented. Most members of the American Society for Quality Control fall into this group. One of the main reasons why members of ASQC are not interested in quality of services is simply that it is not an engineering field.

Service industries which are non-engineering include banking, insurance, health, retail trade, personal service, business services (with exceptions), most of the federal government, most of local and state government, hotels, and restaurants. Service industries that have engineering aspects include public utilities (gas, water, electric light and power, telephone), transportation, and government construction of all kinds (streets, roads, drains, buildings, dams, bridges).

---

[3]H.A. Poling, "The State of Quality in U.S. Today," *Quality Progress,* April 1985, 31.

Division of Responsibility for Quality

It is very important for management to make clear who is resonsible for various aspects of the quality of a product or service. If quality is everybody's business, then everyone has some responsibility for quality. The specific form of this responsibility varies widely. Individuals are responsible for the quality of the work they perform, or work which comes under their authority or jurisdiction.

Management is not only responsible for personal errors and mistakes, but for system or company-wide errors, defects, and deficiencies. From the beginning, management is responsible 100 percent for practically every aspect of the business: space, equipment, machinery, arrangements, organization, hiring of employees, furniture, supplies, processes, methods, and much more. If these are not adequate, then supervisors, professionals, specialists, clerks, blue-collar workers, and others cannot perform at an acceptable quality level. Obstacles to quality performance exist right from the beginning.

Once the agency or company is operating and the initial defects and deficiencies have been eliminated, how is the responsibility for quality divided? It is still divided in two ways:

1. Defects, errors of the system: management's responsibility;
2. Specific errors, defects: individual worker's responsibility.

The percentage division of this responsibility varies, but in the factory all writers seem to agree that most of the responsibility lies with management; three estimates are 90-10, 85-15, and 80-20. These estimates apply to factories, although perhaps not to those where dangerous products (e.g., chemicals) are being produced and where one employee error may be dangerous, destructive, or fatal.

In certain services like health and transportation, where one employee error can be not only dangerous but fatal, *these ratios do not apply.* In these industries many employees are technicians, professionals, or specialists who are employed because of their technical knowledge, special skills, or professional abilities. If they make serious errors, they must be held responsible. They should engage in safe practices without being told to do so. Examples of these specialists are as follows:

1. In health agencies: doctors, registered nurses (RNs), medical technicians, licensed practical nurses (LPNs), dentists, dental hygienists;
2. In transportation: engineers, pilots, navigators, captains, drivers, conductors, controllers, brakemen

Examples of errors of this type are described in a later chapter. The range of error therefore should be from 0-100, where the employee is totally responsible, to 50-50, where both are equally responsible, depending upon the circumstances, to 100-0, where management is totally responsible.

THE FALLACY OF THE COMPUTER AND HUMAN ERROR

Despite the many advantages of the computer, the history of the computer in practice is full of glaring errors, mistakes, faults, and disastrous failures. The major reason is that we have never imposed adequate quality control over the input, over the operation of the computer, and over the output of the computer. In addition, we have not insisted on quality control applied to all computer programming and software. Hence it is easy for serious errors to creep into the computer operation.

The computer has become the 20th Century's Number One alibi to cover up human error. These alibis, cited from actual practice, take the following form:

- The computer blew up;
- The computer made a mistake;
- The computer is obsolete; it is too old. We need a new computer;
- The computer read the wrong number;
- The computer delayed 20 minutes in giving a warning signal;
- The computer made a mistake in telling the workers that the leak was contained (The computer wasn't programmed for this chemical).

Closely related to the computer as an alibi is the practice of covering up human error. The following are some of the justifications given to excuse human error:

- It's nothing but human nature;
- We all make errors;
- It shows we are human;
- It cannot be helped;
- It doesn't happen very often;
- Our error rate is only ½ of 1 percent (base was 37 million financial records);
- Human error is not to blame—it is complex technology.

More Examples

1. "The county's computer system is outdated and overloaded. Software to expand its use is no longer being made." It is estimated that replacing the system will cost in the neighborhood of $1 million. It is used for a county's payroll, personnel records, taxes and assessments, election tabulations.

Comment: The word "outdated" should not be taken seriously. This is not buying an automobile, where interest lies in the latest model. For example, the HP-9810 is no longer made but this desk calculator with Stat Rom and 115 programs is still an excellent, fast, and reliable calculator for numerous statistical and mathematical problems. The fact that the computer is "overloaded" may simply mean that it needs more memory, which could easily be added, depending upon the computer. The fact that software is no longer being made simply means that the county doesn't have a computer programmer. If it did, he or she could easily write a program for the necessary operations. This shows how county officials who obviously know little about a computer and how it operates become the easy victims of the latest sales pitch of the computer and software manufacturers, and waste millions of dollars of tax money.

2. A Social Security official complained that their computer system was a "rambling wreck," causing errors of $1 billion a year. A new system was installed which was supposed to improve accuracy and efficiency. It is now claimed that most of the computer's ills are cured. Another official boasts that the annual benefits of 37 million recipients of Social Security are reported with an accuracy of 99.5 percent—"that's purer than Ivory Snow."—referring no doubt to the 99 44/100 in the advertisements. The Government Accounting Office, however, has surveyed these computer operations in 34 reports and tells a different story. A $115 million contract of 1800 computer terminals failed because the company never tested the system in operation. Also, it is not pointed out that a 0.5 percent error rate means 185,000 accounts in error. Nor is it pointed out that accuracy and efficiency come from programmers and operators, not automatically from the computer.

QUALITY CONTROL IN SERVICES IS NEITHER NEW NOR LIMITED TO CLERICAL WORK

Quality control applied to services did not begin in recent years. It began in 1940, when Dr. Deming applied it to the keypunching and other operations involved in processing the 1940 U.S. Census. Ballowe in 1945 used a large wall time chart to exhibit the daily error rate made by the department filling mail orders at Aldens in Chicago. In the 1950s Jones and Magruder applied quality control and other related techniques to telephone operations. At the same time Lobsinger applied these ideas and techniques to the operations of United Airlines. Later Peach applied quality control to a large retail store (Sears), while Connell applied it to the processing of insurance claims filed with Blue Cross of Western Pennsylvania. These are only a few of many examples that can be cited.

Neither is it true that there has been a sudden growth in the number and employment of companies classified in this area. For decades the number of persons employed in services has greatly exceeded the number employed in manufacturing; the ratio of three to one has existed for over 10 years. Much of the sudden interest in applying quality control to services has arisen out of the publicity that the concept of "quality" has received in connection with products manufactured by the Japanese and imported into the United States. This has led not to a study of past quality control in this country, but to a study of what the Japanese are doing. Hence the widespread adoption of "quality circles" and the techniques associated with them, which involve very elementary statistics.

There is more to services than clerical work, which usually is taken to mean the simpler office jobs of typing, filing, mailing, billing, and the like. Using the term "office work" is no better because office work can be supervisory, managerial, technical, or professional. We show below how clerical work is only one small aspect of the field of service operations. We should not let ourselves be boxed in by terms such as "quality circles" and "clerical work."

Services Involving More Than Clerical Work

Quality measure	Examples
1. Errors, error rates	1. simple clerical work: typing, filing
	2. laboratory tests: blood and urine
	3. laboratory tests: water, air, soil pollution
	4. laboratory tests: industrial
	5. complex records: tax returns, waybills, freight bills, insurance claims, mail orders
	6. computer programming
	7. computer operations
	8. service components: health, transportation, personal service (hotels, restaurants), retail trade, government, insurance, finance
2. Time (too slow)	1. transportation
delay	2. health
idle	3. repairs
down	4. mail orders
lost	
wasted	
service	
unnecessary	
3. Faults of personnel	Every service company
	1. lack of courtesy, consideration, concern, helpfulness
	2. indifference, carelessness
	3. unqualified
	4. shortage of numbers
	5. work not done right

Quality measure	*Examples*
4. Prices too high, charge too much	1. automobile repair 2. medical service, drugs
5. Human variability excessive	1. tax assessors 2. insurance policies 3. laboratories: 29 laboratories studied by Youden 4. chemists
6. Failure	1. airline crashes 2. railroad accidents, collisions 3. structures: dams, buildings, bridges, overpasses

CORRECTING FALLACIES BY EMPIRICISM—BY OBSERVING DIRECTLY SERVICE OPERATIONS

Quality of services suffers from an almost complete lack of direct observation and study of the various operations of service organizations. This direct approach is prevented because we are following the wrong road map. Several places where we go wrong are described below:

- Substituting factory notions about quality for first-hand observations of services in a company or organization;
- False reasoning by analogy from manufacturing ideas and practices instead of observing what is going on in the various operations of a service company or organization;
- Substituting opinions, conjectures, and esoteric theories about human behavior for empirics dealing with services;
- Reluctance, if not refusal, to collect acceptable-quality data that describe significant aspects of services and their components;
- Falsely classifying all service companies and organizations in the same pigeonhole;
- Creating conventional barriers to an empirical approach to services, such as the intangible syndrome, the "irrational customer" syndrome, and the institutional syndrome.

Chapter 5

What Price Human Error?

The nation is plagued with errors, mistakes, and blunders. They are found everywhere: in business, in industry, in government, in private organizations. They are found wherever people are found, whether working or playing, regardless of their activities.

The consequences go far beyond any money losses incurred by the seller and buyer of poor-quality products and poor-quality services. The full extent of the economic and social costs cannot be measured, not only because of the chain effects of errors, mistakes, and blunders but because of the human beings who are lost or injured and maimed, sometimes for life.

Errors, mistakes, and blunders include not only the errors made by a typist but the faulty judgments and decisions made by a top-level executive or professional. The latter can be much more damaging to the company or agency than the former. In some industries, however, such as health, transportation, power plants, and chemicals, employee errors can be very critical, since one error cannot only be dangerous but fatal. Employee errors in these industries are much more critical and dangerous than are employee errors made in a retail store, a bank, or the post office.

At the heart of this situation is the refusal to face up to the difficulties and dangers of the technological civilization in which we live. To meet this challenge requires both knowledge and discipline—two things that rate very low nationwide. The educational system is not interested in either one as an educational goal. The schools are not going to teach knowledge of important life-saving concepts and topics such as speed, centrifugal force, carbon monoxide, electric safety, gasoline vapor, dangerous chemicals, destructive drugs, and risky weather conditions. This would mean teaching everyone some physical science as described in physics and chemistry. Such a series of courses emphasizing important knowledge, together with accuracy, judgment based on sound principles, and ability to think in terms of the real physical world would go a long way toward preventing many of the errors, mistakes, and blunders that are committed every day, and the tragedies that result.

In this chapter many errors, mistakes, and blunders are described, some briefly but others in detail. The purpose is to show that human errors are a major cause of poor-quality performance and high costs of business and government operations. Later chapters are devoted to a description of the nature and scope of human errors; their detection and measurement; their sources; their relation to quality, productivity, and reliability; and finally, the development and implementation of an error prevention program in particular and a non-quality prevention program in general.

BANKS AND MONEY

We start with a wide variety of actual experiences of the customer-buyer of services. These show that quality of service does exist, that it is real, that it can be observed and identified, that the difference between acceptable and unacceptable quality service is readily determined, and that the customer-buyer knows when he or she is not receiving service of acceptable quality. There is no mystery about it.

Case 1

A businessman deposits $1,842 in his checking account in a large bank. It is recorded by the bank as $18.42, and consequently the customer is penalized for overdrawing his account. He explains to the bank clerks what happened, but no correction is made. He spends considerable time trying to convince the bank that they made an error, all to no avail. Finally he sues the bank for wasting his time by being away from his business, and wins.

Case 2

In buying a house through a realtor, a party borrows a large sum of money from a large mortgage company. In the final settlement the real estate company includes the first month's payment of $314 in the settlement. The mortgage company's computer, however, is not programmed this way. The householder receives notices of non-payment and penalty statements. It takes repeated calls to the real estate company and the mortgage company—and months of time—to correct the error.

Case 3

A customer goes to a bank where he has a checking account and asks for $300 in connection with a withdrawal. He requests ten $20 bills and ten $10 bills. The teller gives him three $100 bills. The customer has to explain a second and third time that $(10 \times 20) + (10 \times 10) = 300$. The teller clearly is unfamiliar with this way of asking for $300. Was she listening or was she ignoring the customer? Or was this a case of "doing your own thing" and the customer be hanged? One thing was clear: the teller didn't understand simple arithmetic.

Case 4

Because of improper handling of billing errors, Citibank of New York City has agreed to pay damages to all customers who have been subject to inconvenience, embarrassment, and suspension of credit card privileges.[1] State Attorney General Robert Abrams says that Citibank will pay damages of $50 to any Visa or MasterCard holder who can document that his or her complaint of a billing error was not properly handled. Abrams says that about 100 customers are now entitled to the payments and that the number is expected to rise to 500, resulting in an estimated $25,000 liability for the bank. Citibank has agreed to pay $50 to each customer whose rights under the law are violated in the future. All documented complaints must be forwarded to the bank within 90 days.

This situation raises several questions. What strikes one is the mere pittance and the identical amount that Citibank is paying to compensate customers for all kinds of errors by the bank, regardless of the magnitude and seriousness of the error.

The bank has "agreed" to pay damages. The State Attorney General is not enforcing a law that apparently is on the books and which should provide for damages commensurate with the magnitude, seriousness, and lost time that the errors create. This sounds like the usual "slap on the wrist" kind of treatment for large and influential parties to a court case.

The customer has to prove that his or her rights under the "law" are violated, and the individual has only 90 days to make a documented report. Obviously the entire case is loaded in favor of the bank that made the error, not the individual. It may very well be that the law needs to be changed so that the individual receives ample protection and compensation for loss of time, inconvenience, and other penalties imposed because of the error by the bank. The least that can be said is that this decision is a move in the right direction. Companies should be required to compensate customers for the errors by the company even if it requires a law to force them to do so.

Case 5

Canceled checks can save the customer from the errors made by the faulty accounting systems of both private business and government. In the following examples, canceled checks were a life saver. They show why the customer should fight to the bitter end any attempt by banks to abolish the bank-check system:

- An insurance company threatens to cancel health insurance because it claims that premiums already paid are in arrears. It takes three canceled checks to convince this company that they have made a major error.

---

[1] *The Denver Post,* January 22, 1982.

- A well-known book jobber double bills for books which have already been paid for. The customer also has to make a detailed accounting of the books bought in order to convince the company that all of them have been paid for—by check.
- A well-known magazine does not mail a gift subscription which is already paid for by the advance payment requested.
- A canceled check saves a substantial part of a man's Social Security. When this individual checks with the local Social Security office, he discovers that the self-employment Social Security tax of about $500, paid as part of his 1972 income taxes, has not been credited to his account. A copy of Form 1040, a copy of Form SE, and a copy of the canceled check sent to Internal Revenue Service are necessary to clear up the matter and correct the Social Security account.

RETAIL TRADE

Case 1

A change has taken place in a characteristic of men's clothing that is important to many people: comfort in hot weather when temperatures are between 90 and 100 degrees. Apparently lightweight summer clothes for men went out decades ago. There was a time when men could purchase lightweight shirts, lightweight hose, summer oxfords, and Palm Beach suits, but no more. Now we have "all-weather" clothes for men, permanent press, polyester shirts, tight stretch socks, and "one size for all." Comfort as a quality characteristic has disappeared. Even in the hot, sultry climates of United States, stores do not sell any special lightweight clothing for summer. Apparently it is assumed that men will spend all of their time in air-conditioned rooms, automobiles, and offices, but there are thousands, if not millions, who do not live under these ideal conditions.

Case 2

One might think that the quality of foods is not observable and hence is intangible. Not so. It is true that the word "crisp" has a vague and ethereal meaning when used by salespeople to convince the customer that whatever is "crisp" must be good-quality foods. It is difficult, if not impossible, for a customer to distinguish crisp lettuce, crisp carrots, and crisp apples from lettuce, carrots, and apples that are not crisp. To many, this is an example of the "intangible," but it is a sales creation, not a perception of the customer.

An old-time favorite that has gone down in quality and up in price in many stores, bakeries, and restaurants is apple pie. The evidence is clear: chunks of apple that are partly raw because they are not cooked enough, a poor grade of apples including what appear to be chunks of tough and tasteless dried apples, lots of filler, a dearth of apples, and usually a tough crust.

The specifications for a good quality apple pie can be listed; there is nothing intangible about them:

- made from good ripe apples, e.g., Jonathans;
- finely sliced—no chunks;
- plenty of apples and no filler;
- baked until the apples are done—not raw;
- no tough, rubbery crusts.

It is very easy for a customer to identify an apple pie of acceptable quality, but not without eating a piece of it. The customer cannot tell by looking at the outside of a pie whether it is of acceptable quality or not although a keen eye may see a difference. The same is true of other prepared foods such as fried chicken (none of this deep dried stuff where very little chicken meat is left), and strawberry shortcake (this is not a half a dozen strawberries on a fluffy cake).

If a person has never eaten good apple pie, fried chicken, or strawberry shortcake, he or she is likely to consider acceptable quality the very inferior product now being sold at numerous hotels, restaurants, fast-food places, and other establishments. This is the illusion that whatever is being sold, especially in large quantities, must be acceptable quality. Just because something is sold does not mean that it is any good. People buy this food and even think it is wonderful because they have never eaten anything better.

Case 3

A customer buys a pair of comfortable shoes which are padded and are the most comfortable shoes he has ever purchased, in view of a problem with a broken big toe. He discovers when the heels wear down a little and need some repairing that this $35 pair of shoes cannot be repaired! Surprise! Fortunately, the heels are not worn down too much, so that nylon heel plates can be attached. This is an eye-opener to the customer. Hereafter before he buys a pair of shoes he is going to make sure that they can be repaired. Was this drastic change based on a customer survey? On the manufacturer's superior perceptions?

Case 4

A customer buys a $16 necklace at a well-known department store. Later, when she attempts to wear it, she finds that the clasp is broken and that the two parts are fastened together by transparent tape. Someone, either in the factory or in the store, had patched up a piece of damaged merchandise. She took it back and received a replacement.

Case 5

A customer at a cafeteria of a well-known chain asks for a double serving of mashed potatoes. The person serving doesn't understand, so the customer has to explain what "double" means. At another time a customer asks for the same order as the person ahead of him. Again, the server doesn't understand what "the same" means. It has to be explained. Are these servers functional illiterates who don't understand the meaning of words "double" and "the same"? Is this the thorny road to quality that Dr. Deming refers to? It seems so.

HOTEL ACCOMMODATIONS

Case 1

A couple checks into a well-known hotel in a large city. The weather has been cold, and the room reflects it. The heat is turned on, but apparently the individual unit is not working very effectively. A call is made to the engineer, who comes up and adjusts the controls. The next day the room is still cool. A call is made, and another engineer comes up. The temperature doesn't improve, so the boss of the engineers comes up. He asks the occupants what they want. "A comfortable room" is the answer, with a temperature of about 72°. Apparently the installation needs a complete overhauling, if not replacement. The fan doesn't work very well, so it takes hours to heat the room. The customers are the guinea pigs. The engineers can do nothing because the trouble is a fault of the system. Only a higher-level decision could correct this situation. To the question "Wasn't this room checked out to see that the heating system worked?" there was no answer. Regardless of the very good intentions and pleasant attitudes of all the employees, there was nothing they could do to satisfy the customer. The heating facilities in each room obviously had not been checked out.

Case 2

This is a situation similar to that in Case 1, except that in this case the room was heated by a hot-water radiator during the winter in a large city hotel. The engineer worked on the radiator and the rest of the system for two days. Meanwhile, the occupants went elsewhere to keep warm. On the last day, when they were about to leave, the engineer finally got the radiator to work, so the room was quite warm when the guests left. Once more the guests are the guinea pigs who report the trouble, although they are paying a high price for which they should receive a comfortable room.

Case 3

This is the case of a hotel room that was in a cul-de-sac so poorly lighted that the keyholes in that end of the corridor were hard to see. A key had to be used by blindly feeling around in order to unlock the door. This was a very expensive hotel, but apparently nobody considered in the design of the hotel that locks should be illuminated. The convenience of the customer was ignored.

HUMAN VARIATIONS IN LABORATORY TESTS

Case 1

Clinical laboratories which operate across state lines come under federal regulation because of the power of Congress to regulate interstate commerce. It is estimated that between 10,000 and 15,000 laboratories are subject to some kind of regulation or inspection by federal, state, or private medical agencies. The Health Care Finance Administration within the Health and Human Services Department has federal authority over regulated laboratories. (It is estimated that tens of thousands of laboratories in private doctors' offices, or laboratories connected therewith, are outside any and all control by any agency.) The Bureau of Laboratories of the Center for Disease Control in Atlanta conducts the laboratory tests for the Health Care Finance Administration.

The latest report issued in 1980 shows that the error rate found in the testing of urine, blood, and other laboratory procedures was 14 percent, based on about 3,000 laboratories. While this sounds like a shockingly high error rate, and is high for such critical health tests, it is a great improvement over the 25 percent error rate found in 1970! No evidence is given to tell what these errors are, or how serious. The five reasons cited for the 14 percent error rate, however, were given:

- Incompetence of laboratory personnel;
- Bad management;
- Sloppy supervision;
- No quality control; and
- Bad reagents (very likely faulty or impure chemicals used for test purposes).

With these serious faults, one wonders why the laboratories were allowed to operate. CDC can close down a laboratory until the cause or causes are eliminated. The least CDC can do is to insist upon the following:

- Qualified laboratory personnel;
- Quality control procedures and practices;

- Competent managers and supervisors; and
- Pure reagents.

Case 2

The late W. J. Youden of the National Bureau of Standards used two different materials to test the precision and bias of 29 different laboratories. The measurement for Material A and the measurement for Material B constituted one point on rectangular graph paper. (If the two materials had been random samples of the same material, which they were not, then the points would have tended to fall on a 45-degree line.)[2]

The 29 laboratories would create 29 points which would tend to fall, in theory at least, on a line drawn through the origin $(x = 0, y = 0)$, and would be equally distributed within four quadrants formed by the intersection of two perpendicular lines through the mean or median. This would be true if the measurements made by the laboratories differed only because of random variations, and if the biases or constant errors due to various causes were zero or negligible.

Furthermore, if the two measurements for each laboratory, x and y, were independent and normally distributed, then the points would tend to fall within a circle drawn with an appropriate radius depending upon the probability assigned, using the means as a center. This is what Youden did except that he used the medians, not the means, of the two measurements.

By using the medians and the mean differences, Youden found that 11 laboratories fell outside a circle representing the 95 percent limit. By using the means and analysis of variance, the author found that 10 laboratories fell outside the 95 percent limits. Four laboratories were so bad that Youden eliminated them from the analysis. The author did the same. The 10 and 11 that fell outside the circle include the four extreme outliers.

Deviations perpendicular to the line through the means showed imprecision: the same methods and procedures were not being applied to the two materials. Points near the line but beyond the circle indicated bias—high values if above the circle and low values if below the circle.

Youden concluded that there was no substitute for careful work in the laboratory. He showed that human error was a very serious problem that needed to be carefully controlled, along with other factors, if laboratory tests were to be accurate, and measurements were to vary only with the allowable limits of random variation.

---

[2] W. J. Youden, *Industrial Quality Control*, Vol. XV, 1959, pp. 24–28. A. C. Rosander, *Applications of Quality Control in Service Industries*, (New York: Marcel Dekker, 1985), pp. 316–318.

POWER PLANTS

Case 1

Several human errors were involved in the Three Mile Island disaster, which occurred March 28, 1979 at the nuclear power plant near Harrisburg, Pennsylvania.

- Several cooling systems were closed down for repairs or maintenance but only one of them was turned on. Why the others were not turned on has not been determined. Clearly, no one checked after the repair or maintenance crew finished to see that everything was back in working order.
- Valves on an emergency pumping system were closed when they should have been open. Why they were closed and not open has not been made clear.
- It is also reported that an operator turned off the plant's emergency cooling system, which cooled the core of the reactor, at the wrong time. Why there were no instructions as to the proper time to turn it on and off has never been made clear.

There seemed to be no care or concern for safe operations. There was no monitoring or follow-up on repair or maintenance work to see that systems were set for operating, and, if possible, were operating correctly. Operators were not trained properly with regard to several specific operations, including how to handle critical values.

Case 2

A writer concludes, three years after the Three Mile Island disaster, that the role of the operators at the time of the accident and their role in its occurrence and prevention *has shifted emphasis from equipment reliability to human reliability* (emphasis added).[3]

The accident was initiated by a minor valve malfunction of a type which is correctible by operator action. The severity of the accident arose from failure of complex operations involving inadequate instrumentation on the one hand and several errors or deficiencies of operators on the other.

Two important issues are raised here. The first involves changes in the design of the reactor and modifications of equipment so as to reduce the probability of such accidents by improving control over operations. The second issue

---

[3]F. R. Mynatt, "Nuclear Reactor Safety Research since Three Mile Island," *Science* 235, April 9, 1982.

is that operator training, procedures, aids, and other steps are needed to improve human performance. The accident showed that operators interact with machines and may introduce additional faults by errors of omission or commission.

The NRC is giving greater emphasis to research on operator performance, human factors, and operational aids. Requirements have been tightened, including larger operating crews, more difficult examinations for licensed operators, and improved procedures, as well as other steps.

While there is general agreement that it is advantageous to have well-trained and qualified operators, good procedures, and effective instrumentation and controls, there is substantially less agreement on the use of computers for control. Arguments fly back and forth; one side claims that human operation is more desirable, while those advocating computer control claim that computers are more reliable than human beings. (The latter is true only if the computer is properly programmed to meet any emergency encountered. One should not forget that the computer on Apollo 11 would have landed the ship on a moon rock pile if Armstrong had not taken over controls and landed in a safe spot. A computer cannot tell the difference between boulders and level terrain.)

Case 3

The disaster at Three Mile Island revealed the critical role of the individual operator and the need for emphasis on human reliability if the power plant is to operate safely. It also revealed striking differences of opinion as to the seriousness of what actually happened.

Al Hazle, chief radiologist of the Colorado State Department of Health, stated on April 4, 1979 that the health effects of the Three Mile Island accident have been greatly exaggerated. He stated that the exposure of persons living in the Denver mile-high area is about double the amount every year to which residents were exposed near Three Mile Island.

According to reports, persons in the neighborhood of Three Mile Island are being exposed to about 100 millirems on an annual basis, whereas those living in the Denver area are receiving at least 200 millirems year in and year out. This means that there are thousands of persons living at higher altitudes in Colorado and elsewhere who are receiving much more than 200 millirems per year—places like Aspen, Telluride, Leadville, Vail, Estes Park, and Flagstaff. To what extent this amount of radiation affects health has not yet been determined.

Hazle states that an exposure of 200 millirems does not pose any major health hazard. The implication is that as of today, it poses no health threat at all, since hundreds of thousands of people have lived at these high altitudes for centuries.

Statements by specialists like Hazle clearly show that the mass media, including the press, TV and radio, as well as politicians and "activists," have magnified the Three Mile Island accident into a horror scenario. They have done this by preying on people's fears and the trauma associated with the atomic bomb.

This is all the more reason why human errors should not be tolerated in nuclear power plants, and why human reliability as well as mechanical reliability must always receive top priority. A safe operation is a "must."

Case 4

The Virginia Electric and Power Company has a nuclear plant called North Anna Unit I, apparently run under contract by the well-known engineering firm Stone and Webster. A man cleaning the floors in the control room apparently caught his shirt on a circuit breaker while he was working. In yanking the shirt free, he opened the breaker and shut off current to a control mechanism, which in turn shut down the entire reactor.

This is the way the press reported the accident. If the report is true, it raises some serious question about the care that should be taken by persons when they are working in the proximity of circuit breakers and other delicate control mechanisms. Indeed, it raises a whole host of questions: Should all controls be screened in with limited access? Should cleaning personnel be furnished with coveralls to eliminate loose clothing? Should only special persons be allowed in the control room? Shouldn't employees be trained in safety to avoid accidents of this kind? Shouldn't more care be used to screen applicants when hired, and in training them after they are hired?

Case 5

The Tennessee Valley Authority (TVA) has been testing the Sequoyah nuclear power plant, which they operate, according to a report issued during September 1981. In nuclear power plants rods made of special material are inserted into holes in the radioactive core in order to control the speed of the atomic reaction or to stop it. It is reported that not only at Sequoyah but also at another nuclear plant in Alabama, trouble has been encountered in trying to insert these rods into the core. It is stated in the press that the rods get stuck, making it almost impossible to control the speed of the reaction or to stop it. When this occurs, it is necessary to shut down the plant or else take emergency steps to stop the chain reaction.

It is not explained how these control rods get stuck, nor what conditions give rise to the problem. Is it the rod or is it the core that is defective, or are both of them defective? Apparently the rods get stuck whether electromagnets are being used or whether operators are trying to insert them manually. This raises serious questions about the design, manufacture, and use of these rods and cores. It also indicates that reliability of the equipment is even more important than the reliability of the operators. When the equipment is imperfect, operators cannot expect to do a safe and effective job.

Case 6

Two hydroelectric plants were closed down by human errors within a week of each other in the western part of United States, cutting off electricity to more than 450,000 people. Both plants are run by the federal government.

Two generators at the Parker Plant on the Colorado River were shut down when workers accidentally threw a switch, which in turn powered a safety device that closed down the generators. Power was cut off from about 200,000 people in the Imperial Valley in southeastern California and southwestern Arizona.

Earlier in the week a communication circuit was interrupted in a Pacific Northwest hydroelectric plant, causing the shutdown of generators at the Grand Coulee Dam in eastern Washington. More than 250,000 customers were affected.

Case 7

A nuclear power plant that has a long history of trouble in reaching a full-capacity operation is surveyed by an independent firm of experts. They report the following:[4]

- "The plant has a long standing problem with workers failing to follow procedures. . . . Yet company managers seem reluctant to discipline workers for such mistakes, arguing it's just 'human nature.' "
- The company writes too many "corrective action requests," many of which go uncorrected for years.
- Overall the training is inadequate. "The personnel responsible for developing training programs don't have the skills to produce effective training programs."

In other words, "human nature" is used as an alibi to excuse errors made by employees, corrective actions are not taken immediately but some are delayed for years, and the teachers don't know how to teach or to lay out appropriate training courses. These statements indicate that the company did not hire competent managers and competent employees to start with, nor did they institute training courses and orientation courses to correct these shortcomings. These statements also strongly suggest that the company never heard of quality con-

[4]*Rocky Mountain News,* August 10, 1985, p. 24.

trol applied to these operations; if they did, they did not put a program of quality control into effect.

ERROR IN BILLING A HOUSEHOLDER

A monster of an error is illustrated by copies of two monthly water bills received by a householder, who had had a water meter installed the previous April. Besides the meter in the ground, a water meter was installed on the side of the house, which measured water used to the nearest 100 gallons. This wall meter was connected to a small generator on the ground meter, but the terminals were very close together. Thus any water running down the connecting wires could easily short out the generator or at least reduce its voltage so that the wall meter would not register. The latter happened every time the lawn and junipers were watered, or when it rained. When this happened, it was reported to the water department and to the billing department, but these two groups worked quite independently of each other, being several blocks apart. If the meter on the wall was reported as not reading, the water department would fix it but not report it to billing. This is what accounts for the horrendous bills shown here.

On May 1, 1981 the wall meter read 49, while on June 1, 1981 it read 3; the unit was hundreds of gallons. When the meter reached 49, it conked out. The water department was informed so they came and fixed it and reset it to zero. When the meter reader came, it read 3. When the billing people saw these numbers, they assumed that 49 had advanced to 9,999 and started to read from zero again. This gave a total of 995,400 gallons for a monthly bill of $1,333.34!

$$
\begin{array}{r}
4,900 \\
+\,995,100 \\
\hline
1,000,000
\end{array}
\qquad
\begin{array}{r}
995,100 \\
+\,300 \\
\hline
995,400
\end{array}
$$

The householder called up the billing department and explained what had happened, including the fact that the usual monthly consumption was about 6,000 gallons. Despite this, the error was carried forward to the June bill. Only when the householder took the bills to the billing office and showed how ridiculous they were, was the error corrected.

HEALTH SERVICES

Case 1

An elderly man fell in a nursing home where he was a resident, and broke a bone. Four days later he was taken to the local hospital. He also suffered from emphysema. At the hospital they saw fit to put him on oxygen, so he had to be hooked up to a cylinder of oxygen. It was necessary to go to a dimly lighted storage room of some kind and move in the cylinder of oxygen. This was done, and it was connected to the system. Within 15 minutes the attendants noticed that something was wrong; in three more minutes they discovered that the man was dead.

An examination showed that the person who had gone to obtain a cylinder of oxygen had mistakenly selected a cylinder of carbon dioxide! It was alleged that these cylinders looked alike—they were both grey—and that one was mistaken for the other. The result was a statement that it was an accident, that nothing would be done to the person making the mistake. The hospital held meetings to instruct personnel how to avoid such an accident in the future, the coroner issued a statement that the man died of natural causes, and no damage suit was brought against the hospital. Was this fatal error handled in this cavalier fashion because the man was over 90 years of age or because it was thought the hospital had to be protected? The above is taken from a press report so we do not really know all of the facts, including how the two cylinders of gas happened to be in the same storage space and how they were labeled. Was this error due to the employee, to management, or to both? After this accident, the hospital is reported to have started employee classes in how to handle gases!

Case 2

This case came to light after a $1 million damage suit was filed in a federal court. According to the press, the following are the basic facts. A man who was undergoing surgery was supposed to be put on 100 percent oxygen as soon as the operation was finished. The tank holding the pure oxygen, however, had been partly filled by a supplier, not with oxygen but with nitrogen. After the operation the man was supposed to be on pure oxygen but was placed instead on a highly diluted mixture of oxygen and nitrogen, in a proportion even less than exists in air. It was claimed in the damage suit that as a result of this dilution, brain damage was incurred and that the patient died later. The suit was directed to the supplier and not to the hospital, which had no method of checking what the supplier was doing. Who was to blame—the system, the individual filling the tank, or the individuals using the gas from the tank?

Case 3

It was reported that a military hospital had an oxygen line to which a contractor was supposed to attach a tank of oxygen as the need arose. After two patients died, an investigation was started to try to find out the cause. During the examination it was found that the supplier had attached a cylinder of argon to the oxygen line by mistake. What was the cause? The system? The supplier? The people using argon when they should have been using oxygen?

The preceding cases all deal with the substitution of the wrong gas for oxygen, which clearly is used only in the most stringent circumstances. The cases show that it was possible to substitute carbon dioxide, nitrogen, and argon for oxygen and that no one discovered the mistake until it was too late. These cases indicate very strongly that steps need to be taken to insure that an oxygen tank or line is delivering oxygen and nothing else.

Case 4

A 12-year-old girl who was suffering from severe pains was taken to the emergency room of a hospital. She was given drugs to relieve the pain. One drug was lidocaine. The other was supposed to be phenobarbital, but the emergency room nurse, in mixing the oral preparation, used the last of one bottle of phenobarbital and part of another bottle that was supposed to contain the same drug. The girl's condition worsened, so the nurse injected more lidocaine, which only made her condition worse. She lapsed into a coma and died.

Investigation showed that the drug in the second bottle was not phenobarbital but cocaine. Both were kept in a locked narcotics drawer in the emergency room. According to a statement, both are clear reddish liquids and were in amber-colored bottles, but were correctly labeled. Who was to blame? The system? The emergency room manager? The employee who got the two bottles mixed?

A suit was filed against the hospital for wrongful death. Another suit was filed against the police for illegal search of the girl's home on the assumption that she was a cocaine addict! But a blood test showed that she entered the hospital with no cocaine in her blood; hours later another test showed the existence of cocaine, although no cocaine had ever been prescribed.

Case 5

This is the case of a man in his 70s who was in a hospital, suffering from cancer. Two tubes were connected to him: one a food tube and another for intravenous injections. These tubes were separated until the behavior of the man, largely from pain he was suffering, led him to interfere with them. To get them out of his way, the staff tied the two tubes together and placed them behind and above him. An LPN (licensed practical nurse) who was assigned to him was instructed to give him Pepto-Bismol, but instead of pouring the medicine in the food tube, she poured it in the intravenous tube. As a result, he died in a very short time. Who was to blame? The system? The person who tied the tubes together without putting an identification tag on the food tube? The supervisor, who didn't instruct the LPN which tube was which? The LPN, who didn't ask which tube was which?

Case 6

This case involves two anesthesia machines of the same model made by the same manufacturer. They had been used for years in the regular hospital operating room until they were moved to a one-day unit. On May 29 a woman patient undergoing surgery unexpectedly died while being administered the anesthetic. It was concluded that an overdose of the anesthetic may have contributed to her death.

On June 30 another woman, age 59, was having a pin removed from her ankle under an anesthetic from this same type of anesthesia machine. She died of heart arrest, clearly from an overdose of the anesthetic.

Examination of the machines indicated that *both had faulty valves* governing the flow of oxygen so that the patient received an overdose of the anesthetic. It was discovered that these valves were known by the company to be faulty and had been replaced in at least one machine.

In this case the cause was a faulty valve due to faulty design, faulty operation, or both. The personnel in the hospital were led to believe that the machines were in proper working order, especially after prior factory maintenance. No tests were made to determine whether the valves were operating properly or not. Should the company have warned the hospital to test the machine to see that the valves were working properly before trusting a person's life to them? To what extent is the hospital personnel to blame for not testing these machines before using them? After the first machine failed, why wasn't the second one tested immediately to see if it might fail for the same reason? Were hospital officials and technical personnel guilty of negligence for not doing this?

Case 7

Two operations were switched in a Philadelphia hospital. One woman (age 54) was scheduled for back surgery, and the other (age 58) was scheduled to have parathyroid glands removed. The report issued by the State Department of Health, according to the press, cites all 17 people in two operating rooms as guilty of a series of errors, including not checking identification tags or recognizing the patients. Nor apparently did anyone ask either one what her name was. The report adds that the surgeons realized the error after the first incisions and sewed them up. One gland, however, was removed in the wrong woman.

Is the system to blame? Management? The surgeons? The individuals in control of scheduling surgery? Or are all of them to blame? They need more than identification tags as though these two women were pieces of merchandise. The employees in control should have verified their names by asking them; the surgeons should have done likewise. The latter would have avoided the error if they had asked the names of the women and explained the operation. Clearly they did neither.

Case 8

This is the case of an 89-year-old woman who was in a hospital because of her weak condition as a result of a severe case of arthritis. She was unable to speak above a whisper. She shared a room with another elderly woman but a curtain separated their beds. She wore a diamond ring of great sentimental value; it was set with two large diamonds. Because of arthritis and because of its sentimental value, the ring was not removed from her finger, but someone who is suspected of being an employee entered her room and pried loose the two large diamonds. Since she was too weak to cry out or resist, there was nothing she could do. Apparently she was unable to ring for help. Suspicion falls on an employee rather than anyone else since an employee could easily notice both the diamond ring and her feeble condition.

Case 9

A rancher was injured and went to a nursing home to convalesce, for which he paid $500 a month. When he recovered, he had a hard time getting out. He complained to the head nurse that he was all right. Meanwhile he folded towels for the nurses and did other odd jobs. Finally, after two months of unnecessary residence, he was released; the extra cost, however, was $1000.

While he was in the nursing home his wallet, clothes, and shaving kit were stolen. He saw other residents wearing his clothes. He asked for a lock on his door, but the request was refused.

When he returned home, the medical people insisted that he see a doctor once every month ($20), and have a nurse visit him every Tuesday to take his blood pressure ($5). He was in good health and his blood pressure never changed much, so he saw no need to measure it weekly. A neighbor convinced him to disappear every Tuesday to avoid the nurse and to forget about the monthly visit to the doctor. Even so, the nurse hunted him down on Tuesday and gave him a hard time. However, he refused to budge.

The rancher was being bled to death. The medical and nursing home people were forcing him into unnecessary medical services, which were absorbing all of his life savings. As it was, he was forced to sell his ranch and cattle for $75,000. This money was just about gone. He asked a neighbor a question, for which the answer is not only difficult but sad: "What am I going to do when all of my money is gone?"

Case 10

In a nursing home waffles and syrup are served to 10 elderly patients. The syrup, however, turns out to be oven cleaner. It is admitted that the syrup and the oven cleaner are contained in identical jars and stored in the same place. Furthermore, the jar of oven cleaner is not labeled. The extent of the injury or illness of the patients is not known, or it was not revealed. The nursing home officials blame the situation on inadequate help because the state does not reimburse them enough under Medicaid. Of course Medicaid has nothing to do with storing syrup and oven cleaner in the same place and in identical containers, nor with the fact that the container of oven cleaner was not labeled.

PUTTING HUMAN ERRORS INTO THE COMPUTER

The term "computer errors" is very misleading, and will not be used here because the computer and not people are making the errors. Experience shows that errors due to the failure of the computer mechanism are extremely rare compared to errors made by people working with the computer or having any connection with computers.

The computer has become the Number One alibi to hide human error because of a very primitive notion, innocently started by the pioneers of the computer, to the effect that the computer was a "brain" when it was nothing of the kind. Hence human traits are attributed to the computer, and there they remain to this day.

The alibis take the following forms:

- The computer made a mistake;
- The computer is obsolete;
- The computer system is antiquated: we need a new computer;
- The computer is overloaded;
- The computer read something wrong;
- The computer blew up ("convulsed");
- The computer has a "kink" in it.

People make and blame the computer for the following errors:

- The input information is in error: numbers, addresses, names, codes.
- The computer program is in error: wrong codes, formulas, instructions.
- The computer program is incomplete: vital classes and groups are omitted.
- The file is not updated, is not kept current: money is sent to ineligibles.
- The output is in error for one or more of several reasons: input, program, console operation.
- The computer memory is not large enough to do all the jobs.

• Additional computer programming is necessary, not new hardware or software.

Case 1

Social Security officials report making monthly overpayments averaging about $5,000 to between 1,300 and 2,000 persons all over the country. The checks were supposed to be offset by the current earnings of the recipients, submitted by the latter to Social Security. The computer was not programmed to make this adjustment, so the computer read out the entire amount, which was sent to the individuals. This error in programming the computer was explained away by stating that because of a software problem the computers "convulsed." The real reason: someone did not correctly program the computer, or the software was faulty.

Case 2

Social Security discovered that about 8,000 persons listed as dead on Medicare records were still being mailed Social Security checks. Even three months after this discovery, there is no indication that this is the entire number; about 1,700 were still receiving checks because there was no verification as to whether they were dead or alive.

This is an example of human error because no effective way exists in Social Security to keep the Social Security file current. One would think that an effective procedure would have been developed decades ago to insure that checks would be stopped immediately to Social Security recipients no longer alive.

Case 3

A person received a demand notice from a collection agency acting in behalf of a hospital. The person was very surprised that the hospital had not billed the insurance company; neither had they sent a bill. A call to the hospital elicited the answer that they had sent a letter, but it was returned as undeliverable. An investigation revealed the trouble: some hospital employee had entered the wrong address in the computer.

The wrong address in the computer explained why the hospital's letter and bill were returned as undeliverable. In cases such as this one, where billing is involved, it is imperative that all names and addresses entered in the computer are correct, and a verification system is needed to ensure that no error gets into the computer.

Case 4

Repairmen did not enter into the computer the correct nature of the repair job that had to be done. The customer wanted an FM antenna and an FM hookup from a cable TV company. The first repairman entered "repair" in the computer; the second repairman entered "done" even though nothing was done. This was a case of lack of specifics entered into the computer. It was not only "repair"; it was installing an FM system. Apparently this was not made clear from the beginning. Neither was there any communication between repairmen and the original installer. Without clear instructions, false information goes into the computer.

Case 5

In this case the computer caused trouble and distress because someone did not know how to convert the software of a previous system to the software of a new system. The changeover caused the delay in the issuance of checks to thousands of persons. Expressions used to describe the human errors were "computer kink," "computer glitch," "computer woes," "computer foul-up," "computer mix-up," and "systemwide glitch." It was claimed by the official in charge that some of the data included in the old software were not readily converted to the new system. The organization was implementing a whole new software package. If the data did not match properly, the document was placed on hold.

Apparently a new computer system was installed without determining whether the new software was compatible with the old software. The organization converted to a new system without making sure that the new system and the new programs (software) would do exactly what the old system did. This carelessness led to the kink, the woes, the foul-up, and the mix-up mentioned above. Someone made a serious error because he or she did not understand computers, did not understand software, did not understand computer programming. This situation sounds as though all the software was purchased, and that no one on the staff was an expert enough computer programmer to see that the new system could be programmed to handle all the documents and data and projects handled by the previous system. The system lacked the necessary computer planning and computer programming capability.

Case 6

The error rates made by the states in connection with administering the federal child welfare and Medicaid programs have resulted in billions of dollars being overpaid for these programs. The Secretary of the Department of Health and Human Services (HHS) reports that the average error rate for all states has dropped from a high of 16.5 percent in 1973 to 7.6 percent in 1981. The targets set are a 4 percent error rate for 1983 and a 3 percent error rate for 1984. Federal penalties in the millions of dollars are being imposed on states to force down high error rates. These rates indicate sloppy management and lack of control of operations. Why settle for an error rate of 3 percent, which, when applied to $10 billion, gives an "acceptable" total error of $300,000,000? Pressure should be put on the states to progressively lower the error rates still more; they should not stop at 1 percent, let alone 3 percent. We should reject this common idea that an error rate of 1 percent or 0.5 percent is acceptable when these rates are being applied to a base figure that is in the tens of millions and tens of billions. The next case is an example of this kind of illiteracy about small percentages.

Case 7

A federal official in the Social Security Administration is quoted in the press as stating that an error rate of 0.5 percent in the annual tabulation of totals was a great achievement. The base, however, was 37 million, so 185,000 accounts were in error. We should look not at the 0.5 percent, but the 185,000 accounts and the 185,000 people whose records were messed up. There was no mention of the work load involved and the inconvenience caused by the 185,000 incorrect records. The error rates on these records should be zero. Banks do not allow a 0.5 percent error in their money records.

AIRLINES AND PRIVATE AVIATION

Case 1

A flight lands at the National Airport in Washington during snowy, icy weather. The plane is serviced with antifreeze to remove the ice from the wings or keep it from forming. Another pilot on an incoming plane reports that there is ice on the wings. The plane is on the ground 45 minutes; apparently no attempt is made to determine whether there is any ice on the wings or whether the amount of ice is dangerous.

The plane is cleared for flight and takes off. It climbs no higher than about 300 feet before it plunges onto the 14th Street bridge and falls into the Potomac River, hitting some automobiles as it does so. Only five passengers out of 75 survive. Four on the bridge are killed. Who is to blame for this strictly weather-related accident? The individuals? Management? The system? The official cause is ice on the wings.

Case 2

At New Orleans Airport there have been reports of wind shear in the vicinity of the airport. In wind shear, winds are moving in opposite directions; they can move in any direction vertically, horizontally, or anywhere in between. The net effect on a plane is that there is no even flow of air over the wings and therefore a greatly reduced lift, if any. Despite these warnings, a plane takes off but cannot get any lift, so it crashes in a residential area. Who is to blame? Individuals? Management? The system? It is later reported that the weather information about shear winds was not given to the captain or the crew.

Case 3

During a winter day a DC-10 is approaching Logan International Airport at Boston. The pilot asks for the condition of the runway; he is given an all-clear report. The runway, however, is not clear but icy or snowy. The plane is unable to stop within the length of the runway but runs beyond the end into the bay. Two lives are lost and at latest reports were never found. The tower reported later that they had not really checked the runway for two hours. Therefore, when the DC-10 pilot called in, he was not given the status of the runway on which he was going to land in a few minutes. Who was to blame? Some individual? The tower? The person responsible for knowing the conditions of runways? The entire system?

Case 4

Passenger flights between Anchorage, Alaska and Seoul, Korea are supposed to fly over the Pacific Ocean hundreds of miles from U.S.S.R. For some reason not yet clearly established, Korean Air Lines Flight 007 from Anchorage to Seoul flew over Soviet territory north of Japan and was shot down by a Soviet fighter with a loss of 279 lives.

The major question still unanswered is: Why was the plane more than 100 miles off course? A reasonable explanation, suggested by a pilot familiar with the route, was that erroneous data were entered into the computer system at Anchorage. One published explanation was that the figure in error was the longitude of Anchorage—139 instead of 149. Some such explanation sounds plausible since the computer system obviously had been working correctly on the flight to Anchorage from the east coast of the United States. If a similar error had occurred on this leg of the flight, the airplane would have found itself over northern Alaska instead of over Anchorage. The question still persists: How can such an error be prevented in the future?

Case 5

A private plane with two occupants tried to fly over the Rocky Mountains from Denver to Seattle. For some unknown reason the pilot chose to fly over the Continental Divide by flying up Fall River Canyon in Rocky Mountain National Park, west of the mountain resort town of Estes Park, Colorado. The altitude of the latter is 7,500 feet. The altitude at the top of the canyon is 12,200 feet, so the plane had to climb at least 5,000 feet in 10 miles. This, however, was not the real problem; what was critical was the plane's ceiling. A park ranger told the author what happened. The plane climbed to within 300 feet of the top, but could climb no higher—it had reached its ceiling at about 11,900 feet. Before the pilot realized what was happening, the plane was flying horizontally, not climbing. It plowed into the canyon wall and burned. The ranger said that the pilot had plenty of space in the canyon to turn around and go down if he had realized in time that the plane's ceiling was too low to fly over the top. Articles found near the site revealed that the couple lived in Seattle. (Colorado has 53 mountains with altitudes over 14,000 feet. It is much safer to cross the mountains at lower altitudes in Wyoming and Montana.)

Case 6

A private plane carrying a family, which took off outside Colorado, was headed for Aspen. It crashed on the side of the 14,000-foot Mt. Yale during a snowstorm which had already left deep snow in the mountains. What saved the family was this deep snow, which tended to absorb the shock of a crash landing. They carried no emergency equipment, food, or clothing for this mountain country and weather. The family did the right thing by staying at the plane and waiting to be spotted and rescued. The father, however, without proper clothing or equipment struck out in the deep snow for help. An airplane search together with alpine volunteer rescue teams finally rescued the family. The father perished, and his body was not found until spring. He made the mistake that mountaineers are always warning against.

Case 7

This is the case of a military plane flying in from the East to an airfield in Nevada. It crashed on a mountain in Utah. From press reports it was subject to three difficulties: it appeared to be off course, it was flying too low, and it encountered severe weather conditions. Flying in mountainous country is quite different from flying at lower levels in the East, although there are times when the weather, with rain and snow at about 32 degrees or lower, can be dangerous for flying, even in the East. The dangers are greatly multiplied when flying in the Rockies where there are 53 mountains in Colorado alone with altitudes over 14,000 feet.

Case 8

Complaints Against the 10 Largest Airlines—August 1987. The total number of complaints and the number of complaints per 100,000 passengers for August

1987 are reported by the U.S. Department of Transporation and summarized in the table below.[5]

The complaints of poor quality service take three major forms:

1. Flight problems including cancellations, delays to start, parking on runways, waiting for a space to park, mechanical failure;
2. Baggage problems: delays, loss, damage, difficulty in locating correct carousel;
3. Customer service: rude and indifferent behavior of attendants, unhelpful employees, inadequate meals, poor cabin service.

Northwest gets most complaints

Northwest Airlines moved to the top of the Transportation Department's list of consumer complaints against airlines during August. Complaints against all airlines totaled 7,280, up from 5,995 in July. August complaints against the 10 biggest airlines:

Airline	Total complaints	Per 100,000 passengers	Flight problems[1]	Baggage[2]	Customer Service[3]
Northwest	1,585	47.36	912	182	211
Continental	1,343	38.60	551	225	168
TWA	606	26.96	273	86	86
Eastern	913	24.33	505	103	103
Pan Am	310	23.08	102	72	45
United	607	12.60	244	139	74
American	398	7.89	167	68	56
USAir	143	6.45	67	13	10
Piedmont	98	4.65	45	12	15
Delta	183	3.62	84	25	23

1 - Flight problems include cancellations, delays.
2 - Baggage problems include claims for loss, damage or delays.
3 - Customer service includes rude or unhelpful employees, inadequate meals or cabin service.

This table does not tell the whole story. It shows only the troubles encounterd in the *airline segment* of transportation of the customer from origin to destination. It does not include the problems of quality of service in trying to get to the airport and in departing from it.

Origin	Airline segment	Destination
>	>	>

---

[5] *USA Today,* Sept 8, 1987, p. 3A.

In the first segment of this journey the problems of quality are 1) getting timely transportation from home or office or hotel to the airport; and 2) finding parking space at the airport. This is becoming so difficult that people are having their friends or relatives drive them to the airport. In the last segment of this journey the problem of quality is getting timely transportation from the airport to destination.

Getting to the airport with enough time to check in calls for careful planning of time schedules. Arriving in time to meet a scheduled limousine service for destination or for a return trip may also be risky. It is very difficult now to mesh time schedules of various modes of transportation with scheduled meetings for business or other purposes.

Airline transportation managers are not interested in getting customers from their origin to their destination; nor is anyone else.

HUMAN ERROR, POOR QUALITY, AND SAFETY IN OTHER TRANSPORTATION

Case 1

The Office of Technology Assessment made a study of the problem of safety in various modes of transportation—trucks, railroads, and ships—and came to the conclusion that safety can be improved in two ways: by improving the technology involved and by using the quicker method of reducing human error through better hiring and training.[6]

It was found that the transportation of gasoline accounted for more injuries, dollar damage, and deaths than all other hazardous materials combined. The public alarm over the danger of radioactive material shipments, fed by the press and television, is completely unfounded. The public ranks nuclear fuel at the top of the list but experts rank it Number 20. Deaths due to nuclear materials to date have been zero because of better designed and constructed shipping containers. It would also be possible to build a safer gasoline tanker, but this would not prevent jackknifing and turnovers due to entering and leaving highways at too high a speed.

Local persons who respond to emergencies of this nature need to be better trained. Very often the first person on the scene is a volunteer firefighter.

Most transportation accidents involve trucks and the errors made by the drivers. These errors include driving too fast, lack of careful driving in mountains, driving on and off a high-speed highway too fast, and careless driving on ice and snow. These errors lead to turnovers, throwing a load, and jackknifing.

---

[6]P.H. Abelson, "Transportation of Hazardous Materials," *Science* 234, Oct. 10, 1986, p. 125. Data from Office of Technology Assessment, Report on Transportation of Hazardous Materials, July 1986, Government Printing Office, Washington, DC.

A study made in Washington State revealed that 70 percent of the truck accidents occurred on a straightaway, not on curves. This suggests some form of inattention and loss of control. Shell Oil Company reduced preventable accidents by 58 percent by introducing special instructions and field training. It also installed an automatic device which monitors the actions of the driver. These are sound attempts to protect the individual against making serious errors as well as to obtain objective data about the driver's behavior in case of an accident.

The solution to safe driving seems to be a continuing program of group and individual instruction plus exposure to a substantial number of significant field demonstrations.

Case 2

On single-track railroads, engineers of trains going in opposite directions must be familiar with sidetracks onto which one train must pull in order for another train to pass. Railroads control these movements to avoid collisions. Trainmen are supposed to stop at certain sidetrack stations to obtain orders or directions from a log book or other records, with regard to other trains on the track.

A southbound train with two locomotives and 32 cars was on such a track north of Denver. A northbound train with three locomotives and 49 cars was supposed to move onto a sidetrack and wait for the southbound train to pass. For some reason which may never be determined, the northbound train stopped at the sidetrack station only briefly, apparently read the order incorrectly, and then proceeded northward.

About eight miles north the two trains collided head-on at a curve at the U.S. 36 highway overpass. Five trainmen were killed, three on one train and two on the other. The only survivors were the two conductors, who were in their respective cabooses. The damage to the locomotives, the freight cars, and the overpass amounted to $10 million. In addition, damage suits were brought by the families of those who died.

A total of 36 freight cars were damaged in addition to five locomotives. Some of the freight cars were still burning two or three days later. How this will affect the shippers is not hard to guess. This is the second head-on collision of freight trains in Colorado within a year.

These costly accidents suggest once more the need to give top priority to the prevention of human error. This subject is discussed in greater detail in a later chapter.

Case 3

A national survey of new automobile buyers regarding the number of complaints per 100 automobiles shows that Japanese cars head the list with the fewest number of complaints made during the first 90 days after purchase.[7] The complaints include stalling, rough idling, oil leaks, overheating, poor radio reception, gauges that do not operate, and malfunctioning of power windows, doors, and locks.

All of these defects and faults, except possibly overheating, appear to be the kind that can be easily avoided with careful workmanship, installation, and testing, and they show that the problem of quality is far from being solved. They seem to indicate either that there is no quality improvement program or that if there is one, it is not being implemented on the factory floor. They also show that it may be necessary to work more closely with vendors to make sure that purchased parts such as gauges and radios are working properly before they are installed in the automobile.

Complaints per 100 Cars Made within 90 Days of Purchase:

Low		*High*	
Toyota Camry	109	Chevrolet Corvette	386
Toyota Cressida	122	Dodge Charger	399
Toyota Tercel	127	Chevrolet Camaro	407
Toyota Corolla	133	Chrysler New Yorker	408
Honda Accord	143	Pontiac Firebird	415
Ford Crown Victoria	171	Renault Fuego	491
Chevrolet Citation II	173	Peugeot 505	532

Case 4

A school bus carrying elementary school children collapsed when loose bolts on the rear axle caused the axle and rear wheels to fall off. The bus fell on its side, injuring five children and two adults.[8]

This accident led to an immediately beefed-up program of inspection and maintenance, applied to the entire fleet of 353 buses. As a first step, 122 buses were pulled off the street because of the problems discovered in inspection. As the listing below shows, 12 major types of defects were discovered, many of them serious.

Problem	*Number of Buses*
1. Worn fanbelts	4
2. Flywheel, transmission, clutch	8
3. Springs, suspension, shocks	45

---

[7] *USA Today,* December 13, 1985, p. 6B.

[8] *Rocky Mountain News,* October 7, 1985, p. 13; November 5, 1985, p. 7.

	Number of
Problem	*Buses*
4. Brakes (4 with leaks in tubes)	12
5. Front-end shimmy	2
6. Body poorly attached	12
7. Engine mounts	5
8. Lubrication leaks	2
9. Steering	9
10. Tires	5
11. Electrical	2
12. Rear end misaligned	1
	107
Wrecks	4
Not Inspected	11
Total	122

Fleets are inspected for safety by the state three times a year. Buses are inspected every 2000 to 3000 miles and replaced every 10 to 15 years. The problem is maintenance. Interviews with mechanics and others brought out the following important points:

- For four years preventive maintenance was slack.
- "I have been doing a mechanic's job without the necessary training."
- New mechanics are not trained properly and their work is not reviewed by the foremen.
- There is no training on tires and no measuring to insure tires of the same size.
- A mechanic was told, "Safety is none of your business."
- Helpers and service employees who are less qualified are put on to do mechanics' work.
- Favoritism existed.
- Mechanics are blamed, not management.
- The accident has brought about changes—upgrading and renewed professionalism.
- A mechanic with 14 years' experience said, "They've put pride back into our work."

Three of Deming's 14 points are mentioned directly: Point 6, which deals with training on the job, Point 7, which deals with supervision and leadership, and Point 12, which deals with pride in workmanship. Another very important piont brought out in the interviews is that mechanics are blamed for troubles for which management is responsible.

It is very clear that a quality improvement program instituted by the top supervisors would improve the mechanical features of these buses, promote safety, reduce costs of maintenance, improve the morale of the mechanics, improve performance of the fleet generally, and reduce the amount of capital investment in new buses.

Case 5

Denver's Regional Transportation District (RTD) officials announced that buses recently purchased were performing above expectations.[9] This statement was issued after experience with 30 new buses, the first ones received in a contract for 167 buses awarded to the lowest bidder. Several important aspects are relevant to the quality of performance of these buses, as well as how these companies view quality.

Fifteen of the new buses have been operating nearly around the clock without any trouble. This means that some kind of trouble developed or was discovered in the other fifteen.

Some unanticipated "bugs" developed in these first buses, but officials called these defects minor by industry standards. They claim that other major transit companies have bought buses from several companies and found them worse than the ones RTD bought.

The flaws were corrected in the factory and in RTD garages. RTD quality control people are located at the factory, but no explanation is given as to what they are doing. Buses are not accepted until they are debugged at the factory. The number of problems is stated to be less than that which usually occurs in a new bus. A union official stated, "I haven't heard any drivers complaining." A company official said, "We now have an above-average bus."

Comments. Expectations of RTD officials are such that they accept poor-quality products that should be rejected. They see defects and "debugging" as inevitable, and accept these defects as the industry standard. They are not interested in eliminating these costly defects during the manufacturing process. As long as they expect poor-quality buses, they will get them. It is rather obvious that neither the company making the buses nor the RTD officials understand what quality control, quality management, and quality improvement are all about. They do not realize the tremendous savings involved and the reduced maintenance that results if these buses are made so that all of the "debugging" can be eliminated. The meaningless "above-average bus" is used

---

[9] *Rocky Mountain News*, July 19, 1986, p. 17.

to justify the poor-quality buses RTD is buying. (This is an example of Dr. Deming's Point 4: buying from the lowest bidder and ignoring quality.)

OTHER EXAMPLES

Case 1: Specifications That Failed

On October 3, 1985, while eight 60-ton girders were being put in place for an overpass on a main street in Denver, the western column sheared off, allowing the girders to fall to the street below. One man was killed and four others injured.[10]

Three parties were involved: the engineering firm that designed the project, the construction company, and the State Highway Department. An independent engineering consulting firm that investigated the failure held all three parties responsible. Other findings included in the firm's report were the following;

- A 10-inch slab of reinforced concrete was never laid on top of the pier table.
- The designer's instructions were not clear and unambiguous.
- Technical terms such as "pier table," "pier cap," and "deck slab" may have been confusing to the construction workers.
- The statement that the top deck was supposed to be poured "monolithically" may not have been understood.
- No engineer ever visited the site to check the construction sequence or to review the progress of the work.

The consultants made three recommendations:

1. Construction sequences should be explained and described in plans and drawings;
2. Contractors are to submit a detailed sequence approved by a professional licensed engineer;
3. A competent engineer should periodically review the progress of bridge construction.

The construction company insists that the overpass was built according to the plans and specifications obtained from the designer.

There was a failure of communication between the designer and the construction company: Specifications were not clear and understandable, the construction sequences were not described and arranged in proper order, and there was

---

[10]*Rocky Mountain News,* November 21, 1985, p. 7.

no monitoring of the construction by an engineer from the designer's office, who was familiar with the project.

Case 2: Using Percentages to Deceive

Two very misused words from elementary arithmetic are "percent" and "average." They are commonly used to mislead the public not only by what is said, but by what is omitted. People can be fooled by these words because schools do not explain with examples their uses and misuses. The following example shows how "percent" is used to deceive the American people about unemployment.[11]

| Month/Year | Number Employed | Unemployment | | | Labor Force |
		Number	Adjusted Rate	Actual Rate	
Sept. 1985	107,519,000	8,271,000	7.1%	7.14%	115,790,000
Sept. 1986	109,891,000	8,329,000	7.0	7.05	118,220,000
Change	+2,372,000	+58,000	−0.1	−0.09	+2,430,000

Between September 1985 and September 1986 the estimated *number* of unemployed persons *increased,* but the seasonally adjusted *percentage* of unemployed persons *decreased.* The percentage, not the number, is announced by Washington and emphasized by the press and television networks. A decline in unemployment is what the administration wants, so percentage is used rather than the actual number.

Actually, the number of unemployed increased during the year by 58,000. The estimates, however, are made from nationwide samples and therefore are subject to sampling variations, so the 58,000 may or may not be a significant change. If it is significant, there was an increase in unemployment. If not, then there was no change in the number of persons unemployed.

Percentage is determined by a number and its base. In this case the base is the total labor force, or the sum of the employed and the unemployed shown in the last column above. If the increase in the number employed is much larger than the increase in the number unemployed, the percentage unemployed can easily decrease while the number of unemployed is increasing. This is what the above figures show. The table also shows how tricky the use of percentages can be; percentages can actually conceal the real facts. (Note that the actual percentages are practically the same as the adjusted percentage.)

[11]Data are taken from U.S. Bureau of Labor Statistics and appeared in *USA Today,* October 6, 1986, p. 4B.

Case 3: Zero Errors

"Zero errors" is not a fancy slogan. It is not a delusion. It is not a will-of-the-wisp. It is a "must" in numerous situations. Some examples are summarized below:

1. The fingerprint records of the FBI or any other similar agency must be free of errors. Such an office is not stupid enough to "stabilize" the error rate at 2 percent, or 1 percent, or even 0.5 percent.

2. Airlines aim at a 100 percent safety record. They want no errors that lead to crashes. They do not "stabilize" crashes at 2 percent, 1 percent, or even 0.5 percent. The goal or the standard is zero percent and nothing else.

3. In health services, human errors that can be fatal to patients cannot be tolerated. They do not say that 2 percent of the time, 1 percent of the time, or 0.5 percent of the time an error can be tolerated whereby carbon dioxide (CO_2) is substituted for oxygen, nitrogen is substituted for oxygen, or argon is substituted for oxygen, although errors of these three kinds have resulted in deaths. (These cases were described above.) Zero error in these cases is life; otherwise it is death.

4. If quality is taken seriously (and there are far too many places where it is not), you do not substitute something lethal for something that should be non-lethal: cocaine for phenobarbital (hospital emergency room), arsenic for flour, or oven cleaner for pancake syrup (nursing home). These are actual cases. You do not set "standards" for these kinds of mistakes, nor try to "stabilize" them at some level such as 1 percent. You take steps to prevent them. You reject factory-type thinking.

Chapter 6

The Nature and Scope of Errors

Human error is a major factor determining quality and productivity of individual performance, as well as the performance of machinery, equipment, apparatus, and processes. The word "error" is used very broadly to include mistakes, blunders, delays, accidents, and other behavior which influence quality, productivity, efficiency, and effectiveness of operations, as well as related activities described below.

Human errors are both simple and complex and arise from a great variety of causes. In the following pages they are discussed from several different angles which reflect this complexity. The kinds of errors are not necessarily independent, but are described in different contexts because this is the way they are encountered in practice.

ERRORS AS DEVIATIONS

1. Errors as Deviations from Correct Values

Correct values are found in the applications of both language and number. They are found in spelling, grammar, arithmetic, mathematics, statistics and in all kinds of counts and measurements, including time. These standards of correct values are found in the dictionary, grammar books, the telephone directory, other directories, books of standard classifications, spelling books, mathematical tables, arithmetic tables, and tables of scientific constants.

2. Errors as Deviations from Recorded Facts

Recorded facts are found in the *Statistical Abstract of the United States, The World Almanac,* encyclopedias, atlases, guidebooks, standard textbooks, federal censuses, and handbooks.

3. Errors as Deviations from Correct Methods, Processes, and Procedures

These methods, processes, and procedures include mathematical formulas and equations, statistical formulas and equations, chemical and physical tests and processes, industrial tests and processes, probability sample designs, experimental designs, quality control techniques and quality technology, engineering designs, processes, and procedures, accounting and auditing procedures, the *U.S. Pharmacopoeia,* and other scientific tests and processes not covered above. Errors include misunderstanding of terms, expressions, percepts, concepts, equations, and sequences.

Other examples are deviations from sound and careful practice which cause trouble, such as the following:

- Defects in contents, such as a book, caused by opening packages with a knife;
- Making the wrong selection in filling a mail order or in selecting a drug or medicine;
- Duplicate billing or sending a false notice;
- Poor packaging, causing damage in shipment.

4. Errors as Deviations from Rules, Regulations or Laws

These errors are numerous because of lack of controls, lack of enforcement, lack of adequate records, faulty computer operations, and no doubt many other factors:

- Overcharging Medicare;
- Overcharging Medicaid;
- Falsifying charge under Medicare and Medicaid;
- Charging for services not rendered, medicines not used, tests not made;
- Making payments to ineligible persons;
- Overpaying eligible persons;
- Not paying eligible persons;
- Paying Social Security to persons no longer alive;
- Refusal to repay federal loans;
- Delay in repaying federal loans;
- Misuse of federal loans and other payments (use for trips, vacations, etc.);
- Stealing by employees;
- Shoplifting by customers;
- Passing bad checks.

5. Errors as Misuse of Correct Procedures and Incorrect Applications

In these cases the correct method is used or a sound procedure or process is followed, but errors are made in implementing the method, procedure, or process. For example, a probability sample study is based on a sound and efficient design, but it is invalidated by errors in putting it into effect. Careless and unsound questionnaires or data sheets may result in data from an otherwise sound study that are ambiguous, inaccurate, and misleading. In a Midwestern factory an inspector was applying Mil. Std. 105 to measurements and using four times as much inspection as necessary. This latter is a case of an incorrect application. Other common areas of incorrect application are probability sample studies and the design of experiments.

6. Errors as Deviations from Safe Procedures and Safe Behavior

These are errors made by departing from safe procedures and safe actions in connection with services, products, and industries. These include health services, transportation, power plants and their operations, electrical machinery and devices and circuits, dangerous drugs and chemicals, dangerous gases and liquids and products, construction, and mining.

Mistakes made in these areas can be not only dangerous but fatal. Some behavior in these areas often leads to accidents, but these are invariably due to lack of knowledge, a faulty attitude, faulty judgment, or careless behavior. Several deaths have been reported in the Denver area from cave-ins of trenches, something that could easily be prevented by shoring up the sides of the trench.

7. Errors as Rejection of Improvements, Better Methods, More Efficient Techniques

Examples are rejection of improved processes, techniques, methods, procedures, or products. These include quality control, probability sampling, an efficient computer installation, an improved industrial process, a better procedure, a new product, and a better type of service. These are opposed even though opposition leads to waste, high cost, loss of market, inability to meet competition, delay, or a poor quality product or service.

8. Errors of Judgment, or in Making Decisions

This error is one of the most far-reaching of all types because it can exist at all levels and for all persons, and can affect all operations. It can be clerical, technical, professional, supervisory, or managerial. It can affect policy, planning, people, operations, quality, finance, appraisal, implementation, interpretation, or actions. It can be very costly or not, depending upon the impact of the error on quality, operations, products, services, customers, employment, finances, and competition.

9. Errors Arising from Faulty or Incorrect Diagnosis of a Situation or Problem

These errors occur not only in medical agencies and in medical services, but everywhere. Such an error can be a mistake in identifying the real problem because data are lacking that are relevant, accurate, and sufficient; it can be a false reading of appearances; it can be based on data that are thought to be adequate but are not; it can require knowledge that the individual does not have; or it can arise from inexperience in diagnosis. It can apply to products and services, to operations and research, to machinery and equipment, to processes and procedures, to management and supervision. It can lead to faulty repairs and maintenance, to faulty tests and treatments, to wrong and ineffective corrective actions.

ERRORS AS DELAY AND NEGLECT

1. Delay as Inability to Act

This is a case in which a situation requires action but a mistake is made by delaying action: inability to act, slow response, procrastination, hesitancy to make a decision, fear of taking responsibility, the need to call a conference, the need to clear first with an official or a committee. Delays can be costly, dangerous, and even fatal, depending upon the circumstances.

An example is the railroad control tower operator who failed to throw a switch. The result was an accident. Failure to act as needed may be a very serious error.

This raises the question as to how much delay can be tolerated in any given situation. It all depends upon the situation, as the following list shows:

Tolerable Duration of Delay	*Situation*
No delay	Emergency situation: fire, accident, spilled chemicals, poison gas leakage
Seconds	Emergency situation: fire, auto driving situation, shock, accident (serious)
Minutes	Time required for a fire department to get to a fire, an ambulance to get to a person, a helicopter to get to an accident; deviation from transportation departure and arrival times; time required to see a doctor once person is in doctor's office
Days	Important data, important reports, meeting shipping schedules, important mail or package

Tolerable Duration of Delay	*Situation*
Weeks	Reports, mail, and shipping that are not critical

Tolerated delay is directly related to the seriousness of the situation to the extent that *time* is directly related to the quality of the service and to the nature of the outcome or outcomes, such as fire, sickness, collisions, or accidents.

2. Delay as Wasted Time

Wasted time in its various forms is a major cause of poor quality and high-cost service. Wasted time is not only very costly but is a direct factor in reducing productivity. Examples are numerous:

- Idle time or absenteeism, which retards or prevents the work of others;
- Downtime of equipment, machines, computers, production lines, or processes;
- Interrupted or blacked-out service, e.g., electricity or telephone;
- Waiting for work, supplies, parts, repairs, service, maintenance, or service personnel.

3. Errors as Neglect

Neglect is a form of deliberate waiting to do a necessary job. It may be justified erroneously as a way to save money or cut costs. Examples are neglecting repair and maintenance and letting critical materials deteriorate and decay. Examples of objects and operations that are neglected relative to maintenance and repair are railroads, roads, buildings, streets, machinery, equipment, apparatus, automobiles, trucks, buses, airplanes, airlines, ships, bridges, dams, computers, and typewriters. The neglect of repairs and maintenance, including preventative maintenance, may lead to a wide variety of operating failures, some more or less minor but others very serious and costly: accidents, wrecks, disasters, collisions, fires, failures, floods, collapses, or breakdowns.

4. Delay as Faulty Time Planning and Estimating

These errors and mistakes are caused by poor time planning and by ignorance of operations, leading to delays and lost time. The final results are inefficient operations, wasted time, increased costs, poor service, dissatisfied customers, and discontented employees. Examples include the following:

- Poor synchronization, timing, and coordination of operations and sequences;
- Faulty work scheduling;

- No time schedules, or an incomplete time schedule;
- Setting unrealistic and absurd deadlines for various jobs, tasks, and projects;
- Faulty service time estimates;
- Overloading, service overload, or understaffing, leading to long lines and delays or excessive overtime and driving up costs;
- Overstaffing; too many employees for the work load.

ERRORS AS UNNECESSARY OR EXCESSIVE SERVICE AND SERVICE EQUIPMENT

Unnecessary or excessive service and service equipment add to the price of the service to the customer, demand extra time from the customer, and increase costs to the seller. This may mean nothing to the seller, who can simply raise prices to absorb the additional costs, but it is an effective way to lose customers, especially the more alert and experienced ones. Examples of this situation include unnecessary drugs and medicines; medical examinations; tests and treatments; surgery; days in the hospital; repairs (auto, radio, TV, other); maintenance; items for which insurance premiums are paid; software; X-rays (teeth, chest, breast); and auto tests: safety, pollution.

ERRORS AS OBSTRUCTIONS, HINDRANCES, AND BUILT-IN CONFLICTS

These are internal conditions that lead to poor performance, low productivity, high costs, inability to meet competition, and low-quality products and services. Examples include the following:

- Poor working conditions: heat, light, ventilation, space, facilities, noise;
- Adversary relations between employees and management;
- Conflicts among employees;
- Conflicts and feuds among managers;
- Inefficient methods, processes, equipment, machinery, or apparatus;
- Opposition to new and improved methods, processes, and procedures such as quality control, probability sampling, random time sampling, statistical techniques, computer facilities, automation, and quality management;
- Lack of recognition of talent, superior performance, original work, or successful applications of new and improved methods and techniques.

ERRORS AS THE DESTRUCTION OF SIGNIFICANT DATA AND RECORDS AND UNNECESSARY REPLACEMENT

This type of error applies to reports, files, documents, punch cards, materials, and equipment. It includes erasing computer tapes that should be saved, or scrapping a computer system as obsolete and antiquated when it is not obsolete. A new generation of computers does not mean that the previous generation is inefficient and useless, although computer salesmen may attempt to convince people that this is the case. What the organization or company needs may be more memory, new programs, and a good computer programmer.

This error of destroying useful records usually is made inadvertently, but it can be made because an individual or group does not understand the importance or value of what they are destroying or replacing. This is very often due to the lack of a company-wide policy and time schedule with regard to the disposal of past records. It raises the crucial question of record security, how long records are kept, classification, and disposal. The increase in liability cases and tax audits makes accurate record keeping and maintenance much more important now than in the past.

ERRORS AS LACK OF UPDATING RECORDS

Neglect and delay in updating records, files, and computer storage are a common and sometimes difficult problem. Examples are as follows:

- Social Security records are not kept current because of the difficulty of determining when a recipient died. It may take months, if not years, to keep the files current. Meanwhile, thousands of checks are mailed out monthly to persons no longer alive. The problem is to delete the deaths and add the survivors.
- A problem arises in connection with the patient control file in a hospital. The problem is to keep this file current by immediately deleting discharges as they occur and by adding admittances just as quickly as they occur. If there is much delay, all kinds of trouble can arise in connection with telephone calls and deliveries for patients which have been discharged or admitted.
- Computer files and records must be updated continuously; otherwise a serious problem may arise if a complete run is made or if a sample is selected from the computer file.

ERRORS DUE TO LACK OF COMMUNICATION AND UNDERSTANDING

These errors are encountered almost daily in business, in conversations, in telephone communications, in letters, and in memoranda. They are not serious because in most cases the correction may be made on the spot. They are, however, a source of inconvenience and annoyance. Examples include the following:

- A customer goes to the bank and asks the teller for $100 in five 20-dollar bills. The teller starts to count out 20 five-dollar bills until she is stopped.

- Another customer goes into a bank and asks for $300 in ten 20-dollar bills and ten 10-dollar bills. The teller counts out three $100 bills.

In these examples, what does the teller hear? Is the teller listening to the customer? Is the customer asking for something that is too difficult for the teller to understand? Is the simple arithmetic involved too difficult?

It is stated in the press that when the rate of inflation decreased from 12 percent to 5 percent, the cost of living declined. This is not so. The 5 percent did not erase any of the 12 percent; it just added something on top. This percentage change meant that the price level was still increasing, but at a decreasing rate. The idea of something increasing at a decreasing rate is too complicated for the press, TV reporters, commentators, and tens of millions of others to understand. That is why one never reads or hears any explanation of what "inflation" and its change really mean. For political purposes it is better to let people think that a decrease in inflation rate means a decrease in the cost of living. This is a deliberate attempt to deceive.

"Education Called a Key to Prosperity" is a headline in a newspaper. From this headline one might reasonably assume that the article shows the importance of elementary school, high school, and college education in developing and maintaining a prosperous economy. It does nothing of the kind. The article describes how states that have many high-tech colleges prosper, such as Massachusetts and California. If the headline truthfully reflected the content of the article it would be something like one of the following: "High-Tech Colleges Aid States' Economy," "Colleges High-Tech Programs Aid States," or "States Profit from Their Colleges' High-Tech Programs." The lesson is that if a state wants to strengthen its economy, it had better develop stronger programs in high technology in its colleges and universities.

A questionnaire in a youth survey contained a sentence aimed at discovering cases of juvenile delinquency. The sentence was "Have you ever been in trouble?" This question received so many sexual interpretations from the interviewed youths that the question was finally eliminated from the questionnaire. This case shows the need for a pilot test of a questionnaire or data sheet on a wide variety of potential respondents before it is put into final form. Another question in an entirely different study involving only adults inquired about opinions on a subject that involved the word "profit." After receiving many strange answers, the interviewers discovered that the persons being interviewed were answering a question about "prophet."

TYPES OF ERRORS

There are many types of errors with which managers and supervisors have to be familiar if they are to correct and eliminate them by adequate planning, training, coaching, and error prevention programs. Several types are discussed below.

1. Simple Clerical Errors

These include typing errors such as transposed letters and digits, misspelled words, skipped lines, uneven margins, strikeovers, and many more. Typists themselves can and should be able to prevent such errors if they are familiar with, or have readily available, a standard typing manual and a dictionary.

2. Difficult Clerical Errors

These include filing, coding, and transcribing errors. These are more serious because they affect accuracy of data, waste time in hunting for misfiled documents, and require quality control techniques to keep errors close to zero. In many cases zero error rate is required, as in filing fingerprint records.

3. Difficult Processing

These include errors made in processing important documents such as insurance claims, mail orders, tax returns, health records, job applications, invoices, bank checks, personnel records, freight bills, and mortgage payments. Accuracy is imperative.

4. Calculating Errors

Calculating errors are easy to discover and probably the easiest to correct and prevent. They take many forms ranging from simple arithmetic errors to errors made in complex mathematical problems and equations.

- Simple arithmetic errors: errors in simple addition, subtraction, multiplication, and division and in decimal points and zeros;
- More difficult calculations: percentages, discounts, sales tax, individual income tax, property tax, conversion problems, averages, postage;
- Wrong formulas or equations: simple interest, compound interest, speed and distance, areas and volumes, surveying;
- Errors in solving right formula or equation: any of the above;
- Errors in programming mathematical or statistical equations or in selecting a replicated sample or other sample from computer tapes or memory;
- Errors in running tabulations;
- Errors in operating a calculator or computer;
- Errors in selecting or summarizing numerical data;
- Substituting a complicated set of calculations when a simple set is all that is needed.

5. Recording Errors, Including Interviewing

These errors are made in recording data of various kinds and from various sources. They include errors in reporting the data to be recorded, errors due to faulty memory or recall, errors made on the original records, errors due to using the wrong record or source, errors due to some fault of the interviewer such as misunderstanding or bias in recording, transcribing errors, and misunderstanding instructions or oral statements.

6. Observational Errors, Including Inspection

These include errors made by an observer, whether counting, measuring or just making observations. They also include errors in reading instruments, whether accidental or deliberate, such as "drawing in" measurements that are near specification limits, tending to read only even numbers, or avoiding odd numbers in counting or reporting (e.g., age). In addition, they include errors made by observers, whether they are inspectors or not.

7. Errors of Judgment

These serious errors are made at all levels of organization but especially at the top, where faulty inferences, opinions, and decisions can be very harmful. These faulty judgments and decisions take a wide variety of forms and can arise from various sources:

- Decision to make wrong product e.g.: in automobile manufacturing making Edsels, gas guzzlers, and autos that are not competitive with foreign-made cars;
- Acting on hunch, bias, past practice, or past philosophies;
- Refusal to listen to those with knowledge, know-how, and new ideas;
- Opposition to better methods and techniques;
- Faulty and contradictory top-level views, plans, and decisions;
- False assumptions about the market, quality, and finances;
- Lack of experience with people, operations, and problems;
- Refusal to collect adequate information;
- Lack of control data and controls;
- Refusal to act on knowledge or on pertinent information;
- Faulty interpretation of available data and information;
- Faulty communication system; key information for decision making is stopped before it gets to the decision maker;
- Misunderstanding of what sound management data and information mean.

8. Computer Errors

A major job is to keep errors out of the computer and to have a foolproof system at all points that does just this. Sources of error are numerous:

- Programming errors;
- Errors made by tape librarian;
- Errors made by console operator;
- Faulty software;
- Uninformed programmer;
- Computer memory not updated;
- Use of incomplete file;
- Failure to correct records in error: failure to use computer edit;
- Errors in input data;
- Errors in output data;
- Hardware failure;
- Software failure;
- Programmer lacking technical help;
- Printer failure;
- Failure to debug program completely.

EXAMPLES OF HUMAN ERRORS BY TYPE

1. Technical Errors

- A computer programmer used the wrong formula for the standard error of a subclass aggregate.
- A factory manager used a sample of one employee to obtain an average of the amount of material used by machine operators for each unit of output.
- An inspector in a large Midwestern factory used a sample plan from Mil. Std. 105 for testing a *measurement* of an incoming part and does four times too much testing.
- In two large nationwide sample studies, very faulty and inefficient sample plans were proposed. One was actually used but the better one was prevented from being used.
- A test was run to determine if a significant difference existed in radioactivity due to plutonium in an area in one state compared with that in an area in an adjoining state. Not a single basic principle of a designed experiment was used.
- In setting up a system for a national draft lottery, selections were not made in a strictly random order so that all birth dates had an equal chance of

being selected at any one draw. This occurred for World War II as well as for later wars.

2. Performance Errors Due to Negligence, Failure of Operating Routines, No Verification

- Four reels of tape were omitted from the final tabulation of a nationwide sample study, amounting to 17,000 documents. If excluded, they would have invalidated the entire annual tabulation and report.
- At Three Mile Island it was reported in *Science* that four cooling systems had been turned off for repair and maintenance, but that only one was turned back on. It was alleged that this was one of the major causes of the disaster.
- At one nuclear power plant in the Southeast, an employee working on maintenance and cleanup accidentally caught his shirt in a switch and pulled open the switch, thereby closing down the plant.
- At a Northwestern electric power plant it is reported that an employee pulled the wrong switch, thereby blacking out a large area.

3. Performance Errors of an Individual Character Which Can Be Costly

- Typing errors;
- Coding errors;
- Transcribing errors;
- Observer errors;
- Interviewer errors;
- Inspection errors;
- Calculating errors;
- Filing errors (paper and products).

4. Errors in Computer Operations

- Four reels of tape were omitted from a nationwide sample study tabulation. An independent daily sample receipts control system showed that the sample had been running about 230,000 documents annually. When the computer came up with a total count of 212,000, the chief immediately asked for a check of both the computer run and the sample receipts records. As a result it was discovered that these four reels, or about 17,000 documents, had not been run, which checked very closely with the sample receipts control figure.
- A programmer used the wrong equation for the sampling variance of the

estimate of a subclass aggregate. As a result, about 26,000 calculations were printed in error in the final tabulation.

- Due to a lack of specific instructions to the programmer or an absence of clear instructions to his boss, a programmer included a class of persons in a tabulation where they should have been excluded. As a result, $48 million were paid out in error.
- The computer people changed the specifications laid out by the chief statistician and approved as part of the plan for the original study, with the results that the very values at the extreme right tail of the frequency distribution which were required to answer a basic question were eliminated.
- A mortgage document in connection with a home sale was not filled out to match the way the central computer was programmed. As a result, a payment of $314 on the document was not recognized by the computer. After four months of letter writing and telephone calls, during which the home buyer received penalty letters (off the computer), the computer was corrected to match the original mortgage document. A vice-president did not correct it; the real estate people did not correct it. It was corrected only after a 100-mile visit to the bank and finding a computer operator. This case shows how long it takes to correct an error in a computer in a big company.
- A lump sum payment to reduce the principal on a mortgage resulted in the mortgage company showing $300 less than the amortization schedule. This error was made by the company, but like the case above, several telephone calls and about five months were required before the computer was corrected to match the amortization schedule and eliminate the $300 error.
- A motorist with license plate BT 8828 was entered in Denver computer as BT 8820, where it stayed uncorrected for two years. For over two years the motorist received overdue traffic violation notices for the BT 8820 automobile, despite repeated calls and explanations of the error and equally insistent answers to ignore them or statements that the error had been corrected. What happened was that the error made in the Denver computer was transferred to the Colorado Motor Vehicle computer, but the correction was not. Thus the error remained in the state computer for over three years and accounted for the fact that the motorist received so many traffic violation notices. This case again indicates how difficult it is to correct a simple error in a computer despite repeated explanations over a period of years that an error exists. It took Denver two years to correct an error that should have been corrected as soon as the motorist called attention to the fact that he was being sent someone else's overdue parking tickets, and proved it.

5. Recording Errors

- A businessman deposits $1842 in a Denver bank, which records it as $18.42. He writes checks against the $1842 but receives overdrawn notices with penalties. Efforts to have the bank correct the mistake are futile. He finally sues the bank for the time lost in getting them to correct the error. The court rules for him and orders the bank to pay him for his lost time.

- A deliberate recording error is the "pulling in" of readings near a critical value, as in the inspection of steel rods and other forms that have to meet a lower limit of 60,000 pounds per square inch (psi). An example is recording as 60,000 psi an actual test reading of 59,500 psi.

- During World War II the Truman Committee, in investigating war plant operations, uncovered a situation in a large steel plant where physical and chemical tests of steel plates were faked in the record book. In this case the actual test results were changed when they were recorded.

6. Reporting Errors

- During World War II companies submitted to the War Production Board (WPB) the amount of carbon steel required for their operations for the coming quarter. These values were tabulated for all companies in a specific industry, and together with other figures, were used as a basis for authorizing steel to each individual company. In one case a small company requiring 4,000 pounds of carbon steel actually entered 4,000 pounds on the form submitted to WPB, when it should have been entered as 4 because the unit to be used was 1000 pounds. When processing this data sheet, a WPB clerk entered this as 4,000,000 pounds, obtaining a quarterly total of about 23 million pounds from a 100 percent tabulation. This error was discovered by the Materials Requirement Section, which was using an excellent probability sample to estimate the quarterly requirements for carbon steel. This quick procedure gave a total of about 18,500,000 pounds. As a result the 100 percent tabulation was examined data sheet by data sheet, and in this way the above error was discovered. When this error of almost 4 million pounds was subtracted from 23 million, the sample and the 100 percent tabulation agreed within sampling errors. In this case a sample gave better results than the original 100 percent tabulation, and was used to discover an error in a 100 percent coverage. It served as a sample audit.

- The Federal Census Bureau finds numerous examples of reporting errors in certain characteristics. One of these is the reporting of age, where the tendency is to use even numbers, or numbers ending in 0 or 5. In certain groups an excessive number of persons reported being 100 or more years old. Also, there were more people age 50 than age 31.

- Errors arise from omissions due to memory failure in interviewer-type surveys. In a large nationwide study of family income, check interviewers found that the first interviewer omitted asking about various sources of income such as newspaper route, working in a store at Christmas, and government payments. In this check the actual source of additional income was listed, so the addition was not just a matter of opinion. In one city the income obtained by the check interviewer averaged *20 percent higher* than the income obtained by the first interviewer. In the same study errors arose because many families with higher incomes ($50,000 and over) refused to be interviewed because of invasion of privacy (it was a federal government study). Another reason was fear of gangsters, who had kidnapped a rich banker in the Midwest and held him for a $200,000 ransom.

7. Errors in Appraisal

Two cases are described in some detail because they illustrate how top level officials make a very serious mistake in appraising an agency's nationwide sample studies. The reasons for these mistakes are described in detail. These cases illustrate why and how the most serious mistakes in an agency can be made by the highest officials. It also shows the failure of top level planning.

- A nationwide sample study of rail carload traffic was criticized because it did not yield state data, but only nationwide data. The planning committee never intended the sample to yield state data because of the much larger sample and higher cost required to obtain data in such detail. Whether the top officials were aware of this at the time is unknown, but about 18 months later, when the final study was issued, they took a position that the planning committee had never even considered.
- Another nationwide sample study was criticized because the study did not show monthly data, but only annual data. Here again, the planning committee never intended the sample to yield monthly data because of the larger sample and higher cost required. The top officials had different ideas about the nature of the tabulation and the details that the study should show, but only the final results were issued.

These two cases were very similar although they involved different years, different people, different studies, different executives, and different organizations. Neither group knew anything about the other. A detailed analysis of these situations is given below.

- The top executives differed among themselves about the final form of the data desired.
- There was no top-level written statement as to what the major specifications were.
- The executive planning committee did not pin down the top executives in writing as to the exact kinds and forms of final results desired.
- The executives forgot what had been decided a year, 18 months, or two years before. With nothing in writing, no one could be held responsible at the top level.

- The chief statistician had designed the sample and written the specifications approved by the executive planning committee and had carried them out, but this did not prevent the top officials from criticizing the chief statistician and the sample study.
- Actually, the top officials changed the specifications after the study was completed.
- The planning committee did not plan to collect state and monthly data because of the greatly increased size of sample and a corresponding larger cost, which the chief statistician had pointed out during the planning stage.
- In each case the sample could easily have been designed to obtain the more detailed data.
- This is an example of the decision makers being unable to agree on the specifications and to stick to them. It reflects a serious flaw in top-level planning.

A MORE DETAILED STATEMENT ABOUT THE TWO PRECEDING CASES

In these two studies, three levels of organization were involved in the planning and execution of the nationwide sample studies: 1) top executives, 2) the executive planning committee, and 3) the technical staffs, especially the chief statistician and his staff.

The executive committee asked the chief statistician to develop a feasible sampling method. One of three different sampling approaches was recommended and accepted.

The real problem centered on 1) how detailed the data should be to serve the purposes of management, and 2) how large a sample was required to obtain the data specified. The chief statistician pointed out that the more detailed the data, the larger the sample would have to be, although the most efficient sample design would be used. The executive committee kept bringing up the cost factor. It is not known to what extent, if any, they sounded out the top executives on this point. The point was that if management wanted detailed data, it would have to pay the price. Finally the specifications were settled, a sample plan designed, the detailed specifications laid out, and the sample study implemented.

About two years later, however, the top executives using the study wanted data from a more costly study of data by states and data by months. By this time the executive planning committee was disbanded, but the chief statistician and his staff were still intact. He was now caught between the top executives and a nonexistent planning committee. He was stuck in the middle between the executive committee, for whom he worked, and the top executives, who made the final decisions.

The committee and the executives did not plan and agree to a clear-cut study or put the major decisions in writing. *Planning at the top failed.*
In summary:

- The executives and the executive planning committee worked at cross-purposes.
- Two years later the executives wanted data from a more costly study, which the executive committee opposed.
- Two years later, the planning committee no longer existed, but the statistician and his staff were still on the job.
- Criticisms of the sample studies two years later were not sent to the chief statistician, but they were sent to others. He heard about them and saw them when a colleague showed him the memorandum.
- The chief statistician should not proceed until a written statement of the specifications has been approved by top executives.

What are the lessons to be learned?

- Be sure decisions at the top are put in writing.
- Be sure top planners agree on the basic specifications.
- Be sure the chief statistician knows what the final specifications are.
- The chief statistician should not proceed until a written statement of the specifications has been approved by top executives.

THE SERIOUSNESS OF ERROR

In connection with the prevention of error it is necessary to distinguish between errors that are serious and those that are not. In fact, the seriousness of errors extends over a wide continuum from personal inconvenience to fatality. We may arrange the seriousness of errors in a continuum or scale with regard to the human effects involved and the degree of money loss involved:

Human Effects	*Money Loss*
Inconvenience	None, slight
Frustration	Slight, little
Minor suffering	Minor amount
Minor injury	Minor amount
Major suffering	Moderate amount
Serious injury	Considerable amount
Major injury	Very large amount
Crippling injury	Lifetime loss
Fatality	Heavy, very serious amount
	Too great to measure

These rankings are illustrative; other people may have a different set or may disagree with these. The main objective of these lists, however, is to emphasize that there are human losses involved in errors, mistakes, and blunders as well as money losses, which may or may not compensate for the seriousness of the human effects. If inconvenience and frustration last long enough, the money loss may be much larger than that indicated above.

THE CONSEQUENCES OF ERRORS, MISTAKES, AND BLUNDERS

The consequences of errors, mistakes, and blunders are many and varied; some are minor while others are fatal. The following list shows this variety and the differences in their significance:

- Inconvenience, frustration;
- Increased costs of operation, of production, of services;
- Increased prices of products and services due to wasted time;
- Poor-quality goods;
- Failure of equipment;
- Poor-quality services;
- Dissatisfied customers;
- Alienated customers, lost customers;
- Human suffering (e.g., accidents, unemployment);
- Loss of property;
- Inability to meet competition;
- Employee unrest and conflict;
- High insurance premiums;
- Bankruptcy;
- Lawsuits;
- Business failure;
- Danger;
- Accidents;
- Injuries;
- Crippling effects;
- Fatalities.

These may be divided into a number of broad classes:

- Money losses of all kinds, including insurance premiums and lawsuits;
- Dissatisfaction and alienation of both customers and employees;
- Poor quality of goods, services, performance, data, decisions;
- Fatalities;
- Other suffering and injuries;

- Non-money losses: sentimental items, souvenirs, mementos, photographs;
- Failure of equipment, machinery, and apparatus; failure of facilities.

PSYCHOLOGICAL ASPECTS OF ERROR

Errors, being human, are psychological in nature and origin. The quality manager and supervisor have to understand the psychological nature of these errors if they are to develop ways to reduce, if not eliminate, them. This is no easy task, as the persistence of human errors indicates. Even so, the current notion that errors are human, and therefore should be condoned and accepted, should be rejected. Human errors can be prevented, as numerous studies and extensive experience have shown. At this point some of the major psychological aspects of human error are discussed. The emphasis is on nature, not on prevention, which is discussed in a later chapter, though some preventatives are mentioned. The aspects are sensory motor skills, learning knowledge, attention, memory, reasoning, emotions, behavior, and social interactions.

Sensory Motor Skills

These involve the five senses—sight, hearing, touch, taste, and smell—and the associated sensations, as well as the motor or muscle reactions connected with them. They involve such functions as perceptions, which are an awareness and an interpretation of sensations, and reaction time, which is the time required for a sense organ to react to a stimulus. Ability to perceive and to react varies widely among individuals and has to be recognized in both education and training.

Sight is the most important sensory function because it encompasses all of the visible world, its outward structure, its mobility, and its interaction. It is the key to knowledge because knowledge is recorded and preserved in printed matter of all kinds. No doubt a message can be conveyed better for most people by sight presentation than by voice. One reason is that written sentences are usually much more carefully constructed than are sentences in speech or conversation. Written records have an accuracy that coverage oral records do not have.

The five senses may need testing to determine if they are functioning properly. Tests may show that a person needs glasses or a hearing aid, that the light is too dim, or that glare is interfering with clear vision. Tests also may show that the noise level is too high or that the air is polluted with smelly gases.

Sensory motor functions include many basic abilities: reading, writing, talking, spelling, typing, skating, playing musical instruments, playing physical games, driving an automobile, riding a bicycle, and riding a motorcycle. Learning in these fields requires constant practice, following methods, techniques, and coaching that lead either to successful performance or to a high level of performance.

Perceptions, the interpretations of sensations based upon knowledge and experience, are very important in learning these abilities. Perceptions of speed, distance, motion, and position are very important in driving an automobile. Perceptions of shape, color, size, fit, and weight are important in buying many articles. Perceptions relative to smell of gas, gasoline odor, forces associated with high speed, dangers of lightning and electricity, and how carbon monoxide accumulates are all needed to practice safety in home, office, factory, and recreation.

Learning Knowledge

This area deals with the psychology of learning, especially the mastery of important knowledge. The emphasis is on understanding the meanings of words, sentences, paragraphs, chapters, and topics. These include the important terms and principles of special fields of subject matter such as history, geography, science, elementary mathematics, literature, or a foreign language. The mastery of content provides the substance of writing, thinking, forming ideas, and appraising them. It provides the basis for critically appraising the content of newspapers, magazines, reports, television news, and other sources of events, news, reports, opinions, and conversations. The latter is very important if the American people are not to be brainwashed by opinion, bias, conjecture, and suspicion peddled as news and comment.

Two systems have to be learned: the *language system* based on the 26 letters in the alphabet, and the *number system* based on the 10 digits. Both of these are vital for business, industry, government, and other institutions and for rational and intelligent communication. Both are necessary in the educational system if people are to learn how to think intelligently both as citizens and as workers.

Many factors enter into the learning process. The first items listed below relate to the individual; the last items listed relate to a teacher or a coach.

- Repetition; practice to strengthen memory, neural bonds;
- Divided rather than concentrated practice over time;
- Well-written, accurate, easy-to-understand books, manuals, and instructions;
- Writing out main points of a subject;
- Outlining a book, talk, or seminar;
- Working problems and writing daily (pencil and paper work);
- Explaining main points to others;
- Presenting a summary of a book, talk, seminar, or conference;
- Relating new material to something already learned (association);
- Testing learning on a topic, problem, or subject;
- Correcting errors, as in spelling, grammar, and mathematics;
- Explaining applications to real life;

- Coaching;
- Explanations and exposition by teacher.

Learning consists of understanding both percepts and concepts. The former involve an awareness and understanding of sensory perceptions, as described above. The latter include an understanding of the abstractions and constructs which characterize concepts. These include words which we use daily, yet we haven't the slightest idea what they really mean in terms of the five senses. Numerous examples can be cited because most of our world is conceptual and abstract rather than perceptual. These include force, cost, time, mind, energy, electricity, price, space, gravity, power, quality, profit, control, velocity, effort, management, productivity, efficiency, acceleration, motivation, competition, measurement, inflation, interest, and magnetism.

Attention

Attention refers to the concentration of the senses or mind on a very specific area, subject, object, or situation. It is a selection process in which the individual is forever engaged. We are surrounded by stimuli, but we select that which interests us; this means selection and concentration. The importance of attention is reflected in saying, "Keep your eye on the ball."
"A stitch in time saves nine."
"Don't put off until tomorrow what you can do today."
Attention can be concentrated by getting rid of distractions that divert the mind and thought, by concentrating on problems and activities of interest, by emphasizing goals and purposes, and by developing permanent interests and hobbies and avocations as well as an occupation or profession. Interests are excellent examples of concentrating attention on a restricted or special set of activities.
Attention is gained in many different ways:

- Sight: motion, movement, changes, flashing lights, colors, pictures, posters, sex appeal, strange objects;
- Sound: loudness, varying pitch (siren), strange and different sounds;
- Repetition: repeating an appeal many times;
- Something that appeals to people: big money, sales, getting rich quick, sex appeal, the unusual, sports, adventure, music, exotic science;
- Something new, novel, and interesting: a story, an anecdote, an adventure;
- A demonstration or experiment: scientific experiment, puzzle, invention, computer demonstration, something strange that works.

Attention is a key factor in all education, regardless of the level. Without the attention of the individual, the teacher will not succeed in *teaching* the topic or subject because without the student's concentration on what is being said or done, there will be little or no *learning*. Not only attention is necessary; *sustained attention is required*. This sustained attention to a problem or subject over a long period of time—years or decades—accounts for inventions, innovations, new ideas, new techniques, original discoveries, and creativity.

Memory

Memory no doubt is the most important human characteristic. It enables people to remember the past, to learn from experience. We remember what was, and this has tremendous advantages, even if it does have unpleasant overtones. Together with retention, recognition, and recall, memory makes learning possible. This is a miracle that no computer can ever duplicate.

Memory has a capacity without limits. The retrieval is amazing, and includes events that happened decades ago. There is a tendency to question the accuracy of memory, especially if it goes far back into the past, but this is not necessarily justified. It all depends upon the person and the circumstances.

Memory of events is strengthened and fixed by circumstances such as these:

- How shocking the event was (fire, flood, storm, blizzard);
- How unusual the event was (a trip to a big city, an ocean voyage);
- How personal the event was (being in a runaway, shipwreck, disaster);
- Personal injury (an accident);
- Novelty or newness of the event (when the A & P store arrived);
- Written record, such as a diary, a letter, naturalization papers, or a diploma.

Recall is facilitated in many different ways:

- Written records: letters, record books, bookkeeping records, official documents, diaries;
- Association of one event with another event that happened at about the same time;
- Cues and clues of various kinds;
- Births, deaths, and anniversaries;
- Repetition of the original event.

Retention, recognition, and recall of knowledge and events are not only facilitated but almost guaranteed by a wide variety of activities: skills used constantly, skills once mastered but not often used, knowledge and skills used in one's work, knowledge and skills that one teaches, knowledge and skills that one writes books about, persistent reading of magazines, newspapers, and books, knowledge used constantly, and first-time experiences: telephone, auto, movie, radio, television, concrete roads, electric lights, street car, bus, truck, railroad, phonograph, airplane.

Many factors enter into determining the accuracy of memory, not only of past events but of knowledge. Several of these factors are as follows:

- Intelligence, native mental ability;
- Stress on accuracy in such basic skills as spelling, writing, and arithmetic;
- Strength of initial impressions;
- Association with other ideas and symbols;
- Clear explanations and expositions;
- Physical demonstrations and experiments;
- Tie-in with related ideas;
- Repeated applications of knowledge and skills;
- Tests of knowledge and skills;
- Periodic recall to prevent forgetting;
- Continuous study, lifelong learning;
- Continuous practice;
- Use of cues and other devices to facilitate memory.

Reasoning

Reasoning is a thinking process involving use of percepts, concepts, and other verbal material as well as numerical language to understand, make inferences, draw conclusions, and make judgments. The process involves such concepts as the following:

- Similarities and differences;
- Comparisons and contrasts;
- Cause and effect;
- Relationships: some quantity y varies as some quantity x varies;
- Connections and networks;
- Reconciling one thing with another.

Knowledge is the content with which this thinking is done. Major sources of knowledge include the following:

- Scientific and engineering characteristics and principles;
- Logic;
- Mathematics, statistics, and probability;
- Other specialized knowledge of all kinds.

Reasoning therefore is difficult and subject to error for many different causes, such as faulty data, faulty diagnosis, faulty analysis, faulty inference, faulty reasoning by analogy, false similarities and differences with both past and present, faulty knowledge, incomplete knowledge, lack of knowledge, lack of research, and lack of a critical, questioning attitude.

Here are several examples of reasoning by analogy, along with an appraisal of each:

• The computer is a brain.	False
• Electricity is analogous to water in a pipe with pressure, current, and resistance.	True
• A human being has memory and can be intelligent. A computer has memory; therefore it is intelligent.	False
• Make a clock that reads the time directly, as does an odometer on an automobile (digital).	This was finally done.
• A substance that causes cancer in an experimental test animal can cause cancer in people (Delaney Clause of the Food, Drug and Cosmetic Act).	Not true most of the time
• High grades in high school mean high grades in college.	Not at all. Depends.
• If quality control applies to telephone parts, it applies to other products.	Proven to be true
• If quality control applies to products, it can also be applied to services.	Proven to be true, with qualifications
• If a sample and a population have similar average and percentage compositions for a few characteristics, the sample is a good reflection of the population.	False (demonstrated by Neyman)
• A person who is a good specialist will make a good manager.	Only in some instances

Emotions

Emotions and feelings are at the heart of the attitudes, behavior, and motivation basic to supervision, quality improvement, and the environment of the workplace. Quality is as much a feeling by individuals as it is their intelligence. Supervisors have to deal with individual problems involving feelings and emotions as often as they have to deal with problems involving intelligence and understanding. Indeed, the problems involving emotions and feelings may be much more difficult to resolve. For this reason they deserve careful observation, study, and consideration.

The following are some of the important feelings to cultivate or promote, depending upon whether the individual or the supervisor is concerned: self-esteem, pleasure, satisfaction, recognition, excellence, self-confidence, accomplishment, achievement, challenge, competition, cooperation, teamwork, team spirit, pride in work, attention, security, justice, fair play, credit, and freedom to improve.

By contrast, other emotions or feelings create conflict and trouble. These affect personal relationships involving people at all levels of the organization. They can cause serious problems and will have to be prevented, ameliorated, or eliminated if the organization is to operate a quality improvement program or any other kind of program. These emotions include envy, jealousy, anger, fear, feuds, vengefulness, hatred, antagonism, rebellion, sense of injustice, refusal to follow instructions, hurt, pain, negativism, plotting psychological war against someone, harassment, dislike, opposition, skepticism, suspicion, inferiority complex, personal insecurity, desire for attention, aggressiveness, abrasiveness, plotting and intrigues.

One aspect of human behavior that is closely related to emotions is what psychologists call "mental mechanisms." Mental mechanisms are the various ways which we use to justify what happens to us or to others. They are very often a way to justify failure, loss, why something should not be done. It is a way to justify to ourselves what is going on. They are very important to identify in connection with development of a program for quality improvement because mental mechanisms are usually nonproductive, negative, and destructive alibis or excuses to justify errors and mistakes. Examples are given below, with comments:

- Sour grapes: It wasn't any good anyway.
- Pollyanna: All's well with the world. Everything is fine. No problems.
- Silent treatment: Avoidance; keep quiet. Say nothing,
- "This is not the proper time": Another "avoidance" technique. Fear of taking action or making a real decision; concealed opposition.
- Blaming others: The fault lies with others.
- Negative attitude: Rejection complex; always vote *nyet*.
- Discrimination: Favoritism toward some others.
- Exaggeration: Discrediting others by distortion or exaggeration.
- "Everyone does it": This excuses away faults and failures.

Psychology and psychiatry show that there are no sure-fire methods to deal with the problems of emotions and feelings. The therapeutic field is well developed, but applications are meant for professionals, not for managers and supervisors in organizations. There are remedies that work for some, but not for others. A feud between two departmental managers is not easy to resolve, for example. In many, if not most, organizations these smoldering conflicts are simply accepted and lived with.

The following preventatives may help moderate some of these conflicts: rewards, recognition, encouragement, assistance, commendation, encouraging self-development, seminars and courses in human relations and supervision, personal conferences and talks, explaining the importance of the work and company policy, shifting to other positions, eliminating competition between departments, cooperating "or else," learning from failures, facing realities, accepting what can't be changed.

Behavior, Attitudes, and Social Interaction

Quality in services, according to a nationwide survey by the Gallup Organization and revealed by the experience of customers everywhere, is determined by the behavior and attitudes of employees.[1] Behavior and attitudes are revealed in many different ways, both positive and negative. Negative behavior includes the following:

- Is discourteous, impolite, rude, curt;
- Ignores customer;
- Doesn't like to wait on older customers;
- Doesn't wait on customers in order;
- Shifts company's error onto the customer;
- Doesn't communicate with or talk to customer.

There are other indicators:

- Performance on the job;
- Knowledge of the job;
- Knowledge of what to do in a situation extending beyond the job;
- Knowledge of what to do if the situation is not routine;
- Conflicts among the employees; feuds, jealousies;
- Self-control under stress, criticism, or serious problem;
- Employee engaged in a transaction with a customer does not inform others what to do in case of her absence; leaves customer high and dry.

This raises the question of what type of person to hire in the first place:

- Those who like and get along with people;
- Those who accept teamwork and cooperation;
- Those who can talk to people pleasantly and to the point;
- Those who know how to talk over the telephone;
- Those who are emotionally stable and mature (This is not easy. Use verbal test situations as well as the person's past record);
- Those who are willing to work with customers with a wide variety of habits and attitudes, and who may be demanding and critical.

---

[1] The study by the Gallup Organization is described in detail in Chapter 3.

Managers, supervisors, and employees who want to get along with other people need to exhibit daily behavior and attitudes of certain kinds. People like other people who are kind, courteous, considerate, polite, friendly, fair, honest, truthful, trustworthy, helpful, accommodating, humble, and not boastful or snobbish.

Those who have the following characteristics are also well liked:

- Have no favorites or "teacher's pets";
- Are ready to defend those unjustly accused, especially their own employees;
- Are competent and "know their stuff";
- Are willing to admit mistakes;
- Do not cover up or blame others for their mistakes;
- Are always available to talk;
- Are ready to admit that they "don't know"; are never know-it-alls;
- Are clear and honest, with straight talk;
- Give credit where credit is due;
- Make people feel important;
- Are good listeners with an understanding attitude;
- Are interesting to talk to, good storytellers;
- Recognize the abilities of others;
- Do not hold grudges;
- Are willing to work anywhere when a critical situation arises;
- Recognize work and accomplishments of others.

Chapter 7

The Characteristics of Quality and Their Measurement

Once the nature of quality is understood, the next step is to identify the characteristics associated with quality and how to measure them. Both of these steps—identification and measurement—call for a careful analysis of operations so as to reveal or disclose the various situations or problems involving quality. Once this is done (and with careful observation and examination it is not difficult), the next step is the very critical one of collecting data about these characteristics.

Data are important for several different reasons: they solve problems, reveal a problem that management did not realize it had, show the magnitude of the problem, reveal new problems, or throw light on a situation that may become a problem.

QUALITY CHARACTERISTICS

Quality characteristics encountered in services are of three kinds: measurable, observable effects and conditions, and observable behavior traits and attitudes. The quality characteristics of purchased products are included wherever they belong. Many, if not most, will be measurable, but many quality characteristics will be observable.

Measurable Characteristics in Services

1. Time: delay, waiting, service, idle, downtime, access, lead, wasted, excessive, shipping, delivery, repair, unnecessary.
2. Price and cost: excessive price, high cost, loss, gain, unit cost, unit price, life cycle cost, cost of quality, quality and price, price tag, lowest bidder, contracting out, service cost.
3. Laboratory tests for health: blood, urine, tissue, feces.
4. Instrumental tests for health: temperature, pulse, sight, hearing, blood pressure, glaucoma pressure, electrocardiogram.

5. Laboratory and field tests: air, water, and soil for pollution, chemicals, and radioactivity.
6. Other laboratory tests: business and industrial (retail stores, e.g., Sears); electrical apparatus.
7. Performance tests: e.g., EPA test of gas mileage for automobiles.
8. Errors: number, rate, trend, distribution, cost, learning curve based on errors.
9. Production: volume, total per day, amount per person per day, acceptable quality, unacceptable quality, production curve.
10. Distribution of identicals: distribution of persons performing the same task or operation), testing same samples, assessing the same property, premiums on same insurance policy.
11. Measurable characteristics that affect the quality of purchased products.
12. Reliability of equipment; failures.

Observable Effects and Conditions

These are indicators of poor performance and poor service. They are dichotomies such as yes or no, suceeded or failed, worked or did not work, right or wrong diagnosis:

- Trouble eliminated or not, e. g., radio, television, automobile repair;
- Illness eliminated or not;
- Medicine or drug helpful or not;
- Treatment helped or did not;
- Food satisfactory or not;
- Room satisfactory or not;
- Device, equipment, or apparatus worked or did not;
- Clothing or shoes fit or did not;
- Products defective or not;
- Defects in service or not;
- Postal service satisfactory or not;
- Transportation comfortable or not;
- Transportation convenient or not;
- Transportation on time or not;
- Diagnosis correct or not: X-ray, CAT scan, ultrasound, glaucoma test, Pap smear;
- Installation defective or not, works or does not, work done right or wrong.

These are examples of incompetence, failure to fix, faulty results, failure to satisfy customer, and service failure.

Observable Behavior Traits and Attitudes

These traits are positive and contribute to quality, or negative and detract from quality or contribute to non-quality or anti-quality. As stated before, the results of the nationwide Gallup survey for the American Society for Quality Control show very clearly that customers have no difficulty in identifying these non-quality characteristics in persons who are performing services:

Characteristics That Are Good Quality, Pro-Quality	*Characteristics That Show Poor Quality, Are Anti-Quality*
• courteous	discourteous
• helpful	indifferent
• careful	careless
• polite, mannerly	rude
• kind	curt
• sympathetic	critical, antagonistic
• considerate	abrasive, arbitrary
• prompt	slow, procrastinating
• cooperative	self-centered, egotistical
• accurate	inaccurate, error-prone
• honest	dishonest, deceiving
• encouraging	negative, discouraging
• reliable	unreliable, untrustworthy
• assisting	ignoring
• understanding	indifferent, avoiding
• interested, concerned, caring	unfair
• competent, qualified	incompetent, unqualified

It should be noted that the characteristics of quality listed above are virtues which are highly regarded among people generally. They are some of the marks of the highly civilized and socially acceptable individual. They rate high on the list of desirable characteristics when the customer appraises the service rendered by employees, supervisors, and managers.

Quality of service to the customer is determined by the reliability of equipment. The quality of service to the customer is determined mainly by two major factors: 1) the employees who wait on or serve the customer, and 2) the reliability of all kinds of equipment. The first has already been described, but will receive more attention in later chapters.

The reliability of equipment falls into two categories: 1) the reliability of equipment owned by the customer as householder and 2) the reliability of equipment of companies and organizations that serve the customer. Examples include the following:

- Equipment owned by the customer: automobile, appliances, truck, lawn mower;
- Equipment owned by outside companies or organizations:
  - Public utilities: gas, electricity, water, telephone;
  - Transportation: buses, airlines, trucks, trains, ships, taxis;
  - Medical equipment;
  - Lighting, heating, air conditioning, plumbing in hotels, motels, restaurants;
  - Repair and testing equipment.

The goal is to maintain reliability of equipment at a 100 percent level. The public utilities meet this goal year in and year out with only a rare failure, and often that is due to weather or other conditions beyond their control.

Reliability of equipment should be subject to continuous data collection and study to discover problems before they become serious. Sources include maintenance records, repair orders, failure records and studies, replacement orders, service records, and maintenance and repair and failure records by age.

THE MEASUREMENT OF QUALITY CHARACTERISTICS

Three Forms of Data

The status of quality is determined by collecting data through one of three methods: 1) making measurements, 2) counting, and 3) observations.

The importance of collecting good quality data at the very start cannot be overemphasized. This is because data give an objective evidence of existing quality problems or difficulties, and may even suggest what to do about some of them. Obviously when an inference is made about good or poor quality, substantial and correct evidence should exist to support it. Data therefore should be based upon a careful analysis of problems, or should be collected in connection with an important situation that requires careful study. We therefore turn next to the basic procedure to follow in order to insure that quality is built into the data, the inferences, the actions, and the decisions.

The Quality Information Action Cycle

The cycle diagramed in Figure 7–1 and described below is an effective and universal approach to problem solving regardless of what the problem is and regardless of what kinds of data are collected. Problem identification and analysis are essential preliminary steps to planning a study and laying out the methods to be followed in collecting and interpreting the data.

Problem analysis reveals the characteristics to be studied and the classes and subclasses into which the data are to be divided. Problem analysis also reveals

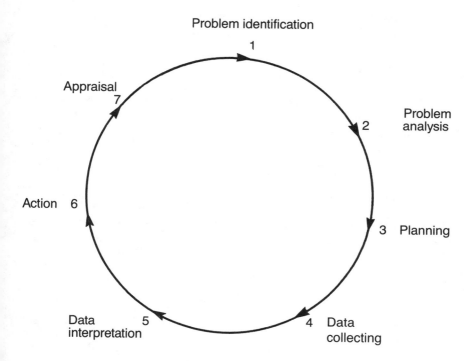

Figure 7–1. **The Quality Information Action Cycle**

the questions to be answered and the hypotheses to be tested. This analysis is carried to the point where the kinds, forms, and amounts of data to be collected are specified. The data have sense because they arise from an analysis of the problems to be solved and the questions to be answered.

The cycle can be modified in the initial stages for a study which is simply an exploration of some situation, subject matter, or topic of interest. There is no problem and little or no analysis of the situation, or detailed planning of the method of data collection. The study plan for the collection of data may be sound, but the basic purpose of the study is to *discover problems, not to solve them.* When the study is finished and the results have been analyzed, it is time to start a serious attack on one or more problems, as shown in the figure.

It should also be noted that while the first cycle may uncover and solve a problem of great importance, it may give rise to some other problems so that another cycle or other cycles are needed. For example, the United States Treasury Department carried out a nationwide sample study that gave them a very good estimate of the amount of non-compliance (tax error) on Form 1040, the individual federal income tax. Once they had a firm figure of non-compliance, the question immediately arose: How should audit resources be allocated to take advantage of the new information?

Each cycle consists of seven consecutive parts, as follows:

1. Problem identification or situation identification;
2. Problem analysis: problems to be solved, questions to be answered;
3. Planning: laying out procedures for attacking the problem;
4. Collecting data: putting the plan into effect;
5. Interpreting the data: reducing data to information, inferences, findings, conclusions, decisions;
6. Taking action based on findings and decisions: substantive action as well as action on procedures and methods;
7. Appraisal: taking note of the progress made, what succeeded and what did not, what worked and what did not, whether problem was really solved or not, what was omitted, what more needs to be done, were the final results of acceptable quality, does the sample or experiment need to be improved.

Examples of False Data and Conflicting Plans that Led to False Decisions

In *Quality is Free,* Philip Crosby tells about a company whose field data had *not* been analyzed and used. It was suggested in a conference that the field data might be the starting point of a quality improvement program. This raises the question: Why had the field data been collected in the first place if it was not going to be used? Other examples of the non-use and misuse of data can be cited to illustrate once more how critical data collection and use are. Some of this criticism of data was due to faulty planning at the top.

- When the sales of a company drops, the top official immediately jumps to the conclusion that the sales department is at fault, that they have been lying down on the job. He substitutes hunch, conjecture, and intuition for actual data relating to the problem. His hunch is wrong.
- A manager of a textile mill comes to the false conclusion that employees are stealing $1 million worth of hose. His false inference is based on data obtained from a test run of one of the best machine operators. The data therefore were highly biased and invalid. The employees are not the problem; he is.
- A large-scale nationwide biased sample of public opinion led to a false conclusion as to the winning candidate in the 1936 presidential election. The same was true of the 1948 presidential election.
- A very poorly designed plutonium test comparing Rocky Flats (Colorado) with a site in Nevada led to a false conclusion which was headlined in the press. The analysis of the data was faulty, incomplete, and not made by a

technically trained person; otherwise the false conclusion would have been discovered immediately.

- A nationwide sample study is planned and executed under the direction of an executive planning committee. After the study is completed and the report is in the hands of top officials, they criticize the sample and those who planned and executed it because the data were not shown on a monthly instead of on an annual basis. This was the result of faulty planning and decision making at the top.
- A similar study made many years later in an entirely different organization was criticized by top-level officials because it showed only U.S. data, not state data. This was due to faulty planning at the top.

Warnings Aimed at Improving Data Collection

Actual practices are cited below, which can serve as warnings in collecting data so as to avoid defects, errors, and other troublesome aspects that characterize poor-quality or rejectable data.

- In a family income study, interviewers do not probe for secondary or short one-time incomes such as newspaper routes, Christmas sales job, or odd jobs.
- Inspectors do not record accurate values when these values are near a tolerance limit, but they "pull in" the value so that it falls within the limits.
- Computer people forget to run four reels of tape for a sample study, thereby eliminating 17,000 records from the study. A manual sample receipts control system catches the error and saves the study.
- In a field office, the person in charge of sampling forgets to sample one cabinet of records. Another person samples at the wrong sampling rate.
- A carload waybill shows sheep being shipped in a tank car. A person records 450 tons being carried by one freight car. These are impossible values.
- The federal census shows that persons report age most frequently with digits ending in even numbers, 0, and 5. In one case there were more persons 50 years of age than age 31.
- In an opinion or attitude questionnaire, the changing of only one key word in a sentence can change the nature of the answers very markedly.
- A bank enters a deposit of $1,842 as $18.42, thereby causing no end of trouble for the businessman who made the deposit. He finally takes the case into court and sues the bank for wasting his time.
- A mortgage company makes an error of $314 in connection with the settlement of a loan to a householder. The latter paid the real estate company the $314, but the mortgage company's computer was not programmed to handle such a transaction. It took months to get this error out of the computer system.

Data Collection Devices

These devices are used to elicit and record original data. Extreme care must be used in designing and using them if accurate and valid data are to be obtained. As described in detail below, there are always two basic problems to consider and resolve: 1) how best to *design* the device and 2) how best to *use* the device to obtain accurate and sound data.

Written Questionnaires: Design

The trouble with just about every written questionnaire is that those preparing it make the serious mistake of assuming that it is a simple job of asking a few questions, but it is nothing of the kind. A sound questionnaire must be carefully designed and based upon an analyzed purpose and a specific goal. This requires more than asking a few conversational questions. Questions aimed at objective facts, as in a census, are easier to formulate than those aimed at opinions, attitudes, or preferences. The following specifications must be observed:

1. Make questions simple and short.
2. Make questions single-barreled; don't combine two questions into one.
3. Use nonemotional words.
4. Use neutral questions; avoid loaded questions because they bias the results.
5. Allow all shades of opinion; avoid questions which restrict replies.
6. Do not use double negatives.
7. Use purpose-related questions; avoid irrelevant questions.
8. If the answer to one question depends upon the answer to another, explain this very clearly.

All questionnaires should be pretested and revised so that they are free of obvious faults: ambiguities, misunderstandings, confusing words, conflicting interpretations, high non-response rates.

Written Questionnaires: Application

There is an art and a science to the use of questionnaires. It is not the simple clerical task that many think. The interviewer should be trained in the following:

1. How to interview;
2. How to ask questions;
3. How to interpret answers (this is vitally important);

4. How to probe without biasing the results;
5. How to report and record objectively;
6. How to keep personal feelings out of questions, especially out of interpretations of what is said;
7. How to ask questions exactly as prescribed. Changing one word can change the answers;
8. How to handle deviates: refuses to answer, listens but has no opinion, listens but objects to the way the question is phrased;
9. How to identify an accurate opinion or view in a long rambling conversation, and ask person to verify or change it.

Oral Interview With a Set of Questions

Face-to-face interviews with a set of questions are often used to conduct market surveys in shopping malls. What was discussed above about questionnaire design and use applies to this situation as well. The real problem in crowd interviewing is that of sampling. Persons to be interviewed are picked out of the passers-by, so there is no way of telling what kind of sample is obtained or how biased it may be in favor of some group. Using a quota system is not acceptable, as numerous opinion polls have shown.

Telephone Interviewing

Today a common way of interviewing is by telephone. In more scientific studies names are drawn at random from telephone directories covering the entire United States. What was described about the design and use of the questionnaire also applies here. In addition, several serious questions arise with regard to the response to a telephone call. For example, what is done about the following?

1. No answer. How many recalls are made? How are "no answers" recorded, if at all?
2. Whom do you want an answer from? What do you do if children or relatives answer?
3. What if the call results in a refusal to answer?
4. What if the call results in listening but no opinion?
5. What if the call results in an objection to using the telephone this way?

Reports on opinion polls give no counts or percentages for those not at home, those who were eligible but unobtainable, or those who refused to answer for any reason whatever. With no report on these, the 3 or 4 percent variation in percentages due to sampling is invalid.

Rating Scales

Rating scales are used extensively to obtain information about quality in a wide variety of services: airlines, hotels, retail stores, auto repair shops, and restaurants. The usual ratings are poor, fair, good, and excellent, sometimes with another class inserted in the middle. These ratings are applied in a hotel to persons such as the telephone operators and the front desk clerk, and to the appearance of the room.[1] The rating scales have several weaknesses with regard to useful information for quality control purposes.

1. The specific activities and conditions on which the rating is based are missing. Management therefore has no problem to examine, diagnose, and take action on. This is especially true of "poor" and "fair" ratings. Management is also in the dark as to why certain activities and conditions are rated "excellent" or "good."

2. The same rating given by different guests or by different persons may represent widely different activities and performances.

3. What some persons like, other persons dislike, so that the same service, performance, or condition may receive a wide range of ratings. If specifics were available, management might be better able to decide what to do. This is a situation where frequency of occurrence is important, so that a sample survey over a period of months might be necessary.

4. Ratings based on widely different experiences are not comparable and therefore cannot be added or quantified in any meaningful way.

What is needed is not a rating scale but a service report. This form provides for listing specific instances of unsatisfactory conditions and behavior. Each instance would give date, place, time, person or persons, and a description of the poor service, faulty condition, delay, poor selection, lack of choice, failures, and other details. In this way management knows what the trouble is and where it is.

Data Sheets

Data sheets take countless forms and are often thought to be associated with clerical work. That does not mean that they should not be carefully designed. Most data sheets are a combination of words, terms, and instructions, as well as places for numerical entries. The number of the latter may run into scores, if not hundreds. If it gets too large, punched cards or other means are used for computer processing.

For manual operations a convenient tabular form which has stood the test of

---

[1] For detailed examples see A. C. Rosander, *Applications of Quality Control in the Service Industries* (New York: Marcel Dekker and Milwaukee: Quality Press, 1985), Chapters 7 and 10.

time is a sheet of paper twice typewriter size (8½ x 22 inches) which can be folded in the middle for easy filing. It can also be torn in half for use in smaller jobs. There are 21 columns and 45 lines, with plenty of space at the top for titles, units of measurement, and other data.

Data sheets should show clearly, together with an explanation, that there are two parts to fill out: identification information and numbers. Identification data should be appropriate for the type of data being collected, and will vary according to purpose. Identification information often includes date, time, place (e.g., department) product or part, name of person, and nature of service.

Detailed information should be given either on the form or separately with regard to the exact nature of the data wanted and where the various figures should be entered. If the numbers have to be entered under several categories or classes, the sheet should explain what characteristic is identified with each class, and what the unit of measurement is.

Three examples of data sheets used in actual practice are given in a quality control book:[2]

- Auto pollution inspection sheet;
- Water quality data for state laboratory testing;
- Blood and urine health laboratory test record sheet.

Four additional data sheets are given in another book:[3]

- Traffic study abstract;
- Random time work sample data sheet—Example 1;
- Random time work sample data sheet—Example 2;
- Record of truck pickup and delivery trips.

What a number stands for should always be indicated together with time and location, if these are applicable.

Special data sheets will have to be prepared for making studies of *administrative records*. Here it is necessary to summarize and analyze the data even though the data required may be run off by a computer. The administrative records in which questions or problems of quality are involved include records from the following departments:

- Personnel: payroll, turnover, absences, sick leave, other leave, length of service;
- Financial: costs, sales, profit, rate of return, market share;

---

[2] *Applications of Quality Control in the Service Industries,* pp. 62, 63, 71.

[3] A. C. Rosander, *Case Studies in Sample Design* (New York: Marcel Dekker, 1977), pp. 69, 263, 284, 302.

- Shipping: delivery time, turnaround time, costs, damage, complaints, defective containers;
- Marketing: market surveys and tests, preferences for competing products, new products;
- Customer complaints: defective product, damaged product, failure of product, poor service, non-delivery, erorrs.

Control Charts

A badly neglected problem in connection with control charts is how and in what form the original data are to be recorded for easy calculation and plotting. The multi-purpose chart shown in Chapter 8 combines a tabular form for a minimum of 100 values, spaces for calculated values, formulas for calculating limits, and cross-section paper for plotting the chart. Everything is conveniently located. With a clipboard to hold the data form and a hand-held calculator to make the computations, it is easy to plot these charts on the factory floor or in the place of work. This method may turn out to be much more effective and faster than a computer since the time-consuming task is the collection and recording of the data. This has to be done whether the calculations and chart are made manually or by a computer. Furthermore, if the computer is located at some distance and has other programs to run, the time required to get the job done by computer may take longer than doing it by the method described above.

The most common control charts are those for $\bar{x}$ (the mean), R (the range), p (percentage), np (the binomial count or frequency), and c (the Poisson count or frequency). All of these can be handled by the chart and the table given in Chapter 8. This latter form can also be used to record paired values x and y for correlation and regression analysis. In addition, it can be used to record and plot a frequency distribution. If all of the data cannot be recorded on one sheet, two or more sheets can be used.

Making Observations of Human Behavior

It is not difficult to observe human behavior in the workplace. The real problem is how to describe it, interpret it, label it, and classify it. Psychology has not developed the vocabulary, the techniques, and the operational definitions which make this permissible, let alone easy. It should not be overlooked, however, that Gallup's nationwide poll of 1005 persons for the American Society for Quality Control showed that individuals could identify the reasons for poor quality services just as easily as they could identify the reasons for poor quality products. Poor quality services concentrated on human behavior and attitudes; poor quality products did not, except in the term "poor workmanship." A few cases illustrate the problems involved in the human behavior and attitudes associated with services.

1. A customer was wrongly charged $166 on her monthly bill, but she kept records of her purchases so she knew the company had made an error. She reported these facts to the credit department of the company. In a telephone conversation, the person in the credit department tried to brush the whole affair aside, saying that the customer had forgotten that she had made the purchases or had let relatives or friends use her credit card. These were obvious attempts to discredit the customer, to suggest that she didn't know what she was talking about.[4]

The customer insisted that she had records to prove what she said, that she had no relatives, that she never lent her credit card to anyone. Finally the company traced the transaction to its main store and found that the sales slip did not show the customer's signature but someone else's; it did show the customer's 10-digit identification number. Furthermore, the customer had never shopped at that store; when the sale was made on a Saturday, the customer was at home, 60 miles away. The customer was right; the company was wrong. How do you classify human behavior in this case? The company's behavior? The following might apply: arrogant, insulting, browbeating, trying to intimidate, self-righteous, falsely accusing and refusing to apologize for their mistake. The company's own record of the transaction showed that the employee at that store made a mistake. How the 10-digit number got on the sales slip was never revealed. It may be that the credit department deliberately shifted a non-collectible account to an innocent customer, believing that it would never be detected. If so, they were fooled. The company never made a written explanation, let alone a written apology.

This company needs to teach its employees some civilized behavior when dealing with customers. It needs to train its salespeople so they know how to handle a transaction correctly. It needs to teach its top-level management to trace down this problem and resolve it, and then explain to the customer what was done to prevent another such error. Top-level management should also learn how to get rid of the incompetents who are talking to customers, or shift them to loading and unloading trucks. Best of all, they should never have been hired in the first place. They should also learn that a case as clear and brazen as this one was requires an apology from the top. Result: a dissatisfied but not a lost customer. The store was too good otherwise.

2. The man in a television repair shop told the customer that the TV set requires a new switch which would have to be ordered. Many weeks passed, but the customer found that the set was not yet fixed. Finally the customer was called to pick up the set. He discovered that the switch was repaired, not replaced with a new one. Conclusion: This was deception. This man could not be trusted; he did not live up to what he promised. Result: a lost customer.

3. A customer asked a gas station operator why the pump price was higher

---

[4]The source of this highly significant case is Margaret G. Rosander.

than the price advertised on the sign. The man asked curtly, "Why are you so uptight about that?" This was a shocking answer to a steady customer. Conclusion: this was not only rude and arrogant but a very uncivilized answer to a legitimate question. Result: a lost customer.

4. A customer ordered three dozen carnations from the flower department of a supermarket. When they were delivered to the store, they were small and sickly looking. The flower clerk considered them inferior quality and refused to accept them. She telephoned the florist about 50 miles away to deliver his very best carnations the next day. This was done, so the customer received the best carnations at no extra cost. Conclusion: Here was an employee who was alert, thoughtful, concerned, sympathetic to what the customer wanted, and took prompt action. Result: a pleased and lasting customer, and a pleased and happy employee who was complimented by the customer for her prompt and thoughtful action.

Examples of Techniques and Data Interpretation

The critical importance of good-quality data in identifying and solving problems was pointed out earlier. Inferences, decisions, and actions relative to quality, or to any other subject, are no better than the data on which they are based. If the data are faulty and defective, so are the inferences, decisions, and actions made therefrom. This applies to everyone from the lowest-level worker to the highest-level executive. Even so, it is much better to operate on the basis of data than on the basis of hunch, beliefs, prejudices, and intuition.

It was pointed out above that a critical part of data collection includes the proper preparation of documents, techniques, and procedures: designing an appropriate sample; designing a sound questionnaire; designing an adequate data sheet; preparing a set of clear instructions; designing an effective set of controls; training interviewers in the art and science of interviewing; training observers in the art and science of observation; training those who take part in processing data; adequate direction, planning, and management.

These steps assume that adequate data are not available. The first step is to explore and examine all of the sources of data now being collected by the company or agency. This means examining data in all departments: personnel, financial, production, purchasing, sales, transportation, marketing, customer service, and others. It may be found that important data are missing, data are not in right form, data are insufficient, data are incomplete, data have to be added or otherwise compiled. Action depends on what is found. In this section, additional techniques and their interpretation are discussed.

Time Chart

This is a simple chart that shows trends in which time is plotted horizontally and the characteristic is plotted vertically. Time may be expressed in minutes, hours, days, weeks, months, or years. The characteristic is some quality measure such as idle time, downtime, delay time, delivery time, waiting time, service time, overtime, absenteeism, number of errors, error rate, number of defects, defect rate, number of customer complaints, production volume, cost per unit, volume of acceptable-quality production, departure from schedule or standard, time to do a job, time to complete an operation, and time to learn a job.

This chart is the simplest and best chart to use as an exploratory device. These plots can reveal out-of-control situations and problems not otherwise apparent because the chart shows variability over time, which is the key to quality control.

A few characteristics may be quite stable over time even though they are not subject to formal control. A schedule may be enough control. For months an express bus arrived at a specified street at about 7:25 a.m. Deviations were explained by rain, snow, fog, or an early start. A computer edit reads out consistently about 5 percent of the total records processed, but action is taken on only 30 percent of the readouts. This raised the question: How to reduce the 70 percent on which nothing was done? Without the plot, this situation would never have been discovered.

Care should be taken in arriving at conclusions unless the quality of the data is known; the data have to be relevant, accurate, clear, and sufficient, with known sampling and non-sampling errors and biases. Extreme deviations may be due to bias in the data, and may have nothing to do with some fault in the operation or some people problem.

This chart can be the basis for starting a quality improvement program of stabilizing characteristics that need to be controlled at acceptable levels, and of driving to zero those characteristics where zero is the ultimate goal. Examples of the latter are given in Figures 7–2, 7–3, and 7–4.

Figure 7–2 shows how the error rate in mail orders was reduced from about 5 percent to less than 1 percent in three weeks. This was done on a departmental basis using a random sample of 100 daily. Figure 7–3 shows a similar decline in error rates in processing insurance claims. Figure 7–4 shows the amazing performance of a key punch operator over a period of 11 weeks. The question was: Could the secret of her performance be discovered and used by others? The results are not known.

Ratios and Percentages in Measuring Quality of Airline Service

Table 7–1 shows five measures of the quality of airline service as derived from data submitted to the United States Department of Transportation for September 1987. This information illustrates how relatively simple measures can be used to indicate the quality of service received by the customer. It should be emphasized, however, that these five measures are only a few of the quality

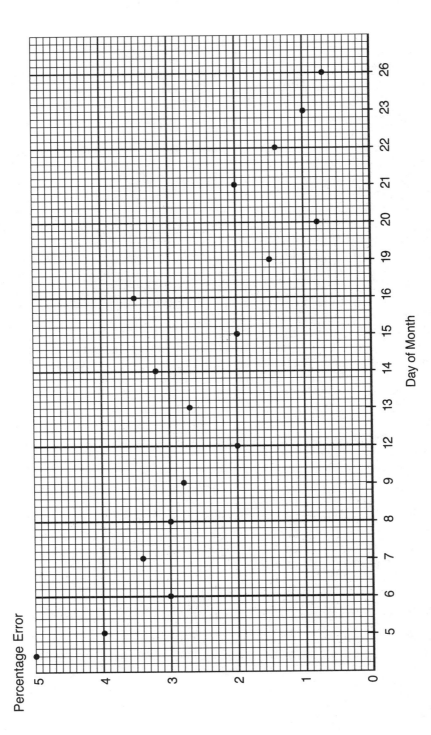

Figure 7-2. Daily Error Rate on Order Tickets for a Mail Order House for Three Weeks

154

Table 7–1. Measures of Quality of Airline Service.

Airline scorecard

Airport rankings

Here, ranked from best to worst, is a list of 27 airports and the percentage of on-time departures during September.

Airport	On-time
Tampa International	91.0
Dallas-Fort Worth	89.5
Atlanta Hartsfield	89.2
St. Louis Lambert	88.8
Orlando International	88.7
Las Vegas	88.6
Houston International	87.9
Salt Lake City	87.9
New York LaGuardia	87.1
Washington National	87.0
Denver Stapleton	86.4
Chicago O'Hare	86.1
Miami International	85.2
Minneapolis-St. Paul Int'l	84.6
Newark International	84.5
Seattle-Tacoma Int'l	84.4
San Diego International	83.6
Los Angeles International	83.0
Charlotte Douglas	82.8
Memphis International	82.7
Boston Logan	82.4
New York JFK	82.1
Phoenix Sky Harbor	80.3
Philadelphia International	77.9
San Francisco	77.8
Detroit	77.5
Pittsburgh	74.9

Baggage complaints

Here is a list of the number of complaints of lost and mishandled baggage per 1,000 passengers received by airlines in September.

Airline	Complaints
Northwest	13.06
United	10.77
Alaska	9.84
American	8.23
America West	8.19
Continental	7.34
Trans World	7.06
Delta	6.98
Piedmont	6.51
Eastern	6.30
USAir	5.94
Pacific Southwest	5.39
Southwest	4.12
Pan American	4.06

Late flights

Chronically late means that a particular flight was more than 15 minutes late more than 70% of the time. The table lists the total number of regularly scheduled flights covered by the report and the percentage of times that they were chronically late.

Airline	Flights	Late (%)
Pan American	179	6.1
America West	526	5.1
Delta	2,112	4.7
Pac Southwest	526	4.6
Southwest	791	4.2
USAir	1,092	3.8
Northwest	1,313	3.4
Continental	1,500	1.6
Eastern	1,287	1.6
American	1,871	1.3
Alaska	224	1.3
Trans World	812	1.0
Piedmont	1,304	0.8
United	1,778	0.6

On-time performance

This table shows the percentage of flights arriving on time. That is defined as arriving within 15 minutes of the scheduled time.

Airline	Percent
American	84.5
Southwest	82.4
Continental	81.1
Eastern	80.4
Piedmont	80.3
United	79.2
Trans World	78.4
Pan American	74.3
America West	73.4
Delta	72.3
Pacific Southwest	70.5
Northwest	69.0
USAir	67.4

Overall complaints

This chart shows the number of overall consumer complaints about each airline, per 100,000 passengers carried by that airline.

Airline	Complaints
Northwest	17.78
Continental	15.11
Eastern	13.25
Pan American	12.82
Trans World	9.59
Hawaiian	7.09
United	5.49
Midway	5.28
American Trans Air	4.76
America West	3.85
USAir	3.61
Braniff	3.29
Piedmont	3.28
American	2.98
Jet America	2.61
Delta	2.17
Alaska	2.13
Pacific Southwest	2.04
Southwest	1.52
Aloha	0.00

Rocky Mt. News 11/11/87 p.3　　　**ASSOCIATED PRESS**

155

Percentage
Error

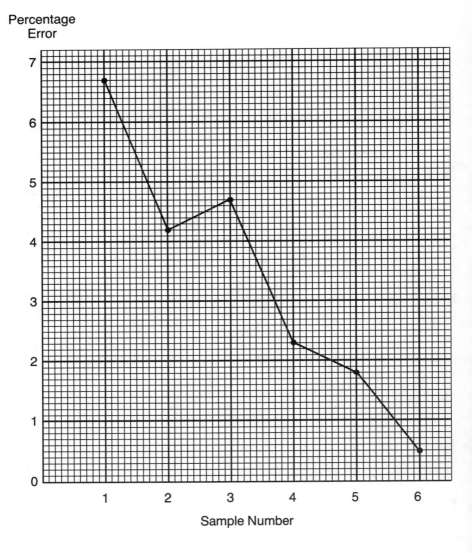

Sample Number

Figure 7–3. **Error Rate for Insurance Claims Coding**

characteristics that are required to indicate the total quality picture of an airline. These characteristics and the unit of measurement are as follows:

Quality Characteristic	Unit
1. Baggage complaints	Number per 1000 passengers
2. Overall complaints	Number per 100,000 passengers

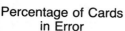

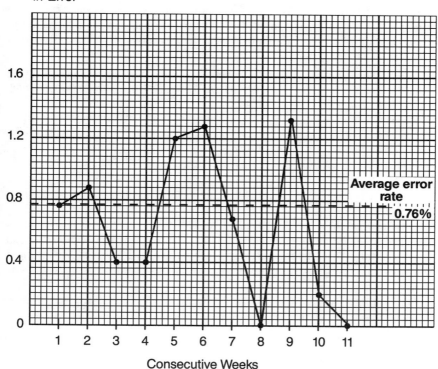

(Percentage of cards in error)
Total number of cards punched = 49,535
Average number punched per week = 4,500

Figure 7–4. **Error Rate for a Key Punch Operator for 11 Consecutive Weeks**

Quality Characteristic	Unit
3. Arrivals on time	Percentage arriving within 15 minutes of scheduled time
4. Late flights	Percentage late 15 minutes or more, 70 percent of the time
5. Departures on time at 29 airports	Percentage of total departures

Care must be taken in interpreting these lists. The best-quality performance is found in those airlines at the bottom of Items 1, 2, and 4, and at the top of Item 3. The best airports relative to departure times are at the top of Item 5.

Frequency Distributions of All Kinds

The frequency distribution shows the composition and variability (scatter) of some aggregate number. It can represent a sample of a 100 percent coverage or census. The frequency can be expressed as a count or a percentage. On a graph it is plotted vertically. The frequency applies to a class or subclass. On a graph it is shown horizontally. The class or subclass can be a characteristic which is a measurement or an attribute and can be divided into three types:

1. Measurements: individual error rate, number of cards punched per day, income, delivery time, salary or wage level;

2. Counts: size of family or household, number of visits to doctor annually, number of times computer failed in one year;

3. Categories or classes: kinds of errors, kinds of illness, kinds of defects, items on a form, reasons for failure, customer complaints.

A table and graph of the third group is called Pareto analysis; it allows one to concentrate on the major sources of trouble. The principle has been in common use for a long time. Internal Revenue agents use it to concentrate on major sources of tax error; an insurance company attacks claim items with the most errors.

Four different ways of recording or presenting the frequency of errors or other measures or counts are the following:

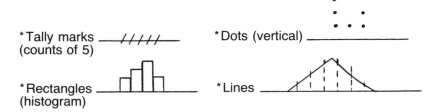

A frequency distribution has many uses. It can be used to show the most frequent errors, the most frequent defects, the variability in error rates in volume of production, and numerous other characteristics. It shows extreme values: a low value on an error distribution needs to be examined to find the improved method that the operator is using. A high value on a production distribution needs to be examined to find the secret of that operator's performance. Extreme values also need to be examined for errors (outliers) in the data. (See Figure 7–5.)

The production distribution for the group shows its present capability. This

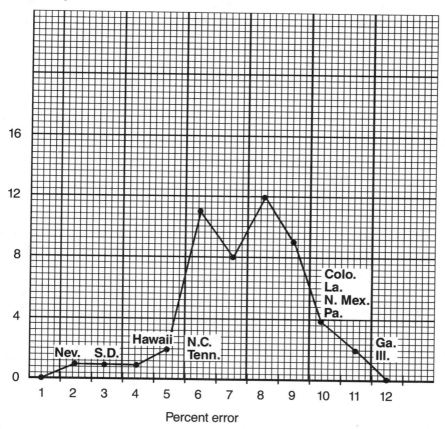

N = 51

Frequency

Source: National Forum Foundation, Washington, D.C. in USA TODAY, November 22, 1985, 12A

Figure 7–5. **Food Stamp Errors in Percentages—1984 by States, including District of Columbia**

does not mean that the capability cannot be improved with further training and the use of better methods.

A frequency distribution of identicals—such as individuals independently performing the same job or task—may reveal that the individuals are not using the same criteria, methods, or basis of judgment, and therefore need to be trained to use the same standards and criteria. Examples are tax assessors appraising the same residential property independently and chemists making the same test on the same sample.

There are two ways to present a frequency distribution: in tabular form (a table) in which the first column shows the item, numerical interval, class, subclass, or category, and the second column shows the number of times each item or class or interval occurs. The number or count is also called the *frequency of occurrence*. The second way is some graphical form such as those mentioned above: a dot diagram, a histogram, a line diagram, or a bar chart.

Sampling

It is unfortunate that sampling is so often neglected and misused. It is a powerful technique which will pay off generously if carefully studied and applied. There is more to sampling than a table of sample plans such as those in Mil. Std. 105D or Mil. Std. 414. Cookbook rules are no substitute for a knowledge of basic principles.

Sampling for most effective results is not as simple as it sounds. In lot sampling, units must be drawn at random, but in the x control chart they are drawn in order of production. Sample surveys, especially if the frame sampled is large (such as those consisting of millions of customers, bills, or claims, or tax returns, or transactions), should be designed, planned, and managed by those who understand both the theory and the applications of *probability sampling*. This usually requires the services of a statistical practitioner. Saving masses of paper from being collected and processed is one road to quality control.

A sample design for one purpose is usually not effective for another purpose. A sample for lot control is not the same as a sample for a control chart. A sample for a customer survey is not the same as a sample for a financial, inventory, or quality audit.

A sample can be used in many different ways in connection with the quality of services; applications include an exploratory time chart; accepting or rejecting a lot of a purchased product; process control, using lots; control charts; sample surveys of customers; sample surveys of lost customers; sampling computer tapes or other records for administrative information or process data; quality audits; financial audits; inventory control; market surveys.

Control Charts

The purpose of control charts is to stabilize random variation (obtain statistical control) by getting rid of assignable causes. This process stabilizes some measurement at the desired level and gives predictive value to both the data and the chart. Once a measurement is in control, any improvement must come from a change in the system, not from the individual worker.

Control charts are beneficial in services for at least three situations: 1) to control production of purchased products to meet specifications; 2) to control measurements of quality characteristics of services within a company, such as percentage utilization of equipment; and 3) process control of errors where the reject number is the upper control.

The best way to start a control chart is by means of a time chart. Stability is reached and setting controls limits are justified only after enough samples are taken to ensure that all assignable causes of extreme values are eliminated.

One of the major advantages of the control chart is that it tells us when to stop tinkering with the equipment, machine, or process once it is in statistical control. It tells us when to leave the process alone as well as when to take action. Once the situation is in control, only changes in the system will improve it.

Four common charts are the following; the reference explains how to construct them:[5]

- $\bar{x}$ for measurement levels in terms of the mean or average;
- R for the variation around x in terms of the range;
- p for proportions or percentages from two classes; "heads or tails" model;
- c for a count of defects, errors, etc. which are independent and rare.

These charts are not to be used to stabilize human errors which are met in the service industries. The goal is to drive these errors to zero, not stabilize them at some value such as 5 percent, 3 percent, or even 1 percent. The assumption that all human errors are random occurrences should be rejected. There is too much evidence to show that most, if not all, of the human errors encountered in the service industries are not random but are due to assignable causes. We need much more experience and more in-depth studies in a wide variety of situations and service industries.

Evidence given in Figures 7-2 and 7-3 shows that it is not hard to drive errors from 5 and 7 percent down to 1 percent or below in a relatively short period of time. We need to know how small can these error rates become under a continuation of the methods used in these situations. So far as is known, no strong pressures were used on these workers to obtain the results shown in the two graphs. In fact, in one case no control was exerted on individuals at all; it was set as a goal for the group that the error rate was too high for customer satisfaction and that an attempt should be made to reduce it.

Random Times Sampling (RTS)

Costs are reduced and productivity is increased by preventing defects in products. Similarly, costs are reduced and productivity is increased by eliminating wasted time in services. Random time sampling based on probability

---

[5] *Applications of Quality Control in the Service Industries,* Chapters 19 and 20.

number
of
pages

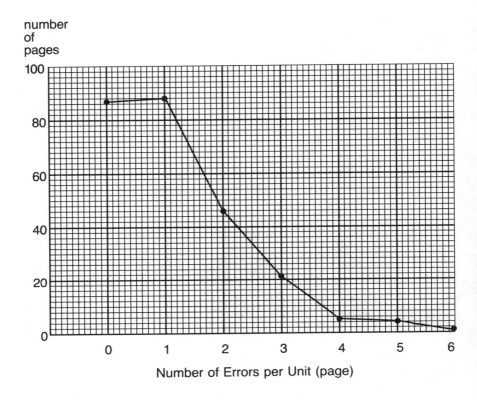

Number of Errors per Unit (page)

Figure 7–6. **Distribution of Errors on 252 Units of Galley Proof for a Book (sentences omitted or repeated are excluded)**

sampling and on the minute model makes traditional work sampling obsolete. It estimates not only proportions but also aggregates, totals, averages, and ratios. It uses the method of estimation inherent in the sample design and therefore eliminates the need for intuitive "commonsense" methods of estimation.

This method is applicable to any working or behavioral situation where time is a factor. It applies to machines, equipment, computers, and other devices and apparatus, as well as to all levels of employees. Usually sampling is limited to time, but areas and employees can be sampled as well.

The method of sampling is simple. For each office or work area, one or more random times are called each day, using a table of random minutes. All minutes in the working day, and sometimes in the lunch hour, are subject to sampling. At each instant, a data sheet is checked for each person—whether at work or not, code number of the activity engaged in, salary or wage, and other information. The data may be collected on an anonymous basis or by an observer. Similar information can be collected for a piece of equipment.

Random time sampling serves at least four important purposes which no other method can do as well:[6]

1. It estimates various forms of wasted time: downtime of equipment, idle time of employees, waiting times of all kinds such as waiting for work, parts, supplies, etc.;
2. It decomposes joint activities by time and cost: e.g., quality vs non-quality;
3. It costs out work activities regardless of their nature and magnitude;
4. It provides an efficient method of estimating parameters and their sample errors.

These advantages are not obtained without sound technical knowledge, careful and persistent management, and the cooperation of both supervisors and employees. Considerable preliminary planning, discussion, and orientation are necessary for a successful application. A pilot run or test of about one week is highly recommended to test the sampling, data sheet, recording, activity codes, and other procedures, as well as the response of employees and supervisors. Successful applications are described in the references.

Relationship Analysis

This is the study of the relationship between two characteristics called *variables* or *variates*. It is also called *correlation* or *regression*. The data consist of pairs of values, one plotted horizontally (x axis), the other vertically (y axis), so that these two values represent one point $P(x,y)$. The data are first recorded in a table; one column represents x values and an adjacent column the corresponding y values. Examples are as follows (see Figures 7–7 through 7–9);

x values	*y values*
employment	production of acceptable-quality product
employment	number of persons serviced
lab test Sample 1	lab test Sample 2 (for k pairs)
salary or wage	hours or days absent
input man-hours	output volume (number of units)
length of training	error rate
length of training	volume of acceptable-quality product
time in use	downtime on specified equipment

---

[6]*Applications of Quality Control in the Service Industries,* Chapter 24. See also A. C. Rosander, *Case Studies in Sample Design* (New York: Marcel Dekker, 1977). See Chapters 14, 15, and 16 for more detailed descriptions of several actual applications, including data sheets.

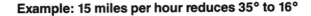

Example: 15 miles per hour reduces 35° to 16°

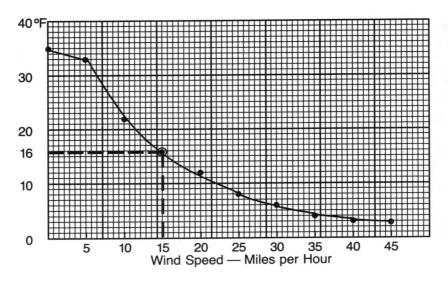

Figure 7–7. How Wind Chill Reduces Apparent Temperature When Actual Temperature is 35°F

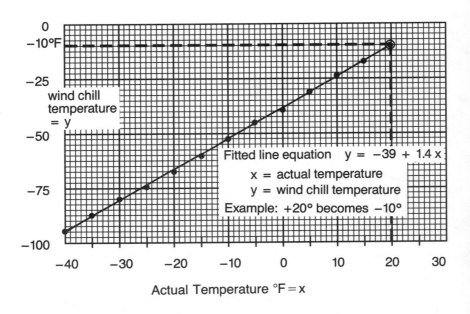

Figure 7–8. Wind Chill Temperatures When Wind Speed is 20 Miles per Hour

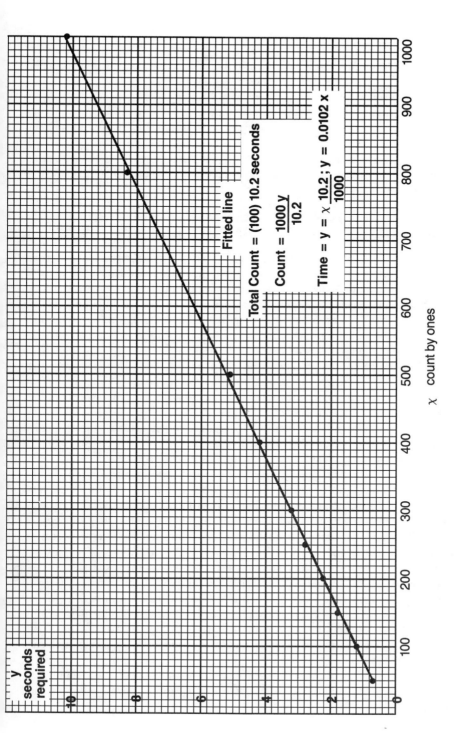

Figure 7-9. Unit Counting Time Required by Program on a Desk Calculator

165

x values	*y values*
duration of health treatment	measurable characteristics, e.g., blood pressure
successive weeks	percent utilization of equipment
successive weeks	percent utilization of employees
time (days)	salary cost per acceptable-quality document

An appropriate straight line is used to interpret the data: $y = x$; $y = a + bx$ fitted by the method of least squares, by eye, or by other approximate methods. A curve is used for nonlinear data.

HOW THE LEARNING CURVE AFFECTS QUALITY CONTROL AND QUALITY IMPROVEMENT

Every quality control program, especially the quality improvement program, includes training and education, sometimes in massive amounts, as steps to take to meet quality goals. Clearly these concepts imply that the new learning, relearning, and repeated learning are necessary. This point brings into consideration the learning curve of both the individual and the group, an aspect that has been neglected if not ignored.

The learning curve takes at least four forms:

1. Volume of correct production as a function of time. This is a curve that rises at a decreasing rate, and is similar to a growth curve.

2. Number of errors, or error rate, as a function of time. This is a curve that decreases as time increases.

3. Number of man-hours required to produce an acceptable unit of quality product, as a function of time. This curve decreases as time increases.

4. Unit cost curve. This curve decreases as time increases.

Examples of the first type of curve are curves of the increase in the volume of correct typing for a given period of time, say five minutes, as a function of time, and the increase in the number of correct letters and symbols received in radio telegraphy for a given period of time, say five minutes, as a function of time. These are increasing curves because errors are reduced, correct reaction times are reduced, and the necessary motions and recognitions of sounds become more automatic. Factory production curves are another example.

Examples of the second type of curve are the plot of the number of errors per unit of work, or the error rate in a unit of work, as a function of time. As the number of errors is reduced by practice, by better understanding, and by eliminating waste time, the error curve decreases as time increases. These data may be collected at the same time that production data are being collected under Item 1.

An example of the third and fourth types of learning curve is the number of man-hours required to produce a product, which may be made hundreds if not thousands of times. World War II furnished some excellent examples in building bombers such as the B-24, and ships such as the Liberty Ship. These curves are decreasing curves, like error curves, but obviously they represent a much more complex situation. As man-hours decrease per unit, so do costs.

Types of Learning Curves

The learning curve should receive more attention because it measures a person's capability to master a job by getting rid of errors and unnecessary time. It also measures the capability of a group to do a specific job under existing working conditions. The learning curve enables management to set goals in harmony with the training and abilities of the persons doing the job. A vice-president once wanted to set an initial daily goal for 2000 transcribed documents. A learning production chart showed that this level was not reached until the 18th day, despite a three-week training course and an excellent supervisor who was an expert in the subject matter and a very good teacher and coach.

The learning curve applies to four situations graphed below. All of these curves are subject to plateaus, or level stretches, so one must be alert not to mistake a temporary plateau as evidence that statistical control has been reached.

1. Errors as a function of time:

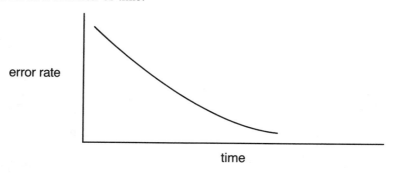

2. Production as a function of time (number of acceptable-quality units):

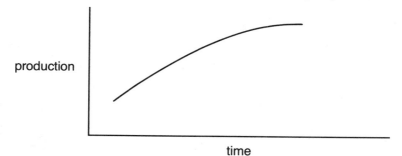

3. Productivity as a function of time:

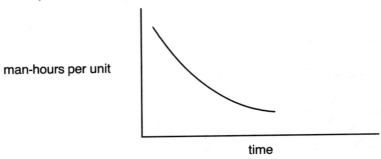

man-hours per unit

time

4. Cost per unit:

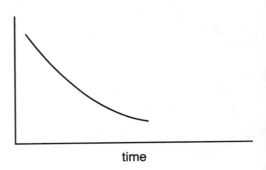

time

Examples of Learning Curves

The first two examples are taken from World War II because that experience provided an abundance of sound learning curve data from plants in a wide variety of product manufacturing. These employees were housewives, students, the unemployed, rejected draftees, younger women, and older men and women.[7]

Case 1

B-24 Bomber plant, Ford Willow Run:

Month	Employment	Production	Employees per Plane
June 1943	42,331 (max)	107 planes	396
Aug 1944	26,560	428 (max)	62

---

[7] The sources of the data for Cases 1 and 2 are official War Production Board data in the author's files.

This plant ignored learning effects and overhired. Production went up; employees were reduced continuously during 13 months.

Case 2

Liberty Ship, Oregon Shipbuilding Co., Portland, OR:

Ship Order	Date	Manhours per Ship	Productivity
1st	Dec 1941	1,100,000	1
35th	unknown	600,000	2
285th	Oct 1943	280,000	4

After building 284 ships this yard built the next ship with one-fourth the manhours that were needed to build the first one. This fact shows how learning effects improve productivity—by eliminating wasted time, unnecessary steps and processes, and errors, and by performing necessary operations faster. This trend shows a common characteristic: most of the gain is made during the early part of the process. In this case the gain made during the building of the first 35 ships was about the same as that made during the next 250 ships.

The gain made in these two cases was *not* due to quality control. It was due to learning effects and the improvement of the operation under repetitive conditions. Quality control was used in some munitions plants, but not in the above-cited bomber plant and shipyard. The next example shows improvement due to both quality control and learning.

Case 3

This large-scale data processing project required persons to transcribe about 100 items of information from rail carload waybills (which differ widely) to a standardized format. This manual operation had to be applied to over 125,000 documents so that the information could be input to a computer. The employees, who were housewives, students, and others, were inexperienced, so they had to be given a three-week course using a 95-page procedural manual. Each employee had to pass a written test before being allowed to transcribe. The supervisor had to coach and instruct continually on difficult and problem items. The results for four days are as follows:[8]

---

[8]The complete record of data is given in *Applications of Quality Control in the Service Industries.* p. 114.

Day	Production per Person (acceptable quality)	Transcriber Cents per Acceptable-Quality Document
1st	64 documents	26 cents
5th	109	15
25th	126	13
45th	213	8

Productivity increased over three times in 45 days due to process control and learning effects. Lot process control accelerated the reduction of errors by rejecting high error lots, making employees redo their rejected lots 100 percent, and by assistance, coaching, and group teaching by the supervisor.

About one-half the gain made in 45 days was made during the first five days! This is similar to the shipbuilding case, where 50 percent of the gain was made during the first 12 percent ($\frac{1}{8}$) of the operation; the 35th ship is about $\frac{1}{8}$ the total of 285 ships.

These cases show that the increase in productivity comes from learning curve effects, in which errors and wasted time are eliminated without any formal quality control. Case 3 shows how quality control in the form of process control can also be a major factor in reducing errors and in improving production and productivity.

Case 4

Learning to solve a complex equation by desk or hand-held calculator:
The graph (Figure 7–10) shows that the time required to solve the equation given is reduced by each of the following methods:

- By repeating the calculation several times (four to seven trials);
- by putting the value of x in memory;
- by using a hand-held calculator where x is in the stack (temporary memory).

The time required is also a function of the order in which the several calculations are made. The best way is not to proceed from left to right in the numerator, but from right to left. (The calculations were performed by the author; all times were taken by a stopwatch. The desk calculator was an HP9810-A with stat rom; the hand-held calculator was an HP25).

Learning Curve Plateaus

A critical part of the learning curve is what psychologists in this field call the *plateau*. At this point learning seems to level off; hence the curve flattens out.

$$y = \frac{3.2\,x^2 - 1.53x + x\sqrt{(2x + 5)}}{x + 2.12}$$

$$y = 1.9573$$

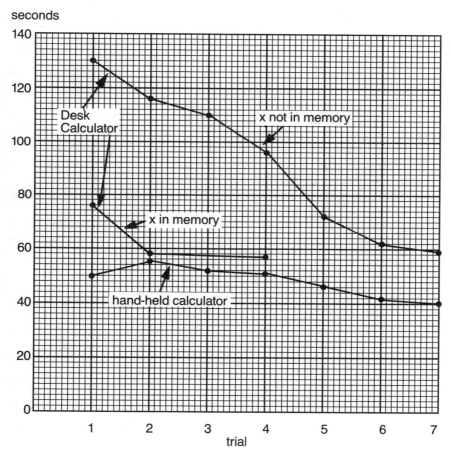

Figure 7–10. **Time Required To Solve Following Equation Given** $x = 1.261$

It is easy to misinterpret a plateau. The learning process has progressed. A control chart shows that the process is in statistical control. A real improvement had been made. We assume that this is the best that the system can do.

The only trouble is that we may be completely wrong. Learning may have stabilized temporarily at the first plateau, but teaching and learning are far from over. Learning still has a long way to go. There are second, third, and fourth plateaus. Learning may have just begun.

Use of the learning curve is required to measure where the worker system really is. There are numerous examples of learning curves from the past, in a wide variety of fields, that have several plateaus. In a recent case involving the transcription of data from a document to a standard format for computer processing, plateaus existed in the learning-production curve at the 120-acceptable-document level, at the 150 level, and at the 200 level. Nor was there any evidence that the 200 level was the best the employees could do. (See Case 3 above.)

This brings us to the crucial question: What teaching process is necessary not only to reach a learning plateau, but to rise above it? Who is qualified to teach? What materials are needed? What kind of instruction is needed? How much *individual* coaching, assistance, and instruction are necessary? Is the teacher able and disposed to do such coaching? Without the proper teachers, materials, and attitudes massive training and education can be a huge disappointment; it will fail to accomplish what we now assume it will accomplish without question; it may even be counterproductive. Effectiveness of learning will depend largely upon the teacher, and in most cases the teacher will have to be the supervisor. This brings up the question: How many supervisors are qualified to teach what needs to be taught so that individuals and groups keep moving to progressively higher plateaus on the learning curve? Implementation will not be as easy as setting the goal.

The Learning Curve and Statistical Control

As stated above, there are four kinds of learning curves: the error curve, the unit cost curve, the time or manpower per unit curve, and the production curve. The first three decrease with time; the last increases with time.

Both research and experience show that a common characteristic of the learning curve is the plateau. While there may be steady improvement in learning in some cases, in other cases learning may fluctuate and stay on a plateau for some time until it moves to a new level and a new plateau. Early work showed that plateaus existed in learning typing, railroad telegraphy, and radio telegraphy. Later experience showed that they existed in wartime production of a wide variety of products, including dry cells and ships, as well as in the errors made in transcribing difficult documents.

The plateau, however, is only temporary except in the last stage, but in quality any of the early plateaus may be mistaken for statistical control. It is quite possible to move to one, two, or even three levels before learning reaches anywhere near a peak. The question that has never been answered is this: How far can this learning with improvement progress? It is easy to conclude at an early point in learning that statistical control has been reached, and that this is the best the individual or group can do, when it is nothing of the kind. Continued practice, coaching, and teaching can very often improve performance far beyond what is expected. For years many people thought the four-minute mile was the limit of human performance, but events since then have shown how wrong they were.

Dr. Deming gives an example of a person learning to play golf. Without instruction he performs aimlessly: under instruction he stabilizes his golf score. This level may be no more than the first plateau on the learning curve. With further instruction and practice he may be able to move to lower and lower levels. What is needed to show the progress of learning is a plot of the daily golf scores over several months of training.

The experienced golfer who took lessons and did not improve simply shows either that he could have improved his score but that the lessons were inadequate, or that he was so advanced on the learning curve that no lessons of any kind would ever be of any help. It may be that the right kind of lessons have not yet been invented. Consider the lesson of the four-minute mile; for decades no one could break the "barrier." Since it was broken, one second has been eliminated every two years. What is the reason?

The Japanese example of a person learning to walk illustrates the plateau effect. This person improved at two levels, but there is not the slightest evidence given that the person could not have moved to an even better level. The person certainly was performing at plateaus which could easily be confused with permanent statistical control.

Plateaus are not limited to learning curves involving primarily motor-sensory skills. In a learning production situation involving the transcription of data on carload waybills to a standard format, the production curve of acceptable-quality documents had at least three well-defined plateaus—one at about 120 documents daily, one at about 150 documents, and one at about 200 documents. These occurred over a period of 45 working days; errors were subject to process control by lots, with 100% re-do of rejected lots by the persons who transcribed them.

OTHER METHODS FOR COLLECTING AND INTERPRETING DATA

Customer Information

Customer information takes two forms: that which the customer volunteers and that which the company collects from the customer. Information is volunteered on rating scales or distributed questionnaires, or is otherwise made available by the company, and is obtained through customer complaints made either in writing or verbally. Two types of form are used: one is a rating scale with space for comments, and the other is a combination questionnaire, rating scale, and open-ended commentary.

Rating Scales and Service Reports

The fatal weakness of *rating scales* is that low ratings such as "bad," "average," "poor," or "fair" provide no basis for taking action, since the specific fault, deficiency, or reason is missing. What is needed is not a rating scale but a *service report* where faults, deficiencies, errors, and complaints are described in specific language, with location and identification. Then management will know what the actual problem or situation is and where it is, and can take whatever action is needed. In a hotel or motel, pads of these blank reports can be placed in every room, so that the occupant can leave a filled-out report at the registration desk when he or she checks out.

Customer Complaints

These are very valuable, but they do not tell the complete story of how all of the customers feel about the product or service. Complaints can be a source of new products, better service, and improved methods and products. They can alert management to problems and situations that might otherwise be overlooked. The management of a large supermarket chain with over 50 stores reports that 90 percent of the customer complaints are justified, and that its policy is to give personal attention to every complaint. The reason is simple: a complaining customer who is not satisfied is very likely to become a lost customer.

A much more serious problem is the dissatisfied customer who never complains. Meeting this problem requires a survey of every customer, preferably on a personal basis (although a telephone call may be satisfactory), every few months. Only in this way can management find out what is bothering the non-complainer.

Information can be collected from the customer by conversation, telephone, interview, or survey, using a questionnaire. This method can be applied to all customers if the number is small and to a designed sample if the number is large: in the hundreds, thousands, or millions. The study should be periodic and continuous, and should be tailored to special groups such as old customers, new customers, lost customers, or big-purchase customers.

The purpose is to keep abreast of what customers believe and expect, and to measure their satisfaction with products or services. Measurement of satisfaction also sounds out customers and users for new ideas about improving products and services. This means that the content of the questioning and conversation should stress the customer's attitude and views toward possible improvements, needed changes, simplifications, better methods, possible ways to do the job better, and behavior and attitude of employees.

In measuring customer satisfaction it is necessary to find out what there is about a product or service that a customer likes or dislikes. Evidence of satisfaction can be measured by determining if the following are true:

- the trouble was eliminated;
- the repair corrected the problem;
- the product the product works fine;
- the service was courteous and friendly;
- the service was prompt;
- the cost of the service was reasonable;
- the product is reliable and inexpensive.

Employee Information

Employees are interviewed or otherwise contacted for the same reasons as customers are contacted—to discover better ways to render services such as these:

- possible improvements;
- needed changes;
- simplifications;
- better methods;
- new ideas;
- better procedures;
- saving time;
- better arrangements;
- how to do a better job;
- need for detailed instructions and explanations.

Another reason for talking to employees periodically is to discover hidden talents and abilities as well as difficulties in personal relationships. This information may reveal innovators, originators, improvers, champions, original thinkers, idea people, self-starters, doers with ideas, trouble shooters, or employee differences and conflicts that obstruct cooperation and teamwork.

Employees, including supervisors and middle managers, are on the firing line. They are where the work is being done; they are where the problems of operations are faced daily. They are the best source of ideas and information for improvement of products, processes, and services.

The improvement suggestion box can be very effective if management supports it and spends time discussing suggestions with employees personally. The trouble with the suggestion box is the cavalier and arbitrary attitude that management often takes toward the whole matter. The appraisers of the suggestions will not like suggestions that affect them or the system. A negative attitude toward ideas with substance reduces the suggestion system to dealing only with minor, if not trivial changes.

Sample Studies and Other Studies for Management Information

The subject of sampling has already been discussed. At this point sample studies are discussed as a major source of significant information for management. These studies are based on designed samples of large-volume files and records, including computer tapes. If the volume is not large, a 100 percent study can be made. A small sample can be used for exploratory purposes. Examples of these specific sources of information include personnel (sick leave, paid leave, etc.), payroll, inventory, finance, customers, purchases, sales, accounts receivable, billing, traffic, shipping and receiving, transportation, and warehousing or storage.

Examples: A railroad with over three million waybills on computer tape for one year ran all of them through the computer, although a probability sample of only 10,000 was needed for the information required.

A computer tape file of about 230,000 records was sampled to obtain 9,000 records divided into 10 replicates, which were ample for the problem at hand. Copies of the 9,000 records were sent to the railroads for additional information needed for the study. The 9,000 copies, but not the 230,000, could be mailed to the railroads.

Tests and Experiments

Tests and experiments are the source of significant information in many aspects of services and service industries. Examples include health services, retail trade, public utilities, business services, and environmental quality control involving both private industry and governments.

Examples of specific applications include the following:

1. Laboratory tests:
    - Health services: blood, urine, tissue;
    - Control of errors in laboratory tests;
    - Reduction in variation between laboratories testing the same thing;
    - Retail goods for wear, length of life, failure, etc.;
    - Calibration of measuring instruments, e.g., for measuring carbon monoxide;
    - Testing purchased products to see if they meet specifications.
2. Field tests:
    - Air pollution: carbon monoxide, nitrogen, oxides, ozone, particulates;
    - Water pollution;
    - Soil pollution;
    - Radiation pollution of air, water, soil, food;

- Sampling sources of city drinking water for contaminants;
- Testing water in public swimming pools.
3. Experiments:
    - Comparisons of the same type of equipment, machinery, or apparatus such as computers, desk computers, hand-held calculators, business software, mathematical and statistical software, quality control software, personal computers, educational and school software;
    - Plutonium effects using test cattle or animals in different places;
    - Testing different laboratories, measuring the same characteristics in the same samples;
    - Testing chemists or others running same test on the same samples.
4. Medical tests:
    - Effects of drugs on people; effects of different dosages;
    - Effects of treatments on people;
    - Effects of environmental factors on health: sun, air, weather;
    - Effects of social and economic factors on health: job, income, etc.

HOW METHODS USED BY QUALITY CIRCLES HAVE CHANGED THE VOCABULARY OF STATISTICS

Quality Circle	*Statistical Use*
1. Pareto chart	1. A composition or distribution table. Idea was in use long before Juran invented the term.
2. Stratification	2. This is the same as Shewhart's "rational subgroups." Means collecting data by classes, subclasses, groups, categories, etc. which may differ widely in quality characteristics. No need for a new word.
3. Check sheet	3. This is the well-known tally sheet which has been in use for generations. No need for a new term.
4. Histogram	4. Histogram does not convey the meaning. The concept involved is the frequency distribution. There are other ways of presenting frequency distributions; call it what it means.
5. Scatter diagram	5. This term has no meaning. All kinds of "scatter" exist in other connections. Call this a "relationship chart" if you do not like the term "regression."

Quality Circle	*Statistical Use*
6. Control charts and graphs	6. Apparently this is the only concept and technique whose name has not been changed.

It is claimed that these six statistical techniques, plus the "cause and effect" diagram, "solve problems," but it is rare that these statistical techniques, or any others, 'solve" problems in the real sense of the word. Rather, statistics discovers problems or problem situations, and helps and assists in the solution of problems as a means of collecting acceptable-quality data.

Statistics indicates the presence of defects, errors, wasted time, and unacceptable behavior, but others who are specialists in the subject matter must find the causes and eliminate them. For example, the control chart indicates that trouble exists, but it does not tell what the solution is. The cause of the trouble and the solution to the problem are discovered and applied by others.

Quality circles suffer from three weaknesses:

1. They keep statistics at a kindergarten level. Many powerful techniques are ignored, such as random time sampling, sample surveys, and learning curve analysis.
2. They cannot correct faults of the system. A major improvement cannot be made.
3. They may create conflict because they are considered a competing group by those in the existing organization.

It should be pointed out, however, that quality circles have been successful in many companies.

Chapter 8

The Eight Vectors of Quality

When a concept, such as quality, is multidimensional, it is easy to seize upon one dimension or aspect and conclude that this alone explains the entire concept. This is what we have been doing in the field of quality. At one time or another attention has been concentrated on management, statistics, people, inspection, quality circles, and process control. A balanced treatment is nonexistent.

The poem about the six blind men and the elephant illustrates this tendency very clearly.[1] Each man generalized from the part of the elephant he touched:

What he touched:	*What he inferred an elephant was:*
Tail	rope
Tusk	spear
Knee	tree
Trunk	snake
Side	wall
Ear	fan

Each was partly right, but all were in the wrong. The elephant was more than the sum of its parts; it was a unitary structure—a *gestalt,* to use a psychological term.

Quality can be described in terms of eight vectors, dimensions, or aspects: *management, supervision, statistics, psychology, economics, time, processes,* and *subject matter.* No program for quality improvement can be complete or effective without making adequate provision for each of these major factors. There is not an important aspect of quality in manufacturing, in service operations, or in service industries that is not covered by one or more of these eight vectors.

Each of these is discussed in some detail in this chapter, but many related ideas and topics are described in later chapters.

To thoroughly understand quality it is necessary to understand the basic con-

---

[1] John G. Saxe, "The Blind Men and the Elephant."

cepts of the eight vectors of quality. This requires the mastery of a wide variety of knowledge. "Knowledge" as used here includes much more subject matter than Dr. Deming's use of the word or Dr. Ishakawa's use of the term "thought revolution." The eight vectors may be characterized as follows:

Vector or aspect	Characterization
1. Management	Overall direction;
2. Supervision	Specific direction;
3. Statistics	Techniques, data;
4. Psychology	People;
5. Economics	Costs;
6. Time	Scheduling, sequencing;
7. Processes	Processes, system;
8. Subject matter	Corrective action, remedy.

First a word about psychology, a subject which permeates quality but which receives very little attention as a field of knowledge. We simply do not have knowledge of psychology and its role in human relations, people problems, and quality improvement.

Psychological gimmicks such as brainstorming, esoteric theories such as Theories X, Y, and Z, and other esoterics such as group dynamics and motivational analysis and transcendental meditation represent largely futile efforts to get at the essence of human relations in quality. What we need are more case studies, more specific instances, more successful experiences of managers and supervisors, more empirics, more real-world problems of employees and supervisors on the job.

You cannot resolve situations involving psychological aspects such as fear (Deming's Point 8), barriers (Deming's Point 9), or pride (Deming's Point 12) by teaching courses similar to the courses taught in management, engineering, and statistics. Of the eight vectors of quality, psychology is most critical. Yet we know the least about it and tend to ignore what knowledge we have.

MANAGEMENT

Major Functions

Top management holds a critical key position because it has to do the following:

- Make a commitment to quality if there is to be a *total or comprehensive* quality improvement program;
- Support and push this program daily if it is to have *continuity;*
- *Correct common causes in the system* that are responsible for poor quality.

To attain these and other goals, management has the responsibility for several major functions:

1. Setting Policy

This mean formulating statements of position to guide and determine present and future decisions and actions. Examples are policies relative to quality programs, growth, new products, new services, customers, warranties, employees, vendors, competition, costs, investments, and profit.

2. Setting Company Objectives

These are goals toward which the company or agency works continuously. Hewlett Packard's seven objectives relate to profit, customers, fields of interest, growth, our people (employees), management, and citizenship or community relations.[2]

3. Making Final Decisions

These are decisions that only top-level management can make. They often resolve conflicts that occur at lower levels, or involve such significant aspects that only top management can make the final decision. Examples are decisions involving expansion, contraction, new products, new services, correcting common causes of poor quality such as worn out machinery, equipment, and other facilities, new projects, new surveys, and organizational changes.

4. Allocating Resources

Only top-level management has the power to allocate resources to functions, departments, divisions, products, services, expansions, and quality improvement program for the entire company or agency. This is accomplished by means of the budgetary process. Division or department heads submit annual budgets but top-level management makes the final determination of how resources are to be allocated.

5. Delegating Authority

It is necessary to delegate authority to lower-level officials so plans can be developed, projects can be implemented, and operations can be carried out effectively. Even when this is done, top-level officials who should concentrate on policies and long-range plans may interfere with officials in operations and

---

[2] W. G. Ouchi, *Theory Z* (New York: Avon Books, 1982), pp. 193–199.

cause considerable trouble. De Lorean describes examples of this in General Motors.[3] A highly recommended type of organization is to centralize policies and objectives but to decentralize operations. This gives officials in charge of operations freedom to run the shop in the most effective ways without interference from the top.

An official may hesitate to delegate authority to a lower-level official or staff professional to engage in an important job for several reasons:

- He is afraid the person may succeed;
- He is afraid the person may receive too much recognition;
- It may mean a promotion for another person;
- He believes it may hurt his own personal goals and ambitions;
- He may be one of those officials who likes to keep his hands on all of the details of the jobs of officials under him;
- He is afraid to delegate authority for other reasons.

On the other hand, it is agreed by experts in management that delegation of authority is necessary for effective leadership. Indeed, the official who delegates power to others may find his reputation as a manager enhanced because he is capable of developing strong and capable leaders. Hence he as well as the lower-level official may receive recognition when the latter does an excellent job.

Delegation of authority is directly related to the opposition of top-level officials to new and better methods of operations, such as quality control, probability sampling, design of tests and experiments, and other techniques of statistical science. Until they are granted authority and power to act, lower-level officials and staff professionals cannot apply these techniques except in a very limited and restricted area which does not involve top-level management.

6. Formulating and/or Approving Broad Plans and Programs

One of the functions of top managers is to lay down long-range plans, to push for quality improvement of both products and services, to make a commitment for excellence in performance at all levels, to keep abreast of market developments and customer needs, and to develop programs for new products and services which will promote growth and meet, if not surpass, competition.

It is very possible for management to get so immersed in short-time activities, day-by-day operations, and putting out fires that they never seem to have time for what is significant and what is required in long-range planning. Hence it is easy for them to be caught flat-footed when the market makes a slow but drastic change or when the competition produces a better product.

---

[3] J. Patrick Wright, *On a Clear Day You Can See General Motors* (New York: Avon), 1980.

Any such undesirable or critical situation can be avoided by supporting and pushing a quality improvement program, by taking all of the steps needed to insure the continuity of such a program, and by deliberately planning to take appropriate and timely actions to correct the common causes and the defects in the system which are the sources of poor-quality products and services.

7. *Evaluating or Appraising Company Performance*

Management is responsible for seeing that the company or the agency is run successfully, that the company operates at a profit, that customer needs are met in a satisfactory manner, that customers are treated in a courteous and pleasant manner, that employees are happy in their work, that employees are given every opportunity to grow and develop their talents, and that vendors are performing their function effectively. To do this, management must know what is going on. They must have information flowing to them so that they will be able to evaluate what is going on in terms of policies and objectives. This will include appraisal of the performance of divisions, departments, branch establishments, profit trends and share of the market, quality costs and the improvement of quality, the gains obtained therefrom, and productivity and how the company stands with regard to competitors as to sales, profits, customer complaints, and quality of product and services.

8. *Directing a Team of Specialists*

Experience and observation show that one of the most difficult and baffling tasks facing management is how to direct effectively a staff, team, or department of specialists. Some managers are just unwilling to accept that fact that a specialist knows more than they do. Some distrust and downgrade them. Some try to overrule a specialist in his or her own field. Some, like Clarence Randall of Inland Steel, are highly critical of all specialists as rigid, narrow-minded spouters of a "jargon"; he expressed this view in *The Folklore of Management*.

Specialists are here to stay; it is up to management to accept them and to learn how to direct them as an effective team. This means that management eliminates feuds, and breaks down barriers between departments and divisions—between design, engineering, manufacturing, purchasing, sales, accounting, personnel, training, customer service, marketing, quality assurance, finance, planning, data processing, and all of the others. That is because these feuds and barriers are due to differences between managers and top professionals in these different departments: there are envy, jealousy, ambitions, deep-seated conflicts, jurisdictional disputes, personality differences, and different basic philosophies and views.

One example of the problem is a task force that was set up to plan, implement, and direct a large nationwide sample study to obtain information for top-level decisions. The task force consisted of two laywers, two accountants, one economist, two statisticians, a rail traffic expert, an operations research specialist, and a computer unit head. One of the lawyers headed the group. This caused a lot of unnecessary friction and wasted time because the lawyer favored the accountants and the computer unit head. This meant that the statisticians, who had the responsibility for designing the sample and for laying out the sample controls and the procedures and formulas for tabulating and analyzing the data, were ignored. The specialists who knew how to design and conduct the sample study were overruled at every step. This is an example of the wrong person heading the task force.

Another example is that of a director who did not want to direct and lead, but wanted to dominate all operations in the division. He tried to dictate to the computer section, to the data preparation unit, to the sampling staff, to the people in tabulation, to the section on economic analysis. This caused resentment among all of the heads of these sections and staffs. The resentment surfaced and became a topic of comment, but only one person had the courage to explain to the director that he was hired to run the staff and that it was unnecessary for him to get involved. That person had to leave.

9. Striving for Adequate Communication and Information Throughout the Company

Management and professionals cannot function unless they are informed about what is going on. Management cannot plan, direct, decide, appraise, or take action unless they know what is going on. The same holds true of professional staff members and supervisors and employees; they need to be kept informed.

This requires establishing a two-way communication and information system between top management, lower-level management, supervisors, and operations. Information flows upward, telling management where operations stand relative to progress, company goals, and problems that need attention. Decisions and actions flow downward (or should) as a result of this information. This two-way communication is a "must," but it rarely exists.

Similarly, supervisors should be in two-way communication with their bosses, and with professional staff members who advise them. Employees should be kept informed by their supervisors about all relevant matters that concern them. Employees should keep each other informed, as needed. When one employee takes the place of another during the day, whether at lunch or not, the second employee should be full informed about all current matters by the first employee. There is nothing more distasteful for a customer than to make an arrangement or conduct a transaction with one employee, only to find on returning that a second employee is in charge who knows nothing about what happened earlier. This can often occur when arrangements are made by telephone.

It is up to top-level management to see that these employees, and all those at higher levels, are properly instructed about how to carry on conversations with customers and how to maintain a continuity in communication among employees so as to keep everyone properly informed as to what is going on. To accomplish this may require that a log book be kept by every supervisor and by every professional, and that every telephone call or other customer conversations be recorded by date, time, and subject matter by the person receiving the call.

It is imperative that useless layers of organization be eliminated so that communication is direct and fast, so that shunting and delays will be avoided. Organization should be limited to three to five layers, and no more. The temptation to create four or five additional layers of organization, to give someone or some group a fancy title and a promotion but very little work, should be stopped in its tracks.

10. Providing Leadership

Tom Peters asserts that what is needed in American business is not management but leadership. He claims that management does not provide the leadership needed for the company to operate in a healthy fashion and to meet competition. This is taken to mean that top-level managers need to be more alert to market changes, customers' needs, and continuous quality improvement of both products and services.

The leader is out in front, breaking the trail. The leader does not necessarily follow the old paths. The leader is not afraid to go in new directions. The leader sets the pace, but makes sure that everybody is together. The leader has to be careful that he does not get too far ahead or behind his people.

Townsend gives 10 characteristics that the boss has to have to be a leader.[4] The boss must be available, humble, inclusive, objective, humorous, fair, tough, effective, decisive, and patient. The meaning of all of these qualities is clear, except possibly "inclusive." This seems to mean that the boss takes an interest in every employee to the extent that the employee is given useful information and advice with regard to professional people, and is referred to helpful books and papers and articles. Everyone is included in this personal assistance. A leader should also be "supportive." He or she should support both professionals and other employees against unjust and unfair criticism.

The Positive Side of Good Management

Examples of management out of control will be given later. Current leaders in the field point out that most of the responsibility for poor-quality products and services is due to management, not to the individual employee. (There are some serious exceptions in health, transportation, and other industries, how-

---

[4] Robert Townsend, *Further Up The Organization* (New York: Knopf, 1984), pp. 249–251.

ever, where one employee error can be fatal.) At this point the positive side of
management is outlined, giving in positive terms the characteristics of good
managers:

- Long-term thinking;
- People-oriented, customer-oriented; customer is interested in operation;
- Employee-oriented—uses their talents;
- Humane, nondictatorial supervision;
- Respects professional people and their knowledge and judgments;
- Exerts leadership, coaches as needed;
- Knows operations, keeps in touch;
- Bases decisions and actions on facts, sound data, accurate information;
- Few layers of organization, clearances;
- Quality- as well as money-minded;
- Pushes constantly for quality improvement;
- No privileged classes;
- Plays no favorites;
- Approves better methods;
- Knows what is going on;
- Not afraid to meet competition.

Errors Made By Top Management, or Management Out of Control

In quality control, all writing and talking deal with a process, an operation,
or a job being out of control, and with a need for an employee or supervisor
to correct the defect. No one ever mentions the fact that management at higher
levels can also be out of control. The following examples are described in
detail.

Case 1

A New England company is losing sales and has been doing so for some
time. The president calls in the sales force and chastises them for not being
more aggressive, for not doing their jobs as they have in the past. The sales
people are taken aback, and protest that they have been doing their usual alert,
aggressive job. One of the salesmen suggests that a survey be made of the lost
customers to find out why they are no longer buying the company's product.
The president finally agrees to have such a study made. The study showed that
the lost customers stopped buying when the quality of the product deteriorated.
An investigation showed that the poor quality appeared at the same time that a
major vendor was dropped in order to reduce costs. Quality was sacrificed to a
price tag, and the company suffered. (This illustrates Deming's Point 4.) When
the company changed back to its former vendor, quality improved and sales
began to increase.

This is the case of a top executive jumping to a conclusion without any evidence. It is based on the false assumption that salesmanship is the key to success. This is management by hunch, not based on facts, objective evidence, or sound information. Only a survey of lost customers could reveal what happened. All companies, whether selling products or services, need to make continuous surveys of lost customers, and of all customers, in order to reveal some serious defect or error that might not otherwise be uncovered. The usual practice of paying attention only to customer complaints is not enough; it is only the tip of the iceberg. Overlooked are the customers who are dissatisfied but who never complain. Like the lost customers in this case, they may simply drop one product and buy another without the company knowing anything about it.

Case 2

The manager of a textile mill making women's hose with semi-automatic machinery accuses the employees of stealing $1 million worth of hose. He calls in detectives, but they find nothing. Then he calls in a firm of psychologists who bring in cameras, one-way screens, and other paraphernalia. Despite all of their efforts, they, too, find nothing. When about to leave, one psychologist asks the manager: "How did you arrive at the million dollars?" This question revealed what had happened. One of the best operators in the shop had been selected to run a test. From this test the average amount of yarn used per pair of hose was estimated. This figure was divided into the total amount of yarn consumed during the year, and resulted in a volume of hose $1 million more than had actually been sold or was in inventory. Further checks showed that the test operator used much less yarn per pair of hose than the average of all of the operators, despite the semi-automatic machinery. The $1 million was the loss that the company was incurring because operators on the average were not performing as efficiently as the test operator. This shows the need for an immediate, effective training program.

This is management by false inference from biased data. The manager used data from a sample of one operator to make an estimate, and then drew a false conclusion from the calculations. At least three different ways were available to avoid the mistake he made:

- Trend charts could be plotted for each operator, showing daily the total amount of yarn divided by the total number of pairs (total yarn/total pairs).
- A better estimate could be obtained by using a random sample of 10 or 15 operators selected at random from the group and calculating total yarn divided by total number of pairs.
- The annual output y could be plotted against the annual input x for each of the past five years, and a line could be drawn through each point and the origin (0,0). Dividing output by input would have shown the real character of the operation. This is input-output analysis, and the easiest to use.

The real problem was the manager, not the employees. The company lacked management control data. It lacked information about operations. It was flying blind. It had no technical capability. It lacked not only the capability to collect sound and significant data, but how to analyze and use the data as well. It needed one good professional statistical practitioner to set up a control system and teach employees and management how to use it. This system would include quality control, sample and test design, input-output analysis, statistical analysis, and error prevention. This company needed one good statistician, not a bunch of detectives and psychologists. It also needed a training program for all operators based on the test operator's method as an effective way to reduce the $1 million "loss."

Case 3

An example of management ignoring its own industry data is illustrated by the automobile industry between 1966 and 1979. The following data show the trend of automobile imports from West Germany and Japan, and the proportion of retail sales in the United States accounted for by foreign cars.[5]

Year	U.S. Imports of One Thousand Automobiles		Foreign Cars as Percentage of U.S. Retail Sales
	W. Germany	Japan	
1966	527	56	6.1 for 1965
1968	708	170	10.7
1970	675	381	15.3
1972	677	698	14.8
1974	620	792	15.9
1976	350	1129	14.8
1978	416	1563	17.7
1979	496	1617	21.8

The Volkswagen sounded the warning when it penetrated the United States market to the extent of over 700,000 cars in the late 1960s. It was West Germany, not Japan, that showed what a large market there was in United States for foreign automobiles. Japan simply moved in on the heels of West Germany and replaced it as the largest supplier of foreign cars. By 1976 Japan was exporting over a million cars into this country, and both the number and percentage were to increase.

The oil crisis of the 1970s and the hard times of the early 1980s turned more and more American auto buyers to smaller, less costly, more efficient auto-

---

[5] *Motor Vehicle Facts and Figures, 1985* (Detroit: Motor Vehicle Manufacturers Association of the United States).

mobiles. Japan had the high-quality product which met the preferences and pocketbooks of millions of Americans, who were also fed up with what they had been buying from Detroit for decades. With the very high gasoline prices, the increased cost of living, and higher taxes, it was necessary for lower- and middle-income families to turn to a less expensive and more reliable automobile. This is what they did, and are continuing to do. Apparently foreign cars will continue to take from 25 to 30 percent of the American retail sales, despite tariffs and quotas.

American auto manufacturers had plenty of warning, but they did not heed it. Some attempt was made to meet this competition. Ford brought out the Falcon in 1965, but it was not a high-quality car; it suffered from a number of defects, so it never made any positive impression on buyers. Other small cars ended up as failures; they simply lacked the quality construction and performance that millions wanted. John DeLorean at General Motors saw the trend and strongly urged that a small car be designed and built to meet foreign competition. This move finally resulted in designing the K-Car in about 1970, but it never succeeded. Eventually it was shelved.[6]

The automobile manufacturers could make more money per car by making large cars, and this is what they have continued to do. The result of this decision not to meet foreign competition resulted in massive unemployment not only in the Detroit area but over the whole nation as the chain reaction of plant closings spread. The waste in unemployment, welfare, continued refusal to build a car to meet foreign competition, and turning to Washington to find a false solution in quotas and tariffs have resulted in losses of hundreds of billions of dollars to the American people.

With the aid of Dr. Deming and Dr. Juran, who introduced quality control and its management into Japan, the American auto industry is trying to stage a comeback. Even so, it has permanently lost millions of customers. The reason is plain, but has been overlooked: the loyalty of a buyer or customer for a product. Millions of Americans are now loyal to a Japanese car, and they are going to stay that way. The irony of the situation is that Detroit, which has relied heavily on product and model loyalty for over 50 years, ignored the real possibility that Americans by the millions could shift their loyalty to a foreign car.

Case 4. Lessons from the Challenger Disaster

The various reports appearing in the press and in *Science* reveal not a situation that is new and startling, but one that is well known to many experienced officials and professional specialists. It can be stated in one sentence: Those with power lack know-how, while those with know-how lack power.

---

[6]*On a Clear Day,* Chapter 12.

The situation is common, although it does not always involve the lethal consequences of the Challenger disaster. The situation has the following characteristics:

- Those with important relevant knowledge, know-how, and experience are overruled by officials higher up.
- Important knowledge is stopped before it reaches the officials making the final decisions.
- Specialists with the key knowledge are buried in so many layers of organization that they can never deal directly with top decision makers.
- There is no communication system that allows the key knowledge of those below to be communicated directly and quickly to top decision makers.

These characteristics exist not only in a large hierarchical organization, but also in a relatively small organization. Technical information of a critical nature may have to be relayed through one or more layers of organization by officials who have not the slightest idea what the information is all about. This information can deal with such technical subjects as physical and chemical tests, sampling, quality control, computer programming, and computer operations. In this relaying process, changes can be made, misunderstandings can arise, important parts can be omitted.

In the case of the Challenger, the decisions of engineers and others in three different places were overruled and ignored, although the decisions were made independently and were the same. The decisions of the engineers and others were stopped. Although higher-level officials knew about these decisions, they never told the top decision makers about them. The decisions of the engineers were never communicated to the top.

The use of a circular radial type of organization is suggested as one possible way to overcome some of these difficulties: it eliminates useless layers of organization and establishes communication between specialists and top decision makers. (See Figure 8–1.)

Improving Management by a Simple Organizational Structure

Management is made more difficult, and costs of operations are greatly increased, by an excessive number of layers of organization. We read about companies with 15 to 20 layers of organization. This practice grows out of the pyramid or hierarchy created by a military or church type of organization inherited from ancient and medieval times. This type of organization creates a huge overhead structure on top of those who do the work. These are the planners, coordinators, liaison makers, spokespersons, and assistants. The waste from this type of organization is due to several factors:

- Some layers are really not necessary to get the job done. (Only three to five are needed, according to Tom Peters.)[7]
- Officials in some layers are merely paper shufflers, extra attendees at conferences, relayers of jobs and assignments to lower levels.
- The level was created to give a host of lower-level officials promotions without disturbing those higher up.
- Extra layers create communication problems: they may distort sound data and information coming from professional people or specialists.
- They may actually prevent data and information from getting to the top, or to the higher level where they are needed.
- These extra layers may delay the flow of essential information when delay is costly and even dangerous.
- These extra layers may be "reviewers" and "editors" of technical subject matter, such as probability sample designs and statistical quality control systems and computer programs for statistical or mathematical problems, when they haven't the slightest ability to do such reviewing or editing. They are superfluous and should be abolished.

One factor that contributes to a "bloated" bureaucracy, whether in private industry or in government, is these unnecessary layers of organization that provide thousands of useless jobs.

Another change that is necessary when useless layers of organization are abolished is to insist that all top-level people, whether managers or professional specialists, cease being general planners and talkers at conferences and go to work to produce something specific and useful. Insist that they get their hands dirty working on real problems.

The following is an actual example of how a communication has to move through eight levels before it is answered:

- Constituent writes a letter to Senator Ribicoff, who sends it to the proper agency Secretary of Treasury, who sends it to the Assistant Secretary, who sends it to the Commissioner, who sends it to the Deputy Commissioner, who sends it to the Assistant Commissioner, who sends it to the Division Director, who sends it to the Branch Chief, who sends it to the Section Chief, who sends it to the Unit Chief, who answers the letter.

This is called "going through channels." It is also called "red tape." It is a huge waste of people, time, and money. No doubt the Food and Drug Administration, which has to report to the Public Health Service, which in turn reports to the Department of Health and Human Services, faces a worse situation.

---

[7]Tom Peters, *Thriving on Chaos* (New York: Knopf, 1987), p. 359. This agrees with author's view, cited earlier.

The Circular Radial System of Management

A simplified system of organization, called the circular radial system, is diagrammed in Figure 8–1. There are only three divisions or levels of organization:

1. The inner circle: the management-specialist team or council;
2. The second circle: the supervisory managers;
3. The third circle: the employees.

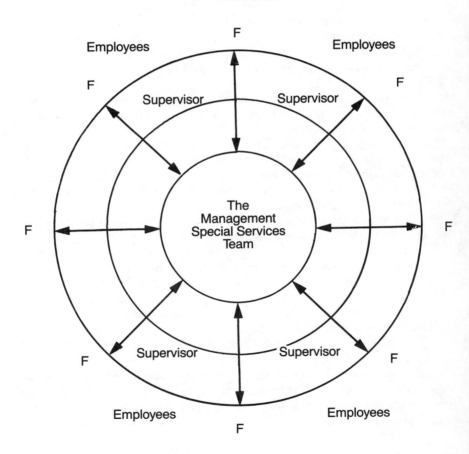

F = functions

Figure 8–1. **The Circular Radial System of Management**

Extending out from the inner circle are radials representing permanent functions to be performed or one-time jobs or projects that have to be completed. The radials also stand for two-way communication between the three circles.

The inner circle is a working team consisting of a few managers and a representative from each of the major specialties and functions. The chairman of this team is the top manager. Line and staff distinctions disappear. This team sets policies, plans, directs, implements, and monitors all functions and operations through supervisory managers and employees. The contact is direct and personal. The inner circle therefore is constantly in touch with the problems facing managers and employees. The team is not isolated from what is going on. Each representative on the team or council knows what others are doing in other parts of the company or agency. Communication is total and comprehensive. Implementation is not divorced from planning, but is an integral part. Plans therefore are put through the wringer before they are cast in final form. The inner circle facilitates teamwork, and develops and implements a continuous quality improvement program.

The specialties and functions represented on the team might be the following; for some functions and projects, not all of these might be needed to form the function or project team: management, design, production, sales, finance, personnel, marketing, purchasing, accounting, legal, customer relations, data processing, training, statistics, and quality assurance.

Management and the Customer

It is very easy to get so immersed in the internal problems, situations, and relationships of the organization that management loses sight of the customer.

A recent report of a survey of top-level officials showed that 70 percent measured the quality of the company's business by looking at customer complaints. This practice shows not only a lack of understanding of the importance of quality programs, but also a very inadequate conception of the role of the customer in the success of the company.

Management needs to put the customer at the top of the list of priorities, at the top of the list of people to talk to; listen to; get ideas from; find out what is wrong; find out what is right; find out why lost customers are lost; find out why pleased customers are pleased; and find out why dissatisfied customers do not complain.

Continuous contacts by mail, telephone, and interviews are necessary to keep currently informed of customer attitudes and behavior. Staggered sample surveys are one way to survey a large number of customers. These are carried out by mail and personal interview. Telephone talks should be included at the convenience of the customer. These should take a relaxed conversational approach, not a high-pressure dictatorial type of salesmanship.

The customer buys a sample of one. There is no mean and no variance. The customer has no evidence of the quality of the purchase. He or she is flying blind. They rely on the trustworthiness of the seller. Their interest is in how a product *operates*.

Management Summary

1. Management deals with people; it directs or relates to their activities for specified goals.
2. People include employees, customers, vendors and competitors.
3. Employees carry out operations.
4. Customers buy and use products and services.
5. Vendors sell products and services to companies or agencies.
6. Therefore management must be familiar with operations, products, and services.
7. Customers want acceptable quality and affordable products and services; also courtesy, consideration, attention, and timeliness in services.
8. Employees want fairness, challenge, personal goal growth, assistance, direction, leadership and rewards.
9. To build quality into products and services requires appropriate techniques, processes, knowledge, abilities, skills, and action.
10. Management must correct system causes of poor quality. Employees must correct special causes of poor quality. Where one error can be dangerous, if not fatal, management and employee are at least equally responsible for poor quality.
11. Management must lead, inspire, coach, and push daily for the quality improvement program.
12. Provide an organization and structure with a minimum number, say three, of layers and clearances. Eliminate useless layers of organization. An alternative to the orthodox hierarchy is the circular radial system, with only three levels of organization.

Therefore, in developing a quality improvement program, management must become concerned with and strike a balance among the following seven factors:

1. Supervision: directing human efforts toward specific objectives and goals;
2. Statistics: utilizing techniques of measurement and data collection to control variability of human performance;
3. Psychology: studying and directing human behavior for benefit of all;
4. Economics: keeping costs and prices such that products and services are affordable and profitable;
5. Time: minimizing delay time, idle time, service time, wasted time, lost time, and all other significant aspects of time;
6. Processes: utilizing methods and procedures and processes that are needed to make products and render services of acceptable quality;

7. Subject matter: providing for the capability to take corrective action, for prevention of errors and defects and delays.

SUPERVISION

The Nature and Types of Supervision

Supervision means to direct, guide, coach, lead. It also means to oversee, administer, superintend. It arises as soon as one person oversees or directs the activities of another. Top-level managers usually supervise only a few persons; they have few subordinates. Middle managers may supervise a few people or many. The first-line supervisor may supervise a relatively small group, say 25, or a very large group consisting of hundreds of employees. While this discussion is aimed primarily at these first-line supervisors, the characteristics of a good supervisor apply to all levels.

Two types of supervision are described. These types seem to cover what exists today, what is undesirable, and what types seem to be needed. They are based on present-day experience, observation, and recommendation.

The Dictatorial Type

This supervisor is bossy, domineering, overbearing, even oppressive. The job is like that of a policeman: keeping watch on employees to see that they are busy at what they are supposed to do. Employees are to be criticized but not helped. They may be required to do an arbitrary amount of work with an arbitrary level of accuracy. Employees are supposed to be seen and not heard. They are not to complain or make suggestions for improvements. Communication is rare; where it exists, it is curt and critical. The dictatorial type can also be a negativist. Every attempt to explain an improvement or to suggest a change is met with a resounding "No" and with a barrage of reasons why nothing should be done. There is never any deviation from this negative attitude. Employees are like robots or marionettes to be used and manipulated for the benefit of the supervisor.

This type of supervision can easily grow out of a prevailing notion that leadership in schools, colleges, and elsewhere is characterized by bossiness, talkativeness, extroversion, and a tendency to dominate other persons. In an extreme form it can lead to self-righteousness and even arrogance. The sooner we stop confusing dictatorship with leadership, the better. The good news is that in management, in theory at least, the dictator school is condemned. Alas, however, it still exists in practice.

The Participative Type

Participative management or supervision refers to the extent to which lower-level officials and employees participate in the functions performed at higher levels. These functions may be few or many; the participation may be slight, full, or partial. It is only fair to point out that good supervision has always respected the ideas, suggestions, and contributions made by lower-level people.

Slight Participation. This is illustrated by the use of the suggestion box by a company or agency. Employees at all levels are invited to submit in writing any ideas or specific proposals they have for the improvement of the work. These proposals are dropped in the suggestion box (there may be several boxes) and later appraised by an official or committee at a higher level. It shows that management is on the right track: that they recognize that employees have valuable ideas and suggestions if only management gives them a chance to express them.

The suggestion box idea suffers from a number of weaknesses. Management may not take it seriously. Suggestions are not discussed with employees or supervisors. If an idea or suggestion represents too drastic a change or could affect higher-level officials if put into effect, it can easily be dismissed and rejected. An example is the suggestion to use sampling on a particular project; this would adversely affect higher-level managers, whose work might be drastically reduced.

There is a tendency, based on observation, to accept suggestions which are simple and which do not rock the boat, but which represent real savings. Examples are reduction in the number of carbon copies typed, the number of names on a distribution list, the use of one form instead of two or three, the change in the layout of a data form or questionnaire, a change in the filing system, a change in the way things are stored.

The system has delays built into it as it is usually administered. It may be months before an employee hears what happened to his or her suggestion. It may remain in the box for weeks and it may take the appraising individuals or group weeks, if not months, to act. As administered, this system is too slow, arbitrary, and cumbersome to be effective.

Full Participation. This form of supervision can take at least two different forms: lower-level officials may participate in higher-level functions, and employees may participate in supervisory and related functions. At both levels the functions involved may include several of the following:

• Isolating problems	• Planning
• Solving problems	• Training
• Making decisions	• Measuring quality
• Setting goals	• Using statistics
• Setting standards	• Improving quality of data
• Improving performance	• Personnel problems
• Measuring progress	• Inspecting or verifying.

Where these groups are small and work as a team, they can be similar to but more effective than quality circles. They should avoid the following limitations and defects of quality circles:

- Employees lack technical capability, so they accomplish little.
- Quality circles are limited to problems that only employees can solve.
- They do not touch the faults of the system, where many (if not most) of the important problems are.
- Numerous applications to improve quality are never made because authority, functions, and capabilities are sharply limited.
- Capable people are not hired, and as a result considerable time and money are spent on training, facilitation, fruitless discussion, and other overhead activities.
- Highly specialized training and experience that are necessary may be missing, such as ability to design a nationwide probability sample that can be implemented with the available people and staff, the technical ability to design an appropriate random time sample for work analysis, or an experiment to answer an important question.
- Sharing ignorance may be confused with sharing knowledge.

Partial Participation. Good supervision has always been characterized by partial participation of lower-level officials and employees. This participation is based upon some important characteristic or ability of the employee:

- The employee knows operations and can make suggestions relative to their improvement.
- The employee has technical knowledge that others do not have and knows how to apply it. Examples are probability sampling, quality control, and computer programming.
- The employee has special knowledge of great value (e.g., rules, regulations, laws, procedures, cost accounting, traffic management).
- The employee holds a key position which makes participation obligatory.

What Participative Supervision Is Not. Participative supervision is effective if teamwork operates and if relevant knowledge, abilities, skills, and attitudes are pooled and directed toward solving a problem, conducting a study or survey, or performing some other necessary function or task. It is *not*

- Management by consensus. There is no inherent validity or superiority in "togetherness."
- Nontechnical people making technical decisions.
- Egalitarianism. Everyone is not equal, is not alike, is not the same.
- Group decision making. This is not the way to operate if decisions are based on votes. Political decisions are not the way to get work done effec-

tively. *The group may be doing no more than sharing ignorance.* The group, the majority, may and can be wrong. It may be more political than rational. Where knowledge of a technical or specialized nature is involved, scientific, engineering, technical, or specialists' decisions should govern.
- Group problem solving by brainstorming. What applies to group decision making applies here also. There can be a lot of talk but little substance. Verbosity is no substitute for knowledge, ability, or skills. Problem solving comes from those who have the necessary knowledge and insight. This is an individual affair, not a mass affair. Innovations, inventions, and improvements are made by individuals, not by committees, circles, or task forces.

Effective technical work does not require a crowd. It requires one competent person trained and experienced in the problem area. The following types of probability sample studies were designed by one professional person with a few comments from another technical person: a nationwide audit control sample for tax returns, a nationwide sample for corporation income tax returns, a nationwide sample for each of the following: carload circuity, household goods moving, rail shipment routing, shortage of freight cars. All of these sample studies were designed and implemented for the first time, and therefore required persons with experience in designing nationwide sample studies and how to implement them. A crowd of people unfamiliar with this kind of technical work would have been a hindrance and obstruction, regardless of how many "brainstorming" ideas they had. This excludes interaction among knowledgeable people, which can be very productive.

The Technical Team

This is a multifunction team pooling the capabilities of several specialists which were needed to develop a plan, implement a plan, or solve a problem.

Example: One team required for a nationwide sample study of freight car shortages included two lawyers, two accountants, two statisticians, two computer specialists, one traffic specialist, and one economist, a total of 10 people.

Example: Another team for an entirely different nationwide sample of an audit type consisted of an economist, a computer manager, an accountant, a statistician, an auditor, and a financial specialist, for a total of six.

As stated above, in probability sample studies the responsibility for designing the sample and managing its implementation falls on one or two experienced professionals who know how to design probability samples, control their collection, and analyze the results. Unless the other members of the team and top-level officials follow the advice and procedures of the sampling and statistical experts, the study may be seriously flawed. Examples of such studies can be cited. Teamwork is much easier to talk about than to attain in practice.

The Nontechnical Team or The Basic Work Team

This is a group of the lowest-level employees working with a supervisor and receiving technical and special assistance as needed. With a civilized, enlightened, and people-oriented supervisor and with technical instruction and assistance, a group of this kind can identify, define, and solve problems peculiar to their work. In this way they can make improvements in quality without becoming a formal quality control circle. This means that *every organizational unit becomes a cell for the improvement of quality*. If the units are too large, they can be divided into smaller functional groups of about 10 each, which now become quality cells in their own right.

Why Supervision?

Supervision grew out of division of labor and the specialization of work inherent in such a division. It arose as soon as products could no longer be made by one man or one woman. As long as the shoemaker made the entire shoe, as long as the tailor made a complete suit of clothes, as long as the baker baked all of the bread and other bakery products, there was no need to hire additional help and therefore no need for supervision. Just as soon as the artisan, skilled workman, or professional person needed additional help, the problem of supervision arose.

Those who know more have to direct those who know less. Those who are more skilled have to direct those who are less skilled. Those who have special abilities have to direct those who lack these abilities.

In any subject matter field such as chemistry or mathematics or statistics, or in any professional field such as law or medicine or accounting or engineering there are many levels of difficulty and many levels of application. In any of these subject or professional fields, the federal civil service system has 15 GS levels which represent 15 levels of difficulty and complexity. Salaries ranging from the lowest to the highest correspond to these 15 levels.

Closely related to difficulty and complexity is the characteristic of the size of the project or job. Designing and implementing a sample of personnel records in an office for local use is a relatively simple job, but designing and implementing a probability sample survey that covers the entire nation is an entirely different matter. It requires a much more complex sample design, detailed planning, a series of controls, and very careful management and supervision. The need for direction, guidance, and a compass is much greater.

The Processing-Supervisory-Feedback Loop

The basic unit for quality performance and quality improvement is the processing-supervisory-feedback loop. The essential features are shown in the diagram (see Figure 8–2). It applies to all levels of a company or agency. It is

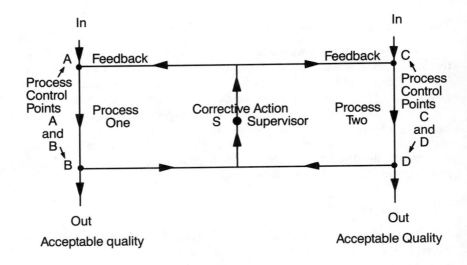

Figure 8–2. **The Processing-Supervisory-Feedback Loop**

assumed that the group consists of employees and a supervisor working on a problem or project which requires following a process or procedure. This process can be technical and complex and require considerable knowledge and experience, with attention to detail. Examples of such processes are purchase orders, tax returns, insurance claims, carload waybills, audit procedures, records of medical care in a nursing home, and transactions in a bank.

It is assumed that the supervisor

- knows what acceptable quality work is and what it is not.
- has sound measures of quality at hand which will indicate errors, error rates, time required, defects, or out-of-control situations. This means understanding of control chart methods and how to use them.
- knows what knowledge and abilities employees need to do an acceptable quality job.
- knows what the goals of the work are and how to guide the employees so that these goals can be met.
- knows the job and job description of every employee.

At key points in the process (Points B and D in the diagram) there are verifiers, reviewers, or inspectors who separate acceptable quality work from unacceptable work by using appropriate methods which indicate quality that is not acceptable. The unacceptable quality work goes back to the source person via the supervisor so that the latter can take appropriate action.

Examples of corrective action that can be taken by the supervisor are as follows:

- Showing employee how to read and interpret a document;
- Showing employee how to do an arithmetic calculation which is in error, e.g., a conversion units problem;
- Explaining an instruction that seems to be misunderstood;
- Demonstrating how an operation should be done, e.g., sample selection;
- Showing how to use a code book to code actual information;
- Coaching employees on points where performance is weak.

Feedback of poor quality work and corrective action are carried out *immediately* without any delay—within the same day or by the next day. If process control is by lot sampling, rejected lots are returned to the person processing them for reprocessing the lot 100 percent. This type of process control has been found both practical and effective.

Criticisms and Faults of Supervisors and Managers

The following are some of the criticisms and faults which employees find in supervisors, managers, and top-level officials. For good management and supervision all of these are to be avoided.

Supervisors:

- Are impatient with employees who have questions and difficulties.
- Do not explain or assist. Cannot explain work or jobs clearly.
- Use threats, warnings, police tactics.
- Their behavior reflects envy, jealousy, and discrimination.
- Injustices exist. Show favoritism. Take credit due to someone else. Refuse to give credit where credit is due.
- Oppose new ideas and better methods.
- Show dictatorial attitudes and behavior.

Officials:

- Oppose new ideas and better methods.
- Overrule technical decisions of specialists.
- Distort by editing technical material they know nothing about.
- Waste time on trivia in staff meetings.
- Set absurd and unrealistic deadlines.
- Set arbitrary rules.
- Show envy and jealousy; practice favoritism and discrimination.

- Take credit due someone else. Deny credit where credit is due.
- Blame lower-level people for their own mistakes.
- Lack understanding of operations.
- Base decisions on hunch and feeling rather than on sound data.
- Carry on a psychological war against those they want to retire, get rid of, etc.
- Show dictatorial attitudes and behavior.

Traits of a Good Supervisor

It is not difficult to enumerate the qualities which a good supervisor should have. The following list is long, but experience and observation show that a good supervisor will have most of these traits. The sad news is that there are far too few supervisors who meet these criteria.

- Keeps close to every employee; knows each job and explains it.
- Recognizes individual differences and acts accordingly.
- Knows where he or she is going; is a good guide.
- Sees that every employee knows his or her job; develops specific job tasks with employee; knows acceptable quality work from unacceptable quality.
- Coaches employees on their weak points.
- Explains to each individual how important his or her job is.
- Roves around and talks to every employee where each works.
- Praises and rewards good work; recognizes ability.
- Promotes from within to the maximum extent.
- Fosters innovation and improvement.
- Has no favorites or teacher's pets.
- Keeps everyone informed about what is going on, using various means.
- Encourages employee self-development.
- Expects results from everyone and shows each person how to attain them.
- Listens to any and all complaints, troubles, and grievances and takes action as needed; knows how to solve problems.
- Levels with every employee; is honest and truthful; no deception or alibis.
- Shows patience toward all those who are slow to learn or need to correct a fault.
- Keeps calm and collected in the face of stress, crisis, or criticism.
- Defends employees against undeserved and false accusations and treatment.
- Gives credit where credit is due; does not claim credit for work others do.
- Updates every job description after talking with every employee.
- Uses job descriptions to cover every function and task, prevent conflicts, and form a basis for appraising individual work.

STATISTICS

Periodically over the decades we in read in papers and books or hear the statement that too much emphasis is being placed on statistics in quality of products and of services. It has been so from the beginning. At early meetings of the American Society for Quality Control and its divisions, both statistics and statisticians were criticized. As time has passed, the indifference toward statistics has grown. First the word was dropped from "statistical quality control"; then "control" was dropped. The recent use of "statistical process control" seems acceptable.

We have never accepted the word "statistics" because it does not have the public image that the word "engineering" has. Quite the contrary. This attitude persists despite the fact that Walter Shewhart solved the problem facing Western Electric by applying statistics and probability where engineering and management had failed.

There are those who think that we should curb the use of the word and the techniques associated therewith because they turn off top-level management as well as lower-level management and professionals. No doubt there are those who have used technical statistics in presenting information to these officials, when the latter had no understanding of statistics.

Overcoming Opposition

You do not talk technical statistics to top-level management, middle-level management, professional specialists, or any other group that has no understanding of what technical statistics is all about. There are several ways to explain statistics:

1. State that quality is concerned with the variability of human performance—its extent and its control. Statistics is the science of variability. Therefore statistics is intimately connected with quality and its improvement. (This is the point that needs to be emphasized, not "number crunching.")

2. Point out the benefits of applying statistical techniques to the problem of management; it is not necessary to reduce these to monetary terms. The following benefits will be obvious to most managers: saving paper, saving people, better quality data, better decisions, reduced errors, more timely data, increased productivity, cutting costs, fewer defects, and more and better work at the *same* cost.

3. Cite examples and case studies of successful applications of statistical methods. Tell how other companies and agencies have succeeded in using statistics. Good examples of successful applications of statistics to problems of management can be found in several books, including the following:

Deming, *Sample Design in Business Research* (Wiley, 1960);
Burr, *Statistical Quality Control Methods* (Dekker, 1976);

Rosander, *Case Studies in Sample Design* (Dekker, 1977);

Rosander, *Application of Quality of Control in the Service Industries*, (Dekker and American Society for Quality Control, 1985).

4. Another approach is to point out and explain by talking and writing that managers have problems with statistical aspects which can be solved only by applying statistical science. Examples of such problems are as follows:

- Problems calling for the collection of good quality data. These include the design of sample studies, sample surveys, sample audits, tests, and experiments.
- Analysis and interpretation of data collected from such samples.
- Detection of out-of-control situations and other sources of trouble that need attention and possible correction.
- Collection of acceptable quality sample evidence for legal proceedings. This requires proper design and implementation of a sample study.
- Determination of the idle time of both employees and equipment by using random time sampling.
- Determination of work costs by various activities, organizational units, and other classifications by means of random time sampling.

Much of the antagonism toward statistics and its applications comes from a fear and dislike for anything mathematical. This dislike first appears in the elementary grades and continues into high school and college. Much if not most of this dread comes from the fact that few teachers can teach the number system and its characteristics in an interesting and meaningful fashion. Indeed, some of the teachers are only one step ahead of the best students, and some (alas) are not even that well versed in arithmetic.

It is not understood by professionals in the field of quality that it is much easier to solve statistical problems than to solve psychological or economic ones. For example, it is easier to design a sample study, lay out $\bar{x}$, R, and c charts, program a computer for statistical analysis, select a sample, construct a frequency distribution, or analyze sample data than it is to solve human relations situations involving fear (Deming's Point 8), breakdown of departmental barriers (Deming's Point 9), or pride (Deming's Point 12).

These problems involve feelings and emotions that are not easily changed. For example, breaking down barriers between departments usually means breaking down barriers between top individuals, including both managers and professionals; it is difficult to overcome these barriers because they are based on jealousy, envy, fear, empire building, ambition, and personality conflicts.

It is much easier to solve statistical problems because they are much more objective and do not involve feelings or emotions. Where differences exist, it is not very difficult to resolve them. This statement refers to specific problems such as those listed above. Furthermore, professionals in quality improvement and quality technology are versed in how to solve problems of quality involving statistics; they are not trained in how to resolve psychological problems or situations.

Statistics As a Powerful and Versatile Science

The evidence is found in the record of successful applications in every field of study, in research and in operations, in private industry and in government, over a period of more than 50 years. The applications of probability sampling, statistical quality control, the design of experiments, and statistical analysis *improved the quality of something*—the quality of data, the quality of performance, the quality of decisions, the quality of actions, the quality of products, the quality of services.

The basic knowledge, both theory and application, can be found in a number of books, such as the following arranged in time order.

Statistics:
> R. A. Fisher, *Statistical Methods for Research Workers;*
> Snedecor and Cochran, *Statistical Methods;*

Quality Control:
> Grant and Leavenworth, *Statistical Quality Control;*
> Shewhart, *Economic Control of Quality of Manufactured Products;*
> Shewhart and Deming (eds.) *Statistical Method from the Viewpoint of Quality Control;*

Design of Experiments:
> R. A. Fisher, *The Design of Experiments;*
> O. Kempthorne, *Design and Analysis of Experiments;*

Probability Sampling:
> Cochran, *Sampling Techniques;*
> Deming, *Some Theory of Sampling;*
> Hansen, Hurwitz, and Madow, *Sample Survey Methods and Theory;*
> Yates, *Sampling Methods For Censuses and Surveys.*

Applications:
> Tippett, *Technological Applications of Statistics;*
> Deming, *Sample Design in Business Research;*
> Rosander, *Applications of Quality Control in Service Industries;*
> Rosander, *Case Studies in Sample Design.*

Statistics In a Nutshell

Statistics, like the sciences, can be explained in terms of a relatively few concepts. The 12 statements below describe briefly these basic concepts. The key words are underlined. It is quite possible to develop these basic ideas and to obtain some idea of what statistics is all about without resorting to any but the simplest mathematics.

1. Statistics is the science of *variability,* or variation, of characteristics.
2. This variation can be *random, non-random,* or both.
3. This variation is displayed in a *frequency distribution,* in a table or graph.
4. The data are collected by means of a sample, which is usually a *probability sample* selected from a defined *population or universe or frame,* or from a designed experiment.
5. The data are in the form of *counts* or *measurements,* or both.
6. *Estimates* are made from these *variates,* either point or interval.
7. The sample counts, measurements, and estimates are subject to *sampling variability,* which can be calculated.
8. The characteristics of a few *probability distributions* can be used to design samples and interpret sample data.
9. The data are interpreted in terms of *levels, variability, differences,* and *relationships.*
10. *Bias, or non-random error,* exists, and must be reduced, measured, or eliminated to guarantee the validity of using formulas based on random variation.
11. *Statistical hypotheses* are tested as part of the analysis of the data.
12. The *central limit theorem* justifies the use of the normal distribution in sample design, the analysis of estimates, and in control charts, regardless of how the original data are distributed.

Downgrading Statistics

Nothing is more apparent from observation, reading, and experience than that statistics is still *not* recognized as the powerful and versatile science that it really is. The trouble is not that statistics is being used too much. The trouble is that it is being used too little. The reasons are not hard to find:

1. Colleges and universities concentrate on training in esoteric and advanced theory of statistics. They avoid training in statistical practice.
2. Managers and professional specialists oppose statistics because they do not understand its value and merits.
3. Many of those who are applying statistics have only a very limited knowledge of the science and how to apply it. In their work it is of minor importance.
4. Quickie courses greatly limit the use of statistics because those who plan and give them are interested only in a few cookbook ideas and procedures. They are not interested in having anyone master even the rudiments of the subject.
5. The same is true of quality circles. The seven so-called problem-solving techniques are very elementary, and give only a superficial treatment. Furthermore, these are not problem-solving techniques; they are problem-

finding techniques. Statistics seldom really solves any problems. It only helps in the solution.

6. Many people stop attaining knowledge of statistics when they have learned about the normal curve and the x̄, R charts. This is arrested development; this is graduating at the kindergarten level of statistics.

The books listed above (and there are many others) describe in detail a wide variety of successful applications of statistics to the problems of management. The many benefits of statistical science applications have been clearly demonstrated for decades. There is no reason why statistics should not be applied more widely in both private industry and government to help management solve its problems.

The Multi-Purpose Chart

The multi-purpose chart is designed to simplify to the maximum extent the recording of data and the calculations. With a hand-held calculator that has programmed into it linear regression, the correlation coefficient, and the mean and standard deviation, tedious calculations are eliminated. All one needs to do is to record the values of basic estimates. An example of such a calculator is the HP 32 E.

The chart provides for the graphic presentation of the data and the results as well as the analysis associated with several statistical techniques.[8] (See Figure 8–3). Provision is made for the following:

- x̄ and R charts for $n = 5$, for 20 samples;
- The p chart;
- The c̄ chart;
- A straight line $y = a + bx$ for a maximum of 100 pairs of values. With fewer pairs, space can be used for residuals or deviations from the fitted line.

In addition the chart can be used for the following:

- Frequency distribution: y = frequency, x = characteristic measure, count, or interval of values;
- Input (x) output (y) analysis;
- Time chart: y = characteristic, x = time;
- Learning curve analysis: y = production, x = time of employment;

---

[8] For examples of the applications of the 11 techniques listed, see *Application of Quality Control in the Service Industries.*

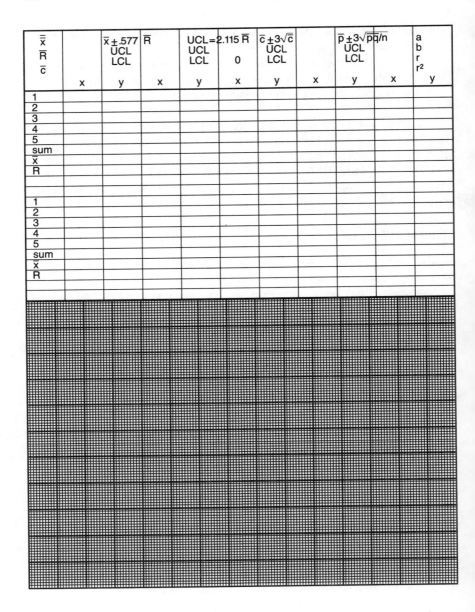

$\bar{\bar{x}}$ $\bar{R}$ $\bar{c}$		$\bar{x} \pm .577\,\bar{R}$ UCL LCL		UCL=2.115 $\bar{R}$ UCL LCL 0		$\bar{c} \pm 3\sqrt{\bar{c}}$ UCL LCL		$\bar{p} \pm 3\sqrt{\bar{p}\bar{q}/n}$ UCL LCL		a b r r^2
	x	y	x	y	x	y	x	y	x	y
1										
2										
3										
4										
5										
sum										
$\bar{x}$										
R										
1										
2										
3										
4										
5										
sum										
$\bar{x}$										
R										

Figure 8–3. **The Multi-Purpose Chart**

- Error curve analysis: y = number of errors or error rate, x = time;
- Man-hour production curve: y = man-hours, x = time, sequential units, or batches of equal sizes;
- Unit cost curve: y = unit costs, x = time.

Sampling

The development of a rigorous science of sampling based on probability was one of the great achievements of the past 50 years. This development is recorded in the basic textbooks by Yates, by Cochran, by Hansen, Hurwitz, and Madow, and by Deming. The unique characteristics of *probability sampling* are the following:

- Each element in the population or frame is given a known non-zero probability of being selected.
- The variation introduced into the sample data is random because a random process, such as random numbers, is used to select the sample.
- The mathematics of random variation can then be used to process and interpret the data.

Types of Probability Sampling

There are several types of probability sampling. In practice the problem is to select that type of sampling which is most appropriate and feasible for the situation at hand:

- Simple random selection (using a table of random numbers);
- Systematic selection with a random start;
- Stratified frame or population with random selection;
- Stratified frame or population with systematic selection;
- Replicated sample with random selection;
- Replicated sample with systematic selection with random start;
- Cluster sampling with or without stratification.

Two types of simple random sampling that require special attention are random time sampling (RTS) and random area sampling (RAS). In RTS the unit most commonly used is the minute because the minute model is applicable, making it possible to estimate aggregates and totals as well as percentages. Other time units that can be selected at random include hours, days, and weeks. In RAS, small, defined areas constitute the frame or population, and a random selection of these units is the sample.

Simple random sampling is used where the variability of the characteristic is not great, as in proportions or percentages, or in a highly restricted measurement such as the height of adults. Stratified sampling is used on frames or populations where the variability of the characteristic is very great; examples are sales, income, taxes, number of employees, size, and volume of production. Replicated sampling can be used on a simple or complex frame or population to simplify calculation of estimates and their sampling errors.

Other Methods of Sampling

There are other methods of sampling, of which three appear to be the most common forms of non-probability sampling:

1. Ordered Sampling. Selecting samples of elements (products) in the order in which they are produced. This is the method which has to be used in process control charts, such as the $\bar{x}$, R charts. Shewhart stressed this point and demonstrated that if random sampling were applied to the entire aggregation of units, this procedure would destroy the extreme variability that we are trying to detect. Random variation in the characteristic was attained or approximated by the elimination of the assignable causes of out-of-control variation.

2. Judgment Sampling. This type of sampling may be, and is, used in scientific work, but it may be subject to unknown biases which make generalizations suspect until they have been verified by other sound and independent studies. Judgment sampling has been very effective in past scientific experimentation and testing largely because of the homogeneity of the materials tested and the constancy and universality of the phenomena observed (e.g., electromagnetic induction).

This type of sampling can be very effective in pretesting questionnaires, data sheets, and sets of instructions. This pretest is run for the purpose of exposing any faults in the words, phrases, questions, and sentences. The draft is tested on the type of person it is being prepared for; hence persons are selected from those with widely different experiences, educational levels, income, ethnic backgrounds, and other similar factors. The pretest is for the purpose of eliminating misunderstandings, ambiguities, and different interpretations.

The customer uses judgment sampling as an everyday practice whether in buying an automobile or a camera or getting two prices for a job from two different contractors or repair firms. It is ever-present in the buying of fruits such as apples and oranges, or vegetables such as potatoes and onions. Avoiding poor quality merchandise of any kind often requires careful and minute inspection for effective judgment sampling. The customer always buys a sample of one item. He or she wants to know how a product operates.

3. Accessibility Sampling. In this kind of sampling, selection of the sample is limited to what is near at hand, what is convenient, and what is nearby. In all testing and experimentation in agriculture with crops and plants, the soil used is that which is near at hand. Many studies are made in which the persons selected in the sample are limited to those in a clinic, a hospital, or a nursing home. Studies of students, teachers, or other persons may be limited to one or a few schools, colleges, and universities. A study may be limited to a low-income area of a city, to an area inhabited by a certain ethnic group, or to an area characterized by "poverty."

All of these sample studies suffer from very serious defects:

- The common practice is to generalize from this limited group to a much larger population. In some cases this generalization has been extended to include the entire United States. Obviously this broad-brush generalization is unjustified, misleading, and unwarranted.
- Not having a well-defined population or universe from which the sample is drawn, the area to which the sample findings apply is unknown. The conclusions have to be limited to the area sampled. This is not the case. The person who conducts the study always wants to generalize far beyond the limits of the study.
- Generalizing to a wider population is not warranted until many other independent studies of a similar character in other parts of the country arrive at the same conclusions. No one pays much attention to this aspect of the problem: those who conduct sample studies of this kind rarely ever try to get others in different parts of the country to duplicate their studies and verify their conclusions.

The problem can be put more pointedly. Just because an agricultural experiment in England gives increased yields of wheat does not mean that this same result will be obtained in Kansas or Saskatchewan. Just because youth 16 to 25 years of age have certain characteristics in Maryland does not mean that youth in the other 49 states will have the same characteristics. Just because older persons in a few nursing homes in New York State have certain characteristics does not mean that everyone over 65 years of age has these same characteristics. There is a practice in this country, where age bigotry is widespread, to study a few "elderly" persons and then assert that the 27 million over 65 years of age have these same characteristics, usually of a derogatory nature: feeble, weak, senile, forgetful, emotionally unstable, helpless, unable to take care of themselves. Figures show that no more than 5 million are in this class. Putting 27 million in the same pigeonhole is a vicious type of generalization arising from biased samples in hospitals, nursing homes, doctor's offices, clinics, and elsewhere.

Basic Questions in the Use of Sampling

For the most effective use of sampling it is necessary to obtain clear-cut answers to several questions:

• What is the sample to be used for?

It can be used for exploration, estimation, detection, control, auditing, and comparing. In general a sample designed for one of these purposes is not the best sample to use for a different purpose. Each purpose has its own peculiar sample design.

Sample sizes can vary widely within each of these purposes. We require a larger sample to estimate a highly variable characteristic, such as sales and income, than to estimate one with limited variability, such as adult height. We require a larger sample to detect a rare event, such as is found in cancer research, than to detect an event which occurs frequently. We require a larger sample to detect and measure a small difference than to detect and measure a very large difference. Because a percentage can vary only from 0 to 100, it is quite easy to obtain a satisfactory national estimate of proportion or percentage with a random sample of less than 2,000 individuals or families.

• To what population or frame do the results from the sample apply?

The dangers of not having a specific population or frame, from which the sample is drawn, have already been pointed out. It is necessary to define, circumscribe, and isolate the frame or population to be sampled as one of the first steps in the planning and design of a sample study. Otherwise, there is no specific domain to which the generalizations from the sample can be applied.

When time is the population being sampled, as in RTS, it is necessary to decide what the objective is. If estimates are needed for a year, then time will have to be sampled for a year in order that seasonal variations are properly represented in the estimates. If estimates are not affected by seasons or by months, then a shorter time population may be sampled: the test to use is to ask how stable are the daily or weekly estimates over time. When values are stable, or are far out of line as percentages of idle time, then sampling over a few weeks or months may yield useful information.

• How was bias eliminated or reduced to a negligible quantity?

The Number One problem in collecting data for any purpose whatever is getting good quality data at the source. This requires eliminating bias or nonrandom error regardless of the source; it includes all possible sources: the sample, the individual response, the interviewer, observer, reader, or user of instruments, the one who counts, or any other. If this is not done, the use of such concepts as standard error and confidence limits is unjustified and invalid.

Half a century ago (1934) Gosset, better known as Student, the first great statistical practitioner, put the problem in one sentence:

"The whole art of statistical inference lay in the reconciliation of random mathematics with biased samples."[9]

Random variation, by using appropriate statistical theory, can be controlled by the proper sample design or by a proper control procedure. Non-random variation or bias arises from conditions in the real world: from the behavior of people, from the operation of machinery, from a wide variety of "assignable causes," to use Shewhart's term. Controlling and eliminating bias in the data are done for the purpose of building quality into data. This is crucial because the decisions and actions based on the data are no better than the quality of the data. If the data are suspect, so are the decisions and the actions.

Some comments are in order in connection with some common methods of collecting data by sampling: questionnaires, opinion polls, data sheets, and telephone polls. In a mail questionnaire, opinion poll, or data sheet, two major sources of bias exist: the framing of the questions or items and non-response or no attitude.

Faults in phrasing questions or items include

- Use of loaded questions;
- Restricting the answers;
- Use of emotionally toned words;
- Use of modifiers;
- Not allowing complete answers;
- Misleading questions;
- Double-barreled questions.

In a mail questionnaire sent to a random sample selected from a population, non-response is a major problem. (It is also a problem if the population is covered 100%.) One way to handle it is to use second and third mailings, and of the non-respondents remaining, select a random sample and interview them.

This procedure, if properly handled, will eliminate the bias due to the original persons not responding. A fatal mistake is to assume that those who do not respond are like those who do.

In a telephone survey based on a random sample of telephone numbers, several serious situations arise which can greatly bias the results:

- The telephone is no longer in use. (Has telephone been disconnected? Do they have another number? Are they in the process of moving?);
- Busy signal. (Do you call again? If so, how many times?);

---

[9] *Student's Collected Papers*, edited by E. S. Pearson and John Wishart (London: Biometrika Office, University College, 1942), p. 220.

- No one answers. (Do you call again? If so, how often?);
- Wrong person answers, e.g., a child or youth. (Do you try to get the right person?);
- Eligible person is not at home. (Do you call later?);
- Right person answers but refuses to cooperate. (This is non-response);
- Person answers but is ineligible. (This person is not in frame or population).

Here are seven cases or situations which can bias the results if there is no follow-up. This is bias due to persons in the sample not being included because of inaccessibility or refusal to answer. Note that any bias due to misunderstanding the questions asked, giving answers which the interviewer misinterprets, giving vague answers, or any other faulty reply, is an *additional source of bias* which may be just as important, if not more important, than the bias due to sampling.

The fault with all telephone polls, and especially those reported in the press, is that the numbers in the sample which fall in the categories given above are never given. Simply obtaining a sample size desired (e.g., 1500) and ignoring hundreds who fall in the categories given above is introducing an unknown bias into the results. In such a case, figures given for the magnitude of the sampling variation area false and invalid.

Some Cases Involving Sample Unit, Sample Size, and Stratification

The following examples show why detailed technical knowledge about probability sampling is necessary if a sample study is to be efficient and effective. It shows the sad results which obtain when persons do not know what they are doing.

Case 1. The sampling unit in a large nationwide sample study was a block or bundle of 100 documents, which was the way they were blocked to facilitate handling and filing. It was claimed by high-level officials that selecting these block units at random was cheaper and better. The statistician, however, proved that the variation in the basic characteristics was very great *between* blocks, and that therefore these blocks should be used as strata, not as sampling units. A sample of individual to documents was finally selected at random from each block. This resulted in a reduction of the volume of paper included in the sample as well as better estimates (estimates with reduced sampling variation).

Case 2. The manager of a textile mill came to the conclusion, based on a sample of one operator, that employees were stealing $1 million worth of hose a year. This figure was obtained by having one operator run a test to determine how much yarn was used per pair of hose. Output was estimated by dividing total yarn consumed by this factor. The test operator, however, was one of the best operators in the mill and used much less yarn than the average for all employees, even though semi-automatic machines were employed. This led to an inflated estimate of output. The sample of one operator led to some highly biased data, which in turn led to a false decision, wasting thousands of dollars on "corrective action" for a "problem" that did not exist. The real problem was the manager, who lacked the necessary technical capability to obtain accurate data about the operations of the factory. The million dollars was the additional cost the company incurred because the operators, on the average, were not performing as efficiently as the test operator. This experience clearly pointed to the immediate need to put all the operators through a training course which would reduce the amount of yarn they were wasting in making a pair of hose.

Case 3. Waybills are a record of the movement of commodities (shipments) by railroads nationwide. The volume of specific commodities varies widely. Coal and iron ore move in very large quantities, while many other important commodities move in very small volumes. A simple random or systematic sample of these waybills nationwide will reflect these large differences in volume. This means that a 1 percent sample of waybills nationwide will greatly oversample commodities with large volumes and greatly undersample those with small volumes. This is the kind of sample that was used for decades.

Stratification of the population of waybills with lower rates for high-volume commodities and higher rates for low-volume commodities would have reduced the volume of paper required, cut costs, and improved the estimates for many important commodities. All of this could be accomplished with very acceptable levels of sampling variation in the estimates for coal and iron ore. This improvement, although proposed, was never made.

Books on Sampling

The following few books describe basic concepts and theory of probability sampling, together with applications. The last two books deal exclusively with sampling, especially replicated sampling, applied to real-world problems facing managements of business, industry, and government.

W. G. Cochran, *Sampling Techniques* (Wiley, 1953). There are later editions.

W. E. Deming, *Some Theory of Sampling* (Wiley, 1950).

W. E. Deming, *Sample Design in Business Research* (Wiley, 1960).

A. C. Rosander, *Case Studies in Sample Design* (Dekker, 1977).

Making Statistics Work for Quality

We describe briefly several steps that need to be taken to insure that statistics contributes most effectively to the improvement of quality.

• Identify statistical aspects of problems. Management is faced with all kinds of problems. One of the jobs of the statistician, or the professional familiar with statistics, is to study every one of these problems for the purpose of determining the statistical aspects of these problems, if such exist. This requires someone who is thoroughly familiar with statistics and how to apply it. It cannot be done by someone with only a superficial knowledge obtained from a few "quickie" courses.

• Make a survey of the entire company or agency to discover where statistics can be applied. The purpose of this survey is not to create a large volume of unnecessary statistical work to do manually or run on a computer. The purpose is to improve the quality of performance, data, products, and services. The purpose is to contribute to the improvement of quality throughout the company or agency. This means that such a survey should be made by a statistician or some other professional who is familiar with a wide variety of statistical techniques and how they can be applied to improve the quality of operations. A check list for this purpose is given at the end of this section.

• Stress collection of high quality data to discover problems. Two approaches can be used to discover and identify problems: the shotgun approach and the rifle approach. In the former a survey may be aimed at a general problem situation but in the process several other specific problems may be revealed by the data.

Examples

A random time sample (RTS) was conducted to estimate time and money spent by a division on "outside" projects, that is, work requested by those outside the division which was not part of the regular work. During the test week, however, it revealed that idle time in the graphics unit was 9 percent, in another unit it was 5 percent, and in the files unit it was 4 percent. The director called in the supervisors, showed them the findings, and requested that they take immediate steps to reduce these high levels of idle time to less than one percent, where all of the other units stood. The major purpose of the study was to estimate, but the first use made of the data was control over idle time, a problem they did not know existed.

A nationwide audit sample was used to estimate the total amount of tax error on federal individual income tax returns. In carrying out this study it was discovered that many persons were claiming aliens as personal exemptions, something the tax law does not allow. Taxpayers were not understanding the instructions, which admittedly were not very clear. As a result, corrective action was taken in two directions: more detailed reporting of data on form 1040 relative to each exemption was required, and the several criteria that a personal exemption had to meet were listed in the instructions.

• Stress the analysis of problems to determine the specific kinds of data needed. This step may follow the foregoing step or be independent of it. The initial emphasis is on a problem, *not on data*. It will be observed that this is contrary to the current emphasis on data analysis, data banks, and data management, in which both problems and the quality of the data are ignored. This is a serious mistake. Analysis is futile, a waste of time, and very misleading if the data are irrelevant, ambiguous, inaccurate, biased, meager, or intractable.

Data are a means, not an end, resulting from analysis and identification of a problem. Data are defined and limited only to those which result from problem analysis, and which bear directly on the problem. Collecting large masses of marginal or useless data, which is not uncommon, is eliminated. This is a real advantage of the predesigned sample study aimed at a definite problem. Many examples are found in the books on sampling cited above. These examples include problems involving accounting, rail traffic, household goods moving, freight car shortages, tax error, unemployment, family expenditures and income, airline passenger traffic and revenues, and household purchases.

• Talk and write about the benefits and advantages of statistics. It is futile to talk or write technical statistics to executives, managers, and professional specialists who know little or nothing about the subject—and this is the usual situation. The approach to use is to stress *benefits and advantages* to the company or agency, such as the following:

- Saves paper;
- Saves people;
- Gives better data;
- Insures better decisions;
- Better performance;
- More effective actions;
- Less time is wasted;
- Fewer errors;
- Fewer defects;
- Costs are reduced;
- Money is saved and used more efficiently;
- Yields more timely data.

A warning is needed. These benefits should not be claimed unless they can be produced. It is not hard, however, to produce these benefits if one understands the subject, especially sampling, and knows how to apply it successfully to real-world problems.

Example: A top-level official is very skeptical of the value of statistics. At a budget meeting which is held once a year, the chief statistician explained in his presentation how in one study many thousands of pieces of paper were eliminated from both collection and processing. This struck the official so that he changed his attitude completely. He liked "saving paper," resulting from a well-designed sample study.

• Develop an adequate statistical capability. Experience shows that a large staff is not necessary for an adequate statistical capability unless the statistical load is such as to warrant such a staff. All that is needed, especially at the start, is two or three professional statisticians who are good practitioners, who have the necessary knowledge, and who have had experience successfully applying statistics to the problems of management. In most places this does not require, certainly at the initial stages, any advanced statistics at the Ph.D. level. Elementary and intermediate-level statistics are quite adequate. It is not advanced knowledge that is important, but ability to successfully apply statistics to the problems at hand.

There is a need to apply a wide variety of techniques because the range of problems encountered requires them. An $\bar{x}$ chart and a histogram are not enough. Other techniques include

- Random time sampling (RTS);
- Random area sampling (RAS);
- Learning curve analysis;
- Frequency distributions of identicals;
- Input-output analysis;
- Man-hour analysis;
- Design of experiments;
- Analysis of variance.

It is often overlooked that a successful application of statistics to real-world problems almost automatically improves the quality of something—data, performance, decisions, actions, products, services. It was not the $\bar{x}$ chart that improved chemical manufacturing but the use of techniques that Shewhart did not describe—design of experiments, analysis of variance, multiple regression, evolutionary operations.

Example: The quality assurance department of a large company issues a monthly report on the status of quality of various operations. It contain tables of data, but the titles are obscure, units of measurement are missing, and there is no analysis. Sampling is used but the methods are not described, nor are any indications given of the sampling variations in the estimates. Frequency distributions are not properly constructed, nor was it possible to verify the means (averages) which were given. Technical material was not separated from the outstanding developments of the month. Problem spots were not indicated, nor was the need for any corrective action. This one detailed report was for everyone from the technical people to the top-level officials.

This company was swamped with statistical problems in their quality assurance report, but they had no capability to handle them. Obviously those who prepared the report had not had even a beginning course in statistics. The report needed to be drastically changed and improved. First the company needed to improve its sampling, presentation, and analysis. It needed to pinpoint where trouble spots were. It needed to issue this report weekly, not monthly. By the time this report reached the officials who were responsible for corrective action, six weeks could elapse. The company needed to prepare three different reports: a one-page report to top-level officials, a substance report to those in charge of operating divisions, and a detailed technical backup report for those who did the technical work and presented explanations of sampling, frequency distributions, calculations, sampling errors, and analysis of the data.

This company suffered because it lacked statistical capability, it lacked a quality policy, and it lacked an understanding of the need for a quality improvement program and how to attain it. Management understood neither quality, statistics, nor any other aspect of a quality improvement program.

The Statistician and Quality Management

Statistics is a broad and versatile field and statistical practice reflects it. We distinguish two different roles: 1) the statistical practitioner and 2) the consultant: academic, salaried company, or private. It is now proposed that the statistician get involved in management and total quality control. This "total statistician" is discussed later.

The Statistical Practitioner

This is the statistician who works in, or with, the operating divisions to help management and professional specialists solve their problems. As Frank Yates put it, "An expert acting in an advisory position is no substitute for the statistician on the job responsible for the planning, execution, and analysis of the data." [10] Statistics is brought to bear to discover problems as well as to aid in their solution, throughout the entire company or agency. Statisticians are closely associated with operations and operating people and their problems. They concentrate on areas and conditions and aspects that can be improved by application of statistical methods. The competence of these statisticians is much more important than their number. Two or three good statisticians with some clerical assistance are all that is necessary. To be most effective, however, they should be allowed to rove all over the place, hunting for operating problems to be resolved and operating conditions that can be improved.

The emphasis is on the problems of management and professional specialists or on discovering problems they don't know they have, not on showing how much the statistician knows about statistics. Gosset ("Student"), Tippett, and Yates are role models for the practitioner.

The job of the lawyer is to help management with legal problems. The job of the accountant is to help management with accounting problems. Likewise,

---

[10] Frank Yates, *Sampling Methods for Censuses and Surveys*, 4th ed. (New York: Macmillan, 1981), p. 6. This statement was in the 1948 edition.

the job of the statistician is to help management with statistical problems and all other aspects of a statistical nature. Management can easily recognize legal and accounting problems. The real challenge to the statistician, however, is that management doesn't know what a statistical problem is, nor does it recognize a situation where statistics is applicable. The statistician will have to use every means he or she can muster to inform and enlighten management as to the scope of the field. The checklist given below can be helpful in showing how broad the field of application is, and in shedding light on the problem. There is nothing like a successful demonstration of the application of sampling, quality control, experimental design, random time sampling, and statistical analysis to an important problem or situation.

The Consultant

The practitioner is in the midst of operations and is a part of the operating organization, or should be. The consultant is not. This makes a world of difference. Passive consultants wait to be consulted. They act in an advisory capacity. They are isolated from problems facing management. Their advice may be heeded or ignored. They cannot explain to management, because of this isolation, what problems are statistical and what are not. This is where management and professionals really need assistance and enlightenment. If successful, this type of consultant may develop a sizeable clientele, and may be effective. Experience shows, however, that there are cases where they are ignored most of the time and live a lonely existence.

The active consultant takes a real part not only in planning, but in implementing and monitoring studies and experiments. The consultant insists on this role right from the beginning. This insures that the application of statistical theory is not invalidated by inept implementation.[11] This approach insures positive, effective, and successful results, something that may be missed by passive consultation.

The Supervisory Statistician

The supervisory statistician is in charge of a unit, section, or division. He or she plans and directs the work involved in a statistical program for the entire company or agency. This includes all work connected with probability sampling, statistical quality control, design of tests and experiments, sample audits, sample evidence, and statistical analysis of data including estimation and inference. Also included are related activities such as design of data sheets and questionnaires, preparation of both technical and non-technical reports for man-

---

[11] For an excellent example see A. C. Rosander, *Case Studies in Sample Design* (New York: Dekker, 1977), Chapter 19.

agement and others, providing technical assistance as required, and giving in-service courses in statistical principles and applications as needed. He or she supervises employees, including professional statisticians, as assistants. The position, because it involves people in operations as well as higher-level management, is both managerial and technical.

The purpose of this group is to bring the full power of the science of statistics to bear on the problems of management—the statistical problems and the statistical aspects of problems. One of the major jobs of the professional statistician is to convince management by demonstrations, case studies, and other means that these statistical problems do exist, and that they can be solved by powerful techniques with substantial benefits to both management and the company.

The functions include planning, design, implementation, and appraisal. They also include determining for management what problems are statistical and what are not. This job is the most important of all for the simple reason that executives and managers simply do not know what is statistical and what is not. They did not get to high-level positions because they studied mathematics, statistics, and probability. Indeed, some of their ideas about statistics (e.g., sampling) are obtained from newspapers and cause more harm than good.

This requires a roving and active supervisory statistician who hunts for statistical problems and situations as well as existing applications that can be improved. Wherever statistics can be applied, there is, in some form or other, an improvement. In this way statistics can be applied to *correct many of the faults of the system,* not only faults due to employee performance. Actual cases of how this was done, or could have been done, are discussed in detail in another chapter.

It is usually necessary to go much farther. It is necessary to demonstrate to management by actual applications that there are better techniques than the ones that are being used. This may mean designing a better sample study or a better experiment. It may mean showing how a random time sample can be used to disclose as well as measure the amount and cost of idle time and downtime, something management may know nothing about.

In this connection one does not talk technical statistics to high-level officials and professionals who are not familiar with the subject. One talks about the *benefits and advantages,* about saving paper, saving people, better data, quicker data, fewer errors, fewer defects, better and quicker decisions, and reduced costs.

There will be conflicts between statisticians and other professional and managerial groups over the introduction of these improved methods, such as probability sampling and quality control. Sampling may reduce sharply the amount of paperwork, and hence may reduce the chances for promotions based on the number of employees supervised, or the size of the study. Two examples are cited.

A nationwide sample study was proposed to measure the extent to which truckers in interstate commerce violated federal laws. The lawyers said it was a legal problem, not a statistical one, so they made a sample plan of their own on the basis of "intuition" and "common sense." Result: a useless study that cost at least $250,000, according to a high-level official. The lawyers did not see that while the content of the study was legal, the method of collecting meaningful data efficiently was not. Sampling specialists were readily available within the agency, but they were never consulted. This illustrates barriers between departments, and the difficulties involved in breaking them down (Dr. Deming's Point 9). This is also an example of the fault of the system, which could also be resolved at a higher level. It shows how statistical knowledge of sampling could correct a fault in the system, but how those with that knowledge were not allowed to do so.

The Federal Communications Commission (FCC) holds hearings based on sample evidence submitted by corporations such as American Telephone and Telegraph Company (AT&T) and Western Union. They had one mathematical statistician, but no specialist in sampling and sample evidence. A President's Commission recommended that they hire a professional statistician familiar with probability sampling theory and practice, who could advise them on problems of sample evidence. Their reply was: "We call in the statistician when we need him." This statement was both evasive and misleading. Since all of the five members of FCC were lawyers, it is obvious that they didn't know what a statistical problem was. Clearly, sample evidence was not a statistical problem to them. They had a statistician, but they didn't know how to use him; they didn't know when they "needed" him. They should never have hired a statistician until 1) they had a better idea of what a statistical problem was and 2) they were aware that their cases involved statistical knowledge of sampling and statistical analysis of sample data. Even if they had a top-notch statistician who was an expert in sample evidence, he or she would be so far removed from the Commission as to be unable to convince them that they had a wide variety of statistical problems and that sample evidence was only one of them. An iron curtain of organization layers would exist between the statistician and the Commission, which could be breached only by some high-level official who understood the statistical problems facing the Commission. A statistician cannot explain to managers and executives what a statistical problem is, or what a statistical aspect of a problem is, if the statistician can never communicate with these officials because too many layers of organization separate them. No doubt improvements can be made on both sides.

The Total Statistician

What appears to be a modification in the two roles described above is now envisaged for the statistician.[12] The word "appears" is used because the spe-

[12] R. D. Snee, *Youden Memorial Address,* ASQC-ASA Conference, Corning, NY, October 1985.

cifics are not spelled out. It may really be, in the main, the same as the effective practitioner described above. This new role, if such it is, seems to have at least four aspects:

1. Learning Organization Development Techniques. These are neither illustrated nor explained. Neither is it explained why statisticians should be concerned in any large way with what is called "organizational development," whatever that is. The statistician is primarily a builder of quality, not a manager of quality, although the supervisory statistician has to be both.

2. Learning Methods to Influence an Organization. The job of the statistician is to influence managers with regard to application of statistics to their problems. Statisticians can influence managers most easily by doing an effective job in helping them solve their problems and improving operations. It was not made clear what "influence" meant in this context.

3. Helping Organizations Use Statistical Tools More Effectively. The statisticians, if they are doing their jobs, are already using statistical tools effectively and helping others as needed. It is not clear how this changes the role of the statistician. To help as indicated may mean that the statistician will have to instruct an unknown number of persons. Will he do this in addition to performing his regular job? Does this "help" mean that the major job may very well be convincing the rest of the organization that statistics is powerful and versatile and should be applied across the entire company or agency? The most effective statistical work will be done by the statistician as a practitioner, not by others who have only a superficial knowledge of statistics and how to apply it. Before you train anyone in statistics, you have to convince them that statistics is worthwhile.

4. Focusing on Total Quality Control Rather than on Statistics. Practitioners as described above focus on statistical problems to be solved and conditions to be improved. Statistics is a means to help management and professional specialists. It is not an end in itself. The job is not to show off our knowledge of statistics. The focus should be on solving statistical problems facing management, and should not be limited to total quality control, however it is defined. The checklist on p. 224 shows this wider scope of the work of the statistician.

PSYCHOLOGY

The most critical aspect encountered in a quality improvement program is not management, supervision, statistics, or eonomics. It is psychology. This is because such a program calls for a change in human behavior, attitudes, ideas, thinking, beliefs, and ways of working, and psychology deals with human behavior, attitudes, traits, emotions, and thinking.

A Checklist to Use in Making a Study, Survey, or Audit

	Sample survey		Random Time Sampling	Statistical Quality Control	Experi- ments	Design of Labora- tory tests
Item	Facts	Opinions				
1. Problems to solve, questions to answer						
2. Purpose of sample experiment						
3. Sample design, experimental design						
4. Population, lot						
5. Frame						
6. Stratification						
7. Replication						
8. Sample unit						
9. Sample size						
10. Random selection, random assignment						
11. Classes and subclasses						
12. Basic characteristics						
13. Experimental factors						
14. Experimental units						
15. Nature of the data						
16. Procedural manuals						
17. Quality controls						
18. Quantitative controls						
19. Random variations, standard error, experimental error						
20. Non-random variations						
21. Data collection methods						
22. Method of estimation						
23. Data tabulation						
24. Decision rules						
25. Statistical analysis						
26. Interpretation of data						
27. Presentation of results						
28. Appraisal of study						
29. Actions taken						
30. Execution and management						
31. Pilot tests, pretests						
32. Training						
33. Staffing						

"Facts" means counts or measurements, including numerical judgmental data such as numerical ratings.

Lectures, books, and seminars by Deming, Juran, and others aim to change the minds of executives, managers, and others—to get them to adopt new goals, new policies, new concepts, new attitudes, new procedures. Deming and Juran recognize that these psychological changes are difficult to bring about, and that improvements are made slowly. Deming[13] states that a long thorny road lies ahead, while Juran[14] states that management's progress in quality during the next 15 years will be at a pace that is agonizingly slow.

The early practitioners who applied probability sampling, statistical quality control, and other techniques to the problems of government and industry met with strong opposition from high-level officials and professional specialists, from 1940 to 1960. The acceptance of these new and better methods was a slow process in any company or agency. The time required to convince management and technical professionals, even under persistent efforts including successful demonstrations, was five to 10 years. This experience has been documented in detail.[15]

This experience is in harmony with what psychology tells us: people do not like to change attitudes, ideas, methods, procedures, techniques, or beliefs which they have held, followed, and applied for decades. Officials and professionals can think of more "reasons" why changes should not be made: a change is not needed, it will cost too much, the present methods have been used successfully for 20 years, this is not the proper time to change, we already have the best method, it is too refined, it will upset operations.

Psychology gives us cues, but no sure-fire methods, for bringing about these changes in people. The crucial ingredient of any approach is that the changes benefit and appeal to the individual in ways that are clear, specific, and immediate. Deferred benefits are usually not as effective as immediate ones. Deferred or indirect benefits have to be tied directly to the understanding and interest of the individual. A quality improvement program that is aimed at improving products and services, meets competition, and insures continuous employment (if not expansion) of job opportunities will be more convincing than talking about market share, higher profits, and increased productivity, which may be of little or no interest to the individual.

These benefits can vary greatly and can take on one or more of many forms. One official became very interested in a nationwide sample study when he discovered that he would have to accompany the statistician on field trips to explain to those offices selecting the sample how the sample data would be

---

[13] W. Edwards Deming, *Quality, Productivity, and Competitive Position* (Cambridge: Massachusetts Institute of Technology, 1982), p. iii.

[14] J. M. Juran, "Catching Up: How is the West Doing?" *Quality Progress,* November 1985, p. 22.

[15] A. C. Rosander, *Washington Story* (National Directions, 500 26th St, Greeley, CO, 80631, 1985).

used. He liked to travel to field offices and to explain to the field people how they were to handle the data.

A top-level official became enthusiastic about a regional sample study when he was told that the new sample design would eliminate collecting and processing about 24,000 documents which hitherto had been collected. At the same time, this improved sample would deliver better quality data than the data they were now collecting. He liked the idea of "saving paper."

Individual Freedom Versus Social Controls

A psychological problem of major importance is the reconciliation of individual freedom with social controls and discipline which are inherent in the job or workplace. This aspect has a direct bearing on the quality of product and of service. The interests of the individual have to be harmonized with the demands of the job. The solution calls for doing things that satisfy the worker but at the same time meet the basic requirements of the job as determined by the company. The company, by doing the hiring in the first place, can set the conditions, qualifications, and kinds of behavior which have to be met for quality performance. The employee may receive only a few of the benefits that he or she would like, but enough to be satisfying.

An actual situation which involved about 20 employees and a supervisor brings this issue into sharp focus. A unit in a private firm had a government contract to process about 150,000 documents from a nationwide sample. The documents were complex (they were rail waybills) and were not standardized, so that they had to be transcribed onto a standard format for key punching. This was a production job, but before any work could be started all of the employees had to take a three-week course using a procedural manual of about 95 pages. It was difficult, requiring close study of each document so that items could be properly identified, coded, and copied. Some arithmetic conversions of units had to be made. It was not a simple clerical job. Furthermore, there were time limits on the contract. An acceptable quality level of performance was required so that the error rate would be low.

Individual desires and individual freedom had to be restricted so that the demands of the job could be met. The following list shows major areas of sharp disagreement between individuals and their freedom on the one hand, and the requirements of the job on the other:

Individual Desires	*Requirements of the Job*
No clock on the wall; Eating on the job;	Clock on the wall; employees paid for eight hours' work; no eating on the job could be allowed because of space, distraction, waste of time.
Personal radios;	They could not be allowed because of distraction, interference with coaching by supervisor, noise.

Individual Desires	*Requirements of the Job*
Determining own hours;	This could not be allowed because of the work load, supervisory problems, extra controls, built-in delays; fixed time schedule required.
Togetherness;	Work was individual in nature; transcription was not a group effort; neither were inspection and typing.
Country club atmosphere.	This was a production job, not a social seminar.

Most of these employees were unfamiliar with the discipline of the workplace, especially one under government contract which called for daily production of acceptable quality and quantity so that the contract could be met on time.

Most of the employees accepted these restrictions, although there was some grumbling at first. Only a few left after they found out how demanding the job was. None of them was familiar with the discipline, rules, and restrictions in the working world. These restrictions did not stop many of the employees from becoming highly productive workers in the ensuing months. A few admitted that they were glad they had been through this work experience.

Accommodating the individual to the group (company), and vice versa is not easy. In some instances the individual needs to change and adjust. In other instances it is the group (company) that needs to change its ways. This is illustrated by the following chart.

Views of Individual or Company	Direction of Change ←――――――――――――― ―――――――――――――→	Views of Company or Individual
1. Improvements;		No improvements; maintaining status quo
2. Innovation;		Against innovation;
3. Teamwork, cooperation;		Adversarial attitude prevails;
4. Preventing errors, defects, delays;		Corrects and explains away errors, defects, delays;
5. New ideas;		Opposition to new ideas: rigid attitude;
6. Personal growth and development;		Indifference to personal growth and development;
7. Recognizing and rewarding achievement;		Ignoring achievement; no recognition or it is very restricted;
8. Effective training program;		No training program;
9. Quality-mindedness everywhere;		Quality not taken seriously;
10. Participative and humane supervision.		Dictatorial supervision.

Some Actual Cases

Some human traits, especially those related to knowledge and subject matter, can be changed without great difficulty. There are other traits, however, which have strong emotional tones and are very hard to combat and change. These include fear, envy, jealousy, anger, rigidity, intolerance, negativism, self righteousness, dominance, snobbishness, and dictatorship.

Fear

A woman in a nursing home is suffering from a physical disability but is normal mentally. She is placed in a room with another woman who is a mental case. She becomes very frightened with the woman's rambling and meaningless talk and aggressive attitude. She reports this to a daughter who is visiting the home. The daughter explains the situation and insists that her mother be moved to better surroundings. This was done, so the source of fear was removed. Not all cases of fear can be solved as easily as this one, but it does point up a serious problem that can exist in a nursing home. Insane persons should not be admitted to a nursing home.

No, Nyet, and Negativism

A very difficult attitude to combat in an official is the attitude of negativism—of reacting to every proposal for improvement or change with a resounding "No." It is similar to the "Nyet" vote of the Soviet Union in the United Nations. We cite three actual cases encountered during World War II. 1) An official opposed the use of probability sampling in making quarterly estimates, even though the method was demonstrated in one industrial division to be vastly superior to other methods. 2) Another official was strongly opposed to the use of a data form which would have greatly improved the collection of data necessary for production control. 3) A group of officials steadfastly opposed collecting labor data on the same form with production schedules and material requirements. They represented "labor," so labor data had to be collected on a separate piece of paper and at a different time. War or no war, these officials were opposed to using the methods necessary to make decisions required by the war production program. They continued this opposition right up to the end of the war. This was not just a case of opposition to what the chief statistician was proposing. The statistician was on a team with two other high-level officials who did most of the talking, but over a period of a year all the conferring and talking ended in complete failure.

Envy, Jealousy

A high-level official didn't like a highly capable young man who had been hired by a lower-level official. He thought that the young man was advancing too rapidly, even though there was not the slightest evidence to support such a view. Whenever he could, he gave the young man a hard time, even though he was not the young man's supervisor. Eventually the young man had to leave.

Years later this same official became very jealous of a lower-level manager who was receiving considerable professional recognition from his talks and papers. Numerous invitations to give professional talks didn't help matters. Their personal relationship, which had been good for years, turned sour. He began to harass the lower-level manager in a wide variety of ways. Eventually the latter, realizing that the situation was hopeless, left for a better job elsewhere.

High-level officials and professional specialists with these characteristics invariably force others to adjust to these kinds of behavior. It is rare to find any of them penalized, demoted, or fired because of these undesirable traits and the effects they have upon lower-level staff members and the quality of the work being performed.

Unhappiness in Job

A competent typist was hired and placed in a large office as a helper. She was shy and new to the ways of a busy, indifferent office. She needed a friendly supervisor to take her in hand and help her adjust to the new environment, but no one took the slightest interest in her. She became very unhappy in her job. Through a mutual friend this situation came to the attention of a high-level official. He called a colleague in another agency who had an excellent record in training new employees. As a result, the typist transferred to the other agency, where eventually she became a very successful high-level secretary. Often employees need a friend to bring out the best in them and to help them over obstacles to quality performance. The alert and effective supervisor will recognize the individual differences in employees and take steps to assist each one of them. Often all that is needed is to take a friendly interest in the individual's work and problems, including personal problems.

Revolt

Opposition arose from a supervisor when it was proposed to transcribe an additional sheet of important information that the agency greatly needed. This information had been collected as part of a nationwide sample for years, but despite its importance nothing had ever been done to use it. The data occurred on only about 5 percent of the sample documents, so the additional work involved was really quite small. This, however, was not the way a supervisor looked at it. She spoke out openly against it. It was too much work. It couldn't be done. It would cut into the regular work. It was not in the job descriptions.

The manager called a meeting of those involved in the sample study and its processing. He explained the value of the data to the agency and the relatively small volume of additional transcription that would be necessary. The information would be much more valuable than some of the data they were now issuing. He then opened the meeting for discussion. Some people agreed that the additional work could be absorbed very easily. The supervisor, however, insisted that the additional job could not be done. Finally the manager resolved the issue with a simple statement: "If the job is too big for you, maybe I'd better assign it to someone else."

This hurt the pride of the supervisor. She completely reversed her former position; the job certainly was not too big for her. Obviously she didn't like the idea of having to step aside in favor of someone else. Furthermore, she didn't like the person who was likely to be selected to head the job. Subsequent events showed that the job was not too big for her or for the staff. They were able to do an excellent job on the new information without in the least affecting the quality of their regular work.

What could have been an ugly confrontation that would have gone to higher levels was neatly resolved with no ill feelings anywhere. It showed that this group could increase its productivity and maintain an acceptable level of work without any additional motivation other than the fact that the agency needed some very important information and they were the only ones who could produce it.

Plots and Intrigues

One enemy of quality is the barriers between officials in different offices and departments. In one case two entirely different groups of officials deliberately tried to discredit the work of an official in another department. The latter had been highly successful in solving nationwide sample problems facing management and in rendering technical assistance to other officials and professionals.

"Intrigue" is the proper word, since both moves were secret and unknown to the official under attack and were made quite independently of one another at widely different times. The official was unaware of what was afoot until he found himself in a meeting and his work being criticized.

In the first case a meeting was called with a large number of high officials in attendance, apparently for the purpose of hearing an outside sampling expert review the sampling program. The outside expert was there by invitation. Only two or three people in the room understood the technical aspects of a sampling program and how to implement it. The expert explained the major problems involved in a nationwide sample design and its implementation. Finally, after some questions and answers, he threw a bombshell into the meeting by asserting that the official under criticism was quite competent to handle these problems. (They had known each other for years as speaking acquaintances). The chairman tried to save something from the meeting insisting that the official under fire be required to make periodic reports to the expert to insure that the work was being done correctly. This was agreed upon, and the meeting was adjourned. Actually, the expert didn't want any reports so after a few weeks they were dropped. The insulting move by top level managers backfired and resulted in total failure.

In the second case, one division arranged secretly to have representatives from an outside, highly prestigious agency attend a meeting. The purpose was to appraise a set of plans and specifications prepared for a nationwide sample study by the division under fire. The manager knew nothing about what was going on until he attended the meeting and discovered what they were doing. The plans were discussed. They were so detailed and so comprehensive that no decision was reached at the meeting. The outside people wanted to study them further. Later these people reported to the complaining division that this was one of the best specifications for a study they had ever seen. That put an end to the matter. Another attempt to pull the rug out from under an official had backfired.

Two different groups of officials had played dirty pool and had lost. The official under fire said nothing in his defense in the first case (he was not allowed to talk), and very little in the second case. Another person really spoke for him in the first case, and the detailed plan was the evidence in the second case.

These cases show that breaking down barriers between departments and people (Deming's Point 9) is not as simple as it sounds. Barriers are not fixed and static. They can arise where they never existed before, due to changes in methods, personnel, managers, successful performance, and many other factors. While barriers are being overcome in one place, they could be rising somewhere else.

Institutional Barriers

Barriers may be derived from organizational and institutional differences in purposes, goals, and philosophies. We cite two examples from World War II.[16]

The AFL and the CIO, the two national labor union organizations, had to have two separate offices within the War Production Board. They refused to cooperate and unite as one office, even during a war. This barrier created a lot of useless overhead expense as well as conflicts over war production policies.

The War Production Board (WPB), in order to control war production, needed to relate labor needs to production schedules in the same plants and in the various industries. The War Manpower Commission (WMC) people, however, had other ideas. "Labor" had to collect its own data on its own forms. This was in harmony with the long-established belief that workers and employers were enemies and adversaries even during wartime. Conferences were held

---

[16]The author of this book was an official in the CIO office under Clinton Golden, and was one of three committee members from WPB trying to work out an effective data collection system with the War Manpower Commission.

between officials in WPB and WMC for over a year in order to try to have labor data collected on the same form as the production schedule. Despite all of these meetings, which continued until the end of the war, nothing was ever accomplished—all efforts by WPB failed. A rational approach to war production control was blocked.

Feuds

Feuds develop between executives and managers and between managers and professional specialists. These are serious conflicts, which are the enemy of quality. If the boss is engaged in such a feud, you can neutralize its influence so far as your work is concerned by staying out of it and by remaining neutral. If required, explain this to the boss. In this way you keep your credibility, you remain friends with everyone, you create trust, you foster respect, and you make it easier to gain support for quality improvement programs. Maintain the professional approach and keep personalities and personal feelings out of it.

An Informer Spying for Management

An employee in a section becomes an informer, aided and abetted by top management. This happens when the chief of a section is promoted to a top-level job and another person takes over as head of the section. This tattle-taling should have been stopped when it started, but it wasn't. It creates a vicious and destructive atmosphere; it is an enemy of trust, integrity, cooperation, and morale. Informing can be combated in a number of ways, short of firing the person. Move the person to another room where meetings, conversations, and talk cannot be overheard. Advise everyone to stick to the job and avoid office gossip. Have everyone keep a record of all important conversations and meetings, with exact times and names of participants. Hold meetings where all complaints and grievances are openly discussed and settled, except in the case of something that is highly personal and should be confidential.

Emotionally Disturbed Employee

In this case a man had been promoted too fast, so that he was out of his depth. The job was entirely too difficult; he had been promoted to the "level of incompetence." Apparently this was the real cause of his emotional problems on the job. This situation could not be solved very easily, short of firing him. He wanted to stay on at the high salary level, but he couldn't perform the work successfully at that level. He had to be convinced that this was true. The solution was to give him a job at which he could succeed. This would not be easy for him to accept, because it meant demotion. The people who promoted him made a very serious mistake, as a careful examination of his record would have shown.

The "Yes" Man

This is the little Sir Echo of the boss's party line. He is an expensive nuisance. He may be the boss's hatchet man, delegated to carry out any criticism, rebukes, reprimands, and other punishments the boss has in mind. He is the enemy of rational dialogue, discussion, and new ideas. He may devote his time and that of the staff to trivia when he is not a sounding board for the boss. If the boss takes a strong stand for quality, this man may be of considerable help. Otherwise he may be just another obstacle to overcome.

Psychology of People in Quality

In any quality improvement program the behavior of eight groups of people is involved: top management, managers, supervisors, employees, customers, vendors, competitors, and government regulators. All of them get into the act at some time and at some place, although government inspectors and other government people are more directly involved in some industries than in others. The word "customer" is used in the ordinary sense as the ultimate buyer and user, individuals who can be either children, youth, or adults. It does *not* mean persons in a factory or office who are recipients of the output of some preceding sequence of work activity.

Quality involves the traits, behavior, attitudes, and activities of each of these groups. There are not only relationships between individuals within groups to be considered, but the relationships between individuals in different groups. The nature of these interactions is very important since it has a direct influence on whether or not quality improves.

In view of the critical importance of these relationships and the need to change behavior and attitudes to develop and implement a quality improvement program, it is surprising that so little attention is paid to the psychological aspects that relate to quality. The 1985 nationwide Gallup survey of 1005 consumers for the American Society for Quality Control, reporting reasons for poor quality products and poor quality services, was a real contribution and a step in the right direction.[17] (See Chapter 3.)

Since there is a dearth of information about the psychology of several of these groups, the following discussion will be limited to the groups about which the most is known: management, customers, employees, and vendors.

---

[17]*Consumer Perceptions Concerning the Quality of American Goods and Services,* conducted for the American Society for Quality Control, The Gallup Organization, Princeton, NJ, September 1985.

Management

Management Roles

Management has five roles in running a company or agency: leadership, planning, directing, delegating, and appraising. The psychology of management, as well as the psychology of individuals, is revealed when they start dealing with people. Some positive characteristics which are identified with these roles are listed:

1. Leadership: sets goals and policies; has a clearly defined road map; inspires staff and employees; keeps eye on what is important; sets an example by doing, not just by talking; leads the way.
2. Planning: emphasizes long-range planning to improve quality and stay in business; short-range plans grow out of long-range plans; sees that planning staff spends its time on planning.
3. Directing: positive, low-key style, participative approach, teamwork, respect for technical and special knowledge and abilities; expects results, stimulates innovation and new ideas; knows how to direct a team of specialists; has direct communication from top to bottom and back.
4. Delegating: is not afraid to delegate authority; allows people freedom to develop new ideas, new methods, and new applications.
5. Appraising: sees that an effective results measuring system is in place and operating; holds managers and specialists strictly resonsible for running their operations effectively and efficiently, including making improvements; rewards superior and innovative performance that results in quality improvements, breakthroughs, and other significant contributions.

There is another role that top management has to play, which is not directly connected with the production or service operations of the company. This involves external community affairs. The company sponsors or helps finance TV shows, sports tournaments, and community events. Executives and managers are spokesmen and speakers not only for the company but for the industry and even for the United States business world. All of these outside activities are for the purpose of creating good will toward the company and the industry. To what extent these activities create good will or ill will is unknown. It is very likely that the ultimate buyers or customers are much more influenced by the experiences they have with the company's products than by any media reports of speeches or sponsorships.

Trends in Management

Management is undergoing substantial if not revolutionary changes, with the movement being accelerated by Japanese competition. Most of the new approaches to management have already been practiced by some American firms for decades. Quality control has gone through the same history: it originated in this country but was given a new push after the Japanese demonstrated how it could improve quality of products, increase productivity, and greatly improve competitive position in the world markets. Like so many other important concepts, it is much easier to talk and theorize about what constitutes good management than to practice it. The following is a tabular arrangement of the old and the new interpretations of several aspects of management. These are broad-brush statements: not all of the old was bad, nor is all of the new as good as is painted:

Aspects	Old	New
Attitude toward lower-level managers	Inferiors, subordinates, master-servant	Team workers, co-workers, assistants
Attitude toward employees	Master-servant, adversaries	Team workers, co-workers key to quality
Attitude toward specialists	Contempt for their jargon, one-track minds	Team workers, key to improvements
Attitude toward customers	"Bloody nuisance," resistance has to be overcome	Persons to be satisfied, listened to, catered to
Attitude toward vendors	Find the cheap one, ignore quality	Cooperate; vendor to meet quality specifications
Attitude toward quality	Increases costs, expensive luxury	Lowers costs, required for productivity and profits and meeting competition
Attitude toward competition	Sales department took care of competition	Forced to meet competition relative to quality, reliability, lifetime costs
Attitude toward inspection	Quality obtained by inspection	Build quality in; reduce inspection to minimum
Attitude toward computer	Blind acceptance, costly use	Moving toward more rational use for specific purposes, not for storing masses of useless data
Attitude toward goals	Short-term, long-term; neglected or ignored	More emphasis on long-term goals and planning

The Psychology of Management

The following list shows three different approaches to management of people. The management creed is different in each case, and is based upon three different psychological views of the relationship between a leader or supervisor and the employees under his or her direction or guidance. In Type 1 the individual supervisor is dictator. In Type 3 the group dominates and dictates. In Type 2 a balance is struck between the leader and the individuals, so that the knowledge and experience of the leader are fully utilized, as well as the ideas and ambitions and idealism of the individuals.

Type 1	Type 2	Type 3
Supervisor as dictator	Supervisor as coach Supervisor as leader	Employees are in control Employees make decisions
Issues orders	Guided by company goals and policies	Supervisor is a chaperone Employees dominate
No discussion	Employees as contributors Employees as doers	Employees discuss, solve problems
Control by orders	Employees make decisions	Control by consensus
No improvement	Supervisor assists employees solve problems	Technical capability can be very limited
Status quo maintained	Supervisor as technical expert and advisor Mutual controls	Internal harmony esential Improvements restricted Individual subordinate
Hidden fear, conflict	Good communication	Individual must give way to group
Domination by and submission to an individual	Employees encouraged to grow, improve Employees are important, recognized, rewarded "No-conflict" atmosphere Teamwork from everyone	Group domination Peer pressure tends to develop conformity and mediocrity

Type 1	*Type 2*	*Type 3*
	Differences recognized, respected, exploited. Employees as human beings whose potential is to be developed and promoted	

The Customer

Changing Attitudes Toward the Consumer and Customer

The customer in our economy faces an eternal battle to obtain acceptable-quality goods and services at an affordable price. A few historic events show this:

- Dr. Harvey Wiley's fight for a pure food law. Passed Congress in 1906 as Pure Food and Drug Act. Meat Inspection Act also passed.
- Vigorous consumer movement of the 1930s:
  - Books: Chase, *The Tragedy of Waste;*
    Chase and Schlenk, *Your Money's Worth;*
    Kallen, *100,000,000 Guinea Pigs.*
  - Formation of Consumer's Union, Chicago Consumer Council.
  - New regulation: truckers, finance (Security and Exchange Commission), Federal Communication Commission, Federal Aviation Administration.
- Consumer movement since the 1960s
  - Nader influence
  - Federal legislation
    - Consumer Product Safety Commission (CPSC)
    - OSHA (workers' health and safety)
    - legislation affecting the automobile.

Under the Constitution, Congress has the power to regulate interstate commerce. Early legislation dealt with regulating business practices. It was assumed that this would help the individual consumer. If it did, it was not observable to the ordinary consumer. Direct legislation affecting the individual came with the creation of CPSC, OSHA, and EPA (Environmental Protection Agency).

The more recent movement has been dubbed "consumerism" by critics of a better deal for the consumer. The word has a derogatory connotation; the assumption is that the customer is ignorant and irrational. The manufacturer is Big Brother, who knows best. American business is based on a huge sales establishment and on a tradition that the customer is the enemy who has to be defeated, the person "whose resistance has to be overcome." The customer is someone who has to be manipulated by using the latest psychology. This philosophy is completely expressed in the book *How to Sell Anything to Anybody*. If salesmanship can sell anything to anybody, why worry about quality of the product or service? Why worry about the price? Why worry if the product is a lemon? Use every trick in the book to sell.

As stated earlier, Shewhart recognized the importance of the *subjective aspects of quality*. His belief that quality products should be made to meet "human wants" showed that he recognized the importance of the ultimate customer or consumer, a point long overlooked.

The answer to the consumer revolt in the 1930s was application of quality control to the manufacturing of products. The anwer was really not an organization such as the Consumers Union and the consumer testing of products, despite their benefits to the consumer. The real answer was quality control at the source.[18]

During the mid-1930s the author attended a lecture given by Dr. Shewhart. Despite the large number of people asking questions, the author was able to ask him, "What is being done to apply quality control to the manufacturing of consumer products?" Shewhart's anwer was, "Nothing so far as I know. I hear Proctor and Gamble are doing something, so you might get in touch with them." That was all.

At that early date very few people in manufacturing had heard of quality control despite Shewhart's 1931 book and the ASTM Manual of 1933, so it is not surprising that nothing was being done in the manufacturing of goods sold directly to the ultimate consumer.

There is no doubt, however, that the human wants of the ultimate consumer were always in the background as the final goal and purpose of quality control. This purpose was completely lost sight of as attention was shifted more and more to the statistical techniques and management needed to make quality control work successfully in the factory.

Since about 1970 there has been a growing attitude that favors the customer. It is seen by more and more businesses and business leaders that the customer should be listened to, not ignored. While many businesses have had this respect for the customer for decades, some have only grasped its importance in recent years. This has been due to the growth in sales of Japanese and other foreign products, the rise of the concept of quality control, and its key role in increasing productivity, cutting costs, and improving competitive position.

Japanese automobiles smashed the myth that the customer could be ignored. Foreign car sales are 25 to 30 percent of the annual sales in this country, and they are expected to stay at this level. Loss of this market has had devastating effects on the entire country, and will continue to do so until we learn how to make a better car than those that come from foreign countries. Millions of

---

[18] The author took this position in the middle 1930s after his experience as a member of the Chicago Consumer Council. The author attended the four lectures given by Dr. Shewhart during March 1938 in Washington, and one previous lecture.

Americans have shifted brand loyalty to foreign products, and every indication is that they will continue to do so.

It is not only automobiles; it is TV sets, radios, cameras, shoes, clothing, and other products. American manufacturers must wake up and face the challenge. Running to Washington to obtain tariffs, quotas, and subsidies will not solve the problem. Only by going back to the drawing boards and building a better product can they meet foreign competition and stand a chance of regaining the domestic markets which they have lost.

Tom Peters is currently an outspoken champion of the customer. In his first book, co-authored with R. H. Waterman and titled *In Search of Excellence* (1982), one chapter was devoted to the customer. In a later book, written with Nancy Austin and titled *A Passion for Excellence* (1985), five chapters are devoted to the customer. In his latest book, *Thriving on Chaos* (1987), he devotes 10 chapters to the customer and 12 points to quality and its improvement. This progressive change over a period of five years reflects the increased recognition that is now being given both to the customer and to quality.

Many well-known companies have built a reputation for quality of service to the customer. In the retail field it is Sears and J. C. Penney, in the electronic field it is IBM and Hewlett-Packard, in the communications field it is the Bell Telephone System. It is no accident that many companies which exhibit a high growth rate are those which are customer-oriented.

A tabular summary is given below to show the old and the new attitudes toward the customer for several key aspects affecting the customer. These are extremes. Not every business followed the old practices, nor are all of the present businesses following the new practices. The shift from the old to the new, however, seems to be the desirable trend that many authorities, business leaders, and quality managers approve.

Item or Aspect	Old	New
• Role in market place	"Bloody nuisance"	Buyers to satisfy
• Attitude toward customers	Break down sales resistance, ignore them, they're irrational	Try to please, courtesy, consideration, listen to them, meet their needs
• Quality of product sold	Made according to manufacturer's specifications	Meet buyer's specifications needs; long life; reliability
• Lost customers	Could care less	Plan to avoid, very concerned about
• Sales	High-pressure sales talks, sales ads, gimmicks	Use high quality to sell product
• Quality of services sold	Indifference, anything goes, customer a guinea pig	Customer satisfaction, care, courtesy, manners, consideration

Item or Aspect	Old	New
• Defects and errors	Fix up errors and defects after they occur, let customer discover them	Prevent defects and errors, correct any to satisfaction of customer
• Time	Delays are common, make customer wait	Promptness, fast service, keep promises for deliveries
• Quality	What company perceives as quality, customer doesn't know what quality is	What the customer perceives as quality, company adjusts to customer's need
• Price	Products and services priced for profit regardless of quality	Acceptable quality and affordable price, low life-cycle costs
• Customer's complaints	Sometimes ignored, sometimes corrected, no attempt to find causes	Correcting complaints not enough, continuous customer contacts and surveys, survey to find out why customers are lost
• Employee attitudes and behavior	Sometimes indifferent if not hostile toward customer, no employee training in how to interact with people	Training courses in how to behave toward customer; stress on courtesy, friendliness, helpfulness, service customer wants, not what employee thinks customer should have

The new approach to better repair service reflects several innovations of considerable convenience to the customer:

- Installing and using modern equipment;
- Using trained and certified technicians;
- Seeing that employees reflect better attitudes, e.g., courtesy, helpfulness;
- Finding out what specific troubles are bothering the customer;
- Following up every repair with a call within two or three days; showing concern;
- Furnishing bus service to employed customers to and from place of work (automobile repair);
- Using a beeper service for paging customers (automobile repair).

A Scale of Management's Attitude Toward the Customer

The attitude of management toward the customer, and the way in which this attitude is conveyed to the employees, are reflected in the way the customer is treated and bear directly on how the customer looks at the quality of service. The customer wants quality goods and services; if courtesy and kindness are added, so much the better.

Neglect	Consideration	Flattery
• Indifferent to complaints	• Settles complaints satisfactorily	• Attempts to please customers with flowers, letters, thank-you notes, phone calls
• Customer is dumb, ignorant	• Customer is treated with courtesy	• Customer is always right • Taking elaborate steps, going to extremes

Most customers would be satisfied if the company took the middle position and treated the customer with courtesy and respect. It should be clear that no flowery words or flattering behavior are a substitute for quality of product or quality of service.

Quality must come first. The customer will not be pleased with flattery and a lemon. The customer will be pleased—very pleasantly—if the flattery is accompanied with good quality service and a good quality product.

A smart company will not use flattery or fawning as a substitute for quality of goods or services. Otherwise the customers will discover sooner or later that they are being "taken," that flattery is nothing but a way of making deception seem acceptable.

Customer buying is social and psychological as well as economic. This is overlooked by management of services; it is true because a face-to-face encounter between two persons is involved. There is communication and interaction because a shopping mall is a meeting place, a recreation center. Shopping is a diversion for many persons. Therefore the behavior and attitudes of those waiting on the customer set the tone and quality of the meeting and the service.

The salesperson or clerk is not just selling, explaining, or correcting. He or she is someone to talk to not only about merchandise, prices, and problems but about related matters such as sales, the weather, and changes in the store. A mutual "Have a good day" is always a welcome parting. The salesperson or clerk may become an acquaintance, if not a friend, of the customer.

These personal contacts between customers and service people can make the meeting a pleasant experience for the customer, and go a long way toward guaranteeing a steady customer. The brief time spent in a pleasant conversation is a gain for everyone.

This friendly atmosphere should exist throughout the organization. Everyone should be oriented toward it. It should be a permanent policy. All hiring and training should be aimed to promote this practice.

Customer Complaints No One Hears About

Customers are subject to all kinds of ill treatment, about which they complain to others but not to the company. Many of these may seem of little consequence to the company, but they leave a bad feeling with the customer because of the injustice or indifference shown by clerks or salespersons.

- While serving a customer, a clerk takes a telephone call and makes the customer wait.
- While serving a customer, a clerk lets another customer barge in with one or more questions and makes the first customer wait. (Need to enforce a number system.)
- While talking over phone to a customer, clerk takes another call and makes the first customer wait.
- Clerk makes an error and blames the customer.
- Customers are not served in order of arrival. (Need a number system.)
- Merchandise in a supermarket is moved, but where is it? There is no indication. This is a constant gripe since it takes months to learn where specific items are located.
- Store is out of an item and it may take days, if not weeks, to be restocked. Sales staff is vague about when they will have it.
- A clerk doesn't know how to calculate a simple percentage reduction in the price of an item, e.g., 30 percent reduction on $19.95.
- A clerk doesn't know how to calculate a new price with two percentage reductions, e.g., 30% plus 50% reduction: $12 $\rightarrow$ $8.40 $\rightarrow$ $4.20.
- Clerks are talking among themselves and ignoring customers.
- No one is in sight when the customer arrives at charge-out area or counter, with articles.
- A householder or apartment dweller has to wait all day for a repair man to show up or for a delivery to be made.
- Bottles cannot be opened without a screwdriver or a pair of pliers. Child-protected bottle tops that only the children are able to open.
- The fast lane in the supermarket can be the slowest. No one explains what "6 items or less" really means. To some it may mean 12 or more. Are four cans of the same thing one item or four? Is the number of items the number of records that has to be itemized on the sales ticket?

The Employee

The behavior and attitudes of employees determine directly the quality of services in most service companies. It is imperative for supervisors and higher-level officials to set an example, to show employees the kinds of behavior expected of them. These are not arbitrary standards of conduct. These are the kinds of behavior and attitudes customers expect and deserve if they are to continue buying from a company. Specifics that management and supervisors should push for continuously include the following:

- Make the individual feel important. Everyone wants to feel important.
- Tell them individually how important their jobs are. If they aren't important, then the job should never have been created in the first place.
- Talk to them where they work, and listen.
- Stress personal growth; encourage and reward it.
- Explain the importance of quality improvements to the future of the company and to all of the employees.
- Reward achievement, accomplishment, and superior performance.
- Give credit where credit is due. Be fair about credit.
- Keep employees informed about what is going on. Have open communication.
- Stress the need for teamwork as well as a high level of individual performance.
- Explain the cost and harm done to everyone in the form of defects, errors, and delays.
- Encourage new ideas and improvements; have weekly reviews of new quality ideas.
- Challenge everyone to do better and to make improvements.
- Insist that supervisors and managers at all levels set an example for new ideas, improvements, helpful assistance, and excellence.

There are at least four aspects of employee behavior and attitude that require careful attention:

- Behavior and attitude toward supervisor and manager;
- Behavior and attitude toward other employees;
- Behavior and attitude toward professionals and specialists;
- Behavior and attitude toward customers, as in retail trade.

For a healthy emotional and mental atmosphere to exist in the workplace, it is necessary to avoid some common practices; some of the most common are various injustices to which not only employees but individuals generally are very sensitive:

- Favorites and favoritism;
- Having a "teacher's pet";
- Denying credit where credit is due;
- Giving credit to someone who clearly does not deserve it;
- Ignoring employees;
- Engaging in office gossip;
- Destructive conflicts and feuds.

The negative needs to be matched with the positive, as in the following examples:

- All contacts and communications between individuals should be kept on an objective, professional basis; personalities are out.
- Everyone wants fair treatment, regardless of position.
- No one likes to be ignored. Keep everyone informed about what is going on. This applies to managers, professionals, and employees.
- Lean over backwards to explain something clearly. Do not assume that people understand what you say or write. Test them to make sure they understand. People will say they understand when they do not. Make sure they understand instructions, procedural manuals, directions, and the like.
- What the entire company needs is a training course in exposition (explanatory writing), because this is an area where everyone, regardless of his or her position, can make improvements. This applies to executives, managers, supervisors, professional specialists, technicians, and employees. Write instructions, directions, and procedural manuals so that employees and others can understand them. Talk the same way.

The old practices and ideas toward employees are contrasted with the new practices and ideas. This does not mean that the newer ideas were not accepted and practiced in the past, nor that all of the older ideas have been abandoned.

Item	Older Idea or Practice	Newer Idea or Practice
• Supervision	Dictatorial	Participative
• Work attitude	People don't like to work.	People like to work if properly led.
• Communication	Keep employees in dark.	Keep them informed.
• Personal growth	Ignored	Promoted, stimulated
• Troubles, grievances	Ignored	Listened to, resolved
• Improvements	Neglected, ignored	Fostered, invited, promoted

Item	Older Idea or Practice	Newer Idea or Practice
• Innovations	Frowned upon	Promoted, stimulated
• Errors	Accepted, corrected	Prevented, zero errors
• Defects	Accepted, corrected	Prevented, zero defects
• Delays	Accepted, corrected	Reduced, eliminated, zero delays
• Training	Absent or sporadic	Continuous for improvements
• Recognition	Very limited, restricted	Emphasized

Education, Learning, and Teaching

Everyone agrees that training and education are the ways to bring about the changes in behavior, attitudes, and knowledge necessary for a quality improvement program. Dr. Deming's Points 6, 7, and 13 deal with training, retraining, and education. Others call for a massive education program. No one points out, however, that it is much easier to talk and write about training and education than it is to implement them. That is because four basic factors are involved: the curriculum, the teacher, the learner, and the appraisal.

The Course of Study—the Curriculum. Who will select the courses to be taught? Who will select and organize the subject matter? Who will lay out the content so that it will meet the needs of the various employees, managers, supervisors, and specialists? Are the materials such that a teacher can teach them and the learner can learn them? Who will put these materials in printed form? The job of laying out courses of study is not as simple and easy as it sounds.

The Teacher. Dr. Deming states that good teachers of statistics are rare. Good teachers of any subject are rare; we do not hire persons in companies or in agencies because they are good at teaching. If a good teacher is hired, it is indeed a rarity. The belief that anyone can be a success at teaching is a myth. We have seen too many poor teachers in public schools, colleges, and universities. Those of us who have been through college and who have taught in high schools and universities may be more aware of the difficulties than those who have not. How to find good teaching is a serious problem. We cannot expect too much from those unfamiliar with effective methods of teaching. "Teachers" may be those who are much more interested in impressing others with what they know than in imparting knowledge to the students.

Both teaching and learning are mental processes which need to be understood. Teaching is using words, numbers, and other symbols to convey meanings, ideas, and relationships to students. Teaching skills is imparting correct hand movements and other movements. Individual differences in ability and rate of learning must be the basis of teaching.

Some principles which facilitate learning and which teachers use are the following:

- Repetition: oral, verbal, written, presenting same idea in different ways;
- Proceeding from the concrete to the abstract;
- Proceeding from the specific to the general;
- Proceeding from the known to the unknown;
- Using demonstrations with objects, instruments, apparatus, graphics to present and develop percepts, concepts, and ideas;
- Starting where the individual is relative to knowledge, vocabulary, etc.;
- Relating instruction to the jobs and problems of the students;
- Making generous use of real-world examples, cases, specific instances;
- Making generous use of explanations and elaborations;
- Testing for understanding and mastery. Teaching, testing, and reteaching. Using different approaches, if necessary, to facilitate understanding of those who do not grasp new concepts and ideas quickly.

The Learner. Besides an orientation course in quality for everyone newly hired, classes will be needed for four different groups: top-level executives, managers and professional staffs, supervisors, and employees.

Special classes may be needed for employees with the most serious problems, or for those who need to be retrained. These special classes will be given in addition to regular classes.

This raises the question as to who will receive training and who will select them. Is everyone to be included in some class? Who will determine what training is to be given to whom, when, where, and for how long? Is training to be voluntary or compulsory? Note that the various courses of study will have to be tailored to these various groups and to these special needs. This is why it was stated above that it will not be easy to develop an appropriate set of courses.

Learning is hearing and seeing words, numbers, sentences, and other symbols, and trying to understand what is being said and written. If the material is at all strange, learning will require not only reading but study and analysis to determine the main ideas and their connections. Questions, discussions, and writing will facilitate learning and retention. In learning skills, what is required is following the motions and sequences as described and demonstrated. Practice is required for mastering both motor skills and subject matter. This practice may continue, as in writing.

Appraisal of Training and Education. It is necessary to appraise the value of these courses in improving the work of the recipients. Course work may not carry over into practice. This is why the courses should be given with stress on job-oriented problems and situations. Appraisal can be and should be given both in the form of written tests after each course is completed and in the form of surveys of performance on the job to see whether improvements are being made. In cases where improvements are not being made or improvements are slight, a diagnosis of the situation is called for. As a result of this study, courses may be changed, or a special course may be given to employees who are still having difficulties in making improvements.

The Computer and Training

The key to training on a computer is software. Software is critical because it determines four very important aspects:

- The content of the course;
- The order of presentation;
- The difficulty of the material; and
- The method of presentation.

The software is the "teacher." When software is used,

- The teacher abdicates.
- Some unknown person X, or persons X, Y, and Z determine content, order, difficulty, method. They make the decisions.
- There is no evidence that the software is appropriate for any of these four aspects.
- There is no evidence that these unknown persons have the answer to the company's training and educational problems.

It is likely that due to the lack of know-how about courses of study, teaching, learning, and testing, officials will, in desperation, seize upon some expensive software which is advertised for training purposes.

The points made above apply equally well to the use of the computer in schools and colleges. The students are now being "instructed" by means of these unknown persons rather than by a teacher on the spot, through the use of materials and commands in the memory of the computer. The software can easily be inadequate and ineffective.

It may pay a company or agency to hire a good programmer and write its own programs. This is highly desirable where the company or agency needs a wide variety of programs ranging from payroll and personnel records to a nationwide probability sample study and extensive statistical analysis of data with a large volume of tabulation and publication.

Software for Tabulation, Calculation, and Analysis

Whether software is being used for training, education, tabulation, calculation, or analysis, it is necesary to make a careful study of needs before attempting to buy any software. Unless such a study is made, money may be wasted and operations adversely affected. Some of the pitfalls to avoid in buying software are the following:

The software is a package which contains an excessive number of programs. This means that the software package may contain a large number of programs which are never used, or it may contain programs which are seldom used and for which a program may not even be necessary. The problem may be more easily solved by a hand-held calculator such as the HP-32E, which costs less than $100.

The program of interest may sound as though it applies, but it really does not. This is because the structure of the data calls for a different program or for the modification of an existing program. The program is not applicable to the data. An example is the nested design of an experiment, where the appropriate analysis of variance has to be used.

The program may solve only part of the problem of data analysis. In this case the program is incomplete. A program or important parts of a program are missing. This means that flexibility in programming is missing. The company or agency is stuck with a rigid set of programs.

Analysts and others can avoid these pitfalls by writing their own programs. In this way they can avoid wasting the time of both the programmer and computer, and can obtain more useful results for the money and time invested.

The Vendors

Vendors or suppliers play a very important role in the quality of products and services. This is especially true if the vendor furnishes a critical part or component. Examples are spark plugs, door locks, transistors, drugs, and medical equipment. Relationships between the buyer and vendor have never been close because so many companies have hundreds, if not thousands, of suppliers. The trend today is to have fewer suppliers and to maintain a close and continuous relationship with them. It should not be overlooked, however, that there were instances in the early days (e.g., the 1950s) when a big company would help a supplier improve the quality of a product. An example is the Ford Motor Company rendering technical assistance to Houdaille to improve the quality of the automobile door locks being made for Ford. Ford's quality control engineers went to the Houdaille factory and helped them install a quality control system. As a result, the percent defective decreased from about 25 percent to about 3 percent.[19]

Some of the major trends regarding vendors are shown here:

---

[19] From a talk given by Ford representative William Smith at a Middle Atlantic Conference of ASQC, a talk heard by the author.

Item	*Older Practice*	*Newer Practice*
• Number	Many, not very selective, ones with lowest prices	Selective, reduced number, a few high-quality ones
• Relationship	Often remote	Close, cooperative working relationship
• Technical assistance	Rare	Considerable, help as needed, discuss specifications
• Certification	Started, aware of need	100 percent certification, a few high-quality performers
• Rating	Started	Severe rating, must meet needs
• Specifications	Try to meet them	Close cooperation to see that specifications work, are met
• Receiving inspection	Inspect most if not all incoming lots, screening	Goal is to get rid of receiving inspection
• Vendor guidelines	Lowest-priced vendor	Quality, not lowest price governs
• Communication	Sporadic, businesslike	Person-to-person, close relationship

Example

This is a true story showing why ''a long thorny road lies ahead of us'' in quality and productivity, to quote Dr. Deming. A city transit company ordered over 100 new buses to update its fleet. When the first deliveries were made, a test run on several of the buses revealed defects in fuel lines and in other parts. Instead of insisting that the manufacturer correct the causes of these faults immediately at the plant, the defects were corrected at the shop of the buyer.

The officials of the transit company then made three statements in connection with the finding of these defects:

- The buses were better than we expected;
- The new buses were ''above average'';
- Other transit companies encounter even more trouble than we have encountered with new buses.

By not only accepting a poor-quality product but actually defending the poor quality, these officials are guaranteeing that the company (the vendor) would continue to make poor-quality products.

If these buses were better than expected, then the officials need to raise their expectations sharply—and quickly. They should not only set acceptable quality standards for the buses they purchase but see that the manufacturer meets these standards. (This transit company awarded the order for the buses to the lowest bidder, without any specifications about quality. See Deming's Point 4.)

Did the statement that the buses rated "above average" mean that they were of acceptable quality? Not at all. The words have no meaning in this context. If the words meant anything, they were a justification for the low-quality product that the company had purchased.

Nor could the transit company find a justification for what they were agreeing to, by pointing out that other vendors were worse than the one they were doing business with. These officials had not the slightest idea what quality meant in purchasing a fleet of buses; they made no attempt to avoid the extra expense that these defective buses created, or the possible extra maintenance cost that these buses might create in the future.

ECONOMICS

In Shewhart's classic work on statistical quality control, *Economic Control of the Quality of Manufactured Product,* there is no chapter on the economics of quality but there are at least six references to economic aspects:[20]

- Reduction in cost of inspection and rejections;
- Statistical control as an aid to engineering design;
- Importance of subjective notions of quality to commercial interests;
- The three sigma limits on a control chart;
- References in economics; and
- Variability that does not exceed that which is economically desirable.

Shewhart showed that by building quality into a product, important economic advantages are obtained such as reduction in inspection, reduction in rework of rejections, and improved design.

Cost of Defects

The cost of defects includes more than just the rework and salvage needed to eliminate the defect. But trying to correct the defect by reworking can be very costly, as the following example shows. It is fictitious, but not unrealistic. It is assumed that one unit out of eight is rejected because of defects. If the

---

[20] Walter A. Shewhart, *Economic Control of the Quality of Manufactured Product* (New York: Van Nostrand, 1931; reprinted by American Society for Quality Control, Milwaukee, 1980), pp. vii, 26–34, 54, 276, 430–436, 477.

defects are eliminated in production, costs go down 20 percent and productivity goes up 25 percent, as follows:

Under Conditions of Zero Defects	*When ⅛ of Units are Rejected Because of Defects*
400 units produced	400 units produced
8 hours	8 hours
$25 per hour	$25 per hour
Defective = 0	Percentage defective = 12.5 percent
	Number defective = 50
Rework = 0	Rework = 50 units
	2 hours to rework
	Cost to rework = $50
Total time = 8 hours	Total time = 10 hours
Total cost per 400 units = $200	Total cost per 400 units = $250
Cost per unit = $0.50	Increase in cost = 25%
Productivity up 25% (50/hr)	Cost per unit = $0.625 (40/hr)

Defects create a whole series of costly situations, including at least these five:

- Cost of rework. This is the major cost due to defects.
- Cost of inspection. The more defects, the greater the variability, the less control of critical dimensions, the more inspection needed, and the more time spent on hunting for trouble and trying to correct it. The better the control, the less inspection.
- Cost of customer complaints. The more defects, the greater the number of customer complaints, the more time spent on handling and resolving customer complaints, and the greater the burden on customer service.
- Cost of the lost customer. The cost of the lost customer is unknown but can be very large; it may put a company out of business. Customers may be lost because of defects and their consequences; they are lost because of a poor-quality product or service.
- Cost of recalls, warranties, and lawsuits. Defects in a product may result in huge losses due to recalls, excesively large numbers of warranties to make good, and even damage suits that may be fatal to the company.

This list shows why eliminating defects is a major goal in the quality program in manufacturing. This is why the goal is to keep driving the number of defects and the rate of defects down toward zero. There is more than one reason for zero defects.

The Cost of Human Errors

The cost of human errors, mistakes, and blunders can be even greater than the cost of defects. Errors can create a whole series of costly situations. These are some of the major ones:

- Cost of correcting minor errors such as those in typing, billing, calculating, transcribing, or coding. This can create a large volume of work.
- Cost of customer complaints due to errors made by employees and others. Errors create a larger work load for customer service. Customers may be lost.
- Cost of serious errors. Where one error can be dangerous, if not fatal, damage suits can arise which may amount to tens of millions of dollars and be just as costly as a product liability case. The loss of equipment and capital structures may also amount to millions of dollars.

The Cost of Wasted or Lost Time

Another source of high costs is lost or wasted time as in these examples:

Idle Time

A random time sample study showed that the drafting unit was idle 9 percent of the time due to poor scheduling of work, and that those in the files were idle 5 percent of the time. This study covererd a division of about 350 employees at all levels. When these levels were discovered, immediate action was taken to reduce them.

Downtime on Equipment and Machinery

A study of records shows that a computer is being used only 60 percent of the time. A failure of computer equipment cuts off all long distance telephone calls from a state for about 12 hours. Downtime of equipment and machinery can be very costly.

Lost Time

A random time sample study for 26 months in the federal government shows that in a division of about 350 employees, 75 percent of paid-for time is worked while 25 percent of the time is used for sick leave, annual leave, vacations, and idle time. This means that four persons had to be hired in order to have three persons working full time—40 hours a week. Other studies made in private industry and in service companies showed lower as well as higher percentages for effective working time.

Delay Time

Shipments of critical and highly needed parts, components, and products that are delayed can be very costly. Shippers ordering freight cars for wheat and plyboard may have to wait 20 days for freight cars, according to a national study by the Interstate Commerce Commission. Often this delay forces farmers and elevator operators to dump thousands of bushels of wheat on the ground. Delay times in emergencies which occur in police, fire, health, and transportation may also be very costly.

Wasted Time

Time can be wasted by not using the most efficient methods and instruments. An actual example is a case of a professional who was fitting a straight line to some data. The method he was using required four hours to complete the job. With a calculation form, the time could have been two hours. With a hand-held calculator like HP-32E, the calculation could have been completed in 30 minutes, showing the tremendous improvement in productivity by using the appropriate hand-held calculator.

Time also may be wasted because of poor conditions of work. An example is excessive heat and humidity—no air conditioning in factories or offices.

Excessive Time

Repair work may take an excessive amount of time. Absenteeism in factory and office may be excessive. Various kinds of shipments from mail to freight may require an excessive amount of time and run up costs for the customer.

The Cost of Economical Purchasing

Purchasing to save money, such as buying from the lowest bidder (Deming's Point 4), can be disastrous because quality is usually ignored. An excellent example is a company that steadily lost sales. The sales deparment was blamed, but a survey of lost customers showed that when the company changed vendors to save money, the quality of the product deteriorated and the customers bought a better competing product. The company immediately shifted back to the original vendor, and when they did this sales began to increase. Both quality and price have to be considered, but especially quality, when making purchases.

The Cost of Quality

The cost of quality as now defined includes steps taken to prevent poor quality, to appraise quality, and to correct internal and external failures. The cost of correcting internal defects and errors has already been described as has the cost of settling customer compalints of various kinds. Prevention of poor quality includes costs of staffing, training, and applications. Appraisal includes inspections, audits, and other measures used to appraise whether the prevention plans are working. Cost of quality is a necessary expense in order to implement a quality program. The aim is to keep the cost of this program only a small percentage of total sales.

The Cost of Undesirable Employee Behavior and Attitudes

The cost of employee behavior and attitudes that turn off customers and send them to other companies is no doubt large but unknown. No one seems to have made an intensive study of lost customers and what they cost a company. Gallup's poll of customers' reasons for poor-quality products and poor-quality services shows that the latter are due primarily to employee behavior and attitudes: indifference, incompetence, and lack of courtesy, kindness, consideration, friendliness, helpfulness, and manners.

The Cost of Useless Overhead

Many companies suffer from too many layers of organization. De Lorean at General Motors eliminated three levels of management in the manufacturing operations: city managers, plant managers, and works managers. There were no less than five levels of management between De Lorean and the plant manager.[21]

There are also too many levels of organization in agencies of the federal government. These slow down communication, delay responding to requests, build in excessive time, and increase costs.[22] Three to five layers are enough. (This topic has already been discussed.)

Peters and Waterman report that the best-run companies in United States have a lean staff.[23] These reports suggest that a company can be overorganized with too many layers of organization, so that it becomes very difficult to manage for quality and quality improvements.

The Cost of Business Catastrophes

The economics of quality would not be complete without a mention of the catastrophes which can beset and overcome a business. Five are listed:

---

[21] J. Patrick Wright, *On a Clear Day You Can See General Motors*, pp. 137–138.

[22] A. C. Rosander, *Washington Story* (Greeley, CO:, National Directions, 1985).

[23] *In Search of Excellence* (New York: Harper and Row, 1982).

- Stealing by employees: this has to be controlled in stores, nursing homes, etc.
- Shoplifting: this is controlled to a limited extent in some retail stores but not very seriously, since such losses can be deducted from the income tax return.
- Unemployment: this can incur a huge social cost from taxpayers and customers nationwide.
- Bankruptcy: many businesses declare bankruptcy but recover and stay in business, apparently none the worse for taking this step.
- Business failure: this means closing out the business with all of the money loss plus the unemployment which follows.

The Cost of Useless Data

The cost of useless data is unknown, but observation and experience show that it must be tremendous. Data that are useless, of questionable value, of very little use, and so huge as to be unmanageable are found everywhere—in business and in government, in research and in operations. The reasons are several:

- Data once useful are no longer needed.
- Data of different kinds and amounts are now more important.
- No one now remembers why the data were collected in the first place.
- The data are seldom, if ever, used.
- The special interest that prompted the data collection in the first place no longer exists.
- Better methods of collection can be used, such as probability sampling, thereby eliminating unnecessary paper and getting better quality data.
- Collecting large masses of data is unnecessary.

Data on the cost of this situation are nonexistent, but the loss is there, as observation and experience show. The following facts reflect this situation:

- Excessive amounts of data are put in computer memory.
- Data banks contain data never used or rarely used.
- Data banks are full of useless data.
- Data banks are full of adjusted data that defy ordinary statistical analysis. Hence costs are high and benefits are few.

TIME

Time is a very important quality characteristic. If time can be saved, it affects directly a whole series of significant operations and traits:

- Time is related to production.
- Time is related to productivity.
- Time is related to costs borne by the company.
- Time is related to the prices charged the customer.
- "On time" is a very important goal in many operations: it reduces inventories.
- Promptness is a characteristic defining one aspect of quality of service.
- A business can be built on "quick service."

The cost of wasted time has already been described in detail. Other important aspects, with detailed listings, are described or given below.

In *My Fair Lady* there is a song titled "Get Me to the Church on Time." There are numerous occasions where "on time" is important, if not critical. It is reported that with airlines, "on time" transportation means scheduled time plus or minus 15 minutes. "On time" is one of those rare characteristics in a service company that is, or should be, controlled and stabilized in value. Plotting individual deviations from scheduled times (departure or arrival) against time will show to what extent the 15-minute deviation is being attained. (There is no need to use an $\bar{x}$ chart since the 15-minute tolerance applies to individual flights, not to an average.)

An example of the importance of time and how service operations are time-designed is the mail service. Different classes of mail travel at different speeds. Fast mail advertised as over night mail is carried by U.S. Express Mail, Federal Express, Purolator, and others. Special delivery and priority mail speed up delivery. Parcel post to London is about 43 days from a specified place in Colorado; air mail requires eight days. Time is directly related to the class of postage—first, second, third, or fourth class.

Another situation where time is very important is banking. When interest rates are 10 percent, 15 percent, or 20 percent, a bank does not want $1 million, let alone $100 million, in transit or delayed, even one day or two. Delays in depositing money so it is available for use are very costly. Bankers call this problem "float."

Some specific data are given by the State Controller of Colorado. He points out the losses in cash flow which are caused by delays and excessive inventories:[24]

Item	*Savings*
• Getting federal funds one day earlier:	$449,000 in interest annually;
• Collecting accounts receivable one day earlier:	$58,371 in interest annually;

---

[24] *Rocky Mountain News*, July 25, 1986, p. 24.

Item	*Savings*
• Setting a three-day limit for employers to deposit income tax withholding:	$5,500,000 in interest annually;
• 10 percent reduction in inventories:	$5,300,000 in savings annually.

Delays in paying federal income tax refunds are also costly because if the refund is not paid by about June 1, the IRS has to start paying interest on all refunds issued after that date. This can amount to millions of dollars.

Time is also very important in other financial matters. Premiums on insurance policies have to be paid before the expiration date of the insurance, or protection lapses. Some companies carry forward the protection, assuming the premium will be paid. Usually, however, a company will not do this unless an agreement is arranged beforehand.

Certificates of deposit need to be renewed before the date of maturity. Otherwise the holder will lose interest on the days lost after the date of maturity. This means that a new certificate will have to be prepared dated the day after the date of maturity.

So it pays the individual, as well as banks and governments, to be time-conscious when it comes to financial affairs.

Examples of Time-Saving Devices

There are several time-saving devices which have arisen during the past few decades which reduce the time necessary to do a job and increase productivity. A few examples are as follows:

MICR

This stands for "magnetic ink character recognition" and is used for identifying and processing bank checks. A six-digit code number in magnetic ink is printed on all checks and forms for each individual. It is now used universally across the entire country. It helps the bank, however, more than it does the depositor.

UPC

This stands for "universal product code" and is used in grocery stores and supermarkets to identify packaged goods. It is used with a laser scanner to read the product identification and write it on a tape. UPC has probably helped the store more than the customer in speeding up service. This is because at the check-out station the delaying factors which have *not* been eliminated are the writing of checks, the use of food stamps, making change, credit cards, and bagging. What the customer does receive is a much better itemized account of what he or she has bought, including cost of fruits, vegetables, and meat, which the clerk enters into the machine by hand; weighing is automatic and is registered on the sales slip.

Hand-held Calculators

The hand-held calculator increases output per person (productivity) five to 10 times. For the solution of mathematical and statistical problems by an individual, it has no equal. This breakthrough in calculation is due to at least four major factors:

- Common functions are programmed into the calculator: reciprocals, squares, square root, logarithms, trigonometric functions, powers, and normal distribution. Use of tables is eliminated.
- Interpolation in tables, as in log tables and trig tables, is eliminated.
- No intermediate values need to be recorded.
- Many statistical functions are programmed into the calculator: e.g., arithmetic mean, standard deviation, correlation coefficient, and linear regression.

A hand-held calculator capable of performing all of these operations is the HP-32E. It is a waste of time to use a computer and software costing thousands of dollars to solve problems that a $65 hand-held calculator can solve quicker and more easily. This gain, however, cannot be made unless the user has the proper mathematical knowledge and knows how to use it.

The Computer

The computer can be very effective in many service operations if certain specified conditions are met. Millions if not billions of dollars are wasted on computers and software because these conditions are not met:

- A feasibility study that matches a computer with needs and load;
- A feasibility study that matches software with needs and load;
- The services of a competent full-time computer programmer;
- A competent computer specialist who knows how to manage and run a computer system efficiently;
- A critical in-depth examination of all sales claims made by those who sell computers and software.

The Copier

The copier has been very effective in reducing the cost of making large numbers of copies of all kinds of typed, printed, or written materials. It saves typists from making 10 or 20 carbons on a typewriter. It makes copies of materials available to a wide variety of people and thereby improves communication by keeping them properly informed. It is fast and cost effective.

Examples of Specific Time Characteristics Relating to Quality

- Delivery time:
    Mail, parcels, mail orders, truck shipments, rail shipments, air shipments, shipper's orders for freight cars, factory orders, hospital and doctor's orders for medicines and drugs and equipment, home deliveries by retail stores, "just in time" deliveries.
- Time to do a repair job:
    Factory repair, office repair, home repair, auto repair, TV-radio repair.
- Waiting time:
    Waiting time to get an appointment, waiting time to get service, waiting time at post office or bank, checkout at a supermarket or to get a tax refund, waiting time to get transportation.
- Downtime and idle time:
    Downtime of machinery, equipment, apparatus, computers, desk computers; idle time of employees in various jobs, projects, departments.
- Deviations from scheduled times:
    Transportation schedules, giving medicine on time in hospitals and nursing homes, shipments and deliveries that do not arrive at a scheduled or promised time.
- Emergency times:
    Fire alarm, pollution alarms, police calls, ambulance calls.
- Length of life:
    Length of life, life cycle costs, failures, reliability.

PROCESSES: COMPONENTS OF SERVICE

Processes include the means to manufacture a product or to render a service. In services the total operation can be broken down into *components of service*. These components include all of the various divisions of the total operation. They are the parts that have to be planned, designed, supervised, and appraised. Quality of service is reflected in each of these components, which are the different sets of activities which go to make up the total service. Invariably employees are directly associated with the quality of service in each of the several components.

Components of service in an office include the following: editing, reviewing, calculating, coding, filing, transcribing, key punching, storing, tabulating, listing, billing, summarizing, programming, typing, mailing, word processing, and accounting.

The components of service in connection with airline travel can be listed as follows:

- Making reservations and payment;
- Checking in at counter with baggage; getting seat assignment;
- Waiting at proper gate;
- Boarding plane and finding seats;
- Waiting on ground;
- Takeoff;
- Instructions on board;
- Food and drinks service; other services;
- Landing and preparing for discharge;
- Going from plane to baggage carousel;
- Waiting for baggage;
- Getting all pieces of baggage;
- Reporting any damage to baggage;
- Finding transportation;
- Waiting for transportation.

SUBJECT MATTER

Experts in the subject matter of the problem are needed to locate and resolve causes of trouble, out-of-control situations, failure, and sporadic operations of machines and processes. Examples of this need for special knowledge or new data to correct faults and solve problems are the following:

Coors Brewery uses automatic fillers to fill bottles. Control charts are used to control the fill. When the filler goes out of control by filling too much or too little, the filler is stopped and a special mechanical engineer is called in to adjust the filler in question.

Grant describes a case of a factory product being out of control. Only after someone who knew heat treatments studied the situation was it resolved. The method of quenching the metal had been changed; they company had changed from quenching in water to quenching in oil.

A company began to lose sales and was at a loss to know why. Only after a study of lost customers was the answer found: vendors had been changed to cut costs, but at the expense of quality.

Chapter 9

The Experts on Quality

The purpose of this chapter is to describe the views of five experts in the field of quality management: Crosby, Deming, Ishikawa, Juran, and Peters. The major aspects, the topics emphasized, and aspects omitted will be described. How these views and programs can help managers and others initiate, develop, and implement a program of improvement of quality in services concludes the chapter.

CROSBY ON QUALITY

Crosby in his book describes 14 steps in a quality improvement program.[1] The 14 steps are given below with a brief statement on the theme of each.

1. Management Commitment: Top level management participates in and sets policy for a company-wide quality improvement program.
2. Quality Improvement Team: This team, composed of representatives from every department, runs the quality improvement program.
3. Quality Measurement: Collecting data in both manufacturing and service areas to 1) show trends (progress) and 2) identify problems. Cites field failure information which was never analyzed; could be used as a starting point for a quality improvement program. (Why wasn't field failure data ever analyzed?)
4. The Cost of Quality: The cost of quality is the cost of doing things wrong. It shows where corrective action is most profitable. This is the job of the comptroller using detailed information on what constitutes cost of quality.
5. Quality Awareness: Showing both management and employees the cost of nonquality and the need to be constantly concerned with identifying problems of nonquality and working toward their elimination.
6. Corrective Action: Corrective actions are taken at four levels of organization by groups of engineers and supervisors, by managers and staffs,

---

[1] P. B. Crosby, *Quality Is Free* (New York: McGraw-Hill, 1979; Mentor paperback, 1980).

by task forces, and by senior management. The goal is to resolve problems permanently.

7. Zero Defects (ZD) Planning: An ad hoc committee from the quality improvement team studies the ZD concept and lays out plans to implement it throughout the company. ZD means that everyone should do things right the first time. It is a defect prevention program. Part of the plan is to get employees to voluntarily sign a Zero Defects pledge.

8. Supervisor Training: All levels of management should receive training in all aspects of the quality improvement program, including the Zero Defects program.

9. Zero Defects Day: A special day when all employees realize through personal experience that a real change has been made.

10. Goal Setting: Following ZD day, supervisors meet with employees for the purpose of setting specific individual and group goals to reduce defects.

11. Error-Cause Removal: (This is misleading.) This step calls for employees to report all kinds of troubles, hindrances, and situations which they encounter on the job that prevent them from carrying out the zero defects program.

12. Recognition: Recognition of those who meet their goals or turn in outstanding performances. This means not money awards but recognition by higher-level officials.

13. Quality Councils: These councils are for the purpose of bringing together on a regular basis the professional quality people and managers, mainly for communication purposes.

14. Doing It Over Again: This step emphasizes that quality improvement never ends. Measures have to be taken to guarantee continuity of the quality improvement program despite changes in personnel, management, organization, products, and services.

Some ideas basic to this plan are the following:

- Quality is conformance to requirements.
- The cost of quality is the cost of doing things wrong.
- The purpose of quality improvement is to prevent defects and errors.
- A quality management program should be established in every department.
- Quality improvement is a continuous activity that takes time to develop.
- Zero Defects is for the purpose of preventing defects.
- Cost, schedule, and quality are the basic areas of performance.
- The quality maturity grid shows where an individual or company stands relative to the five stages of development of attitudes toward quality: uncertainty, awakening, enlightenment, wisdom, and certainty.
- The Make Certain program is to help employees identify problems and work toward eliminating them.

Remarks

Advice on how to collect good-quality data is missing. Techniques involved are ignored.

Errors are hardly mentioned. Human error is much more than a question of inattention.

Nothing is said about how to prevent human error.

Not enough is said about how workers and others prevent defects.

Several important nonquality characteristics are omitted:

- Defects in purchased products
- Human errors, mistakes, and blunders
- Wasted and lost time
- Unacceptable human behavior and attitudes
- Customer complaints
- Lost customers
- Damages, losses, lawsuits, recalls
- Excessive cost
- Poor-quality data
- Failure to mention safe operations and performance

"Doing the job right the first time" is never described or analyzed.

- Unless the worker has all of the tools and knowledge required to do the job, the job can never be done at all, let alone done "right."
- For many jobs it is not a question of right or wrong. It is a question of efficiency. It is a question of using the best method or a better method. This includes all jobs involving technical and special knowledge. Examples are a better computer program, a better sample survey design, a better-designed experiment. Something can be done "right" but still be very wasteful.
- Is there a "right way" to make a bed, to sweep a floor, to prepare an order in a restaurant?

Quality as conformance to requirements does not specify who is setting the "requirements" or how "conformance" is determined. Is it determined by the company? The engineers? The customer? It is hardly the latter.

The cost of quality is not only the cost of doing things wrong. It is the cost of wasted time, unacceptable behavior, and lost customers.

Further Remarks

Nine problems are reported by employees as needing attention because they prevent workers from doing their job. The real question is: Why wasn't something done about these problems by the supervisor? Why wait for a big ZD company program?

1. Dim light on instrument: Why wasn't the boss told a long time ago?
2. Screwdriver is too short: How long has operator been waiting for the proper tool?
3. Different typewriter ribbons: Why buy ribbons that don't match?
4. Filled out field service forms are illegible: Why weren't they mailed back pronto?
5. Needed oil is stored in another building: Why? Why close down to go get some oil?
6. Drawings are too small to read: Let somebody know it immediately. Why wait?
7. Soldering iron is worn out: Was any soldering done, or did operator just wait?
8. Improper tools are used to open wooden boxes: Did anyone ever open any boxes, or did they wait?
9. It's too noisy for computer programmer: Why not ask the boss to move him?

These represent sloppy operations that should have been corrected immediately by the supervisor or foreman and the employee. If they need a Quality Council to correct these faults, or a Zero Defects program, then something is radically wrong with the employees who are not complaining, and with the supervisor for not taking steps to correct numerous faults in the current operations in the system.

Zero defects cannot be approached, let alone attained, by exhortations and sales gimmicks. The employees need to have the tools and the coaching necessary to drive defects toward zero. The same is true of human errors, wasted time, and other costly non-quality characteristics. There has to be a continuous prevention program aimed at the elimination of all sources of anti-quality.

The most serious shortcoming is that the customer is ignored. The customer is discussed in less than two pages under "consumer affairs" in connection with customer complaints and how to handle them. The emphasis is on internal operations of the company, with special attention to managers and employees. Outsiders such as customers, vendors, and competitors are not listed in the index.

Customer perceptions, preferences, needs, demands, and specifications are ignored. The plan is company- and management-oriented, not customer-oriented. It does not meet one of the major requirements for a quality improvement program in a service company or industry.

There is no indication that "customer complaints" are the most important part of the customer's role in a quality improvement program. *All customers* have to be contacted and surveyed if the company is to keep informed of what is going on: the dissatisfied customer who does *not* complain, the indifferent customer, the lost customer, the pleased customer, the customer who complains, the missing customer. Customers want to know how a product *operates,* not how it is made.

DEMING ON QUALITY

Deming's 14 Points

Deming's 14 Points constitute a plan for top-level management to accept and implement if they want to improve productivity, competitive position, and stay in business.[2] The plan is different from other plans aimed at the same general objective. Deming's plan is grounded in Shewhart's statistical quality control. It is based on decades of experience in a wide variety of jobs, functions, and activities in both private industry and in government while acting as a consultant and advisor. It is based on analyzed observations, not on some academic theory of management or human behavior. The language is not that of group dynamics. It is not based on Theories X, Y, or Z. It is based on experience. It is empirical. It is pragmatic. It is eclectic.

As in all other plans, the real test comes in trying to implement such a revolutionary plan, whether in manufacturing, government, service industries, or other industries. Implementation will take more than convincing a few officials at the top that quality improvement is a necessary condition for the success and improvement of their companies. Everyone, at all levels, not only must be convinced but actually must practice daily quality improvement. The reasons why implementation is doubly hard are clear when one analyzes the 14 Points, since they run counter to the following:

- Price tag practices of the purchasing department;
- Short-term profits desired by executives;
- Standard times and costs of the industrial engineers;
- Rating practices of the personnel department;
- Training programs of the training department;
- Numerical goals of managers;
- Vendor practices of the purchasing department;
- Inspection practices of the receiving department;
- Hiring practices of the personnel department;
- Accounting practices of the accounting department;
- Attitudes toward quality and statistics in all departments.

---

[2] W. Edwards Deming, *Quality, Productivity, and Competitive Position,* (Cambridge: Massachusetts Institute of Technology, Center of Advanced Engineering Study, 1982).

The Analysis and Implementation of Dr. Deming's 14 Points

The 14 points can be combined into seven groups:

Group 1. Purpose and problems:
   Point 1. Constancy of purpose to improve quality of product and service.
   Point 2. New philosophy for a new economic age.
Group 2. Problem finding:
   Point 5. (Find problems in the system for constant improvement).
Group 3. Vendee-vendor relations: purchasing and inspection:
   Point 3. Cease mass inspection.
   Point 4. Select vendors on basis of quality as well as price.
Group 4. Training and education:
   Point 6. Use modern methods of training on the job (employees).
   Point 7. Use modern methods of supervision (supervisors, foremen).
   Point 13. Institute program of education and retraining.
Group 5. Psychological problems:
   Point 8. Drive out fear.
   Point 9. Break down departmental barriers.
   Point 12. Foster workers' pride of workmanship.
Group 6. Numerical goals:
   Point 10. Eliminate numerical goals and slogans.
   Point 11. Eliminate work standard with numerical quotas.
Group 7. Continuity:
   Point 14. Push every day on the above 13 points.

Additions

The 14 Points are the responsibility of top-level management because it alone can furnish the leadership, approval, and support needed to promote and attain quality in products and services across the entire company or agency.

Eleven more points are added for various reasons: important points that need more emphasis, points that are just as important as some of the 14, points that are characteristics of quality in services but are ignored or do not apply to manufacturing. Each of the eleven is described briefly; many of these points are treated in detail elsewhere.

1. It is strange that *time* as a characteristic of quality has never received any special attention. Time is at the heart of productivity, cost of production, cost of operations, prices, wages, salaries, and cost of services. It is at the heart of job, project, and production schedules. It is the basis of all transportation schedules. It enters into all kinds of emergency situations. Promptness is one of the characteristics that the customer wants in quality of service.

Lost and wasted time can be just as costly as defects in products and errors made everywhere, as in the following:

- Idle time of employees, e.g., waiting for work.
- Downtime of equipment, apparatus, machinery.
- Delay time, e.g., repairs, shipments, emergencies.
- Excessive time to do a job, make repairs.
- Unnecessary time in doing a job.
- Lost time from work, e.g., absenteeism, sick leave, drugs and alcohol.
- Wasted time of inefficient methods, e.g., 100% study instead of a sample.
- Wasted time making defective parts or rendering a useless service such as featherbedding (firemen on diesel locomotive).
- Stolen time, e.g., using work time for personal business, employee stealing.

Quality improvement means that people not only work smarter but that they make better use of their time.

Time also includes synchronization of the various components designed into the system, components such as products, services, sequences, operations, processes, subprocesses, procedures, and movements.

2. *Safety* is a very critical quality characteristic in several service industries but especially in health, transportation, power plants, including nuclear power plants, and construction, whether under government contracts or not. Quality control people in manufacturing never even mention safety, but this attitude has to be rejected in the service industries, especially those named above.

Safety is directly related to human errors since so many fatal accidents in services are due to mistakes and blunders, even when the accident is due to defective materials or equipment and not to an error in human performance or operations. It may be that an accident has been due to a serious error of judgment relative to testing and maintenance of equipment. Sometimes the situation could have been prevented if an easy human-behavior alternative had been followed.

The tragedy of so many of these fatal accidents is that they are preventable with a little more care, concern, alertness, and knowledge. These accidents are not like non-preventable earthquakes, floods, and tornadoes which we have to accept and live with.

3. *Keep close to customers and non-customers.* Even though the current attention is on the customer, it is necessary to emphasize it in connection with services. The need here is for continuous customer and non-customer surveys so as to keep in close touch with preferences, interests, variations, and differences. Neither customer complaints nor orthodox market research are enough. There are many markets, not *a* market. Various groups have to be surveyed to insure that an important group, even though small, is not being ignored or neglected. Both the customer and the non-customer are not only sources of complaints but sources of new ideas, new products, new services, and improvements generally.

4. *Keep close to the employees* on the one hand and to operations on the other. Management needs to keep in close touch constantly with all of the various operations. This means keeping in contact with employees at all levels. The roving manager listens, learns, and helps. Employees, too, are a source of problems and ideas because they are where the work is being done. They should be encouraged to report problems and suggest solutions and improvements. They should receive recognition, credit, and rewards for making improvements.

5. *Collect and analyze good-quality data.* Put an end to the persistence of useless data. Concentrate data collection on the most important problems. This means continuous collection of good-quality data from employees, customers, and non-customers. Recognize always that the design of data sheets, questionnaires, probability sample studies of all kinds, tests, and experiments requires the services of professional people who not only know the theory involved but know how to apply the theory to real-world problems. Conclusions, decisions, and actions, regardless of who makes them, are no better than the data on which they are based.

6. *Apply statistical techniques which Shewhart did not use or emphasize.* These include the use of random time sampling for work analysis and cost estimates; the use of probability sample surveys to study employees, customers, and non-customers; the use of learning curve analysis to ascertain capability of an individual or a group, the reduction of errors, the reduction of unit costs, and the increase in acceptable quality production; the use of input/output analysis; the use of designed tests and experiments.

7. Develop a continuous program at all levels to reduce if not *prevent human error.* The terrible price that is being paid for all kinds of human errors, mistakes, and blunders has already been described in detail. It is imperative to have a prevention program that starts with hiring personnel and is applied throughout the entire company or agency on a continuous basis.

8. Recognize that *employee attitudes and behavior* determine the quality of services in practically all agencies and companies. That these determine quality was shown very clearly by the nationwide Gallup poll of 1005 adults' perceptions and reports on poor quality, made for the American Society for Quality Control in 1985. This poll verified nationwide what millions of people already knew. Attitudes and behavior cannot be ignored or overlooked.

9. *Promote innovation,* invention, and implementation of better methods, techniques, and processes. There is a real need to stimulate, promote, and foster the invention, development, and application of new and better methods and techniques to the problems of the company or agency. This program should apply to everyone in the organization, not just to the professional technical persons or the highly specialized people. This means supporting, defending, and assisting the innovators and improvers rather than opposing and criticizing them, which is so often the case. Foster and reward originality and creativeness

so as to discover new and better ways, methods, techniques, processes, products, and services.

10. *Stress simple, sound, and effective communication,* both oral and written, at all levels. Conduct continuous training in both oral and written communication. Keep everyone informed of what is going on. Teach everyone not only how to improve their speaking and writing but how to use the telephone.

11. Keep emphasizing that *a quality improvement plan is not enough;* talk about the many advantages of a quality program is not enough. All of these plans and words mean nothing unless they are put into effect. Top-level managers have to realize and admit that it is the workers at the operating and working levels who will make a quality program work.

There are several other aspects of management that affect quality of products and services, but they will only be noted here:

- Contracting out a job, project, or function rather than forming an in-house capability. Experience shows that contracting out can be worse as well as better.
- Automation of certain processes or operations.
- Office layout or a service company layout: locations, arrangement.
- Personnel policies and practices.
- Computerization.

Responsibility for the 14 Points

The major responsibility for each of the 14 Points is tabulated below. All departments are involved directly or indirectly in all 14 points, but the major responsibility for each is concentrated in a single department or level of management.

Item or Point	*Responsibility*
1. Constant purpose	Top-level management
2. New age	Top-level management
3. Mass inspection	Inspection, purchasing
4. Price tag	Purchasing department
5. Finding problems	All departments
6. Training on the job	Training department, all departments
7. Modern methods of supervision	Training department, all departments
8. Driving out fear	All departments
9. Breaking down departmental barriers	All departments
10. Eliminating numerical goals	All departments
11. Eliminating numerical work standards	All departments

Item or Point	*Responsibility*
12. Removing barriers to pride in work	All departments
13. Instituting a vigorous program of education and retraining	Training Department, all departments
14. Creating management structure to push the above 13 points	Top management

The 14 Points concentrate on internal operations that affect management, supervisors, and employees. Vendors are involved in Points 3 and 4 but the emphasis is on the purchasing and inspection departments, and what their new functions should be.

Implementation

The 14 Points are a mixture of goals, problems, activities, and assignments. The real problem is not developing a plan but implementation. The real problem is putting the plan, whatever it is, into effect. The reason is simple: the 14 Points represent a drastic departure in thinking from conventional wisdom, and a sharp deviation from established business and industry practices.

We have already listed 11 areas where one or more of the 14 Points runs contrary to beliefs and practices not only of executives but of various departments such as purchasing, training, personnel, receiving, and industrial engineering.

The psychological aspects are very difficult because they involve conflicting attitudes, feelings, emotions, and values which cannot be changed easily, nor can they be changed in most cases by rational arguments, reasons, or appeals. This is especially true of Points 8, 9, and 12, which deal with fear, barriers, and pride. It is also true of Points 1, 2, and 5, which deal with purpose and the new philosophy. Top-level managers are no doubt convinced more by the success of the Japanese in domestic and world markets than by any elaborations of what quality and quality control and quality improvement mean. These psychological problems cannot be solved like statistical problems.

Training and education are difficult to implement because officials, managers, supervisors, and professional specialists are *not* hired for knowing how to teach (Points 6, 7, and 13). Rarely will any of them be good natural teachers. Dr. Deming states that it is hard to obtain good teachers in statistics. He might have added that it is hard to obtain good teachers, period. We expect training and education to prevent defects, eliminate errors, improve skills, and strengthen knowledge so as to improve quality, but we do not explain how these highly desirable goals are to be attained. We expect improvement by applying a program of massive education, but we can easily be disillusioned because we do not have the capability to make massive education effective.

Receiving inspection, selection of vendors, and purchasing involve vendee-vendor relations, which appear to be the easiest to resolve but may turn out to be much more difficult than anticipated (Points 3 and 4). Vendor certification and vendor rating are not new. What is new is reducing the number of vendors of acceptable-quality products and services. What is new is buying according to quality and price, not price alone.

It will be difficult to put the brakes on numerical goals and work standards, let alone get rid of them. Progress could be made relative to numerical goals if learning curve analysis was used to measure the progress and capability of individuals and groups. Work standards and standard costs could be eliminated if random time sampling and the minute model were applied to work situations. The trouble is that neither of these methods of collecting and analyzing data is well known. Random time sampling (RTS) involves a knowledge of probability sampling which few have. With RTS, standard costs could be eliminated in favor of actual costs, while at the same time working toward elimination of wasted time (allowable time), which is accepted under orthodox methods.

The 14 Points require an understanding of statistics, and an ability to apply it, that exist only rarely in companies and agencies. Over 40 statistical problems are used in *Quality, Productivity, and Competitive Position* to illustrate various concepts, conditions, and situations. Statistical techniques used include the binomial distribution (both the binomial count and the binomial proportion), the Poisson distribution, the $\bar{x}$, R, p, and np charts, and the square root approximation of the Poisson distribution. It is not explained why the binomial is used, why the Poisson distribution applies, and how the square root approximation is handled. More knowledge of statistics is assumed than any executive, top manager, lower-level manager, professional, or supervisor has. It is true that the reader can gain an idea of the main purpose and meaning of many of these points by observing some of the charts and skipping the mathematics. This means, however, that the reader will not understand why and how certain mathematical calculations were made, or the assumptions behind them. The heart of quality control is missed.

Of the 500 registrants for the April 1983 seminar held at the Utah State University, 10 percent were top executives, 40 percent were other management people, and the other 50 percent were quality managers, engineers, personnel and administrative people, and others. Half came from Utah and half from outside the state. Even though the course was aimed at top management, only one out of 10 of those attending came from this group. Half of the group were not management people at all. This may be much more desirable than it sounds; at this stage, the more people are exposed to the new approach to quality, the better, whether they are top management people or not.

The 14 Points may be considered a road map for management and others to use to improve quality. Four conditions must be met if the map is to be used effectively:

- Individuals must be able to read and understand the map.
- Individuals must know where they are.
- Individuals must know where they are going.
- Individuals must be able to select a desirable route from origin to destination.

If these conditions are not met, a road map will be of little value.

The persistence of inefficient methods and processes, and of useless data, often characterizes a company or agency. These have to be reduced and eventually eliminated before there can be any real improvement in quality. Top-level management cannot do this. These changes have to be made by persons, usually experienced professional persons, who are very conscious that the methods are inefficient and that the data are useless, and who know how to improve the situation.

In implementing a quality program, it is imperative that the two major sources of poor quality be sharply distinguished: special causes or assignable causes, for which the individual worker is responsible, and chronic or common causes, which are faults of the system and for which management is responsible. Use of statistics is necessary to bring a process or operation under control. Once it is under control, further improvement can be brought about only by changing the system. This is why careful and proper use of statistics is so important; there are also other reasons, such as the collection of good-quality data.

The 14 Points and Services

1. *Create constancy of purpose to improve.* Manufacturers who face strong foreign competition are able to see the need for better-quality products. This is not true of service companies. Their competition is domestic, not foreign, if they have any competition. They will not render better services simply because the Japanese are making better products.

They have to be *convinced* that getting rid of poor-quality performance reduces costs, saves people, increases productivity, satisfies more customers, strengthens their competitive position, and ensures that they stay in business. They need to be made aware of the high cost of poor quality services, of doing things wrong. They have to *accept* quality before they can have a firm purpose.

These are other objections that can be raised and will have to be overcome:

- We are already giving high-quality service.
- Improving the quality of services will cost too much.
- Quality of services cannot be improved like the quality of products.
- We cannot improve quality of service with the kind of employees we have.
- We already have 99.9 percent reliability of services (or better) e.g., telephone, gas, water, electricity.

This means that there has to be a drastic change in attitude and purpose, not only of top level officials but in all those down below. The real question is: Who is going to bring about this change, and how?

2. *Adopt the new philosophy for a new economic age.* Proclaiming a new age will not improve the quality of services. It will take more than pronouncements and exhortations.

Quality must be learned. It requires a whole new set of attitudes. It calls for the understanding and acceptance of a new set of concepts and ideas. Quality means applying a whole new set of methods, techniques, practices, and processes. It requires an understanding and a balanced application of the eight vectors of quality.

We will live with delays, errors, mistakes, and blunders until we insist that they are not acceptable. We must show people how to move toward zero defects, zero delay, zero errors, acceptable quality attitudes and behavior, and better methods, techniques, and processes. The real task is how to move toward quality improvement. The basic ideas have to be introduced into both the educational and economic systems. They do not exist in the former, and very little in the latter.

3. *Cease dependence on mass inspection.* This does not apply to service industries to the same extent as it applies to manufacturers. Quality control people have worked for decades on vendee-vendor relations, vendor certification, and vendor rating to improve the quality of purchased products. Service companies and agencies are concerned about *the quality of purchased products,* just like a manufacturer.

Service companies should work closely with vendors to see that they understand the products wanted, can produce them under adequate quality and quantitative controls, and can certify to the same. This will relieve the service company of expensive receiving inspection, or at least will reduce inspection only to highly critical items.

There are also many situations and operations within a service company where inspection or review is used. Exploratory time plot should be used to determine if inspection or review can be reduced, if not eliminated, by effective use of process control. If inspection, review, or verification is required as part of a companywide error prevention program, so be it. (This subject is treated in detail in a later chapter.)

4. *Cease buying solely by the price tag.* Quality control people have known for decades that quality has to be a major factor in purchases. This accounts for the longtime interest in vendee-vendor relations. Examples abound of the dangers of buying cheap: tensile strength is inadequate, defects have to be corrected before machine can be used, customers are lost due to reduced product quality, risk of failures increases. The purchasing department of a service company has to learn that quality is even more important than price because buying cheap and saving money may easily lower the quality, increase costs, lose customers, and compromise safety. What is important is the vendor's tech-

nical capabilities, manufacturing ability, quality control program, and success in producing products according to the specifications and needs of the customer. The purchasing department and others need to work closely with vendors to make sure that they understand the products wanted and the functions to be performed, and that the suppliers are equipped to produce what the vendee wants.

5. *Constantly improve the system of production and service.* Before improvements can be made in a service organization it is necessary to locate the places, problems, situations, jobs, projects, procedures, and operations where improvements are needed. It is also necessary to determine the nature of these improvements and who will make them. Special causes of poor quality can be corrected by the employees. Chronic causes and faults of the system have to be corrected by first-line supervisors or by higher-level managers.

It is necessary to make a survey of the entire organization to locate and identify these problem areas. This survey can be facilitated by using an audit plan and form developed by the author for surveying both statistical and non-statistical situations and problems.[3] (See checklist in Chapter 8.)

Once more the question arises: Who will make these studies? Who will identify the problems? Where will the suggestions and recommendations for improvements come from? Top-level management will not do these things. They will have to be done by those lower down who know the work, who know the operations, who know what needs to be changed and improved. These people obviously include the employees and the first-line supervisors, as well as professional staff specialists who are familiar with the technical aspects of the work.

6. *Institute training on the job.* Training on the job should deal with those aspects of the job that are peculiar to the company and the industry. It should *not* include teaching employees how to read, how to do arithmetic, how to answer simple questions, or how to talk over the telephone. Employees who cannot meet these qualifications should never have been hired in the first place.

Training is necessary to orient employees into quality policies and practices, into what their job consists of, into instruction manuals or procedures and what they mean so there will be no misunderstandings, into what is acceptable quality work and what is not, into any special rules and regulations the company has that are set by the company or by government, into the importance of individual behavior in connection with services involving face-to-face relationships with customers. Employees need to be tested to ensure that they understand these points clearly.

7. *Institute leadership to help people do a better job.* (This is a revision of "Use modern methods of supervision.") Points 5 and 7 seem to have the same

---

[3] A. C. Rosander, "Conducting Audits," *Federal Statistics,* Report of the President's Commission, Vol. 1, 1971, pp. 158–169. Superintendent of Documents, U. S. Government Printing Office, Washington, DC 20402. Set of 2 volumes $4.

meaning, or certainly a lot in common. The system is improved by helping people do a better job. Quality is built into products and services by those who do the work, by those who make the products and render the services. These are lower-level managers, supervisors, professionals, and employees. Top-level management does not do this. Their role so far as quality is concerned is to build quality into policies, plans, decisions, and actions.

For technical guidance and assistance, competent professional people are needed. Top-level or middle management cannot do this. What is needed is one or two professional practitioners who know quality technology and how to apply it. These are people who recognize a situation involving quality when they see it, who know how to design and implement a probability sample program, and in general know how to apply the science of statistics to solve the problems of management. This is necessary because management in services is faced with many more statistical problems than they realize. Very often the push to do a better job and use a better method will come from these professionals with experience in making improvements, not from top-level management.

8. *Drive out fear.* This refers to the fears of production employees. There is more to this situation than the fears of these employees. It is just as important to do something about the fears and frustrations of supervisors, professional specialists, and middle managers. These people can also be rebuffed whenever they discuss troubles, suggest changes, or recommend improvements. New ideas are seldom received with favor for the simple reason that they may change the organization, administration, procedures, operations, or practices.

Opposition to better methods and procedures comes from higher-level officials and professionals who are not familiar with the technical nature of many of the improvements recommended, such as probability sampling, statistical quality control, and design of tests and experiments. Behind this opposition are fear of change, jealousy, feuds, and even intrigues.[4]

Fears and frustrations are symptoms of a sick organization. Communication is faulty. Significant information from professional experts is stopped. It never reaches the top decision makers, or the decisions of professional specialists are overruled. The Challenger disaster is an excellent example, although many other examples of the same kind can be cited.

There is no positive meaningful dialogue between management and those supervised. People at all levels are discouraged from reporting their troubles, problems, and grievances, Communication is prevented rather than encouraged. Only management can change this faulty communication system. Managers should have three plaques on their desks:

I LISTEN. I ANSWER QUESTIONS. I ASK QUESTIONS.

---

[4] See Rosander, *Washington Story,* for a wealth of examples and experiences to support these statements. See also Wright, *On a Clear Day You Can See General Motors,* describing John DeLorean's experiences.

This practice should reassure all employees that managers will listen and try to understand their problems and suggestions. This change in attitude will help to reduce, if not eliminate, the fears and frustrations that exist at the present time.

9. *Break down barriers between departments.* It is not enough to break down barriers *between* departments; barriers *within* departments also must be broken down. This is because barriers are due to people: to conflicts, to differences of opinion, to different personalities, to different ways of thinking and operating, to different abilities to communicate, to feelings and prejudices, and many other reasons.

Breaking down the barriers between departments means breaking down the barriers between people in these departments, but especially the barriers existing between the top-level officials and professionals in one department and those in another. In a service company this means that the various specialists have to cooperate: accountants, auditors, statisticians, quality specialists, computer specialists, marketing specialists, and customer service people. This means teamwork on task forces, and it is up to top-level management to see that this teamwork is put into effect and that it works smoothly and effectively. Managers of different departments should be hired with an emphasis on ability to cooperate with other departmental managers. It will be up to top-level management to resolve serious conflicts between departments. It will be up to departmental managers to resolve serious conflicts within their departments.

10. *Eliminate numerical goals and slogans.* The trouble with numerical goals in services is that

- they are not applicable;
- they are not helpful in improving quality;
- they are not realistic even when set;
- they are premature because of lack of a wealth of experience;
- the worker lacks the knowledge, material, equipment, procedures, and skills to do the jobs implied in the goals.

The only numerical goal in service industries such as health, transportation, and power plants, where one employee error can be dangerous if not fatal, is zero. You do *not* set acceptable levels in services for defects, human errors, wasted time, unacceptable behavior, fatal accidents, dissatisfied customers, customer complaints, lost customers, or poor-quality data. You drive these levels to zero, and see that every worker is equipped with the knowledge, resources, and means to move in that direction. We are now at the stage of pph (parts per hundred or percent). The next stage is parts per thousand (ppt). Finally, the goal is parts per million (ppm).

In many services 100 percent reliability is a numerical goal which is attained daily. The householder expects the water to run when he turns on the faucet. He expects the bulb to light when he snaps on a switch. He expects the gas stove to operate anytime. He expects the telephone to give a dial tone when he wants to communicate. He expects the garbage to be collected on schedule. He expects electricity to be available constantly so the furnace, the refrigerator, the stove, the radio, the television set, the electric typewriter, the electric toaster, and many other appliances and devices will operate on demand. A numerical goal of 100 percent reliability is constantly on the minds of those who run our public utilities.

11. *Eliminate work standards.* The trouble with work standards is that acceptable levels of error, defects, wasted time, and other non-quality characteristics are built into the standards. This is directly contrary to what we have just described. The way to correct this situation is to use modern work sampling— that is random time sampling (RTS with the minute model)—to estimate actual time and cost of performing a task, doing a job, or carrying out a project. In this way one obtains an objective measure of idle time, downtime of equipment and machinery, waiting time for work or parts or supplies, lost time, and what this wasted time is costing the company or agency. Then steps can be taken to identify the sources of these wasteful practices and eliminate them. This means quality improvement and reduction in costs. In the process a new set of actual times and costs is obtained, which take the place of fictitious standard costs. RTS is repeated so that time characteristics are kept under control and reduced to the maximum extent possible.[5] The snap reading and tour methods of work sampling are now obsolete.

12. *Remove barriers to pride in workmanship.* Obviously "pride in workmanship" refers to physical products produced in a factory or elsewhere. It does not apply literally to those who work in service companies or agencies. The equivalent in these organizations is one or more of the following:

- Satisfaction from doing a good job;
- Satisfaction from doing something that pleases a customer;
- Pleasure from solving a tough problem;
- Resolving a problem that is bothering a customer.

This employee satisfaction can come with or without the support of higher-level management. It may be no more than doing a good job every day. It will be enhanced through provision by management that doing a good job is officially recognized in some manner, though not necessarily in a monetary way.

Doing a good job means that the employee, regardless of level, has the following:

- Adequate knowledge to do the job;
- Experience in solving tough problems;
- Desirable personal attitudes toward customers and others;

---

[5]The basic paper is Rosander, Guterman, and McKeon, "The Use of Random Work Sampling for Cost Analysis and Control," *Journal of the American Statistical Association*, June 1958, vol. 53, pp. 382–397.

- Clear understanding of what his or her job is;
- Clear understanding of what constitutes an acceptable quality job and what does not;
- Clear understanding of how his or her job is related to the jobs of others, to the work of the department, and to the purpose of the company.

It is up to management to see that the person has the basic qualifications for the job when hired, that the person is oriented after hiring into the policies and practices of the company, that the supervisor or another person explains in detail what the job is and what it is not, what acceptable quality work consists of, what constitutes unacceptable work, and how doing a poor quality job affects others in their work. The importance of this particular job to the work of the division and department should be explained and emphasized. It is well for the employee to know right from the start that he or she has an important job, and that others rely on him or her to do an acceptable quality job.

13. *Institute a vigorous program of education and self-improvement.* The serious problems that are encountered in training and education in service companies have already been discussed. Briefly, officials, professionals, and supervisors are *not* hired because they know how to teach, instruct, train, or educate. Yet we count on these persons to plan, direct, and implement an effective education and training and retraining program. Such a program is easy to talk about and include in a plan for improving quality, but it is very difficult to put into effect.

It is not just a question of employees including supervisors and of professionals and managers attending classes. The situation is much more complicated than that. A wide variety of sound and relevant courses has to be planned, the content has to be selected and organized, the material has to be presented so that it can be understood and mastered, and individuals have to be tested to see that they are learning what is intended. Furthermore, it is necessary to test individuals on the job to see if they have improved quality by applying what they learned. Massive education will be very costly and wasteful, if not ineffective, unless it is carefully planned and run by people who know what is appropriate and know how to teach, coach, and test.

14. *Form a structure to maintain continuity. Put everyone to work improving quality.* The challenge of this plan is not only to start a quality improvement program but to plan and execute it in such a way that continuity is maintained. Steps must be taken by management, professionals, and supervisors to see that the program is built on a solid foundation, that people are hired, oriented, and trained in quality improvement, and that quality is a continuous aspect of the work ethic.

The 14 Points and Health

1. Health services do not need a constant purpose. They need a new purpose. They need a new purpose encompassing a comprehensive approach to the quality of health and related services rendered to patients.

A Senate investigation, many studies, numerous press reports, and personal observations reveal an alarming absence of any notion of what quality of health services really means or what management of quality entails, or any recognition that grave faults exist in the system. The major trouble is institutionalism.

If the question of quality is raised, one of two responses results: A proclamation that quality already is excellent, or an assertion that the quality of service desired is impossible because it is too expensive.

2. Health services are *not* in a new age. They will not be in a new age until they create it themselves. To create this new age they will have to get rid of the following:

- Unnecessary surgical operations (40% according to a Rand study);[6]
- 14 percent error rate in laboratories testing blood, urine, tissue (Center for Disease Control study);
- "Warehousing" of older persons (U.S. Senate investigation);[7]
- Blackout of accessible medical services on Saturdays, Sundays, and holidays (no one dares get sick on these days or need medical help);
- Mixups of drugs, gases, and patients (too many examples reported in press);
- "Quality" determined by government inspectors and state health officials;
- Inhumane and cruel treatment of persons in nursing homes;
- Stealing by patients, employees, and administrators in nursing homes;
- Reducing food to patients to cut costs and make money, resulting in malnutrition;
- Employees who can't tell the difference between a valve on an oxygen line and a valve on a heating system, and the managers who hire them (Denver case);
- Hospitals, nursing homes, and doctors who put profit above quality performance;
- Fear peddlers and their scare tactics and false alarms;
- Dictating that *everyone* over 65 (28 million) should have a flu shot.

3. Health agencies purchase a wide variety of important products such as drugs, medicines, instruments, equipment, supplies, food, beds, linens, and gases. They need to cooperate closely with vendors and suppliers to insure that quality programs are in place and working, so that nothing is defective and no errors are made.

If purchases call for 100 percent inspection of critical drugs and medicines, and 100 percent testing of equipment and instruments to insure safe usage, so be it. When lives are at stake, no one can afford to make errors. A continuous error prevention program should be in place and working.

---

[6] Study by Rand Corporation of 1132 adults not under Medicare. *USA Today*, Nov. 13, 1986, Section D.

[7] *USA Today*, May 22, 1986, Page 1.

4. In health services it is wise to buy on the basis of quality as well as price, and not award business to the lowest bidder or buy at the lowest price. Buy from vendors who have their production processes under statistical quality control and who can certify that products are made to meet operating specifications.

We should go further. Eliminate receiving inspection as much as possible by using vendor certification of the quality and indentification of the products bought. Screen vendors and deal with the best. Certain tests may be needed on critical items, although every effort should be made to have the vendor do these tests. These should include tests for labels, contents, composition, and conformance to orders.

The purchase operation includes more than just buying acceptable-quality products. Store products so that serious mixups are avoided. Store bottles, containers of drugs, medicines, and gases in separate cabinets or rooms to avoid mixups in use. Clearly label cabinets, drawers, shelves, cylinders, bottles, other containers, and storage places. This is for foolproofing and preventing errors.

5. Health services cannot work for the constant improvement of services until they first understand and accept what quality and quality improvement mean. They have to make a start before they can make an improvement. They have to be able to identify all kinds of anti-quality situations, and know how to go ahead and correct them. Finally, they need to know how to isolate all kinds of problems that need attention, involving the system, employees, food, medicines, patients' complaints, treatment of patients, housing, security, and more.

6. Many if not most health agencies will not do much, if any, training on the job. This is because they have neither the time nor the staff to do this training. Indeed, training employees on the job is the last thing they have in mind. Those agencies that hire qualified persons who are competent, careful, accurate, and considerate of sick people will require very little training on the job unless some special problem or situation arises. Other agencies that do not have highly qualified persons will need to plan training courses in these desirable traits, but are not likely to do so.

Regardless of the qualifications of employees, it is necessary to give training in labeling and storage to avoid mixup errors. This means that all critical items must be carefully labeled and separately stored. Training should be given in reading names of patients, reading labels on medicines, drugs, and cylinders of gas, and checking out equipment and instruments before use to insure that they are working properly.

Hire qualified people in the first place. Train by example, demonstration, and use of records, charts, and complaints. Train for safety, for zero error, promptness, and zero delay. Train for humane behavior and humane care. Train for cooperative attitudes and teamwork. Hire for these traits but train for them if needed.

7. Institute supervision and leadership to help people do a better job. The

first thing that both employees and supervisors in a health agency have to learn is what constitutes a "better job." One easy way to learn is to observe the poor-quality jobs that surround them, such as those listed above.

The purpose of supervision in a health agency is to insure that the employees are doing the acceptable quality jobs they are hired to do. This means acceptable types of performance such as humane behavior, safety, zero error, and zero delay time. It means giving medicines to individual patients correctly and on time. It means prompt answers to calls. It means honesty, alertness, care, concern, compassion, and communication with patients. It means you don't treat patients as though they were pieces of merchandise. You can't scrap and rework people.

8. In health services it is *not* the fears of employees that loom large; it is the fears of the patients, as in the following list:

- Stealing of personal belongings by employees: wigs, robes, jewelry, food;
- Stealing of monies by administrators: Social Security checks, other monies;
- Fear of ill-treatment from certain employees;
- Fear of ill-treatment from supervisors, including nurses;
- Stealing of personal belongings by other patients: clothing, wallet, shaving kit;
- Fear of insane patient, who may be a roommate;
- Fear of running out of money to pay the bill (in a nursing home);
- Fear of fire (nursing home may be a firetrap);
- Fear of a surgical operation;
- Fear of a treatment, such as chemotherapy for cancer;
- Fears inculcated by scare tactics;
- Fear of doctors.

9. In health services the barriers to break down are not so much those between departments because daily health services in institutions are interconnected and closely sequenced. The relationships between purchasing and administration, between admissions, surgery, discharges, and patient control should be close and cooperative. There also are other relationships where barriers should not exist:

- Between employees and patients;
- Between nurses and patients;
- Between doctors and patients;
- Between medical technicians and patients;
- Between supervisors and patients;
- Between the front office and patients;
- Between doctors and nurses.

Break down dictatorship, condescending attitudes of Big Brother and Big Sister, brutal frankness of doctors and nurses, the arrogant attitude that the patient is dumb and knows nothing about his or her health, refusal to believe the patient, and refusal of doctors and nurses to talk and explain.

10. Eliminating slogans does not apply to health services as such, and numerical goals may exist but are not publicized. For example 100 percent reliability of people and equipment is imperative. What health services suffer from are not so much slogans as cries from dictatorial fear peddlers and broad-brush generalizations from poor quality medical research. Examples are:

- Everyone over 65 years of age should have a flu shot
- All men should get tested for colon cancer
- All women should be tested periodically for breast cancer
- Every federal employee should be tested for AIDS

In health services 100 percent reliability, accuracy, timeliness, and humaneness are paramount. The goal is to drive human errors to zero, delay times and wasted time to zero, and objectionable behavior of employees and health professionals to zero.

11. Work standards and standard costs are not necessary in health services, if modern work sampling (random time sampling with the minute model RTS) is applied. This method gives actual time and actual costs for jobs, tasks, projects, operations, functions. It detects and identifies sources of idle time, down time, delay time, excessive time, etc., so that they can be eliminated thus improving productivity and reducing costs. These random time samples are taken throughout the agency periodically so that there is continuous elimination of wasted time and improvement of operations. (The snap reading and tour methods are now obsolete.)

In health services there are some characteristics which have numerical implications. Examples include idle time, delay time, down time, length of life, reliability, laboratory tests, repair costs, time to failure, life cycle costs.

12. Pride in workmanship does not apply to services. Pride in building a product does not exist. Here the problem is pride in rendering a health service. The following are possible ways this can be done:

- doing a good job
- pleasing a customer
- solving a difficult problem
- getting rid of some serious trouble a patient has
- correcting a chronic fault
- talk more to patients
- make patients more comfortable
- make correct diagnosis
- improve some procedure or practice

The service person has to like people, like to help people, has to understand individual differences and peculiarities, has to be tolerant of customers' reactions and criticisms.

13. There is not much need for massive education in health services at the basic service level (patient control, admissions, discharges). The need for education and additional training arises in the technical areas as new methods, drugs, medicines, treatments, and instruments are developed and put into practice. Examples include the CAT scan, chemotherapy, sonar methods, a new instrument for measuring pressure in glaucoma, and the like.

Where there is need for a more thorough education is in nursing homes and similar institutions. This is because there are no technical requirements that have to be met by employees. Apparently registered nurses (RNs) are not required; perhaps only licensed practical nurses (LPNs), if anything. Until states require hiring qualified persons in nursing homes, there will not be any great improvement in quality of service. Since nursing homes in most instances are run for profit and not by a non-profit religious or secular organization, there is little hope that quality improvement in the performance of employees will be forthcoming.

14. This point deals with putting everyone to work to improve the performance of the company or agency. Quality cannot be improved until people understand what quality means. From the above it is obvious that before you can put everybody to work to improve quality, you have to put *somebody* to work to start to improve quality of performance. Clearly, quality has to be started before it can continue. The crucial problem in the above discussion is that of starting a program, understanding and accepting the basic ideas of a quality program, and implementing the plan once it is understood and accepted.

The problem is further complicated by the fact that the states, even though they are allotted federal taxes for health care by the federal government, fail to insist on hospitals and nursing homes meeting acceptable quality practices. They all work on the false notion that government inspection means quality control. No state as yet has set up comprehensive quality control programs for hospitals and nursing homes and monitored them at least quarterly to see that acceptable-quality services are being rendered.

ISHIKAWA ON QUALITY

The source of the following material is a book by Professor Ishikawa, who has been a leader in the field of Japanese quality control since the 1950s.[8] Six topics are discussed: quality control, total quality control, quality circles, qual-

---

[8] Kaoru Ishikawa, *What is Total Quality Control?—The Japanese Way,* translated by David J. Lu (Englewood Cliffs, NJ: Prentice-Hall, 1985).

ity control in subcontracting and purchasing, quality control in marketing, and statistics in quality control.

Quality Control

Quality control and its implementation require special attention to several factors:

- Satisfy the true requirements of customers. Study the needs of consumers and consider them in design and production.
- Consider not only the quality of product but the quality of work, quality of service, quality of information, quality of process, quality of people, and quality of the system.
- There has to be control of cost and the control of production.
- There must be figures on amount of production, defects, scrap, and re-work.
- Satisfy true requirements of consumers, not national standards.
- Quality is hard to express. Products have more than one quality characteristic. We need a consensus on what are defects and flaws.
- It is necessary to expose hidden or latent defects.
- Use statistics and process control to reduce variability.
- Products have to conform to quality of design.
- Six steps are needed to complete the control circle:
    1. Determine goals and targets.
    2. Determine methods of reaching goals.
    3. Engage in education and training.
    4. Implement work.
    5. Check the effects of implementation—check the causes and effects.
    6. Take appropriate action—prevent recurrence.

Hindrances to Control and Improvement

There are several obstacles to quality and quality improvement that have to be overcome:

- Apathy of top executives and managers;
- Those who feel that there are no problems;
- Those who feel that their company is best;
- Those who oppose new methods;
- Self-centered people;
- Those who refuse to learn;
- Despair, jealousy, envy;

• Narrow-minded people;
• Those who live in the past.

Total Quality Control

Total quality control means that everyone learns quality control, not just a few professionals. There is no quality control department with a quality specialist assigned to each department. Specialization in quality is downplayed, so staffs do not exist or are weak. Line officials and personnel dominate the decisions and the action. Teamwork must exist among all departments, groups, and employees. Massive education in quality tends to weaken the staff arrangement.

Total quality control is companywide, is management with facts, puts quality first, combines knowledge with action, is consumer-oriented, is based on a long-term view, and utilizes employees' abilities. Management must strive to satisfy customers, make people happy, and provide adequate income to employees and profits for shareholders.

Cross-function management must be used. This is brought about by cross-function committees, which are top-level management committees with permanent standing. Their functions include quality assurance, cost control, quantity control, and personnel control. Task forces or project committees operate below these executive committees.

Quality Circles

In the beginning the purpose of quality control circles or groups was education in quality control techniques and tools. It was easier to teach foremen and employees in groups than to attempt to teach them individually. Furthermore, the employees felt more at ease in a group.

Start quality control first, not a quality control circle. Managers, division heads, section chiefs, and those responsible for quality control must be the first ones to study quality control and quality control circles.

The way to start is to select a person to be responsible for quality circle activities in the entire company. Recruit circle leaders. Initially, foremen already on the job can be the most suitable quality control circle leaders. In fact, they are naturals for this leadership because they are in charge of employees and are familiar with the problems encountered by the group.

At the start, membership in the quality circle is voluntary; this is done deliberately in order to avoid any appearance of pressure or force from top levels. Eventually full participation by everyone is expected, with full utilization of quality control techniques. It is recommended that the number in a circle be limited to 10 or less. If the number exceeds 10, other circles are formed. As stated above, the circle is a group method of learning a strange subject, in which leaders teach the members.

A quality circle operates by following these steps:

- Decide on a theme, goal, or area of study.
- State reasons why this particular theme or goal is chosen.
- Assess the present situation.
- Analyze—probe into causes.
- Determine and take corrective measures.
- Evaluate the results.
- Prevent recurrence; standardize; prevent slipups.
- Consider remaining problems.
- Plan for the future.

These nine steps are now used as a problem-solving process. In this connection quality circle members not only learn how to use the seven tools mentioned later but also learn additional subjects such as physics, chemistry, electronics, and other fields in which their work lies.

In a quality circle the supervisor is the leader. He or she studies quality control, attends circle conferences, approves themes, helps employees get started, helps assemble and prepare data, enhances individual abilities, and instructs them in quality control.

It should be pointed out that quality circles limit and pervert the sound use of statistics. There are many reasons for making this statement, including the following:

- There is no need for a new, misleading vocabulary. There is no point in accepting the Japanese version of standard terms in statistics. They are not authorities in statistics, whatever else they may be.
- The seven tools described later ignore the significant problem of *collecting* good-quality data.
- The seven tools ignore the significant problem of *analyzing* good-quality data.
- There is no evidence that they master the basics of probability sampling.
- The seven tools do not include several very significant techniques used in quality improvement:
    - Random time sampling to discover, measure, and prevent all kinds of wasted time: idle time, downtime, delay time, waiting time, and the associated cost.
    - Probability sample surveys for management data about customers, employees, markets, and administrative problems.
    - Learning curve analysis to measure three basic trends: error curve, production curve, and unit cost curve, as well as the capability of a group.

There is more than one danger in this band-aid approach to statistics. With a superficial knowledge of elementary statistics, performance will be slow and inefficient. There is the danger of malpractice because there is no emphasis on what is acceptable quality data and what is not. The circle is at a very low managerial level and therefore is restricted to immediate problems of the workplace. The circle cannot deal with problems concerning the faults of the system or with inefficient methods and procedures because of its limitations in jurisdiction and knowledge. In many respects the quality circle may actually become a barrier to quality improvement because everyone will become satisfied with its successes at a very elementary level.

Quality Control in Subcontracting and Purchasing

In manufacturing the question arises: What should be made and what should be bought? At one extreme the company produces everything; at the other extreme the company buys everything and simply assembles the final product. Professor Ishikawa states that in manufacturing the Japanese buy 70 percent from others, while in the United States only 50 percent is bought outside. He believes that buying more outside and making less by the company improves quality and reduces costs. No doubt this large volume of purchases is a major reason why the Japanese work so closely with their vendors; they must, if there is to be acceptable quality in the finished product.

In this country, even if persons do not agree with this view, they still consider it an open question, with a wide range of proportions possible for an efficient operation. How much a company produces and how much it buys will depend on many factors including the quality of the work of suppliers, the cost of buying versus the cost of making, the function involved, and the capital investment involved.

In a service organization the question is this: What services should be in-house and what services, if any, should be contracted out or purchased? Obviously, functions are not contracted out which are at the heart of daily operations. The only jobs eligible to be contracted out are highly specialized ones in which the contractor has an obvious capability which the organization does not have. Even here, there is a question whether the organization should develop the capability; it should, if the jobs are recurring.

In services there is no evidence that contracting out is better than qualified in-house capability. The latter has several advantages: easier control and supervision, better communication, more efficient operation, reduced cost of coordination. Four actual cases of contracting out show how this arrangement made things worse:

- Contracting out the cleaning of a seven-story office building—contract canceled.

- Contracting out a nationwide sample study in the U.S. Department of Commerce—canceled.
- Contracting out a nationwide sample study in the U.S. Department of Transportation—used three contractors and still didn't receive an acceptable quality job.
- Contracting out data processing to a computer firm—very unsatisfactory service reported by the official responsible for contracting out.

The relation of vendee (buyer) to vendor (supplier) with regard to quality involves the following decisions and actions:

- Vendee should select vendors carefully, taking into consideration management competence, technical capability, sales trend, quality history, sales, reputation, suppliers, delivery history, and reliability.
- Both parties agree to cooperate and communicate.
- Both parties should have quality control systems in place and operating.
- Vendee submits detailed information on what vendor should make.
- Vendor submits data to vendee.
- The parties fill out contract as to quality, price, quantity, and delivery.
- Both parties agree on how to settle disputes.
- Vendee audits vendor's quality control.
- Vendee helps vendor develop quality control, if and when needed.

Quality Control in Marketing

Marketing is defined to include both the distribution and sales of manufactured products and the "soft" products which come from service industries. Marketing must develop customer confidence and trust. It is more than just selling products. It has the function of discovering the needs and wants of customers and pushing for better products to meet these needs. It is necessary to educate, define clear objectives, and control the process. Some of the major activities required before sale, at time of sale, and after sale are given below. These are applied to products, but many of them also apply to services.

Before sale:

- Analyze needs of customers;
- Plan new products;
- Research product;
- Prepare instructions on use, repairs, service, operation.

At time of sale:

- Educate sales people in quality control and quality;
- Determine if customer knows how to use product;

- Call attention to warnings to be followed in using;
- Make sure the product works at time of sale.

After sale:

- Analyze and correct complaints;
- Note warranty period;
- See that manuals are clear and complete;
- Determine reason and frequency of products returned;
- Study and record adjustments and repairs during warranty.

Control orders received, sales, accounts receivable, profit, inventory, delivery dates, hours spent with customers, packaging, and shipping. Use sales experience to improve product.

Statistics in Quality Control

Emphasis is on the seven tools, six of which are statistical. These are stressed because they are the elementary techniques used by quality circles. The words in parentheses are the ones used by the Japanese.

1. Distribution of defects, causes, factors, etc. (Pareto analysis);
2. Use of rational subgroups and divisions (stratification);
3. Tally count (check sheet);
4. Frequency distribution (histogram);
5. Relationship and correlation analysis (scatter diagram);
6. Graph and control charts;
7. Cause and effect diagram.

The first six items are statistical; the seventh is not. Graphs and control charts are words used in quality circles, and are the same as our terminology. It is claimed that in Japan 96 percent of all quality problems can be solved by these seven tools, and that all levels in the company use them.

Other statistical techniques which have limited use are theory of sample surveys, sample inspection, estimation and testing hypotheses, sensory tests, and design of experiments. In addition, a very limited number of engineers and technicians use advanced design of experiments, multivariate analysis, and operations research (OR).

This is an area where it is dangerous to generalize from the factory to the office or from manufacturing to service. There are several powerful statistical techniques that can and should be used in services but are rarely, if ever, used in the factory. One big difference arises from the huge volume of paper that service organizations have to produce, process and file. Actual examples are the following:

- Use of *random time sampling* with the minute model (modern work sampling) to estimate time and cost of idle time, downtown, waiting time, and to service time, etc., and to take appropriate action;
- Use of designed *probability sample studies* for customer surveys, non-customer surveys, administrative studies for management information, making sample studies from computer tapes, employee surveys, marketing studies;
- Use of *learning curve analysis* to measure capability of individuals and groups and to obtain significant information about error trend curve, production trend curve, unit cost trend curve, and time per unit curve.

JURAN ON QUALITY

Dr. Juran is pre-eminent in the field of management for quality. No one has been in the field longer. No one has written about it more extensively. No one has shown keener insight into the problems of quality now facing management in the United States. The sources of the following material are selected books, papers, and publications issued by the Juran Institute.[9]

Quality is defined in several ways:

- Fitness for use;
- Conformance to manufacturer's specifications;
- Conformance to customer's requirements;
- Characteristics derived by analysis of customer's needs.

Management for quality includes many aspects but especially the following:

- Quality is the responsibility of top-level management.
- A quality program must start with the top management officials.
- Senior managers need to learn how to manage for quality. Managing for profit and production is not enough.
- Management needs to adopt the trilogy—the three-part program: quality planning, quality control, and quality improvement.
- Management should support and push a continuous program of quality improvement.
- Management should provide the leadership that insures that everyone in the organization is guided by quality and quality improvement.
- Management of quality requires teamwork of managers, supervisors, professional staff, vendors, and employees.

---

[9] J. M. Juran, editor, *Quality Control Handbook,* 3rd edition. (New York: McGraw-Hill, 1974); *Quality Progress* Nov. 1985, Aug. 1986; Juran Institute; "Quality Improvement for Services," 1986.

- Management of quality means that top priority is given to the desires, preferences, requirements, and needs of customers and users.
- Management has the sole responsibility of seeing that chronic problems are solved and that faults of the system are corrected.
- Management needs to take the steps necessary for self-education and self-development to enable them to assume the leadership of a quality improvement program across the entire company.

Organizing for quality calls for changes. New groups are formed and old functions are revised. Quality is no longer concentrated in a quality control department but takes the following forms:

- Quality improvement council at the executive level;
- Quality improvement councils at other senior executive levels;
- Quality improvement teams of an interdepartmental character;
- Quality improvement teams at the departmental level;
- The quality function shifted more and more to line people;
- The Quality Control Department no longer runs the show. This staff advises, helps, trains, assists, develops better techniques and methods, and monitors to see that techniques are implemented properly.

These councils and teams are the means for carrying out a continuous company-wide quality improvement program. This requires knowledge, and ability to use this knowledge. Here is where the Quality Control Department or staff can be of invaluable assistance: quality policies, quality goals, quality concepts, quality techniques, quality costs, quality characteristics, quality planning, quality improvement, and quality measurement. These changes call for a new approach to hiring, to training, to promotion, to evaluation of individual performance, and to supervision of employees.

Quality Improvement

Quality improvement is an ongoing process planned every year as part of a total quality budget. The following activities are involved:

- Preparing an annual quality improvement plan;
- Estimating cost of poor quality;
- Identifying quality improvement projects;
- Selecting quality improvement projects for current program;
- Training and educating for implementation;
- Applying diagnostic methods, e.g., Pareto analysis;
- Finding the remedies and taking corrective action;
- Institutionalizing quality improvement to insure continuity;
- Engaging in strategic planning for quality.

What to Avoid

Dr. Juran warns us about the limitations of certain aspects of quality now receiving attention. Some aspects have received too much emphasis, have been perverted from their original purpose, have retarded quality improvement, or cannot produce what their users think.

Quality Circles

These can correct only the special problems at the employee level. They are limited in scope and restricted in their application. They cannot solve the faults of the system. Only management can do this at higher levels.

Statistical Quality Control (SQC)

Instead of being used to improve quality, SQC is being used to freeze the status quo. It becomes an obstacle to quality improvement. Admittedly, this is a very narrow view of SQC, apparently due to lack of understanding of the techniques and their application. There are too many examples where SQC was responsible for or led to quality improvement. This is really poor practice due to ignorance of the techniques.

Exhortation

Exhortations and slogans at all levels do not improve quality. Simply exhorting officials and others to "do their best," "to improve quality," or "to make quality Job One" does not improve quality. Words and pep talks do not improve quality. People must have the proper tools if they are to improve quality, and the inclination and ability to use them. Slogans, gimmicks, and sales talks are no substitutes for knowledge, abilities, understanding, and desire to make improvements.

Quality Costs

A narrow view of the cost of poor quality is not enough, if the purpose is to increase profits and ignore quality. Quality cost is but one aspect of a company-wide quality improvement program. Stressing increased profit is not the main purpose of an analysis of quality costs. The purpose is to improve quality, and if this is done, profit will take care of itself.

Comment: A Revised Model

The Juran model consists of a three-part sequence called the trilogy: quality planning, quality control, and quality improvement (see Figure 9–1).[10] During quality planning, the cost of poor quality is endured. At Time Zero the characteristic is brought under control, but there is chronic waste. During quality control some cost of poor quality is eliminated, but the cost of chronic waste remains. During the third stage, quality improvement, there is a breakthrough to an improved lower level, which is brought under control. This eliminates most of the chronic waste. There is no mention of improvement beyond this second zone of quality control, although it is the next logical step in the sequence.

This model is applicable to characteristics which are improved when they move from higher to lower values. An example is coatings of all kinds. The example of coating paper at Nashua is described in detail by Dr. Deming in Chapter 1 of both of his recent books. This example follows Figure 9–1 very closely, with a few exceptions. During what is designated "quality planning" Nashua struggled with the problem without knowing what to do. They made progress at Time Zero by applying SQC to the coating data. Apparently there were no "spikes," but only a breakthrough to a thinner and stabilized coating level. They are working on further breakthroughs which go beyond Figure 9–1.

The model does not apply to two broad classes of characteristics:

* Measurements which are stabilized at some level and need no "improvement" because they have to be held "constant." Examples are resistance and capacity. Improvements come not by changing levels, but by using new materials and better methods to obtain the same target value and the same narrow variability. There is no change in the zone of control.
* Characteristics which are discovered by sound data collection methods very quickly after Time Zero and which are not acceptable in value or in practice. Examples are excessive fills by weight or volume, overcount and undercount, error rates, excessive amounts of waiting time, and illegal practices.

These characteristics are *not* stabilized except the first. Rather, steps are taken immediately to reduce, if not eliminate, the cause. Improvement takes place with no stabilization, or very little. Examples from practice illustrate this latter type of situation.

The Juran model breaks down in the middle state—quality control—at Time

---

[10]J. M. Juran, "The Quality Trilogy," *Quality Progress,* August 1986, pp. 19–24.

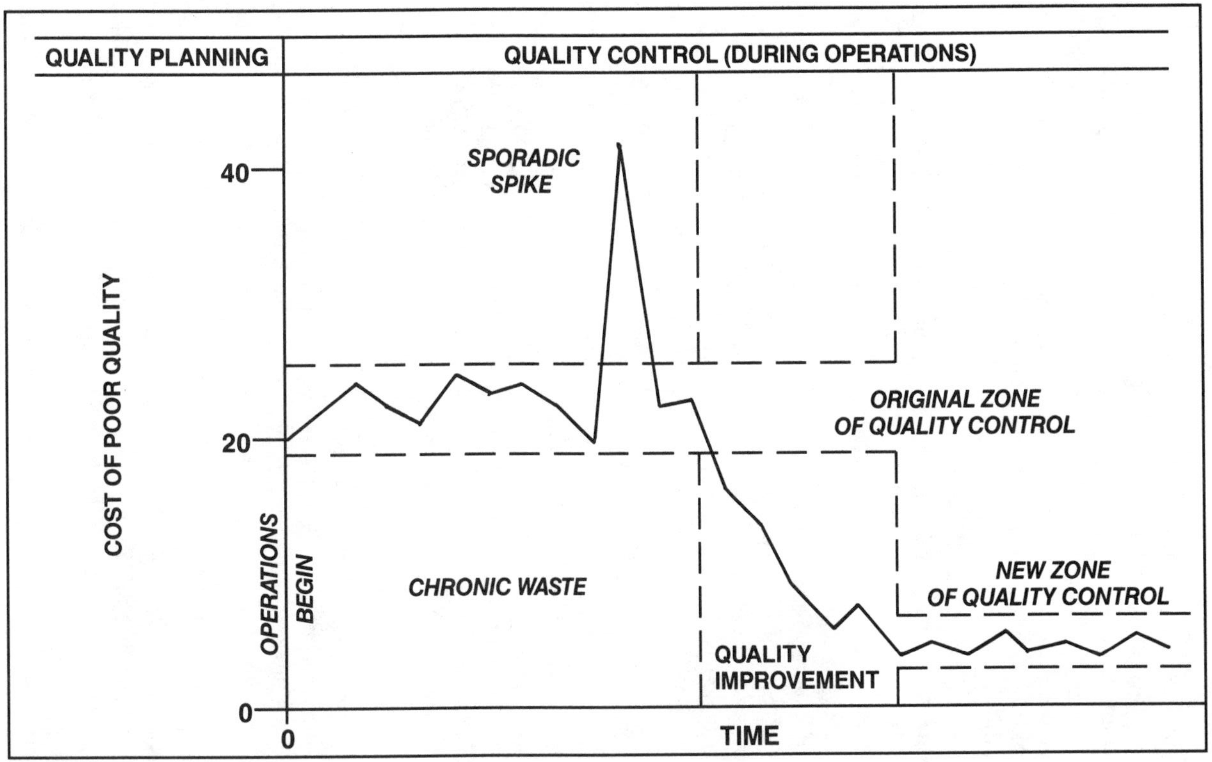

Figure 9–1. The Quality Trilogy

294

Zero for some factory and service operations. In this situation as soon as some data are available, a serious deviation is found that requires immediate action or improvement. A variety of actual examples illustrates the point. (See Figure 9–2.)

Case 1

A canning factory packs and sells 12-ounce cans of sauerkraut. Collection of data shows that the fill is running much higher than 12 ounces—14 ounces and even higher. Steps are taken to examine the method of packing the material to see if the weight can be brought nearer to 12 ounces. This is done, and the amount of excess is reduced. The goal is to put the fill under control with the lower limit at about 12 and the upper limit at about 12½ ounces. When they attempt to put the can weight under control, they discover that it would be absurd to stabilize the fill around 14 ounces when they are selling it as 12.
(Source: Speaker heard by author at quality conference University of Maryland)

Case 2

A steel mill produces and sells ingots which weigh 5200 pounds. That is, they are supposed to weigh 5200 pounds. Collection of data shows that the actual weight is averaging 200 or more pounds above 5200. Steps are taken to push the weight closer to 5200. There is no point in stabilizing the weight at 5400 pounds if it can be brought down to 5250. These steps were successful in bringing the average much closer to 5200, at a saving of $175,000.
(Source: Wade Weaver, Republic Steel, in *Industrial Quality Control*)

Case 3

The above examples dealt with fills and weights. This example deals with errors in the order filling department of a mail order house. A random sample of 100 orders is selected daily from all orders filled, and the number of orders in error is recorded. This error rate is posted daily on a huge wall chart where everybody can see it. The purpose is to reduce the error rate by simply calling the group's attention to the need. There is no control over individuals. The initial error rate was about 5 percent, the error rate continued to drop until, at the end of three weeks, it was 0.75 percent. Obviously there was no point in stabilizing the error rate. In fact, the goal was to drive the error rate toward zero, and this was the way it moved. How much closer to zero the error rate could move we will never know. This example shows that all you need is some good data. Control charts are often unnecessary.
(Source: Paper by James Ballowe, Alden Mail Order House)

Case 4

This insurance company (Blue Cross) introduced statistical quality control and formed a statistical quality control department for the purpose of reducing the number of errors on documents which are input to a new computer system. The purpose was not to stabilize errors at some level, as some dimension of a product is stabilized in a factory, but to reduce or eliminate them. Statistical quality control techniques were used to improve processing and output, not to freeze the status quo.

They used designed samples, sample inspection, frequency distribution of errors, and Pareto analysis. There was close cooperation between the quality control department and the supervisors and managers. They used conferences, retraining, coaching of individuals, and revision and clarification of instructions. All kinds of tools were used to help employees reduce the number of errors they were making.

They succeeded very well in a number of operations. In claims coding, the error rate dropped over a period of six weeks from about 7 percent to about 0.5 percent. Unacceptable subscriber refunds were reduced from 8.3 percent to 2.4 percent. In hospital claims an error rate of 8.4 percent was reduced to 1.1 percent. In all areas there was a drastic reduction in error rates. This not only saved time and money, but improved quality and productivity and reduced subscriber complaints. Other valuable by-products were use of sample checks instead of 100 percent verification, improved training by the supervisor, and more objective evaluation of employees' work.

(Source: Paper by F. M. Connell Jr. reproduced in A. C. Rosander, *Case Studies in Sample Design*, Dekker, 1977, Chapter 10)

Case 5

A data processing division of 350 employees in an agency of the federal government was faced with the problem of measuring how much time was being spent on projects requested from the outside, which were not included in the budget. For this purpose a random time sample was designed to cover the entire division during 480 minutes of every working day. To test the sampling methods, data sheet, coding instructions, and other procedures a test run was made over five consecutive days. Eight random minutes were called on each employee from the messenger boy to the director for each of these five days. A summary of the initial data revealed some surprising results and situations no one was aware of. In the graphics unit 9 percent of the time was spent waiting for work; in three other units the figures were 4, 6, and 7 percent respectively.

The director took immediate action. He called in the supervisors and explained what had been found. He asked them to examine their work schedules, find out why the employees were waiting for work, and take the necessary steps to eliminate the problem. If they needed any help from the director, they should call him.

This is a case where a type of data never before collected revealed a serious problem which needed to be corrected. Chronic waste existed because no one knew it existed; it took the use of random time sampling to discover it. This shows why data collection methods and technical knowledge are so important. A quality circle with its six so-called problem-solving statistical methods would never have discovered it because the members do not have the knowledge and experience required. This was a situation that had to be eliminated, not stabilized.

(Source: Data and papers in the author's files)

Case 6

The U.S. Treasury Department has published the results of an audit of federal individual income tax returns based on a designed nationwide probability sample. This audit control program was a real breakthrough because it showed for the first time the actual magnitude of three very significant characteristics:

- The size of the problem of noncompliance;
- The location of tax errors (the range of occurrence); and
- The magnitude of tax errors.

This meant that they now had a much more complete picture of where the major sources of error were so that audit resources could be allocated in a more rational manner. Pareto analysis had been followed for decades, but now they had a much more complete analysis. This is another example in which collection of good-quality data is the key to improvement.

We cite one example of an improvement that was made. It was discovered in this audit that many taxpayers were claiming aliens living abroad as personal exemptions, something not allowed by tax law. Two steps were taken to correct this situation: a new schedule was added to Form 1040 (it is still there), and more detailed instructions were added, explaining who can be claimed as a personal exemption and who cannot.

(Source: *The Audit Control Program* issued by the U.S. Treasury Department)

Case 7

This company had a federal government contract involving a large data processing project. The job consisted of transcribing over 100,000 complex documents to a standard format for computer input. The transcribers were inexperienced and required about three weeks of training, using a 95-page procedural manual. The supervisor was an expert in the subject.

To keep the error rate down, process control in the form of lot acceptance based on a sample was applied to every block or lot of 300 documents. When a block was rejected it was returned to the individual who had processed it. The block then was redone 100 percent and was put through the sampling process again. The sample and rules were such that the error rate was kept below 5 percent, which was deemed acceptable with a later computer edit. Without this process control and error prevention coaching the error rate would have been between 15 and 20 percent. A consultant handled the sampling, quality control, and other technical problems. Process control by lot sampling was feasible and acceptable to the vice-president. Control charts were not.

While the error rate was kept below a certain level, there were several very significant improvements over a period of 45 days:

- The time required per acceptable document *decreased* from about eight minutes to about 2¼ minutes.
- Production of acceptable documents *increased* from about 60 to about 210 per person per day.
- The unit cost per acceptable document *decreased* from about 26 cents to about eight cents.

The error rate decreased for some individuals, but process control prevented it from getting out of control for others. This was necessary because the employees, most of whom had never worked before, were not accustomed to the discipline of an office or to emphasis on accuracy in their work. On this project improvements came from the learning curve and from the excellent work of the supervisor in preventing errors, mistakes, and wasted time.

(Source: Data and reports in the author's files)

Summary

These seven cases are summarized as follows:

Description	*Stabilize or Not*
Case 1. Data show excess fill.	Stabilize at improved fill.
Case 2. Data show excess weight.	Stabilize at improved weight.
Case 3. Data show high error rate.	Do not stabilize.
Case 4. Data show high error rate.	Do not stabilize.
Case 5. Data show idle time.	Do not stabilize.
Case 6. Data define serious problem.	Do not stabilize.
Case 7. Data show learning curve improvement.	Do not stabilize.

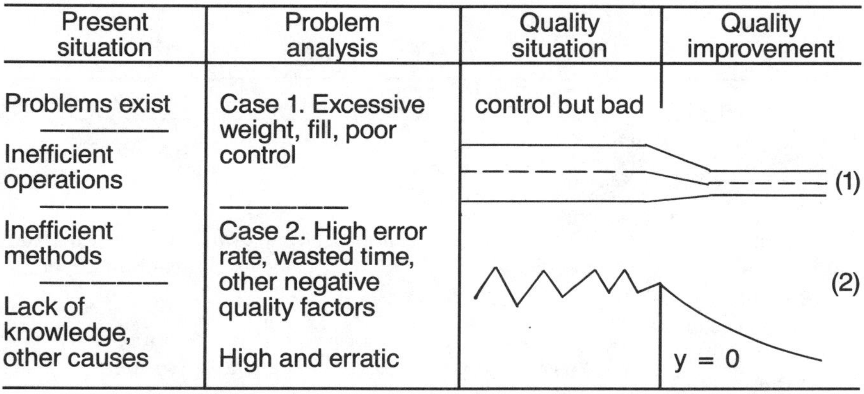

Present situation	Problem analysis	Quality situation	Quality improvement
Problems exist ——— Inefficient operations	Case 1. Excessive weight, fill, poor control	control but bad	(1)
Inefficient methods ——— Lack of knowledge, other causes	Case 2. High error rate, wasted time, other negative quality factors High and erratic		(2) y = 0

(1) Measurement is stabilized but much nearer to goal.
(2) Characteristic is driven downward toward zero (0).

Figure 9–2. **A four-stage model**

The crucial step is the collection and analysis of accurate, relevant data. It is amazing that this key step receives little or no attention. In all of the cases above, simply examining the data with little or no analysis revealed a serious problem or situation.

In the Nashua example described by Dr. Deming, the situation stayed in confusion until they decided to collect data on the coating level and its variability (presumably with x̄ R charts). Then they found that the level was under control. This meant that only a basic change could improve the situation. (See Figure 9–2 for a modified four-stage model reflecting the foregoing realities.)

TOM PETERS ON QUALITY

Tom Peters has discovered the vital importance of quality and the need for a continuous 12-point program.[11] There is an immediate need for a quality improvement revolution to meet competition, especially foreign. This means providing top-quality goods and services to meet the perceptions of customers, both individual and organizational.

Quality may be even more important than price in the market-place. The

---

[11] Tom Peters, *Thriving on Chaos* (New York: Knopf, 1987), pp. 70–81.

A Three-Stage Quality Improvement Process

Stage 1	Stage 2	Stage 3	Remarks
Exploration	Data Collection Data Analysis Diagnosis	Improvement	
Study problem Study situation Do research Plan data collection Design sample Other planning	*Case 1.* Characteristic must be stabilized at $\bar{x}$.	Improvement at the same level $\bar{x}$.	Improve materials, technique, etc.
	Case 2. Characteristic is subject to progressive stabilization.	Improvement at *lower* or *higher* levels which are stabilized.	Improve the system.
	Case 3. Characteristic is not stabilized.	1. Improvement at a stabilized level. 2. Improvement by driving value to zero.	Improve the system. Take immediate action.

Examples of Cases 1, 2, and 3 above:

Case 1. Physical measurements that are "constant"	Voltage, frequency, resistance, capacitance, wave length
Case 2. Physical characteristics that can be changed	Coating of paper, other kinds of coatings, soldering, welding
Case 3. A characteristic that is an immediate problem	Errors, error rate, idle time, illegal practice, unacceptable behavior, overfill, underfill, overcount, undercount, overweight, underweight

customer defines what is important. After 15 years, many do not give quality top priority.

Peters describes four findings from his observations and studies:

1. Customers will pay a lot for best quality.
2. Firms that provide this quality thrive.
3. Workers want the opportunity to provide top quality.
4. No product has a safe lead in quality.

His 12-point quality program comes from observing companies that reflect these traits. The points are paraphrased below:

1. Management must be intensely committed to quality.
2. There is a guiding plan, following plans by Crosby, Deming, Juran, or some other similar plan.
3. Quality is appraised by data collection.
4. Quality ideas and performance are recognized and given appropriate compensation.
5. Everyone is trained in statistical techniques for assessing quality.
6. Quality is implemented by inter- and intra-departmental teams.
7. Quality ideas and projects can involve a simple problem—they do not have to be large or companywide.
8. Quality is stressed on all occasions.
9. There is a parallel organizational structure concentrating on quality.
10. Quality involves everybody—managers, employees, customers, and vendors.
11. Getting rid of non-quality reduces costs.
12. A quality improvement program is continuous.

There is nothing new in these 12 points that was not included in the quality improvement programs proposed by other experts. Peters, however, is making a real contribution by bringing them to the attention of a wider audience.

A few comments are in order. Point 9 does not represent the views of some other experts. The trend seems to be to train line or operating personnel to identify and solve quality problems. The role of the quality staff is to instruct, coach, assist, advise, and monitor. Their job is to see that line people use quality techniques and technical knowledge most effectively.

There is also the question about how to start a program. Peters's quality program starts with top officials and covers the entire organization. It may be easier and better to start with a single problem in one department, where getting everyone's cooperation is easier. Without this cooperation a project can easily fail. This is a major obstacle to starting a program across the entire company at once.

IMPLICATIONS FOR SERVICES

We have already pointed out changes, modifications, and additions that have to be made to these plans in order for them to apply to a quality improvement program in services. We have stressed that while developing a plan is important, it is futile and ineffective unless it is properly interpreted and implemented. It is a lot easier to talk about a plan than to put it into effect. This is doubly true in service industries, where the concept of quality is misunderstood or ignored, and where quality is not as obvious as controlling the dimension of a physical object.

Let us summarize some of the major aspects of quality of services that have been overlooked but are of vital importance. Some of these aspects arise because some service industries are sharply different from others.

1. *Safety is a Number One quality characteristic* in service industries like health, transportation, power plants (including nuclear power plants), and construction, whether under government contract or not. These are operated by companies or organizations where one employee error can be not only dangerous but fatal. (This assumes that unreliable equipment is not the cause)

Technically trained individuals such as doctors, nurses, airplane pilots, engineers, and technical assistance must be held responsible for the safety of any potentially dangerous service rendered to the customer. If the equipment and conditions are judged to be unsafe, then the individual should refuse to perform. The goal has to be zero errors and zero failures.

2. *The only standard or goal for a certain class of non-quality characteristics is zero:* errors, defects in purchased items, failures, lost time, customer complaints, ill-mannered behavior toward customers, lost customers, waiting time for something needed. This means an emphasis on the zero goal at every point: hiring, promoting, training courses, error prevention courses, and safety courses.

3. *The quality of service that the customer receives comes from the bottom, not from the top.* The customers do not buy services (or products) from the CEOs. Neither do they buy from other top-level executives or from management at any level.

They buy or are served by whatever clerk or salesperson waits on them. These employees are usually the lowest-paid persons in the place. They are more likely not to be trained in how to handle the various inquiries, questions, and problems of the customer with intelligence and feeling. No one explains to them what quality of service means. Furthermore, top-level policies, purposes, and plans relative to quality of services may never permeate to the employee level that is directly responsible for the quality of service.

The CEO talks quality; he doesn't build quality into products or services. All of the fine-sounding words about quality expressed by the CEO and his associates mean nothing unless put into practice five (or more) layers of organization below, at the employee level. Hence the quality of service *actually received* by the customer comes from the bottom. It does not come from the top and never will.

Quality of service received by the customers is therefore determined by the behavior, attitudes, and competence of the clerks, salespersons, or others who wait on them. It is the performance of these persons, and these persons alone, that determine the quality of service received by the customer. Since quality is determined by human behavior and attitudes, it is psychological, not statistical.

An *exception* is a situation where the quality of service is determined by the reliability of equipment, as in public utilities, transportation, health, and other industries. Poor-quality service due to unreliable equipment and poor maintenance is not caused by employees but by higher-level management. Poor maintenance appears to be caused by top-level management trying to save money rather than by poor performance of employees, although the latter can happen.

4. *Poor quality characteristics in the customer's view are not the same as the poor quality characteristics in the organization's view.* Poor quality to the customer involves such characteristics as behavior and attitudes of employees, the time factor reflected in promptness, and the price factor reflected in affordability and safety. The organization usually is not interested in any of these from the viewpoint of the customer. The organization is interested in reducing (if not eliminating) defects in purchased products, human errors everywhere, failures of all kinds, downtime on machinery and equipment, idle and lost time of employees, and customer complaints.

In any quality improvement program planned and implemented by an organization it is very important that full consideration be given to the quality characteristics with which the customer is concerned. It is recommended that before any program is started, a survey be made of all customers to determine in some detail just what quality characteristics they are concerned about.

5. *It is just as necessary to calculate the cost of poor quality to the customer as to determine the cost of quality to the organization.* Cost of quality to date has been concentrated on and limited to a company or organization. No one is interested in determining what poor-quality products and poor-quality service cost the customers. This is understandable. The purpose of calculating quality costs is to justify the existence of a quality program, of a quality department, of quality professionals. Quality cost experience shows that this program is cost-effective: the savings made in eliminating or reducing internal and external failures of all kinds, including defects, errors, and failures, are considerably greater than the cost of the quality program.

It is time, however, to calculate the cost to the customer of poor-quality products and services. These costs would include such items as loss of time, extra transportation costs, extra telephone costs, extra correspondence, extra travel, absence from work, unnecessary repair, and cost of injuries due to unsafe equipment and unsafe services.

6. *Some characteristics in services need to be stabilized and improved; most non-quality characteristics need to be driven to zero.* Examples of the first kind are

- time measurements that cannot be zero;
- absences;
- turnover;
- promotions;
- downtime on equipment and machinery;
- shipment time;
- time to do a job.

Examples of the second kind are

- human error;
- defects in purchased products;
- idle time;
- waiting time;
- unnecessary time;
- customer complaints;
- accidents;
- disasters;
- failures of equipment;
- unsafe conditions and equipment.

7. *We need to follow an empirical approach in implementing a quality improvement program in services.* This approach avoids wasting time on hunches, conjectures, assumptions, esoteric theories, or fallacies. It means collecting significant data and information at all key points, on each of the service components, at all customer contacts, and on all employees. Information can be obtained in many different ways:

- Direct observation of every service component;
- Customer appraisals—written and oral;
- Surveys of all customers;
- Surveys of all employees;
- Interviewing customers;
- Interviewing employees;
- Interviewing vendors;
- Observation of competitors' operations;
- Failure of equipment.

This should be a continuous process so that quality improvement is grounded in the realities of services—in behavior, activities, interactions, events, and incidents.

8. *Psychological aspects of quality, including fear, pride, and barriers, cannot be resolved by the usual methods.* Managers, supervisors, and professional specialists are not hired because they are good teachers or can solve psychological problems. Changes have to be brought about in a different way, not by the usual subject matter training course. To resolve these problems calls for changes in conditions, attitudes, behavior, supervision, communication, and relationships from adversary to co-worker. Solving these problems will not be easy. It is questionable whether some of them are ever "solved." Conflicts exist or arise which will be resolved with no more than a truce.

9. *Training and education have to be planned and implemented to reflect the unique aspects of service quality.* These aspects include the following:

- Psychological aspects are as important as managerial, economic, and statistical aspects.
- Quality of many services is determined by clerks, salespersons, technicians, and assistants.
- Quality of some services is determined by the reliability of equipment, so 100% reliability must be the goal and standard.
- These aspects call for specially designed courses and treatment as well as special teachers. The usual instructional courses are inadequate; they do not apply in many situations.

10. *Control time, cut costs, and please the customer.* Time is a major quality characteristic of service. The customer wants promptness: reduction in waiting and delay times and service times, elimination of excessive and unnecessary times. The company wants elimination of downtime on equipment, idle time of employees, and waiting time for work.

11. *Apply powerful techniques not used by Shewhart.* There are several very powerful techniques which were not discussed by Shewhart. These techniques are very important because they help correct faults in the system. They reveal problems hitherto undetected. They provide significant information never before available. These techniques include the following:

- Random time sampling (modern work sampling);
- Probability sample surveys and studies;
- Learning curve analysis;
- Exploratory time trends;
- Design of tests and experiments;
- Input/output analysis.

By these means problems are discovered. Problems are solved. They help make quality improvement an effective and never-ending undertaking.

12. *The place to start a quality control program is in a situation where nonquality may exist, or does exist.* A quality program can be started at one of many different places, such as one or more of the following:

- Where the work is being done;
- In a component of service operations;
- At customer contacts with the organization;
- Where failures occur;
- Where data are collected, compiled, analyzed, tabulated, or processed;
- Where managers, supervisors, and employees complain about problems or situations.

13. *Quality is determined by people, not by the type of organization.* If people are educated, oriented, motivated, and cooperating for quality, the usual

supervisor-employee structure will work successfully. The attitude of people is more important than the organization chart. With the proper attitudes the usual organization will improve quality, providing it has the technical assistance, guidance, and stimulation that it needs. With the proper attitudes and assistance in knowledge that it lacks, the usual organizational unit can become a quality improvement cell.

14. *A plateau on a learning curve may be mistaken for a condition of statistical control.* Where a job or task is new to the employee or employees and requires learning the job over a period of weeks or months, the learning curve situation exists. This means that as learning continues, errors are reduced and excessive time is eliminated.

Periods of no improvement occur, resulting in a plateau on the learning curve. This level stretch of time may be mistaken for a condition of statistical control. Experience with learning curves shows that there may be more than one plateau; more often there may be two, three, or even four, depending upon the length of the learning period. One 45-day learning-production curve had three plateaus.

Chapter 10

The Management of Quality

INITIATING A QUALITY PROGRAM

It is trite to state that quality cannot be managed until there is a quality program in existence. The first questions to ask are Who will start a movement toward quality? How will it be started? What form will it take? Where will the first steps be taken? What role does top management have in starting it? Once interest in quality develops, what steps will be taken to continue interest in quality and a quality program?

Quality is a new and revolutionary idea. It is not the old concept of something high-priced. It calls for new ways of thinking, applying new techniques, running a business a different way. It calls for new knowledge. It requires changing minds, adopting new concepts and ideas. This is bound to be a lengthy process. It means that the function of management itself has to change so that the goal is not just profits, but profits and quality.

Top management as well as senior managers may become interested in quality in many different ways. They may hear or read about it from the following sources:

- A newspaper such as the *Wall Street Journal* or *The New York Times;*
- A business magazine such as *Fortune* or *Business Week;*
- Literature on quality conferences conducted by Drs. Deming and Juran.
- Other top executives or managers;
- News of some successful quality project.

Some prevailing views that have to be overcome, or least modified, before a quality program can be started include the following:

1. *Quality increases costs.* This view confuses quality with high costs and high prices. The quality program reduces costs by getting rid of sources of costly non-quality operations, activities, and characteristics.

2. *Quality should not be too good because short life means more sales.* This is a common-sense view that backfires. Customers soon learn that short life means high life cycle costs, that the product is shoddy and of poor quality. They start buying a better-quality product. Sales decline; they do not increase.

3. *We already have the best-quality product or service.* The organization needs to survey customers, market, products, and services to prove it.

4. *Quality applies to products but not to services.* The first part of this book shows that while services are different from products, quality applies to services just as much as to products. The organization needs to survey its operations to discover how errors, wasted time, faulty data, customer complaints, and other sources are increasing costs.

5. *We do not need to be concerned about quality. Our sales department will take care of that.* Quality is built into products and services. This is not the job of the sales department.

6. *Quality is not cost-effective. It will cost more than the benefits received.* Numerous examples can be cited to show that this is not true.

7. *We do not have the additional resources needed to put such a program into effect.* What is needed is knowledge, not expensive capital investment.

Somehow these objections, and any others, have to be overcome before a start can be made in developing a quality program.

More than top-level officials must become interested in quality if an effective program is to be developed. Everyone will not only have to become interested in quality and make it an integral part of the management structure, but apply it daily to the improvement of company operations. Top-level management must take the lead in seeing that quality performance is "everybody's business." Even to make a start requires a lengthy process of exposure, orientation, training, and education.

The quality message must be carried to all five levels of the internal organization and spread throughout all levels:

- Top-level executives;
- Senior executives;
- Middle-managers;
- First-line supervisors;
- Employees.

The management of quality must be concerned with 11 groups of people— six inside the organization and five outside. All of these groups must be considered in organizing, planning, designing, and implementing a quality program. Clearly the most important outside group is the customers. The customers' needs, preferences, and specifications must be satisfied by the quality control program. The chart shows how the internal organization must be concerned with these five outside groups. (See Figure 10–1.)

Starting at the Top

It is necessary for top-level management to be committed and convinced if a quality improvement program is to apply to the entire company. They have to

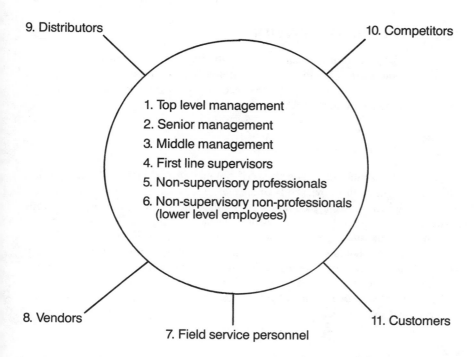

9. Distributors   10. Competitors

1. Top level management
2. Senior management
3. Middle management
4. First line supervisors
5. Non-supervisory professionals
6. Non-supervisory non-professionals
   (lower level employees)

8. Vendors   11. Customers

7. Field service personnel

Figure 10–1. **Eleven Groups of People Involved in Quality**

do more than approve. They have to push the program. They have to exert constant quality leadership. They have to see that quality thinking and action permeate every level of the company. This will require years of persistent effort. Without it the program stands a very good chance of failing.

Starting at the Bottom

A logical place to start applying quality concepts and quality control is at the working level, where problems are faced constantly, or places where customer contacts occur.

A significant problem that concerns an interested and cooperative supervisory group is a good place to start. These persons are conscious not only of problems but of ways that might be used to resolve them. Success here shows that quality works, and demonstrates what might be done on other problems and situations in other departments. These successful demonstrations are one of the best ways to convince doubting Thomases.

QUALITY ORGANIZATION

The quality function is organized in many ways. There seems to be no standard procedure, nor should one be expected because of the wide differences existing among organizations and the recent development of the field. Several forms of organization are described here briefly.

Quality Control Department

This is the traditional, older way of organizing for quality. It concentrates the quality function in the hands of specialists or trained professionals familiar with the quality control techniques of Walter Shewhart. In the beginning this was a natural way to handle the problem because of the highly technical nature of Shewhartian quality control, the fact that managers were not trained and not interested in mathematics or statistics, and the fact that only technically trained people could show that Shewhartian quality control worked successfully in the real world. Once this demonstration had been made in a wide variety of industries, it was easy to ignore the role of technique and start emphasizing engineering and management.

Quality Assurance Department

This was an extension of quality control but with the emphasis on the entire company and on the entire quality program. The purpose was to ensure that the quality program was not only in place but that it was operating according to plan and prescription. This led to a program of quality audits. There are examples showing where stress on quality assurance has led to the neglect of quality control.

Quality Council or Committee

The quality council is a recent development growing out of the emphasis on total quality control and encompassing the entire company or organization. It usually consists of senior managers appointed by top-level management. The duties of the quality council include the following:

- Setting quality policies for the entire company;
- Seeing that quality improvement teams are set up at lower levels;
- Giving constant support and encouragement to those at lower levels;
- Taking steps to see that the company has the technical capabilities and other resources to carry out a quality program;

- Seeing that quality improvement projects are part of a continuous plan and budget of the company;
- Taking steps to institutionalize quality improvement—seeing that the program has continuity.

Quality Teams

Quality teams have been introduced in connection with quality councils and the total quality control movement. These teams usually are interdepartmental but they can also be formed at each organizational level, such as a division or department. They can also be formed for special purposes. Some are similar to the usual task force, being disbanded once the project or problem is completed.

Teams work on problems with quality aspects. These problems can be interdepartmental and hence initiated by the quality council. In this way these teams work on correcting the faults of the system which only management can resolve. Members of the team are selected who can make a contribution and who have expertise in the particular area in which the problem falls. They meet regularly for the purpose of noting progress, discussing new problems, and hearing reports.

The functions of the team are similar to those of any organizational unit with specific functions:

- Identifying problems;
- Collecting data;
- Analyzing data;
- Diagnosing problems, or getting aid if problems are highly technical;
- Finding causes of trouble;
- Finding remedies which will remove causes; taking action;
- Following up to see if remedy is effective.

Quality Task Forces

These are groups which are set up to tackle and resolve an important company or organization problem or situation. They are always interdepartmental, consisting of one or more qualified members from each of several departments. The authorization comes from top-level officials. The task force is aware of the general problem but may lack detailed aspects, which may require more information from the top officials. The task force, headed by a chairman, plans the study, directs the collection of data, analyzes the data, summarizes the findings, and makes a report to top-level management. With qualified people and expertise to handle the technical aspects, the task force can be as effective as a quality team formed for the same purpose.

Quality Ideas

Quality ideas are really an outgrowth of the old suggestion system, but with radical changes with regard to how it is conducted and how suggestions are appraised and rewarded. The trouble with the suggestion box system was that management did not take an active part in it, did not publicize its importance, neglected its relation to quality, and concentrated only on how much money or time the suggestion would save.

When quality becomes everybody's business, suggestions for improving the quality of products and services at every level are of paramount importance. Under the new approach, quality ideas come from quality teams, from quality task forces, or individuals. These ideas may be the same as those that might have come from the old suggestion box, but management reviews each one, separates the better ones from the poorer ones, and takes steps to implement them. Some of these do more to save money than to improve quality of the product or service. They usually improve quality of performance by eliminating wasted time. In many offices this elimination of time may greatly improve the production of both product and service, and may lead to results in a more timely fashion.

Under a policy of quality ideas, employees at all levels are encouraged, stimulated, and rewarded for ideas that improve the quality of operations, data, performance, decisions, products, and services. Deliberate attempts are made to obtain ideas from those at the working levels where the work is done, where problems are frequent, and where ideas for improvement are most likely to occur. The people on the job are the ones who are most likely to have ideas about how to improve the procedures, methods, processes, and techniques being used. The problems beyond their scope are the technical ones, which require much more knowledge and capability.

It should not be overlooked that while a large number of quality ideas at the lowest level may be very productive and cost-saving, there is a limit to what can be accomplished this way. Problems of a complex technical nature cannot be solved in this way: only qualified professionals or technical specialists can do this.

MAJOR QUALITY GOALS FOR MANAGEMENT

Quality is to be managed with several basic goals or objectives in view. Nine are given below; every one of these is of great importance and calls for balanced attention. Top-level management and senior managers all must work toward the realization of these objectives by giving each one constant daily attention.

- Quality means strong and constant leadership from management.
- The company's goal must be to satisfy and please customers whether they are buying products or service.

- Quality means fostering and promoting employee growth and development at all levels. This means mastering both old and new knowledge relating to the job.
- At all times the emphasis must be on cooperation and teamwork at all levels.
- Everyone learns and applies quality control.
- There is a policy and practice of close cooperation with vendors (suppliers).
- It is assumed that everyone shall learn the basic statistical and non-statistical techniques and methods, and be able to use them effectively.
- A major policy of the company is continuously to promote innovation and better methods.
- Everyone shall be informed of all the major changes and events that are taking place in the company.
- An effective quality program has to be based on the collection and analysis of sound and accurate data and information at key points and for all kinds of quality characteristics.
- Steps shall be taken at all levels to see that the quality improvement program has permanence and continuity.

THE LIMITATIONS OF QUALITY CONTROL CIRCLES[1]

Quality control circles are subject to severe limitations. They have some serious built-in weaknesses. The "successes," such as those illustrated by the items listed below, greatly exaggerate the importance of the accomplishments. They were selected from the literature in no special order. They are divided into two groups where they would ordinarily fall: supervisory functions and office operations.

1. Supervisory functions:
   - Updating job descriptions;
   - Upgrading jobs;
   - Improving poor employee attitude;
   - Clarifying job instructions;
   - Processing new job requests;
   - Dealing with personal telephone calls.

2. Office operations:
   - Combining operations;
   - New training schedules;
   - Eliminating reports;
   - Choosing rubber bands vs. staples;

---

[1] Sources: A seminar on quality control circles attended by the author; articles and talks on the subject.

- Correcting teller machine failure;
- Reducing paper costs;
- Compiling glossary of bank terms;

- Processing bank checks;
- Handling customer inquiries.

These "projects" show that the emphasis is on minor, even trivial situations. A few could be significant, but on the whole they represent the simple comments that come from the suggestion box: type 10 carbons instead of 20, distribute five copies instead of 12, combine three forms into one. These "problems" no doubt represent changes and improvements that should be made, but they are of minor importance compared with the real quality problems that the company faces. These are small changes that could be made under any properly run organization without incurring the expense of installing a quality circle program with consultants, steering committees, facilitators, and leaders, and the disruption that such a program entails. The quality control circle program, however, suffers from many more weaknesses, such as the following:

1. It is restricted to special problems and situations within a local area. It cannot do anything about correcting the faults of the system, where the real problems lie.

2. It lacks the technical capability to deal with problems. It therefore has no capability to identify problems, let alone analyze and solve them.

3. It lacks statistical capability. It has to be taught simple statistics, which employees should know when they are hired. Learning simple statistics does not mean that they know how to apply them.

4. The organization should not have to waste time and money training employees in statistics and how to apply them to the company's problems. They should be hired with this knowledge. If this is done, then there is no need for a quality circle.

5. This means that employees lack both depth and breadth in the field of statistical techniques and therefore can be of no help in solving more difficult problems involving quality. Examples are sample surveys and random time sampling, input/output analysis, learning curve analysis, and process control of clerical work.

6. There are conflicting jurisdictions. It is not the job of a quality control circle to write or revise job descriptions for anyone. This is the job of higher-level people who know the policies, goals, and specific functions on the one hand, and the job requirements to meet these goals on the other.

7. The job descriptions of those who are members of a quality control circle are never mentioned or described. It appears as if all of their jobs are the same, although probably they are never put in written form, or that the work in the circle is entirely separate from the work listed on a job description. There are a lot of unanswered questions here. Why are eight to 10 persons needed in a quality circle when only one, two, or three could do the same job?

8. The quality circle idea is clearly based on the assumption, which may be

false in many if not most instances, that the present organization is wrong, that the supervisor is incompetent, and that the employees are being squelched.

9. Finally, quality circles, with their emphasis on six statistical methods plus cause-and-effect diagrams, are not applicable as such to a large number of industries which do not use the common Shewhartian statistical techniques. These industries include chemicals, paper, rugs, wire, textiles, carpets, job shops, and bulk commodities. These industries never could use the $\bar{x}$ and R charts and other charts described by Shewhart. Instead they had to turn to other statistical techniques which Shewhart did not describe or did not emphasize. These techniques include the following:

- Design of tests;
- Design of experiments;
- Multiple regression;
- Analysis of variance;
- Evolutionary operations;
- Probability sample studies and surveys;
- Random time sampling (modern work sampling);
- Learning curve analysis;
- Input/output analysis.

THE RISE AND DECLINE OF QUALITY CONTROL CIRCLES

The most recent information on quality circles is not very encouraging. Juran[2] states that quality circles in this country are on a decline for three reasons:

- The quality control circle is a separate entity, not integrated with the management structure or function.
- Managers are not trained in quality and hence are unable to make effective use of the quality circle. Responsibility is delegated to facilitators, leaders, and consultants.
- There is no central coordination or guidance relative to quality circle concepts, implementation, applications, and problems.

Juran concludes, however, that as managers learn how to manage quality, there is likely to be a revival of interest in quality circles.

Another source reports that 70 percent of all quality circles eventually fail for several major reasons:[3]

---

[2] J. M. Juran, "QC Circles in the West," *Quality Progress,* September 1987, pp. 60–61.

[3] T. C. Bagwell, "Quality Circles: Two Keys to Success," *Quality Progress,* September 1987, pp. 57–59.

- Lack of preparation: resistance, opposition, objection;
- Lack of appropriate technical knowledge;
- Lack of appropriate materials: confusing content, factory examples;
- Lack of appropriate instruction: teaching is inadequate;
- Too drastic a change from current routines and practice;
- Facilitators and others create conflicts with managers and supervisors; the latter may get the feeling that they are "outsiders";
- No initial survey of attitude toward quality circle and its acceptance;
- Persons involved including managers and supervisors are not convinced of its value, especially on a continuing basis.

What this shows is that setting up some parallel or competitive organizational structure has inherent weaknesses that almost doom it to failure from the start. This is because quality is a people-intensive problem, and people are the key to success or failure.

Until the people involved are convinced, trained, educated, and motivated in quality, no structure of any kind will work. People have to accept quality, recognize its value, and work continuously to attain it if a quality improvement program is to succeed.

When the people problem is solved, the usual organizational structure will work just as well, if not better, than some different and more complex structure.

Form Versus Substance

Organization stresses form or arrangement. It is not the form of organizational units, administrative divisions, or special groups such as a quality control circle, a quality council, a quality team, or a quality task force that really counts. It is the substance. When substance is missing, forms are ineffective shells of people. That is why they fail or are mere substitutes for the real thing.

What is needed is people with attitudes and knowledge, with appropriate skills and abilities, with drive and motivation, with innovations and improvements, with effective techniques and methods and processes—the substance of quality. Both Dr. Deming and Professor Ishikawa stress that quality is concerned with knowledge and is a knowledge revolution. This is the substance of quality and a quality improvement program, but it is always people who have the knowledge, who have to use it, who have to apply it to problems, who have to build quality into products and services. There is no special reason why a new form of organization or a new form of organization chart has to be used to start, develop, and maintain a quality program. There is no reason if managers, supervisors, and employees are properly trained and educated in quality improvement and how to attain it.

QUALITY PLANNING

Quality planning means laying out the series of steps for a quality program. It is a set of guidelines, like a blueprint. It is a road map that lays out the route from origin to destination. The following is a general form; the special planning needed for quality improvement is discussed later:

1. Determine quality *goals* or objectives.
2. Base these goals on identification of *customer needs.*
3. Lay out the *process* required to meet these goals.
4. Provide the *resources* needed to carry out this process.
5. Measure *progress* made toward meeting these goals.
6. Identify *problems* or trouble spots in the process.
7. *Diagnose* problems and isolate causes.
8. Take *action* needed to resolve problem.
9. *Follow up* to see that remedy or action is effective.
10. Plan for *continuous quality improvement.*

Dr. Deming uses a very abbreviated plan that is simple but effective, the PDCA plan:

1. Planning;
2. Doing;
3. Checking;
4. Action.

This plan can be described in more detail in connection with quality planning for a service company (See Figure 10–2):

1. Identify the specific character and variety of customer needs.
2. Translate these needs into specific goals.
3. Lay out the components of each service operation.
4. Identify the activities of each component.
5. Plan to have the resources necessary for each of these activities.
6. Provide for measuring progress toward goal in each component.
7. Plan to identify problems and troubles in each component.
8. Provide for taking immediate action to remedy any situation.
9. Follow up to see that the situation has been corrected.
10. Plan for continuous quality improvement by service component.

PUTTING THE QUALITY PLAN INTO EFFECT

The quality plan should be put into writing with detailed explanations so that the operating people can put it into effect. This will be greatly facilitated if operating people have representatives on the quality planning committee.

Figure 10–2. **Quality Management in Services**

Regardless of the type of organization used, the first step of supervisors and managers is to make a survey to identify problems and troubles that need attention. This will not be hard since they are already aware of some of these problems and troubles. A section or departmental survey will reveal a list of chronic and special difficulties that need attention. A similar companywide survey will reveal interdepartmental problems that require the organization of a task force or a quality team to handle them. Actually, the task force or the quality team may make the survey in the first place.

The second step is to list these problems in order of their importance so that the most important can be tackled first. An alert manager or supervisor will be aware of some of these problems and troubles even before any study is made. Some of them will already be receiving attention from managers and supervisors.

The third step is to concentrate on an important problem and allocate the required resources to it. This means analyzing the problem, designing and implementing an effective method of collecting good-quality data, interpreting the data, and isolating critical findings. Then it is necessary to determine causes, propose remedies, take appropriate actions, and find those steps which eliminate the cause if the cause is not obvious.

In many cases the collection and interpretation of the data will not only answer a significant question (e.g., how big is it?) but will reveal a new problem that management did not know existed before (such as excessive waiting time). This new problem may require immediate action from both the supervisor and the higher-level manager.

In any event the purpose of the quality plan will be to get rid of non-quality characteristics such as defects, errors, wasted time, unacceptable behavior and attitudes, customer complaints, lost customers, biased and misleading data, and failures.

Some Basic Requirements

Before an organization can be fully operative in putting a quality program into effect, certain conditions and requirements must be met. The major ones are as follows:

- Managerial capability;
- Statistical capability;
- Nonstatistical technical capability;
- Supervisory capability;
- Problem-solving capability;
- Provision for collection of good-quality data;
- An effective communications network;
- Surveys of customer needs and preferences;
- Provision for surveying lost customers;
- Provision for analyzing customer complaints and resolving them;
- Provision for close, cooperative relations with vendors;
- Provision for employee growth and development, for discussion and resolution of all grievances, for reporting new ideas and improvements.

Management Modes of Operation

The functions of management, as usually defined, are four in number, and they apply to the quality program just as to other programs: to plan, to direct, to delegate, and to appraise.

Over the years some special formulas have been invented to stress a certain approach to management:

- Management by exception (MBE): This means that managers concentrate on deviations from rules, regulations, expectations, and standards. This can mean managers that are spending most of their time putting out fires. Quality suffers.

- Management by objective (MBO): This means setting up a list of objectives and concentrating attention on these. They may include sales, profits, share of the market, reducing costs, or buying by the price tag. Quality can easily be ignored.
- Management by wandering around (MBWA): This expression seems to have originated with Hewlett Packard. It means that managers and officials walk around where operations are going on and talk with the employees. This practice is effective if problems are discussed and if workers are commended, stimulated, and listened to. It is not effective but only a waste of time if managers simply walk around observing what is going on and nodding to workers here and there.
- Management by personal association (MPA): This includes the walking-around manager, but with a big difference. The purpose is not just to observe what is going on but to take a personal interest in each worker, to talk with them, and to ask for their suggestions for changes and improvements. MPA is for the purpose of letting workers know that managers do care about what is being done, and that cooperation and two-way communication are imperative for an effective operation.

An effective management mode or style aims at leadership. Leadership means getting others to do the following:

- Understand the route that the company is taking to reach company goals;
- Work toward these goals;
- Innovate, originate, invent, and improve;
- Get results that are important and pertinent;
- Work as a team by cooperating, helping, and sharing;
- Strive toward improvement and betterment.

Qualifications of Managers, Professionals, and Supervisors

The success of the quality plan depends upon the managers, professionals, and supervisors who engage in the day-by-day processing and technical work. Qualifications of major importance are the following abilities:

- To explain what quality means;
- To identify quality problems;
- To collect and analyze good-quality data;
- To assemble and allocate the resources needed;
- To diagnose problems and find causes;
- To find remedies and correctives;
- To hire and train competent assistants;
- To survey customers and identify their needs and views;
- To stimulate employee growth and teamwork;
- To reward and commend employee accomplishments and achievements;

- To resolve employee complaints and grievances;
- To promote good, clear communication everywhere;
- To avoid conflict by promoting good personal relations;
- To give credit and recognition where credit is due.

QUALITY CONTROL

The concept and principles of statistical quality control, or more simply, quality control, originated with Walter Shewhart of the Bell Telephone Laboratories in 1924. The purpose was to devise a method which made it possible to separate chance causes in manufacturing from assignable causes which could be eliminated. Eliminating assignable causes meant that the characteristic was now subject only to random variations, which could be measured and could create a predictable situation. The emphasis was on stabilizing a measurement because the value of this measurement was prescribed in the manufacturing specifications.

In manufacturing, quality control means taking the steps necessary to stabilize a count or a measurement at an acceptable level. In services there are also measurements or counts, but in many cases the goal is not to stabilize the measurement or count at some acceptable average but to drive the value down to zero. Examples of measurements are absenteeism, delivery time, time to do a job, service times, and billing time.

In connection with defects in purchased products, human errors, lost and wasted time, unacceptable behavior and attitudes, customer complaints, losses, and damages, the goal is not to stabilize a value at some level but to drive these values continuously toward zero. The only acceptable goal is zero, even though it is never reached. These sources of waste are controlled by getting rid of them.

Techniques used for statistical control include the following, which are used most often:[4]

1. $\bar{x}$ chart for control of means;
2. R chart for control of variability;
3. p chart for the control of proportions or percentages;
4. np chart for the control of a binomial count;
5. c chart for the control of a Poisson count.

APPRAISAL

First goals are set, then plans are made to attain these goals, then the plans are put into effect. The next step is to ensure that everything is working as

---

[4]For a detailed discussion of these charts see E. L. Grant and R. S. Leavenworth, *Statistical Quality Control*, Fourth Edition (New York: McGraw-Hill, 1972).

planned. This brings management to the final step—appraisal or evaluation. The function of appraisal involves taking such steps as the following:

- Comparing actual results with expected results;
- Determining what progress has been made;
- Studying the extent to which non-quality characteristics and quality costs have been reduced;
- Examining trend of volume and quality of output;
- Observing what improvements have been made;
- Observing actions that should be taken;
- Examining growth of managers and supervisors;
- Examining improvement of processes;
- Seeing whether things are being done right;
- Examining performance of persons at all levels: managers, supervisors, employees;
- If some new procedure has been introduced, such as quality circles, determining what they have accomplished and achieved;
- Examining the trend and nature of customer complaints; improvements;
- Examining the nature and trend of relations with vendors; improvements.

Provision has to be made to obtain data on a periodic basis and to see that goals are being reached, that plans are being carried out as formulated, and that critical problems are being solved. The methods used to obtain the necessary information include the following, mainly management reports, departmental reports, and personal observation.

Reports:

- Production reports;
- Quality reports;
- Progress reports;
- Inspection reports;
- Financial reports; cost of quality reports;
- Quality audit;
- Financial audit;
- Other audits.

Personal contacts:

- Customer complaints;
- Employee surveys;
- Management by personal association;
- Management by wandering around;
- Personal customer surveys;
- Vendor surveys;
- Personal observation.

QUALITY IMPROVEMENT

Management needs to plan for a program of continuous quality improvement. At the present time these improvements take two general forms:

1. Improvements brought about by applying conventional numerical or statistical techniques. This approach can unearth all kinds of problems and critical situations that management does not know it has.

2. Improvements that are procedural and organizational in character and require little or no technical knowledge. They deal with simple routine procedures, structure, organization, and arrangements.

Examples of these two approaches to improvement are given below.

Numerical or Statistical

These methods require not only technical knowledge but how to apply them to the problems of management. The most common are the following:

- Time charts of errors, defects, waiting times, etc.;
- Control charts for measurements;
- Control charts for counts or frequencies;
- Probability sample surveys;
- Designed tests and experiments;
- Frequency distributions;
- Frequency distributions of identicals: variability doing the same thing;
- Regression control, including input/output analysis.

Nonquantitative Procedural and Organizational

These are simple changes in routines and organization as follows:

- Reduction in number of copies of memos, letters, reports, etc.;
- Reduction in number of clearances, approvals, signatures, etc.;
- Elimination of excess layers of organization;
- Shifting inspectors and others to direct production;
- Changing physical arrangements: rooms, equipment, space, lighting;
- Changing the organization: simplification, streamlining, etc.;
- Introducing preventive maintenance on all equipment, other facilities;
- Making better use of space.

Planning for Continuity

Management needs to plan for continuity in the quality improvement program. This calls for the annual provision and support of such a program. Several steps can be taken to insure this:

1. An annual quality improvement budget, including specific projects and resources required to support it;
2. A list of quality improvement projects or problems from each department, with a proposed time schedule;
3. A comprehensive survey of *all* customers to improve customer service, to reduce customer complaints and dissatisfaction, to interview lost customers, and to learn the reasons for losing them;
4. Review of all training courses, including provisions for new courses to improve quality performance at all levels;
5. Considering appraising managers and supervisors, in part at least, in terms of their contributions to quality improvement;
6. Developing a better system of estimating costs of non-quality and taking steps to reduce, if not eliminate, all such sources;
7. Continuing to take steps to reduce errors, defects, lost and wasted time, poor-quality data, and unacceptable behavior and attitudes toward customers and employees;
8. Reducing the cost of defects in purchased products and services;
9. Cooperating more closely with vendors on products so that receiving inspection can be reduced if not eliminated;
10. Providing for the necessary permanent human and equipment capabilities that are required to tackle these problems, carry out these projects, find causes, and apply remedies. Continuity requires permanent high-class capabilities.

THE QUALITY PERFORMANCE BUDGET OFFICE

Deming's 14 Points call for top-level management to establish a constant purpose aimed at a continuous improvement of quality of products and services. A management structure has to be set up to maintain continuity of the constant purpose and its implementation. Juran calls for continuity of the quality improvement program by the institutionalizing of what he calls the quality trilogy—quality planning, quality control, and quality improvement. Juran wants quality to be given the same attention and place in the company that financial planning receives.

The quality performance budget office is one way to serve this purpose. It gives quality high-level recognition and guarantees the continuity of the quality improvement program. Its major functions may be listed as follows:

1. It represents top-level management although it may be under a top-level quality council or quality committee.
2. It works closely with all departments and offices in planning, developing, and implementing quality improvement plans, programs, projects, and improvements.

3. It coordinates the quality improvement plans and projects of all departments and offices.

4. It receives, analyzes, and summarizes all problems, situations, and projects that are submitted as candidates for the overall company quality improvement program for the next year.

5. It estimates, in cooperation with heads of departments and offices, the resources needed for the various programs and projects.

6. In cooperation with heads of departments and offices, it sets priorities on quality improvement programs and projects.

7. It works with the financial budget office to obtain approval for the top-priority projects agreed upon.

8. It makes costs of quality studies with the cooperation of department and office heads, so that the financial budget office will have actual evidence of the direct money value to be saved by implementing the proposed quality projects.

WHY STATISTICIANS HAVE DIFFICULTY WITH INFLUENCING TOP MANAGEMENT

A paper discussing Dr. Deming's 14 Points calls attention to the implications of these points for the professional statistician. The major obligation of the statistician is to develop a new climate in management and to transform management as laid down in the 14 points.[5]

Dr. Deming says, "A long thorny road lies ahead." A thorny road lies ahead for the professional statistician who tries to reconstruct top-level management to stress not only the commitment to quality but its attainment. The following observations are based on actual experiences in trying to convince top-level management and top-level professionals that probability sampling and quality control on the one hand, and statistics on the other, work successfully in the real world.

1. Top-level managers and professionals are opposed to probability sampling, statistical quality control, and statistics. To them, statistics means not a science but a compilation of numbers, such as baseball statistics. To them, sampling means what the pollsters have been doing since the 1930s and what they read in *The New York Times* or *The Washington Post*. To them, quality control is something strange, something they have never heard of before. Like people generally, they do not like to accept something new and strange. Several very effective applications have to be made before they will accept these new concepts and this new science.

---

[5] B. Joiner, "The Key Role of Statisticians in the Transformation of North American Industry," *The American Statistician*, August 1985, Vol. 39, No. 3, pp. 224–234.

2. The opposition to probability sampling takes many forms. "It is a refinement that we do not need. It will upset our operations. It will not give the detailed data we now have. It will be too costly. It will be difficult to teach to our employees."

3. The opposition to statistical quality control is even stronger, making it much more difficult even to get one project started. Quality control meets the problem of error head on, and management doesn't want to do this. "Errors cancel out. Errors aren't important. As for quality control, that's all right in manufacturing telephone parts or even in steel mills, but it doesn't apply to our company or to our agency. We already have quality control." (They confuse inspection and review with quality control.) "This is not the proper time to introduce quality control." (Of course the proper time never comes, although quality control is needed immediately.)

4. The statisticians have to compete with other specialists for attention, budget, space, manpower, and facilities. These other specialists include lawyers, accountants, economists, engineers, computer people, and a host of others. The statisticians are far down on the totem pole; the older and better-established professions and specialties rank higher and have more clout. All of these represent competition that will have to be overcome. Are statisticians equal to the task? Are they equal to the challenge?

5. Statisticians are usually three, four, or five layers of organization below the top. These layers are a real barrier. They prevent the statistician from ever communicating with top-level officials directly. All communications have to be relayed through two, three, or four layers of organization. This means that communications may never get anywhere near the top officials. All the statisticians can do is what was often done in the past: develop and apply probability sampling and quality control to various projects which come under their jurisdiction. They can also spread the advantages of these techniques to higher levels; the best way is successful demonstrations that these concepts and techniques apply to the problems of the company or agency.

6. The fact that statisticians are placed at lower levels of the organization shows the low value placed on the statistician's services, and the poor image he or she has relative to other professions. It should be noted that high-level officials and professionals do not get to the top or even near it because they studied mathematics, statistics, or probability in college. Indeed, high-level executives are the ones who avoided all such courses when they were in college. The statistician already has two strikes before he or she even begins to try to make a change and an improvement in what management is doing. This is not surprising. Many people in the quality profession itself believe that statistics has received far too much attention. They believe that management is the most important factor in quality control. Very few refer to Shewhart's statistical quality control anymore. Even in quality work itself there are those who want to get rid of statistics.

7. The effectiveness of the statisticians will depend upon how the job is

defined and how the statistical work is carried out. Three different approaches to the job are described: 1) the sitting consultant, 2) the roving consultant, and 3) the statistical practitioner in operations.

Many statisticians are hired to act as consultants to managers and professionals. If the consultant sits in an office waiting to be called, he or she will not be able to accomplish much in the way of influencing management. The Federal Communications Commission, in response to a recommendation by the President's Commission on Statistics, wrote, "We call in the statistician when we need him." The entire commission consisted of lawyers. How can they call in a statistician when they don't know what a statistical problem is? This is what can happen to a statistician, especially to a consultant. He can be hired as a consultant and then seldom be consulted. Another very significant weakness of a consultant is that his advice can be ignored; management is under no obligation to accept the consultant's recommendations.

If the consultant is to be effective, he or she needs to roam all over the place hunting for statistical problems, identifying projects with statistical applications, and spreading the advantages of probability sampling, quality control, and other aspects of statistics. The job should be that of the roving consultant hunting for problems which management wants solved or doesn't even know about. Here, as elsewhere, the statistician works on management's problems, not on the statistical problems of the statistician.

The statistical practitioners in operations are in a much better position to influence what management is doing. They are in the midst of the work. They see and hear about the problems that management faces. They work directly with others—managers, professionals, and specialists. They are on task forces. They are designing samples to get good data so management can make better decisions. They can demonstrate that statistics work. They can demonstrate the advantages of sampling, quality control, and other aspects of applied statistics. Thus they are in a position to influence many ways in which management operates.

8. If statisticians want to play around with data that interest them, techniques they have a special attachment for, or problems in mathematical statistics they would like to work on, this is not the place for them. This is not the climate that management needs. The statisticians' work has to be not in their interests, but in management's. It has to be not in esoteric theory, but in everyday statistical practice. Many of those who take advanced degrees in statistics may not find this type of work to their liking. Certainly this type of work is not reflected in current statistical journals.

9. The climate to which Dr. Deming refers will certainly include the following. Hence the statistician, to the maximum extent possible, will work toward attaining the following on a continuous basis:

• Quality performance for everyone: prevention of errors, defects, faults, and mistakes;

- Separating and distinguishing system errors and defects from individual errors and defects;
- Seeing that corrective action is taken for system errors and defects. Seeing that appropriate corrective actions are taken for special errors and defects;
- Working continuously for the acceptance and use across the entire company or agency of probability sampling, statistical quality control, and other parts of statistical science;
- Isolating, identifying, discussing, and helping to solve statistical problems wherever they exist in the company or agency;
- Describing the acceptable-quality data that have to be collected and analyzed as a result of problem analysis;
- Stressing the need to start with an analysis of management's problems, not with data; that the data arise out of problem analysis;
- Emphasizing the importance of collecting acceptable-quality data. Otherwise inferences and decisions may be false, and actions ineffective, if not futile and misleading;
- Identifying areas, problems, and projects where sampling and quality control and other techniques can be used effectively. Designing and implementing sample studies, quality control programs and applications, tests, and experiments. Showing how these methods can be used effectively and successfully in a manner superior to what management is now using.
- Using data collection, such as random time sampling and sample surveys, to discover problems.

10. Personal conflicts will have to be resolved. Personal relationships will be a real problem. In trying to influence management, conflicts are bound to arise from several sources. There is no guarantee that all of the statisticians will agree with the Deming program. If the computer unit has an interest in statistics, and many of them have, a jurisdictional dispute will arise immediately. Fears that the new approach may affect status and promotions will lead to strong opposition. Opposition will increase as the influences and the power of the statistician grow. Envy and jealousy from professionals and managers will need to be faced. Personality clashes are to be expected. There will be those who will fight to stop the program, both openly and secretly. It will take time—considerable time—to obtain the acceptance, confidence, and cooperation of others. The statistician will have more than departmental barriers to overcome. Patience and good-natured acceptance of rebuffs will be needed. The statistician will have to demonstrate several successful and important applications to management's problems. He or she will need to present the program and its merits by talking on every available occasion. He or she will need to present success stories in writing on a continuous basis and on every occasion. The approach and the emphasis should always be on a cooperative teamwork basis. The last thing the statistician wants to do is claim credit for any

success; the best approach is to keep silent or give credit to the team, where it properly belongs.

STATISTICS IN QUALITY MANAGEMENT

The statistician's role in quality improvement has attracted considerable attention since Dr. Deming has written two books and given periodic seminars on statistics in quality control and the need for a new managerial climate in quality.[6] These papers and others describe the role of the statistician and how he or she should change management, but there is no discussion of the problems and difficulties that are encountered when the statistician tries to put these ideas into practice. The real problem of implementation is ignored. Some of these difficulties which arise in actual practice will now be described briefly. The approach is that of the statistical practitioner who has had decades of experience as a supervisory mathematical statistician.

1. The statistician's job is to help management solve statistical problems anywhere in the organization. This cannot be done until management is convinced that statistics is a useful and powerful science that can solve management problems successfully. First the statistician has to convince management by actual performance that statistics should be accepted and applied to statistical problems wherever they exist. Not only managers but nonmanagerial professionals have to be convinced to the extent that they accept statistics as desirable. This is not easy to do, as those who have tried it know.

2. It is not the statistician's job to spend time trying to make everyone in the organization "statistically minded." Get them to accept statistics as useful and better than what they are now using. The statistical practitioner should explain statistics only to the extent that it is needed to do the job for which he was hired. He should not waste his time teaching simple statistics to employees, supervisors, and managers. His time is too valuable and costly to the organization. Some other less costly ways should be used if this is deemed important. The reality has to be faced: large numbers of managers, supervisors, and employees are not interested in "statistical mindedness" or in anything connected with a course in statistics. They have their own subject matter specialties. The goal of the statistician is to show these people by example and demonstrations that it is to their advantage to accept statistics, if not to appreciate it.

---

[6] G. J. Hahn and T. J. Boardman, "The Statistician's Role in Quality Improvement," *Amstate News,* March 1985, pp. 5–8. Hahn and Boardman are chairman and vice-chairman respectively of the ASA Committee on Quality and Productivity. See also B. Joiner, "The Key Role of Statisticians in the Transformation of North American Industry," *The American Statistician,* August 1985, Vol. 39, No. 3 pp. 224–227.

There is another danger in teaching everyone statistics, a danger encountered in practice. A few persons with a little statistical training become "experts" and go out on their own, creating a statistical mess that a competent statistician has to clean up. A little learning is a dangerous thing, wrote the poet.

3. The statistician can rarely influence decisions made by high-level officials. The exception is the case where the top-level decision depends upon data and information from a nationwide or key sample study, from a critical experiment, or from other data where statistical interpretation is necessary.

Otherwise top-level officials couldn't care less about statistics. The reasons are obvious. Their thinking is dominated by money (financial officials), figures (accountants), legal matters (lawyers), sales trends (sales manager), production (production managers), and future conditions (economists). It will be exceedingly difficult for the statistician to find a place in this management style. It will not be easy to get them interested in variability, quality, and even quality costs, let alone sampling and other aspects of statistics. To get their attention will require one or more demonstrations that statistics saves money, reduces costs, improves production, or solves a problem which is very important to them.

4. The statistician can have direct influence on several of Dr. Deming's 14 Points. Quality today is dominated by a discussion of plans and how they change, or should change, the attitudes and behavior of top-level management and those at lower levels. Nothing is said or written about how these plans are to be put into effect. Nothing is said about the countless problems encountered when a practitioner tries to implement these plans. Any top-level manager, middle manager, supervisor, or professional, whether a statistician or not, will encounter a host of extremely difficult problems and obstacles.

The following points appear to be those of Dr. Deming's 14 Points about which a professional practitioner in statistics can have some direct influence, if he or she is allowed the freedom to observe, study, and analyze.

Point 3. Mass inspection:	This involves sample inspection of lots or 100 percent inspection.
Point 4. Buying by the price tag:	This involves quality as well as price. This involves purchasing and the vendor, with emphasis on quality control.
Point 5. Discovering problems across the organization:	The statistician periodically makes surveys to discover statistical problems.
Point 6. Training employees:	Teaching use of statistics on the job.
Point 7. Training supervisors:	Teaching use of statistics in supervision.

Point 11. Abolishing work standards: Using random time sampling to obtain estimates of actual work time and costs.

Point 13. Education: Teaching new and better methods in statistics as applied to production of products and services.

5. The statistician is very limited in his or her ability to create a new management climate. Creating a new management climate is a fine-sounding objective, but very difficult to attain. The reasons are not hard to find, and are as follows:

- It calls for revolutionary changes.
- Management has to change its goals, attitudes, thinking, and behavior.
- Management has to change its thinking about sales and profits.
- Management has to change its attitude toward customers.
- Management has to change its attitude toward design and production of a product or service.
- Management has to change its attitude toward the role played by employees.
- Management has to learn a new way to manage: to lead rather than give orders. It has to learn a new mode of operation.

The practitioner in statistics has a new job, but not the one usually propounded. The practitioner has to aim at gaining acceptance for statistics and an appreciation of statistics as a powerful, versatile science that is useful to management. This is done by a series of successful projects and problems: a nationwide sample study, a probability sample to improve sample evidence in legal proceedings, collecting good data instead of bad, designing an effective test or experiment, doing a statistical job much better than it is now being done in the organization.

A new management climate is not enough. Such a change must be accompanied simultaneously by a new professional climate. Opposition to quality improvement can be just as strong from professional specialists as from top-level and senior managers. The value and success of quality and statistics must be demonstrated successfully to these professionals, just as they are to others.

6. Knowledge of the basics in some other subject matter may or may not be necessary. If the statistical work of the practitioner is limited to one narrow field and if all of his work is in this field, it pays to become familiar with the subject matter of this field. Biostatistics is an example.

In many organizations and in many jobs, the statistical problems may range over a wide variety of subject matter fields. An example is the problem of freight car shortages, which involves law, finance, transportation, traffic, economics, and accounting.

In another situation the statistical problems do not involve knowledge of the subject matter involved, since the statistical problems can be solved with little or no help from subject matter specialists. The field of taxes is an example. The statistician simply learns how to ask the right questions of the experts in the field. (This applies to any field.) The experts usually do not have the information the statistician needs to design probability samples and analyze the data. One basic characteristic which is always missing is a measure of variability. Nothing is available but averages, totals, and percentages. These are the measures on which professional specialists concentrate; measures of variability such as the frequency distribution, the variance, the standard deviation, and even the range are missing.

The worship of the average and the percentage has led to this sad state of affairs. This is the established practice of economists and others in the media. Average salaries are given, but never the distribution by amount of salary. The same is true of other characteristics such as wages, ages, cost per mile to own and run an automobile, taxes, income, sales, price of a house, and numerous other variables.

7. Statistical quality control has led, and can lead, to improvements. It is misleading, as now stated, to limit the use of statistical quality control to the detection of erratic and unimportant sources of variation. Statistical quality control charts improved quality from the start. This is why it was successful. This is why the periodical *Industrial Quality Control* is full of examples of improvements made by using the control charts. The diagram shows why (see Figure 10–3). Statistical quality control brought order out of the chaotic inspection systems that were used previously. We cite three cases which show how these quality improvements were made.

Case 1. The use of a control chart in a cannery showed that a 12-ounce can of sauerkraut was really being filled with 14 to 15 ounces. Action was taken to change the method of filling these cans so that the fill would be nearer to 12 ounces. A possible goal was to shoot for an average of 12.5 ounces with a greatly reduced variability. (Source: Quality conference at the University of Maryland)

Case 2. A study at a steel mill showed that considerable excess weight was being put into the steel ingots. A quality control chart was used to study the problem and to eliminate causes of this excess weight. As a result, the average weight of the ingots was brought closer to about 5200 pounds. The savings was $175,000. (Source: Wade Weaver, Republic Steel, in an article in *Industrial Quality Control*)

Case 3. The president of Deere and Company, manufacturers of agricultural implements, reported that they had an elaborate inspection system for the purpose of building quality into their products. They collected and accumulated a mass of inspection reports, but nothing seemed to be done with them. These reports

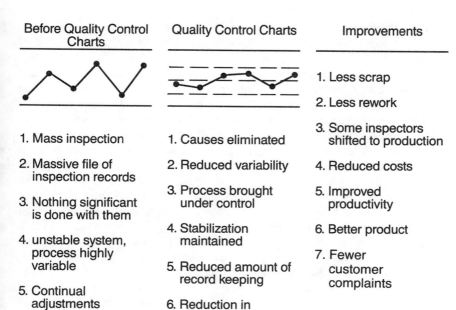

Before Quality Control Charts	Quality Control Charts	Improvements
1. Mass inspection	1. Causes eliminated	1. Less scrap
2. Massive file of inspection records	2. Reduced variability	2. Less rework
3. Nothing significant is done with them	3. Process brought under control	3. Some inspectors shifted to production
4. unstable system, process highly variable	4. Stabilization maintained	4. Reduced costs
5. Continual adjustments	5. Reduced amount of record keeping	5. Improved productivity
	6. Reduction in inspection	6. Better product
		7. Fewer customer complaints

Figure 10–3. **Statistical Quality Control Charts of Purchased Products Lead to Improvements**

did not result in any actions to reduce the defects. They simply went into the files with little or no action. When statistical quality control charts were introduced, all of this changed. Inspection records from the charts were studied to identify causes and eliminate them. As a result the processes were brought under control. Scrap and rework were reduced. Fewer inspectors were needed; some were shifted to production. Costs were reduced and the quality of the product improved. The president was very enthusiastic about how statistical quality control had improved their system of inspection. (Source: a talk and a paper in *Industrial Quality Control*)

8. The difference between enumerative and analytic studies is blurred in practice. A one-time sample, the enumerative study, may field significant management information even though that information is out of date as soon as it is selected. These one-time samples include health studies, tax audits of Form 1040, freight car shortage studies, studies of those 65 years of age and older, and many more. The results may be useful for future years for several reasons:

- The frame changes very little from year to year.
- The situation or practice needing correction will continue regardless of the frame or population. An example is claiming aliens as exemptions on federal income tax returns.

- The characteristics under study change very little, even though the frame or the population changes. An example is freight car shortages in the Midwest.
- The relationship between two variables x and y does not change even though conditions change drastically. During World War II scores of commodities followed a pre-war pattern, much to the surprise of some economists.[7]
- Management can operate much better with data subject to possibly 5 to 10 percent error than with no data at all, where errors in decisions may be 25 to 50 percent or even 100 percent. For example, a well-designed nationwide sample study of those 65 years of age and older would put to rest a whole host of conjectures, suppositions, misinformation, and false statements. The study would reveal significant differences; now all of these persons (about 30 million) are put in the same pigeonhole. Something like the following would give the needed data; one well-designed sample study is all that is needed. Working for pay: living in own house, apartment, other. Not working for pay, able to take care of self: living in own house, apartment, other. Not able to take care of self: living in nursing home, with relatives, with friends, at home using home care, other. This factual information would put to rest most of the broad-brush generalizations of gerontologists, geriatricians, and millions of others.

HOW A COMPANY'S ERROR AND EMPLOYEES' BEHAVIOR LED TO A LOST CUSTOMER[8]

1. The Situation:
    - This transaction involves a large retail store with branches in several cities.
    - The customer, who has been doing business with this store for 12 years, purchases hundreds of dollars' worth of merchandise monthly.
    - The customer has a company credit card with a 10-digit identification number.
    - Purchases are made in one branch store, not in the downtown store.
2. The Problem:
    - The customer is charged on her account for $166 of clothing she never bought. The customer knows this because she keeps a record of all her credit card purchases.
    - The customer tries to convince the credit department that an error has been made, but fails.

---

[7] A. C. Rosander, *Elementary Principles of Statistics* (New York: Van Nostrand, 1951), pp. 414–416.

[8] Source: Margaret G. Rosander

- The company keeps billing the customer for $166 plus interest, but the customer refuses to pay.
3. Reaction of the Main Credit Department:
   - In a telephone conversation the customer is told that she must have forgotten what she bought. (The customer had her own records.)
   - She is also told that she must have allowed some member of the family to use her credit card. (No family existed.)
4. Follow-Up by the Credit Department:
   - The company hunts down the sales slip for the bill and duplicates it.
   - The sales slip shows that the customer did not sign it. Someone else signed it, whose first name sounded a bit like part of the customer's name.
   - The sales slip shows (typed or printed) the customer's 10-digit credit card number.
   - The purchase was made at Store No. 6, where the customer never traded.
   - The purchase was made on a Saturday, when the customer was at home 60 miles away.
   - Five items of women's clothing were purchased, which accounted for the $166.
   - An affidavit is sent to the customer, who is asked to swear before a notary public that the 10-digit account number was used fraudulently. This was done, although how the 10-digit number was printed on the sales slip at Store 6 obviously was never investigated.
   - The company continues to bill the customer for $166 and the customer continues to refuse to pay.
   - Finally the customer requests that the account number be canceled and the account closed.
   - The company finally issues a new account number, but it is doubtful whether the customer will ever use it.
   - There is no letter from the company admitting that they made an error and that they regret what happened. They keep concentrating on the customer, and ignore the failure within their own system.
5. Possible Sources of This Trouble:
   - The trouble could arise at any one of four different places. The first is the clerk at Store No. 6, who did not obtain from the purchaser all of the necessary information, including a legible signature. The key question is: Was the 10-digit number entered on the sales slip in Store 6, or not?
   - Another source might be some clerk or other employee at the branch store where the customer usually shopped, since these persons had access to the 10-digit number.
   - The main credit office might be responsible, since these employees had access to the 10-digit number.

- The computer system people might be the source, since these employees had access to the 10-digit number.
- If the 10-digit number was put on at Store 6, then somebody had obtained the 10-digit number from an employee in the branch store.
- If the 10-digit number was not obtained by the clerk at Store 6, then the credit office or the computer system, or both working together, put the number on the bill so they could collect $166, even though from the wrong customer. The credit office could be covering up for what happened at Store 6.

6. Appraisal:
   - The customer was treated in an insulting manner by employees in the main credit office. In effect, they were accusing her of lying.
   - These employees jumped to false conclusions before they had any facts about the purchase and the customer.
   - They did not obtain a copy of the sales slip before they started to jump to false conclusions.
   - There is no evidence that the company is carrying out an in-depth investigation along the lines indicated above. It is doing nothing to correct the faults in the system.
   - It shows once more how hard it is for a customer to get an error out of a computer system, especially when the company insists it did not make an error.
   - It shows the utter incompetence of both management and the computer people to apply quality control to all aspects of computer work: error-free input, error-free programming, error-free output, a quick way to correct errors once they get into the system.
   - It shows the incompetence of both the employees, who treat customers in this high-handed manner, and the management, which allows it. Obviously these employees need special training in how to treat customers, and if they do not learn how to treat them in a civilized manner they should be fired. Or put them in a job unloading trucks.
   - It shows the incompetence of management in having an employee in Store 6 in the very important position of selling women's clothing, who does not know how to handle a credit card transaction. This is another employee who needs to be trained in how to do her job, and to report immediately any irregularity she discovers.
   - Management centers its attention on an innocent customer they think they will lose, rather than on their sales, credit, or computer system (whichever one it was) that failed. Obviously they do not want to admit that they made a big mistake, or explain to the customer what actually happened. The customer has no evidence that the company is investigating the case, is aiming to find the real cause, and is taking steps to prevent it from happening again.

QUALITY WITHOUT A NEW ORGANIZATION CHART

If quality is everybody's business, then quality performance and quality improvement are not an organizational matter but a psychological problem. This means that quality is based on knowledge, abilities, attitudes, orientation, motivation, cooperation, courtesy, reliability, trustworthiness, and credibility.

If managers and supervisors have employees with these characteristics, or if they develop these characteristics in their employees, then there is no need for some special organization, a new organizational chart, "streamlining" the organization, quality circles and the like, or promotional gimmicks. The problem becomes one of changing people rather than changing the organization. This assumes, of course, that persons at all levels have the necessary attitudes and capabilities, as stated above.

An Organizational Unit as a Quality Improvement Unit

There is no reason why any organizational unit, regardless of what it is called, cannot be a quality improvement group. This is because quality of service and quality performance are a question of what the supervisor and the employees do, not what they are called. A number of conditions have to be met, however, before any unit can take on this role.

1. It has a function to perform and goals to be met which are clearly understood by everyone in the unit.
2. Employees must have the appropriate skills and abilities.
3. A supervisor is required who knows how to supervise, lead, and direct a quality program.
4. Human errors have to be faced, identified, corrected, and prevented. It is the supervisor's job to help employees to learn how to avoid errors.
5. Problems have to be identified and solved using efficient techniques.
6. Employees work on special causes of non-quality, while the supervisor works on chronic problems which are faults of the system. Some can be solved directly; others have to go to higher levels in the organization.
7. Problems are discussed at least weekly, and the progress made toward meeting the goals is discussed.
8. Supervisor coaches employees as needed, and helps improve use of techniques to solve problems.
9. Employees are encouraged to submit ideas that will improve the quality of the work, and to hunt for problems and situations that can be improved.
10. Employees are encouraged to improve their personal knowledge, abilities, and skills. Training courses are set up for this purpose. Supervisor

will conduct some of these courses with job-centered problems and situations.
11. Everyone is kept informed of what is going on.
12. Improved performance is recognized.
13. Personal grievances are aired and discussed with supervisor, who takes appropriate action.
14. Supervisor talks with employees at their workplaces.

This is the substance of quality control and quality improvement, so it doesn't make any difference what the group is called. People performance is what counts.

GUIDELINES TO THE MANAGEMENT OF QUALITY IN THE SERVICE INDUSTRIES

1. Survey components of service operations intensively to identify problems, troubles, and situations that need improvement.
2. Analyze services and their components into basic characteristics that determine quality.
3. Recognize two different aspects of quality: quality of service rendered to customers, and quality of products purchased that are needed to render this service.
4. There are many ways to start a quality improvement program. Use the one that best fits your situation.
5. Balance the quality improvement program by using all eight vectors of quality. Do not be misled by what is being done in factories.
6. Roam all over the company or agency, hunting for problems to be converted into projects for improvement.
7. Reject the notion that errors are "human" and can be tolerated. Set zero errors (ZE) as the goal. Stress procedures, training, etc. that help persons reach this goal.
8. Reject the notion that wasted time is "human" and can be tolerated. Take steps to make zero delay time (ZD) a realistic goal.
9. Push forever for good-quality data as the basis for all decisions and actions.
10. Where one employee error can be dangerous, if not fatal, as in health, transportation, chemicals, and power plants, make the division of responsibility for poor quality at least 50/50, but set zero errors as a "must."
11. Develop customer-employee face-to-face relationships that are friendly, cordial, and harmonious.
12. Stop neglecting time as a major characteristic of quality of services.
13. Bring the full power of statistics to bear on problems. The six simple methods used by quality circles are only the beginning.

14. Statistics can be used to correct faults of individual performance as well as the faults of the system.
15. Management doesn't know what a statistical problem is, nor how it is related to quality of products or services. The identification of statistical problems is the job of the statistician or someone who is familiar with statistical practice.
16. Eliminate receiving inspection. Put the responsibility for quality of products and services on the producer of these products and services.
17. In services that involve face-to-face contacts between employees and customers, stress and train for courtesy, accuracy, promptness, efficiency, and reliability.

Positive Action Concepts for Supervisors and Managers

Given below is a list of positive action words or concepts which should be used often both by supervisors and by managers. A periodic review of these words may suggest new ideas and ways of supervising or managing.

A. assist, advise, achieve, accomplish, apply, accuracy, alert, appraise, analyze, act, assign, audit
B. build, brainstorm
C. control, certify, correct, challenge, clarify, communicate, cooperate, construct, confirm, coach, check, collect, contribute, courtesy, care, consideration, change
D. decide, delegate, develop, describe, discuss, diagnose, deliver, design, do
E. educate, explain, explore, encourage, evaluate, expedite, examine, estimate, evolve, efficient, effective
F. find, fix, foster, flexible, fair
G. give, grow, grade, gage, guide
H. help, hold, hire, honor
I. improve, innovate, invent, inspect, inspire, instruct, inquire, illuminate, initiate
J. judge, judicious, just
K. know, kindle, knowledge
L. lead, listen, learn, locate, light
M. manage, master, measure, monitor, motivate, meet, maintain, modify
N. nurture
O. operate, observe, outline, organize
P. plan, perform, produce, promote, provide, please, praise, prevent, pride, prompt
Q. quality, question, quantify
R. review, rate, reward, relate, report, record, reform, reliable, recognize, remedy, research

S. supervise, serve, specify, survey, support, study, stimulate, save, solve, satisfy, synchronize, sample, share, safety
T. train, teach, tutor, test, trust, time, talk, think
U. undertake, utilize, use, urge, upgrade, urgency
V. verify
W. weigh, warn, work

Negative Concepts and Words to Avoid or to Correct

There are concepts to avoid, correct, or ameliorate:
A. apathy, accident, antagonize, arbitrary, avoid, arrogance
B. blunder, blemish, barriers, berate
C. carelessness, costly, corrections, conflict, confusion, conjecture, condemn
D. delay, downtime, defect, defective, dissatisfaction, dangerous, disaster, destructive, disregard
E. error, envy, excessive, egotistical
F. failure, fault, faulty, fear, fatal, foolhardiness, false, falsify
G. gouge, goof
H. haste, harmful, harm, harsh, hate
I. idle, indifference, ignorance, inaction, ignore, inefficient, ineffective, illiterate
J. jealousy
L. loss, liability
M. mistake, misunderstanding, misuse, misinterpret, misjudge, malpractice, mixup, mislabel, mislead, misrepresent
N. neglect, negative, noncooperative, noisy, nullify
O. obstruct, oppose, object, offend, omit, overbearing, offensive
P. procrastinate, postpone, paralysis, plotting
Q. quit
R. reject, rude, rigid, reckless, rip off
S. silence, stubborn, self-centered
T. temper
U. unsafe, unreliable, useless, uncooperative, unkempt, unnecessary
W. waste, wasteful, willfulness, warfare, wait

LEARNING ABOUT THE UNKNOWN

All kinds of important knowledge about the customer—the ultimate customer—are unknown for the simple reason that companies have been organized and run without any regard to these aspects. As one editor wrote, the customer is considered a "bloody nuisance." Furthermore, American business is grounded in salesmanship and advertising. You do not contact the customer to find out what product or service is desired. You make the product or offer the service, and then rely upon salesmanship and advertising to sell the product or the service. Salespeople boast about how many million dollars' worth of something they sell every year. They couldn't care less about quality or what the customer wants. The extreme of this sales philosophy is reflected in a paperback book titled *How to Sell Anything to Anybody.* When you can do that, why worry about quality or any other desirable characteristic? The unknown is deliberately built into American business. It is a false creation. The unknown can very easily become less unknown if companies will only take the time and effort to find out what customers prefer, like, want, and dislike.

Given below are five projects and five questions that need to be thoroughly surveyed by companies to which they are applicable, namely all of the large companies and most of the others, except the very small ones which do not have the resources.

Projects

1. Study the effect and the loss due to dissatisfied customers. This can be done easily by a properly designed and executed sample survey of customers if the sample is very large. Otherwise cover them 100 percent.

2. Study the effect and the loss due to lost customers. It is known that one company did just this and found that the cause was changing vendors to save money at the expense of quality (Deming's Point 4 on buying by the price tag). This means keeping a close control on the names and addresses of lost customers and following up immediately after they are lost to discover the specific reasons.

3. Study the effect and gain due to the satisfied and pleased customer. This requires a carefully designed questionnaire to discover what products and services were pleasing, and why. Probe for reasons.

4. Study the effect and loss, if any, due to those who do not complain. This study requires some very careful design to discover why the customer does not complain, what aspects satisfy the customer, and what aspects do not. There is a need to probe for any adverse effects of keeping quiet: did they ever shift buying to a competitor? If so, to what extent, and for what specific products and services?

5. Study the effect of well-known persons advertising or endorsing a product or service on television or radio. This study is for the purpose of determining whether advertising on TV is better or worse than advertising in the newspaper, magazine, or direct mail, and whether use of popular persons makes any difference.

Questions to Ask Persons Interviewed

The following five questions are the kind about which the company needs to have facts, not opinions or conjectures. These data can be collected only by a well-designed and well-managed study.

1. Have you ever bought a product (service) because someone told you it was real good?

2. Have you ever *not bought* a product (service) because someone told you it was poor quality?

3. Have you ever been so dissatisfied with a product (service) that you changed stores (company)? What was the reason? How much buying did you shift?

4. Have you ever been dissatisfied with a product (service), but have done nothing? What was the reason? What was the product (service)?

5. (For owners of foreign cars) Why did you buy a foreign car? How does its quality compare with a domestic car if you have had the latter? Will the next car be a foreign car? The same kind you now have? Why?

THE MANAGEMENT OF PEOPLE

Personnel Policy

Human errors, mistakes, and blunders are major causes of poor-quality products and services on the one hand and faulty operations on the other, whether committed by top management, other supervisory personnel, or nonsupervisory personnel. These may be due to one or more of many causes: lack of knowledge, lack of skill and ability, ignoring critical data, poor judgment, carelessness, attitude, motivation, substituting opinion for factual information, misunderstanding of procedures and techniques, or refusal to follow safe and efficient procedures and techniques. Regardless of the cause, a continuous quality program is needed to eliminate all causes of critical and major errors, and to reduce the causes of minor errors commensurate with their seriousness. Personnel policy includes such working guidelines as the following:

1. Quality performance applies to everyone.
2. Do the job right the first time. Make zero errors and zero defects an ideal to work toward. Eliminate service failures.
3. Keep operations running safely and effectively. Avoid mistakes and accidents.
4. Minimize delay times, service times, and interrupted service.
5. Employee satisfaction is just as important as customer satisfaction.
6. Provision should be made for continuous growth, challenge, and recognition through a continuous program of education, training, assistance, and rewards.
7. Superior compensation is to be given for superior performance.

The Role of Management

The role of management is the key factor in the development and implementation of a successful quality program for the entire company, even though the initial application of quality controls and assurance may be limited to one operation or part of the company. This is because management determines quality policy, the nature of the quality program, its direction, its priority, its rate of implementation, and its success. The responsibilities include the following:

- Developing and supporting a quality policy;
- Taking the corrective actions that only management has the power to take;
- Setting an example for quality performance;
- Supporting the lower-level managers in their quest to improve quality;
- Supporting the first-line supervisors in their goals to attain better quality;
- Encouraging managers to make observational tours to bring the quality message to lower-level supervisors and employees. Stress the roving manager.
- Providing a work environment that fosters good-quality performance.
- Verify that the combinations of materials, equipment, machinery, procedures, instructions, and supervision are capable of meeting requirements.

The Vital Role of Personnel Behavior in Service Quality

Attainment of quality in service is dependent upon understanding, influencing, directing, and improving human factors in service operations. The following aspects require careful consideration and top priority:

1. Services involve behavior, attitudes, judgment, conclusions, decisions, and actions.
2. The quality goal includes the objective to have behavior, judgments, conclusions, decisions, and actions of such excellence that all service operations are continuous, effective, efficient, and safe.
3. The quality problem is one of continuous monitoring to detect trouble and deficiencies arising from human factors.
4. The first step in solving a problem is to make a correct diagnosis of the trouble whether it is an illness, a TV set, a radio, an automobile, an operating failure, or a product failure.
5. The second step is one of finding and applying the correct remedy.
6. The third step is verifying the effectiveness of the remedy. Behavior, judgment, conclusion, decision, and action are measured in terms of whether they are acceptable, appropriate, accurate, safe, adequate, sound, and relevant, and whether the remedy works and the trouble is eliminated.

Personal Attitudes

Personal attitudes are of vital importance in developing and maintaining quality performance at all levels of the company. Examples of major attitudes that are highly quality-oriented include the following:

1. Cooperation and teamwork. These are necessary because jobs, tasks, and projects require the merging of many different skills and the knowledge of many specialties; worker interaction is required; in a sequential operation, what is done at an earlier stage affects what is done at a later stage. Let your co-workers and supervisor know what is going on whenever this need arises.
2. Concern, alertness, sense of urgency. These are necessary to detect trouble fast and eliminate it quickly; to stop trouble from occurring in the first place; to prevent a small deficiency from growing into a big one; to work toward error-free performance.
3. Consideration for others, courtesy, politeness. These are necessary because of the interdependence of employees and customers, supervisors and employees. Customers deserve special attention and consideration because they are paying the bills. They are the market; they keep the company going.
4. Skillful communication. This is necessary to meet the needs of customers, management, and employees with a minimum of delay time and with an absence of conflict or friction. This means reporting conditions to the proper level of supervision and management as needed. It means effective and efficient communication with customers and any others who make inquiries.
5. Take nothing for granted: assume nothing. This is necessary to avoid trouble and serious mistakes and errors of all kinds. It means follow-through by asking, verifying, checking, inquiring, and confirming.
6. Honesty, integrity, trustworthiness. These are necessary so that the quality system has credibility, that it reflects conditions as they actually exist, and that the data and reports derived therefrom can be trusted.

Personal Growth and Satisfaction

For an effective quality system it is necessary to provide for personal growth, advancement, and satisfaction. Management must provide opportunities, facilities, and an environment that encourage growth even though the desire for growth must come from within, not from without. Growth includes growth in knowledge, skills, abilities, and attitudes which are necessary to do a better-quality job, to make better and more difficult decisions, and to prepare for promotion to more responsible and difficult positions. Aspects for management's special attention include the following:

1. Employee participation: employee-supervisor meetings, quality circles, planning groups, task forces, and staff meetings.
2. Keeping employees informed: through meetings, announcements, and reports. Employees need to keep one another informed.

3. Training: refresher courses, special in-training courses, in-house training program, and outside courses and seminars.
4. Personal help and assistance: discussion groups, talks on personal problems, grievances, promotions, finances, car pools, credit union, employee clubs and activities, career opportunities, and political activity. This helps employees work toward error-free performance.
5. Employee facilities: provision for lounge, cafeteria, snack bar, vending machines, and parking lot.
6. Management observational tours: periodic, often weekly tours of all units by managers and supervisors for the purpose of observing what is going on, becoming aware of what each unit is doing, praising a unit or supervisor for superior performance, stressing the goal of improved quality, if needed, getting a feel of the morale in the different units, and learning about problems and what needs to be done.

WHAT MANAGEMENT NEEDS TO AVOID

If management is to direct an effective quality improvement program, it will have to avoid the following practices, which are based on recorded experiences. These appear in the press, periodicals, and books by DeLorean, Peters, and others:

1. Policy-making officials who try to run operations. Usurping the functions of operating and middle managers.
2. Overruling decisions of specialists and professionals, making technical decisions.
3. Opposing change; opposing new techniques such as probability sampling and quality control.
4. Becoming jealous or envious of lower-level managers, professionals, or specialists.
5. Wasting time in meetings and conferences on trivia or routine matters.
6. Hiring and promoting the incompetent, the unqualified, or the inexperienced.
7. Promoting from without rather than from within when latter is justified.
8. Conducting a psychological war against someone they want to get rid of.
9. Catering to yes-men and yes-women.
10. Showing favoritism in praise, promotions, or rewards.
11. Doing nothing to stop bickering, feuding, conflict. Taking sides in a feud.
12. Stressing conformity to rigid and arbitrary rules and practices.
13. Basing decisions on hunches rather than on facts, data, and realities.
14. Insisting on excessive paperwork and reports.

15. Doing nothing about a planning group that does not plan.
16. Setting unrealistic time limits on jobs and projects.
17. Avoiding collecting key information.
18. Delaying making important decisions.

Chapter 11

The Cost of Quality

Analyzing cost of quality into specific dollar amounts is one way of convincing officials that a quality program has real money value. The cost of quality, wrote Philip Crosby in *Quality is Free,* is the cost of doing things wrong. Stated another way, it is the gain obtained by getting rid of non-quality or anti-quality characteristics. The way to start such a study is to have managers and others find out what all the errors, mistakes, wasted time, inefficient methods, corrections, reruns, customer complaints, lost customers, and other activities of correcting and patching up what went wrong are costing the company.

One company estimated the first time that about $10 million was spent on these wasteful activities. The figure increased to $16 million the first year after they dug deeper into the problem, but remained at $14 million during the second year. Quality improvement—getting rid of non-quality—is the easiest, cheapest, and most powerful way to save money by cutting costs. All that is needed is new knowledge. There is no need to spend huge amounts on capital investments for new equipment, machinery, and processes or on additional operating expenses. The company, however, will have to spend a relatively small amount of money to gain this additional knowledge, if it does not already have this know-how.

THE FOUR CATEGORIES OF QUALITY COSTS

The four categories of quality costs are those developed by the Quality Cost Committee of the American Society for Quality Control.[1]

Prevention costs are those costs which are incurred in order to prevent poor-quality products from being made and poor-quality services from being rendered. This includes such activities as hiring qualified persons at all levels, orientation courses, training, special prevention programs, and planning quality

---

[1] *Quality Costs—What and How,* second edition, (Milwaukee: American Society for Quality Control, 1971).

1. *Prevention*	Quality staff, planning, training, improvement, data collection and analysis plans, quality reports planning	Good 40–50% Poor 10%
2. *Appraisal*	Inspection, review, verification, checking, audit, sampling, testing, equipment used for foregoing, data collection and analysis	Good 40–50% Poor 20%
3. *Internal failure*	Making errors and mistakes, correcting errors and mistakes, computer reruns, waste created by errors and mistakes, errata sheets, downtime on computer, downtime on equipment, idle time of employees, waiting time for supplies and parts and repairs, inefficient methods, techniques, and processes, poorly written manuals and instructions, faulty explanations, doing work over, poorly trained employees, loss due to absenteeism and turnover	Good 0–10% Poor 40%
4. *External failure*	Customer complaints, lost customers, returned goods, warranties, error adjustments, lawsuits, failure to fix or repair, correcting faulty repair job, correcting errors and mistakes found by customer, loss due to dissatisfied customers, fieldwork costs, failure of product to work as claimed or advertised, failure of service	Good 0–10% Poor 30%

control and improvement programs. These include allocating adequate resources to prevent sources of non-quality or anti-quality from ever arising.

Appraisal costs include all those costs incurred to determine by data collection and other means whether non-quality products or services have been prevented from being made or rendered.

Internal failure costs include those incurred in correcting all the errors, mistakes, blunders, faults, and failures made within the company. These include costs involved in improving (correcting) a faulty method, process, or technique.

External failure costs are those which arise once the product or service is outside the company. These are discovered or reported by the customer or user,

Examples of Cost of Quality by Categories

Cost Category	Manu-facturing[a]	Banking[b,c] Latzko	Banking[b,c] Aubrey	Insurance[d] Townsend	Printing[e]	GE	Ideal
Prevention	15%	2%	14%	45%	2%	2%	60%
Appraisal	50	28	46	25	45	14	40
Internal Failure	24	41	4	18	51	14	0
External Failure	11	29	36	12	2	70	0
Total	100	100	100	100	100	100	100

Dollars or percent of work time: 44%

[a] *Quality Costs—What and How,* second edition (Milwaukee: ASQC, 1967), pp. 27–28.
[b] W. J. Latzko, *Quality and Productivity for Bankers and Financial Managers* (New York: Marcel Dekker and Milwaukee: ASQC Quality Press, 1986), p. 88.
[c] C. A. Aubrey II, *Quality Management in Financial Services* (Wheaton, IL: Hitchcock, 1985), p. 31.
[d] Patrick L. Townsend with Joan E. Gebhardt, *Commit to Quality* (New York: Wiley, 1986), pp. 126–129.
[e] *Quality Control Handbook,* edited by J. M. Juran, third edition (New York: McGraw-Hill, 1974), pp. 5–8, 5–9.

and represent some defect, fault, or failure of the product or service sold by the company.

The ideal goal is to drive the two groups of failures toward zero by increasing the resources allocated to prevention and appraisal, but especially to prevention. The goal is to prevent non-quality or anti-quality sources from arising.

These percentages vary greatly for several reasons:

- Differences in the number of items included;
- Differences in the items included;
- Different ways of classifying the same items;
- Differences in methods of costing;
- Differences in allocating resources;
- Differences in quality patterns and practices.

Combining categories throws light on the proportions of resources used to prevent failures:

Prevention and Appraisal	$\frac{1}{65}$	$\frac{2}{30}$	$\frac{3}{60}$	$\frac{4}{70}$	$\frac{5}{47}$	$\frac{6}{16}$	$\frac{7\text{(ideal)}}{100}$
Failure	$\frac{35}{100}$	$\frac{70}{100}$	$\frac{40}{100}$	$\frac{30}{100}$	$\frac{53}{100}$	$\frac{84}{100}$	$\frac{0}{100}$
Total							

Clearly the more is spent on prevention and appraisal, the less the amount that appears in the failure category. The ideal would be to drive the failure costs to zero. What is needed is more experience on how close to zero the external and internal failures can be driven; how far an increase in prevention and appraisal pays off. A recent paper analyzes the cost models involved.[2]

It is shown that a zero failure cost is not only a possible model, but that it is a model implied in a continuous evolutionary quality improvement program. Apparently there is no reason why failure costs cannot be driven toward zero. An example is cited where defects are reduced by a factor of 250, not just a factor of two or three. This means that defects and errors are expressed in parts per million (ppm), not in parts per hundred, as is the common practice. IBM, Hewlett-Packard, Sony, and Toyota are cited as believers and practitioners of a continuous reduction in the rate of defects. There is no apparent reason why human errors cannot be reduced in a similar manner, especially in those companies and industries such as health, transportation, chemicals, and nuclear power plants, where safety is paramount because one employee error cannot only be dangerous but fatal.

Executives Uninformed about Quality Costs and Quality

In the official newsletter *On Q* for November 1986, the American Society for Quality Control reported the results of a Gallup poll of 698 senior executives. The results were both startling and challenging—startling because they were not expected and challenging because they show that quality is neither widely understood nor accepted.

With regard to costs of quality, 23 percent didn't know the costs associated with producing a quality product or with rendering a quality service. Obviously they were not familiar with the high costs of producing poor-quality goods and services.

Even worse, 70 percent estimated that the cost of poor quality was 10 percent or less of gross sales, showing that they were not familiar with the real cost of producing non-quality products and services. Actual costs based on studies and experience of experts put the figure much higher—usually between 25 and 40 percent.

No doubt one of the reasons why costs of quality are ignored or greatly underestimated is that 64 percent of those answering measure quality only in terms of customer complaints. This shows a complete misunderstanding of the seriousness, magnitude, costs, and benefits of quality and quality improvement. Clearly these officials are not concerned about prevention of poor-quality products and services because they are unaware of the high cost of defects, human errors, wasted time, and other characteristics of non-quality.

---

[2] Arthur M. Schneiderman, "Optimum Quality Costs and Zero Defects: Are They Contradictory Concepts?" *Quality Progress*, November 1986, pp. 28–31.

These officials are not interested in any quality or quality improvement program, in a quality department, in quality improvement teams, or in making quality everybody's business. They show what some of us have been claiming for years—that it is those managers, professionals, and supervisors in middle and lower levels who are really aware of the need for, and the advantages of, quality improvement programs. Drs. Deming, Juran, and Ishikawa are right— the place to start educating people in the company in quality is at the very top.

A Checklist for Determining the Quality Costs of Failures

Quality costs, according to the standard system, are created by internal and external failures, including failure to use better techniques and processes. The following list is suggestive rather than comprehensive. The most detailed list of items for all four quality cost categories is given by Harrington.[3] No attempt is made to point out the number of persons, amount of resources, and amount of time required to correct, meet, avoid, or resolve these situations.

(Internal Failures)

1. Typing errors	24. Poor sample design
2. Misfiling	25. Excessive calculation time
3. Delayed filing	26. Defective print job
4. Downtime on typewriter	27. Pages omitted in report
5. Downtime on computer	28. Page numbers interchanged
6. Other downtime	29. Sample documents lost
7. Failure to fix or repair	30. Sample not selected
8. Supplies not in stock	31. Sample misselected
9. Waiting for work	32. Excessive repair time
10. Waiting for repairs	33. Excessive service time
11. Waiting for supplies	34. Waiting for service
12. Waiting (other)	35. Reviewing
13. Reruns	36. Sorting, classifying
14. Jobs done over	37. Misleading data sheet
15. Idle time (employees')	38. Error in accounts
16. Absences	39. Error in bank deposit
17. Work delayed due to absences	40. Biased sample creating false data
18. Turnover	
19. Payroll error	41. Mixup of two drugs ⎤ FATAL RESULTS
20. Shipment time	42. Mixup of two gases ⎦
21. Computer program error	43. Airline pulling wrong ticket
22. Computer program debugging	44. Flight canceled
23. Error by computer librarian	45. Customer wrongly billed

---

[3] H. James Harrington, *Poor-Quality Costs* (New York: Marcel Dekker and Milwaukee: ASQC Quality Press, 1987), pp. 167–184.

(Internal Failures)

46. Error in mortgage transaction
47. Unnecessary sample adjustments
48. Billing error
49. Invoice error
50. Railroad waybill error
51. Accidents
52. Disasters
53. Injuries
54. Illness
55. Employee stealing
56. Shoplifting
57. Error in personnel record
58. Error in amortization schedule adjustment
59. Customer complaints (on the spot)
60. Breakage in stores and elsewhere
61. Damage due to unpacking, etc.
62. Error in travel voucher
63. Company loses sales slip
64. False billing
65. Proofreading by two persons
66. Canceled letter, memo
67. Rewriting letters, memos, reports
68. Retyping letters, memos, reports
69. Correspondence to correct field errors, etc.
70. Internal mail misrouted
71. Internal mail not delivered
72. Mailroom errors
73. Telephone calls to correct errors
74. Special publications
75. Travel to field to explain work
76. Late arrival of people
77. Late arrival of supplies
78. Sample receipts control
79. Collection of useless data
80. Biased data
81. Lack of data
82. Poor physical arrangements
83. Special training and assistance
84. Rewriting instructions
85. Following wrong instructions
86. Rudeness
87. Loss due to fire, wind, flood
88. Loss due to vandalism
89. Damage due to customer handling
90. Equipment failure
91. Collecting, analyzing error data
92. Inadequate sample design
93. Coding errors
94. Faulty sampling
95. Unnecessary calculations
96. Misunderstanding instructions
97. Defective communication
98. Wasting talents
99. Using substitute help
100. Inaccurate counting
101. Inefficient methods
102. Tax error
103. Employee complaints
104. Baggage damage

(External Failures)

1. Double billing for book sales
2. Double billing for insurance premiums
3. Double billing for magazine subscriptions
4. Missing items in sewing kit
5. No holes in sequins
6. Buttons poorly sewed on shirts, coats, jackets
7. Voltage regulator set so high it burns out generator
8. Trouble not eliminated on first trip, first attempt
9. Trouble within warranty time

(External Failures)

10. Self-employment Social Security tax not recorded for one year
11. Defect in printed bank checks
12. Page missing in a book
13. Two pages interchanged in a book
14. Damage due to transportation, in transit
15. Customer time and travel to correct company error
16. Failure to repair first time
17. Goods have to be returned
18. Damage lawsuits
19. Product liability lawsuits
20. Professional or business loss-of-time lawsuit
21. Customer complaints—price, not in stock, service, etc.
22. Letters and telephone calls by customer to correct company errors
23. Waiting time for service
24. Prescribed drug or treatment ineffective
25. Company refuses to correct its own errors
26. Time to make and settle insurance claims
27. Spoiled food item
28. Spoiled milk
29. Leaky canned item
30. Person cannot open bottle, container
31. Food not edible
32. Contaminated food
33. Dispenser doesn't work
34. Product does not work as advertised
35. Concentration on label not effective
36. One foot on panty hose reversed
37. Misleading instructions for use
38. Lost customers
39. Dissatisfied customers
40. Insurance companies fail to explain how premiums are arrived at, size of credits
41. City water meter fails to work
42. City water meter read in error
43. Business double billed for sales tax already paid
44. Disasters

THE COST OF NON-QUALITY

We turn now to a discussion of non-quality, a departure from the traditional cost of quality. The cost of non-quality is the cost of doing things wrong. Quality cost is what remains when we get rid of the cost of non-quality. This sounds trite, but it has a deeper meaning. The approach to the cost of quality is negative, not positive. How often do we make excellent products without defects which satisfy the customer? How often do we render a satisfactory service without errors, that satisfies and pleases the customer?

We get partial progressive quality by reducing the sources of non-quality. Progressively better quality results since this reduction of sources of non-quality is progressive and time-consuming.

For purposes of discussion and understanding, it is helpful to divide the total cost of quality into three broad components (see Figure 11–1):

C = total cost of quality

C_1 = cost of what is done right with best processes and performance. This is

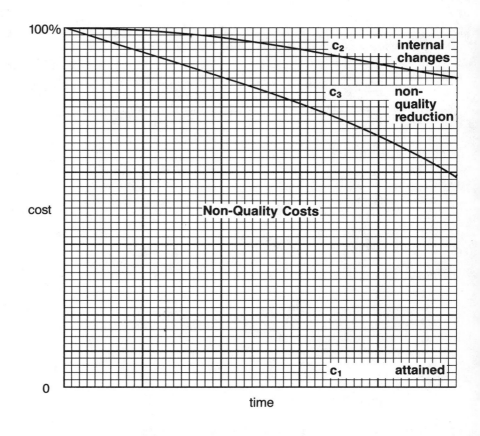

Figure 11–1.   **Three Kinds of Costs**

the best that can be done with the present state of the art and science. Quality already has been attained. Something new, however, may come up which can result in quality improvement. Must keep watch on new developments.

C_2 = These are organizational and related changes which can result in reduction of costs: eliminate one or two layers of organization, eliminate duplications and overlapping of functions and duties, get rid of all those sources that generate an excessive amount of paper, eliminate unnecessary jobs, combine units, change physical arrangements.

Note that these are quite different from reduction of costs due to manufacturing better products and rendering better services. These activities and changes are not included in the field of quality as we define it. Where a question box system exists, these are the kinds of ideas that usually dominate the questions submitted.

C_3 = This is the cost of the non-quality characteristics which have already been mentioned and which are listed below. These are the costly sources that we plan and work to get rid of, or at least progressively reduce in magnitude and effect.

The situation where things are done right but very inefficiently is included here. Methods, techniques, and process are out of date. There is a better way. This situation is included here because it is often the source of the poor quality.

This is primarily a fault of the system. Only rarely would an individual have the power to introduce an improved method even if he or she is familiar with it.

The total cost of quality, then, is

$$C = C_1 + C_2 + C_3.$$

Very little can be done about reducing the value of C_1. However, management should be on the lookout for developments which may make it possible to improve quality even more.

C_2 can be the source of large savings because of the waste that is built into the organization and its operations. This source of reduced costs is not included in conventional quality control, but certain aspects of organization and operations can be related to quality aspects and quality improvement. This is true where some aspect can be traced more or less directly to poor-quality products or poor-quality service.

C_3 involves non-quality aspects which increase costs and decrease quality, and which we try to reduce the effects of, if not eliminate:

- Defects in purchased products;
- Errors and mistakes;
- Wasted time;
- Accidents and disasters;
- Unacceptable behavior and attitudes;
- Customer complaints;
- Dissatisfied customers who do not complain;
- Lost customers;
- Faults and failures that are endured;
- Useless data;
- Biased data;
- Shoddy products; inadequate products;
- Failures in performance;
- Products with prematurely short life;
- Services that do not last;
- Faulty communication system.

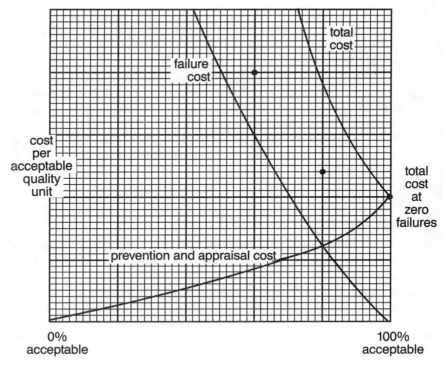

Source: A.M. Schneiderman, *Quality Progress*, November 1986

Figure 11-2. **Total Cost at Zero Failures**

Total Quality Cost at Zero Failure

In previous chapters, it was emphasized that the goal with many quality characteristics in services is not to stabilize them, but to drive them to zero. The conventional view is that such a goal is impossible and Utopian. The argument is that optimum quality costs occur at some point below 100 percent acceptance, at some percent defective or some percentage in error. It is claimed that zero defects or zero errors result in an infinite quality cost.

Examples have already been given where error rates have been driven toward zero, and have come close to zero, by using rather simple methods in regular operations. Now, here is some additional evidence that driving these characteristics toward zero does not result in an infinite cost. (See Figure 11–2).

Schneiderman shows that there is no mathematical requirement that the optimum total quality cost occurs at less than 100 percent good quality.[4] The minimum could very well be at 100 percent. Total quality costs are minimized when the slope of the failure line is the negative of the slope of the prevention and appraisal line.

Schneiderman claims that movement toward zero failures comes from a slow evolutionary process rather than from an innovative revolutionary break-through. (In practice we find both of these.) He concludes that a program of continuous improvement "does not necessarily increase costs as the quality level approaches 100 percent."

This analysis supports the thesis described previously and based on experience with non-quality characteristics. It should be pointed out that in the examples cited and in experience, the benefits attained by improved computer operations and in other operations, in reduced customer complaints, and in other ways have more than compensated for the money spent on prevention and appraisal.

The Cost Effects of Customer Attitudes

What many companies overlook is the economic effect on the attitudes of their customers. A non-quantitative analysis is given below.

Customer attitude	Customer action	Effect on company
1. Pleased customer	Praises product or service to others; free salesmanship.	Brings in new customers. Company gains.
2. Dissatisfied customer	Complaints to others. Talks about poor-quality product or service. Starts to buy elsewhere.	Causes hesitation on part of would-be customers. Hearers may buy elsewhere. Reduces customary buying. Company loses.
3. Lost customer	Spreads word not to buy product or service. Buys from competitors.	Results in more lost customers. Company can suffer serious loss.

Some Costs Not in the Textbooks

The following cases show costs which are not included in the conventional four categories. These are costs to the customer due to a company error, cost

---

[4] A. M. Schneiderman, "Optimum Quality Costs and Zero Defects: Are They Contradictory Concepts?" *Quality Progress*, November 1986, pp. 28–31.

to the customer due to poor service, cost of lost time to the nation, and cost of a lost customer to a company.

Case 1. Cost of a Mortgage Company's Error to Customer

1.	Two letters to Denver	$ 2.00
2.	Two telephone calls to Denver	6.00
3.	Professional time lost @ $75 an hour	75.00
4.	Auto trip to Denver, 120 miles @ 20¢/m	24.00
5.	Parking	5.00
6.	Professional time lost, 4 hrs. @ $75	300.00
	Total	$412.00

It cost the customer $412 to correct a $314 error that the company had made but obviously was incompetent to correct. It was an employee, not the vice-president, who finally corrected the error at a computer outlet in less than 30 seconds.

Case 2. The High Cost to a Customer of Repairing a TV Set[5]

Harrington[5] summarizes the costs incurred in California for repair of a television set bought in Cleveland (while on a cross-country trip). The total repair cost was $18.38 ($2.38 for a transistor plus $16.00 for the cost of the repair). The additional costs are listed below:

Additional cost to customer:

• Locate and go to repair shop in Cleveland, 3 hrs. @ $10/hr	30.00
• Travel 32 miles in Cleveland @ 20¢/m	6.40
• 4.5 hrs. TV repair in California @ $10 hr	45.00
• 72 miles travel to TV shop in California @ 20¢/m	14.40
• Loss of tape recorder sale 10% of $298	29.80
	$125.60

The $36.40 was spent in Cleveland, but no work was done because the customer did not have the warranty paper. No warranty paper, no work. If the work had been limited to California, the total cost would still have been $89.20. The only trouble was a failing transistor. The total time elapsed to obtain repair was 15 days. The additional cost to the customer was five times the actual

[5] H. James Harrington, *Poor-Quality Costs* (New York: Marcel Dekker and Milwaukee; ASQC Quality Press, 1986), pp. 131–135.

repair cost, if the situation is limited to California. Telephone calls by the repair shop in California could have reduced the cost to the customer by 30 percent.

Case 3. What a Little Lost Time Can Cost

- There are 70,000,000 people employed in the service industries.
- Assume that 50 percent are subject to some idle time.
- This means 35,000,000,000 are subject to idle time.
- Assume that the idle time is 30 minutes a day, 100 hours a year.
- That adds up to 3,500,000,000 hours per year.
- Assume that the average wage and salary is $8 per hour.
- That gives a total of $28 billion lost each year.

From estimates given by some persons familiar with the subject, this is a very modest figure. It shows, however, that the cost of even a small amount of wasted time daily can add to a tremendous figure.

Case 4. The Cost of One Lost Customer

Assume that a customer spends $100 annually at a store and that the interest rate is 10 percent. If the store loses this customer, what is the loss over five years, assuming simple interest?

1st year	2nd year	3rd year	4th year	5th year
$100	110	231	364	510
	100	100	100	100
	210	331	464	610

At the end of five years the company has lost a minimum of $610. If the interest were figured on a compound basis, the total would be higher.

Case 5. The Cost of Turnover

The cost of turnover does not seem to be included anywhere in the four categories of quality costs. A company or agency may invest considerable amounts of resources in training persons to learn to perform a job—to move them to a higher level on the production curve and a lower level on the error curve. No organization wants to lose employees who have been brought to a high level of productivity and quality performance. This includes professionals, managers, and supervisors, as well as employees at lower levels.

This means that the organization will take steps to prevent this loss of good workers and this turnover of personnel in ways such as the following:

- Individual recognition;
- Some special award;
- Companywide publicity and recognition;
- New and challenging assignments;
- Promotions;
- Additional and special training.

The cost of turnover includes various costs involved in an employee leaving, the cost of training new employees, the slowdown of production and deterioration of quality due to the loss of important employees and supervisors, the cost involved in using experienced employees and supervisors to give new employees the help, assistance, and coaching they need on the job, and other personnel office costs.

Examples of the Cost of Poor Quality

What costs money is not good-quality services. It is poor-quality services. Getting rid of poor-quality service, or better yet, preventing it from occurring in the first place, is a very effective way to reduce costs. Poor quality creates costs both for the company and for the customer. Examples are given below. They can be translated into losses ranging from hundreds to millions of dollars, depending upon the nature of the poor-quality performance.

The Company

Errors:

- Time used to discover errors
- Time used to correct errors
- Time used to process errors
- Time used to correct chain effects caused by an error
- Cost of letters, memos, etc. to correct errors
- Cost of telephone calls to correct errors
- Cost of transportation to correct errors
- Cost of accidents and disasters caused by human errors

Defects in purchased products:

- Cost of discovering defects
- Cost of correcting defects: time spent with vendor
- Chain effects: customer complaints, damage suits
- Cost of accidents and disasters caused by defects

Wasted or lost time:

- Lost time—people cost
- Lost time—equipment cost
- Lost time—machinery cost
- Lost time—cost of repairs
- Lost time—cost of maintenance
- Lost time—cost of lack of materials
- Lost time—cost of lack of supplies
- Lost time—cost of lack of parts
- Lost time—cost of lack of power and energy

Customer complaints:

- Cost of the complaint system
- Cost of receiving complaints
- Cost of answering complaints
- Cost of resolving complaints

Lost customers:

- Annual loss of losing a customer
- Annual loss of all customers lost
- Loss due to chain effect of lost customers

Accidents and disasters:

- Costs arising from errors, defects, misunderstandings, ignorance, careless-ness, violation of safety rules, lack of communication

Attitudes and behavior of employees:

- Lost customers
- Lost sales
- Excessive time
- Unnecessary paperwork

Unnecessary investments due to poor quality:

- Computer
- Other equipment
- Machinery
- Robots

- Consultants
- Specialists
- Managers
- Software

The Customer

Getting errors corrected:

- Loss due to absence from work, business
- Cost of transportation
- Cost of telephone calls
- Cost of letters
- Cost of time used for conferences, talks, explanations
- Cost of other paperwork

Making complaints:

- Time required to make complaint
- Time required to explain
- Time required to resolve complaint

Getting repairs done: auto, TV, radio, appliances, etc.:

- Waiting time
- Time lost from work or business
- Cost of faulty diagnosis
- Cost of faulty remedy
- Cost of finally getting trouble eliminated

Medical care:

- Faulty diagnosis
- Faulty treatment
- Unnecessary examination
- Unnecessary transportation
- Unnecessary medicine
- Unnecessary treatment
- Unnecessary visits
- Waiting time
- Unnecessary time lost from work

Excessive repairs and maintenance:

- Short life
- Low reliability
- Poor functioning
- Excessive repair costs
- Defective design
- Poor-quality parts

The customer is interested in how a product operates or functions, not in how it is made.

Chapter 12

Service System Design

FACTORS AND TECHNIQUES IN SERVICE SYSTEM DESIGN

The service rendered by a service organization requires careful identification, circumscription, and analysis and attention to all of the specific components that enter into the service enterprise. It is convenient to distinguish three broad classes of activities and components:

- Those that involve only customers;
- Those that involve only the company, its vendors, and its employees;
- Those that involve both customers and employees; customer contacts.

Three techniques for laying out a design are described and illustrated:

- A master list of major activities in sequence;
- A flowchart, including customer contacts;
- A main line of sequences with feeder lines.

The design is a detailed plan showing sequences, connections, and relationships. The design must include not only the internal and external activities of the company, but also the activities that involve only the customer and those that involve both the customer and the company. It is easy to get so involved with the quality of the internal operations of the company that the customer is completely forgotten, or at least neglected.

The *master list* of major operations consists of the major types of activities and factors required to render service to the customer. These major types are then broken down into specific components so that the quality aspects and characteristics can be identified and described. Examples of a few of these major items are as follows:

Restaurant		*Nursing home*
Company:	Customer:	Medical: drugs, doctors, nurses
Food planning	Food choice	Food
Food menu	Food ordering	Room and furnishings

Restaurant		*Nursing home*
Food quantities	Waiting time	Personal care
Food purchasing	Food service	Security
Food storing	Price	Treatment: employees, other residents
Food preparation		Activities
Food serving		Sanitation
Sanitation		Management
		Supervision

A *flowchart* shows the major steps and operations from the beginning of a transaction or service to the end. It includes each of the three major classes of components listed above.

Sometimes a flowchart, to be complete, must show significant components beyond what the company provides. This is because the flowchart for the customer includes more than the flowchart for the company. Consider an airline. It has no apparent interest in assisting the customer in any way to get to the airport. The fact that the parking lots are full and the customer has trouble finding a place to park does not concern them. Neither does the fact that the customer may not have any convenient method of getting to the airport. The same is true at the other end of the line. The airline is not interested in whether the customer gets to his or her destination or not. It does not realize that getting to the airport and getting to the destination may be the most difficult parts of the journey.

The concept of total transportation is missing. No airline has a bus service that coordinates with the airline service. The only known instance of such a bus-airline connection is the bus line that Frontier Airlines used to have between Fort Collins, Colorado and the Denver Stapleton Airport. In this case the passenger bought a ticket and checked in baggage not at Stapleton but in Fort Collins, about 75 miles from Denver. It eliminated all of the hassle encountered at a very large airport.

A flowchart is a sequential chart because it shows activities in the order and the relationship in which they are performed. At each sequence, the issue of quality of service arises.

The *main line* is a line representing, at various points, the major service functions from beginning to end. It may or may not be a time line. It may combine both space and time, however. *Feeder lines* representing major or minor contributing services come in from the sides at the appropriate places and times. The main line with feeders serves the same function as the flowchart but is much simpler. The main line represents service to the customer, not some internal activity of the company. Company activities may or may not be side feeders. The main line, however, will show activities and functions which involve both the company and the customer.

The purpose of these techniques is to identify significant aspects of services for several purposes:

- To isolate quality areas;
- To locate where quality problems can occur, e.g., customer contacts;
- To isolate quality characteristics;
- To locate trouble spots;
- To find causes of trouble;
- To find remedies and correctives;
- To take action for quality improvement;
- To use the design or plan to determine kinds and number of persons to hire;
- To use the design or plan to assign persons to jobs, tasks, or function;
- To use the design or plan to improve seating, arrangement, and service of customers.

Limitations of Design

A service system cannot be designated like a physical mechanism, such as an electric motor or a radio receiver. There are too many human elements involved. (See Figures 12–1, 12–2, and 12–3.) The design, however, does include structure, relationships, operations, components, connections, duties, tasks, certain rules of the game, sequences, time relationships, space relationships, and places where customer contacts occur.

Yet courtesy and promptness, for example, cannot be designed into the system. Neither can countless other human traits essential to quality performance. These important quality characteristics have to be a part of the operations and workings of the system, and practiced by all levels of employees. They have to be characteristics of the persons hired and taking part in the operation of the

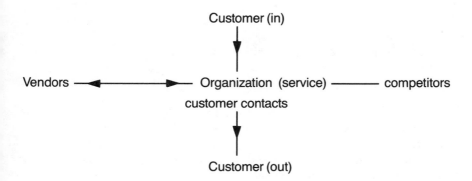

Figure 12–1. **The Service System Sequence**

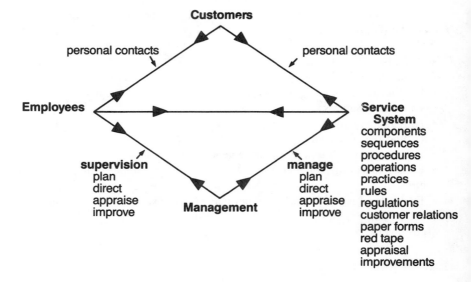

Figure 12–2. **The Service Structure and Process**

system. Hiring, training, conferences, and seminars have to be a part of the system if these human traits are going to contribute to quality improvement.

The customers have needs and demands. They pay the bills so they are entitled to their money's worth. They are entitled to fair and courteous treatment. The organization wants the customer to leave satisfied, if not pleased: it wants the customer to return.

The vendor is the supplier of goods and services to the organization. It wants to supply goods and services that meets the company's requirements. This means that the vendor must plan to meet the levels and standards set by the specifications of the company. Also, the products must satisfy the operating requirements of the company.

The company has employees who use purchased products to render services that meet the quality goals and standards of both company and customer. These services must be performed in a courteous, efficient manner if the customer is to be satisfied.

Competitors must not be overlooked. They make products which compete with those of the vendors. They render services which compete with those of the service company. If competition is to be met, the products of competitors must be of the same, if not better, quality, and must sell at the same or lower price. The same holds true of the services of competitors. To meet service competition, very close attention must be paid to the desires and preferences of customers.

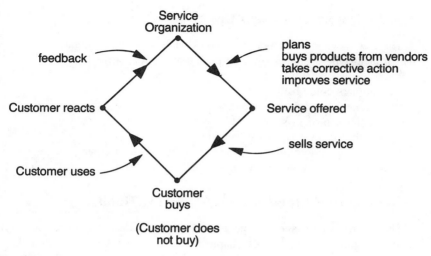

Figure 12–3. The Customer–Organization Service Cycle

Purposes and Advantages of Design

The design of a service system has several purposes and advantages, as follows:

- To lay out a specific structure showing all major functions and components;
- To plan for some definite needs of a customer or group of customers;
- To show the relationships of one component to another;
- To identify places and points where quality performance is involved and where such performance can be improved;
- To show how operations are interrelated and interconnected;
- To identify places where customer contacts occur.

It has to provide a structure which will perform effectively because customer satisfaction is based on how the organization functions, not on how it is constructed.

The Indicators of a Good Design

There are several indicators of a good design of a service organization. Those which please the customer must be placed at the top of the list.

- Customers come back;
- Customers are satisfied or pleased;
- No delays, prompt service;
- Smooth operation of every component;
- Smooth operation: all components or parts work together;
- Nothing the customer wants is omitted or excluded.

Designing to Fit the Customers' Buying Habits

The entire system and its operation have to be designed to fit the buying habits of the customers. These habits vary from one kind of commodity or service to another. Examples of buying habits in retail stores are the following: buys from a list; buys from memory; buys one or two items; buys without a list; impulsive buyer; large-scale buyer; roving customer looking around; Customer with a purpose (searches for one specific item or more). Checkout registers have to be planned for various types of customers, especially in a supermarket. Checkout registers are provided for various types of customers:

- Quick service for those with few items (say, six or fewer);
- Fast service for those with a moderate number (say, seven to 15);
- Service for those with a large number of purchases.

The trouble with specifying number of items is that an item is never defined, so all kinds of counts appear (for example) in the quick checkout counter. Are six cans of pears one item or six? From the viewpoint of the checkout operation they are six, because each can has to be recorded by the laser beam.

Examples of Major Functions

A design must consider all functions which are involved in rendering a service to the customer and to the public. Far too often this major purpose is overlooked. Some examples are given below:

- Airline, bus line, railroad, ship lines;   Transport people;
- Restaurants, cafeterias;   Feed people;
- Hotels, motels;   House people;
- Insurance, police department;   Protect people;

• Banks;	Provide safekeeping for assets;
• Post office, other;	Provide mail and package service for people;
• Doctors, hospitals;	Alleviate or stop pain, sickness;
• Grocery stores, supermarkets;	Sell food to people.

The main function is to service people directly and immediately. A quality improvement program must address this main function and not be diverted into minor internal functions of the company or organization.

Analyzing Major Functions

These major functions are broken down into major components, which are often the basis of departments or divisions in the organization. Fifteen are listed; others may have more or fewer. Regardless of the size of the organization, the common ones are always present in one form or another. Seven are listed here:

- Planning;
- Purchasing;
- Personnel;
- Finance;
- Sales;
- Operations;
- Accounting (bookkeeping).

Smaller companies have to provide at least for these seven functions, even though they may have only one or two persons *engaged* in each function.

The other eight functions will be found in large organizations; they are as follows:

- Legal;
- Marketing;
- Traffic and transportation;
- Auditing;
- Data processing;
- Research and development;
- Customer service;
- Quality assurance.

Most of these functions are supportive: they do not deal directly with the quality of the product or service, or with the customer. Those that have any fairly direct connection with quality of service to the customer include purchasing, personnel, sales, operations, and customer service. This does not mean that the quality of performance in connection with the other activities and functions is not important. It simply means that quality performance does require a lot of necessary overhead expense.

Each one of these functions needs to be decomposed into its various components, and quality must be applied to each one of them. For example, the personnel function can be divided into the following components (this is not necessarily a complete list):

- Individual personnel file;
- Absences, leave;
- Hiring;
- Promotions;
- Discharges;
- Resignations, transfers;
- Retirement;
- Classification;
- Job descriptions;
- Vacancies, job openings;
- Training, seminars, conferences;
- Payroll, taxes, withholding;
- Employee guidebook;
- Grievances, complaints;
- Ratings.

The Role of Customer Contacts

Customer contact means any contact that the customer has with people in the organization which may have a bearing on the quality of service. The customer contacts and the service component are basic elements in the design of a quality service system. A flowchart is laid out as a first step to show these components and these contacts.

Some service components have customer contacts; others do not. The latter are not visible to the customer. Examples are buying and preparing food in a restaurant or cafeteria, the selection and preparation of food for airline flights, the people who work behind the scenes in a public utility, and the accounting department in a bank or insurance company.

The quality of service is judged by the customer on the basis of the contacts he or she makes with the employees of the company or organization. The customer's contacts provide the only information he or she has to form a judgment of the quality of service rendered. Some contacts may lead to a favorable attitude, others to an unfavorable attitude, still others to complaints.

The organization, however, must be concerned with all aspects of the service components whether they involve customer contacts or not. Indeed, the components which are not visible to the customer may be and usually are very vital to the quality of the service that the customer receives. Hence the company must go beyond what the customer perceives, and must stress quality of product and quality of service of every aspect that makes up the service system of the organization.

The organization, however, needs to keep in close touch with customer contacts so as to be informed about what the customer perceives to be the quality of performance of the organization. This means obtaining information about the following:

- The location of these customer contacts;
- The number of these customer contacts;
- The duration of such contacts;
- The favorable ones, and where they are;
- The unfavorable ones, and where they are;
- Those from which complaints come, and where they are.

Once management is aware of an unfavorable response from some customer contact, it is necessary to find the cause. This may involve employees, supervisor, or some component operation behind the scenes. In any event, the situation needs to be resolved to everyone's satisfaction, if it is at all important.

Designing to Reduce Variability of Human Performance

Designing a system fulfills the purpose of reducing variability of human performance. Consider three actual examples. One hundred forty-eight tax assessors assessed the value of the same residential property. The values ranged from about $4000 to $21,000, with an average of about $11,000. Dr. Youden of the National Bureau of Standards sent samples to 29 laboratories for testing. The purpose was to discover how much laboratories varied among themselves in testing presumably the same thing. Four values were so erratic that they had to be thrown out of the analysis; the remainder varied considerably. It is observed that the behavior of salespersons in the same store varies greatly in the way they approach and talk to customers. Customers don't like to hunt for salespersons.

How do you design a system that reduces the variability of tax assessors, the variability of laboratory chemists and other scientists, and the variability of the performance of salespeople? There are two approaches: 1) at the time of hiring employees should be screened to avoid extremes of performance, and 2) once they are hired, the following steps can be taken to reduce the variability:

- Tax Assessors: They need training in a standard set of criteria to use in appraising the value of residential property. The training should be followed by actual applications, with coaching as to where performance can be improved.

- Laboratory tests: These chemists clearly are not using the same methods. They are not using the same care in testing; they are not subject to close supervision as what to do and how to do it. The method will have to be described in detail in writing, and scrupulously followed if the extreme variations Youden found are to be greatly reduced.
- Behavior of salespersons: These persons need to attend classes in sales behavior, how to meet and talk to customers, how to talk about stock in hand, and how to be available.

Procedures have to be built into the system in the manner described above if wide variations in the behavior of persons is to be avoided, and if an improved quality of performance is to be guaranteed.

Designing Out the Faults of the System

A quality program or a quality system requires more than designing components to correct chronic troubles of the system and special causes connected with the employee. These are the hidden faults of the system. They exist because all kinds of quality characteristics are ignored or overlooked, because important aspects, components, or techniques are neglected or are not considered worthy of attention, or because it is assumed that they will be taken care of. Very often these faults have to be discovered after their absence or neglect causes trouble; examples are the following:

- No data at all: relevant data are not collected in an important area or situation.
- Biased data: these data can be worse than no data at all because they lead to false decisions; they may lead management to think it has a ''problem'' that does not exist.
- Inadequate data: the data may lack quantity and coverage and therefore lead to wrong inferences and decisions.
- Inefficient collection of data: this is due to a poor sample design, to an inadequate sample design, to lack of knowledge of sampling principles and practices, or to collecting too little or too much data. The result: waste, excess, and useless data.
- Inefficient analysis of the data: collection and analysis have to go together. Organization must have capability not only in how to collect data but how to analyze them in terms of quality control and improvement.

To design out the faults of the system due to poor-quality data requires at least one good professional statistician who understands probability sampling for surveys, sampling for quality control charts, and sampling for design of experiments. This person will also know how to analyze the data. Supervisors and employees need to be taught not only the basic techniques of sampling but its vital importance. One good professional statistician is all that is needed to design and implement adequate sampling plans and surveys, analyze the data, and teach others who lack knowledge about sampling.

Wasted Time, Lost Time, Down Time, Excessive Time, Idle Time

A comprehensive program needs to be planned to collect data to identify, locate, and reduce (if not eliminate) wasted time, lost time, and excessive time. This means keeping records on amount of time to answer a letter, to answer a telephone call, to ship an order, to wait for a job to be done, to do an internal job. This means using random time sampling to measure downtime on machines and equipment, idle time of employees waiting for work or for other reasons, amount of time to do a job or project; it means using the minute model to cost out these situations and projects. This requires training in better use of time and better work scheduling, preventive maintenance, and setting reasonable and realistic time goals.

Unacceptable Employee Behavior, Attitudes, and Appearance

One component of quality of service that can easily be overlooked is employee behavior, attitudes, and appearance. It should take top priority at the time of hiring. Those who do not like to work with people, who do not like to be kind and courteous to people, who have a low boiling point and who cannot handle calmly a situation involving trouble and conflict should never be hired in the first place. If they are hired, and if these attitudes are discovered, the person should be advised to seek employment that fits his or her behavior and attitudes. These characteristics, which are so important in quality of services, have already been described in some detail in Chapter 3. At this point the purpose is to emphasize that these characteristics cannot be overlooked in designing the components of a quality service system.

In order to develop the appropriate behavior, attitudes, and appearance, it is not only necessary to hire employees with these traits, but to have periodic seminars and conferences to maintain, reinforce, and set examples of these desirable characteristics. It would be well, in view of the personal nature of these characteristics, to allow the employees to develop their own standards and rules of conduct and dress on the job. Management should lead by persuasion, example, and experiences from other companies. They should emphasize that the way for the company to stay in business is to satisfy and please the customer; this involves personal relationships as much as, or even more than, the nature of the product or service being sold.

Errors and Error-prone Situations

In designing components it is well to try to anticipate where errors are most likely to arise, and to set up measures that will prevent them. This means that all kinds of foolproofing devices have to be used. Examples are the following:

- To prevent mixups of drugs, etc. use separate storage and distinctive labels.
- To prevent computer programming errors, have programmer work with statisticians or other specialists, and require a test run approved by them.
- Introduce verification techniques: checking, redundancy.
- Use safety devices and alarms.
- Use past levels to avoid major errors.

A Case: A Challenge to Management to Design Service Components

This is a description of what an expert found by observation while walking through a large number of stores.[1] An ex-general manager of a large retail store walked through Denver downtown stores to observe how they were operating in regard to customer service. This is what he found.

- Out of the 67 stores, no one spoke to him in 35 stores.
- He saw broken store fixtures.
- He saw dirty windows and doors.
- He saw incomplete window displays. Items sold had not been replaced.
- He noticed that some stores closed before 6 p.m.
- Some stores were poorly staffed during the lunch hour.
- In 35 stores he observed the following:
    - Employees engaged in lengthy personal telephone calls;
    - In 32 stores, 26 salespersons were chewing gum;
    - In one shoe department, the sales clerk was slouched in a chair.

He also made the following observations: Economic conditions shouldn't affect the quality of service. Retailers should set higher expectations for their employees. They're hiring clerks when they need salespeople. Inability to sell cost one store $200 in sales, the amount this expert was willing to spend on some clothes.

Suffice it to say that there were objections to what the expert observed, as well as those who agreed that he was right on target in stressing quality of service to the customer. He pointed out faults of the system as well as situations that the employees themselves could correct.

Once an employee understands the requirements of the job and performs well, the responsibility for quality performance shifts from management to the employee. When it hires each employee, management should make the rules of the game very clear not only in conferences and conversations but also in writing. These rules should cover specific aspects of behavior such as the following:

---

[1] *Rocky Mountain News,* April 19, 1987, p. 64.

- Making personal telephone calls;
- Chewing gum on the job;
- Smoking on the job;
- Coffee breaks and rest periods;
- Covering telephones during lunch hours;
- Hours of work and punctuality;
- How to talk to customers;
- Relationships with other departments;
- Lunch hour;
- Staffing during lunch hour;
- Working during rush periods;
- Sick leave;
- Paid-for leave;
- Unpaid-for leave;
- Absences;
- Promotions;
- Grievances and complaints;
- Political activities on the job;
- Attendance at professional conferences;
- Training classes: in-house, outside.

EXAMPLES OF FLOWCHARTS AND CHECKLISTS

The use of flowcharts and checklists is illustrated in the following pages. They show how the components of the service system are identified and placed in the proper relationships. They illustrate the kinds of activities to be included in flowcharts and checksheets. These are a blueprint for the entire service operation. In all cases the emphasis is on the customer. In some instances the components which are important to the organization, but invisible to the customer, are shown. In one case, the customer contacts with employees and with the system are indicated.

Examples of flowcharts:

- Flowchart for a restaurant;
- Flowchart for an airline flight;
- Flowchart for service in a doctor's office;
- Flowchart for service in the outpatient department of a hospital;
- Flowchart for the operations of a supermarket;
- Flowchart for a nationwide sample study of freight car shortages.

Examples of checklists:

- Checklist for a nursing home;
- Checklist for auto repair;

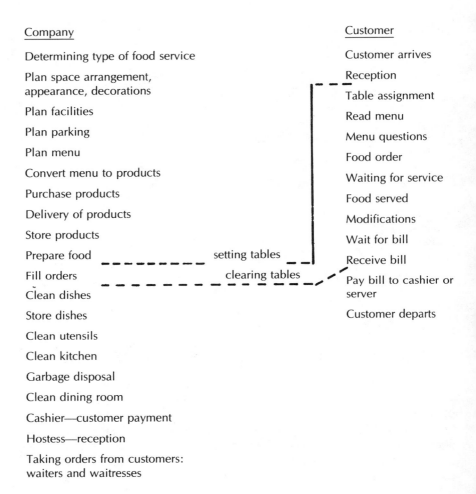

Company	Customer
Determining type of food service	Customer arrives
Plan space arrangement, appearance, decorations	Reception
	Table assignment
Plan facilities	Read menu
Plan parking	Menu questions
Plan menu	Food order
Convert menu to products	Waiting for service
Purchase products	Food served
Delivery of products	Modifications
Store products	Wait for bill
Prepare food setting tables	Receive bill
Fill orders clearing tables	Pay bill to cashier or server
Clean dishes	
Store dishes	Customer departs
Clean utensils	
Clean kitchen	
Garbage disposal	
Clean dining room	
Cashier—customer payment	
Hostess—reception	
Taking orders from customers: waiters and waitresses	

Flowchart for a Restaurant

- Checklist for hotel and motel;
- An STR action chart: checklist for spotting trouble.

SERVICE SYSTEM DESIGN: A SUMMARY

Design of Service Systems

The quality system should assure that all components of the system are identified, are analyzed into their quality characteristics and goals, and planned to

Company's activities	Customer's actions
Fueling plane	Origin of customer
Preparing plane for flight	Reservations
or	Transportation
Waiting for plane to arrive	Parking, if possible
Loading food	Checkin
Loading baggage	Safety check
Other loading and unloading	Waiting in lounge
Closing plane for departure	Waiting on plane
Towing plane into position	Takeoff stage

Safety lecture, demonstration

On-board service
food, liquor, music, magazines, movies,
captain's comments

Prepare for landing

Landing

Waiting to disembark

Travel to baggage pickup

Finding the baggage pickup

Waiting for baggage to appear

Finding all baggage

Finding outside transportation

Waiting for transportation

Transportation to destination

Baggage damage

Lost baggage

Tickets not correct

Cancellation of flight

Passenger bumped

Transfer to another line

Flowchart for an Airline Flight

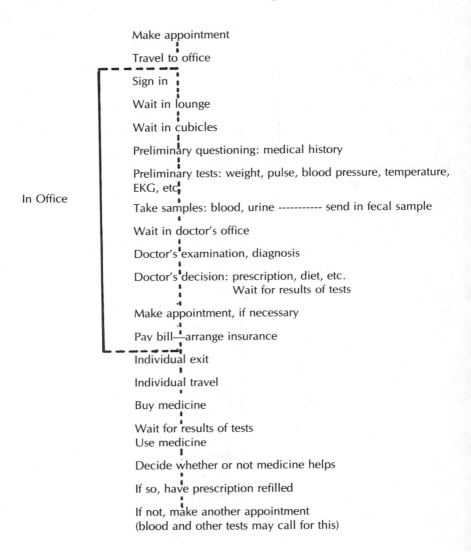

Make appointment

Travel to office

In Office

Sign in

Wait in lounge

Wait in cubicles

Preliminary questioning: medical history

Preliminary tests: weight, pulse, blood pressure, temperature, EKG, etc.

Take samples: blood, urine ---------- send in fecal sample

Wait in doctor's office

Doctor's examination, diagnosis

Doctor's decision: prescription, diet, etc.
                   Wait for results of tests

Make appointment, if necessary

Pay bill—arrange insurance

Individual exit

Individual travel

Buy medicine

Wait for results of tests
Use medicine

Decide whether or not medicine helps

If so, have prescription refilled

If not, make another appointment
(blood and other tests may call for this)

Flowchart for Service in a Doctor's Office

operate effectively and harmoniously. For service systems in place, the goal is to improve the quality of the component operations and integration of the components, as needed. For an entirely new service system the goal is to design the various components and their coordination for maximum-quality performance consistent with customer satisfaction.

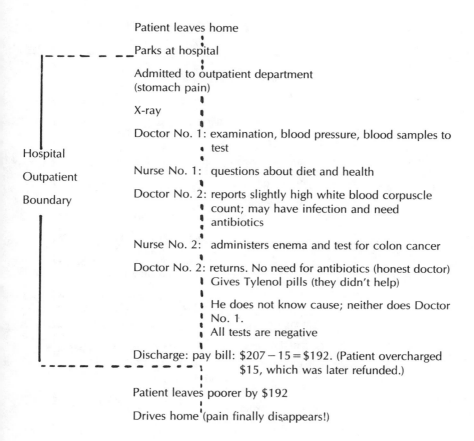

Patient leaves home

Parks at hospital

Admitted to outpatient department
(stomach pain)

X-ray

Doctor No. 1: examination, blood pressure, blood samples to
test

Nurse No. 1: questions about diet and health

Doctor No. 2: reports slightly high white blood corpuscle
count; may have infection and need
antibiotics

Nurse No. 2: administers enema and test for colon cancer

Doctor No. 2: returns. No need for antibiotics (honest doctor)
Gives Tylenol pills (they didn't help)

He does not know cause; neither does Doctor
No. 1.
All tests are negative

Discharge: pay bill: $207 − 15 = $192. (Patient overcharged
$15, which was later refunded.)

Patient leaves poorer by $192

Drives home (pain finally disappears!)

Hospital
Outpatient
Boundary

Flowchart for Service in the Outpatient Department of a Hospital

Service Components

A service component is an identifiable series of activities or operations, or a sequence of events or behavior, which is an integral part of the service system. These constitute the elements to be planned, designed, coordinated, and unified whether they are closely related or sequential, or whether they are independent. Physical appearance, arrangements, and attractiveness are important components.

Integrating Service Components

Whether components are sequential or independent, each should be designed considering interrelationships so as to create an effective total system that pro-

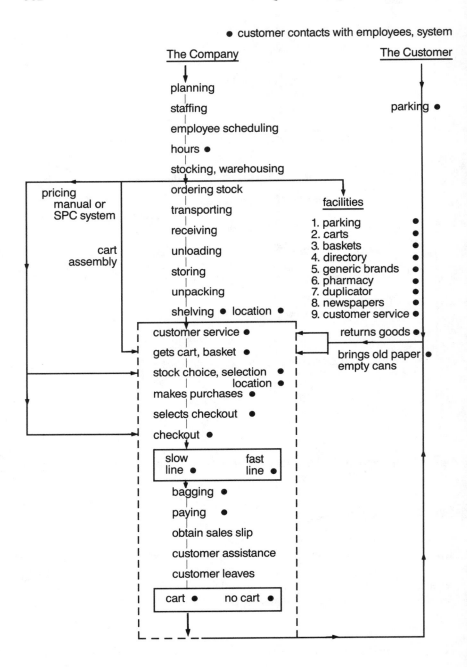

Flowchart for the Operations of a Supermarket

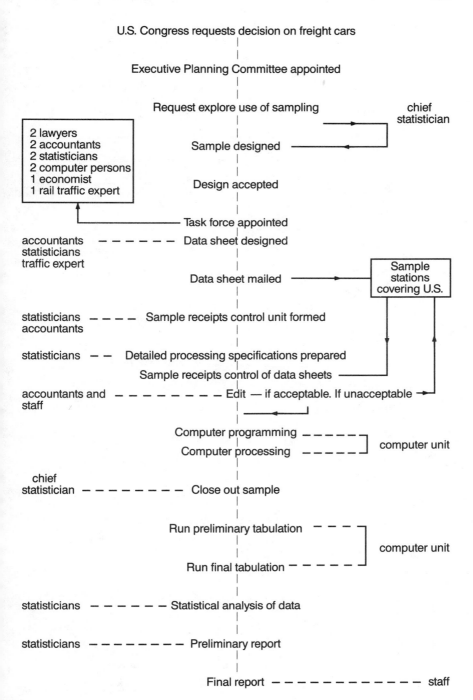

U.S. Congress requests decision on freight cars

Executive Planning Committee appointed

Request explore use of sampling — chief statistician

2 lawyers
2 accountants
2 statisticians
2 computer persons
1 economist
1 rail traffic expert

Sample designed

Design accepted

Task force appointed

accountants — — — — — Data sheet designed
statisticians
traffic expert

Data sheet mailed — Sample stations covering U.S.

statisticians — — — — Sample receipts control unit formed
accountants

statisticians — — Detailed processing specifications prepared

Sample receipts control of data sheets

accountants and — — — — — — — — Edit — if acceptable. If unacceptable
staff

Computer programming — — — — —
Computer processing — — — — — — computer unit

chief
statistician — — — — — — — — Close out sample

Run preliminary tabulation — — —
computer unit
Run final tabulation — — — — —

statisticians — — — — — — Statistical analysis of data

statisticians — — — — — — — Preliminary report

Final report — — — — — — — — — — staff

Flowchart for Nationwide Sample Study of Freight Car Shortages

Checklist for a Nursing Home

---

1. Food

    as prescribed by doctors _____

    on time _____

    sufficient _____

    nutrition _____

    any malnutrition _____

    eating assistance _____

    eating arrangements _____

    personal service _____

    other _____

2. Medical

    as prescribed by doctor _____

    right drugs given _____

    given on time _____

    response to calls _____

    nurse's care _____

    doctor's care _____

    medicine control _____

    right amounts of drugs given _____

    other _____

3. Room

    pleasant _____

    clean bed _____

    comfortable bed _____

    accessible signal _____

    clean linens _____

    roommate _____

place for personal belongings _____

pictures _____

other _____

4. Personal care

    bath _____

    hair _____

    clothes _____

    jewelry _____

    calls for help _____

    bed sores _____

    bathroom assistance _____

    needed assistance _____

    personal cleanliness _____

    other _____

5. Security

    against stealing _____

    against other patients _____

    against fire _____

    against employees _____

    of money, including

        social security _____

    of personal possessions _____

    blocking corridors with wheelchair

        patients _____

    other _____

6. Employee attitudes

    helpful _____

attentive _____	compassionate _____
concerned _____	indifferent _____
indifferent _____	profit-oriented _____
ignore calls _____	no concern for patients _____
cruel, brutal _____	employee training _____
thieving _____	hiring _____
other _____	supervision _____
7. Activities	facilities _____
exercise _____	kitchen _____
reading _____	sanitation _____
radio, television _____	wheelchairs _____
religious programs _____	dining room _____
games _____	heating _____
trips, tours _____	ventilation _____
visitors _____	air conditioning _____
other _____	housekeeping _____
8. Management	safety _____
humane _____	other _____

duces customer satisfaction at minimum cost. This calls for a detailed analysis of the activities involved in each component once it is identified and bounded, as well as the identification and implications of all interrelationships.

The Role of People

Service system design must consider the vital role of all the persons involved in the functioning of the service system:

- personnel: management, other supervisory personnel, nonsupervisory;
- customer-buyer: individual, company or agency.

With personnel the problem is not only to define what quality performance means but to provide the facilities, conditions, and relationships which will

Checklist for Auto Repair

Directions: This is to be filled out for every repair job or for a well-designed sample of such jobs. A summary of the data for the various questions and items will show how effective the design of the quality system is.

1. Waiting time of the customer to get service: days _____ hours _____

2. Customer travel time to service: hours _____ minutes _____

3. Date of service _____

4. Customer's description of trouble _____
   or

5. Customer's list of items to be checked: oil _____ tires _____ battery water _____

   radiator water _____ radiator antifreeze _____ brakes _____ starting _____

   filter _____ transmission _____ gearshift _____ lights _____ other _____

6. Customer's wait in lounge: hours _____ minutes _____
   or

7. Was customer given ( ) or rented ( ) a car while car was in repair?

   (neither _____)

8. Service time days _____ hours _____ minutes _____

9. Charge for service time _____

10. Charge for repair parts, other _____

11. Were specific services itemized? yes _____ no _____

12. Were all items serviced? yes _____ no _____

13. Were all repairs and changes satisfactory? yes _____ no _____

14. What was unsatisfactory? _____

    _____

    _____

15. If unsatisfactory, was car returned? yes _____ no _____

16. Was it reserviced? yes _____ no _____

17. Length of wait for reservice: days _____ hours _____ minutes _____

18. What was mechanic's original diagnosis of problems? _____

    _____

19. Remedies used _____

    _____

20. Was original diagnosis changed? no _____ If "yes," how? _____

Checklist for Hotel and Motel

1. Making reservations
2. Confirmation
3. Transportation in
4. Parking
5. Check in
6. Baggage handling
7. Is the room ready?
8. Is the room the kind asked for?

Room
1. At least two chairs
2. At least two reading lights
3. Writing table
4. Clock
5. Radio
6. Television
7. Telephone service
8. Room service menu
9. Heat: does it work?
10. Air conditioning: does it work?
11. Bath, shower
12. Hot water
13. Soap
14. Towels
15. Beds
16. Bed linens
17. Extra blankets
18. Closet space
19. Do the keys work easily?
20. Is there a wake-up call?

Other services
1. Room service
2. Restaurants
   Coffee shop
   Dining room
   Sunday service
3. Bars, cocktail lounges
4. Drugstore
5. Newspapers
6. Magazines
7. Ice available
8. Quiet surroundings
9. Is room made up daily?
10. Courtesy bus
11. Mail service
12. Recreational services, e.g., pool

Checkout service
1. Checkout
2. Baggage handling
3. Transportation out (arrangements)
4. Filling out report on services
5. Were room and service worth the price?
6. Was service satisfactory?

facilitate the attainment of quality performance. With buyers, the problem is to determine what constitutes the characteristics and conditions that lead to customer satisfaction. These conditioning factors should be built into the service system design.

Personnel Performance as a Quality Determinant

Quality is determined by the performance of people at all levels: managerial, other supervisory, and nonsupervisory. The quality aspects of both individual and team or group work should be considered; a team or group may consist of an organizational unit, a task force, a technical committee, or some other group.

An STR Action Chart: Checklist for Spotting Trouble

An STR action chart serves the purpose of identifying sources of trouble (s), identifying the trouble (T), and laying out the remedy to correct the trouble (R). It can use data from a detailed check sheet.

Source	Trouble	Remedy
*Food		
*Room		
*Medicine		
*Personal care		
*Security		
*Employees		
*Supervisor		
*Medical care		
*Nurse		
*Doctor		
*Other patients		
*Dining room		
*Assistance		
*Recreation		
*Communication		
*Religious		
*Visitors		
*Administration		
*Sanitation		
*Housekeeping		
*Management		
*Reservations		
*Transportation		
*Mail		
*Billing		

Service Goals

A service system should specify, wherever possible, service goals or levels such as zero error rates, minimum delay times, acceptable service times, 100 percent service reliability, regulatory requirements such as those relating to safety and sanitation, customer satisfaction in terms of ratings or complaints, costs such as affordable and life-cycle costs, and other measures. Careful attention has to be given to the subjective aspects of customer satisfaction and customer perception of quality of both products and services.

Service System Appraisal and Improvement

Management should be appraised in terms of quality policy and plans, support of the quality program, support of quality implementation, and providing means and resources which employees and other supervisors require for quality performance.

Other supervisory personnel are appraised in terms of their understanding of the quality program, effectiveness in motivating employees to meet quality performance goals, quality improvements, and in taking immediate corrective actions where they can do so or reporting need for corrective action to higher organizational levels. Nonsupervisory personnel are appraised in various ways such as employee performance, employee rating, employee suggestions and contributions, employee criticism, customer complaints about employees and quality improvements. Customer satisfaction can be appraised in terms of customer complaints, customer ratings, customer tests and surveys, and trends in customer patronage. In addition to using these appraisals to improve the quality of service, a study of market trends, a survey of successful service firms, and taking steps to improve personnel and customer relations can also improve the quality of the system. A survey of lost customers should be part of a continuous plan to improve quality of services.

Chapter 13

Starting a Quality Control Program

PREREQUISITES

Before a company or agency can start a quality control or a quality improvement program (QUIP), there are certain requirements or prerequisites that have to be met. There is nothing unusual about this. It is universally recognized that this is true in all technical and highly specialized fields. Any stranger to the field needs some orientation, some knowledge, some understanding before he or she can start to work in the field. The field of quality, quality control, and quality improvement is no exception. What do these preliminaries consist of? How are they acquired? There has to be at least one person in the company or agency who has this orientation before anything can be started.

Someone has to know what the word "quality" means. This requires some understanding of what the term "quality characteristics" means, what is meant by "poor quality," what is meant by "quality improvement," and how it is attained. It must be recognized that people (employees, customers, and others) are the key to quality improvement, and that knowledge of supervision and techniques is the way by which this improvement is made.

Several different ways are open to anyone who desires this orientation. One is to take seminars in quality management and quality techniques. Another is to study at least one book in each field such as *Management of Quality* by Juran, *Statistical Quality Control* by Grant or Burr, or Deming's *Quality, Productivity and Competitive Position*. Another is to take college courses in management and statistics, with special reference to quality if this is possible.

Without careful preparation, there may be form but little substance. There may be a lot of talk but little action. There may be fine-sounding policies, plans, and decisions but little or no implementation. The following example shows what happens when a large company has neither the managerial nor the technical capabilities to run an effective quality program. They never really learned what quality control and quality improvement were all about.

A Case Study

This is a description of the quality program of a large service company, although there are others like it. This example illustrates just about everything a company or agency *should not do:*

- It has a quality assurance department.
- It issues a monthly report and apparently nothing else.
- Apparently this report is considered of no greater importance than any other routine monthly report, e.g., payroll, personnel, inventory.
- The tables of data are not clear, the titles are not well worded, units of measurement are missing. Frequency distributions are not properly constructed. Averages could not be verified. Explanations of various tables and charts are not given.
- Sampling is used but the methods are not explained. Sampling variations in the estimates, as well as biases in the data, are not discussed anywhere.
- Something which is akin to standards of performance is shown, but these standards appear to be set in terms of past achievement rather than in terms of some improved level of attainment.
- There is no description of how the data indicate trouble or being "out of control," or how or what corrective action is to be taken and by whom.
- One gets the impression that this report will lead to very little change in the status quo.
- There is no explanation of the functions of the quality assurance department, what the specific purpose of this monthly report is, or to whom it is directed. Neither is there any information as to how the report is prepared, and by whom. There is no mention of what this report has to do with "quality" or with "quality assurance."

What Is the Trouble with This Arrangement?

It is obvious that several things are wrong with this arrangement. It is much easier, however, to point out these shortcomings than it is to correct them:

- The Quality Assurance Department has a big statistical job, including sample design, but no statistical capability to do it.
- No one seems to realize that the quality of the statistical work is not even at the level that is required of those taking the very first course in statistics. They do not seem to realize that they have a statistical problem.
- Those in charge do not seem to understand what "quality control" means, including collection of good-quality data at the source. Neither do they seem to understand the implications of "quality assurance," the name of the department.
- Those in charge do not understand what "management of quality" means, the management or supervisory capability required, or what "management for quality improvement" means.
- Those in charge do not seem to be aware of the need for urgency in isolating, identifying, and correcting sources of trouble or "out-of-control" situations. By the time the monthly report reaches an official who can take corrective action, five or six weeks may elapse.

- They apparently look upon the report as a routine statistical matter and nothing else. More emphasis seems to be placed on whether operations are meeting certain numerical levels or "standards" already set than upon whether any improvements have taken place. They may be more interested in maintaining the status quo, which seems to them to be quite satisfactory, than in making any improvements or desirable changes.
- The entire report suffers from a dearth of explanations. Methods, data, tables, calculations, and charts need to be explained. Analysis and exposition are missing. The report is not tailored to the needs of the various levels of officials and others for whom it is intended.

What Do They Need to Do to Improve Quality?

The first step is to realize that they have to start from where they are now. They have an ongoing quality assurance department, so the word "quality" is not new to them. This is where to start. This is where to begin thinking about improving quality and quality assurance in the company. Identify the important quality characteristics, such as errors and delay time.

Begin by cleaning up the monthly report. This report is a major source of important problems and projects, involving both operations and a presentation and analysis of problems with corrective actions. Use them to start making improvements. Get managers more interested in quality and in its improvement. Get them involved in identifying, analyzing, and solving significant problems. Move toward a program of continuous quality improvement. Get top-level management to make this a company policy and commitment.

To clean up the monthly report requires technical capability and ability to prepare and make effective presentations in written form. All that is needed to do this is to hire one good practitioner in statistics who knows quality control. He or she can begin immediately to implement an improved technical approach in a series of steps, covering each of the following:

Improving the quality of data collected as needed;
Sampling;
Data Analysis;
Explanations;
Tables;
Frequency distributions;
Discovering problems;
Graphs;
Calculations;
Format;
Presentation;
Organization of material.

Action reports should be separated from summary reports and from detailed backup data reports. They should be tailored to specific levels of officials, professionals, and supervisors. These improvements can be made readily without upsetting the existing organization. It is doing better what they are already trying to do. However, the improvement of the monthly report should be seen as only the beginning of a broader program which could lead easily to a drastic change in the reporting system itself.

It is necessary at the start to have a clear idea of the *characteristics* which determine quality of products and services, as well as situations which are related thereto. It is necessary to have a clear understanding of what quality means before one can start a program whose aim is to improve that quality.

In connection with a program to improve the monthly report, the managers and others, with the assistance of the statistics or quality control specialist, can lay the foundation for beginning a continuous program of quality improvement. This will include plans, training, procedures, and actions along the following lines:

- Orientation and redirection for better management, and supervision for the purpose of engaging in a broader and more balanced quality program;
- Technical instruction at all levels for a more complete and effective application of quality technology, including the collection of quality data;
- Emphasis on the concept of statistical process control to improve specific operations in various parts of the company;
- Surveying and instructing employees and managers with regard to what quality performance requires and what quality improvement means;
- Identifying important problem areas and concentrating on solving them first, using management of quality and quality technology most effectively;
- Stressing the need for improved quality data and data analysis.

How do you convince present management and the people in the Quality Assurance Department that they need statistical capability and that the monthly report can be greatly improved? It will not be easy for an outsider to do this. It will be difficult even if the initiative starts from within the company. Once the company is convinced that it needs statistical capability, one of several routes can be taken:

- The best way is to hire a quality specialist who knows sampling and statistics, and can apply them effectively, or a practitioner in statistics who knows how to apply them effectively to quality control problems and situations.
- A less desirable way is to train someone, preferably a supervisor or professional, in statistics and quality control. This person could come from the QA department or from some other part of the company. The danger is

that this training will lack both breadth and depth, and therefore the person will not be able to exploit technology to the same extent as a specialist in quality control or in statistics.

ORGANIZING FOR QUALITY

Quality can be organized and managed in many different ways. The following five ways illustrate actual practice:

1. Vice-president in charge of quality department and customer relations. Department may be called Quality Assurance Department;
2. Quality council consisting of senior officials, with formation of quality teams at every lower level;
3. Regular organization with quality circles in every unit or section;
4. Regular organization with task forces for special jobs and projects;
5. Regular organization with quality orientation of every employee.

The organization takes the following simplified form:

Level	*Function*
Top executives	Head quality council;
Upper-level managers	Compose quality council;
Middle managers	Implement and monitor quality program;
First-line supervisors	Supervise and implement quality program;
Employees	Work according to quality plan; may form quality circles or not.

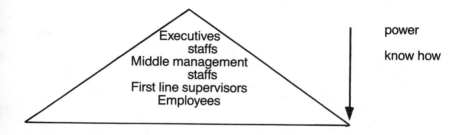

Figure 13–1. **Top-Down Execution of a Quality Program**

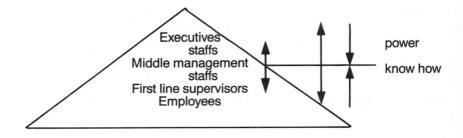

Figure 13–2. Two-Way Execution, Starting in the Middle or Below

Another Approach: Starting at the Working Level

The experts recommend that the quality improvement program start with the top-level executives. Then, by their policies, decisions, and actions, quality improvement will permeate the entire company or agency. Then constant leadership will guarantee continuity of the program. This is hard to implement.

Another approach is to start at the working level, where the know-how and problems are. This includes middle-level managers and professionals, supervisors, and employees. These are the persons to start an improvement project; these are the ones who build quality into services and products:

	Level	*Major characteristics*
	Top	Power
Start here →	Middle	Technical and power know-how
→	Bottom	Work ability, problem awareness

Instead of talking to managers, supervisors, and employees about "quality" and "programs," we talk about improvement: product improvement, service improvement, work improvement. The questions are: How can we improve the work? What can we do better? What needs to be changed? Are there faults to be corrected?

The specific concerns include simplification, better methods and equipment, defective materials, excessive delays, lack of cooperation, high error rates, communication problems, more detailed and clearer instructions, and better-defined goals.

A start can be made by a middle manager, a middle-level professional, a supervisor, or a group of supervisors. Meetings and discussions are held with employees and supervisors to obtain cooperation and to compile a list of important problems. One of these is selected for a pilot improvement project: one in which cooperation prevails and which is not too big, is very important, and has a very good chance of succeeding.

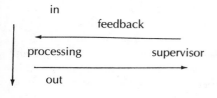

Quality Control Department

designs sample, discusses documents, puts sample into effect, prepares error table, corrects errors, holds conferences with supervisor, sets error levels, prepares reports for supervisor and manager

Example 1. **Quality Control Department Works with Supervisors**

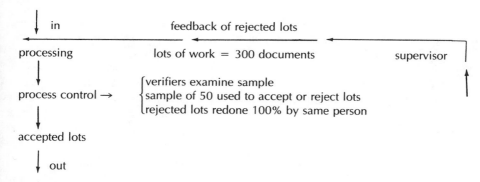

Note: Sample is designed by consultant. The supervisor keeps error and production records for every employee; coaches, trains, and concentrates on frequent errors; is an expert who decides what is right and what is wrong.

Example 2. **Supervisor or Manager Uses Process Control Designed by Consultant**

Starting From the Middle and Going Up and Down—the Past

The example just given illustrates how middle management is used as the origin of and steppingstone to a quality improvement program. This is how the first successful applications of quality control started in both products and services. All of the persons identified with the first successful applications of quality control were in middle management or lower middle management, or were supervisors, foremen, inspectors, staff specialists, or professionals.

This is the way it had to be. Shewhart's books on quality control were based on mathematical statistics and probability. To demonstrate whether his theories and methods would work successfully in the real world required persons who were familiar with basic principles of statistics and probability, and were interested in applying them to specific problems or situations in operations. An application as technical and mathematical as quality control could never be made by executives or managers. They do not get to the top by studying mathematics, statistics, and probability. In fact, these are the subjects they avoid in college. (In the 1930s and 1940s college courses in these subjects were very rare. One had to learn the basics by studying the books available, the ASTM manual of 1933, and issues of the Journal of the Royal Statistical Society. Short courses were given to lower-level employees during World War II by a selected group including Deming, Olds, Knowler, Grant, and Working.) As Clarence Randall of Inland Steel said, the courses that an executive should take are law, accounting, and Shakespeare.

Today, now that Shewhart's concepts and techniques have been demonstrated to work very successfully in the real world of both manufacturing and services, it is easy to be enthusiastic about management and to ignore techniques, as if management alone is all that is needed. No one wants to admit today that it was the failure of management and engineering in the first place that brought the Western Electric problem to Shewhart at the Bell Telephone Laboratories, and resulted in his solving the problem by means of statistics and probability.

Starting from the Middle and Going Up and Down—The Present

This approach is not as unsound today as many people would have us believe. President MacDonald of General Motors states that some middle managers are well ahead of their bosses with regard to quality. President Sperlich of Chrysler also had a good word for the middle manager.[1] This seems to be a warning that while considering the development of a quality improvement program, top-level management and others should not overlook the fact that support for a quality program already exists in middle management.

The Dana Corporation reports that the initiative for a program stressing quality came from division managers. This movement for quality went from the operating groups to top management. Top-level management agreed to support them, and made a major commitment to total quality. Quality went from the grassroots to top-level management and then down again.[2]

These examples show that the importance of quality may reach middle management before it reaches the top. Hence they give support to exploring if not starting in the middle where operations are, and where managers are faced daily

---

[1] *Quality Progress,* April 1985, pp. 30–31.

[2] *The Juran Report,* Winter 1985, p. 109.

with both short-run and long-run problems. It may also suggest that the best way to start a quality improvement program in one company may not be the best way in another. The goal is that regardless of the nature of the original or initial approach, a continuous program of quality improvement is planned and implemented.

Top Down

This is the approach recommended by all of the leading authorities on the subject: Drs. Deming, Juran, and Ishikawa. The quality program is to start at the very top and to move downward through upper management and middle management to supervisors and employees.

The first question is: How will the top get started? They are not accustomed to starting anything as innovative and as technical as quality control. Apparently the authorities mentioned above assume that top-level management will attend the lectures, seminars, or video showings presented by one of these authorities. This is one way to get the top started. But what about those who do not attend and those who are not convinced even after attending? Who will convince these top-level executives that they need a quality improvement program? It will not be as simple as it sounds. Many problems will arise.

Suppose there are differences of opinion among the top officials with regard to a quality program. How will this be resolved? How influential can the top be in initiating technological and managerial changes which quality implies, even after they understand the implications of these changes?

The top is not familiar with operations where most of the problems exist and where most of the situations involving quality arise. Executives bake no bread. They can furnish the stove, the ingredients, the utensils, and the space, but someone else bakes the bread and therefore determines its quality. The top makes policy, final decisions, and plans and allocates the resources, but others must implement them.

For the "top down" to work, there must be formed at the same time a quality council, quality steering committee, quality executive group, or executive quality team. It will be up to this key group to see that the policies, plans, and decisions of the top, relative to quality and its improvement, are carried out. This means carrying the quality message to lower-level managers, supervisors, and employees. This cannot be done until surveys are made to find out the attitudes, opinions, and reactions of these employees to a quality program.

The program may be resented as imposed from on high unless those below are involved, unless it has the approval of most of the managers and employees, and unless, at the same time, those below are solicited for their attitudes, views, and problems. Not all layers of organization may accept quality as defined by the top. It will be necessary to obtain large areas of agreement before any real start can be made.

It is not the top that is aware of problems, inefficiency, and waste. It is those below, who do the work. It is the supervisors who struggle with operations daily; it is middle managers who plan, measure, appraise, and implement. These are the ones who can see most easily where improvements can be made and what forms they should take.

The top knows only when sales go up or down, when profits are good, when competition is a threat, or when the rate of return falls. They are money-oriented. Quality requires a change in thinking, and the understanding of new concepts.

How will top officials learn about quality control or total quality control? There are several ways:

- From experts, e.g., Drs. Deming and Juran;
- From the media, e.g., *The New York Times, The Wall Street Journal;*
- From the competition, e.g., the Japanese;
- From top officials in other companies;
- From their own top-level officials, middle management, staff professionals;
- From someone in operations who demonstrates that quality control works.

This change can be a slow process because quality control and total quality control are new and strange ideas and concepts. Management has never heard of them before. It is much easier for management and high-level professionals to accept a computer system with whirling reels of tape, flashing lights, and high-speed printer. A machine is much easier to sell than an idea.

Weaknesses of the Top-Down Approach

The weaknesses of this approach can be summarized as follows:

- Difficulty in getting all managers and departments to cooperate;
- Slowness with which the top level accepts the idea of quality;
- The length of time it takes for quality concepts to trickle down through the organization;
- That the technical knowledge required is missing;
- That a balanced approach to quality is difficult and takes time;
- That the top doesn't know where the real problems are;
- That the top doesn't see itself as responsible for its own quality of performance; it concentrates on the employees.

Examples of a Quality Program Started at the Top

Examples of starting a quality program at the top are described and diagrammed below.

1. A bank. A vice-president was put in charge of starting and developing a

quality program. He was not familiar with the subject nor how to start. The first step he took was to talk to the several managers and discover what they thought about quality, what standards they had if any, and related information. The managers didn't have definite ideas; on the whole they were vague. Then he surveyed employees to obtain their views on quality. As a result, steps were taken to

1. explain quality
2. define quality characteristics
3. develop standards and goals
4. learn problem detection, diagnosis, and remedies
5. develop the quality concept companywide, and form quality circles to put program into effect
6. start training classes

2. Insurance. We cite two insurance companies which started quality in entirely different ways.

1. This company started with the formation of a quality council consisting of upper level managers. They directed and guided the program. A quality staff was formed which assisted quality teams which were formed to identify and resolve quality problems. Middle managers monitored quality while supervisors worked with employees to implement the program.

2. In this company quality control was introduced to reduce the errors in the claims which were the input data to a new computer installation. Top officials recognized that unless errors were sharply reduced the use of a computer would be very expensive if not a failure.

A quality control division was formed which guided, trained, advised, and assisted the supervisor in all technical aspects including sampling and quality control charts and analysis of errors and their prevention. Time trends and control charts were used to control all of the major kinds of errors. As a result all sources of error were driven down to one percent or below.

Case 1: A Public Utility

The chief executive officer of this company read about quality control and later went to Japan to observe how the Japanese applied it to their industries.

A quality council was formed, with quality improvement teams organized at every lower level. A quality improvement team found that the billing department was making 60,000 errors a year. With the aid of the quality improvement team, this rate was reduced to nearly zero. One wonders what kind of sloppy supervision existed in the billing department during the previous decades. Was it necessary for someone to go to Japan to find out these errors were massive and needed to be prevented?

Case 2: Company A

1. Chief executive officer reads Crosby, hears Crosby.
2. CEO has a senior executive go to Crosby College.
3. Senior executive holds meetings with middle managers.
4. Middle managers hold meetings with first-line supervisors.
5. Supervisors put quality plans and program into effect.

Case 3: Company B

1. Program was started at the top of a fundamental unit or department.
2. They found one man who knew how to apply quality control to the problems of the department. The purpose was to make a successful demonstration in one area.
3. They ran a quality project in one area before spreading out across the company.
4. The managers have to direct the quality teams and see that the quality improvement programs are well managed.
5. The "facilitators," whose job is to teach, coordinate, and lead, are the line managers.
6. The manager of the department has to make sure that resources needed are available.
7. The employees are encouraged to join the quality teams and participate in the quality improvement program. (In this case membership in quality teams was voluntary. In other cases it is compulsory.)

STEPS

1. Quality survey:
   - Quality situation;
   - How managers viewed quality;
   - How quality was measured;
   - Quality objectives.

Vice-President for Operations
|
Vice-President for Quality Assurance and Customer Relations
|
Quality Assurance Division
Quality Staff

Figure 13–3. **How a Bank Organized for Quality**

2. Develop quality program:
   - Specific measurements of quality;
   - Develop standards;
   - Develop quality assurance concept companywide;
   - Define deviations from desired quality;
   - Employee meetings and participation;
   - Identify deviations;
   - Apply Pareto analysis;
   - Diagnose problem;
   - Identify causes;
   - Find remedy;
   - Take action;
   - Introduce quality cost program;
   - Develop reports;
   - Develop training courses to improve quality.
3. Refine program:
   - Issue quality assurance report monthly; prepare other reports;
   - Collect data and analyze quality costs;
   - Engage in long-range planning;
   - Give more attention to customer relations.
4. Introduce, organize, promote, and expand use of quality circles.
5. Develop a long-range quality improvement program.

Figure 13–4. **How an Insurance Company Organized for Quality**

Fig. 13–5. **How a Public Utility Organized for Quality**

Program Steps

1. Define quality.
2. Set quality goals.
3. Measure quality characteristics by sampling.
4. Identify deviations from goals.
5. Compare obtained measures with standards.
6. Find causes of deviations.
7. Take corrective action.
8. Plan for continuous quality improvement.
9. Inaugurate quality cost studies.
10. Be sure quality program includes everyone.
11. Implement plan for continuous quality improvement.
12. Plan organization and operations for continuity of program.

Starting at the Top, in the Middle, and Below at the Same Time

In this approach a start is made simultaneously at the top, where the final power is, and in the middle and below, where the knowledge of troubles and problems is. This means that the lower-level people receive the green light to go ahead with a quality program at the same time that the top-level officials are making a commitment to total quality.

This approach sounds good on paper, but whether it can be attained in the manner stated is another question. It requires that middle management be ready to push an initial quality improvement program, and that all they need from the top is approval, commitment, and constant purpose.

Two conditions must be met: acceptance and support from the top, and the statistical and other technical capability in the operating divisions. This means the understanding of a wide variety of sampling, quality control, and related techniques, and how to apply them effectively. It means the ability to survey operations, identify problems, isolate quality characteristics, measure and control them, and implement an effective quality improvement program. Making policies and decisions at the top is only one step. They mean nothing if the managerial and technical capabilities do not exist to put content and substance into a quality program.

BASIC QUESTIONS

A quality program involves several basic decisions at the start:

- *Who* will start the program?
- *Where* will the program start?
- *When* will it start?
- *How* will it start?
- *What* will start the program?

Who?

It can be started at any level in the company, or by an outsider:

- Top-level managers: president, vice-president;
- Middle managers;
- Professional staff members;
- Supervisor or foreman;
- Consultant;
- Conductor of a training class.

Who Starts It?

- An individual: official, manager, technical professional (e.g., a statistician). This is someone who is interested in quality, or someone who is familiar with quality control techniques and problems. This person may be in one of the operating divisions.
- A group, team or task force: This can be a group selected by a higher-level official who is in a position to authorize the formation of such a group. Some lower-level official or manager may be appointed to head this group. It should include anyone in any of the divisions who has interest or knowledge in quality.

Where?

A quality program may start anywhere in the company or organization. Hence it is necessary to select the place most likely to succeed with a big payoff.

- In an operating division;
- In connection with a purchased product;
- In connection with inspection or verification;
- In a specific situation;
- Where a problem exists or is found;
- Where some chronic problem or situation exists;
- Where a serious customer complaint is found.

When?

Several important conditions have to be met before a quality program can be started:

- The idea of a quality program is accepted, approved, and supported.
- Teamwork and cooperation among all those involved can be counted on.
- The necessary approval has been obtained.
- The necessary technical capability is available.
- The necessary managerial and planning capability is available.
- A suitable project is found.

How?

The several steps followed in carrying though a quality program from beginning to end are applicable as follows:

- Identify the problem.
- Analyze the problem.
- Identify the quality characteristics.
- Collect the necessary data.
- Interpret the data.
- Isolate cause or causes.
- Find the solution.
- Take action.
- Measure improvement.

How Does the Organization Start It?

- Obtain internal knowledge:
  Survey managers, supervisors, employees, and customers for problems, troubles, and ideas for improvement. Find out what quality of products and quality of services means to them.

- Obtain external knowledge:
  Hire someone to conduct conferences on quality and on quality management and techniques. Read books, view videotapes, and learn quality from experts such as Deming and Juran.

What Can Start It?

A situation or a problem may arise which can start a program or the first application in such a program. Actual cases are as follows:

- Need to control high error rate of input into a new computer system;
- Need to control error rate arising in transcribing data from documents to a standardized format for input into a computer;
- Realization by manager that 100 percent verification is unnecessary;
- Manager attends a class in quality control;
- Foreman attends a class in quality control;
- Statistician applies quality control to errors made by coders and key punch operators;
- High-quality data are required by government regulations (e.g., insurance).

What Does the Organization Do Next?

- Isolate and identify quality characteristics associated with quality:
  Defects;
  Errors;
  Delay time;
  Lost time;
  Employee complaints, attitudes, ideas, troubles, knowledge;
  Customer complaints, attitudes, ideas, troubles, knowledge;
  Lost customers: Why were they lost?
  Unsafe conditions and practices.
- Separate poor quality due to system from poor quality due to employee.
- Select a problem or situation to start on.
  - Make a list of problems involving quality and select one to start on: one that is important, full of interest, highly visible, with high probability of success, relatively easy to solve or improve.
  - Plan and implement this problem as a project.
  - Appraise this project and use experience to develop a quality program.

DEVELOPING A QUALITY PROGRAM

There is no quick and easy road to a quality program or to a quality improvement program. The experts in the field are agreed that it takes several years to get a program off the ground, for the following reasons:

- It is a knowledge revolution.
- It involves the entire company or agency.
- It represents a large volume of new ideas, concepts, and techniques.
- It calls for a drastic change in thinking.
- It calls for a drastic change in behavior.
- It is not a new product; it is a new idea, and many persons do not like new and revolutionary ideas.

This is more easily seen when the details of the new creed are laid out:

- Quality is everybody's business.
- Do the job right the first time.
- Quality is built into a service, not inspected in.
- Improving quality is a constant goal.
- Satisfy the customer by stressing accuracy, promptness, and politeness.
- Where the employee renders the service directly to the customer, the employee is responsible for the quality of that service.

Management's job is to make sure all employees and officials understand that specific quality goals include the following:

- Defects go to zero.
- Human errors and mistakes go to zero.
- Lost and wasted time go to zero.
- Unacceptable human behavior goes to zero.
- Customer complaints go to zero.
- Lost customers go to zero.
- Damage and losses go to zero.
- Unsafe conditions go to zero.

Management's job is also to see that managers, supervisors, and employees have whatever is required to move toward these goals:

- Tools;
- Facilities;
- Equipment;
- Knowledge, know-how;
- Resources;
- Guidance, leadership;
- Technical capability.

Quality Planning

Planning is part of a cycle of steps which are expressed in different forms. The following is a general form:

1. Plan goals or objectives.
2. Apply the various means necessary to reach goals.
3. Measure progress toward goals.
4. Identify problems or trouble spots.
5. Take action.

Dr. Deming uses four general steps, which are applicable to services:

1. Plan
2. Do
3. Check
4. Action

These can be applied in more detail to services, as follows:

1. Plan the service operations and their components.
2. Put the plan into effect or into place.
3. Render the services to customers.
4. Test and appraise each component of service.
5. Take the necessary actions to eliminate sources of trouble and to resolve any problems.

The following are examples of specific plans which are involved in quality planning:

1. Plan a quality improvement project budget.
2. Plan to improve customer services and to reduce customer complaints.
3. Plan to stress quality in all training courses; plan new courses in quality management and quality techniques.
4. Plan to survey lost customers and find out why they were lost.
5. Plan to improve services in critical areas.
6. Plan to work on appraising managers and supervisors in terms of their contributions to quality.
7. Plan to develop a better system of estimating quality costs.
8. Plan to improve quality of products from vendors so that receiving inspection can be reduced, if not eliminated.
9. Plan to reduce further the cost of defects in purchased products, errors, lost and wasted time, and unacceptable behavior toward customers.
10. Plan to develop and implement safety programs in all operations.

Quality Control

Quality control means taking steps necessary to stabilize a count or a measurement at an acceptable level. In services this does not mean stabilizing a measurement at some acceptable average but driving levels down to a minimum. Examples are absenteeism, delivery times, times to do a job, and service times.

In connection with defects in purchased products, human errors, lost and wasted time, unacceptable behavior, customer complaints, and losses and damages, the goal is not to stabilize some level but to continually drive these values toward zero. The only acceptable level is zero, even though it may never be reached. These sources of waste are controlled by eliminating them.

The responsibility of management is to see that the technical capability is available and is actually working toward these goals. Quality control will be the goal and aim of both the local quality improvement teams or quality circles and the interdepartmental quality improvement teams whose function is to get rid of the faults of the system and to solve problems cutting across two or more departments.

What Is the Scope of the Project at the Start?

The scope initially covers the entire company, but this approach has serious limitations unless steps are taken to overcome obstacles. At this point we assume that the program is started in a very limited fashion so that the chances of success are maximized. This limited approach takes the following form:

- Start with a single problem.
- Use this problem for a quality improvement project.
- Start with a problem or situation that has a high probability of success.
- Use this project as a demonstration that quality improvement is real, that it can be attained, and that it succeeds.

There is a very real advantage to selecting a project which can demonstrate that quality can be improved. It is hoped that such a demonstration will convince the doubting Thomases, the skeptics, and the critics that quality improvements can be attained in the real world under actual working conditions. If one project is not enough, then two or three may be necessary to convince the doubters.

Taking Bearings—Finding Out Where People Stand on Quality

Two actions are necessary to take bearings and to find out where managers, supervisors, and employees stand relative to quality:

1. Making a survey of *attitudes* toward quality and its improvement; and
2. Making a survey to discover and identify *problems*.

The Attitude Survey

The survey of attitudes toward quality is preferably made by personal interview by a high-level manager or professional staff member. The personal interview is preferred to a questionnaire because the interview can obtain evidences of feelings and attitudes (pro and con) which a questionnaire never reveals. People interviewed should be told beforehand and assured that the survey is being made anonymously, that it is not being used for rating purposes, and that it is being used to improve the position of everyone in the company or agency. This assurance is necessary in order to obtain frank and honest opinions from everyone interviewed. It is necessary to determine which groups and departments are favorable, which ones are critical, and which ones have no strong feelings one way or the other.

At the 40th ASQC Congress, G. W. Connell described how a quality program failed because of lack of teamwork. His report carries a lesson for all who are about to start a quality program, or who have one underway.

The president of the company supported the program. Managers were required to read up on total quality control in services; they attended seminars on total quality. They did all of the right things—but overlooked the vital need for cooperation and teamwork among the several departments. There was lack of teamwork among the top management group, and the president was unable to resolve the differences of opinion. Three heads of departments were supportive, but two heads of departments were resistant, and this division existed even after 18 months. The program failed for lack of teamwork.

Connell explains that teamwork means working harmoniously for common goals. The conditions necessary for this relationship were missing, and were directly related to three aspects of the organization:

* Organization climate or atmosphere: The atmosphere was not that which fostered cooperation and teamwork. It was implied that there were conflicts, tensions, isolation, and deep-rooted differences.
* Lack of leadership: The president was unable to resolve differences of opinion, to modulate conflicting attitudes, or to get opposition managers to bury their differences and work for the larger good of the company.
* People not working together: There were no open discussions, trust was missing, there was silence and isolation, and communication was highly restricted.

Why Teamwork is Necessary

It is necessary to show that the quality improvement program requires cooperation and teamwork, for the following reasons:

- Problems and projects are rarely limited to one narrow subject.
- Problems cut across many specialties even in the same department.
- The most important problems are usually inter-departmental.
- The faults of the system involve the entire company.
- Finding causes of trouble and eliminating them require special knowledge, skills, and abilities.
- Once a situation or a problem involves more than the specific task of one person, others are involved and cooperation in resolving it is necessary.

After an Attitude Study, What?

If the attitude study shows a favorable attitude toward a quality program, or if the questions raised can be readily answered, then the next step is to make a problem survey.

If the attitude study shows misunderstanding of what quality means, indifference, doubt as to its value, or open opposition, then the problem becomes one of orientation, explanations, and holding meetings and discussions. There is no point in going ahead with a program until there is widespread agreement that such a program will not only improve the position of the company but the position of managers and employees as well. Approval is necessary; otherwise cooperation and teamwork are all ineffective, if not impossible.

Several steps can be taken to try to convince the skeptical:

- Point out gains made in eliminating errors, defects, wasted time, etc. (Convert gains into money savings.)
- Describe success stories in other companies.
- Bring in experts to explain advantages of a quality improvement program.
- Consider setting up a demonstration project in a department which is favorable to a quality program.
- Circulate materials on quality of services that relate directly to the work of the departments involved.

Three Surveys of Views about Quality: Managers and Supervisors, Staff Members, and Employees

Three different surveys are made to determine where the three major groups of employees in the company or agency stand relative to quality and quality improvement. These surveys are necessary to reveal views, opinions, and attitudes toward quality. These have to be the starting point. These show what the first steps have to be, the nature of such steps, and whether a different approach is needed for each of the three groups.

One approach that has been used is to have a high level official interview the several managers to find out what "quality" and "quality performance" and "quality improvement" mean to them. Do they have goals or standards?

Are there levels of performance to be attained? Have they heard of "quality control" or "quality assurance"? The findings between companies and within companies may vary widely. Some have heard about quality, others have not. Those who have heard about quality may not think that it applies to them. The purpose is to reveal attitudes, views, and opinions. It is not to pass judgment.

A similar survey is made of supervisors. If there is no great interest in quality then the first step is to hold lectures and seminars for the purpose of explaining in detail what quality and quality improvement mean in practice. Indeed the first step may be to set up an educational program in quality and quality improvement for all three groups: managers and supervisors, professional staff members, and employees. The program will have to be tailored to the specific needs of each group although there will be many common elements and topics.

A survey of the professional staffs will aim to discover to what extent, if any, they are familiar with quality and quality control. Examples of questions to ask are: Have you heard about quality control or quality assurance? Are you familiar with any of the techniques used in quality control? Have you ever used any of these techniques? Are these techniques applicable to any of the problems you are familiar with?

A survey of employees is made by each supervisor, or it can be made by managers and supervisors working together. A short questionnaire may be used to survey everyone, rather than a sample study. This would consist of a few printed statements and questions, something like the following:

> The company's goal is to reduce customer complaints, reach new customers, meet competition, improve our sales through improved services, and stay in business. Improving the quality of our products and services is the way we plan to do this. This involves everyone in the company.

- Do you favor these goals?
- Do you believe that quality of products and services can be improved?
- Do you know of any jobs or projects that can be improved?
- Are you aware of any problems that need more attention?
- Are you in favor of training courses that would help employees advance? do a better job?
- Describe your problems on the job.

The Problem Survey

The problem survey may not be the very first step, but it has to be near the top of a list of priorities. This is because tackling and resolving problems is at the heart of the quality improvement program. Isolating and identifying these difficulties, obstacles, and problems therefore must be one of the initial activities in starting the program. These are the situations where errors can be reduced, if not prevented, where failures are discovered and avoided, where delays are identified and reduced, if not eliminated, where complaints come to light, and where attempts are made to prevent them. Here is where the quality of services is improved, costs are reduced, and productivity is increased. The company discoveres whether customers are satisfied or not, whether customers are being satisfied or not, whether customers are being lost, and why.

You begin, as Dr. Juran reminds us, with a problem-oriented project.[3] In addition, quality improvement progresses on a project-by-project basis. The problem survey is an integral and vital part of any quality program. Furthermore, there are several advantages to starting a program on a problem or project basis, rather than trying to apply quality control to the entire company or agency at once. These advantages are as follows:

- An initial problem can be selected which has a high probability of being solved successfully.
- It debugs the procedures. Defects in the plan and procedures can be more easily corrected without involving the entire company.
- It tests how employees and supervisors react. It is easier to meet criticisms and objections that may arise.
- It shows where improvements—desirable changes—should be made in the approach, procedures, techniques, and supervision.
- It shows where more training and education may be necessary.
- It shows what problems and difficulties will be encountered as applications to new problems and projects are made. It suggests what has to be done to expand this program to other parts of the company.

The problem survey covers the entire company or agency and is conducted for the purpose of isolating and identifying problems and situations which can be the basis of a project-by-project quality improvement program. The following list shows that it is not hard to find such problems or situations; this list is not comprehensive.

1. Purchased products:
   - Errors in specifications, orders, billings, and invoices;
   - Defects in products;
   - Vendor errors and misunderstandings;
   - Receiving inspection and its elimination;
   - Delays in receiving shipments;
   - Rating vendors;
   - Vendor certification.
2. Operations where errors occur:
   - Billings;
   - Payroll;

---

[3] J. M. Juran, "Catching Up: How is the West Doing?" *Quality Progress,* November 1985, p. 19.

- Complaints;
- Auditing;
- Claims;
- Accounting;
- Sales;
- Data collection;
- Invoices;
- Sampling tax returns; .
- Data analysis;
- Specifications;
- Purchase orders;
- Computer programs;
- Test methods;
- Data processing;
- Coding;
- Transcribing;
- Computer editing;
- Tabulations;
- Typing;
- Word processing;
- Calculations;
- Sampling plans;
- Personnel records;
- Customer service.

3. Operations where time is lost or wasted:
   - Downtime of equipment, etc.;
   - Downtime of computer;
   - Employee idle time;
   - Waiting for work;
   - Waiting for parts, materials, supplies;
   - Waiting for repairs;
   - Excessive time for repairs;
   - Delayed shipments;
   - Absenteeism;
   - Data collection;
   - Inefficient sample design;
   - Untrained employees;
   - Delays in outgoing transport.

Problems are discovered in many different ways: by interviews with managers, supervisors, staff members, or employees; by examination of available data of all kinds; by talking with managers and supervisors in operating divisions; by using a staff professional familiar with quality control and quality problems; by applying data collection methods; by a study of customer complaints; by a survey of customers; by a survey of lost customers; by talking with vendors and their professional staffs and employees.

Problems divide into two groups: those which supervisors and employees can resolve at the working level (these are local and sporadic problems which employees can correct); and those which are interdepartmental or involve faults of the system which can only be resolved by the supervisor, high-level officials, or an interdepartmental team or task force.

There are numerous problems of the system which the supervisor can and should correct. Examples are repair of typewriters and other equipment, computer trouble, trouble with heating, lighting, and air conditioning, and repair and adjustment of furniture. Many faults of the system can be settled by the supervisor or by the official one level higher. A procedural manual of the faults of the system that can be corrected at lower levels should be prepared in detail and approved by top-level management.

Usually there are so many problems of each kind that a list of priorities is prepared to insure that the most important and most troublesome problems are tackled first, and that nothing significant is overlooked.

Examples of Problem Solving

Two examples of problems and their solutions have been given. The first case involved an excessive number of errors on insurance claims processed by a computer. This involved a fault or weakness of the system. To correct this problem, management created a quality control department with the necessary statistical capability. By working closely with supervisors, this department was able to assist in making this a very successful operation.

The second case involved the control of errors in transcribing data from a difficult shipping document, a carload railroad waybill. The manager-supervisor was in full charge of processing, including process control developed by a consultant, and also coached employees continually to eliminate errors. This also was a successful operation.

In both cases, planning and implementation were carried out by middle-level and lower-level persons familiar with control techniques and with the subject matter involved.

Making a Successful Demonstration

While this approach has already been mentioned under the heading of making a problem survey, the subject is so important that it needs a more detailed description. One way to get top-level management interested in a quality control program is to make a pilot study or studies as a demonstration project. To be most effective, this demonstration should be an outstanding success.

This demonstration is made for the purpose of showing that quality control works and that its benefits of reduced costs, improved productivity, and better customer satisfaction are real. Several criteria can be used for selecting a problem or project:

- A problem that is bothering managers;
- A chronic problem;
- An important or significant problem;
- A problem that can be easily solved;
- A problem with room for improvement that is measurable;
- An application whose success will attract attention.

Judging from past experience, it may be necessary to make more than one successful demonstration. Two or three such demonstrations may have to be made in different departments on different problems and different characteristics. One success may not be enough. It usually isn't.

It is not necessary to obtain approval from the top in order to make this demonstration. It may very well deal with a problem that falls completely within the authority and responsibility of a middle manager. In this case he or she can proceed with the necessary plans, techniques, organization, supervision, and implementation. The necessary statistical and other technical capabilities should be available and should be used. If training of employees and supervisors is necessary, this should be given. If procedural manuals are necessary, these should be prepared. Every step should be taken to insure that this is a successful application.

Making a Sample Study for Improved Data

The road to top-level approval of quality control may be by way of a probability sample study that gives managers some very important information that they lack. Such a study, properly designed and managed, delivers high-quality data in a timely fashion at a greatly reduced cost. The greatly reduced cost is due to the elimination of a census, 100 percent coverage, and a 100 percent tabulation. The reduction of work at every step from the collection of data to the tabulation of the final results leads, in most situations, to great savings of both people and paper. Saving paper appeals to most managers even more than the saving of people, which in reality is much more important. Because of the large amount of time saved, productivity is increased; more high-quality work can be done in the same length of time. Showing that sampling works may pave the way for a quality control program which requires the use of samples for control charts, receiving inspection, customer surveys, market surveys, sample audits, experimental designs, field tests, laboratory tests, nondestructive tests, cost studies, and much more.

Further Remarks on the Faults of the System

One of the points to keep clearly in mind during the early stages of planning a quality improvement program is a clear idea of the division of responsibility for quality and for its accomplishment. This is not so much a question of allocating percentages to each level as of making clear what kinds of problems must be resolved at each level of the organization. It may be wise to enumerate major examples at the various levels and to put them in writing for clear understanding and guidance. The following divisions illustrate this idea. Most problems of the system do not need to go to the top.

Top-level management:

- Approval of departmental budgets;
- Capital expenditures for machinery, equipment, etc.;
- Introduction of new major processes or procedures including a company-wide change or survey;
- Changes in the budget for training, travel, personnel, etc.;
- Sample survey of customers, lost customers, market;
- Change in the computer system;
- Change in basic policies and practices.

Middle management and professionals:

- Putting the quality program into effect;
- Making all kinds of special studies for management and operational purposes;
- Designing and implementing all kinds of sample surveys of customers, lost customers, vendors, employees, etc.;
- Monitoring quality program to see that it is operating as planned and that training is given as required;
- Correcting faults reported by supervisors or going to a higher level.

First-line supervisors:

- Faulty typewriter: call repairman or send to repair;
- Faulty computer: call computer company engineers;
- Faulty duplicator: call duplicator repair;
- Faulty heat: call building engineer;
- Faulty air conditioning: call building engineer;
- Faulty telephone service: call telephone company service.

Most problems of the system do not need to go to the top. Most of them can be solved by the first-line supervisors or by middle management. The first-line supervisor sees that the local special problems are solved by the employees working with the supervisor.

Motivating People

Westinghouse has a presentation for the purpose of motivating employees to develop a quality consciousness. It is called "Do It Right the First Time."[4] This approach to motivation needs considerable modification and analysis.

The way to quality according, to some people, is the following:

Do It Right.
Do It Right the First Time.

This ought to be added:

Continue to Do It Right.

What is the implication of the word "right"? It implies that

- People *know* what is right;
- People *perform* in the right way;
- People *know what to avoid* that would make it wrong.

What further has to be done? The decision and the action must be not only right but also

- The most effective,
- The most efficient,
- The best, and
- Successful.

There may be no point in doing something "right" if it is inefficient, costly, time-consuming, and succeeds only temporarily. For example, a sample design can be "right," but it can be terribly wasteful because it is inefficient. Doing something right involves not only the correct diagnosis of troubles, as in health, repair, and customer services, but also the use of better methods, procedures, and techniques.

---

[4]Wess Smith, CVS Video Publications, Westinghouse Electric Corporation, Pittsburgh, 1987.

What to Avoid: Top-level Management Out of Control

1. Policy is to emphasize earnings and profits, not quality of product or service;
2. Make decisions that should be made at a lower level;
3. Do not understand operations; experience is in other fields;
4. Serious conflicts and feuding between heads of departments and divisions;
5. Override technical decisions of technical professionals;
6. Make operating decisions;
7. Take over or interfere with operations;
8. Internal conflict or disagreement as to policies, plans, or decisions;
9. Tone down or change drastically a talk or paper that an official is to make;
10. Assignments should be made to lower-level officials;
11. Wasting time on lower-level functions, jobs, and responsibilities;
12. Staff meetings are devoted to trivia;
13. Staff meeting subjects could be better handled by memos or announcements;
14. Show favoritism;
15. Foster and promote "yes" men;
16. There is a planning job, but no planning;
17. Conduct psychological wars, e.g., to get someone fired or discredited;
18. Arbitrary opposition to improvements or improved methods;
19. Bullying officials into early retirement;
20. Promoting the incompetent;
21. Inability to diagnose problems and their causes;
22. Teamwork degenerates into a rigid loyalty or subservience;
23. Jealousy over the success of another official;
24. Want to dictate to lower-level officials, not listen to them;
25. Do not know how to collect and use the information they need;
26. Do not take action on the data they have;
27. Do not make adequate study of the market, the consumer, or the customer;
28. Knowingly deceiving the public as to the real nature and quality of the product;
29. Blaming an operating division and official for top management's faulty decision.

SUMMARY

Step 1. Who will convince top officials that a quality program is needed?

- Outsiders: consultants;
- Outsiders: competition;

- Outsiders: other top-level officials;
- Outsiders: newspapers, magazines, etc.;
- Insiders: lower-level officials or professional staff people;
- Others.

Step 2. Who will convince middle management, supervisors, and employees that a quality program is needed?

- Little convincing needed; already aware of quality control;
- By reading books and periodicals;
- By taking courses or seminars in quality control;
- From one professional or manager who already knows quality control;
- Others.

Step 3. Where will the technical quality control capability come from?

- From some professional staff member, such as quality specialist or statistician;
- From a consultant who will teach quality control;
- From some manager who knows quality control;
- From a company statistician who understands quality control and how to apply it;
- From others.

Step 4. After the top-level officials approve, what will be done?

- Set up a quality council; or
- Use one or more of the starting methods given above; or
- Set up a demonstration project to show that quality control works; or
- Make a survey of managers, professionals, and employees; or
- Other; set up seminars and courses in quality control, quality planning, and quality management.

Step 5. Who will develop and plan the quality improvement program?

- Quality council;
- Quality executive committee;
- Quality teams;
- Task forces.

Step 6. Who will implement the quality improvement program?

- Organizational units set up as quality improvement groups or cells;
- Quality circles trained in quality control methods;

- As a starter, a quality task force working on a selected problem or project;
- Quality improvement teams.

Step 7. How will the success of the quality improvement program be measured by top officials?

- Measurable improvements, e.g., errors, delay time, customer complaints;
- Quality costs: prevention, appraisal, failure;
- Monetary: increase in sales, profits, return, share of market, competition;
- Effectiveness of education and training;
- Elimination of costs of non-quality.

Chapter 14

Error Prevention

Chapters 5 and 6 have already shown how the nation is plagued with errors, mistakes, and blunders, that their occurrence is universal, and that their kinds and variety are very extensive. Emphasis has been placed on human error because its prevention is one of the best ways to improve the quality of both services and products. Regardless of how formidable the problem of error is, every attempt should be made to control and reduce it. In this chapter some general methods of prevention are presented first, followed by a description of a wide variety of errors and ways that can be used to reduce if not prevent them. The goal is to prevent errors, not just to reduce them, but this improvement obviously will have to come in a number of stages. Progressive reduction is the road to some kinds of prevention.

METHODS OF PREVENTION

The methods described are used to control and prevent errors, mistakes, failures, blunders, and disasters. A quality improvement program calls for a more widespread, a more intensive, and a more thorough application of these methods than is now being carried out.

Verification

Verification for accuracy and completeness can be done either by self-verification or by another party or person. Verification means to confirm, substantiate, insure correctness, support with evidence, establish truth, accuracy, existence, and make certain. The second person can be a checker, verifier, auditor, inspector, reviewer, monitor, or proofreader.

Redundancy

Redundancy refers to a parallel system of some kind that enables the system or operation to be carried on, even though one system or person is unable to do so. Electric circuits are arranged in parallel so that if one circuit fails, the other takes over. The use of assistants or backup personnel is another example, such as a copilot. Working the same mathematical problem in two different ways is an example of redundancy to detect and eliminate errors. Getting diagnoses from two different doctors is another example; so is submitting the same blood sample to two different laboratories for testing.

Training

Many errors can be traced to a shortcoming in knowledge or to a lack of understanding or knowledge in the form of instructions and explanations. Training is needed in special areas such as safety, emergencies, and unusual situations. Training is needed in error prevention, with emphasis on the kinds of errors that occur on the job. Coaching by the supervisor relative to specific procedures, processes, calculations, and the like is essential to ensure that the work is being done correctly.

Safety Rules and Regulations

This includes wearing proper clothing, hard hats, and the like. It includes rules on how to move trucks of goods safely in a supermarket, piling goods safely in storage and on the shelves in the store. It includes observing "no smoking" signs and rules, if they exist. It includes advice to customers on how to use carts safely, especially if the customer has children along.

Safety Devices

These include all kinds of alarms and red lights. They are especially necessary on railroads, where they have been installed for many decades. They include enclosures of dangerous devices and machinery such as electrical transformers and air conditioning machinery. They also include prominent signs which warn of high voltage and other dangerous electrical circuits.

Prominent Labels

In order to avoid mixups which can be dangerous, it is imperative to label all containers of chemicals, drugs, and the like very prominently, using colored print to attract attention. Storage areas should also be designated by prominent signs showing what they contain. Dangerous electrical machinery and apparatus should be prominently identified. It is obvious that bottles of drugs and other liquids that are dangerous, and can be easily confused, need to have much more prominent and different colored labels so that they cannot be confused.

More and better use of identification tags would prevent errors due to mixed-up identification. Such tags would prevent a case such as that reported in the press, in which the surgeries of two women in the same hospital were interchanged.

Separate Storage

The following examples of serious mixups show the need for separate storage cabinets, chests, and rooms for materials that are potentially dangerous or fatal:

- Phenobarbital and cocaine: similar bottles in the same hospital cabinet: one death.
- Oxygen and carbon dioxide: similar containers in the same hospital room: one death.
- Arsenic and flour: similar containers in the same place: some seriously ill persons in a case that could have been fatal.
- Pancake syrup and oven cleaner: similar containers in the same place: about 10 nursing home residents had to be treated in a hospital.

Separate storage combined with prominent and colored labeling could have prevented all of these mishaps. Both parties were to blame: employees were careless and indifferent; they were not alert to the dangers involved. Management was negligent and careless in not seeing that these containers were in different cabinets, areas, or rooms, and were prominently labeled. It was also careless in not giving these employees training in safe handling of these containers and in the need to read labels carefully in order to prevent a mixup.

Restricted Access

One way to stop errors from being made in critical areas is to surround them in some way so as to restrict access to only a very few knowledgeable and competent persons. This may mean access only to a few designated employees and supervisors, but even this policy has a risk that can be reduced by proper training. According to the press, an employee in a hospital who had a key to a restricted area turned off the oxygen line when he thought he was turning off the heat. One wonders why a person who was so ignorant had access to this critical area. After this accident, which could have been very serious because about 50 patients were connected to the oxygen line, the management built an enclosure around the oxygen valve with a padlocked door. This represented a padlocked area within a padlocked area. Obviously only in this way, with very few persons having a key to the oxygen valve compartment, could they assure themselves that the oxygen line was safe from accidental cutoff.

Protective Knowledge

Lack of knowledge is one of the principal causes of accidents and disasters. Important knowledge about dangerous gases, objects, forces, and conditions can prevent untold errors that result in injury and loss, if not tragedy. Some of these are listed below:

- Ice on the wings of an airplane;
- Carbon monoxide from the exhaust of an automobile, truck, or bus;
- Carbon monoxide from the burning of coal or gas;
- Centrifugal force acting on an auto, truck, bus, or other object moving in a curved path;
- Lightning;
- Electric circuits in the home or apartment;
- Leaking gas from furnace, hot water heater, or gas main;
- Matches;
- Cigarette lighter;
- Lighted cigarettes;
- Weather dangers: snow, ice, rain, hail, wind, fog;
- Dangerous roads and streets.

Attitude Orientation

This is kept separate from training, which is for the purpose of filling in the gaps in knowledge that are causing errors. Attitude orientation is for the purpose of discussing attitudes that lead to error and for substituting a positive, preventive attitude. Some of the aspects to be stressed are as follows:

- The need to have attitudes of care, concern, and alertness on jobs where the safety of every worker depends upon putting safety first. The slogan is always ABC—Always Be Careful. Learn safety measures and put them into practice.
- The high cost of errors, regardless of what kind they are;
- The fact that many kinds of errors may easily turn a customer into a lost customer;
- The need to check and double check all transactions to ensure that no error has been made;
- Taking nothing for granted. Do not assume that something is being done. Go and see if it is being done. Follow up. Do not assume that something is working correctly. Check to see that it is working properly.

Procedural Manual

The procedural manual should be a detailed description of the various tasks involved in the job or project, and how to perform them. It provides the knowledge and procedures necessary to understand the job, and how to do it correctly. It serves the following purposes in reducing and eliminating errors:

- It shows new employees what the job is like and what they have to master in order to perform a satisfactory job.
- It is a constant reference book for employees to use to refresh their memories about how a specific aspect of the process or project should be performed. It is a book to study.
- It shows how specific problems are to be solved. An example is the problem of conversion of one set of units to another, such as cords of wood or drums of gasoline to pounds and tons. It gives advice relative to various forms of coding, such as statistical coding and commodity coding. The manual therefore is a refresher and a review of points that may be causing difficulties.

Legibility and Clarity

Very often errors are made because handwriting is not legible, there are strikeovers in typing, there are misspelled words, there are transposed letters or digits, or there are abbreviations that cannot be deciphered. Something very important may not be identified by number, title, date, or place. This lack of identification may cause a lot of trouble.

A sentence in a set of instructions may be confusing for lack of proper punctuation, or because of a wrong word or phrase. This lack of a clear meaning may have serious effects if it produces an error or a malfunctioning in operations.

Errors can be prevented by stressing and training for the following:

- Legible writing of all letters, words, and abbreviations;
- Legible writing of all numbers;
- Writing names and addresses accurately; distinguishing names that sound alike, e.g., Hurst/Hirsch, Cole/Kohl;
- Verifying to avoid all transpositions of letters and digits;
- Verifying to avoid all misspellings.

It is unfortunate that in recent years a false notion has become quite common in schools that spelling is of minor importance. In fact, some schools do not even teach spelling. If schools were aware of the serious results that result from carelessness in spelling and name recognition, they might take the subject more seriously. Serious errors are made in hospitals, in personnel records, in checks, in billing, in nursing homes, and in credit cards because names are misspelled, names that sound alike are confused, or the spelling is not verified.

Identical Names

Many errors are made in services involving billing and other contacts because of identical first and last names of two persons. These are some actual examples:

Two women have the same charge account at the same store. One can be charged for the purchases of both, one can be charged for the purchase of the other, or the wrong purchases can be charged to both accounts.

Two persons were patients at the same hospital at the same time. The medicine for the one is given to the other. The treatments are interchanged. Surgery can be interchanged. One is billed for the charges against both.

Several methods can be used to avoid this error:

- Add a middle initial in one case or in both cases.
- Add two middle initials in one case, if necessary and acceptable.
- Get the addresses or locations. These will be different. (Use room numbers in a hospital.)
- Use Social Security numbers for each person.
- Use some other ID such as a driver's license.

Proper Hiring and Promoting

The source of errors is the individual. To prevent error means convincing the individual of the advantages of reducing, if not eliminating, errors, and assisting him or her in ways that will bring this error prevention about. One of the first steps a company can take in developing such a program is to hire persons who have the knowledge, abilities, and attitudes that help keep errors at a minimum.

This means hiring persons who are error-conscious and whose work record and attitudes show them to be accurate, alert, careful, concerned, and attentive to details. They should approve and support a program that stresses safety, accuracy, driving error rates to zero, and continuous improvement. They should believe that error rates can be controlled and reduced—"that errors are not human and therefore should be overlooked and condoned." Anyone who insists upon this belief should not be hired, and if already in the organization should be shifted where he or she cannot do any harm. There are already far too many persons, some in responsible positions, who condone errors that are often serious because they are "human." This attitude and this philosophy need to rejected in the strongest terms.

People should be hired who are in favor of a program that drives the error rate to zero, who are flexible, who are promotable, who are not afraid of change and improvement, and who treat the customer with courtesy and consideration.

Preventing Errors as Deviations from Recorded Facts

An excellent example of how people make statements which are erroneous deviations from recorded facts comes from a press report relating to the raising of the Titanic.[1] The statement is made that ship navigation in 1912 was crude and the Titanic did not know where it was. This statement is false in all respects because it is contrary to recorded facts. The writer obviously did not research the subject because much material has been written about it. The facts are recorded in a book entitled *The Story of the Titanic,* edited by Jack Winocur and published by Dover in 1960. The facts are clear:

- The position of the Titanic was accurately known. It was 41° 46′ north latitude and 50° 14′ west longitude
- The evidence is clear. The Carpathia, when it heard the SOS sent by wireless, changed its course and headed for the spot where the Titanic was, a position it reached *exactly* in about four hours.

This showed that Phillips, the chief wireless operator, was sending the correct position as given to him by Captain Smith, and had been sending it continuously for hours. The allegations clearly are based on opinion, conjecture, and ignorance; they are not only false but reflect on the knowledge, integrity, and character of some courageous men.

How do you prevent this kind of error when there is plenty of evidence readily available to refute it? These errors can be avoided by careful researching of the subject and by insisting that those who write memoranda, reports, or any other document have adequately researched the subject for the accurate, basic facts.

Preventing Errors as Deviations from Correct or Standard Values

A tremendous amount of time and money is wasted because of deviations from correct or standard values. These deviations create costly jobs for editors, reviewers, verifiers, proofreaders, and the like. Here are some examples with suggested remedies:

Errors	*Remedies*
• Spelling:	Provide dictionaries. Hire educated employees in the first place.
• Grammar:	Use a grammar book. Hire employees who are educated.
• Physical constants:	Have copies handy of chemical and physical handbooks, and make sure they are used.

---

[1] See my letter on the Titanic featured in the *Rocky Mountain News,* September 4, 1980.

Errors	*Remedies*
• Historical dates, events, time placement, time sequences:	Use historical atlas, encyclopedia, history books, past copies of magazines and newspapers.
• Telephone numbers (wrong numbers have greatly increased):	Use telephone directory: learn how to use it: write down telephone number before making a call. Wrong numbers seem to be due to trying to remember correctly seven consecutive digits. Many persons cannot do it.

General Remedies

The company should have an everyday working policy and practice that everyone is expected to use reference books as needed, to do the research work necessary for any and every job, to get into the habit of using every verification method applicable to the work, to make extensive use of written notes and jottings rather than relying solely upon memory, and to have their own notebooks of commonly used and important addresses and telephone numbers.

The telephone company could be very helpful in reducing the number of wrong telephone calls, which has sharply increased in recent years. It could give classes in the correct use of the telephone—how to make a call, how to use the correct number by writing it down and using the written number while making the call, how to identify yourself when initiating a call, and how to identify the party desired at the other end of the line. Experience shows that there are far too many telephone illiterates using the telephone. Schools could do nothing better than show students how to us the telephone in a civilized and rational manner.

Preventing Errors as Deviations from Correct Methods, Procedures, Processes, and Techniques

Numerous errors are made because of some deviation from a correct procedure. The correct procedure can be a very simple transaction or it can be a complex formula. Prevention in the simple cases given below calls for care in entering a figure and verifying it after entry, or it may call for following established procedures and not changing them in order to cover up an internal error. Several examples are given where the error is due to lack of knowledge, inability, or indifference toward verification or checking with a knowledgeable source. The company should insist that this verification with a specialist or other knowledgeable person be mandatory. Numerous errors could be prevented in this manner.

- A large bank records a deposit of $1,842 as $18.42. Even after proof was submitted, the bank refused to correct the error. The depositor had to sue the bank in court for wasting his time.
- A large department store chain bills a customer for $166 worth of merchandise that she never bought, and for which she had documentary and other proof that she had never bought it. The company not only persisted in avoiding the issue and trying to shift the blame onto the customer, but many have been guilty of trying to shift the loss incurred in a falsely conducted transaction onto an innocent customer. The company refused to disclose what it did in this matter.
- The gas argon is pumped into the oxygen line of a hospital.
- The wrong equation is used to calculate the standard error of an estimate. Result: 26,000 figures are published in error.
- In the inspection department of a factory, Mil Std 105 is applied to variables rather than to attributes, increasing sampling volume four times.
- The formulas for a binomial proportion are used instead of the formulas for a ratio proportion.
- The wrong computer program is applied to the data collected from a nested experimental design.
- The binomial model does not match the physical conditions under which the data are collected.
- A plutonium test is made without using the basic principles of experimental design.

Preventing Errors as Deviations from Rules, Regulations, and Laws

Local ordinances, state laws, and federal rules and regulations have been in effect for many decades to protect the public and avoid not only costly errors but serious departures from what is acceptable performance and quality.

Error	*Remedy*
• Water in milk;	Inspection, legal action.
• Short weight;	Inspection, testing scales, survey, legal action.
• Private planes in prohibited space;	Maps, patrols, severe penalties, pulling license.
• Failure to observe signals; destruction of automatic devices as reported by the Federal Railroad Administration;	Hiring, training, severe penalties, firing.
• Payments to ineligible persons or parties;	100 percent sample audit, audit periodically, quality control.

Error	*Remedy*
• Overpaying eligibles;	100 percent audit periodically, verification sample.
• Not paying eligibles;	Survey of list of potential eligibles; press release as to who is eligible.
• Paying Social Security to the dead;	Continuous updating of the file; setting up an organized procedure to identify these cases.
• Overcharging Medicare, charging for services not rendered, charging for medicines not purchased or used, taking patient's Social Security checks, shoplifting, employee stealing.	Legal action.

Preventing Errors as Misuses of Correct Procedures and Incorrect Applications

The remedy is implied in each statement of misuse or incorrect application. The statement made is a practice to avoid.

Misuse

- Allowing large biases in sample data and then worrying about the variation due to sampling (standard error);
- Errors made by interviewers using a questionnaire or data sheet: poor questioning, forgetting to ask some important questions, no probing for something critical;
- Fitting a straight line to the means of an $\bar{x}$ chart in quality control: running an unnecessary regression analysis using a computer program and testing whether the line could have come from a population line whose slope is zero;
- Poor execution, management, and control of well designed sample. Neglecting to identify each replicate in a replicated sample, or neglecting to tabulate the data as a replicated sample. Neglecting to control interviewers on an ongoing basis so that bias in family income data collected varies from 10 to 20 percent underreported.

Incorrect application

- In a work sample, concentrating observations on workers so as to obtain a "large" sample, say from 1,000 to 5,000 in a few days. The time population is still only a "few days" and that is what the data apply to. Need to spread sample over days, weeks, and months to obtain measure of variability over seasons or other sources of variability.

- Eliminating part of the time population in a work sample. The population is every minute of the working day, and every working day.
- Data analysis requires a ratio proportion, not a binomial proportion.
- Mil Std 105 applies to attributes, not to variables.
- Part of the human population should not be excluded because we think it is not important. Let the sample show whether it is important or not. What is left out may be needed.
- In one analysis, the correlation coefficient was very high because of one extreme value. A graph of the values showed that correlation was practically zero without this extreme value.
- An efficient sample designed for one purpose was very inefficient when used for an entirely different purpose.

Preventing Errors as Deviations from Safe Procedures and Safe Behavior

These practices call for an emphasis on safe practices, safe methods, and safe behavior at all times, These errors usually are fatal. A basic remedy is safety training on a continuous basis in all of these cases. The company or organization needs to stress safety as the Number One quality characteristic in every one of these situations.

Error or danger	*Remedy*
• Trenches or other excavations caving in;	Shore up all sides to prevent cave-ins.
• Ice on airplane wings:	De-ice thoroughly before takeoff.
• Wind shear;	Hold plane until shear disappears or moves away.
• Drug mix-up or chemical mix-up (e.g., cocaine for phenobarbital);	Put dangerous drugs in separate cabinet and in separate room. Do the same for dangerous chemicals. Make and attach large clear labels for every such container.
• Gas mixups (argon, carbon dioxide, nitrogen for oxygen);	Check all gas deliveries. Put large labels on all gas cylinders so users can see them. Keep cylinders of dangerous gases in separate room so carbon dioxide cannot be substituted for oxygen. Identify what gases are in what rooms or compartments.

Error or danger	*Remedy*
• Failure of concrete in building construction;	Monitor so concrete hardens. Prevent pushy time schedule.
• Failure on overpass construction;	Have constant monitoring by professional engineer of construction so that plans and sequences are followed.
• Freight trains colliding on same track; five deaths;	Training, use checkpoints, automatic alarms in each engine, radio communication.
• Anaesthesia machines fail; two deaths;	Test equipment before use to see that it is working properly—no stuck valves, etc.
• Surgical mixup of two patients;	Use identification tags, IDs of some kind.

Another case where zero errors are an absolute necessity is the FBI fingerprint file. An error implicating an innocent man may be a life or death matter, or at least a miscarriage of justice. Police will look for the wrong person.

Preventing Errors as Rejection of Improvements, Better Methods, and More Efficient Techniques

These are of special value in collecting and analyzing data for improving quality in services. They reveal problems and situations that management does not know it has. They are not now being used in the service industries (and some of them are not being used in manufacturing to any great extent) because they are too advanced for the six kindergarten statistical techniques which have become identified with quality circles. Ironically, we are letting the Japanese dictate to us about the use of statistics. As a result, many powerful methods are being ignored.

Technique	*Correcting Faults in the System*
• Probability sampling;	For surveys of lost customers, regular customers, potential customers, employees, vendors, competitor's customers.
• Random time sampling (RTS);	Measuring time and cost of idle time, downtime, delays, waiting time, transit time, joint activities, special jobs, departments, projects, functions.
• Learning curve analysis;	Individual and group capability, production curve, error curve, unit cost curve, unit time curve.

Technique	*Correcting Faults in the System*
• Tests and experiments;	Tests of blood urine, tissue; air, water, and soil tests for pollution and radiation; radiation tests and experiments.
• Input/output analysis;	Using relationship for control and prediction.
• Sample evidence;	Systematic use in a legal proceeding saves a tremendous amount of time, human effort, and money while obtaining better evidence.
• Statistical analysis;	Better interpretation, use, and presentation of data.

All that is needed is to hire one good professional statistician who is a practitioner with knowledge and experience in applying these techniques. An additional two or three assistants are all that is required, except where the statistical work load is heavy. The statistician will conduct classes in statistics, advise and assist individuals, and help anyone who has a statistical problem. A major function will be to explain to everyone, especially at higher levels, what a statistical problem is.

Preventing Errors in Judgment and Decision Making

The errors in judgment and decision making described here are limited to higher-level managers and executives, as well as to higher-level professional specialists.

Error	*Remedy*
• Decision by hunch, conjecture, assumption;	Need to collect adequate data about the problem or situation.
• Decision by biased data (inference was false);	Need to use adequately designed sample, statistical quality control charts on machines, input/output analysis.
• Purpose of study changed after sample study was completed;	People at the top need to get their act together, agree on purpose of sample study before it is started, before it is designed. Need for agreement at the top.
• Nationwide sample study used for purpose it was not designed for;	Need to communicate with those who designed the sample. May need to design a new sample for a new purpose.
• Sales department blamed for lost customers;	Survey of lost customers showed that cause was poor-quality product due to change in vendors to save money (Deming's Point 4). Need good data.

Error	*Remedy*
• New product does not sell;	Need to make an adequate market study, need to study competitor's product, need to make survey to find out why product does not sell.
• Ignoring professional statistician on the staff; errors compounded;	Computer programmer does not confer with statistician, but on his own uses wrong equation for standard error. Result: 26,000 figures are in error. Error compounded when results are published and not rerun on the computer. Action approved by top official even after being told tabulation should be junked and rerun.

Causes of Newspaper Errors

A large newspaper may print an issue that contains over 100,000 words, so that there are numerous opportunities to make errors. Usually newspapers, and magazines as well, from time to time carry corrections of errors that have been discovered or reported from outside.

An editor on a Birmingham, Alabama newspaper made a study of the causes of errors for which the newspaper had printed corrections. He interviewed the persons responsible for the errors and asked them this question: How could the error have been avoided? He asked the causes of 103 errors and classified the answers into eight categories given below:[2]

1.	Needed to check one more source, e.g., telephone directory	37
2.	Incorrect information from "reliable" sources	23
3.	Reporters or editors in a hurry, inattentive	19
4.	Established checking procedures were not followed	9
5.	Assumed information was correct when it was not	6
6.	Faulty editing	6
7.	Composing room error	2
8.	Erroneous information in a clip file never corrected	1
	Total number of errors	103

All of these classes of errors show that a verification step, *the need to make one more check,* was needed in addition to what was done. Errors arose be-

---

[2] *Rocky Mountain News,* October 6, 1986, p. 60.

cause of persons being in a hurry, not following verification procedures when they existed, and assuming that information and sources were correct when they were not. It is clear that the people knew how to eliminate the errors, but there was no policy or insistence that errors be kept at a minimum. Apparently a newspaper expects errors and therefore it gets them, and expects to get by with a certain number of errors which it believes would be too costly to eliminate.

SYSTEM CORRECTION PROCEDURES

System correction procedures should be included in policy, planning, and procedures. These are provisions for correcting the faults, failures, and errors in the system that are bound to exist, and which are beyond the authority and ability of the individual to correct. These procedures should be of such a nature that they tend to reduce, if not prevent, such system errors, mistakes, and failures from occurring in the future. Correcting faults in the system should be only the first step in preventing them.

It is obvious after a careful look at the situation that only certain system corrections need to go to the top officials. The other corrections can be made by middle management and by supervisors, some with top-level approval which may be obtained beforehand. Some examples at each of three levels are given below:

1. Decisions of Top Management

- Budget;
- Capital investment: new equipment and machinery; new computer system;
- Staffing: additional employees;
- New projects: market survey, customer survey, random time sampling applied across the entire company, or even to one department; employee survey;
- New products;
- New services;
- New vendors;
- New processes, change in operations;
- New policies and practices;
- Changes in organization and functions;
- Changes in the budget, e.g., new financial outlays;
- Changes in the training department and training courses.

Any faults of the system that require or involve any of the above cannot be corrected without clearance and approval at the top.

2. Middle Management and High-Level Professionals

These are the key people in any organization. They have the know-how and capability, get the work done, run operations, know where the problems are, and put plans and policies into effect. The major responsibility for improvement of quality rests with them.

- They originate new methods, new techniques, new processes that improve operations.
- They put plans, methods, techniques, and processes into effect.
- They can make minor changes in the work environment.
- They can make changes that do not involve new financing or drastic changes in organization.
- They see that appropriate procedural manuals are prepared and kept up to date by the first-line supervisors.
- They prepare training course contents and materials; they bear the brunt of training on the job all supervisors and many, if not most, employees.
- They prepare technical plans and specifications as needed, e.g., sample design, design of a random time sample, and specifications required to put such plans into effect; monitor implementation.
- They see that quality control policies, plans, and techniques are put into effect, and that they are carried out according to plan. Their job is to see that quality improvement really succeeds.
- Their job is to see that all of the powerful quality improvement techniques are explained, understood, and used throughout the organization. Only in this way can quality improvement be significant and continuous. The simple methods used by quality circles are not enough, and it is the responsibility of middle management and high-level professionals to see that management and others are aware of this. Top-level management is not aware of this. They will have to be shown by some knowledgeable professional or manager.

3. First-line Supervisors

Neither employees nor supervisors should have to go to the top to have every fault of the system and every system quality problem solved by top management. System correction procedures should be established which allow the first-line supervisors (or middle managers) to handle many, if not most, of the faults of the system. These failures must be anticipated and a procedure established which provides the supervisor with the authority and means to correct them. Numerous examples can be cited:

- A typewriter fails and needs repair;
- An unsafe condition exists;

- The heating system is not working;
- The air conditioning system is not working;
- One or more electric lights have burned out;
- The computer or some part of it fails;
- Some fault is found in the training materials;
- A data sheet is difficult to use;
- A questionnaire needs clarification;
- A printing job is unsatisfactory;
- A better sample could be designed;
- In one area data are badly needed;
- One of the procedural manuals needs updating;
- A better test or experiment could be designed;
- Several employees could use hand-held calculators;
- A desk computer is needed with the proper software;
- Certain technical books would save a lot of time.

When a better form, questionnaire, sample, test, experiment, or procedure could be designed, the action to take is to have a report prepared describing the need and the new method, and then send it forward for approval. This action is taken at the operating level; higher-level officials simply approve it if this is required. Otherwise operating people go ahead and put the plan into effect. Often approval is simply perfunctory because the material is too technical, specialized, or difficult for higher-level people to understand. The stress is improvement at the same or less cost, not techniques.

More Examples of Human Errors and How to Prevent Them

Case 1

A high level official of a manufacturing company is worried because sales have been dropping in recent months. He calls in the sales force and tells them that they are not doing a good job. They are very much surprised because they thought they were doing a highly satisfactory job. During the discussion, it is suggested that a study be made of the lost customers to determine, if possible, what happened to cause sales to drop. The study was carried out, and as a result, it was found these former customers were dissatisfied with the quality of the product, and as a result had shifted to another company. Investigation showed that the decline in quality occurred about the time the company shifted vendors in order to save money. They immediately went back to the former vendor, and as a result the quality improved and sales began to increase.

This situation falls under Deming's Point 4 where quality is sacrificed to price, to the lowest bidder. It also related to Point 9 which calls for breaking down barriers between departments. In this case purchasing department, production, and sales were not working as a team. No attention was being paid to quality so Point 1 calling for constancy of purpose with regard to quality was also involved. Other points not listed were involved: the need to keep in close touch with customers and make sure they are satisfied; in this way trouble is discovered before any, or many, customers are lost. Customer complaints are not enough for they may never come. This case also shows the need for collecting good quality data about the quality of the product, as well as good quality data from every customer. Without good quality data, top level management failed to make a correct diagnosis of what the real trouble was.

Case 2

A manager of a textile factory was sure his employees had stolen a million dollars worth of hose during the past year. He called in some detectives who observed the employees and the factory but found nothing, so they left. Then the manager called in a consulting firm of psychologists. They came with cameras, one way screens, and other paraphenalia. They studied the situation for days, but they too could find nothing. They were about to leave when one of the psychologists asked the manager "How did you arrive at the million dollars?" As a result, the entire situation was cleared up.

The manager had run a test on one of the operators (who turned out to be one of the best) and calculated the average amount of yarn used on the semi-automatic machine to make one pair of hose. He then divided this number into the total amount of yarn, and came up with a number of pairs of hose which was valued at a million dollars more than what was produced. It was shown that considerable variation existed in the ampunt of yarn used by different operators to make a pair of hose despite semi-automatic machinery, and that the test operator used much less than the average of the entire work force. The million dollars was the money lost because the average for the group was not that of the test operator! The million dollars worth of hose was not stolen; it had never been produced. The employees needed to be trained in the methods of the test operator.

The problem was not legal, it was not psychological, it was statistical. The problem was not the employees stealing. It was the manager. He was flying blind. He had no information whatever that told him what the situation was in the factory. The necessary information could have been obtained in one of three different ways; his error grew out of the highly biased sample of one on which he based his decision:

- a random sample of 10 operators could have been used instead of one
- quality control charts could have been run on each machine for 10 days
- the manager could have plotted an input-output graph showing amount of hose output vertically against amount of year input horizontally, for each of the past 5 years. A line drawn through the origin and these points would

have given the amount of output per unit of input for each of 5 years. This would have shown him that nothing unusual was happening during the year in question.

This manager needed an adequate information system which showed him what quality of product was being turned out, and what quality of performance was being obtained from each of the operators.

Case 3

A factory operator reports trouble with his machine. A quality control person selects a series of samples for an x̄ chart and takes the data to a computer to process. Sample means are calculated, a straight line is fitted to the means, a t test is run on the slope of the line, and a computer print-out is made. All of this called for a special computer program. The hypothesis of zero slope is rejected so the news is conveyed to the operator that his machine is out of control. This he already suspected.

This is a case of unnecessary statistical analysis and unnecessary use of computer time. A simple x̄ chart with an R chart tests the same hypothesis. The unnecessary work not only added to overhead costs but increased the time wasted by an idle machine and operator, if not defective parts. Furthermore the operator did not have to be told he was in trouble. He already knew it.

This is an example of attention of technical people being diverted, by zeal for statistics and the computer, from a real job—that of locating the problem and getting the machine and operator back into acceptable quality operation *as quickly as possible*. The failure is overlooking the high cost of the delay in using sophisticated statistics, and in the downtime of the machine.

The real goal could have been accomplished on the factory floor by using data sheets, a hand held computer, and graph paper to construct an x̄ chart and an R chart. When out-of-control was discovered, then immediate action could have been taken to find the cause and eliminate it. This would mean calling in a maintenance engineer or other specialist.

Case 4—A Large Company

This is a large company with a central quality assurance department which issues a monthly report of about 100 pages. It contains data on quality characteristics, including measures of time. Operating data are given for all of the operating offices. There are tables and graphs, frequency distributions, and calculations of averages and percentages. Some data are based on samples. This report is circulated to officials, who take whatever action seems to be needed. They receive this report only once a month. No other report on the quality of performance is issued or prepared.

Here is a report that is highly statistical, but the department shows not the slightest capability for this kind of work. Titles of tables are vague and incomplete, units of measurement are missing, methods of sampling are not described. The averages calculated from frequency distributions cannot be verified. The layout of frequency distributions does not follow standard practice. Obviously those preparing this report have not had even the most elementary course in statistics.

This company needs statistical capability, but also much more. It needs to be exposed to the basic principles and practices of statistical quality control. It needs to study intensively Deming's 14 Points. It needs to understand how quality is built into services and products. It needs to be aware of the urgency required, not only to correct but to prevent errors, mistakes, faults, and failures. Under the present system, officials may not be aware of certain troubles until they have existed for four to six weeks. Obviously they are not aware of the tremendous importance of the time factor in preventing poor quality, reducing costs, and improving productivity.

Case 5—A Government Contract

This private management information firm had a federal government contract to process a nationwide sample of over 200,000 documents, which already had been collected. The first major operation was to transcribe data from the sample documents, which were not standardized, to a standard format which would be keypunched for computer processing. Inexperienced help—students, housewives, and others—were hired to do this transcribing, despite the fact that this was no simple clerical job. These employees had to be trained for at least three weeks, using a 95-page procedural manual. The supervisor, who was an expert in these documents, not only gave a test at the end of the training to insure ability to do the work in an acceptable fashion, but assisted and tutored individuals as the work progressed. She also kept production records and carried out the quality control program planned by a consultant.

Three situations involved quality of performance:

- An immediate goal of 2000 documents per day;
- The error rate of each transcriber;
- Writing a computer program for sampling variances.

A production goal of 2000 documents per day was set by the vice-president, despite explanations by the supervisor and consultant that this figure was much too high for such a complex job. In fact the goal was arbitrary and unrealistic, but this is not an uncommon practice of high-level officials who have little or no understanding of operations or what is required to do a satisfactory job. In fact, this goal was not reached until the 18th day—after more than three weeks of actual production. This illustrates Deming's tenth point: eliminate numerical goals. In this case the goal was meaningless and was ignored because it was far beyond the capability of the group. Maximum production of 2,774 was reached on the 39th day; production means "acceptable-quality documents."

Work units or lots of 300 documents were formed for convenience in handling and filing, and these lots were sampled for process control. A systematic sample was drawn from each lot by a reviewer. If the lot was rejected, it went back immediately to the employee who processed it. Then a 100% redo was required. The supervisor assisted or coached the person if this seemed to be necessary, or if difficulty was encountered with a certain kind of calculation or item. The vice-president wanted only review, but he got process control because acceptable-quality data required that the error rate be kept below 5 percent. This rate with a later computer edit was expected to bring the error rate down to about 3 percent. In this case the supervisor was much more concerned about doing acceptable quality work than was the vice-president. That latter was interested only in quantity production. He had no interest in quality.

A computer program had to be written for the calculation of certain sampling variances. This job was assigned to an electronic engineer who was not familiar with the mathematics involved. A statistician was available but was never consulted. The formulas were also included in a report which had been prepared by the consultant. Apparently the programmer thought he could pick up the necessary mathematics in a statistics book. This is where he made a serious mistake. As a result, about 26,000 variances were calculated in error and were printed in the final report: at last word they had never been corrected.

This case illustrates several of Deming's points, but Point 9, concerning breaking down barriers between people, applies to the vice-president and the rest of the staff.

SOURCES OF ERRORS ON FEDERAL INCOME TAX RETURNS

These are errors that occur on the individual federal income tax returns as filed. They do not include errors found by a tax audit by the Internal Revenue Service. This list indicates what has to be done by individuals to reduce, if not eliminate, these sources of error.[3]

Type of Error	*Number of returns*
1. Copied wrong number from tax tables	1,098,310
2. Math error in figuring refund or tax owed	773,252
3. Medical or dental expense itemized wrongly	301,604
4. Mistake in earned income credit	273,586
5. Math error in figuring taxable income	17,004
Total number	2,463,756

---

[3] Source: IRS figures as of August 10, 1985. From *USA TODAY*, Feb. 6, 1986, p. 4B.

In Item 1 the individual copied the wrong number from the tax table. In Items 2 and 5 the individual made an error in calculating a refund, a tax owed, or a taxable income. In Items 3 and 4 the individual may have misunderstood the instructions, made the wrong calculations, or made an error in the correct method.

Item 1 shows that over one million persons cannot take the figure for the taxable income and for the kind of return filed (single, married, filing jointly, etc.) and, using these two items of information, find the correct tax in the tax table. This error has nothing to do with mathematics, arithmetic, or calculations. It involves the ability to use a two-way reference table correctly, given a horizontal value and a vertical class. This is the same ability which is needed to find one's weight in an age-height table, given one's height and age. These persons are unable to do this simple task.

Item 2 is an error in making a subtraction and identifying what it means. It is an inability to make a proper subtraction involving two possibilities:

1. Calculated tax is *greater than* the amount of money paid, in which case you owe the IRS the difference, or
2. Calculated tax is *less than* the amount paid in, in which case the IRS owes you the difference as a refund.

This is simple arithmetic involving one number, which is a correct value or a standard, and another number, which is an obtained or calculated number. This arithmetic is illustrated by problems in profit or loss, gain or loss, surplus or deficit, excess or deficiency, overpayment or underpayment.

In Item 5 the error in the taxable income could occur in at least these places: in calculating the adjusted gross income, in the deductions, whether itemized or not, and in the exemptions. An error can also be made in addition to obtain the gross income and in subtraction to obtain the taxable income.

Paying for errors does not prevent them. Banks are paying their customers for errors that the banks make. The penalty is for the stated purpose of guaranteeing satisfactory service. The customer, however, has to discover the error and present proof of the error to a bank employee. Obviously this arrangement does not guarantee satisfactory service because it does not put the responsibility for the error on the person or persons who made it. *It also makes the customer find the errors that the bank makes.* Not only can this be a very costly practice, but it is no substitute for error prevention methods, including training. The annualized cost for the four banks reported are as follows:[4]

Bank of America, San Francisco	$10,000
Commerce Bank, Aurora, Colorado	200
South Trust Bank, Birmingham, Alabama	5,400
Bank of Boston, Waterbury, Connecticut	50,000

[4]*USA TODAY*, July 17, 1987, p. 1B.

The first bank pays up to $36 for six month of checking account fees. The second bank pays $5 for every error. A major error is misprints on teller receipts and loan statements. The third bank pays $10 for any error on monthly checking account statements. The fourth bank pays $10 credit for any errors on its monthly checking accounts; it had 2,109 errors in about five months.

The three banks which are losing $5,000 a year or more on these penalty payments could do much better by applying quality control to errors on checking accounts and statements. Error prevention methods would not only save money but would give the customers better service than they are now receiving. It is highly questionable whether forcing the customer to find the bank's errors and then paying him or her for it "guarantees satisfactory service," as the banks claim. Obviously this is no way to prevent errors for which bank employees are responsible. Customers should rebel at such a practice.

THE MIXUP TYPE OF ERROR

A rather common type of error is that characterized by a mixup, a switch, or a wrong substitution. Several examples of this type of error are illustrated, with remarks:

	Correct action	Nature of Error	Remarks
1.	$A = A$	$A = A_1$	Wrong size, type, model, strength, concentration, etc.
2.	$A = A$ $B = B$	$A = B$ $B = A$	Switch or interchange of products, orders, operations, persons, addresses, etc.
3.	Brown = Brown	Brown = Braun	Action taken on wrong person.
4.	$O_2 = O_2$ $O_2 = O_2$ $O_2 = O_2$	$O_2 = CO_2$ $O_2 = N_2$ $O_2 = A_2$	Wrong gas put into system and given to patients: carbon dioxide, nitrogen, and argon substituted for oxygen.
5.	$A = A$	$A = B$	Wrong article or product; wrong method or procedure.

Error 1 is prevented by using some method of verification.
Error 2 is prevented by using a better identification system plus verification.
Error 3 is prevented by some method of verification.
Error 4 is prevented by strict controls, testing, and monitoring.
Error 5 is prevented by some method of verification.

All of these are the types of errors that require specific types of training aimed at the cause of the error and ways to prevent it.

SUMMARY OF ERROR PREVENTION METHODS

At this point a summary of error prevention methods is presented. It shows the wide variety of methods which have to be used if errors are to be brought under control and kept that way. The goal, as stated before, is to drive errors toward zero. In many operations and industries zero error is the only goal that can be allowed for specific situations.

1. Operating methods
    - Group daily error chart;
    - Individual daily error chart;
    - Daily accident or safety chart;
    - Inspection of operations, processes, storage, labels;
    - Safety measures and devices;
    - Procedural manuals with emphasis on correct methods;
    - Storage, limited access;
    - Labels, warning signs;
    - Cautions and warnings about taking risks;
    - Clear and complete messages and communications.
2. Verification methods
    - Self-verification and review, edit;
    - Two-person independent verification, review, check, inspection;
    - Verification techniques and methods, e.g., second source;
    - Supervisory review, check, verification;
    - Mathematical verification techniques: cross-check, different orders, different methods, graphic methods, approximations;
    - Data verification: check interviews, past data, other sources, computer edit, data sheet review;
    - Communication verification: insure lower-level technical and managerial approval or disapproval, lower-level clearance at all levels.
3. Training
    - Training in subject matter related to errors, error-related knowledge;
    - Training in all aspects of safety in performing the job: knowledge, practice, actions, behavior, risks, protection;
    - Attitude orientation of employees and others toward errors, safety, customers, other employees, work environment;
    - Periodic error prevention meetings at all levels;
    - Training in the nature, incidence, occurrence, and behavior relative to emergencies: "What to do if . . . ."
4. Recognition and rewards
    - For error reduction;
    - For safety record;
    - For other quality improvement;

5. Control methods
- Sample receipts control;
- Patient control: admissions and discharges;
- Customer order control;
- Computer edit to discover and eliminate errors and inconsistencies;
- Preventing computer errors by controls over every stage:
  - over the input data: very severe controls are needed here because of the impossibility of correcting an error once it is in the computer;
  - over the programming: very severe controls are needed here because an error here is transmitted to the very end of the process (tabulation, calculation, etc.);
  - over the output: the output needs to be in the form required to answer the questions posed by the study for which the data are collected and tabulated;
  - over the calculations: calculations have to be correctly programmed, correctly run, and summarized in handy form;
  - over the tabulations: tabulations have to meet the specifications laid down when the study was planned and the data were collected; correct analysis of the data.
- Updating the files: many errors are made because files are not kept up to date: active and inactive files should be kept current.

MASSIVE TRAINING

The Obstacles to Massive Training

One of the remedies prescribed for making quality improvements is "massive training." The term seems to imply that by the sheer force of a huge volume of training, the problem of quality improvement can be solved. The use of massive training or problem-oriented training to prevent human errors and to improve quality and productivity is not as easy as it sounds; nor will it be as effective, as the term seems to imply. It sounds like a sure-fire method that will give quick results. It is not. The reasons are not hard to find.

1. It assumes effective teaching. Where will the *teachers* come from? Organizations do not hire people because they know how to teach. It is rare that any employee does. The quality—the effectiveness—of the teaching cannot be overlooked.

2. It assumes a carefully planned, structured, and sound *curriculum* or set of courses aimed at error prevention and quality improvement. Who will prepare these materials? Organizations do not hire these kinds of people.

3. It assumes that teachers know how to *organize and present* these courses effectively and that the employees will know how to apply to their jobs what is taught. This assumption is open to serious question.

4. It asumes that certain *individual attitudes* will be changed or inculcated as a result of this teaching:

- The careless will become careful;
- The indifferent will become alert;
- The irresponsible will become responsible;
- The ignorant will become knowledgeable;
- The inaccurate will become accurate;
- The rude will become courteous.

This is a tall order, and one that will not be attained by the usual training course even if it is magnified 10 times. The basic change must come in attitudes even more than in knowledge, abilities, and skills. This will not be easy. It will take time, measured in years, not days or weeks.

5. It assumes not only that attitudes will change but that proper knowledge, abilities, and skills will be mastered and *applied successfully*. We should not expect very much very soon, or we will be sadly disillusioned.

What is wrong with massive education? One view is that massive education should be the major instrument in a wider plan to get rid of professional staff members, specialists, and middle managers. Under this strategy there will be no need for lawyers, accountants, engineers, statisticians, chemists, physicists, and all the other technical specialists. Everyone in production, everyone on the production line, everyone in operations will be his or her own lawyer, accountant, statistician, and engineer.

Everyone on the production line or in operations of any kind will belong to a big happy family which will never be bothered by specialists or middle managers. They will be deceived into thinking that they are sharing knowledge, when all they are sharing is ignorance. Their enthusiasm will disappear once they are faced with some tough technical problems.

Mass education as set forth in this way is a delusion. Too much relevant technical knowledge is needed in quality improvements; too many powerful but efficient techniques require years of study to learn and even more years to apply successfully to complex problems; thus no massive education program can enable ordinary employees on the job to approach, let alone equal this knowledge. Rejection of powerful and extensive fields of specialized knowledge is not the solution to our problems; it is the road to disaster.

Who Will Teach this Massive Training Program?

Current criticisms of quality control in manufacturing companies imply that the present staff and supervisors are failing to do a good job of training and education. If they were not failing, workers would know their jobs; workers would know what is acceptable-quality work and what is not; workers would understand basic working rules and procedures; workers would know what to do about routine problems; workers would know what to do about unusual problems. If this is true, how then can massive training and education improve quality? Who will teach the teachers *how* to teach and *what* to teach?

This is another idea that sounds good in theory but is very difficult to put into practice. What we are *not* doing is spelling out in detail what has to be done in connection with massive training and education to improve quality, to move employees from one plateau of the learning curve to a better one. This is another great idea that can fail.

If you pull foremen and supervisors and professionals off their regular jobs to teach lower-level or new employees, it will be a very costly project, as all of us know who have actually had to do it. The regular work suffers and you never know how effective the teaching is, nor how productive the newly trained employees will be.

Let's face it. Rarely is a foreman, supervisor, or professional a good teacher naturally. How many of them have been brought up to explain in detail the steps in a process, to explain anything clearly, accurately, and simply, or to take into consideration individual differences in ability to learn?

Requirements for Massive (or Any) Training to Succeed

1. Training must be based on the characteristics of the learning curve.
2. It must push the learning curve to the "limit." It must push the learning curve beyond the first plateau.
3. Training must bring about the following:
   • A progressive elimination of the number of errors;
   • A progressive elimination of serious errors, regardless of number;
   • A progressive elimination of unnecessary steps, acts, sequences, or operations;
   • Introduction of better ways, better methods, better techniques, quicker faster steps, shortened methods and procedures. Use of shortcuts;
   • Progressive elimination of any and all external obstructions, distractions, and interferences to learning and improvement;
   • Elimination of situations and arrangements that appear to cause or promote errors, such as complicated data sheets and confusing communications;
   • Reduction of the operation or sequence to the bare essentials;
   • Shifting of all employees, regardless of level, who are prone to make errors, regardless of training and coaching. Shift them to other jobs where errors cannot be made or are not important.
4. Ample time must be allowed.
   • Learning proceeds slowly;
   • Elimination of errors and waste motion is a slow process;

- Allow two to four years to put program into effect for major reduction in errors;
- Allow one year to get started: train for a diminishing error rate;
- Start slowly on one project or operation; use coaching by good supervisor.

5. Learners must move to higher and higher plateaus on the production curve or lower and lower plateaus on the error curve or unit cost curve.

6. *Attitudes require special treatment and special methods:*
   - Use of personal conferences;
   - Small group conferences led by a trusted person;
   - Small group conferences led by another employee;
   - Conferences stressing to everyone the value of safety, zero errors, quality improvement.

COUNTERING JUSTIFICATION OF ERRORS, MISTAKES, AND POOR-QUALITY SERVICE

A major problem in the prevention of errors is to learn how to counter the various justifications which are made for errors and mistakes. This can be very difficult because these attitudes may have been accepted for a long time. Where errors have to be zero or have to be driven to zero, it is wise to make this clear when employees are hired, as well as when they are being given an error prevention course. Examples of the attitudes to be changed are the following:

- Nobody is perfect.
- It is just "human nature" to make errors.
- Everybody makes mistakes.
- It is natural to make errors.
- It shows that we are human.
- It is not the people, it is the computer.
- It doesn't happen very often.
- The error rate is only ½ of 1 percent ("only" meant 185,000 financial records in error).

There are many ways to counter these attitudes. The very first step is to make sure that no one who holds these attitudes is ever hired. Methods that can be used include the following:

- Insist on either 1) hiring people with the necessary attitudes and technical knowledge or 2) training them in what they need to know and have on the job.
- Explain where errors are *dangerous* and can result in harm to both the organization and the individual, including damage suits.

- Explain the high cost of errors and mistakes internally.
- Explain the undesirable effects of errors and mistakes on customers.
- Explain the various methods of checking and verification, and how to use them.
- Explain the need to read carefully all instructions, directions, and procedures, and to ask questions about anything in doubt.
- Explain the need to research all kinds of material to insure accuracy and clarity in all written and oral statements.
- Give courses periodically on prevention of different kinds of errors that are met in the various operations and departments.
- Give courses and demonstrations in safety procedures and emergency situations.
- Explain that in many situations the only acceptable standard for the error rate is zero.
- Explain that it is just as easy to learn to perform an operation error-free as to perform it with mistakes. Learn to do it right in the first place.

The long-term approach to error prevention does not lie primarily with the company or the organization. It lies with the public school system.

The job of the elementary school is to teach reading, writing, arithmetic, spelling, grammar, geography, and other content subjects needed by children so that they will grow up to be intelligent citizens on the one hand and proficient workers on the other.

This means teaching children how to read and answer a simple business letter, to read and understand a set of instructions and directions that are used on the job, to understand oral instructions and explanations given to them by the boss, and to work simple arithmetic problems encountered in banks and stores or required by health insurance and tax returns.

The company or organization should not have to waste time, use high-salaried people, and drive up prices by spending time teaching elementary school subjects to 18-year-olds.

Neither should the company or organization have to teach such desirable attitudes as accuracy, timeliness, care, courtesy, honesty, and fairness, where these attitudes are necessary in order to do a good job or to communicate with other people, including customers.

What needs to be changed is the attitude that has been observed, by which children in school are allowed to 1) spell any way they want to spell 2) ignore rules of grammar, and 3) violate all rules for writing or speaking a clear sentence.

The standards of spelling, grammar, and writing are still in force and need to be emphasized. Creative writing needs to be restricted to that area where it belongs—poetry and fiction.

TEACHING QUALITY IN PUBLIC EDUCATION: THE CRISIS IN EDUCATION

The foregoing implies that there is a crisis in public education relative to teaching quality. Quality cannot be built into products and services by illiterate and ignorant workers. Evidence from all directions shows that the public school system is failing to teach mastery of the important abilities, knowledge, and skills necessary for the production of quality products and services. The following examples illustrate this point:

- "An estimated 13% of the employed adults in this country—15 million people—are functionally illiterate. The problem is that Johnny still can't read" (*On Q*, ASQC Newsletter, September 1986).
- A section of a professional society (ASQC) gives a course in elementary arithmetic to members and other workers in factories—what should be learned by the sixth grade (Northern Colorado Section of ASQC).
- It is reported in the press from time to time that there are 20 to 25 million illiterates in this country.
- A recent report of 250 business and academic leaders states that half of our high school seniors can't read well enough to handle moderately complicated tasks.
- The chairman of the Xerox Corporation reports the following (David Kearns, *USA TODAY*, Oct. 27, 1987, p. 1):
    - Business must spend $25 billion a year to train workers who can't read, write, or count.
    - Only 50 percent of the high school graduates have been satisfactorily educated for the workplace.
    - One-fourth of the graduates can hardly read their own diplomas.
- A company advertises a video training course in basic mathematics for employees. More accurately, the course is simple arithmetic that should have been mastered by the eighth grade.[5]
  The topics listed are real number line, addition, subtraction, multiplication, division, averages, decimals, coded numbers, percentages, plotting points, squares, square roots, and using a calculator.
  If this type of teaching is needed in a factory or an office, then somewhere the teaching of simple arithmetic is failing not only in one grade but in the entire elementary school. We cannot meet competition in business, whether domestic or foreign, with this kind of public education.

The solution to the problem is not more money, more gimmicks, more manifestoes from Washington, more overhead administrators and aides, or more

---

[5] *Quality Progress*, November 1987, p. 14.

computers. The solution to the problem is the teacher—the teacher who knows how to teach important knowledge, abilities, and skills so that the student gains an adequate mastery of them. This would appear to call for a drastic change in curriculum, subject matter, methods, and testing. These changes may be necessary to ensure that the goal of teaching is effective learning by the students.

INNOVATIONS AS QUALITY IMPROVEMENTS

Error prevention is an effective way to improve the quality of services. Another way to improve quality is by introducing innovations or changes in designs, procedures, methods, techniques, and services. Often quality of service to the consumer can be improved by a very simple change.

The following are some new ideas that can improve the quality of service to customers:

1. Post signs in aisles of a supermarket, identifying products or groups. Put signs at a level where they can be easily read.
2. When an item is moved, put up sign to show new location.
3. Give customers with years of patronage an ID card for use in check cashing, writing checks, etc.
4. Mail bank interest statements annually rather than monthly. Only an annual statement is needed for tax purposes.
5. Eliminate insurance premiums for impossible or nonexistent situations, such as lack of income and adjoining buildings.
6. Reduce insurance premiums of low-risk persons such as nondrinkers, nonsmokers, and drivers with no accidents for 25 years.
7. Design padded shoes for comfort and elimination of blisters, etc.
8. Implement a system which takes a traveler from origin to destination.
9. Enclose shopping malls. (This has already been done in many places.)
10. Print blank occasion cards so person can write own message on the inside.
11. Design a bed using the principle of the sleeping bag.
12. Design a kitchen oven in two separate parts—one for small dishes and one for a large job, for the purpose of saving energy and making the use of the oven more convenient and more comfortable.

Chapter 15

Techniques in Services

STATISTICS—A MAJOR VECTOR IN QUALITY

Statistics—the Science of Variability

Statistics is the science that deals exclusively with variability of characteristics. Therefore it is no accident that statistics is a natural to apply to quality which is characterized by variability—its detection, control, reduction, and prevention. Statistics applies whether the variability is associated with the dimensions of products, the performance of individuals, or the characteristics of services. In services this variability can exist whether the characteristics are strictly measurements or not.

Statistics consists of a wide variety of specific principles and techniques that are applicable to a large number of situations, whether they are purchases by a service organization or the human performance required in the rendering of that service. Examples are the following:

- Product: stabilizing a dimension, reducing defects;
- Chemical: performing some test or experiment;
- Insurance claims: reducing both reporting and processing errors;
- Customer attitude: conducting a probability sample survey;
- Downtime on equipment: using random time work sampling to measure frequency and cost.

These and other techniques are described with examples later in this chapter.

The Need to Learn Statistics

The above list shows the need to learn basic statistics so that variability can be detected, controlled, reduced, and prevented. The need will now be described in more detail.

Statistics furnishes the tools to collect data adequate to the problem or situation, to analyze or interpret the data, and to determine whether a problem exists. The role of statistics in quality is not so much solving any of these problems as discovering them so that subject matter specialists rather than statisticians can solve them.

One of the most, if not the most, important contributions of statistics to quality is its use in distinguishing special causes from chronic causes or faults of the system. By use of statistical control over a process, also known as statistical process control (SPC), one determines whether a special cause exists. This is a fault which the employee can correct or is in a position to correct. This brings the process under control, but it still may turn out defective parts or a poor-quality product. The reason is that other factors are operating which are beyond the control of the employee. These factors include worn-out equipment, defective or inadequate materials, faulty instructions, inefficient methods and processes, and much more.

When the cause of the poor quality is the fault of the system, then the supervisor can solve some problems but has to turn to a higher level of management to report other problems and have them solved. As has already been pointed out in an earlier chapter, there are many faults of the system, many of them hidden from view, so that only a professional or specialist familiar with quality control programs can identify them and plan to correct them with the approval of higher-level management. Examples are as follows:

- Designing and implementing a probability sample survey to measure the attitudes of present customers, noncustomers, and lost customers.
- Designing and implementing a random time work sample for the purpose of measuring the amount and cost of idle time, downtime, waiting time, and other situations where time is an important factor in performing a job or project, and where reducing costs and improving the quality of performance are easy to accomplish.
- Designing a system of data collection so that improved quality data will be input into the computer, and so that errors in programming and process will be reduced, if not prevented.
- Using learning curve analysis on a new job where everyone has to be instructed in an entirely new operation, so as to reduce errors and measure the capability of the group under actual working conditions. This means collecting data on both errors and production for each person once the job has been learned.

There is also an immediate need to master basic statistics—to understand Dr. Deming's two books: *Quality, Productivity, and Competitive Position* and *Out of the Crisis*. The emphasis on the 14 Points for management to accept and practice in the management of quality has led to a neglect of the many applications of statistics in the discovery and resolution of a wide variety of problems. An examination of the first book mentioned above shows the frequency of occurrence in the use of various techniques and concepts in statistics:

- Charts and related problems are used 47 times.
- The binomial distribution is used at least seven times.
- The Poisson distribution is used at least seven times.
- Probability is used at least three times.
- Variance and standard deviation are used at least twice.

This gives an idea of the extent to which technical concepts and techniques are used, even though others may obtain a slightly different count (variability is expected). This does not include Chapter 13, which is devoted entirely to inspection of incoming materials, with special reference to the criterion for determining whether to inspect 100 percent or not at all.

This list shows that the reader must know quite a bit about basic statistics to understand fully the calculations which are made in many parts of the book, and why they take the form they do. The book is both statistical and managerial. Actually, it consists of a series of real-world examples which show why management has to use statistics to improve operations, the process, and the product.

At no place are any but simple methods used. This shows that simple methods can be very effective if one knows the problem on the one hand and statistics on the other. This is the secret of making effective use of the binomial and Poisson distributions. They have to be thoroughly understood so that one knows to which real problems they apply and to which they do not apply, and to which problem one distribution is applied and to which the other distribution is applied. One cannot do this without mastery of the appropriate knowledge. This knowledge has nothing to do with management as such. It is used to discover and resolve problems and critical situations.

Statistics and the Computer; Software and Statistical Over-kill

There is another, just as important reason for understanding statistics—the widespread use of the computer, software, and the hand-held calculator for statistical and mathematical purposes. Three kinds of needs of the organization have to be considered: 1) calculation needs, 2) data processing needs, and 3) storage and retrieval needs. Knowledge of statistics is necessary if these needs are to be met effectively and efficiently.

Calculations

There are several ways to make calculations, depending upon the mass of data, the frequency of occurrence of the problem, and the necessity of discovering trouble and taking corrective actions immediately.

Calculations on large masses of data, such as those accumulated in a large sample study, are best programmed into the tabulation of the data. If the statistical calculations are difficult, such as calculating the standard error of a subclass aggregate, then the computer programmer will usually need assistance from a statistician to see that the proper formulas are used.

It is usually necessary on these large jobs to program the calculations necessary because of their special and limited character rather than try to buy a piece of software to do the job. The trouble with software, as pointed out below, is that it usually comes in a package which contains many more programs than are needed.

For simple problems and for problems using a very limited amount of data, the use of a hand-held calculator (such a the HP-32E) is both handy and low-cost, and gets the results immediately. All that is needed for fast work is a clipboard with the multi-purpose table and chart given earlier together with a hand-held calculator. Data are recorded on the form, the proper calculations are made, and the data are plotted on the chart. This is a quick way to produce time charts and tentative $\bar{x}$, R, p, and c charts, so that if trouble exists it can be detected immediately. This method eliminates all the delay inherent in collecting data, running it through a computer somewhere, and printing out a chart with necessary (and unnecessary) calculations. This method can be used at any work site where data are accumulated, or at any other place where data are already available. With a properly trained person it is a big money saver. It makes a huge investment in hardware and software unnecessary.

Data processing

Tabulation of large masses of data, such as those obtained from a large sample study, a census, or 100 percent coverage, requires careful design of the various tables to be run on the computer. These are designed in terms of the purpose of the study, the estimates that are required, and the comparisons that are to be made. Without proper design of the data collection and the tabulations, a lot of costly but useless data and tables will be turned out by the computer.

Data input

By careful analysis of the problem, by use of quality control applied to the input data, and by careful tabulation, calculation, and analysis, useful information will result. A major problem is to insure that only high-quality data are input to the computer. This means putting intensive and effective controls on the quality of the data collected.

Statistical Overkill or Appraising the Advertising of Software

Advertising of software for statistical purposes is full of misleading displays and presentations. It is not so much that what is presented is inaccurate in calculation, but that the presentations and the calculations are not tied up with quality and its improvement, which is the sole purpose of SPC and SQC. The comments below illustrate the situation.

- The goal is quality, not a colored picture on a CRT. The connection is not explained.
- The goal is control of the process or production, not a fancy chart.
- Statistics is a means to an end, not an end in itself. The impression that the advertisers and exhibitors give is that the colored lines, graphs, charts, and tables are an end in themselves, not a way to improve quality. The gap between statistics and pictures, and quality, is not bridged or explained.
- Fictitious $\bar{x}$ charts with control limits are shown on the display. Some of them show runs that clearly make the process suspect without reference to the control limits. The latter are not based on a run of data in which assignable causes are eliminated and the process is stabilized before the limits are calculated. It is not explained that the purpose of the chart is to eliminate causes and maintain variability within the control limits. Where the computer is placed and how long it takes to investigate a point out of control are not mentioned. The *quality* advantages of the computer are ignored.
- Fitting a normal distribution in red or green to a frequency distribution is useless esthetics; it serves no useful purpose. It would serve a useful purpose if the process capability were shown, and whether or not the tolerance (6 sigma) fell within the range of the distribution.
- If the computer and the relevant software are some distance away from the work site, their use may defeat one of the major goals of quality control—finding the trouble quickly and eliminating its cause promptly.
- All calculations are to six decimal places, whether the original data justify such calculations or not. Rarely will a real-world problem in quality, either in manufacturing or in services, justify that many decimal places. The only justifiable place will be certain measurements in manufacturing and laboratory research.
- On a p chart the sample size is not given, even though $\bar{p}$ is shown. LCLs on p or c charts can be zero. The lower limit in such cases is not non-existent.
- Mode, median, standard deviation, skewness, and kurtosis are calculated, even though they are never used. Nor is there any need for them. This is a carry-over from textbooks of concepts that are not used in practice, es-

pecially mode, skewness, and kurtosis. The median is rarely used in quality control work. Neither is the standard deviation, although with larger samples and the new calculators there is no reason why the standard deviation should not be used when it is better than the range.

- In one instance a c chart is constructed from a population in which the mean is *exactly* equal to the variance. This never occurs in practice. Fictitious problems are substituted for those from the real world.
- In one case of an exact Poisson distribution, not only is a c chart plotted but also a p chart, a u chart, and an np chart. There is no explanation for why four charts were constructed, or that all four charts would give the same results if the problem involved were a real-world problem.
- A sharp linear regression is shown within the control limits of an x̄ chart. There are also control limits on the regression line. Obviously constant factors, not chance factors, are operating within the control limits of the x̄ chart. This could run out of control at the upper limit, but why wait? What purpose does this line serve? This inside trend could be due to tool wear or some other constant factor.
- On one chart on a display the frequencies are expressed in decimals. It does not look as if the scales were reversed. Someone made a horrible mistake.
- In some of the problems it is not enough to calculate a mean and a range. A frequency distribution is needed.
- In one demonstration a normal curve is fitted to a histogram. Nothing else is done. What is the purpose? There is no explanation; this is a useless exercise.
- A curved line is used to accumulate values of attributes to 100 pecent, as though they are variables.
- A straight line $y = a + bx$ is fitted to some data without any explanation of why it was done and what it was used for: prediction? interpolation? exploration? The correlation coefficient appeared to be about 0.75, so the fitting of a straight line acounted for only a little more than half the variance in y. The line has no predictive value.
- An x̄ chart had 14 points below a mean of 52, four at the mean, and seven above the mean with one value (out of control) at 54.6. UCL = 54, LCL = 50. There were no explanations of these values. They appeared to be fictitious, not a problem from the real world; 14 points below the mean makes it suspect.
- A straight line relationship between x and y—a linear regression—is called a "scatter diagram," following the Japanese. This is not the only situation in which there is a "scatter" of values (the frequency distribution is another), so the term is ill-chosen. This is one place where there is no justification for accepting something the Japanese invented.
- There is a display where a cubic equation is fitted to data. This is justified as a demonstration of curve fitting. The trouble is that curve fitting and

certainly cubic equations are very rare in statistical practice as applied to quality in products or quality in services.

These displays and examples illustrate statistical overkill in connection with quality. The software has an academic flavor rather than the flavor of the real world. The problems are not real; the meaning is missing; the connection with quality is completely ignored. The programs are excessive in number and overelaborate. The software world needs to get in touch with the real world of quality control and quality improvement.

How to Misuse Statistics to Justify Your Purpose

Two concepts in statistics are used to illustrate the very common practice of employing statistics to justify some purpose that a person has in mind. The two concepts are average and percentage. These are not the only ones, but they will illustrate the point. Average and percentage are used almost daily to mislead the public, to justify some position, to subvert the facts, to create a reality that does not exist, to confuse the individual, or to avoid the real problem.

Average

A view held and fostered not only by educational officials but by governors of states, high-level officials in Washington, and the media generally is that average salaries are too low. The cry is, "If quality of education is to improve, pay the teachers more." (Some do not believe it is a question of money but a question of the teacher's ability to teach. More pay will not change the situation.)

This is a statement by an official in the Colorado State Department of Education: [1]

> "The average teacher salary is getting closer and closer to the (national) average each year, and it will continue to do so if the legislature doesn't increase its spending amounts (for education)."

In this case the national average is being compared with the state average. Some interesting points arise:

> Is the state average moving down or is the national average moving up?

> The averages will become closer if the national average moves up faster than the state average.

---

[1] *Rocky Mountain News,* November 5, 1986, p. 70.

The real question is whether these averages have any relevance to the improvement of education, whose quality is determined by the performance of the teachers in the classroom. Salary averages simply divert attention from the real problem, which is the ability of the teacher to teach reading, language, writing, geography, spelling, and other important information, abilities, and attitudes.

Another example comes from transportation; the details were given in Chapter 5. RTD—the Regional Transportation District—runs the bus lines in the Denver area. It let a contract for 167 buses to the lowest bidder. Of the first 33 buses received from the manufacturer, about half were in such poor shape that they had to be debugged before they could be used. These defects and flaws were corrected both at the factory and in the RTD garages. No one insisted that these defective buses be returned to the manufacturer so they could be put in a workable condition. RTD just accepted the poor-quality product it received. One official was quoted as saying:

"We now have an above-average bus."[2]

One wonders what an "average" new bus is like. These officials are accepting poor-quality products by calling them "average" or "better than average." They are accepting a lot of poor products, increasing the costs required to put them in workable condition, and letting the manufacturer get away with patching up buses rather than manufacturing high-quality buses at the factory. They are not aware of what quality is, nor are they aware that it is the manufacturer's responsibility to deliver defect-free buses.

Still another example of the misuse of the average is in the field of weather. Average temperatures for a day, or some other period, are considered "normals." Actually there is no such temperature as "normal." This is a fictitious calculated number which for a consideration of everyday living has no meaning. What has meaning is not the average but the variability of temperatures and rainfall. Variability represents the real world; an average does not. Some people can get so attached to the "average" or the "normal" that they complain about the variations in temperature or rainfall which represent the real world. They reject reality and accept the fictitious. Weather reports should report not the so-called "normal" from the past but the variability of the temperatures and rainfall from the past.

Percentage

In Chapter 5, actual federal government figures show that in 1985, when the actual estimated number of unemployed persons *increased,* the unemployment in terms of both adjusted and unadjusted percentages *decreased.* Only the percentage unemployed is given wide publicity in the newspapers and on tele-

---

[2] *Rocky Mountain News,* July 19, 1986, p. 17.

vision because this is what the administration in Washington wants to show—that unemployment is steadily declining. The number of unemployed is ignored and has been for years, although this is what defines the real problem; the percentage does not. The number of unemployed persons, running between 8 and 9 million, is actually more than official records showed during the last years of the great depression of the 1930s. This fact is also ignored.

As shown in Chapter 5, the reason why the percentage can decrease while the number of unemployed is increasing is due to the simple fact that the base on which the percentage is calculated increased much more than the number of unemployed—a simple principle that one should learn in elementary arithmetic.

Another situation where the idea of percentage is widely misleading is in connection with the CPI—the consumer price index, inflation, and the cost of living. Since about 1980 the price index has been declining. This is *not* a measure of cost of living for several reasons:

- It does not reflect the *amounts* of goods bought.
- It does not include many commodities which consumers buy.
- It includes commodities that consumers seldom or rarely buy, such as the cost of a home mortgage.
- It excludes such common items as monthly gas, electric, telephone, water, and garbage removal bills. It excludes taxes and insurance.

The media and officials lead people to believe that the reduction in the rate of inflation means that the cost of living is declining. These figures mean nothing of the kind. Inflation figures mean that the *cost of living is increasing,* but *at a decreasing rate.* This is an idea that the press never explains. Apparently it is too complicated for persons who have never had a good course in elementary arithmetic. The best measures of inflation and of the cost of living are the prices and amounts of goods you have bought at the store daily over the past five or 10 years. These, together with your public utility bills and tax bills, show how cost of living is increasing.

This chart shows how quality is improved when management makes a serious effort to reduce errors. The data are derived from a sample of 100 orders selected daily from filled orders. No individual records are kept or displayed, only the group error rate shown above, exhibited on a large wall chart (Figure 15–1).

Notice a tendency for the rate to level off for several days at about 3 percent. This is a plateau on a learning curve, to be discussed later. Finally, more errors are eliminated so a shift to 2 percent and below occurs and holds. The latest available data show that the error rate is now below 1 percent and no doubt with further effort can be reduced even more.

This is a simple time chart of the daily error rate. It measures the improvement in quality of performance, and how long it took to obtain that improvement. No control charts are used, nor are they necessary. The goal is to drive

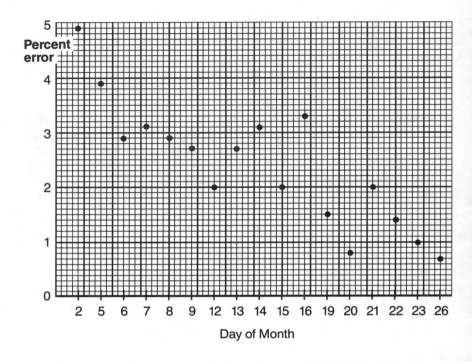

Figure 15–1. **Daily Error Rate on Order Tickets for a Mail Order House for Three Weeks**

the error rate toward zero. This was accomplished in a very striking manner in about one month. The actual number of days shown is 17. The reduction in error rate was from about 5 percent to less than 1 percent during this time.

RANDOM TIME WORK SAMPLING

The theory and application of modern work sampling based on random minutes originated with Rosander, Guterman, and McKeon in 1955.[3] Random time sampling (RTS) for work activities has several unique features which depart sharply from former conventional methods of snap readings and ratio delay:

· RTS is based on the theory of probability sampling.
· It uses the minute model, in which a random minute is both an intsant and an interval or duration.

---

[3] A. C. Rosander, H. E. Guterman, and A. J. McKeon. "The Use of Random Work Sampling for Cost Analysis and Control." *Journal of the American Statistical Association,* June 1958, vol. 53, pp. 382–397.

- Complete time populations are sampled; the working day, the working week, the working year.
- A table of random minutes is used as the source of the random minutes to be selected into the sample. The same table can be used as a source of random days because random days are a subset of random minutes.
- Associating with each random minute the corresponding wage per minute, salary per minute, rental per minute, and cost per minute makes it possible to use the sample to estimate aggregate costs, category costs, and subclass costs.
- An appropriate probability sample is designed for the purpose at hand and for conditions under which the sample is to be selected.

Random time sampling (RTS) has several distinctive merits:

- Estimates can be made not only of time but of costs of delay time, downtime, idle time, waiting time, job time, activity time, lost time, and component time.
- It is the only method that can decompose joint costs of complex activities with validity and accuracy.
- Estimates can be made of the costs of specific jobs and functions or of individuals in groups or in areas, using ratio estimation.
- RTS can estimate time and cost of activities whether they involve work or not.

These data match very closely an actual situation in a graphic arts department. The $20,000 is based on what would have occurred if 1) no random time sample study had been made, 2) the conditions existing had continued for a year, which was not unrealistic, and 3) other conditions remained the same (Figure 15–2).

The data were derived from calling eight random minutes daily on the graphic arts department and observing whether each of the 10 employees was at work or was waiting for work. The chart shows how many minutes employees were waiting for work each day, out of a total of 80 employee minutes. The observed data are as follows:

Day	Total Sample Minutes Daily	Number Waiting for Work	Percent Waiting
1	80	9	11.2
2	80	6	7.5
3	80	5	6.3
4	80	8	10.0
5	80	10	12.5
	400	38 sample minutes	9.5

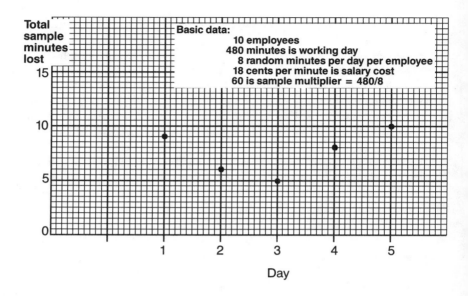

Figure 15–2. **$20,000 potential annual loss due to waiting for work, Graphic Arts Department**

Calculations:

$x = 38/5 = 7.6$ minutes per day

percent $p = 38/400 = 7.6//80 = 9.5$

Note: The minute model is used in which random minute is treated as a duration, not as an instant. As a result of the 9.5%, immediate action was taken to improve the scheduling of work. Cost per minute = $0.18

Weekly cost $C = 38 \times 0.18 \times 60 = \$410.40$

Potential annual cost therefore approximates $20,000.

Example: A Simple Cluster Time Sample

The first example illustrates how a simple cluster sample is used to estimate not only quality costs but non-quality costs and the cost of idle and other time. Table 15–1 illustrates the layout, the raw data, and the intermediate derived data. The raw data come from five individual data sheets. Table 15–2 gives the calculations of costs and proportions with their sampling variances.

For illustrative purposes the time population is only 480 minutes, from which eight minutes are selected at random. The object population is a set of five employees, which is not sampled but is included 100 percent to give a cluster of values for each random minute. The multiplier required to extend the sample

Table 15–1. A Simple Cluster Time Sample to Estimate Quality Costs

1 = quality activity; 0 = non-quality activity; x = idle, other; derived values, quality activities only

Employee	Sample Random Minute								Sample Sum	Cents Per Minute	Total Sample Cents	Estimated Population Cost (dollars)
	1	2	3	4	5	6	7	8				
A	0	x	1	0	0	1	0	x	2	10	20	$ 12
B	1	1	0	0	0	1	1	0	4	10	40	24
C	x	1	0	1	1	0	0	1	4	20	80	48
D	1	0	0	1	1	1	0	x	4	30	120	72
E	1	1	1	x	1	1	0	1	6	30	180	108
sum	3	3	2	2	3	4	1	2	20	100 ($1.00)	440 ($4.40)	$264 (440×60)
p_j	.6	.6	.4	.4	.6	.8	.2	.4	p = 20/40 = 0.5 or 50%			
x_j	$.70	.60	.40	.50	.80	.80	.10	.50	4.40	$\bar{x} = 4.40/8 = \$0.55$		

*The multiplier is 480/8 = 60; for example, 20 cents × 60 = 1200 cents or $12.

467

Table 15–2. **Calculations for Table 15–1**

Quality Activities

Proportion engaged in quality activities   p = 20/40 = 0.50 or 50%

Sampling variance = $\dfrac{1}{8 \times 7} \sum (p_j - 0.5)^2 = 0.24/56$ $j = 1, 2, \ldots 8$

Standard error = 0.065 or 7%

Aggregate quality cost = X = \$4.40 × 60 = \$264

Sampling variance = $s_x^2 = \dfrac{480^2}{8 \times 7} \sum (x_j - 0.55)^2$

Standard error = s_x = \$39.54 or \$40

Non-quality activities

Proportion = 15/40 = 0.375 or 37.5%

Aggregate cost = (40 + 40 + 60 + 90 + 30)60/100 = \$156

Idle and other activities

Proportion = 5/40 = 0.125 or 12.5%

Aggregate cost = (20 + 20 + 30 + 30)60/100 = \$60

Summary

Quality	\$264	55.0%	Quality takes 50% of time, 55% of the cost
Non-quality	156	32.5	
Idle, other	60	12.5	
Total	\$480	100.0%	Check: total cost from Table 15–1: \$1 × 480 = \$4

---

cost to the population cost is therefore 480/8, or 60. This multplier applies to each employee as well as to the total of five employees. Cost (cents or dollars) per minute is assumed for each employee. In a real problem these values are derived from wage and salary rates entered on the data sheets.

The calculations of the aggregate quality cost, its sampling variance, and the standard error are derived from those employees engaged in quality activities at each random minute. The multiplier of 60 is used to extend the sample values to the population value to obtain total or aggregate cost. In this case it is not needed to estimate proportions. The proportion engaged in quality activities and its standard error are also calculated, and are shown in Table 15–2. In addition, Table 15–2 shows the calculations for proportions and aggregate costs for non-quality activities and for idle and other activities, so as to account for the total population cost for both time and employees. The heads-tails binomial model formula PQ/n does *not* apply.

Table 15–1 is a summary of the raw data taken directly from the data sheets with the cents per minute entered for each employee. In this table 1 stands for a person engaged in quality cost activity at each random minute, 0 stands for a person engaged in a non-quality cost activity at each random minute, and x stands for a person who was idle or engaged in other activity. The columns at the right and the three rows at the bottom are derived from the "1" entries, which are activities classified as quality functions. In Table 15–2, calculations are also made for those engaged in other activities.

A Replicated Sample

A replicated sample is one which consists of several independent but equal samples drawn from the entire population. Usually the total sample is divided into four to 10 replicates. This method of sampling has two major advantages: 1) it greatly simplifies the calculations of the estimates and their standard errors regardless of their nature, and 2) it sheds light on the internal consistency of the data by comparison of the several replicates.

Table 15–3 shows a four-replicate sample of time applied to 10 employees for a 480-minute working day. The replicates are balanced so that two random minutes are selected during the first four hours and two from the last four hours. As in Table 15–1, a 1 means that an employee was engaged in a quality

Table 15–3. A Four-Replicate Sample to Estimate Quality Costs

1 = quality activity 0 = all other activities R = replicate

Employee	Replicated Samples (random times) R-1 2:28	R-2 11:34	R-3 3:41	R-4 9:07	Sum (quality)	Cents Per Minute	Sample Total (cents)*
1	1	1	0	0	2	8	16
2	0	1	1	1	3	8	24
3	1	0	0	1	2	8	16
4	0	1	1	1	3	12	36
5	1	1	1	0	3	12	36
6	0	1	1	0	2	12	24
7	1	1	1	0	3	12	36
8	1	1	1	1	4	20	80
9	0	1	1	0	2	20	40
10	1	1	1	1	4	20	80
sum (quality)	6	9	8	5	28	132 $1.32	388 $3.88
cents x_j	80	124	116	68	388 $3.88	$\bar{x} = 388/4 = 97$	
proportion p_j	.60	.90	.80	.50	2.80	$p = 2.80/4 = 0.70$	

*Multiplier to use to obtain population estimate is 480/4 = 120.

Table 15–4. Calculations for the Data in Table 15–3

Quality Costs[a]

Estimate of population proportion   p = 28/40 = 0.70 or 70 percent

Standard error of p:

range method: $s = \dfrac{0.90 - 0.50}{4} = 0.10$ or 10%

Sum of squares method $s^2 = \dfrac{1}{4 \times 3}(.01 + .04 + .01 + .04) = 0.10/12$

$$s = 0.09 \text{ or } 9 \text{ percent}$$

Estimate of total quality cost:
$X_q = \$3.88 \times 120 = \$466$ (120 = 480/4)

Standard error of X_q:

replicate estimates of X   R-1: $X_1 = .80 \times 480 = \$384$
(multiplier = 480/1)   R-2: $X_2 = 1.24 \times 480 = 595$
R-3: $X_3 = 1.16 \times 480 = 557$
R-4: $X_4 = .68 \times 480 = 326$

check $X_q = \dfrac{1}{4}(384 + 595 + 557 + 326) = \$466$

Standard error s_{X_q}:

range method: $\dfrac{595 - 326}{4} = \$67$

sum of squares method: $s^2 = \dfrac{1}{4 \times 3} \sum (X_j - 466)^2 = 4271$
(j = 1,2,3,4)

$$s = \$65$$

Non-Quality Costs
$X_{nq} = 120 (.40 + .60 + .40) = \$168$

Summary

Quality costs	$466	74%
Non-quality costs	168	26
Total	634	100

From Table 15–3 the total cost is $1.32 × 480 = $634 which checks

---

[a] Rosander, A. C., *Case Studies in Sample Design* (New York: Marcel Dekker, 1977), pp. 275–328, appendix.

activity when the random minute was called, while a 0 means that an employee was engaged in some activity not included under the quality function. Cents per minute are assumed to be known for each employee and are shown in the next-to-last column in the table. The raw data are taken from the data sheet.

Table 15–4 gives the calculations of proportions and aggregate costs with their standard errors for quality-classified activities. An estimate of non-quality costs is also shown, as well as a summary. As in Table 15–2, total costs are calculated by two independent methods to verify the accuracy of the arithmetic. It should be observed that total minutes and cents per minutes are constants and therefore are not subject to sampling variations. Costs and proportions, however, being estimated from a random sample of minutes, are always subject to sampling variations.

Table 15–4 shows that while 70 percent of the time was spent on quality activities, 74 percent of the cost was quality cost. While this is only a simple illustration, wide differences can exist between the time distribution and the cost distribution where employees with widely different wages and salaries are engaged in the same kind of work.

Example

This is an example of using RTS to measure downtime of a piece of equipment. It may be a copier, a word processor, a computer, or some other device in daily use.

Eight random minutes are selected from a table of random minutes for each of five days, four in the morning and four in the afternoon. An eight-hour day is assumed: 8 a.m. to 12, and 1 p.m. to 5 p.m. A tally mark is made whenever the device is down or not in use at the random minute. The data are as follows: This shows that Day 5 is suspect and needs investigation. Even without Day 5 the average is slightly above 30 percent, which may be considered too high. Continuation of this sample for several weeks will reveal how frequent these downtimes are, and whether steps taken to reduce them are effective. Someone familiar with costs of downtime per minute can calculate the loss due to this downtime.

Example

The cost of performing Activity A can be estimated as long as it can be identified, observed, and reported. It can be one of a group of joint activities. The situation consists of 10 persons working eight hours a day; a random sample of eight minutes is called, one each day. The 10 persons are a group or cluster, and are not sampled. When a random minute is called, an *observer* determines what every one of the 10 is doing, or *self-reporting* is used, in which each individual reports whether he or she is working on Activity A or not. It is asumed in the latter case that individuals can identify their various activities so that they can report correctly. This sample requires first that a record be made of the occurrences of Activity A and then that these be changed into dollars per minute (cents per minute, if these are easier to work with). The table below gives cents per minute, but these are changed to dollars in the calculations. In this example employees are earning 10 or 12 cents per minute.

Table 15–5. Downtime of Piece of Equipment

Random Times

	Day 1		Day 2		Day 3		Day 4		Day 5		Total for Week
a.m.	805	—	858	1	823	1	924	1	840	1	
	912	—	911	1	845	—	1053	1	942	1	
	948	—	1023	—	1027	—	1117	—	1005	—	
	1150	1	1049	1	1154	—	1124	—	1134	—	
p.m.	109	1	103	—	111	1	131	—	330	1	
	133	—	258	—	218	—	317	—	336	1	
	204	1	310	1	254	—	416	—	423	1	
	330	—	402	—	328	1	440	1	449	1	
Sum		3		2		3		2		6	16
proportion p_j		0.375		0.250		0.375		0.250		0.750	0.40

Calculations Total Sample Size = 40

Downtime or not in use $\bar{p}$ = 16/40 = 0.40 or 40 percent

Sample average = 16/5 = 3.2; 3.2/8 = 0.40 or 40 percent

Sampling variance for 5 days = $\dfrac{p(1-p)}{n} = \dfrac{0.40 \times 0.60}{40} = 0.0060$

$s_p = 0.077$

Variation between samples for week

$s_p^2 = \dfrac{\sum (p_j - 0.40)^2}{5 \times 4} = \dfrac{0.00844}{5 \times 4} = 0.092$

$s_p = 0.092$ 3 $s_p = 0.28$

UCL = .68
LCL = .12

Table 15–6. Cents per Minute for Activity A When a Random Minute Was Called

Persons	1	2	3	4	5	6	7	8	Sum
			Random Minutes (clusters)						
1							10		
2	10	10	10	10		10			
3	12	12			12				
4				10			10		
5		10				10		10	
6						10			
7	12	12	12		12				
8					12		12		
9				10				10	
10									
sum	34	34	32	30	36	30	32	20	248 cents
					cents				

$$x = cents/100$$

Let M = 8 days = 8 × 480 = 3840 minutes; assume 480 minutes in a working day. The sampling rate is 8/480. Hence the multiplier is 480/8 = 60; $\bar{x}$ = 2.48/8 = $.32; m = 8 cluster minutes. Sample Mean for 8 Days

Calculations
The average daily cost C = 60 × $2.48 = $148.80.
Total cost for 8 days = 8 × 148.80 = $1190.40. This is $\dfrac{3840}{8}$ × 2.48.

$$s^2 = 3840^2 \, \frac{\sum (x - .32)^2}{8 \times 7}$$

s = $68.08.

Example: Federal Statistics Division of 350 Employees.[4]

The division had about 20 major classes of projects and over 105 subprojects and jobs in its regular work schedule. The work sample was used to determine time and money spent on these jobs and on projects for budget planning and hearings, for work control and scheduling, and for special jobs and projects requested by outside agencies. The latter tended to be high-priority jobs which the division was expected to "absorb," but at the expense of delaying its reg-

---

[4] Rosander, Guterman, and McKeon. "The Use of Random Work Sampling for Cost Analysis and Control."

ular work. A major purpose of the work sample was to show how much time and money were being diverted to these special jobs. The work sample also provided unit costs of punch card work because production records were kept, as well as information on personnel utilization in each of the 24 organizational units as a basis for costing out new jobs and new projects.

The major features of the work sample, which ran for 26 consecutive months, were as follows:

- The time frame was 510 minutes per day, including a 30-minute lunch period. All employees were included, from the messenger boys to the director—typists, clerks, secretaries, key punch operators, coders, supervisors, economists, statisticians, computer specialists, and graphic artists.
- Different random times were called by telephone from an administrative office to reach each of the 24 organizational units. One of the clerks called random times on the administrative office.
- Anonymous self-reporting was used. At each random minute each employee filled out a data sheet giving the code number of the activity in which he or she was engaged. Salary grade was checked. Secretaries or supervisors verified every data sheet and filled out sheets for absentees. Once the procedure was learned, it required only 10 to 15 seconds to fill out a data sheet.
- Every employee was furnished a pad of data sheets, a book of instructions, the code number of every new job assigned, and codes of all current jobs.
- Eight random minutes per day were used in the test run of one week, but only three random minutes per week were used in the final plan because only monthly and annual data were required.
- The use of the minute model made it possible to estimate aggregates as well as proportions.

Two tables were run, showing the distribution of payroll for major projects for the pilot run of one week and the distribution of working and nonworking time for the 24 organizational units during the same week. Even the pilot run was used for control when four organizational units showed four percent or more of waiting time. Management was highly pleased with the entire project and pointed out the several advantages to management of a random time sample of the type used in this study.[5] As a result of this project, the author constructed two tables, one listing 4000 random minutes and one listing 4000 random days.

After 26 consecutive months it was found that the major estimates and factors developed were highly satisfactory for management purposes, so the project was discontinued. The plan, however, was available for reactivation in case

---

[5] Engquist, E. J. "How Management Can Use Work Sampling." *New Frontiers in Quality Control, Proceedings of Middle Atlantic Conference*, ASQC, March 1962.

it was found necessary to test for changes or obtain new information. This has never been done.

Example: Railroad Accounting Office

In 1967 the Great Northern Railroad (now merged with the Burlington Northern) allowed the author to test whether work sampling could be applied to their accounting office, to freight office, and freight platform. This section describes the former; the next section describes the latter. The accounting office consisted of three separate offices containing a total of 37 employees. Work sampling was applied to each office separately; data were obtained for each office and for all combined. The purpose was to determine the allocation of time and expense to 20 classes of activities, as well as to furnish information on the utilization of employees.

The plan was tested for 10 days, with four random minutes being called on each employee each day. Anonymous self-reporting was used, with a special data sheet showing items required such as code of activity, hourly wage rate, on leave, at lunch, at work assigned, doing related activities, waiting for work, or other, including personal coffee break and present but not working. Wage rate per hour was obtained so that the method of estimation inherent in the sample plan made it possible to estimate both time and wages.

The estimating equation used to obtain the data on salaries and wages by activities is as follows:

$$X_{ia} = \frac{480}{4} \; \frac{(1)}{60} \; \sum m_{ia} \, c_{iah} = 2 y_{ia}$$

Where X_{ia} is the total for activity A, m_{ia} is the number of random minutes identified with activity a and c_{iah} is the *hourly* wage rate for persons performing activity A; 480/4 is the multiplier, the inverse of the sampling rate; and 60 converts hourly rates into dollars per minute. This equation is simpler to use than the equivalent based on dollars per minute:

$$X_{ia} = \frac{480}{4} \; \sum m_{ia} \, c_{ia} = 120_{ia}$$

No difficulties were encountered with regard to the sample plan or its implementation. The plan worked with a minimum amount of interference in the employees' work. The major problem encountered was not a sampling problem or a management problem, but an accounting problem, namely the soundness of the 20 classes of activities. It was discovered immediately that many activities that the clerks were performing did not fit into the classification. Actual work tended to overlap many of the classes. As a result, a major recommendation was to revise the classification so as to reduce to a minimum the number of overlapping classes.

We have already shown how the standard errors of these estimates can be obtained by using the four random minutes per day as a four-replicate sample and by calculating the standard error from the replicate estimates. This is the easiest way to obtain valid estimates of the standard errors of aggregates, proportions, and ratios. We also have shown how to obtain the standard error of a proportion which is a ratio, by means of the appropriate standard error equation.

Example: Railroad Freight Platform

The platform was about 60 by 1200 feet, and the work consisted of loading and unloading boxcars on three tracks. Motorized trucks with three or four carts were used to move the freight. Men or crews could come and go at any time from 8 a.m. to 10 or 12 p.m. These conditions posed problems of how to sample the area and how to sample time.

With the help of the manager of the freight station and a blueprint, the platform was divided into 12 areas easily identified by pillars or other fixed objects. Areas were laid out so that a variety of activity tended to occur in each, and so there was neither absence nor concentration of activity. Because areas were to be sampled, heterogeneity of activity in each area would give the most efficient sample. Furthermore, the areas should not be too large or contain more than about six workers, or the observer would have difficulty in recording the data at any random minute. The test showed that the areas raised no problems in this respect; the observer reported no difficulties.

Three of these 12 areas were selected at random daily, and for each area a different set of six random minutes was selected daily. A table of random areas and random minutes was prepared for each day. The observer studied the list and noted the time order for observing the sample areas. When the first random minute occurred, he observed the men in the corresponding sample area, counted them, and recorded what each was doing. He had two small data sheets to fill out, one for the group and one listing each man in the area. He entered the name of the man's job and his hourly rate, as well as other information. He reported that he had no difficulty in doing this largely because he knew many of the men as well as the work.

In the final plan each day was divided into two eight-hour periods: from 8 a.m. to 4 p.m., and from 4 p.m. to 12 p.m. Each eight-hour period was divided into four two-hour periods and one random minute selected from every two hours, giving four random minutes in each of the eight-hour periods.

In the final plan, sample areas were balanced over the two eight-hour periods requiring a cycle of four days, so that in four days each of the 12 areas was selected once and only once. Each of the areas occurred once in the eight-hour period 8 a.m. to 4 p.m. and once in the eight-hour period 4 p.m. to 12 p.m. Three areas still were selected randomly for every eight-hour period.

In estimating the proportion engaged in a specified activity, a ratio-type estimate is used because in each sample area, both the total number of employees observed and those engaged in a specific activity vary from area to area; in the same area they vary from one random time to another. Hence the standard error of ratio estimate must be used.[6]

Example: Overhead Expense—U.S. Corps of Engineers [7]

In this project a work sampling plan was designed and implemented on a nationwide scale to allocate overhead expenses to 40 classes of activities by districts and divisions. Some of the major difficulties and deficiencies in the study are as follows; employees were not sampled.

The sample plan, instructions, procedures, and methods of preparing the final tables should have been tested on a smaller area and improved before they were applied nationwide. This is recommended practice in any new study of any size, especially a nationwide study.

The sample plan was deficient or complicated in a number of ways. One half-hour was omitted from each day. A table of random minutes was not used, but a longer method of calculating random minutes from random numbers. It was not necessary to recalculate the sample size every month. The method of assigning a random minute to each of the 20 organization units was unduly complicated. Hence an excessive amount of time was used to select and to assign random minutes.

Forty classes of activities were used, but no provision was made for overhead activities not classifiable under the 40. Neither were the 40 described in detail, nor were there any prior tests made to determine the soundness and clarity of these classifications.

Overhead expense could have been estimated directly from the sample, but was not. Instead it was found by multiplying the number of personnel in a

---

[6] Estimate of proportion P_a engaged in Activity A is $p_a = \dfrac{\Sigma x}{\Sigma y}$

where x is number engaged in Activity A and summation is over all random minutes and sample areas, and y is the total number summed also over all random minutes and sample areas.

Variance of p_a: $v = \dfrac{1}{n\,(n-1)\,y^2}\left(\Sigma x_i^2 + p_a^2\,\Sigma y_i^2 - 2p_a\,\Sigma x_i\,y_i\right)$

where x_i and y_i are the paired values from each random area for each random minute, and y is the mean of all of the y_is; n is the number of such paired values.

---

[7] Source: Plan transmitted to A. C. Rosander by H. J. Pilgrim, U.S. Corps of Engineers, September 16, 1959.

salary grade at the end of the last pay period of each month by the middle of the grade salary or wage rate. This method could easily be biased, but an estimate from a sample using actual salaries and wages would not have been biased if properly designed and managed.

The standard error of a proportion engaged in one of the 40 activities was calculated, assuming that the proportion engaged in the specific activity was about the same in all of the subclasses of employees. This is not likely to be the case for all activities. Use of a cluster model with a ratio estimate might have been more appropriate. Replication would have been even better because of its simplicity.

It is not clear why it was stated that some persons, like messengers and custodial workers, would be exempt from the sample when the district determined that their work simply cannot be identified.

The distribution of time to the 40 activities was calculated, ignoring all overhead activities not classifiable under the 40.

The instructions for making calculations from the samples and constructing the final table are far too brief to insure correct calculations and summaries in the field offices.

It seems quite clear that they attempted too large and too difficult a technical job without proper and sufficient preparation, planning, and assistance and without the necessary initial testing and training.

Example: Billing Department of a Telephone Company [8]

The Chesapeake and Potomac Telephone Company of Virginia ran a test to determine whether random time sampling (work sampling) or 100 percent time records was better to determine the distribution of time used by clerks and machines on specified jobs in their revenue accounting center. The results of the test would determine what four telephone companies would do about this problem.

Several hundred thousand customers had to be billed each month. The billing process is fully mechanized, using punch cards, accounting machines, and computers. Several different work operations are performed on a variety of machines. Time reporting 100 percent in these units had always been difficult not only because of the variety of work operations and machines used but also because of overlap operations. A clerk may operate two or more machines simultaneously which are performing different jobs. The operator was required to prorate time over several jobs performed at the same time. Random time sampling was the best way to do this.

A group of accountants and statisticians planned the project. Five random

---

[8]C. E. McMurdo, "Work Sampling for Distributing Machine and Clerical Time." *Proceedings, Middle Atlantic Conference, ASQC*, March 1962, pp. 305–310.

minutes were selected per 510-minute day; the lunch period of 30 minutes was included. Because a machine unit consisted of about 10 clerks and 20 machines, it was estimated that 100 observations of the unit per month would meet their needs. The five random minutes were assigned to subsamples or replicates One through Five, so that the estimates of the standard errors and confidence limits were greatly simplified. This was one of the first work sampling studies to use replication to estimate sampling errors.

The work activities were coded into 17 classes, and the machines were coded into four classes and 10 types. Final results were obtained for each of these classes and types. Mark-sense cards were used to record data at each random time on each clerk and each machine. On each clerk card was recorded the production (activity) code and the type of machine being operated. Each machine card was marked to indicate whether it was idle, out of order, or working, and if it was working, the production code of the job. The date, time of observation, subsample number, clerk and machine identification number, and other information were also recorded. At the end of each month the clerical hours were summarized and distributed by production codes; similarly, machine hours were tabulated showing productive hours, idle time, and out-of-order time, according to job codes.

Finally, the results from the 100 percent time reports were compared with those from the random time sample; 90 percent confidence limits were set on the estimates obtained from the sample. In 12 instances the time from the time report fell outside these limits; nine of these were in machine production, where the time report showed consistently lower figures. In clerical jobs two time report figures were too high and one was too low. 1245 observations were made on clerical work and 3903 were made on machine work. The machines were in production 55 percent of the time; the time sheets showed 51 percent, but this value fell below the 90 percent confidence limit.

The committee concluded that the sample was better: it gave more accurate reporting, it interrupted valuable machine time the least, operators could devote full time to the machines, paperwork for operators was reduced, the problem of overlap operations was solved, reports were unbiased by human judgment, prorating of time by operators was no longer required, and approximately 40 percent of the time formerly required to summarize reports was saved.

Example: Allocating Radiomen in a Naval Communications Center[9]

Work sampling was used to determine how radiomen could be equitably allocated among naval communication centers. The need grew out of the fact that the work load consisted of a variety of work units of varying difficulty.

---

[9]*Navy Management Review*, April 1961, pp. 10–12.

Originally the work was broken down into five broad functional areas and weighting factors were applied to the different work units; the factors were averages of judgments. Certain questions arose which led to the formation of a research team, whose function was to find the reason for the weakness of the present system and to formulate a new work measurement system that would be more acceptable to all personnel.

The research team first suggested that personnel maintain logs, but this was objected to, as was the use of a stopwatch. Finally they laid out a work sampling plan which would yield new weighting factors based on how much time, on the average, was required to process each message. Messages were classified into seven types. The average time required for each type of message was calculated using time spent on each type of message as derived from a random time sample and using the number of messages of each type readily available from operating records. These average times resulted in weights ranging from 1 to 8, as compared with a range of 1 to 5 under the older system. Employees were dissatisfied with the older weights, but accepted the new factors derived from the work sample.

In designing and implementing this random time sample several problems arose, but these were finally resolved satisfactorily:

- A new classification of the functional areas and the work activities had to be developed.
- Agreement on the meaning of terms had to be reached for terms such as "message center" and "message section," and where "routing section," "broadcast section," and "wire room section" fit into these. Considerable differences of opinion existed as to what these terms included.
- It was found that a brochure was needed to explain in clear language the need for the study and the procedures involved.
- At first the supervisors objected to being observers because of the extra work, but several trial runs demonstrated that their fears were unfounded.
- Supervisors also objected to using a table of random numbers because it interfered with their regular work. To resolve this, they obtained a clock which could be set so that a chime sounded at each random minute.

Example: Work Sampling in a Small Business [10]

In this application work sampling was applied to a plant nursery of 42 employees to determine the time distribution of 21 different classes of activities, including personal, walking, avoidable delay, and miscellaneous. The usual tour method was used to observe all employees. The author calculated average

---

[10] Isherwood, J. D. *Journal of Industrial Engineering,* September–October 1960, pp. 417–420.

cost per minute using the method first proposed by Rosander, Guterman, and McKeon (see Footnote 3 and *Industrial Quality Control,* June 1960).

Calculating a proportion and its standard error for one day or a few days applied only to that limited time, not to the future. Only by repeated sampling and testing, as is used in quality control charts, can people be sure whether they are dealing with one population or with several. Without a stable population, estimates can be very misleading.

The author states that the method proposed by Rosander (Footnote 4) is inappropriate for a small business such as this plant nursery. This statement needs to be clarified. The basic principles of sampling, quality control, and design of experiments are applicable regardless of the size or type of business. In designing and implementing a sample plan, however, the plan and operations must be adapted to the physical environment and the type of work. Obviously certain procedures such as self-reporting, which are appropriate to an office where employees are relatively immobile, cannot be used in a factory, on a construction site, or on a truck or railroad platform. In fact, it is easier to apply random time sampling to a small business than to a large business or office because it is so much more simple to design, manage, and control.

In this plant nursery one might use a sample plan in which the working environment is divided into areas; like minutes, these areas are subject to random selection. For example, assuming a five-day week, one could use 60 days x 4 areas x 4 minutes = 960 observations in a year. In the 60 random days, each day of the week would occur 12 times, assigned at random to each month. Areas would be balanced by time; time would be balanced by days and months. A plan of this type would not be difficult to manage, and it would give more and better data than taking the same number of observations in a few days or weeks.

Random selection rather than systematic selection is recommended because this avoids making the assumptions inherent in the latter. Because tables of random minutes and random days are available, it is now simple to use random selection. If systematic selection is used with a random start, it is imperative to use replication in order to obtain a valid standard error of the estimate.

Example: Work Sampling Applied to Inspectors [11]

In this application the quality control manager used work sampling to determine how the inspectors were using their time, and to what extent inspection equipment was being used. The usual problems had to be solved: elements of activity and their coding, designing data and tally sheets, determining the size of the sample, the procedure to be followed in taking observations, training

---

[11] Kazmierski, A. S. "Work Sampling for Quality Control Managers." *Quality Progress,* January 1971, pp. 30–32.

observers, making and recording observations, processing the data, and setting time standards.

In calculating time standards it is assumed that it is possible to obtain the number of unit tasks accomplished or units inspected, marked, or otherwise processed, so that time obtained from the work sample can be matched with actual production. No example is given, or any indication of the difficulties which arose in this connection.

The sample is to be selected from the population, but the population is not defined. Actually, it is all the working minutes in a day, such as 480 minutes, and all the working days in a year. It is alleged that the first and last half-hours of each day are not typical, and therefore presumably should be eliminated. Obviously this introduces an unknown bias in the results because 12.5 percent of the population is thus eliminated. It is stated that one should be careful of rare cases, such as machine breakdown, which give a false picture of the results. Actually, it is the omission that gives the false picture. To be valid, the sample data must reflect what is actually going on—personal judgments as to what is typical or not typical, or what gives a false picture or a fair picture—should not be interjected into the sample plan, its implementation, or the analysis of the results.

USE OF GRAPHICS TO ANALYZE AND PRESENT DATA

Several examples are presented and described, using graphic methods to make interpretation of data simpler and easier. The following are taken from actual problems faced by individuals responsible for interpreting data and making recommendations therefrom:

- Distribution of time required to ship a package between two points (Figure 15–3);
- Distribution of time spent waiting in the waiting room of a doctor's office (Figure 15–4). (This does *not* include time spent waiting in cubicles, time for tests and examinations, time conferring with the doctor, time paying the bill, and arranging insurance.);
- Variability of readings at both ends of a three-minute timer (Figure 15–5);
- Distribution of errors in galley proof for a book (Figure 15–6);
- Input/output relationship for a process in a distillery (Figure 15–7);
- Learning-production plot for an individual over a period of 45 consecutive working days (Figure 15–8).

In each case the situation is explained in detail and the conclusions to be drawn are pointed out. These examples show how important inferences and findings can be obtained from rather simple presentations of data.

This chart shows the actual number of days required to deliver a package by parcel post (third class mail) originating in northern Colorado and destined for

frequency

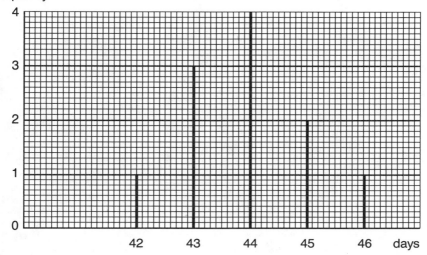

Figure 15–3. **Number of Days of Delivery Time for Parcel Post Package from Northern Colorado to London**

London, England. Allowance of 44 days is usually sufficient, although 46 would be safer. These transit times assume absence of strikes or other work stoppages both here and abroad. This chart is based on actual experience (Figure 15–3).

This type of distribution of transit or shipment times can be used to compare different modes of shipment and to determine which mode is most efficient for different kinds of shipments. It can be applied to different companies to compare the time required to fill and receive an order. This would allow an organization to select those that are most timely in shipping quality products, or in rendering technical or other types of services.

Another distribution approximates one based on known averages and experiences reported by people waiting in doctor's offices. This does not include waiting time in cubicles or waiting for a nurse to take pulse, temperature, weight, and blood pressure. Nor does it include the time required to wait for a technician to take one or more blood samples, a urine sample, or a fecal sample, or to perform some other function, such as taking an EKG (electrocardiogram) or X-rays (Figure 15–4).

Finally, there is the actual time spent with the doctor: questioning, examination, diagnosis, and prescription of treatment, drugs, or further tests.

Frequency distributions (not just averages) of the time spent are greatly needed: 1) sitting in the cubicle waiting; 2) running tests of all kinds; 3) taking samples in preparation to take tests; 4) with the doctor, receiving medical advice and

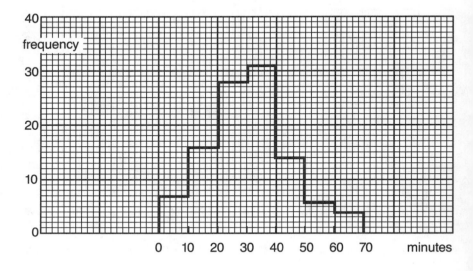

n = 106 persons; average x̄ = 31 minutes

maximum time = 65 minutes

Figure 15–4. **Distribution of Waiting Times in Waiting Room of Doctor's Office**

recommendations; 5) waiting in the waiting room on arrival; and finally 6) waiting before one can get an appointment to see the doctor.

The above distribution has a mean or average of 31 minutes, which agrees rather closely with a published figure of 29 minutes. The range extends from close to zero (very little waiting time) to a figure close to 70 minutes (over an hour).

Figure 15–5 is an example of individual values; the purpose of the test was to determine the stability of each end of the timer and how close each end came to three minutes. A stopwatch was used to measure time. Positions were kept identical in all tests. There was no turning of the timer on its vertical axis because this can change the reading. Tests were run at different times, which may account for some variability. Change in temperature may also be a factor (Figure 15–5).

The mean of A is +1.14 seconds, its range is 1.3 seconds, and its maximum value is +1.7 seconds.

The mean of B is −2.72 seconds, its range is 1.6 seconds, and its maximum value is −3.5 seconds.

The two ends are obviously different. A is closer to three minutes. In practice the variations between the two ends and within each end are not significant,

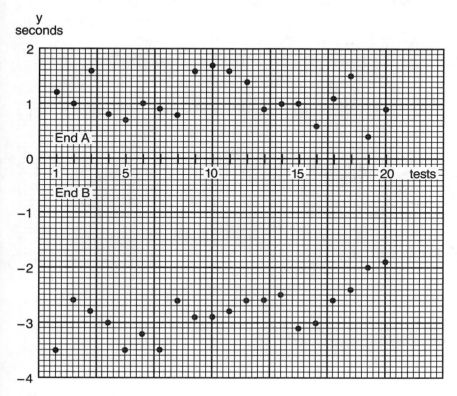

Figure 15–5. Deviations from Three Minutes of Both Ends of a Three-Minute Timer

whether the timer is being used to time boiling eggs or a long-distance telephone call. This is an example in which statistical significance is of no practical value.

The types of errors include errors in words and errors in sentences. The above shows only word errors. These include misspelled words, words omitted, wrong words, words repeated, and correct words changed. (Figure 15–6). Errors involving sentences not included in the chart above were part of a sentence omitted, part of a sentence repeated, sentence structure changed, wrong punctuation, page omitted.

No distribution of these errors was made because *all of them,* without exception, had to be corrected. No such thing as Pareto analysis can be allowed. *Some of the worst errors were the infrequent ones.*

No doubt, costs can be reduced in this kind of operation by holding error

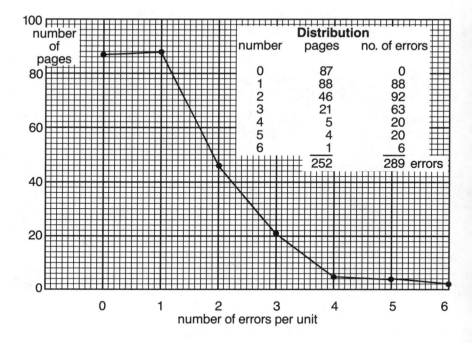

Distribution		
number	pages	no. of errors
0	87	0
1	88	88
2	46	92
3	21	63
4	5	20
5	4	20
6	1	6
	252	289 errors

Figure 15–6. **Distribution of Errors in 252 Units of Galley Proof (excluded are sentences omitted or repeated)**

prevention seminars and discussing every one of the word errors and every one of the sentence errors. Zero errors is the goal and every effort should be made to attain it, even though one or two errors may get through.

These data (Figure 15–7) from the United States Treasury Department show that a straight line is a good fit to the relationship between amount of corn input and amount of whiskey output for a specific distillery.

The correlation coefficient is 0.98, so r^2 is 0.96. This means that 96 percent of the variation in the whiskey output (y) is explained by the corn input (x).

The line can be used as a basis of control by using its predictive value.

- Given the quantity of input, an estimate can be made of the quantity of the output.
- Government regulators as well as distillery people can use the predictive property of the line to monitor records of whiskey output.
- Tests can be conducted monthly, quarterly, and annually to see if the relationship is biased and to what extent. If it is, the coefficients can be changed to reflect any significant change in the process. The line given above reflects a certain set of conditions, and will hold only as long as

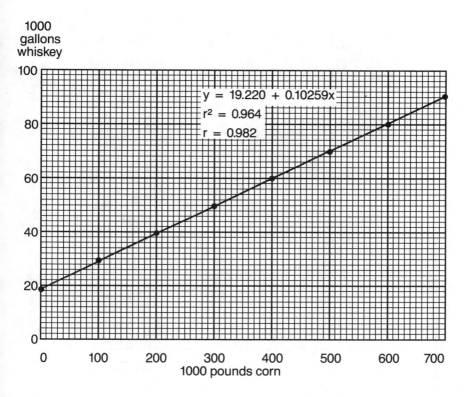

1000 gallons whiskey

$$y = 19.220 + 0.10259x$$
$$r^2 = 0.964$$
$$r = 0.982$$

1000 pounds corn

Figure 15–7. Use of straight-line relation as a control in a distillery

these conditions continue to exist. When they change, a study will need to be made to determine when the process stabilizes so that a new line can be fitted to the data.

Learning Curve of a Superior Transcriber

Figure 15–8 is a plot of the daily production of acceptable-quality documents by a superior transcriber. The plot for 45 consecutive working days shows the gains made due to learning effects.

The working situation was as follows. Over 100,000 carload waybills, which are not a standard form, had to be transcribed to a standard format which could be used for inputing the data into a computer system. None of the transcribers hired for this project had had any experience with this kind of document or this kind of work. For most of them, this was their first job. Knowledge of the job was zero. The supervisor in charge of this project had prepared a 95-page procedural manual which described with examples each step in the operation.

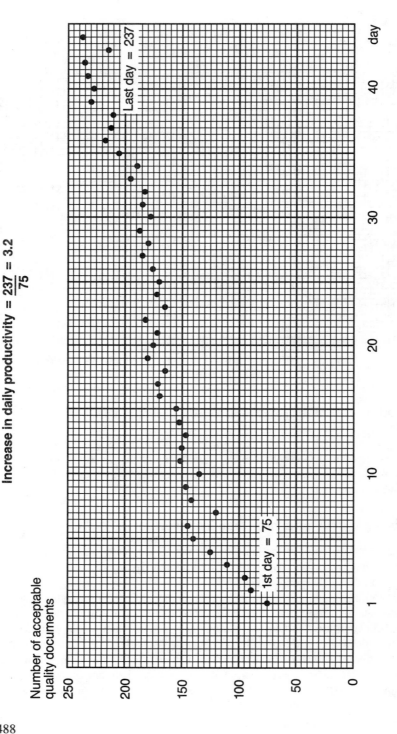

Figure 15–8. Learning Curve of a Superior Transcriber in Terms of Acceptable-Quality Production for 45 Consecutive Working Days

The supervisor was a transportation specialist who was an expert in processing carload waybills issued by railroads. She also had had prior experience in teaching and coaching other persons in this kind of waybill processing. Obviously, all employees had to be put through a training course before they could do any serious work on the project. They were also instructed and coached continuously once the project got under way. On the chart Day 1 is the day on which this particular transcriber started work on the project.

The gains made by this transcriber, as shown on the chart, are due to several factors:

- The personal coaching of an excellent supervisor;
- The 95-page instruction manual, with real-life examples;
- Elimination of errors as understanding grew;
- Reduction in the time required to transcribe as understanding grew;
- Elimination of interference from other employees;
- A quality control system that discovered more than a stated number of errors in a work batch and forced a 100% redo of the entire lot of 300 by the person involved. This feedback was immediate, mostly on the same day.

The learning curve shows the characteristics associated with learning:

- Big gains during the first five or 10 days, or during the early stages;
- Increase in productivity, in this case 237/75 or 3.2, which doubled by Day 13;
- Plateaus where learning levels off: plateaus tend to appear at 150,175,185, and 233;
- The dip on Day 8 was due to a rejected lot. The dip on Day 44 came on a Friday, when several of the employees were leaving because the job was coming to an end.

The danger of a plateau on a learning curve is that it will be mistaken for a stable condition of statistical control, when in fact the plateau is only temporary and the learner can move to higher and higher (or lower and lower) plateaus.

SAMPLE SURVEYS AND COMPLETE COVERAGE

Quality of service means measuring periodically the attitudes, preferences, opinions, and appraisals of customers. It is necessary to see if customers' requirements are being met. It is also necessary to survey lost customers and potential customers to learn why they quit buying or why they haven't started to buy. It is necessary to survey attitudes of employees toward their jobs and work for ways of making changes and improvements. It is also sound practice to sound out vendors from time to time to see what their attitudes are.

There are two broad approaches to this problem: If the number of persons is large, then a properly designed probability sample study is called for. Otherwise a complete coverage of all persons is necessary. This means that names and addresses have to be available for some people who are interviewed but not for others.

In all of these studies and surveys, *the design of the questionnaire is most critical*. The data and information are no better than the care, accuracy, and clarity with which the questions are asked. Far too little attention has been paid to the art and science of asking questions. It is highly recommended that those charged with the responsibility of designing questions for a questionnaire study an old but excellent book by Payne, *The Art of Asking Questions. Pretesting a questionnaire is an absolute necessity in order to debug it, to ensure that words and sentences are simple and clearly understood, and to see that they reflect the purpose of the study.*

The design of the questionnaire is even more difficult than the design of the probability sample because the former is more of an art than a science. The latter is strictly scientific, although some professional judgment may enter into certain decisions such as stratification, how large a sampling variation to take, and with what probability. In a probability sample the most difficult problem is that of control; that is, ensuring that the sample design is carried out and managed as planned.

The details of how to design and implement a probability sample study are described elsewhere, and hence will not be discussed here.[12] Here we give the major steps to follow in designing and executing such a study. Obviously a professional statistician or other specialist familiar with the design and execution of sample surveys is necessary if an effective study is to be carried out.

1. Determine the general and specific purposes of the study; the questions to be answered.
2. Determine whether to use probability sampling or 100% coverage. Both kinds of studies require careful planning, design, and implementation.
3. Determine the information needed and the data wanted; analyze problems.
4. Design a probability sample or lay out a census plan.
5. Design the questionnaire or data sheet.
6. Pretest the data sheet or questionnaire, and revise it.

---

[12] W. E. Deming, *Some Theory of Sampling* (New York: Wiley, 1950);
W. E. Deming, *Sample Design in Business Research* (New York: Wiley, 1960);
Leslie Kish, *Survey Sampling* (New York: Wiley, 1965);
A. C. Rosander, *Case Studies in Sample Design* (New York: Marcel Dekker, 1977, 1981);
Frank Yates, *Sampling Methods in Censuses and Surveys* (New York: Macmillan, 4th ed.);
A. C. Rosander, *Application of Quality Control in the Service Industries* (New York: Marcel Dekker; Milwaukee: Quality Press, 1985).

7. Mail questionnaire or data sheet with explanations and instructions, if mailing is used.
8. Train interviewers to use questionnaire, whether on nonrespondents or on others.
9. Plan and implement controls at every key point: sample selection, sample receipts, performance of interviewers, data source, processing.
10. Plan and execute tabulation and calculations to answer basic questions.
11. Interpret data and summarize findings.
12. Take appropriate action on findings relative to original problem or problems.
13. Redesign sample, questionnaire, data sheet, instructions, and anything else that needs improvement.

Three Common Sample Designs

The following three common sample designs are based on the principles of probability sampling:

- Simple random sampling;
- Stratified random sampling;
- Replicated sampling;

In a simple random sample, the sample is selected (using a table of random numbers) from a known population or frame at a specified rate, so as to give the sample size desired.

In a stratified random sample, the population first must be divided into groups, categories, or classes which tend to correlate highly with the characteristics desired from the sample. Population strata differ in these characteristics or in the frequency of occurrence of important items or classes. Prior knowledge, a prior study, or experience helps in the selection of significant strata. The number may run to five or 10 groups, or as high as 20 or 30. Stratification makes it possible to reduce the sample size or to obtain better data with the same sample size. The reader should be warned that stratification does not improve the estimates of proportions from classes which do not vary widely. This is why stratification is seldom used in a sample study that aims only at proportions or percentages, such as an opinion survey. (Nonresponse is much more important.)

In a replicated sample four or more independent random samples are selected from the same population. (An example was given earlier in this chapter.) This sampling method makes it possible to obtain estimates and their sampling errors very easily. A common method is to use a random start and then to increase these random numbers by the zone width Z, which is kN/n where k is the number of replicates, N is the number of units in the frame or population, and n is the size of the sample desired.

Sampling rate is 1/50.
Let N = 100,000, k = 10, and the sample size n = 2,000. / Then

Zone width $Z = \dfrac{10 \times 100,000}{2,000} = 500$. An example is given below for k = 10.

Z	233	375	171	15	317	268	93	47	422	236
1–500	233	375	171	15	317	268	93	47	422	236
501–1000	733	875	671	515	817	768	593	547	922	736
etc.										

The situation just described can be designed as a stratified random sample if there are four size classes: A = very small, B = small, C = medium size, D = large and very large. The rates are staggered so as to sample lightly for the small units and heavily for the large units. N = 100,000 and n = 2,000, just as in the replicated sample. The replicated sample assumed that stratification was not necessary.

Strata	Frame count	Sampling rate	Sample size
A	40,000	1/200	200
B	30,000	1/100	300
C	20,000	1/40	500
D	10,000	1/10	1000
Sum	100,000		2000

These figures are illustrative. They are not necessarily the best strata or the best sampling rates to use. This design would be used not to obtain proportions but a count or measurement of some kind. In stratified sampling, the total sample size arrived at independently can be allocated to strata in one of three common ways:

- Proportional to the division of the frame or population in the several strata;
- Optimum allocation, where the standard deviation of the characteristic and the size of the frame are known or can be approximated for each stratum;
- Allocation to give about the same or not widely different standard errors in each of the strata.

Replication can be applied to each stratum. It would simply be a repetition of the design given above for a replicated sample, applied to each stratum with different sampling rates.

Sample Sizes

These sample sizes are determined by using the principles of statistics and probability sampling. The details of sample design are not presented here because they are beyond the scope of this book; the reader is referred to the sources previously given.

1. Sample size for mean or aggregate:

1. $n = \dfrac{s^2\, z^2}{d^2}$ where s = standard deviation of x

                               z = normal deviation for
                                            level desired: 1.96 for 95%
                               d = deviation allowed or set

2. $n = \dfrac{s^2\, z^2}{d^2 + s^2\, z^2/N}$ N = frame or population size
                                         (used where n is large relative to N)

3. $n = \dfrac{c^2\, z^2}{p^2}$ c = coefficient of variation $s/\bar{x}$
                              p = $d/\bar{x}$ proportion of mean

4. $n = \dfrac{c^2\, z^2}{p^2 + c^2\, z^2/N}$

2. Binomial proportion:

1. binomial proportion $= p = \dfrac{x}{n}$ where n is a constant, the sample size

2. $n = \dfrac{p(1-p)\, z^2}{d^2}$ (for sample less than 5% of N)

3. $n = \dfrac{p(1-p)\, z^2}{d^2 + \dfrac{p(1-p)\, z^2}{N}}$ (for samples over 5% of N)

3. For ratio $f = \dfrac{\Sigma x}{\Sigma y}$ (when a proportion is a random variable, binomial above does *not* apply)

$$n = \dfrac{1(c_x^2 + c_y^2 - 2\, r\, c_x\, c_y)}{c_f^2} \qquad c_f = \dfrac{s_f}{f}$$

Assume c_f. The values r, c_x, c_y are given. Set correlation coefficient r = 0 to obtain maximum safe value of n, if r is unknown. r is the correlation coefficient between x and y.

Questionaire Design: Examples of Questions

Questionnaire design is just as important, if not more important, than sample design. This is because few persons recognize that there is an art and a science to developing an effective questionnaire for a specified purpose. As has been shown many times, the answers obtained depend upon how the question is phrased, how it is asked, and what probing questions follow. It also depends upon what person in the family or in the company answers the questionnaire.

A pretest of a questionnaire on the kinds of persons it is intended for is an absolute "must." The following are suggestions for questions to ask a customer:

1. Have you bought our Product A during the past month?
   If answer is "yes":
2. Are you satisfied? If "yes," explain why you like it.

   _____

3. If answer is "no," explain why you are not satisfied with it.

   _____

4. If answer is "no," have you bought some other similar product?
   Yes___ No___
5. If answer is "no," have you passed this on to others? Yes___ No___
6. What improvements are needed in the product?

   _____

7. Do you think these improvements should be made?

   _____

8. Would you be satisfied then? Yes___ No___

For lost customers:

1. Why did you stop buying our product? _____
2. What improvements or changes are needed? _____
3. If these changes were made, would you buy the product? Yes___ No___
4. Have you criticized this product to others? Yes___ No___
5. Have others been influenced by your criticism? Yes___ No___
6. Are you buying a competitive product? Yes___ No___
7. What are the advantages of the product you are buying? _____
8. What has to be done to get you to go back to the product you used to buy? _____
9. Is price a factor? Yes___ No___
10. Is service a factor? Yes___ No___
11. Is quality a factor? Yes___ No___
12. Are operating, repairing, and maintenance costs factors? Yes___ No___

QUALITY CONTROL CHART EQUATIONS AND CONSTANTS

Statistical Control Charts

Five kinds of control charts are described, showing the key equations for making estimates and how to calculate the center line and the upper and lower control limits. For more detailed information with industrial examples, the reader is referred to the standard ASTM manual, a classic on the subject of statistical quality control.[13]

Binomial Proportion p

The binomial proportion $p = \dfrac{x}{n}$ is based on the "heads or tails" model of events. Only one of two events A and B can occur at a time; *n is the sample size and is a constant,* and x is the number of events of Type A (or Type B) that occur in the sample n.

It is necessary to stress this nature of the proportion because a *ratio proportion* which is a random variable, in which both numerator and denominator are variables, must be handled in an entirely different way.

The center line of the control chart for p is

$$\bar{p} = x/n$$

where x = number of defects, computer readouts, etc. in the sample
and   n = the size of the sample, which is a fixed number.

The variance of p is $s_p^2 = \dfrac{\bar{p}(1 - \bar{p})}{n}; \quad s_p = \sqrt{s_p^2}.$

The control limits are $\bar{p} + 3\,s_p$ and $\bar{p} - 3\,s_p$.

Binomial Count np

Because in the preceding section $\bar{p} = x/n$, this means that the count $x = n\bar{p}$. The variance of this count is

$$s^2 = n\bar{p}(1 - \bar{p}); \; s = \sqrt{s^2}$$

where the letters mean the same as before. The center line is np.

The control limits are $n\bar{p} + 3\,s$ and $n\bar{p} - 3\,s$.

In actual problems the value of p in the binomial proportion and in the binomial count will be an average value because many samples, or segments of data, will be involved. Hence $\bar{p}$ is substituted for p in every case.

Poisson Count c

In the binomial expressions given above, in cases where the value of p is very small, $1 - p$ is very close to unity or 1. Therefore we can write

---

[13] *ASTM Manual on Quality Control of Materials, Special Technical Publications 15-C* (Philadelphia: American Society for Testing Materials, 1951).

$$\bar{c} = np = \frac{\sum x_i}{n} = \frac{\sum c_i}{n}.$$

Therefore the variance $\bar{s}^2 = np$ so that $s = \sqrt{np} = \sqrt{\bar{c}}$.
This is the Poisson distribution, in which the variance s^2 is equal to the mean $\bar{c} = np$.

The control limits are $\bar{c} + 3\sqrt{\bar{c}}$ and $\bar{c} - 3\sqrt{\bar{c}}$.

This is applied to problems where events are rare and independent, and do not cluster. It is applied to defects, errors, and other events which are important but occur only rarely and independently of one another. It is often assumed that they are distributed as the Poisson distribution, although no study has been made to prove it.

Arithmetic Mean $\bar{x}$

The most common control chart applied to physical measurements is a set of two charts, the $\bar{x}$ chart to control a level or aimed-at value and the R chart to control the variability of the measurements around this mean.

These charts are used much more in factories than in services because in factories there are numerous measurements that have to be controlled and stabilized: length, width, depth, diameter, density, weight, volume, temperature, pressure, resistance, composition, strength, and much more. The reason is that manufacturing specifications call for a specified value for a measurement with a specified tolerance about this value. In services this is not true, except when products are being manufactured for the use of service organizations and specifications have to be met for certain products. Examples are drugs with a certain consistency and instruments which must be valid and accurate.

The arithmetic mean is calculated from actual values x_i from a sample of n:

$$\bar{x} = \frac{\sum x_i}{n}.$$

The range R is the difference between the maximum and minimum values in the sample n. The range is used as a measure of variability in this method:

$$R = x_{max} - x_{min}.$$

The average value of R is $\bar{R}$:

$$\bar{R} = \frac{\sum R_i}{k} \quad \text{where}$$
$$R_i = \text{range of a single sample}$$
$$k = \text{number of samples.}$$

For an $\bar{x}$ chart the center line is $\bar{x}$. The limits are

$$\bar{x} + A_2\bar{R} \text{ and } \bar{x} - A_2\bar{R}.$$

The values of A_2 are constants depending upon the value of n. For a sample of 4 the value is 0.729; for a sample of 5 it is 0.577. Other values are given in Table 15–7.

Range R

The range chart (the R chart) is used in connection with the $\bar{x}$ chart to put limits upon the variation about $\bar{x}$. This is necessary because an out-of-control situation can exist in the $\bar{x}$ chart without affecting the R chart, and vice versa—the out-of-control state can be in the variability, not in the mean.

For the R chart the center line is $\bar{R}$, the calculation of which is given above. The control limits for R are

$$\text{lower limit} = D_3\,\bar{R}$$
$$\text{upper limit} = D_4\,\bar{R}.$$

D_3 and D_4 are constants depending upon the size of n the sample size. D_3 is 0 for both $n = 4$ and $n = 5$. The corresponding values for D_4 are 2.282 and 2.115. Other values are given in Table 15–7.

The range is almost as efficient an estimate of variability for small samples (e.g., $n \leq 10$) as is the standard deviation. Because it is simpler to calculate, it is in standard use where sample sizes are small.

For larger samples, however, the standard deviation is a better estimate of the variability and should be used. Now that hand-held calculators have the standard deviation programmed into the instrument, as in the HP-32E, there is no longer any reason for not using the standard deviation when it is appropriate. Because the standard deviation of the mean (standard error) is

$$s_{\bar{x}} = \frac{s}{\sqrt{n}} \quad \text{where } s^2 = \frac{\sum (x_i - \bar{x})^2}{n-1},$$

the limits for $\bar{x}$ using the standard deviation are

$$\bar{x} + 3\frac{s}{\sqrt{n}} \quad \text{and} \quad x - 3\frac{s}{\sqrt{n}}$$

where n is the sample size.

An estimate of the standard deviation is $s = \dfrac{\bar{R}}{d_2\sqrt{n}}$. For values of d_2 of 10 or less, d_2 is approximately $\sqrt{n}$, so this reduces to $\dfrac{\bar{R}}{n}$. Values of d_2 for various values of n are given in Table 15–7.

Table 15–7. **Factors for Computing Control Chartlines**

Number of Observations in Sample, n	Chart for Averages			Chart for Standard Deviations						Chart for Ranges						
	Factors for Control Limits			Factors for Central Line		Factors for Control Limits				Factors for Central Line		Factors for Control Limits				
	A	A_1	A_2	c_2	$1/c_2$	B_1	B_2	B_3	B_4	d_2	$1/d_2$	d_3	D_1	D_2	D_3	D_4
2	2.121	3.760	1.880	0.5642	1.7725	0	1.843	0	3.267	1.128	0.8865	0.853	0	3.686	0	3.267
3	1.732	2.394	1.023	0.7236	1.3820	0	1.858	0	2.568	1.693	0.5907	0.888	0	4.358	0	2.575
4	1.500	1.880	0.729	0.7979	1.2533	0	1.808	0	2.266	2.059	0.4857	0.880	0	4.698	0	2.282
5	1.342	1.596	0.577	0.8407	1.1894	0	1.756	0	2.089	2.326	0.4299	0.864	0	4.918	0	2.115
6	1.225	1.410	0.483	0.8686	1.1512	0.026	1.711	0.030	1.970	2.534	0.3946	0.848	0	5.078	0	2.004
7	1.134	1.277	0.419	0.8882	1.1259	0.105	1.672	0.118	1.882	2.704	0.3698	0.833	0.205	5.203	0.076	1.924
8	1.061	1.175	0.373	0.9027	1.1078	0.167	1.638	0.185	1.815	2.847	0.3512	0.820	0.387	5.307	0.136	1.864
9	1.000	1.094	0.337	0.9139	1.0942	0.219	1.609	0.239	1.761	2.970	0.3367	0.808	0.546	5.394	0.184	1.816
10	0.949	1.028	0.308	0.9227	1.0837	0.262	1.584	0.284	1.716	3.078	0.3249	0.797	0.687	5.469	0.223	1.777
11	0.903	0.973	0.285	0.9300	1.0753	0.299	1.561	0.321	1.679	3.173	0.3152	0.787	0.812	5.534	0.256	1.744
12	0.866	0.925	0.266	0.9359	1.0684	0.331	1.541	0.354	1.646	3.258	0.3069	0.778	0.924	5.592	0.284	1.716
13	0.832	0.884	0.249	0.9410	1.0627	0.359	1.523	0.382	1.618	3.336	0.2998	0.770	1.026	5.646	0.308	1.692
14	0.802	0.848	0.235	0.9453	1.0579	0.384	1.507	0.406	1.594	3.407	0.2935	0.762	1.121	5.693	0.329	1.671
15	0.775	0.816	0.223	0.9490	1.0537	0.406	1.492	0.428	1.572	3.472	0.2880	0.755	1.207	5.737	0.348	1.652
16	0.750	0.788	0.212	0.9523	1.0501	0.427	1.478	0.448	1.552	3.532	0.2831	0.749	1.285	5.779	0.364	1.636
17	0.728	0.762	0.203	0.9551	1.0470	0.445	1.465	0.466	1.534	3.588	0.2787	0.743	1.359	5.817	0.379	1.621
18	0.707	0.738	0.194	0.9576	1.0442	0.461	1.454	0.482	1.518	3.640	0.2747	0.738	1.426	5.854	0.392	1.608
19	0.688	0.717	0.187	0.9599	1.0418	0.477	1.443	0.497	1.503	3.689	0.2711	0.733	1.490	5.888	0.404	1.596
20	0.671	0.697	0.180	0.9619	1.0396	0.491	1.433	0.510	1.490	3.735	0.2677	0.729	1.548	5.922	0.414	1.586
21	0.655	0.679	0.173	0.9638	1.0376	0.504	1.424	0.523	1.477	3.778	0.2647	0.724	1.606	5.950	0.425	1.575
22	0.640	0.662	0.167	0.9655	1.0358	0.516	1.415	0.534	1.466	3.819	0.2618	0.720	1.659	5.979	0.434	1.566
23	0.626	0.647	0.162	0.9670	1.0342	0.527	1.407	0.545	1.455	3.858	0.2592	0.716	1.710	6.006	0.443	1.557
24	0.612	0.632	0.157	0.9684	1.0327	0.538	1.399	0.555	1.445	3.895	0.2567	0.712	1.759	6.031	0.452	1.548
25	0.600	0.619	0.135	0.9696	1.0313	0.548	1.392	0.565	1.435	3.931	0.2544	0.709	1.804	6.058	0.459	1.541
Over 25	$\dfrac{3}{\sqrt{n}}$	$\dfrac{3}{\sqrt{n}}$				*	**	*	**							

$$*1 - \frac{3}{\sqrt{2n}} \qquad **1 + \frac{3}{\sqrt{2n}}$$

Note 1: for no standard given use A_1, A_2, c_2, B_3, B_4, d_2, D_3, and D_4.

Note 2: for standard given use A, c_2, B_1, B_2, d_2, D_1, and D_2.

Source:

ASTM Manual on Quality Control of Materials, Special Technical Publication 15-C (Philadelphia: American Society for Testing Materials, 1951), p. 115. Used by permission of ASTM.

Four Methods of Process Control Applied to the Same Problem

Four methods of process control are applied to the same project:

1. Lot sampling for acceptance or rejection;
2. The np chart;
3. The c chart;
4. The p chart.

The project has already been described in this and earlier chapters in order to illustrate a number of different aspects of a large-scale data processing operation. The process control actually used on this project is Number 1 above: lot sampling for acceptance or rejection.

The project was a federal government contract to a private company, calling for transcribing a nationwide sample of over 100,000 carload waybills onto a standard format to facilitate preparing the input to a computer.

A lot consisted of 300 waybills used as a work unit. In the process control used, 50 waybills were selected from each lot, using a random start. If five or fewer waybills were found in error, the lot was accepted. Otherwise it was rejected and was redone 100 percent within one day by the same person. Then a different sample of 50 was selected, and the test was made. Rejections were very effective in keeping the error rate down.

The 20 to 25 clerks and the three verifiers, none of whom had any work experience, were trained by the manager-supervisor, who was an expert in carload waybill processing and an excellent supervisor of many years' experience. She prepared a 95-page procedural manual describing in detail, with examples, all of the specific tasks and operations required. Each clerk had a copy of this manual for study and reference. The supervisor did considerable individual coaching and group teaching.

It was planned from the start to keep the error rate below 5 percent. A computer edit was expected to catch other errors so that the overall error rate would be below 4 percent, which was judged satisfactory for data to be used for statistical purposes only.

A summary of the four methods is given below:

1. Lot Sampling

This method was used because it was the only feasible method under the circumstances and the only one that management would accept. No additional employees were needed; they would have been required if a control chart had been kept for every employee. The only procedure that management would accept was review, so it was not difficult to apply lot sampling and tell management that it was review. Management got process control, but everyone called it "review" if asked.

The plan: Accept lot of 300 if $c \leqslant 5$; otherwise reject and redo 100 percent. "c" = number of defective records in sample n = 50.

The estimated error rate, based on 188 processed lots or 56,400 records, was 4.8 percent. The total number of errors, using a multiplier of 6 = 300/50, was 2,682.

The sample plan therefore kept the error rate below the 5 percent set originally as the goal.

2. The NP Chart

The following are the characteristics of this plan. Because the sample of 50 is 1/6 of the lot, a correction has to be made.

1. $p = 0.05$, $q = 0.95$.
2. $n = 50$, sampling rate $f = 1/6$, $1 - f = 5/6$.
3. $np = $ mean $= 50 \times 0.05 = 2.5$. (This is the center line.)
4. $\sigma = \sqrt{npq(1-f)} = \sqrt{50 \times .05 \times .95 \times 5/6} = 1.41$.
5. $3\sigma = 4.2$.
6. $np \pm 3\sigma = 2.5 \pm 4.2$ UCL = 7
                              LCL = 0

3. The C Chart

For the error rate to be 5 percent or less, the maximum mean $\bar{x} = np = 50 \times 0.05 = 2.5$, $\bar{c} = \bar{x}$.

1. $\bar{c} \pm 3\sqrt{\bar{c}} = 2.5 \pm 4.7$ UCL = 7
                                     LCL = 0

4. The P Chart

The values for p, q, n, and f are the same as in 1 above.

1. $p = 0.05$.
2. $\sigma = \sqrt{pq(1-f)/n} = \sqrt{\dfrac{.05 \times .95 \times 5/6}{50}} = 0.028$.
3. $3\sigma = 0.084$.
4. 0.05 ± 0.084 0.14 = UCL
                       0 = LCL

A proportion of 0.14 or 14 percent applied to a sample of 50 gives 7 as UCL, the same as the other two methods. These plans accepted seven errors, whereas the lot sample plan accepted no more than five errors in a sample of 50. This plan accepted a lot of 300, not a lot of 50.

Testing for Variations among Laboratories and Analysts Using Identical Samples

Assume that the pairs of values are independent and form a bivariate normal distribution with means u_x and u_y, with correlation coefficient $p = 0$. Then circular control limits can be set to measure the extent to which bias or constant errors have been eliminated. For example, this method can be used to measure differences between analysts and between laboratories. The equation of the circle is

$$(x - u_x)^2 + (y - u_y)^2 = \lambda^2 \sigma^2 = r^2$$

where r = radius of the circle about the center u_x, u_y and is estimated by λs, and where s is calculated from the data as described above. If departure from a standard is desired, then $u_x = u_y = u$ where u is the standard mean; otherwise the means $\bar{x}$ and $\bar{y}$ are used. Circles can be drawn which, if the conditions are met, will contain 95 percent, 99 percent, or 99.73 percent of all points. The constants necessary are as follows:

Percent within Circle	Center of Circle Standard	Center of Circle No Standard	λ	Radius of Circle
95	u,u	$\bar{x},\bar{y}$	2.448	2.448 s
99	u,u	$\bar{x},\bar{y}$	3.035	3.035 s
99.73 (3 σ)	u,u	$\bar{x},\bar{y}$	3.441	3.441 s

The constant $\lambda = \sqrt{\chi^2_{1-\alpha}}$ where $\alpha = 0.05$ for 95 percent, 0.01 for 99 percent, and 0.0027 for 3 sigma limits, and the value of chi square is taken at 2 degrees of freedom. In an application by Youden the circle was centered at the median values of x and y.[14]

---

[14] For a detailed analysis of the data collected by Dr. Youden from 29 laboratories, see A. C. Rosander, *Applications of Quality Control in the Service Industries* (Milwaukee: ASQC Quality Press; New York: Marcel Dekker, 1985), pp. 316–318.

Chapter 16

Some Case Studies

THE QUALITY OF HEALTH SERVICES

Health service is described in detail because of its importance, cost, and widespread complaints. Judging from experience, earlier reports, and a more recent one (*Quality Progress,* May 1987), quality in health services is in a confusing, paralyzing, and uncertain situation. It labors under myths and fallacies that it needs to get rid of. It needs knowledge, direction, and purpose. First it will have to get rid of the obstacles that are preventing development of a program for quality of service for patients.

The Fallacy of the Factory

The first notion to get rid of is that quality of products produced in a factory is the same as the quality of services rendered in a hospital, nursing home, clinic, or doctor's office. This point has been discussed in great detail in earlier chapters. That the factory syndrome is prevalent and needs to be corrected is reflected in two statements: [1]

"We are just imitating what is being done in industry."

"Industrial procedures for quality control are increasingly being studied as a model for measuring medicine."

Slavish imitation of what is being done in a factory is the worst way to start a quality program in a service company. A quality program needs to be based on a direct and intimate study of services rendered by the organization. A hospital is not a factory; neither is a nursing home. Neither is a clinic or a doctor's office. It has been pointed out that a service organization has to consider the quality of purchased products, just like a manufacturing company, but this is as far as the similarity goes.

---

[1] M. L. Millenson, "A Prescription for Change." *Quality Progress,* May 1987, p. 17.

503

The Fallacy that Quality Cannot Be Defined or Described

Two quotations reflect this view:[2]

"I can't define it, but I know it when I see it."

"Many in health are still trying to define quality."

Persons making these statements obviously are not familiar with the extensive literature of the past decades on the development and applications of quality control as applied to services, and medical services in particular. Ironically, it is the patient who seems to be more familiar with quality of medical care than the professionals in institutions.

We have already described in detail in Chapter 3 the results of the 1985 poll on quality of services, conducted by the Gallup Organization for the American Society for Quality Control. This poll showed that 593 persons out of a nationwide sample of 1005 not only complained of poor-quality services but gave specific reasons for this poor quality. Employee behavior and attitudes topped the list, followed by excessive time and high costs. These respondents can give just as clear and as definite reasons for poor-quality services as they can for poor-quality products. There is nothing elusive or phantomlike about quality of services.

In the same poll, 83 persons gave reasons for poor-quality services received in a hospital within a year or two of the survey. The following are eight major reasons for poor service, in order of frequency:

1. Indifferent personnel;
2. Too slow;
3. Too expensive;
4. Lack of courtesy;
5. Lack of personnel;
6. Unqualified personnel;
7. Work not done right;
8. Poor service (unspecified).

Of these complaints, Items 2 and 3 involve measurements of time and money. Time is very important, and although the customer puts up with delay and waiting times daily, there are times when the waiting time is excessive, performance is too slow, and promptness is not there when it is needed. Excessive time ("too slow") is a complaint brought against many types of services, not just hospitals. "Too costly" is self-explanatory.

---

[2]M. L. Millenson, "A Prescription for Change," *Quality Progress*, May 1987, pp. 18, 17.

Not all doctors, however, are so uncertain about quality and the patient, as the following quotation shows:[3]

> "Patients have been deemed too dumb to know good quality from bad. Most medical authorities have begged the question by contending that we have yet to define 'quality of care.' Lack of a precise definition has never prevented me, or most patients, from judging individual episodes as good, bad, or mediocre. . . . No one is in a better position than the patient to judge value or quality of care."

This position is also taken by many of those who have been working on quality of medical services for decades. It is the position taken here.

The Myth That Quality Has to Be Defined as a Physical Measurement

This fallacy comes directly from the factory, where control over a physical measurement is tantamount to meeting the specifications for the product. In services there is no such situation. In health the nearest situation of the same kind is found in some instrumental measurements, such as temperature and blood pressure, and in laboratory tests of blood, urine, and tissue, all for diagnostic purposes. This view is expressed in the following quotation (see Figures 16–1 and 16–2):[4]

> "Health care industry has had great difficulty with defining medical outcomes in terms of measurable quantities."

As noted above, only time and price are direct measurable quality characteristics of services. Laboratory and instrumental tests and measurements are indirect because they are used for diagnosis. Service quality does not have to be measurable. It can be

- observable (indifferent, rude, abusive behavior of employees);
- distinguishable (qualified personnel vs. unqualified personnel);
- a presence or absence situation:
  - trouble is eliminated or not;
  - diagnosis is correct or not;
  - remedy is effective or not.

---

[3] F. J. Primich, "DRG: A Hazardous Prescription." *Quality Progress,* May 1987, p. 32.

[4] "Health Care," *Quality Progress,* May 1987, p. 15.

time

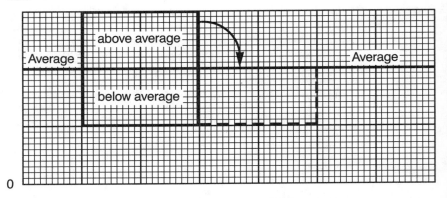

0

Source: *Quality Progress,* May 1987, p. 19

Figure 16–1. **What Happens to the Average If All Patients Are Discharged More Quickly Than the Average Case?**

Institutional Performance Versus Individual Patient Quality

Confusion arises because efficiency of institutional performance is not sharply distinguished from the quality of service to the individual patient. The institution may be emphasized at the expense of the patient because it is in the institutional aspects that cost savings can be made. These so-called quality cost savings can be made at the expense of the quality of service to the patient: hiring fewer nurses, hiring fewer attendants, reducing room furnishings, cutting food costs. There are many opportunities.

The difference is easy to show.

Institutional Performance
(daily, weekly, monthly,
annual basis)

1. Admissions
2. Discharges
3. Length of stay
4. Empty beds; percent occupancy
5. Number of surgical operations; success rate; failure rate
6. Time to make laboratory tests
7. Babies delivered
8. Deaths; ratio to live discharges

Quality of Service to the Patient

Quality of medical service to the patient means getting rid of illness, ailment, or trouble. This includes ailments which can only be ameliorated. Excluded are cases of incurable diseases and permanent disabilities. In these latter cases, quality means taking all steps to make the patient comfortable, free from pain,

frequency

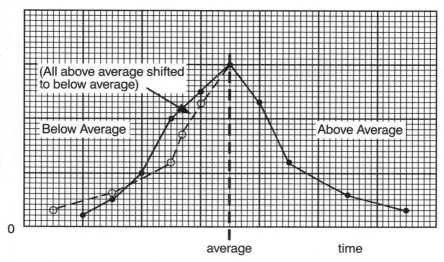

Figure 16–2. **What Happens to the Average If All Patients Are Discharged More Quickly Than the Average Case?**

Institutional Performance (daily, weekly, monthly, annual basis)	*Quality of Service to the Patient*

Institutional Performance:

9. Number of discharges, by ailment
10. Ratio of patients to doctors
11. Ratio of patients to nurses
12. Deaths per 100 patients
13. Surgical operations, by kind
14. Number of meals served
15. Number of patients needing special food or special food preparations
16. Success rate, heart bypass operations

Quality of Service to the Patient:

and as happy as possible.
Quality service means correct diagnosis and effective remedies.
Quality means that doctors and nurses talk to the patients and explain what is going on or what is to take place. It means listening and asking questions.

The mass performance of the institution may be of primary interest to administrators, but systems engineering and delivery systems are no substitute for correct individual diagnosis and treatment. There is always the danger that the individual will be sacrificed to institutional rules, regulations, standards, practices, and traditions.

Service Quality Versus Product Quality Versus Institutional Quality

This situation points up the sharp differences between individual service quality, product quality, and institutional performance.

In individual services, quality is defined as

- Meeting the customer's requirements;
- Meeting the customer's needs and preferences;
- Getting rid of the customer's troubles;
- Making the correct diagnosis;
- Finding and prescribing an effective treatment or remedy;
- Operating safely with zero errors in a timely fashion.

This is a far cry from the factory engineering definition of the quality of a product:

- Conformance to product specifications determined by the manufacturer;
- Making a product that is fit to use;
- Making a product that is durable and reliable.

In manufacturing many supposedly "identical" units of the same product are produced. These units have a distribution, a mean, and a variance. The problem of quality control is to limit this variance around a mean so that the product performs according to specifications, or better.

A Sample of One

In services we have no such situation. Services to individuals are very different; they vary tremendously in nature, type, and duration. Differences exist even where two or more persons are receiving the same service, but quality of service is an individual matter, not a mass affair.

For example, in all repair work, such as repairing an automobile, a radio, a television set, or an electric iron, we are dealing with a sample of one. It is an individual or single unit that has to be fixed. There is no mean, no variance, no distribution. It is not a statistical problem. The findings of statistics may be brought to bear only from outside research, studies, or experience with many similar cases. Quality of service hinges on fixing a particular item or trouble, and nothing else. (See Figure 16–3.)

A sick person desiring medical service is also a sample of one. There is no mean, no variance, no distribution. It is not a statistical problem. It is a medical problem, although it is true that behind the diagnosis and remedy statistics may be applied to medical research.

A sick person wants to get rid of his or her trouble. The job of the doctor and nurse is to to do just that: make a correct diagnosis and prescribe drugs, treatment, or other remedies that get rid of the trouble. When this is attained, there is quality of service, but not otherwise. Exceptions, of course, are incurable diseases, permanent disabilities, and ailments which can only be ameliorated.

Many difficulties and even dangers arise when the patient is not considered a sample of one, but one of millions in the same pigeonhole:

- The drug dosage is too strong or too weak;
- The generalization from medical journals does not apply to this person;
- The drug that is supposed to work on "everyone" does not work on this person (e.g., sleeping pills);
- A blood measurement that falls outside or even inside the "standard" range may not apply to this person;
- A drug such as estrogen may affect a person in a very different way than is held by conventional wisdom (regular doctors);
- A person may *not* show many of the "standard" symptoms of the trouble (e.g., appendicitis);
- The trouble the person complains of is *not* what the nurse or the doctor says "everybody has";
- Doctor does not explain how to use a medicine properly (e.g., eye drops);
- The tranquilizer pill that is supposed to be effective fails;
- The patient's stomach pain is not affected by Tylenol, showing that three doctors were wrong;
- Everyone 65 years of age and over (28,000,000), with no exceptions, should have a flu shot, according to the annual medical decree from CDC in Atlanta.

Doctors make the mistake of treating a patient as one of a large population under statistical control, when that is not the case.

Hospital Quality According to the Patient

One source that can throw light on the quality of medical and nonmedical services in a hospital has been ignored. This is the person going out the door—the discharged patient. (See Figure 16–3.)

All discharged patients should be given a quality appraisal sheet to fill out and mail in later. This gives the patient time to fill it out when he or she may feel better and may be in a different atmosphere. A business-type self-addressed envelope requiring no postage should be furnished to facilitate replies.

This appraisal should be *anonymous* to protect the patient. Some patients may be so afraid of consequences that they will refuse to put their judgments and observations on record, even under the condition of anonymity.

Examples of items to appraise are the nonmedical and the medical:

Remedy

Diagnosis	Remedy		Remarks
	Effective	Not Effective	*Remarks*
Correct	Quality	Poor Quality	Best situation
Not Correct Baffled	Unlikely	double poor quality; failure	Worst situation

Figure 16–3. **The Diagnosis Remedy Quality Square**

Nonmedical	*Medical*
• Front office	• Doctors
• Admittance	• Nurses
• Volunteers	• Medical assistants
• Attendants	• Diagnosis
• Wheelchairs	• Remedy
• Telephone calls	• Treatment
• Mail	• Medicines, drugs
• Flowers	• Pharmacy
• Visitors	• Surgery (if any)
• Discharge	• Attention
• Food	• Assistance
• Room	• X-rays
• Roommates (if any)	• Ultrasound
• Bed	• Other medical technology
• Charges, cost, insurance	• Doctor's examination
• Talking	• Blood, urine, other tests
• Listening	• Length of stay
• Communication	• Talking
	• Listening
	• Communication

The Independence of Health and Biological Factors

Medical practice seems to assume the extensive dependence of one illness or pain on certain behavior or biological conditions. This is attested by the detailed tests and medical history that doctors want from every patient: childhood diseases, cause of ancestors' deaths, operations, defects, and much more.

These factors may be independent of the current trouble and very often are. Yet this long-winded examination is carried out even for some simple trouble such as ear trouble. Doctors are always on a fishing expedition because very few doctors are good diagnosticians. In an actual case, a stomach pain brought about the following in the outpatient department:

1. X-ray;
2. Blood tests (white blood corpuscle count slightly high, but it was finally ignored);
3. Colon cancer test;
4. Diet and eating quiz;
5. Medical examination.

In the end they found nothing and admitted they didn't know the cause. Hence they could not prescribe a remedy. (The Tylenol pills they gave were ineffective.) The bill was $192. The pain finally disappeared, according to a report from the person afflicted.

Quality Control in Laboratory Medicine

Quality control is used extensively in laboratory medicine.[5] It is used not only in connection with laboratory tests and measurements, but also in connection with laboratory safety, purchases control, and infection control.

Variability in Laboratory Measurements

Measurements made on healthy subjects give coefficients of variation (the standard deviation divided by the mean) of the following magnitudes, based on day-to-day variation:[6]

---

[5] J. C. Todd, A. H. Sanford, I. Davidsohn, and J. B. Henry, *Clinical Diagnosis and Management by Laboratory Methods,* 17th edition (Philadelphia: W. B. Saunders, 1984).

[6] *Clinical Diagnosis,* p. 57.

Checksheet for Quality of Individual Medical Service

Time Required

1. An individual is sick, hurt, ailing, injured   ————————
2. Arrangements are made for individual to see a
   doctor:
   Waiting time for appointment   ————————
   Waiting time in doctor's office   ————————
3. Doctor makes examination
   3.1 Waiting time for service in cubicles   ————————
   3.2 Initial tests: pulse, temperature, weight, blood
       pressure   ————————
   3.3 Other tests: EKG, X-rays, ultra sound   ————————
   3.4 Blood and urine for tests   ————————
   3.5 Medical history, diet, etc.   ————————
   3.6 Other   ————————
   3.7 Waiting for results of various tests   ————————
   3.8 Doctor makes examination   ————————
   3.9 Doctor describes what he or she is doing ————————
4. Doctor makes a diagnosis   ————————
   4.1 Diagnosis is correct   ————————
   4.2 Diagnosis is incorrect   ————————
   4.3 Unable to diagnose   ————————
   4.4 Doctor describes diagnosis   ————————
5. Doctor prescribes remedy   ————————
   5.1 Remedy is effective   ————————
   5.2 Remedy is ineffective   ————————
   5.3 Doctor describes remedy   ————————
6. Follow-up to find correct diagnosis   ————————
7. Follow-up to find effective remedy   ————————
8. Exceptions
   8.1 Incurable disease   ————————
   8.2 Permanent disability   ————————
   8.3 Chronic trouble that can only
       be ameliorated   ————————
9. Summary: Measures of quality service as seen by
   patient
   9.1 Correct diagnosis
   9.2 Effective remedy
   9.3 Minimum delay time, no unnecessary waiting
   9.4 Reasonable price, no unnecessary service
       charges
   9.5 Result: cured, helped, recurring, failure:
       Cured ————
       Helped ————
       Recurring ————
       Failure ————
   9.6 Doctor describes diagnosis, remedy

Analyte	Coefficient of Variation
potassium	0.05
glucose	.06
iron	.27
cholesterol	.06
albumin	.03
urea	.12

These measurements were selected to show the wide range of coefficients of variation. This variation will be reflected in the reference values used in any one measurement.

It is stated that "in a clinical setting, group reference intervals based on data from so-called healthy subjects are the predominant type of reference used. A common error . . . is the practice of using the lower and the upper limits of the interval as rigid boundaries within which the patient is considered 'normal' and beyond which the patient is termed 'abnormal' and thought to be suffering from some pathologic process. This approach may be very misleading . . . a value outside the stated interval might be a sign of *good* health rather than a cause for concern, e.g. a patient having a cholesterol value below the lowest reference limit. For another patient, having a value within the stated interval might *not* be a sign of good health, e.g. a patient on Coumadin with a 'normal protein.' "[7]

Laboratory Safety

Laboratory safety is of critical importance not only because of the physical damage that is involved but because of the injuries to technical and professional workers, and the serious effects that these can have on the operations of the laboratory.[8]

Several causes have been found for these accidents:

• Experienced workers taking risks;
• Hurry to meet deadlines (some imaginary);
• Carelessness;
• Fatigue;
• Mental preoccupation: worrying, daydreaming.

One study of accidents showed that they were caused by experienced, not inexperienced operators.

---

[7] *Clinical Diagnosis*, p. 58.

[8] *Clinical Diagnosis*, p. 22.

Accident prevention involves two major factors: the knowledge factor and the emotional factor. It has been found that knowing the rules of safety is not enough. The worker must maintain a constant, cautious, attentive *alertness*. *Concentration* on the job is imperative. Accident and disaster drills are recommended.

Control over Purchases

Control over purchases is exerted by competent and authorized staff familiar with the vendor's quality of service and reliability. Control is exerted by product research, written specifications, testing, on-site visits, delivery schedules, and inventory control.[9]

These controls are applied to equipment, reagents, and supplies. All items received are inspected, and dated where shelf life is very important. While it is recommended that the purchaser work closely with the vendor in connection with written specifications, there is no indication that the vendor is required to assure the quality of the product as ordered so that mass receiving inspection can be eliminated or even sharply reduced. Many items will need to be dated, catalogued, and labeled at time of receipt.

OTHER CASE STUDIES

Thirteen additional cases are described, which deal with a variety of industries, situations, companies, and problems. They relate to the quality of performance of management, supervisors, and employees. They include success stories as well as failures. They illustrate successful management of quality as well as situations where management still has to learn how to manage quality. They illustrate the importance of good-quality data and technical competence in achieving success in starting and developing a quality improvement program. The 13 cases, in order, are as follows (the last case, describing the lessons learned at Three Mile Island and Chernobyl, is the most important of all):

1. Insurance claims;
2. Mail orders;
3. Data processing;
4. Key punching;
5. Public utility;
6. Tax returns;
7. Insurance company;
8. Biased data;
9. Failure of management by hunch;

---

[9]*Clinical Diagnosis*, p. 1388.

10. A quality department;
11. Problems uncovered by random time sampling;
12. Faulty product hidden from user;
13. Three Mile Island and Chernobyl.

Case 1. Insurance Claims—Program Started by Top Management

Stage 1. Preparation:

1. Need for improvement grows out of errors in data input to computer.
2. Management sets up quality control department as staff function.
3. QC department explains quality control to employees and supervisors. The first step is to get them to accept and approve quality control.
4. All basic documents are reviewed. Right and wrong entries are described and identified.
5. Checklist is prepared for supervisors and inspectors (verifiers).
6. Process flow chart is laid out and discussed.
7. Pilot is run in limited area for initial application

Stage 2. Putting program into effect:

1. Quality control department introduces program:
   - Determines sample sizes;
   - Selects samples;
   - Interprets sample data;
   - Counts unacceptable documents;
   - Prepares error table and distribution;
   - Applies Pareto analysis;
   - Concentrates on high-frequency error items.
2. Department discusses results with supervisor, submits report.
3. Concentrates on eliminating assignable causes—major causes of error.
4. Continues sampling to measure whether improvement continues.
5. Makes final report to manager.
6. Continues training and redesigning forms as needed.

Stage 3. Final results: Processing time is reduced; cost is reduced; customer complaints are down; productivity is up; morale of employees is up; error rate is reduced (see Figure 16–4).

Case 2. Mail Order House—Program Started by a Manager of a Department

1. Manager attends class in statistical quality control.
2. Decides to apply quality control to the mail order department.

percent
error

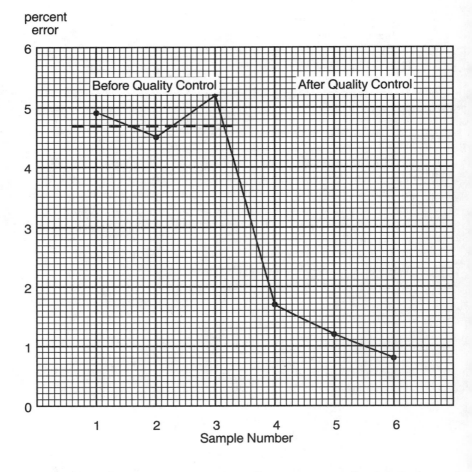

Figure 16–4. **Quality Improvement in Coding Insurance Application Cards**

   3. Explains plan to select sample.
   4. Explains plan to measure group error rate.
   5. Explains plan to plot error rate daily on big wall chart; starts program.
   6. Select sample of 100 orders daily.
   7. Inspectors (verifiers) determine number of orders in error.
   8. Post error rate on wall chart daily.
   9. Examine where errors are made.
  10. Sources of errors are explained to group.
  11. Goal is to reduce error rate.
  12. Error rate declines.

13. Result: steady improvement in performance of the group. (It is not known whether quality control was ever applied to individuals.)
14. This successful application leads to use of quality control in other departments.

Case 3. Data Processing—Program Started by a Consultant

1. The need: to control errors in transcribing documents to a standard format for computer input. Documents were carload waybills, which are *not* a standard form.
2. This private company had a federal government contract to process 125,000 documents.
3. Technical staff was not familiar with project. Hired manager and consultant who were.
4. Manager-supervisor was traffic expert who prepared 95-page procedural manual detailing all steps and calculations needed to transcribe carload waybills.
5. Clerical processing staff consisted of unskilled housewives, students, and others who had to be trained for three weeks; had to pass test before going on production.
6. Vice-president wanted only review of work, not quality control.
7. Consultant with supervisor laid out process control by lots of 300; called it review.
8. Manager-supervisor had three verifiers and 20 employees. She was tutor, coach, decider of what was correct, director, and disciplinarian.
9. Consultant designed subsampling, provided equations for sampling errors, laid out process control plan, and plotted errors and production by individuals and for the group.
10. Process control was by lots of 300. Sample was 50; five errors to accept, six to reject lot. Rejected lots went back immediately to those who did them with 100 percent redo.
11. Goal was four percent final error rate after a computer edit to pick up other errors and inconsistencies. This was acceptable because data were for statistical purposes.
12. Employee problems encountered: eating, use of radios, too much togetherness, dislike of office discipline and controls, opposed clocks, didn't want to get to work at 8:30 a.m., didn't realize they were really trainees, couldn't understand that company had to job to do and they were being paid to do it. Much of this was due to the fact that this was the first job for most of them.
13. Serious problems and defects:
    - 5500 corrected punch cards never got into the final tabulation.
    - 26,000 calculations of sampling errors were wrong.

- Data for one major commodity looked suspicious compared with external data.
- The above three corrections were never made; data were published without them.

14. Without process control by lots, the error rate in the final data would have been between 15 and 20 percent.

Case 4. Key Punching—Program Started by Chief Statistician

1. Staff professional familiar with statistical quality control confers with operations manager about gains to be made by using sample verification of punched cards instead of 100 percent verification.
2. Discusses proposal with the supervisor of the 90 keypunch operators.
3. Studies daily error and production records of the keypunch operators.
4. Discovers that 15 operators consistently have error rate less than 2 percent and punch between 6000 and 7000 cards per day.
5. Proposes that sample verification be applied to the work of these 15 operators.
6. Operations manager approves use of sample verification.
7. A lot sample plan is designed and discussed with the supervisor.
8. A sample of 50 cards is selected from the daily production of each operator and examined for errors: if 0, the work is passed; if 1, the work is verified 100 percent.
9. This meant that 750 cards were checked daily, making it possible for a maximum of 5000 to 6000 cards to be passed daily without verification. Actually, the number was about 4000.
10. Plan works satisfactorily.
11. Due to a reorganization, however, most of these 15 operators were bumped by ex-operators with greater seniority but higher error rates.
12. Error rate of new operators is 10 percent or more.
13. Lot sampling plan had to be abandoned temporarily: training was needed to reduce error rate.
14. Lot sampling was never restored because error rate of new operators was never reduced below 5 percent.

Case 5. A Public Utility—Program Started by the Chairman of the Company

1. Chairman of the company forms a quality management team of senior officers.
2. The team visits other companies.
3. The company brings in outside consultants in quality management.

4. The program starts with a pilot project, which is successful. This project is limited to one department.
5. This success, however, leads the chairman to expand the program to the entire company, requiring participation of everyone at all levels and in all departments.
6. Organization of entire company takes the following form:
   - Corporate—quality council;
   - Division—quality teams (Quality teams are formed for special areas or problems.);
   - Districts—quality teams;
   - Local—quality teams.
7. These quality teams are similar to task forces but tend to be continuous.
8. Functions of the Quality Council:
   - Policies;
   - Plans;
   - Final decisions;
   - Leadership;
   - Encouragement;
   - Constant pushing.
9. Quality engineering and training are part of the quality improvement staff functions.
10. Examples of accomplishments of quality teams:
    - Errors in billing reduced;
    - Chronic equipment problem solved;
    - Better use made of fuel as source of energy.
11. Results
    - 1000 improvement teams formed;
    - Permanent quality group of senior managers;
    - Reduction in customer complaints;
    - A large saving in cost of operations.
12. Unlike quality circles, these quality teams work on eliminating faults of the system for which management is responsible.

Case 6. Tax Returns—Program Started by Senior Management

1. The U.S. Treasury Department released the results of an audit control program based on a nationwide sample of 160,000 individual income tax returns.
2. The purpose of this study was twofold: to determine the size of the nonconformance problem by determining the volume of total tax error and to identify the major sources and causes of these errors. The purpose was to allocate audit resources better across the country.

3. A central task force was formed to plan and direct the study.
4. A probability sample of 160,000 returns was designed to give a nation-wide estimate of tax error, as well as to disclose where the major sources of error were.
5. Once the sample was selected, it was audited in the usual manner.
6. The audited sample was tabulated and analyzed at the central office.
7. The major findings were described and illustrated in a publication distributed to the public as well as to the top officials.
8. Major findings:
   - Noncompliance in form of tax errors totaled $1.5 billion;
   - Major sources of error (in order): unreported income, underreported income, deductions, exemptions, arithmetic.
   - Categories with most errors: business returns, businesses that do not use cash registers, certain cities.
9. The study disclosed that many taxpayers were taking aliens as personal exemptions, which was clearly illegal. Actions taken:
   - Instructions were rewritten and described in detail, making clear the criteria to be met to qualify for a personal exemption.
   - A schedule was added to Form 1040, requiring more details about support of individuals. The schedule is still in use.
10. Results:
   - Management knew, for the first time, how big the noncompliance problem was.
   - Management knew, for the first time, many new areas and sources of error where audit resources needed to be allocated.
   - Management could now calculate each year how much of the noncompliance ($1.5 billion) had been corrected.

Case 7. An Insurance Company—Program Started by Chairman of the Board

A companywide program, "Quality Has Value," succeeded in an insurance company over a period of two years.[10] The highlights of this program are as follows:

- The chairman of the board issues a policy statement on quality and productivity. The company was to be identified with quality in perception as well as in fact. It cites Crosby: quality means zero defects, conformance to requirements, and doing it right the first time. Goals are high quality, high productivity, and customer satisfaction.

---

[10] Patrick L. Townsend with Joan E. Gebhardt, *Commit to Quality* (New York: Wiley, 1986).

- A quality improvement team of eight executives is selected. Chairman is vice-president for operations. Crosby's *Quality is Free* is given to every member. Several months later, employees are first involved with discussion meetings about quality.
- Quality teams are formed and value analysis workshops are held. Knowledge of employees is tapped. Outside consultant helps with workshops. Value analysis is an appraisal of every aspect, function, and level of the organization. Value analysis is concerned with the right things to do, quality teams with doing it right. There is also the question of doing the right thing the right way at the right time. The value workshop includes decision makers from every department. The objective is to redesign every function to meet objectives at the right cost, and to improve functions and operations.
- Examples: Standardize pricing and forecasting methodology, contract out person services, restructure underwriting department, merge two departments of underwriting services. Thirty value workshops had annualized savings of $6 million.
- Quality teams differ from quality circles: they are compulsory, not voluntary. Managers are team members. More ideas are received. It is assumed that everyone can contribute. It is necessary to train team leaders using outside help. Team meetings spend 30 minutes of company time weekly. Natural bosses are selected as team leaders, using boss's expertise and experience. No explanation is given as to how "problem solving" is taught. Examples of practices needing correction: one clerk alphabetizes cards, the next clerk throws them away. Key punch operators knowingly punch errors from coding sheets.
- Various methods are used for recognition, gratitude, and celebration: bronze, silver, and gold pins; printing names and pictures in company papers; holding home office employees' party; special awards for best player and best team.
- Changes in corporate practices and ideas:
    - Quality ideas: number increased from 4100 the first year to 5700 the second year.
    - Basic questions: Does work do what it is intended to do? Is there a better way? Is it repetitious? Is it outdated? necessary?
    - Introduction of PEET: Program Ensuring that Everybody's Thanked. Not the same as MBWA: Managmeent by Wandering Around.
    - Publications: *Quality News* and *Quality Field News*.
    - Surveys by market research department: home employees, field employees, policyholders.
    - Second-year goals: make a new quality cost census; modify quality team efforts.
    - Listening down—and out: emphasis on talking with employees and

getting their ideas, using personal interviews, conversations, and surveys. Applying these ideas to field offices.

Case 8. Management by False Data Proves Costly and Futile—A Case of Biased Data

This is a classical case in which the lack of sound data led management into costly projects and a critical situation.

1. Management ran a test on one machine operator and concludes that employees are stealing a million dollars' worth of merchandise annually.
2. The test consisted of measuring the input of material and the corresponding output (product produced). The input was yarn, the output a pair of hose. From these test data the average amount of input per unit of output was calculated.
3. The manager then divided this value into the total input for the year and came up with a million dollars short on value of merchandise produced.
4. He called in detectives. They observed the employees and operations for days, but found nothing.
5. Next the manager called in a team of psychologists. They came with cameras and one-way screens and observed the situation for days, but they, too, found nothing.
6. Finally one of the psychologists asked how the million dollars was arrived at; this broke the case.
7. This led to further tests, which showed considerable variation among operators although they were using semi-automatic machines.
8. The original test operator was one of the better operators, and produced more output per unit of input than did the average—she used less input per unit of output.
9. Consequently the estimate of the output was $1 million worth of output too high.
10. The $1 million difference was the loss because the average of the non-test operators was not that of the test opeartor.
11. This was not a legal problem or a psychological problem. It was a statistical problem, a sampling problem, and a data collection problem.
12. The problem was management. It had no accurate data on production. It had no accurate data on output in relation to input. It had no data on the variability of the machine operators' performance. It was flying blind.
13. Accurate data could have been obtained in one of three different ways:
    - The simplest would be to divide annual input by annual output for each of the last five years and to compare them.
    - In running the test a larger sample should have been used, possibly a sample of 10 operators selected at random.

- Control charts should have been used on each operator and plotted daily, with input divided by output.
14. Defeat could be turned into victory by finding out the secret of the test operator and having the other operators follow her example.
15. Management needed a data collection system that would enable them to control operations.

Case 9. Management by Hunch Fails—A Case of No Data

This is a case where top management jumped to a false conclusion without any data and then had to reverse an earlier decision when the facts were known. It emphasizes the need for management to have high-quality data on key operations and situations so that false decisions are avoided.

1. The company's sales have been declining for some months.
2. The president of the company is very concerned.
3. He calls in the salespeople and accuses them of not doing their job.
4. The salespeople protest. There has been no letdown; they have been doing their usual job.
5. After considerable talk and protest, the president is persuaded to make a study of the lost customers.
6. A survey of lost customers is planned and carried out.
7. The study reveals that the customers were lost because the quality of the product had deteriorated. The quality of a competitor's product was better.
8. The problem now is to try to discover what happened to the quality of the product, and when.
9. Past production records, receiving inspection records, and vendors are examined and analyzed.
10. Finally, the investigation reveals what happened: Some months before, in order to save money and cut costs, a new vendor was substituted for a higher-priced one.
11. Money is saved, but at the expense of quality. The purchasing department overlooked the importance of quality (Deming's Point 4).
12. When it dawned on the company that customers had been lost because of poor quality, they returned to the original vendor.
13. When they made this change, the quality of the product improved and their sales began to increase.
14. This experience showed that it would be good practice to keep in touch with lost customers and to find out why they stopped buying the product.

15. This means that a company should make continuous studies of customers to discover those which are lost or are about to be lost. The restriction of interest to customer complaints is not enough.

16. This experience also shows that the gain made by buying cheap is easily overshadowed by the loss due to lost customers.

Case 10. A Quality Department—A Case of No Technical Capability

This is about a quality department, as revealed by the monthly report. The information was furnished on the condition that the data would not be revealed. In addition, the name of the company remains anonymous because revealing it would serve no useful purpose.

This case is highly illuminating because, when judged from the voluminous monthly report, it shows what is missing in an effective quality program.

1. What is missing:
   - Companywide attitude and approach;
   - Top-level push for quality;
   - Urgency;
   - Technical capability;
   - High-quality data and analysis;
   - Differentiating employee action from management action;
   - Constant improvement of services.
2. Conclusions drawn from examining monthly report:
   - Tables lacking titles and units of measurement;
   - Poorly constructed frequency distributions;
   - Sampling and sampling variations not described;
   - Five to six week's delay in getting information to management;
   - No indication of critical problems or situations needing immediate attention;
   - No priorities;
   - No reports to different levels of management: no differentiation of technical reports from action reports;
   - Lack of technical capability to collect and analyze data: no statistical capability;
   - Report is more of a status report than an action report on quality improvement;
   - Report is a statistical report, with tables and charts.

What is missing is a report on quality status, quality improvement, and situations that need to be looked into immediately. This should be a weekly report, not a monthly report.

Case 11. Random Time Work Sampling for Control and Costs—A Case of Getting Better Control Than Expected

1. The director of a division of 350 persons engaged in data processing is dissatisfied with the 100 percent work time records that employees are filling out.

2. He finds the data unsatisfactory for costing out projects and budget planning.

3. A staff member suggests that he use work sampling. He asks the chief statistician whether work sampling can be applied to the work of the division.

4. The chief statistician says it can, but recommends a pilot study of one week to test the various procedures that have to be developed: sampling, data sheet, instructions, activity codes, calling random times, etc.

5. The director approves. Three professional members of the sampling staff design sample and data sheets, prepare instructions and activity codebook, and lay out method for calling random minutes.

6. Meetings are held with employees in their organizational units to explain purpose and methods, including when pilot run will be made. Acceptance is very good.

7. A pilot run is made for one week, (five days), with eight random minutes being called on every organizational unit each day. Persons are not sampled; only minutes.

8. As a result, all methods are greatly improved; new plan goes into effect and continues for two years. All 350 persons are included in the study.

9. Under the improved plan random minutes are called in by telephone from central point; lunch hour is included in the sample; activity codes are increased in number and described in more detail; anonymous self-reporting is used with pads of data sheets; and number of random minutes called is greatly reduced. The time sampled is 510 minutes per working day, but not all working days are included in the study—only three days per week. Secretaries or supervisors check every data sheet after a random minute is called.

10. The pilot run reveals that four units have "waiting time" that exceeds 2 percent. When the director sees this, he calls in the supervisors and shows them the data. Immediate action is called for to find the causes and eliminate them. Although the purpose of the study is not to exert control, this is the first use to which the data are put. This is an unexpected benefit.

11. Other results from the final study:
    - Effective working time was 75 percent of total; paid-for leave and idle time occupied 25 percent.
    - Study gave salary costs of different programs and projects.

- Study gave basis for costing out new projects, programs, and jobs.
- Study gave basis for better budget planning.
- Study revealed units and projects where improvements could be made.

Case 12. Faulty Product Hidden from the User

According to reports,[11] a substantial number of the 600,000 pacemakers in use in the United States either have been recalled or are suspect. Users are never informed of these recalls because federal procedures require that the manufacturers inform only doctors or institutions—not the patients. This means that those who have moved or changed doctors or hospitals may be walking around with a faulty pacemaker.

This information comes from the Pacemaker Recall Data Bank of Orlando, Florida. Patients with pacemakers have to contact this agency to find out whether their pacemakers have been recalled and to obtain the Federal Food and Drug Administration report as to when they were recalled and why.

This is another example of the brazen indifference of manufacturers, medical service people, and government agencies toward patients with serious medical problems. The fact that replacements are covered by Medicare or private insurance is irrelevant. This cavalier attitude shows that these patients (and many others) are classified and treated as if they were pieces of merchandise.

Case 13. Lessons Learned from Three Mile Island and Chernobyl [12]

The lesson revealed by Three Mile Island and Chernobyl is loud and clear. It is that *human reliability* is just as critical as mechanical reliability, if not more so. The vital issue facing this industry, as well as other industries, is *human error and its prevention*. With a reasonable amount of human reliability on the part of both management and operators, both of these disasters could have been avoided.

Ahearne points out several significant similarities between the two nuclear power plants:

- Operators and industry were complacent because of the belief that no accident could occur and that no unsafe situation could arise.
- Operators were ignorant of nuclear power engineering and of how the plant actually operated.

---

[11] *Modern Maturity,* American Association of Retired Persons, December 1986–January 1987, p. 16.

[12] J. F. Ahearne, "Nuclear Power after Chernobyl." *Science,* May 8, 1987, pp. 236, 673–79; Richard Wilson, "A Visit to Chernobyl." *Science,* June 25, 1987, pp. 236, 1636–40.

- Operators were never instructed in how the safety system worked, nor were such instructions included in any emergency procedures.
- Operators not only overrode the safety systems but deliberately shut them down or ignored warnings that the safety systems should be operating.

Ahearne concludes:

"Mechanical systems were defeated by operators who did not understand what they were doing and took actions that deliberately overrode safety systems. In both cases, the plants were particularly sensitive to such an override . . . in the TMI accident, a significantly longer period of time went by in which knowledgeable operators could have corrected the actions.

"The TMI reviews led to significant changes in the way U.S. plants are operated. These changes included requiring simulators for plants and simulator training, including accident sequences; increased training for operators and upgrading the quality of operators; and safety review committees . . . great emphasis was placed on personnel issues, one reason being that much of the hardware was already in place."

Ahearne states in response to a criticism of some points in his paper:

"It is also true that the operators had not been trained to handle the events that were developing at TMI (Three Mile Island."[13]

He quotes further from official reports:

"One major review concluded: 'First, the operators on duty had not received training adequate to ensure that they would be able to recognize and respond to a serious accident . . . Second, neither the operating crew nor their supervisors . . . possessed the necessary combination of technical competence and familiarity with the plant. . . .' "[14]

"Nevertheless 'these operating personnel made some improper decisions, took some improper actions and failed to take some correct actions, *causing what should have been a minor incident to develop into the TMI-2 accident*' " (emphasis added).[15]

---

[13] *Science,* October 9, 1987, vol. 238,p. 145.

[14] M. Rogovin and G. T. Frampton, Jr. "Three Mile Island: A Report to the Commissioner and the Public." NUREG CR/1250 Nuclear Regulatory Commission, Washington, DC, January 1980, vol. I, pp. 17, 103.

[15] J. G. Kemeny et al, "Report of the President's Commission on the Accident at TMI." Washington, DC, October 1979, p. 27.

Wilson points out the same basic contributory factors described by Ahearne, but discusses in more detail the weakness of the reactor design and what has been done since to improve the situation.

Design Errors

The Chernobyl reactors have an instability that is especially critical and dangerous at low power output—in this case 20 percent of full power.

There was a belief, similar to one held in United States before TMI, that the design was safe and that no accident could happen. What was overlooked was that in actual operations, there might be a serious deviation from the designer's rules and specifications.

According to Ahearne, Britain warned the Soviet Union that the design had serious defects and placed too difficult a task on the operators.

Management Errors

The Soviet designers specified a set of operating rules which were to be followed in the strictest manner. Management found these rules too difficult to follow to the letter.

Management deliberately ran the reactor below 20 percent power. The rules were not obeyed by the deputy chief engineer. Six important safety devices were deliberately disconnected.

Operator Errors

The operators took actions which increased rather than checked the instability. This was because the rules were not understood. The operators were not educated in what these rules meant in terms of operating the reactor. Neither did the operators understand elementary nuclear physics, or they could have performed more intelligently.

Conclusions

These disasters were due to human errors. What can be done to prevent them?

- Hire technically qualified people.
- Train them in plant operations.
- Train them in safety systems.
- Train them for emergencies.
- Foolproof the design as much as possible.
- Be sure managers and operators *understand* the rules and operations, and *know what to do in any emergency.*

Chapter 17

The Past Is Prologue—and So Is the Present

WHAT IS QUALITY OF SERVICES?

The purpose of this chapter is to answer some key questions about the quality of services. It is not just a summary because it contains new material in the form of amplifications and new ideas. The next section lists 17 specific meanings of "quality of services." This alone shows that quality is multidimensional and that there is no simple answer to the question "What is quality of services?"

Three key elements constitute the general model: the supplier, the service organization, and the recipient. The service organization relies on the supplier for products free of defects—products that meet the requirements of the service organization. It relies on all personnel for the quality of internal operations.

The recipient relies on employees and the equipment they use for quality of service. Quality of service involves physical factors, such as quality of products used for service, as well as the behavior and attitudes of the employees rendering services directly to the customer.

The general model for quality of services can be diagrammed in the following way:

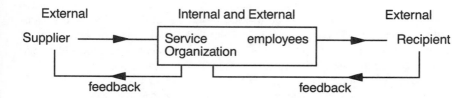

Feedback from the organization may improve the quality of the product from the supplier. Feedback from the customer may improve the quality of the service from the employees. Internal controls are used to improve the quality of performance within the organization.

The customer is a sample of one. Customers are *not* a single population under statistical control. The organization should survey customers using 100 percent coverage or a probability sample. Employees can be surveyed in a similar manner. The purpose of both of these surveys is to uncover views about quality and how to improve it.

WHAT ARE THE 17 MEANINGS OF QUALITY OF SERVICES?

Errors	1. Quality is error-free performance of mechanisms.
	2. Quality is error-free performance of people.
Defects	3. Quality is purchased products that are defect-free.
Diagnosis	4. Quality is correct diagnosis.
	5. Quality is finding the correct remedy.
	6. Quality is getting rid of trouble.
Behavior	7. Quality is courteous behavior.
	8. Quality is being reliable and trustworthy.
	9. Quality is efficient performance.
	10. Quality is safe performance.
Time	11. Quality is meeting a time schedule.
	12. Quality is prompt action and performance.
Cost	13. Quality is getting your money's worth.
Prevention/	14. Quality is preventing errors of all kinds.
Protection	15. Quality is preventing defects of all kinds.
	16. Quality is protection against all unsafe conditions.
Data	17. Quality is sound data for detecting and solving problems.

WHAT IS "TOTAL QUALITY CONTROL" AND WHO IS "EVERYBODY"?

The term "total quality control" came out of the factory. It aimed to break down the isolation between departments, functions, and processes and to substitute an integrated system whereby all were cooperating to produce quality of product. The expression "Quality is everybody's business" seems to have had a different origin; the author used it in a 1958 publication in connection with a service organization.[1] The origin is uncertain, but this expression was used before any attention was paid to total quality control. In the same publication it is stated that "quality mindedness should be developed throughout the organization," so the total concept was accepted in services before 1958.

---

[1] A. C. Rosander, *Statistical Quality Control in Tax Operations* (Washington, DC: U.S. Treasury Department, 1958), p. 26.

A Broader Interpretation

Both "total quality control" and "everybody" should be given a much broader interpretation, as the following bar graph shows:

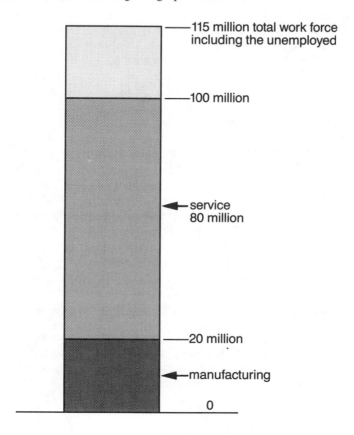

According to the experts, "total" = 17 percent. "Everybody" = 20 million. It is obvious that the experts are putting the emphasis on the factory, not on the entire economy. The narrow factory view should be rejected. Quality must apply not only to services but to the entire work force. Even this chart is incomplete because it excludes customers who do not work or work for pay. This includes millions outside the work force.

What is needed is *comprehensive quality control* (CQC), not just a quality orientation that is limited to the factory. Quality must apply to all work activities, whether paid or not. Therefore it includes the regular work tasks performed by volunteers.

Millions of men, women, and children buy products and services daily. They, too, have a right to receive acceptable-quality products and services for the money they spend. High-pressure advertising is no substitute for quality. In many companies, the millions of dollars spent on advertising might better be spent on improving the quality of the product or service.

This broader interpretation of quality calls for a change in attitude toward the customer. One evidence of this change is found in the work of Tom Peters, who devotes five chapters to the customer in his 1985 book, *A Passion for Excellence*. It is high time to stop blaming "consumerism" for the damage suits, recalls, foreign competition, and other troubles that beset manufacturers.

It is a matter of record that the consumer-customer is overly patient, acceptive, and even docile in regard to the poor-quality products and services that he or she buys. Columns in the press and programs on television attest to the raw deals the customer receives—defective products, mail-order scams, fraudulent services, and much more. The 1985 Gallup poll for the American Society for Quality Control showed that 53 percent of the 1005 respondents complained of poor-quality products—products that fall apart, do not last, fail to perform well, and reflect poor workmanship.

Here is more objective support, if more is needed, for putting a stop to the practice of using "consumerism" to discredit customer complaints and cover up poor quality. If manufacturers make safe, reliable, efficient, and affordable products—if they take quality seriously—there will be no need for recalls and no incentive to start a damage suit. The same challenge applies to a service organization.

WHAT ARE TOP-LEVEL OBJECTIONS TO QUALITY?

The following are objections to quality which have been expressed by officials and professionals at various levels in a company or organization. They give quality proponents cues with regard to how to approach officials and professionals when attempting to convince them of the merits of quality improvement programs in services.

- Quality control doesn't apply to services
- We don't know how to measure quality of services
- Quality doesn't apply to our business, just to factories
- We don't need quality control, only review and inspection
- This is not the proper time to introduce such an idea
- We already have quality
- Quality costs too much; we cannot afford it
- Our employees and supervisors will object to anything like that
- Our middle managers will not accept it
- Our people are already doing a quality job

How to overcome objections. Overcoming objections is not easy and requires time, patience, and persistence, as well as a wide variety of strategies.

- Demonstrate with a successful application using an important problem or troublesome situation
- Make a report in writing on the costs of non-quality or poor quality
- Give a talk on the costs of non-quality or poor quality
- Prepare a series of success stories from the quality literature
- Set up a series of seminars on quality improvement and its advantages
- Have an executive who believes in quality improvement give a talk
- Bring in a consultant to explain quality and its advantages
- Get officials to attend top level seminars on quality
- Conduct training courses using video tapes of Dr. Deming and Dr. Juran
- Lay out and develop a training program in quality and quality improvement for all levels: employees, supervisors, middle managers, senior managers.
- Include in the training program adequate instruction in the basic ideas and techniques of statistics.
- Eventually hire at least one professional statistician who is familiar with applying statistics to problems of management and especially to quality aspects on a broad basis.

DID QUALITY CONTROL PRACTICE START AT THE TOP?

The following list illustrates the problems to which a company or organization first applied quality control. These show the kinds of situations where a quality program can be started. They show how to select a problem to which quality control can be applied successfully. With two exceptions, all of them come from service companies or organizations. Only two in the list were really started by top level officials.

- errors in key punching census data
- errors in key punching sample data
- errors in insurance claims
- errors in filling mail orders
- errors in typing
- errors in billing
- errors in industry coding
- errors in statistical coding
- errors on shipping documents
- errors in filing
- errors in the file
- errors in typesetting galley
- errors in printing bank checks—MICR
- airline reservations
- revenue accounting
- transcribing railroad waybills

- computer edit
- clerical work in accounting
- clerical work in an office
- personnel characteristics and operations
- waiting time: waiting for work
- airport parking
- computer readouts
- repeated laboratory tests
- transcribing tax data
- railroad mileages (shipping)
- bus scheduled times
- testing chemists with same samples
- excess volume
- excess weight in canning
- three minute timer

CAN QUALITY START BELOW THE TOP LEVEL?

Yes, it can and does. Indeed quality control and quality improvement started below the top. Successful applications of statistical quality control (now statistical process control) were first made by a few professional specialists and middle managers. There are several reasons for this:

1. Quality control, originated by Walter Shewhart, was based on statistics and probability. The latter succeeded in solving the problem that management and engineering could not solve. These technical subjects have never been popular with executives, managers, and professional specialists.

2. Top-level managers and executives do not reach the top because they know anything about mathematics, statistics, or probability. In fact these are the subjects they are going to avoid. Clarence Randall wrote in his book. *The Folklore of Management,* that the college subjects for an executive to study are law, accounting, and Shakespeare.

3. It was a few lower level professionals who first successfully applied Shewharts' techniques to real-world problems in manufacturing and services. The reason is that they had studied statistics, or had been exposed to it, so they were able to understand and apply Shewhart's theories to problems where they worked.

4. Shewhart's control charts could be learned and applied successfully by employees and supervisors with a minimum of knowledge. With proper instruction these people could apply quality control successfully, and therefore show that Shewhart was not proposing some more useless academic theories.

5. The role of probability sampling should not be overlooked. It was easier to demonstrate the successful application of probability sampling and the tremendous savings that resulted therefrom, than it was to demonstrate the advantages of statistical quality control. Sampling opened the door to quality control.

Probability sampling also was a technical field that required years to master both theory and practice. Management liked the results, but statisticians had to do the work, had to demonstrate that probability sampling also applied successfully to real world problems and situations.

Another misconception needs to be corrected. These early successful applications of probability sampling and statistical quality control involved more than statistics, more than a narrow minded statistical consultant. The innovator was a practitioner and more often than not, was not a statistician. He had to originate a program and implement it as well. This meant the innovator faced several problems:

1. had to know the statistical aspects and how to apply them
2. had to supervise a group of employees
3. had people problems
4. had to work with professional specialists
5. had managerial problems
6. worked for an expanded use of probability sampling and statistical quality control

Statements such as the following show how advanced thinking was in 1958 relative to the quality program:[2]

- "Develop quality-mindedness throughout the organization"
- "Stress that quality is everybody's business"
- "Put quality control program on a cooperative basis"
  (The three foregoing precede Feigenbaum's total quality control)
- "Quality is built in, not inspected in"
- "Final responsibility for putting the program into effect . . . . lies . . . in the operating sections not with the statisticians"

The latter shows that the statisticians recognized what their functions were—that the responsibility for quality lies with the employees who do the work, and that their function is technical except where they are in a supervisory position.

The criticism aimed at this early approach to quality was that it made no provision for continuity, that it stressed statistics and not management, and that it did not include everyone. These statements are easy to make in the 1980s. They really are neither fair nor valid. Before we could make quality *everybody's* business we had to make it *somebody's* business. It was far from obvious in the 1930s and 1940s that Shewhart's techniques and theories would

---

[2] A. C. Rosander, *Statistical Quality Control in Tax Operations,* U.S. Treasury Department, Washington, Sept. 1958, p. 26.

work in the real world beyond the manufacturing of telephone parts. The real job of the pioneer appliers was to show beyond a reasonable doubt that these techniques could be applied to a wide variety of real-world problems in both manufacturing and in services, not alone to the problems of Western Electric. This took until about 1960. Without this proof in actual industry and business experience, management is futile and helpless. After all, management cannot operate in a vacuum; there has to be content.

Without Shewhart, management has no quality to manage, engineering has no quality to build. Not only that, but management had to be convinced that quality control was a powerful and effective tool in running a business. Quality, it would appear, has developed in three stages:

Stage 1. Application to isolated problems. Statistics and statisticians dominate. Hasn't got to management yet. This is 1930s, 1940s, 1950s.

Stage 2. Application to a wide variety of problems in many industries. Expansion of techniques and their application. Stress is still on successful applications. 1940s, 1950s, and 1960s. (See Industrial Quality Control from 1946 to 1968.)

Stage 3. Application of quality concepts and techniques across the entire organization. Management begins to dominate due largely to Japanese influences. 1970s, 1980s. Movement still has not influenced the service industries to any great extent.

It took until the 1970s and 1980s for management (especially in manufacturing) to realize the competitive power of quality control, and begin to see that quality improvement has to be a significant and continuing part of business planning and operations. Only a few companies in a few service industries are beginning to see and act on the importance of quality improvement as a basic factor in business operations.

ARE THERE STANDARDS FOR QUALITY OF SERVICES?

Standards are not applied to services as they are to manufacturing. The reason is simple. The products produced in a factory have a wide variety of physical dimensions or characteristics which must meet pre-determined values or standards. An example is 110 volts 60 cycles alternating current. All kinds of machines, instruments, and devices must meet this standard. In services there may be a standard which can be non-quantitative in most instances and quantitative in a few.

Non-quantitative standards in services may be defined in several ways:

- As requirements of the customer
- As goals set by the organization
- As civilized acceptable behavior (laws, manners, etiquette)
- As a desired level

• As a desired event or happening
• As a written recipe (which is a specification)

Food preparation is based upon a set of recipes. Many of these tend to be goals or standards. Sometimes such a standard is needed. For example, in a hotel dining room, on four different mornings the oatmeal listed on the menu had four different consistencies—from solid to soup.

Quantitative standards are possible but there is little evidence that they are set, let alone used, for characteristics such as the following in a service organization:

• turnover
• absences
• paid-for leave
• shipping time
• transaction time
• downtime of equipment
• idle time of employees
• waiting times
• deviations from departure and arrival times
• defects in purchased products
• time spent on unacceptable quality purchases
• repair time
• maintenance time
• time required to do a job

For errors, the only standard to set is zero (0). Errors are not to be stabilized at some level. Safety as a quality characteristic in health, transportation, and elsewhere must meet the same standard. Safety must be the number one quality commitment.

WHAT DOES "EVERY CUSTOMER IS A SAMPLE OF ONE" REALLY MEAN?

Every customer's requirement is unique. It is a sample of one. There is no mean, no variance, no distribution. The size distribution of a million pairs of shoes is not going to give the customer a comfortable fitting pair of shoes when he or she goes to the shoe store. The distribution the store has may *not* contain the size including the proper width the customer needs. This means the store cannot satisfy the needs of the customer. As far as these customers are concerned, this type of store cannot meet the quality of service the customer requires.

Satisfaction means satisfying a sample of one. It means satisfying many unique samples of one. Requirements are expressed in terms of samples of one. If the unique requirements of a sample of one cannot be met, the customer may, and often does, accept what is offered or what is available.

In certain industries steps are taken to eliminate the customer as a sample of one. Examples are the ''package deals'' which contain several items, some of which the customer does not want, or does not like, or finds do not apply to his or her particular situation. The ''package'' sandwich at a restaurant illustrates the former, while the ''package'' homeowner's insurance policy illustrates the latter. These ''package'' deals destroy the customer's freedom of choice, and force him or her to accept something they do not want. This type of forced service can hardly be considered acceptable quality service. It forces thousands if not millions of customers into the same pigeonhole, and substitutes profit and even fraudulent practices for quality performance.

EXAMPLES OF QUALITY OF SERVICE WHICH INVOLVE A SAMPLE OF ONE

- individual medical service
- individual purchases in a store
- individual telephone service
- home water service
- individual income taxes
- individual mail service
- individual restaurant service
- individual cafeteria service

- repair service: auto, radio, TV, etc
- insurance policy: home, health, auto
- individual bank service
- home electric service
- individual transportation
- individual hotel service
- individual motel service

For many of these characteristics, especially those dealing with time, we want to take steps to reduce the amount of time involved, to minimize before a stabilized time is acceptable.[3] Examples are:

- downtime of equipment
- repair time—waiting time is involved
- maintenance time—waiting time is involved
- waiting time
- idle time
- turnover
- absence
- time to do a job
- transaction time

---

[3] W. G. Hunter, J. K. O'Neill, and C. Wallen, ''Doing More with Less in the Public Sector,'' *Quality Progress,* July 1987, especially pp. 21 and 22.

Two examples are described in the reference—repair time for a city's motor vehicles, and processing time on a State's word processing operation. On some of these jobs accuracy, completeness, appropriate format, and correct diagnosis of the trouble are as important, or even more so, than the length of time required.

Dangers of using averages as standards. For numerous characteristics the "average" or arithmetic mean is often used as a "standard" or "norm." This is common in weather reports where the average for a given is taken as the "normal," as though this is the value to expect; the variability of the temperature for the day is ignored.

In services, the average has nothing to do with the quality of the service. "Above average" does not mean acceptable quality or superior quality performance. "Below average" does not mean unacceptable quality or inferior quality performance. The use of the word may have no meaning. We have already referred to the official who claimed that the city had "above average buses." Actually this may be a way to avoid the question as to whether all the city buses are of acceptable quality, or that performance could be improved.

In the health field, as well as in other fields, averages are used as norms for large populations both of people and of things. An example in the health field is the use of averages in studying the elderly.[4]

"Most gerontological research however continues to concentrate on average tendencies within different age groups, and to neglect the substantial heterogeneity within such groups."

"The emphasis on usual age-linked tendencies encourages an over-readiness to treat age as if it were itself a sufficient explanatory variable; the emphasis on heterogeneity within age groups compels a search for other explanations as well."

The authors are saying what has been taught in statistics for ages: that the average is not enough and may be misleading. It is the variability that may be most important and lead to a more complete analysis and interpretation of the data and the population to which they apply. Concentrating on averages leads to an over-emphasis on age as the major factor, when a study of variability reveals other variables are operating and may be even more important than age.

A classical example of the dangers of fixing a numerical value near an average, not only as a standard but as a limit, is the 65 years of age written into the Social Security Act of 1935. At that time the expected age was about 60, but 65 was reached by both sexes by 1950.

The present figure (1987) is about 75 but we are limited to 65. Vested interests are so strong that Congress cannot raise it to 67, let alone 70 or above

---

[4] J. W. Rowe and R. L. Kahn, "Human Aging: Usual and Successful," *Science,* (July 10, 1987) vol 237, p. 148.

where it belongs for two reasons: to save the social security fund in the future, and to utilize in government and private industry the tremendous amount of experience—knowledge, abilities, and skills—now being wasted by professionals, managers, and specialists of all kinds who have been shoved out of the mainstream of the economy by a mistaken notion called "retirement."

How does probability sampling create a break-through in quality? An ignored but powerful technique for creating a break-through in quality is probability sampling. Service organizations have large volumes of paper work and data to which probability sampling is applicable if a 100 percent coverage isn't necessary or if it is impractical. Probability sampling should be applied across the entire organization, not alone to some isolated application using Mil Std 105 D such as that employed in a factory.

Sampling in the form of audits, surveys, and studies does more than save volumes of paper. It saves people, who are much more important. It greatly improves the quality of data, and greatly reduces the amount of time required to obtain final results. The cost savings of the examples below amount to tens of millions of dollars annually.

Some examples that show how significant these break-throughs can be are the following from both government and private industry; the first number given is the sample size:

1. U.S. Bureau of the Census
   - 60,000 households out of about 70,000,000 for monthly unemployment and employment estimates. (The household sample has many other applications many of which have been adopted by private business.) This sample survey started in 1943 and has been going continuously ever since.
2. Internal Revenue Service (Source: Statistics Division)
   - 600,000 out of 60,000,000 individual income tax returns
   - 160,000 out of 52,000,000 individual income tax returns for a tax audit
   - 300,000 out of 1,000,000 corporation income tax returns without any appreciable loss of important information
3. Transportation: improved sampling
   - reduction to 46,500 records from 71,000[5]
   - reduction to 155,000 records from 230,000[6]
4. Transportation: motor carrier freight bills (nationwide)
   - 400,000 out of 260,000,000[7]

---

[5] A. C. Rosander, *Case Studies in Sample Design,* New York, Dekker, 1977, p. 270.

[6] Data in author's files.

[7] *Ibid.,* p. 250.

WHY ARE CUSTOMER'S REQUIREMENTS VERY OFTEN NOT MET?

Quality defined as "meeting the customer's requirements" can be very unsatisfactory to many customers. There are many reasons why this definition is not met by many service organizations.

1. The company truncates the frequency distribution of clothing sizes, shoe widths, and other measurements. Many customers fall in the dimensions eliminated. It is really unknown by the customer whether the sizes in question are not manufactured, or whether they are made but the company does not stock them.

2. What the customer wants is not carried or stocked or served because it does not sell very often, it is not the mode, it is not popular, it is not requested very often, it is not a high profit item.

3. What the customer wants is only a part of a "package" and the customer must buy the entire "package," or nothing at all. One example is home insurance. Another is automobile insurance which the customer must buy because it is required by law.

4. A company will not depart from the usual routine to give the customer what he or she wants. It does not sell or operate by exception. The customer must fit into the established routine to receive service.

5. What the customer wants is not carried at the time of the year the request is made. The customer is asked to come back in 3 to 6 months.

6. What the customer wants is "out of date." It used to be made but not any more. The "new and improved" now dominate the market. It may be a repair part. It may be a replacement. It may be a bookcase like one the customer has. If the manufacturer of the bookcase can be located, and is still making these book cases, the customer may be able to get what is wanted.

7. Due to the working hours of the customer, it may be difficult to get service during hours that do not penalize the customer. Time schedules may not meet the customer's requirements, but the organization's.

WHAT ARE THE CAUTIONS AND DANGERS INHERENT IN LEARNING SITUATIONS?

A learning situation can involve a maximum of four time plots or learning curves described below. The chief danger is that a plateau or a relatively level run on a learning curve will be taken as a condition of statistical control when it is nothing of the kind.

A further danger is that a plateau will be interpreted to mean that this is the "best that we can do," when further improvement is easy with a little more learning and practice and instruction.

Instruction may be stopped after two or three plateaus based on the assumption that learning has reached its limit.

There is a danger that top level managers and professionals will expect learning to proceed at a fast pace, and as a result will set unrealistic and arbitrary numerical goals of production levels, including time limits or deadlines.

The maximum benefits will not be obtained unless data are collected on a daily basis for each of the learning curves, and the data used to improve operations:

1. volume of acceptable quality production (increasing number of units of product)
2. error rate (number of errors divided by number of units of acceptable production (a decreasing curve)
3. Unit cost curve (cost per acceptable quality unit of production) (a decreasing curve)
4. man-hours or time per unit of acceptable quality production (productivity) (a decreasing curve)

All of these characteristics are studied on a daily basis: recorded daily, calculated daily, and plotted on a time graph daily.

IS A SUCCESSFUL QUALITY PROGRAM DEPENDENT ON THE MODE OF ORGANIZATION?

No, it depends upon people. It depends upon their capabilities and attitudes, not on the organization chart. It depends upon acceptance, knowledge, and experience of people with the various aspects of quality of services. It depends upon the cooperation of people. Without teamwork, the program cannot even start, let alone succeed. The form of the organization is a very minor factor.

Even so, the people have to have certain characteristics, or the program cannot be initiated, expanded, and continued. These include personal traits as well as technical and other capabilities.

Personal traits	*Capabilities*
• acceptance of quality concepts	• technical capability
• cooperation	• problem detection
• teamwork	• problem solving
• communication	• management of quality
• safety	• ability to apply statistics
• patience	• error prevention
• accuracy	• how to supervise
• acceptance of new ideas	• how to survey customers
• innovation	• how to resolve complaints
• flexibility	• how to cost non-quality characteristics
• courtesy	• how to talk to customers

If people have these traits and abilities, then quality improvement can work effectively under the usual organization of managers, supervisors, and employees. Then there is no need to superimpose on the present organization another one consisting of councils, teams, facilitators, and circles.

HOW CAN LOWER-LEVEL MANAGERS AND SUPERVISORS CORRECT FAULTS IN THE SYSTEM?

There are many specific steps they can take to accomplish this.

1. by correcting local mechanical and related troubles: light, heat, air conditioning, computer, word processing, typing, etc.
2. have an itemized action list approved granting them power to take action
3. introduce better methods such as random time sample, probability sample surveys, data collection, data forms, control records, etc.
4. by training on the job: technical knowledge, updated knowledge, behaviorial improvements, improved supervision
5. by error prevention meetings and seminars
6. by safety training; instruction for emergencies
7. by talking to employees about their ideas about changes and improvements
8. by improving current routine procedures
9. by improved hiring and promotions
10. by introducing awards and rewards for achievements and improvements
11. by getting rid of irksome rules and regulations
12. by obtaining better facilities and equipment
13. by filling a gap in needed technical knowledge
14. by surveying lost customers
15. by surveying all customers
16. by establishing better communication with suppliers
17. by better physical arrangements of offices and work space
18. by surveying competitors

WHY DO WE OVERLOOK SIMPLE BUT SERIOUS ERRORS, MISTAKES, AND BLUNDERS?

One reason is that we are so concerned about building high reliability into complex mechanisms that we overlook the simple causes of failure.

It is easy to assume that simple errors will not happen, or if they do, they will not be serious.

Specialists such as engineers who make critical technical decisions that would prevent an error, are overruled, e.g., the Challenger disaster. In this case earlier evidence of a defect was neglected or ignored because nothing serious happened. The conditions for the defect to be serious had not yet arisen. It is ironic that with all the complex computer systems to protect the mechanism internally, it was the simple characteristic of temperature that did them in.

As we pointed out earlier, experts who have studied the Three Mile Island and the Chernobyl disasters state rather strongly that both of these could have been averted with more careful work by management and the operators. Employees lacked the technical knowledge and alertness needed to avoid what happened. In fact, the operators in both cases overrode the very safety systems which were designed to prevent just such an accident.

These accidents pointed to the need for operators to know how nuclear physics operated, knew the safety steps needed in case of an emergency, and had been trained in how the plant operated. Management was negligent in all three ways. There was a need to have a better trained set of operators who were familiar with safety measures and how to take them when needed.

Another less serious case but still one that had dramatic consequences was a computer program that was written in error because he lacked the statistical knowledge that was readily available on the staff. As a result 26,000 calculations were published in error, which contributed eventually to the downfall of the company.

WHY ISN'T EMPHASIS PUT UPON THE PREVENTION OF ERROR?

There are several reasons:

- Many persons don't like to talk about errors.
- There is a common view that errors are human. Everyone makes them, so why get so concerned about them? Errors are to be forgiven, and even overlooked and covered up.
- We ignore accuracy in spelling and grammar in schools. Even the scope and accuracy of arithmetic appear to be far below the standard required in business, the professions, and everyday work and citizenship.
- It is rare for a high-level official or professional to admit that he or she has made an error, even when it is obvious that an error has been made.
- Large areas of work and study not only do not emphasize accuracy, care, and the need to hew to the truth, but actually foster the opposite. The belief in "creative thinking" in writing, both in schools and in the working world, fosters an attitude that is contrary to describing the real world accurately as it is.
- Stress on errors puts responsibility on the individual who committed the error. Many persons in both the factory and the office resent this.
- Rather than admitting personal responsibility for an error, it is easier to hide behind technology and blame the computer, if it is involved.

This true story comes from the U.S. Bureau of the Census. A Census group was meeting with a Congressional finance committee with regard to the budget for the next federal census. During the meeting a Census representative suggested that some money ought to be appropriated for the purpose of reducing the errors in the census. Whereupon a Congressman jumped up, pounded the table, and exclaimed, "There's not supposed to be any errors in the census!"

WHY IS QUALITY CONTROL AT THE TOP MORE IMPORTANT THAN QUALITY CONTROL AT THE BOTTOM?

- The top has power but lacks know-how: the bottom has know-how but lacks power.
- The top makes far-reaching decisions affecting all employees.
- If the top makes a mistake, not only the entire company but every company and organization connected with it suffers. This mistake may involve a new product, competitors, the market, customers and buyers, managers and employees, processes and methods, finances, or investments.
- Lower-level mistakes affect only a limited area of products and services. These mistakes may be corrected before they become serious. The consequences may go no further than recalls or complaints. Responsibility is limited and diffused.
- If the entire organization is to be changed, only the top-level officials can do it. To do this they have to learn how to manage quality, as Drs. Deming and Juran have been pointing out for years.

WHY DOES SO MUCH OF THE CUSTOMER'S QUALITY OF SERVICE COME FROM THE BOTTOM AND NOT FROM THE TOP?

The customer does not buy from the CEO. The customer is not served by any executive. The customer is served by a salesperson, a clerk, or someone else, who is often the lowest-paid person in the place. These are the persons who determine the quality of service received by the customer.

Executives and other top managers *talk* about quality. They lay out plans, make decisions, and issue orders. They hold conferences and lay down policies. They do *not* build quality into products or services. Their policies, plans, decisions, and orders may filter down and be taken seriously, or they may not. These fine ideas may get lost filtering down through five or more layers of organization.

Starting a quality improvement program at the top may result, therefore, in more talk than action, in more plans than achievement, in orders that are misunderstood if not ignored, in fine ideas that are never implemented.

Therefore the fine-quality service acclaimed at the top is *not* what the customer is receiving. The critical gap between purpose and plans at the top, and actual quality performance at the bottom, can be closed only by *effective implementation*. Customer contacts are made at the bottom, not at the top.

Quality of the service is limited to the face-to-face interaction between the customer and the person or persons contacted, regardless of what service company or organization the customer is dealing with. The server is courteous or not, competent or not, prompt or not, helpful or not. There may be no connection whatever between what this person is doing and what the CEO is talking about.

WHY IS THE COMPUTER THE NUMBER ONE ALIBI OF THE TWENTIETH CENTURY?

The computer was originally called a "brain" by an early computer expert, and the notion stuck. The computer took on human traits. The computer, being anthropomorphic, can be blamed for any errors connected with it.

At the same time, we are not taught in schools and elsewhere that accuracy is significant and that avoiding errors and mistakes is a goal to keep forever in mind. Admitting an error or mistake is too destructive of our egotism, which is greatly overemphasized today. Hence we find some way to excuse or cover up any error we make.

A giant step is made in error prevention when we admit that we individuals made the error. If we are the computer programmer, we admit that we made a mistake in the program. We do not blame the computer. The computer then becomes what it really is—a sophisticated mechanism operating in the way some human being programmed it to operate.

The situation is much more complicated. The computer has been surrounded by a vocabulary that stresses data and machines, not people. Examples include hardware, software, data elements, data banks, and data management. The real culprit is software. People buy and use software as if some superior human being prepared it, who knows all about the problem and the situation involved. They don't realize that distant and unknown persons write the programs—and no one else. It is assumed that these unknown persons know exactly how the data were collected and have written the correct program, when this is not the case at all.

This situation is illustrated by computers in schools. By using software the teacher abdicates his or her position of being responsible for the teaching function. The unknown programmer or programmers become the teacher, determine the curriculum, set the order of presentation, and make the explanations, if any. They may also do the testing. Teaching is absent. The regular teacher is ignored, as are the personal contacts with the students about their difficulties.

Another culprit is the emphasis on the manipulation of data, *not on its quality*. Therefore the critical problem of collecting acceptable-quality data dealing with problems is ignored. Stress is placed on the analysis of the data when the data may be so poor as not to justify any analysis at all. By this we mean that the data may be irrelevant to the problem, insufficient in quantity, ambiguous in meaning, with unknown bias, and with an unknown sampling variability if the data come from a sample. Analysis is worthless unless the data are of acceptable quality.

Since the computer has made "intensive analysis" possible, this can be another serious limitation of the computer. A tremendous amount of computer time and output may turn out to be of little value if the input is not of acceptable quality. With dross as input, gold will not be the output.

WHY IS THE COST OF QUALITY REALLY THE COST OF NON-QUALITY?

What is called "cost of quality" in the standard manual *Quality Costs* is really the cost of getting rid of non-quality. This is because what are described as costs of quality are the costs of failures—both internal and external to the company—plus the cost of detecting and preventing them. It is the cost of doing things wrong.

The reason may be that it is easier to cost out defects, rework, and salvage of manufactured products than it is to cost out their absence. It is easier to cost out the correction of errors, wasted time, complaints, and failures in services than it is to cost out their absence. These defects and errors can be isolated and identified rather easily, and their cost can be estimated.

Quality is never total until we get rid of non-quality. When non-quality is progressively driven to zero, the quality costs approach the total cost of production. The cost of quality then is the cost of making an acceptable-quality product or rendering acceptable-quality service, and nothing else. This is the goal we work toward. (See Figure 17–1.)

WHY ISN'T FACTORY QUALITY CONTROL APPLICABLE TO SERVICES?

Conditions in services are radically different except in the case of products that a service organization has to buy to carry out its service functions. Then the service organization wants the supplier to apply quality control to the manufacturing of the products so that they meet specifications and the needs required to render high-quality services.

By stressing factory employee grievances in the workplace, the fact is overlooked that in most service organizations, it is the employee who determines the quality of the service to the customer. Quality is determined by a face-to-face meeting and interaction of two persons—the employee and the customer. Employee behavior and attitudes define the quality of service received.

percent

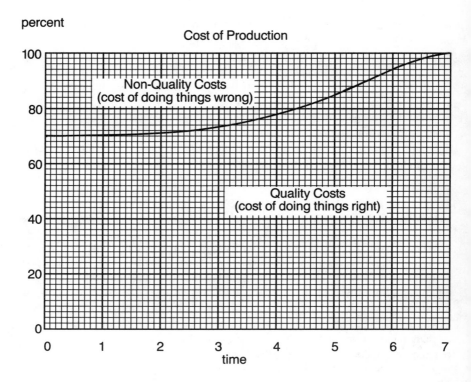

Figure 17–1. Driving Non-Quality Costs to Zero over Time

It would require a wide stretch of the imagination to say that customers are being served by a system that is under statistical control. Individuals serving the customer may and do exhibit widely varying modes of behavior, different attitudes, and different actions.

The general service model may be diagrammed as shown at the beginning of this chapter; it is easy to see how this differs from the operation of a factory, as shown here:

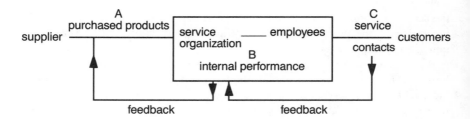

Quality is of major importance at three points: A, B, and C. There is a tendency to concentrate on B and then on A. Point C may be given slight attention. It may even be ignored or limited to customer complaints.

WHY ARE TIME, BEHAVIOR, SAFETY, AND DATA SO IMPORTANT TO THE QUALITY OF SERVICES?

This question relates directly to the preceding question for the simple reason that these four characteristics do not receive *major* attention in connection with the quality of products made in a factory. They are referred to occasionally and given lip service, but they are not given any special attention. In all service organizations, on the other hand, they are of vital importance. The following tabular arrangement shows briefly why they are significant.

Time
- Excessive time of service
- Delay time
- Idle time
- Downtime
- Unnecessary time
- Lost time
- Excessive processing time
- Excessive time to do a job

All of these mean poor performance, poor supervision and management, poor-quality service, and increased costs to the company and higher prices to the customer.

Behavior
- Indifference
- Carelessness
- Incompetence
- Rudeness
- Abrasiveness
- Negative attitude
- Non-cooperative attitude
- Unreliable behavior
- Failure to keep promises

- Dissatisfied customers
- Lost customers
- Internal failurs
- External failures
- Customer complaints
- Poor-quality work
- Loss of sales
- Mismanagement

Safety
- Carelessness
- Indifference
- Neglect
- Ignorance
- Lack of training
- Lack of knowledge
- Faulty decisions, actions

- Breakage
- Damage
- Injuries
- Disasters
- Failures
- Fatalities
- Lawsuits

Data
- No data
- Biased data
- Incomplete data
- Irrelevant data
- Ambiguous data
- Unavailable data

- False inferences
- False conclusions
- False decisions
- Faulty actions
- Financial losses
- Solving "problems" that don't exist
- Missing critical problems, situations

WHAT IS THE ROLE OF EFFICIENCY IN A QUALITY PROGRAM?

It is unfortunate that the word "efficiency" inherited a bad connotation from the past, when the popular thing to do was to hire an "efficiency expert" to improve production and productivity. The word is rarely, if ever, used in connection with quality control.

There is one definition of quality of products that carries the implication of efficiency—quality as "fitness for use." This expression means that the product works. It is suitable and proper for the end, need, or use to which it will be applied. What is missing, however, is that nothing is said about *how well it works*. Nothing is said about the likelihood that *something better* can be used for the same purpose.

Products for the same use may have widely different degrees of "fitness" or efficiency to accomplish that purpose. The concept of how well it works (whatever "it" is), or its efficiency, applies to services as well as to products. Examples are not hard to find. The following illustrate this point:

Machinery:	• Model T Ford vs. a modern automobile. The Model T was fit for many uses: it carried people, milk cans, cream cans, and sacks of wheat to the grist mill.
	• Wheelbarrow vs. bulldozer for moving dirt;
Mechanisms:	• The old desk calculator vs. the hand-held electronic calculator;
	• Early IBM equipment vs. the modern computer for data processing;
Methods, technology	• Probability sampling vs. 100 percent coverage and tabulation;
	• Efficient probability sample survey vs. a judgment sample survey;
	• Efficient sample inspection vs. spot checking.

In quality of services we want to use the better methods, not just any method that works. Hence quality improvement turns out to mean the most efficient actions and operations, although "quality improvement" sounds better and is more acceptable than "efficiency."

Efficiency really means producing a result or attaining a goal without wasting resources—in other words, making the most effective use of resources. With a quality orientation this approach will result in quality improvement. (This is analogous to the technical definition, which is energy output divided by energy input.)

Efficiency means that we use better materials, methods, processes, techniques, equipment, people, managers, and supervisors. In each of the eight vectors of quality we strive for what is better, for what is excellent, for improved quality:

- Management: better leadership;
- Supervision: better supervisors;
- Statistics: more efficient techniques for each purpose;
- Psychology: more effective ways of dealing with people, including employees and customers;
- Economics: better cost reduction measures;
- Subject matter: better diagnosticians;
- Processes: better processes;
- Time: more and better time-saving measures.

With improved quality of services we have

- Better results at a lower cost;
- Better results at the same cost;
- Better results sooner;
- More time-saving methods;
- Better employee and managerial performance;
- Better customer relations.

WHY ARE GOOD-QUALITY DATA SO IMPORTANT?

One of the most neglected aspects of quality improvement is the need for quality data. There are several reasons why collecting and analyzing good-quality data are crucial.

- Good data start management on the right track for solving a problem by 1) finding the problem, 2) defining it accurately, and 3) discovering its scope.
- Good data discover problems that management doesn't know it has.
- Good data put inferences, conclusions, decisions, and actions on a sound basis.
- Good data prevent waste on poor-quality data, biased data, or a lack of sufficient data.

- Good data prevent waste of resources on "problems" that don't exist.
- Good data prevent further damage from a serious problem that does exist and for which data are lacking because the problem is unknown.
- Good data nip a problem in the bud before it becomes serious.

WHY IS QUALITY OF SERVICES RECEIVING SO LITTLE ATTENTION NATIONWIDE?

There are several reasons why this is so.

- Quality of product dominates the quality field despite the fact that employees in manufacturing are only one-fifth (20%) of the total work force. "Total quality control" includes only manufacturing.
- Services are tacked onto quality of products, so they receive only passing attention.
- Quality of service has few champions.
- It has no organization to speak for it.
- Service industries show no interest in quality except in a few isolated instances. Therefore there are very few full-time professionals working on service quality.
- Many companies claim that they already have quality service. To them "quality" does not mean the same as it does to those working in the professional quality field. They do not understand what a quality improvement program means.
- There is a danger that a company will be satisfied with only one or two successful applications of quality improvement. They do not see quality as a companywide or an organizationwide program.

Selected References

These references were selected because of their fresh treatment of important ideas, their emphasis on basic concepts, detailed descriptions of applications, important case studies, applications to service industries, and descriptions of how to start and develop a quality program.

Critical Problems in Quality of Services
Connell, Gale W. "The Human Element in Service Industry Quality." *40th Anniversary Quality Congress Transactions*. Anaheim, CA: American Society for Quality Control, 1986, pp. 323–28.

Flynn, Michael F. "Garbage Out: The Fine Art of Putting Garbage In." *40th Anniversary Quality Congress Transactions*. Anaheim, CA: American Society for Quality Control, 1986, pp. 149–54.

Human Error in Nuclear Power Plants
Ahearne, J. F. "Nuclear Power after Chernobyl." *Science* 236, May 8, 1987, pp. 673–79.

Nuclear Regulatory Commission, "Report on Three Mile Island." *Science* 204, April 20, 1979, pp. 280–81.

Wilson, R. "A Visit to Chernobyl." *Science* 236, June 26, 1987, pp. 1636–40.

Management for Excellence
Peters, Tom. *Thriving on Chaos, Handbook for a Management Revolution*. New York: Knopf, 1987.

Peters, Tom, and Nancy Austin, *A Passion for Excellence*. New York: Random House, 1985. Warner Books, 1985 (paperback).

Peters, Tom, and R. H. Waterman, Jr. *In Search of Excellence*. New York: Harper and Row, 1982.

Management for Quality

Crosby, Philip B. *Quality is Free*. New York: McGraw-Hill, 1979. Mentor edition 1980 (paperback).

Deming, W. Edwards. *Out of the Crisis*. Cambridge: Massachusetts Institute of Technology, 1986.

Deming, W. Edwards. *Quality, Productivity, and Competitive Position*. Cambridge: Massachusetts Institute of Technology, 1982.

Ishikawa, Kaoru. *What is Total Quality Control? The Japanese Way*. Englewood Cliffs: Prentice-Hall, 1985.

Juran, J. M. "Catching Up: How Is the West Doing?" *Quality Progress,* November 1985, 18–22.

———. "The Quality Trilogy." *Quality Progress,* August 1986, pp. 19–24.

Quality Control in Medical Laboratories

Data Recap, 1970–1980. Skokie, IL: College of American Pathologists, 1981.

Henry, J. B., and J. L. Giegel (eds). *Quality Control in Laboratory Medicine*. New York: Masson, 1977.

Todd, J. C., A. H. Sanford, and I. Davidsohn. *Clinical Diagnosis and Management by Laboratory Methods,* 17th edition. Philadelphia: Saunders, 1984.

Quality Control in Services

Aubrey, C. A., II. *Quality Management in Financial Services*. Wheaton, IL: Hitchcock, 1985.

Aubrey, C. A., II and L. A. Eldridge. "Banking on High Quality." *Quality Progress,* December 1981, pp. 14–19.

Florida Light and Power Company, Case Study 39. Houston: American Productivity Center, 1984.

The Gallup Organization. "Consumer Perceptions Concerning Quality of American Products and Services," September 1985.

Juran, J. M. (ed.) *Quality Control Handbook,* 3d edition. New York: McGraw-Hill, 1974.

Langevin, Roger G. *Quality Control in the Service Industries*. New York: American Management Association, 1977.

Latzko, William J. *Quality and Productivity for Bankers and Financial Managers*. New York: Marcel Dekker; Milwaukee: ASQC Quality Press, 1986.

Rosander, A. C. *Applications of Quality Control in Service Industries.* New York: Marcel Dekker; Milwaukee: ASQC Quality Press, 1985.

————. *Case Studies in Sample Design.* New York: Marcel Dekker, 1977.

————. *The Early History of the Administrative Applications Division.* Milwaukee: American Society for Quality Control, 1985. See especially the last 17 pages on lessons learned and obstacles encountered and overcome.

————. *Statistical Quality Control in Tax Operations.* Washington: U.S. Treasury Department, 1958.

————. *Washington Story.* Greeley, CO: National Directions, 1985. Personal experiences in attempting to apply statistical quality control, probability sampling, and the science of statistics to the management problems of the federal government from 1937 to 1973. Full address: National Directions, 500 26th St., Greeley, CO 80631. $9.95 postpaid.

Townsend, Patrick L. and Joan E. Gebhardt. *Commit to Quality.* New York: Wiley, 1986.

Sampling for Service Quality Management Data

Cochran, W. G. *Sampling Techniques.* New York: Wiley, 1953.

Deming, W. Edwards. *Sample Design in Business Research.* New York: Wiley, 1960.

Rosander, A. C. *Case Studies in Sample Design,* New York: Marcel Dekker, 1977.

Statistical Quality Control

These books describe the basic concepts and principles of statistical quality control, even though the applications are to products and manufacturing. The concepts and principles must be adapted to service functions and service industries.

ASTM Manual on Quality Control of Materials. Special Technical Publication 15-C. Philadelphia: American Society for Testing Materials, 1951. An official and classic treatment of statistical data and presentation of variation, with equations and constants for quality control charts. Highly recommended to put meaning into a highly computerized trend today.

Burr, Irwing W. *Statistical Quality Control Methods.* New York: Marcel Dekker, 1976.

Grant, E. L. and R. S. Leavenworth. *Statistical Quality Control,* 4th edition. New York: McGraw-Hill, 1972.

Quality Control Handbook, 3d edition. New York: McGraw-Hill, 1974.

Shewhart, W. A. *Economic Control of Quality of Manufactured Product.* New York: Van Nostrand, 1931. Republished in 1980 by the American Society for Quality Control.

Shewhart, W. A. with W. Edwards Deming (editor). *Statistical Method from the Viewpoint of Quality Control.* Washington: Graduate School, Department of Agriculture, 1939.

Index

A

B

C

$\overline{\underline{Q}}$

R

S

Acknowledgment of Permissions

Quality Resources and Quality Press gratefully acknowledge use of the following materials:

Table, "Northwest gets most complaints," reproduced on p. 102, reprinted with permission from *USA Today*, September 8, 1987, p. 3A.

Table, "Complaints per 100 Cars Made Within 90 Days of Purchase," reproduced on p. 105, reprinted with permission from *USA Today*, December 13, 1985, p. 6B.

Table 7–1. Measures of Quality of Airline Service ("Airline Scorecard"), reproduced on p. 155, reprinted with permission from *Rocky Mountain News*, November 11, 1987, p. 3.

Figure 7–5. Food Stamp Errors in Percentages—1984 by States, including District of Columbia, reproduced on p. 159, reprinted with permission from *USA Today*, November 22, 1985, p. 12A.

The 14 steps in a quality improvement program, reproduced on pp. 261–262, reprinted from P. B. Crosby, *Quality Is Free,* 1979; permission granted from McGraw-Hill, New York, New York.

Figure 9–1. The Quality Trilogy, reproduced on p. 294, reprinted from *Quality Progress*, August 1986, pp. 19–24, with permission from the J. M. Juran Institute.

The narrative example of overhead expense—U. S. Corps of Engineers, reproduced on pp. 477–478, transmitted to A. C. Rosander by H. J. Pilgrim, U. S. Corps of Engineers, September 16, 1959.